Modern Political Systems: Europe

Modern Political Systems

EUROPE

Roy C. Macridis and Robert E. Ward

Editors

PRENTICE-HALL, INC.

Englewood Cliffs, New Jersey

Great Britain

Samuel E. Finer
University of Keele, England

France

Roy C. Macridis
Washington University

The German Federal Republic

Karl W. Deutsch
Yale University

in collaboration with

Rupert Breitling
University of Heidelberg

The Soviet Union

Vernon V. Aspaturian
Pennsylvania State University

Modern Political Systems: Europe

Macridis and Ward

Designed by Walter Behnke

Maps by Liam Dunne

C

Preface

This two-volume series on *Modern Political Systems* is a byproduct of a continuing process of revaluation and theory-building in the field of comparative political analysis that began at an Inter-University Research Seminar sponsored by the Social Science Research Council in 1952. We would like to take this occasion to acknowledge our debt and our gratitude to Dr. Pendleton Herring, the Council's president. We as a group and comparative politics as a discipline are to an unusual degree beholden to him for his unfailing understanding and support of scholarly efforts to advance the level of both theory and practice in this field. We are similarly indebted to the Committee on Comparative Politics and to its chairman, Professor Gabriel A. Almond, and to Dr. Kenneth Thompson, Vice-President of the Rockefeller Foundation, for the personal encouragement and Foundation support a number of contributors received over a period of years.

These volumes represent an attempt to translate our own versions of some of the recent theorizing and writing in the field of comparative politics into a text for American undergraduates. We have retained the traditional "country by country" format, since this fits best the organization and needs of existing courses. While treating each political system or group of systems separately, we have also tried to utilize a common framework of exposition and analysis. We conceive of politics as a system for the identification and posing of problems and the making and administering of decisions in the realm of public affairs. Political systems are part of a larger social system which actually generates the conditions, attitudes, and demands that constitute the basic working materials of politics. In these books, therefore, we have made an especial effort to place politics and government in their appropriate historical, social, economic, and ideological setting.

Such an approach makes little sense if it does not also help the student to understand the more general political problems of our time. It is our hope that these volumes will stimulate interest in and genuine intellectual curiosity about these issues that will extend beyond the classroom. The fate of parliamentary institutions, the challenge of totalitarianism, the politics of emerging nations, the explosive forces of rising expectations and demands among the new nations, the perennial contradictions between stability and change, and the political competition between "democratic" and "totalitarian" models in the struggle to "modernize" the underdeveloped world are problems that will determine all of our lives and shape the kind of world in which we live. If we succeed in introducing such issues to the student and in stimulating some better-informed and more systematic attention to the problems which underlie them, we shall have achieved our major goal.

The editors are grateful above all to the authors for their cooperation and patience. Particular thanks in this case are also due the publishers. Alfred W. Goodyear and James J. Murray III have been sources of constant help and encouragement. But the main burden was assumed by James M. Guiher, Jr., of the Project Planning Department of Prentice-Hall. He has edited the entire manuscript, and his work and criticisms have helped us immensely in the completion and improvement of both volumes. Responsibility naturally lies with the editors and authors. While assuming it cheerfully, we are conscious that the magnitude of the undertaking leaves room for many errors.

R. C. M.   R. E. W.

Contents

Introduction

*Roy C. Macridis
and Robert E. Ward*

page 1

Great Britain

Samuel E. Finer

I.   Introduction, 17

The British Empire and Commonwealth. The Evolution of the United Kingdom. The British Constitution.

II.   The Foundations of British Politics, 26

Public Participation in Government. The Climate of British Politics. Current Factors in British Politics.

III.   Social Foundations, 39

The Political Role of Social Class. Public-School Men and the "Power Elite." Pressure Groups.

IV.   Political Parties and Elections, 50

The History of the Parties. The Conservative Party. The Labour Party. Elections. The Liberal Revival.

V.   Parliament and the Crown, 81

The Cabinet. The House of Commons. The House of Lords. The Crown.

VI.   The Cabinet and the Central Administration, *102*

*The Primacy of the Prime Minister. The Cabinet at Work. The Executive.
The Public Corporations. The Government and the Economy. The Social
Services.*

VII.   Great Britain Today . . . and Tomorrow, *117*

*Questions about Some Political Institutions. Internal Problems. Britain and
the World. Toward the Next General Election.*

Bibliography, *132*

France   I.   Introduction, *137*

Roy C. Macridis

II.   The Foundations of French Politics, *142*

*Historical Foundations. The Ideological Foundations. The Social Founda-
tions. Economic Foundations.*

III.   Social Foundations, *154*

Social Groups. Interest Groups.
—

IV.   Political Parties under the Fourth Republic, *171*

*The Communist Party. The Socialist Party (SFIO). The Radical Socialists
and "Allied" Center Formations. The MRP (Popular Republican Movement). Independents and Moderates. The Rally of the French People
(RPF). The "Poujadists" (UFF).*

V.   The Fourth Republic: 1946–1958, *192*

*The Electoral System. The Governmental Machinery. The "Immobilisme"
of the Fourth Republic. The French Administration: A Countervailing Force?*

Contents

VI.   The Constitution of the Fifth Republic, 207

The President of the Republic. The Cabinet. The Legislature. Other Constitutional Organs and Principles.

VII.   The Evolution of Political Forces under the Fifth Republic, 219

The First Referendum. The First Legislative Elections. The New Political Forces. Government and Parliament. Crisis and Gaullist Victory.

VIII.   Governmental Performance under the Fifth Republic, 244

Independence for the Former Colonies. Algeria. Foreign Policy. The Economy. Education. The Political Institutions.

IX.   The Fifth Republic . . . and the Future, 259

After de Gaulle, What?

Bibliography, 263

The
German
Federal
Republic

Karl W. Deutsch
in collaboration with
Rupert Breitling

I.   Introduction, 269

A Picture of Stability. A Provisional Present.

II.   The German Political Heritage, 274

The Middle Ages. The Beginnings of Political Unity. In Search of State-hood. The Prussian State. German Unification in the Nineteenth Century. The Second German Empire, 1871–1918. The Weimar Republic, 1918–1933. The Hitler Era, 1933–1945.

III.   Germany in Transition, 293

Partition and Allied Military Government, 1945–1949. A Convalescent Republic, 1949–1955. Bonn's Return among the Powers, 1955–1962. The Continuing Division of Germany.

IV.   Ideology and Opinion, 309

The German "National Character." Bonn's Postwar Achievements. Ideological Cleavages and Groupings.

V.   Social Foundations, 322

The Strength of Occupational Groupings. Levels of Education. Income Groups, Status Groups, and Social Classes. Regional and Religious Factors.

VI.   The Basic Law of the Federal Republic, 337

A German Type of Federation. The Guiding Values: Human and Civil Rights. The Predominance of Federal Powers. The Bundestag. The Bundesrat. The Chancellor. The President of the Republic. The Mechanics of Law-Making. The Courts.

VII.   Political Parties and Interest Groups, 361

The Changing Party System. The Christian Democratic Union (CDU). The Social Democratic Party (SPD). The Free Democratic Party (FDP). Interest Groups and Elites.

VIII.   The German Federal Republic
Today . . . and Tomorrow, 387

The Decision about Western European Federation. The Political Dreams of the New German Literature.

Bibliography, 395

The
Soviet Union
Vernon V. Aspaturian

I.   Introduction, *401*

The Soviet Challenge. Soviet Russia as a Former Underdeveloped Country. The Main Features of Soviet Totalitarianism.

II.   The Russian Political Heritage, *408*

The Russian "National Character." The Historical Background.

III.   The Foundations of Soviet Politics, *422*

Economic Foundations. Population. Literacy and Education. Communications Media.

IV.   Ideological Foundations, *438*

The Philosophy of Karl Marx. Lenin: The Emergence of Voluntarism. Stalin: The Hardening of Totalitarianism. Soviet Ideology since Stalin.

V.   The Soviet Social Order, *453*

The Social Transformation of Russia. "War Communism" and the NEP. The "Revolution from Above" (1928–1933). The Stratification of Soviet Society. Social Mobility in the Soviet Union.

VI.   The Communist Party, *473*

The Primary Party Organziations. Regional and Union Republic Party Organizations. Inner-Party Democracy: Party Elections. Inner-Party Democracy: Criticism and Self-Criticism. The Central Institutions of the Party.

VII.   The Social Composition
       of the Communist Party, *492*

Factionalism in Soviet Society. The Composition of the Party. The Social Pyramid of Power.

Contents

xiii

VIII.   The Soviet Constitutional Order, 503

The Functions and Principles of the Constitution.   Soviet Federalism: Theory and Practice.   Soviet Elections.   The Supreme Soviet of the U.S.S.R.   The Presidium of the Supreme Soviet.   The Council of Ministers.   Ministries and Other Departments.   The National Economic Councils (Sovnarkhoz). How "New" Governments Are Formed.

IX.   The Soviet Union Today . . . and Tomorrow, 524

Problems Ahead.

Bibliography, 529

Epilogue
Roy C. Macridis
   page 533

Appendix   General Bibliography, 545

Comparative Tables of Statistics, 547

I. National Populations and Areas.   II. Indexes of Industrialization.   III. Educational Attainment and Circulation of Mass Media.   IV. Gross, and per Capita National Products, 1960.   V. Industrial Origin of Gross Domestic Product. VI. Exports and Imports as a Percentage of Gross National Product.

Index
page 557

Contents

xiv

ROY C. MACRIDIS

and ROBERT E. WARD

Introduction

I

This book in our two-volume set on major political systems is devoted to four European powers—Great Britain, France, West Germany, and the Soviet Union. All four are today, despite the rapidly changing nature of the world, major powers. They are leaders in science, technology, industry, and art. They account for one quarter of the world's total industrial production; their citizens enjoy a standard of living that ranks them among the most prosperous inhabitants of the world. As of 1960, the average income of an English citizen was $1,340 per year; of a French citizen, $1,200; of a citizen of West Germany, $1,170; and of a Russian, $818. These nations—with the exception of Great Britain—have had among the world's highest rates of industrial growth since the end of World War II and the highest rates of urbanization of any countries in the world in the last fifty years. Illiteracy is virtually non-existent, and involvement in politics on the part of the citizenry is widespread. The people in each of these countries are generally articulate about their common purposes and goals, and they share a deep sense of common destiny and nationality with their fellow citizens and abide by common rules through which ideological and social conflicts are settled. In dealing with these four countries, we shall be concerned with the "politics of modernity."

Despite certain common traits, the countries we have chosen differ profoundly in many respects. England, which became the center of the Industrial Revolution that began in the latter part of the eighteenth century, maintained a position of industrial, political, and naval supremacy almost until World War II. In the name of economic liberalism, she acquired a far-flung empire and used her navy to keep the seas free so her merchant marine could import raw materials and foodstuffs and export manufactured goods to every corner of the earth. But, most important, the representative and parliamentary institutions that originated in feudal times gradually secured wide acceptance first among the British nobility, then among the rising middle class, and finally, in the nineteenth century, among the working class.

By the time the Industrial Revolution arrived in England, Britain had developed a political system that carried all the seeds of a healthy democratic state: respect for individual rights, representative institutions, responsible and limited government, and, above all, the art of compromise and gradual change. Largely because the political system was capable of overcoming sharp social conflicts, Britain is the only country that has not experienced a major revolution since the middle of the seventeenth century. The strains and stresses of the twentieth century and her diminished status as a world power have not affected the strength of her political institutions at home.

Even more remarkable, the British system has been able to cope with the independence movements of her colonies. In the nineteenth century, Britain ruled more than a quarter of the population of the world, in an Empire that stretched from New Zealand, Australia, Singapore, Malaya, and India through the Middle East, the Nile Valley and Africa into North America. Some of her colonies were settled by English-speaking peoples who were given their full independence after World War I. In others, colonial rule continued until 1945, and it is only in the last decade and a half that a peaceful "liquidation" of the British Empire has been achieved. But here again the British have shown their genius in political adaptability. Most of the colonies, after becoming independent, have joined the British Commonwealth, a community of member states that are linked together by a number of informal ties and in most cases by a common acceptance of the British Crown.

In a period of declining power and colonial disengagement, Great Britain has been able to give us, like the Scandinavian countries, a genuine example of democratic socialism. After World War II, the Labour Party received a large parliamentary majority and proceeded to overhaul the British economy and social structure: it nationalized a number of key industries, took over the control of the levers of economic activity, established a National

Health Service to provide medical care to all as a matter of right, and attempted to narrow income inequalities. This "peaceful revolution" was accomplished without violating parliamentary procedures and individual rights. What is more, after the defeat of the Labour Party in 1951, the major reforms were accepted by the Conservatives, thus diminishing party strife and accentuating the broad area of agreement that typifies the British political system.

French democracy has not fared as well. The Industrial Revolution hit France just in time to sharpen the already existing ideological divisions that stemmed from the French Revolution. The Third Republic (1871–1940) was unable to cope with urgent problems of social and economic reform. By 1940, it was ripe for the demise that defeat at the hands of the German Army made inevitable. The Fourth Republic, established in 1946 after the Liberation of France, was a projection of the Third Republic and perpetuated and reflected ideological and class cleavages. The result was a stalemate on many basic issues that confronted the country. But even more important, a long colonial war in Indochina and later in Algeria gave to the military the opportunity to assume important powers and to defy the authority of the republican state. It was in the wake of a military uprising in Algeria against the government of the Fourth Republic that General de Gaulle was returned to power and given sweeping powers to overhaul the parliamentary institutions. On September 28, 1958, the French people accepted the new Constitution—the Fifth Republic—under which the old parliamentary government has disappeared in favor of presidential leadership.

Political and constitutional instability has also accounted for the lack of a clear-cut policy with regard to the French colonies. Only in the last years of the Fourth Republic were reforms made toward colonial autonomy, but it was only under de Gaulle, and on the basis of his own personal popularity, that the African Republics were granted their independence. The Army was brought under control and Algeria became independent on July

3, 1962. De Gaulle has returned to play the role of Cincinnatus—to settle the Algerian war with which the republican institutions were unable to cope. In November, 1962, the Gaullist forces won the election and it is likely that the Fifth Republic will continue.

The instability of democratic institutions in France before World War II was symptomatic of a general decline of democracy throughout the whole of Europe in the period between the two World Wars. With the exception of the Scandinavian countries and Switzerland, democracy and parliamentary institutions were abandoned or seriously qualified in every country on the Continent. In Germany, the Weimar Republic (1918–33) gave way to a one-party government. Constitutional limitations were set aside, individual rights were abandoned, and the state, controlled by the National Socialists, claimed total control over the minds, conscience, and lives of German citizens. In the name of racial supremacy, Germany set out to conquer Europe, attacked the Soviet Union, and challenged Great Britain and the United States. In the very heart of Europe, the Nazi movement threatened the most cherished traditions of Western European civilization—individual freedom and limitations upon government. It denied the rational assumptions on which democracy rests and came close to destroying Western civilization.

The defeat of Nazism by the Allied powers was followed by the division of Germany into two parts—the German Federal Republic and the German Democratic Republic. The German Federal Republic, commonly called West Germany, reintroduced constitutional and parliamentary government and in the last decade has enjoyed an unprecedented prosperity and political stability. The German Democratic Republic, under Communist rule, has been unable thus far to rival West Germany in economic prosperity, and its existence depends on Soviet support. At this point, the political future of Germany is a burning issue, and one not confined within the borders of the country. Conflict between the two Germanies, subsumed under the broader conflict between the United States and the Soviet Union, may create tensions that will put an end to the democratic experiment of the Federal Republic. As in the past, democracy and parliamentary government retain a tenuous foothold in the heart of Europe.

The Soviet Union, naturally, presents a special case. Russia was an underdeveloped society governed by a despotic regime until the end of the nineteenth century. In 1917, after some half-hearted reforms had been made in the direction of parliamentary government and democratic freedoms, the Bolsheviks came to power. Inspired by Marxism, they introduced Communism to Russia and established a ruthless party dictatorship—under Lenin until 1924 and under Stalin until 1953. The major effort of the Communist Party has been devoted to the task of industrializing and modernizing what was primarily an agrarian society. This has meant that the Soviet Union has had to concentrate on building heavy industry, on speeding up the process of urbanization, and on improving its educational system. Under an authoritarian government, the Soviet leaders greatly accelerated industrial development in the U.S.S.R. and now claim they will surpass even the United States in the near future. They have thus challenged not only the democratic West, but have provided a new model of development for the former colonial nations of the world.

The Soviet Union provides us with a political system that rivals democratic norms and values. Under Soviet totalitarianism, ultimate authority resides with a small elite within a one-party system, but the whole society is mobilized to attain certain goals. Social and political mobilization is achieved not only through terror but through the manipulation of a number of incentives—income, ideology, social mobility, and others. The Soviet system introduced new political techniques to achieve socialism rapidly, to gain in one generation what the West attained gradually and in the context of democratic values. In accomplishing this rapid modernization, the totalitarian system of the Soviet Union has been a "success," and we are today faced with a number of puzzling questions about the U.S.S.R. Is totalitarianism in the Soviet Union a permanent mode of government? Can totalitarianism be considered a transitional system that can lead a backward society rapidly toward modernization? Is totalitarianism likely to evolve gradually into an open society once the country is modernized and has gained prosperity and the comforting benefits of economic security?

Our task in this volume, then, is to analyze four very dissimiliar systems: the highly stable British parliamentary system, the unstable parliamentary institutions of the French Republic, the very recent development of a successful parliamentary democracy in West Germany, and the outright totalitarian system of the Soviet Union. Why and how shall we attempt to compare these four widely divergent political systems?

II

The whys of comparative politics are many and persuasive for student and teacher alike. Comparison, to begin with, for any student, and more particularly for the American college student, is like a guided tour of foreign lands. It shows that human beings living in different societies differ in their political behavior. They differ in the political values they hold dear; in the ways in which they apprehend each other and the outside world; in the manner in which they solve similar problems. Thus those who study comparative politics come to realize that health services may be a completely nationalized service in one country and based on one's ability to pay in another; that trains controlled and run by the government may be just as efficient as trains run by private companies; that individual liberties are highly valued in one system but that the interests of the group or the state are more esteemed in others. The student who reads about the governments of Great Britain, the Soviet Union, Japan, or China begins to gain perspective on his own political system, to re-examine attitudes and practices long taken for granted, and to scrutinize his own political institutions and those of others. Habit and intellectual conformism give place to critical evaluation and appreciation, the mark of an educated man.

Political differences, naturally, raise questions of "why." Why did Marxism strike such firm roots in the Soviet Union? Why have so many underdeveloped Asian societies flirted with Marxism or established one-party governments? Why has the parliamentary system brought stability to British politics but not to French politics? Why so many parties in France but only two in England or, for that matter, in the United States and Japan? Why do certain peoples accept readily the notion of state ownership and management of their economy and hold this compatible with democracy and freedom, while others do not? Finally, why do some political systems repudiate democracy and representative institutions while others deem them essential? To answer these questions, it is not adequate simply to recognize and list the individual differences that separate one political system from another. Descriptive identification of national differences is important, but not enough. We must also explain them. We must search for regularities and differences in political behavior and try to account for them. We must strive to develop a scientific outlook on politics.

The types of explanation we give to the national political differences we note may vary. In some cases, similarities or differences may be explained in terms of the history of the countries involved. For instance, it may well be that parliamentary institutions developed a remarkable viability in England because they were established before the Industrial Revolution. In France and Germany, on the other hand, industrialization preceded any very significant experience with parliamentary institutions. This is an essentially historical explanation.

Complementing the historical explanation, we have what may be called the structural-functional explanation. It views all political systems both in terms of certain common indispensable functions which must be performed—recruitment, communication, the maintenance of order, adjudication of conflicts, etc.—and in terms of certain structures or institutions which perform them. In different political systems, a given function may be associated with quite different structures and institutions. For example, the adjudication of conflicts may be handled by a formal judiciary in one society and by private mediators, village elders, or a priesthood in others. Such differences may in turn be accounted for by variations in social and economic organization, in value systems and prevalent ideologies or—this approach is far from incompatible with historical explanations—in specific historical circumstances.

If we were to compare, for instance, the political systems of certain underdeveloped countries that had formerly been colonies, a knowledge of the traditions and institutions implanted in each by their former imperial masters would be indispensable to an understanding of present differences. Thus present political differences between Malaya and Indonesia to some extent relate to differences in the histories of the British and Dutch colonial systems. But, beyond this they also relate to differences in social structure, population characteristics, levels of literacy, leadership characteristics, and economic circumstances in the two states. Similarly, differences between French and British parliamentary institutions relate to contemporary ideological variances, relative degrees of industrialization, different configurations of interest groups, and a variety of other factors in addition to historical differences.

The structural-functional approach, in other words, strives toward a sophisticated definition in depth of political systems, the identification of the most important institutions in each sys-

tem, and the classification and explanation of their political differences and similarities. On the basis of such analyses, it hopes ultimately to establish a comprehensive science of politics capable of developing general laws or statements of regularity about political behavior. As in the natural sciences, such laws would be stated in the form of hypothetical generalizations involving a series of conditions. For instance, it might be posited that in societies lacking serious ideological conflicts and possessed of single-member district, majority electoral systems, two-party systems will tend to develop. Or, it might be said that within a given society industrialization and prosperity will, all other conditions being equal, lead to a decrease in political conflicts over abstract or general issues and the development of a political system primarily concerned with the solution of concrete and specific problems. Again, it might be hypothesized that significant and sizable groups which are systematically denied access to positions of status and influence within a political system will, all other things being equal, eventually seek to gain these by violent means.

Such hypotheses can be tested against historical and contemporary evidence and may be modified or rejected accordingly. Research and empirical observation are indispensable elements of valid comparative political studies, just as they are in all forms of scientific inquiry. It is through empirical observation that we enrich our knowledge of conditioning factors, the presence or absence of which lead to the validation or rejection of our hypotheses. For instance, if we propose that wherever there is A (e.g., a single-member district, majority electoral system) that B (a two-party system) will follow, only to find that this is so in one country but not in another, then we must seek empirically the reasons for this disparity. We do so usually through a search for further relevant factors (X, X1, X2, X3, X4, etc.). Once discovered, our hypothesis is then qualified to read that B will follow A, *provided* factors X1, X2, or X3 (e.g., social, religious, or regional factors or others depending upon field observation) also obtain. In this manner, a more comprehensive and refined explanation accounting for the differences between the two systems can be formulated.

It is at this point that comparative political analysis becomes particularly challenging and at the same time frustrating for the student. He would like to be able to identify quickly the regularities and differences between systems and to come up with a simple explanation for them. But rarely, if ever, can this be achieved in practice. All political systems possess certain characteristics which are unique, that is, which cannot be duplicated. In fact, we will find it virtually impossible to verify any hypothesis or develop definitely any generalization that is valid for all political systems at all times. Invariably we will be forced to lengthen the chain of conditioning factors (X's) for each and every political system, and note that the generalizations proposed must be carefully qualified in terms of a variety of individual and idiosyncratic factors. Thus, at the very moment when we propose to develop general laws, we seem to bog down in the enumeration of unique situations. In despair, we tend to fall back on the facile explanation that uniqueness is the only rule of politics, that comparative study cannot really explain political differences, and that

the degree of indeterminancy in political behavior is so great that no generalizations are possible.

It would be a serious mistake to accept such an explanation. We have been careful to point out that, if one proceeded in the manner suggested, political uniquenesses are identified and explained. This is a point of crucial importance. We had to start from the general in order to identify and explain the unique. Unless we started with general political concepts and hypotheses, not only would we have been unable to generalize, even in qualified fashion, but we would not even have been able to distinguish between particular political differences, much less try to account for them. After all, how can one tell what is different and unique without first knowing what is general, or at least first being aware of the existence of a relevant general concept? Power, for example, is a general political concept which is variously manifested in different societies—through, for example, symbols of religion, magic, property, or pomp—to name just a few. But, without first grasping the notion of power as a general concept, we would be unable to relate these symbols to power as particular manifestations. This leads to the heart of our problem, namely, what general concepts shall we use in order to compare different political systems and to explain the similarities, differences, and uniquenesses that we observe.

III

We must begin by stating what we believe a political system to be and what factors we hold to be relevant to the comparison of political systems. This will involve the identification of those qualities and problems which we will treat in the case of the individual political systems under consideration.

A political system is a mechanism for the

identification and posing of problems and the making and administering of decisions in the realm of public affairs, an area which is variously defined by different societies. The official machinery by which these problems and decisions are legally identified, posed, made, and administered is called government. Government provides both an official and authoritative mechanism for the identification and posing of problems and the making and administering of decisions and a means of formalizing and bestowing legitimacy on the products of this process. In practice, it does more than this; by providing a context and an apparatus for the taking of official decisions, it also in time comes to influence the types of problems which are posed and decisions which are taken.

Government—in the sense of society's legislative, executive, judicial, and bureaucratic machinery—is not, however, the sole concern of students of comparative politics. It is only a part of a larger political system. Government interacts continuously with this less formalized and broader social phenomenon called "the political system." This includes government, but also includes such additional informal or unofficial factors that affect the functioning or products of a society's problem-posing and decision-making apparatus in the realm of public affairs as: (1) its historical heritage and geographic and resource endowments; its social and economic organization; its ideologies and value systems; and its political style; and (2) its party, interest, and leadership structure. Government plus these two categories of related and mutually affective factors thus constitute the political system of a society.

The first step in the analysis of a given political system is to ascertain and describe those aspects of a society's historical, geographical, social, economic, and ideological heritage and endowment—listed under category (1) above—which are significantly related to its political decision-making system. This will provide at the same time a picture of the working environment of politics and an inventory of a system's basic problems, resources, attitudes, groups, political alignments, and styles of action which relate in some operational fashion to political decision-making. For this reason, we refer to such factors in the chapters which follow as "the foundations of politics."

In practice, it is not easy to agree, for a given society, on just which of its many characteristics are of present and primary political importance—and, in this sense, "foundational" —and which are of only historical or secondary importance. They are not necessarily the same from country to country, nor are they constant for different stages in the history of a single society. Their satisfactory identification and evaluation in any given case is itself a matter calling for considerable study and sophistication and about which judgments will differ. In general, however, the more unfamiliar, non-Western, and underdeveloped the political system under consideration, the greater the need we find for explicit and detailed treatment of these foundational aspects of politics. American students simply do not bring to the study of Asian politics a fund of relevant information or a semi-intuitive "feel" for the situation in any way comparable to that which they bring to the study of their own or some Western European political system. Finally, it should be emphasized with respect to these "foundations of politics" that, although they are here distinguished one from the other, categorized, and treated separately, in fact they constitute a unified, national, interrelated, and interactive complex. Their dissection here for expository purposes should not lead one to forget this fact.

The interaction between these foundational aspects of a political system and the governmental organs of that system constitute what we call "the dynamics of politics." Social, economic, political, and ideological claims and supports rising from these foundational aspects of a system are constantly being presented to officials and organs of government with the demand that they be converted into public policy. Political parties, interest or pressure groups, and political leaders play the role of conveyor belts between the makers of such claims and the organs of government which make official decisions and establish public policy. They thus serve as active or dynamic agents within a political system, sifting and choosing among its claims which demand action, formulating these in actionable terms, gathering support, and presenting the results in the form of demands for political action. These so-called dynamic factors of politics— political parties, interest or pressure groups, and political leaders—thus bridge the gap within a system between political foundations and the formal decision-making organs of government. Actually, the word "gap," because it implies discontinuity, is perhaps an ill-chosen term. These are all interpenetrative and interactive components of a political system, and the distinctions we are here making between parties, interest groups, and leadership on the one hand and government on the other are more analytical than real.

The third major component of political systems is government, which is the formal and legitimacy-conferring machinery for the identification and posing of problems and the making and administering of decisions in the realm of public affairs. More specifically, it is the legislative, executive, judicial, and administrative or bureaucratic machinery of state, and the constitutional and legal framework within which these operate. While distinctive functions and organs of these sorts are usually identifiable in most non-primitive societies, it should not be assumed that they will be neatly and individually packaged or institutionalized along the lines indicated by these traditional categories or that, if so, they actually perform the functions indicated. Legislative and executive functions, for example, are often combined, while modern legislatures in practice seldom really legislate in any very complete or classical sense of that term. Along similar lines, it should also be noted that where totalitarian systems, such as the U.S.S.R. or the Chinese Peoples Republic, are concerned it is largely meaningless to attempt to distinguish between the governmental roles and powers of the Communist Party and the formal apparatus of state.

In studying any system, we are interested not only in the input aspects of its mechanism but also in its outputs. Consequently, for a given political system, we are interested not only in the above-described input process by which it poses, makes, and administers its decisions but also in the nature, quality, and effectiveness of the decisions taken, that is, in the efficiency and performance characteristics of political systems as well as their mechanics. The output or efficiency of a political system can be gaged by its capacity to survive and its ability to make decisions that are widely accepted. Assessment of the former is relatively simple. Where the latter is concerned, in a democratic system it can usually be determined by the response such decisions elicit among social groups, interest groups, and other associations. In a totalitarian system, the test is similar, though the nature of the groups concerned and the manner of ascertaining their responses are different.

An efficient political system maintains a balance between stability and change. Change is an inevitable consequence of the competing political claims that arise among groups as a result of shifting technical, social, and economic conditions and the demands that such groups press as they struggle to gain access to positions of influence and power. Throughout the nineteenth century in Europe, for example, one major source of political change arose from the claims of the lower middle class and the workers for greater access to political influence, while in the twentieth century the attempts of these same groups to translate their newly acquired political influence into permanent socio-economic benefits have been of similar importance.

Efficiency, therefore, is a function of governmental response to such groups and demands. To be efficient, however, such a response must take place within a context of stable and generally accepted political institutions. Otherwise, emerging groups will attempt to gain power by revolutionary means, and this has disruptive effects upon the entire system. From this point of view, there is no guarantee that a democratic political system is more efficient than a totalitarian one. A totalitarian government might develop mechanisms of representation which can identify and quickly translate into public policy the claims of the most significant new groups. A democratic government might discover that its representative institutions are no longer able adequately to convert the claims of strong and competing groups into decisions on public policy or to provide a satisfactory synthesis of competing claims. It sometimes happens that democratic societies become victims of their own philosophy. By developing organs of representation that register accurately the demands of all groups and by attempting to satisfy the claims of all, it may in effect hand over to each group a veto power that leads to a national political stalemate in which no major political decisions can be made. This happened in France under the Fourth Republic.

In the chapters that follow, we will discuss this question of governmental efficiency primarily in terms of governmental performance viewed in two somewhat different lights. We are concerned first with matters of relatively short-term performance. How do the governments treated define their appropriate spheres of political concern and activity? How do they allocate their attention, funds, and resources among these spheres of concern? What has been the nature and efficiency of their performance with respect to such standard spheres of governmental concern and action as justice, social security, public works, economic planning, national security, and foreign relations? Beyond such relatively specific and short-term issues, however, we are also concerned with certain matters relating to the long-term performance characteristics of these political systems. How efficiently are they coping with the larger problems of political development or modernization? What forms of political organization and action—democratic, authoritarian, or some variant of these—are they finding most appropriate to their needs? In whose behalf is the system operating? These are the underlying and enduring problems of all political systems in our time. Their import and urgency will vary within a particular system as well as from system to system, but some combination of these problems is critical for all societies. Together, they provide major themes for the two volumes of this series. As such, they merit somewhat more extensive comment.

The problems of political modernization differ in important respects between "under-developed" and "developed" societies, but no political system is in a long-term sense free from the need of adapting its structure, attitudes, and practices to changes in technology and social, economic, and political needs and possibilities. In underdeveloped settings, effective political modernization in our time involves almost the total restructuring of the society. Illiteracy must be eliminated and elementary, advanced, and specialized education made available; family and local-centered attitudes and forms of social organization must be replaced by more national and individual patterns; the gap dividing city from village must be narrowed; new and far larger segments of the population must be involved in the political process; a professionalized bureaucracy must be recruited and trained; and the entire process of political decision-making must be rationalized and rendered more representative along lines quite antipathetic to traditional practice. These are formidable undertakings in their own right and, in reality, are rendered even more so by the fact that they constitute but a small facet of a larger modernization process involving an entire range of additional massive and linked changes in fields such as technology and economics. If one makes partial exception of such relatively advanced states as Japan and Israel, all other Asian societies are involved in the earlier stages of such a modernization process. Indeed, this struggle to modernize might broadly be said to constitute the major theme and problem of Asian politics since at least 1945. As such, it will receive a good deal of attention in the volume on Asia.

The problems of political modernization are different for so-called "developed" societies, such as the North Atlantic states, the U.S.S.R., and a few others. They have already achieved relatively high levels of performance in terms of their political, economic, and social systems. For them, the crucial question becomes the continuing adaptation of political attitudes, structure, and practice to the national needs for economic growth and for a more equitable distribution of the national income among all sectors of the population. An examination of the efficiency and performance characteristics of political systems such as these becomes closely linked with questions about the role of the so-called "private" and "public" sectors in the national economy, and the advantages and disadvantages of a free market economy, nationalization, and economic planning. Of great importance also is the role of government as a purveyor of social and economic services and an instrument for the achievement of both social welfare and social justice. Issues of this sort will receive strong emphasis in this volume on Europe.

In both volumes, we are also concerned with one of the most crucial problems of our times—the world-wide competition between democratic and authoritarian forms of government and decision-making. Authoritarianism in this sense includes quite a broad range of political systems, ranging from truly totalitarian forms such as those in the U.S.S.R. and the Chinese Peoples Republic to the less organized and more traditional forms of despotism or oligarchy found in a number of Asian states. Authoritarianism in this context means a political system in which the range of effective popular participation in the political decision-making process is officially curtailed, while that of some relatively small elite group or groups is exalted and maximized.

In practice, this usually involves a system in which a single political party or group representative of but a small segment of the population monopolizes the representative function and controls all organs of government and other social institutions deemed important. In its most modern and extreme form, the totalitarian state, the hallmarks of the authoritarian system are an extreme degree of organization, mobilization, and centralization

of authority viewed as normal qualities of the state. Despite its elitism and extreme authoritarianism, a totalitarian system is also one in which all citizens, young and old, are constantly engaged and activated politically in the service of the national goals of the moment. It is a highly mobilized system which exalts the rights and purposes of the state over those of individuals and recognizes few rights of privacy or non-participation, much less of opposition.

All democracies, on the other hand, despite a variety of forms, have one thing in common—a basic distinction between the individual and the state in terms of personal rights that the state normally cannot invade. These rights may be religious, political, social, or economic, but their "autonomy" is not contested. It is, furthermore, a political system in which dissent, opposition, and conflict between parties and points of view are not only taken for granted but are positively valued as an indispensable means of insuring representative, responsible, and viable government. In such a system, although the sphere of official as opposed to popular decision-making may be both large and expanding, a significant and autonomous sphere of decision and action is always reserved for private individuals and groups.

In our time, the most comprehensive and durable challenge to both the existence and the expansion of democratic political systems has been offered by the success of the Bolshevik Revolution of 1917 and the subsequent development and spread of the Communist type of totalitarian political system. Politically, the Communist system rejects democracy in the name of some of its most important postulates—equality and freedom. Drawing upon the writings of Karl Marx, a great German scholar of the nineteenth century, the Russian Communist leadership and, more recently, Chinese leaders as well, have argued that democratic politics as practiced in the West is simply a device for establishing and perpetuating the evils of a capitalist society under the rule of a minority bourgeois class dedicated to the subjugation and exploitation of the workers. They claim that capitalist democracy, born of class warfare, is also destined to perish through a class war in which the working masses will revolt to establish a society in which productive resources will be used for the benefit of all. This common benefit they identify with the expropriation of private property and the socialization and control of the means of production by the state.

As long as Communist claims were limited to philosophical criticism and advocacy, their danger to democracy, even if serious, was remote. But when they were reinforced by the power of a great modern state dedicated to their world-wide realization, the threat to democratic institutions became immediate and urgent. The Soviet Union under the leadership of Stalin "built" a socialist state and achieved unprecedented economic progress in the course of a single generation. Russia industrialized at a rate hitherto unknown in the West. It was able to survive the German attack during World War II and thereafter to rebuild its war-devastated economy and attain a position of global power second only to that of the United States. To many underdeveloped peoples of the world seeking both independence from colonial status and a shortcut to modernization, this example of the strength and accomplishments of a socialist system became an inspiring and attractive model. But with this model went the central ideas and practices of Soviet Communism: one-party government, totalitarian control of all channels of individual expression, and the ruthless harnessing of the individual to the achievement of state goals.

Thus from a philosophy of social protest and revolution, Communism has become, under Russian leadership, a potent instrument of global strategy in a world beset by an unprecedentedly dangerous conflict between the Communist and democratic systems. Active Communist Parties have been established throughout the world, while, with Russian support, Communist governments have risen to power in all of the Eastern European and Balkan states except Greece and Turkey. In recent years, Communist strength and influence have also spread rapidly in Asia and the colonial world. In 1949, a Communist govern-ment was established in China, while strong Communist parties challenged existing arrangements in India, Indochina, Indonesia, Malaya, and the Middle East. In all these areas, Communism holds forth the promise of quick realization of the local desires for industrialization and economic modernization.

During this period of the rise of Communist power, capitalism and the democratic political institutions with which it is associated have also markedly changed their character. Nineteenth-century ideals of free competition and a free market economy have been gradually replaced by a more socially oriented and responsible philosophy, emphasizing social security, full employment, medical care, and social and economic justice. In some instances, so-called capitalist economies such as England's have gone as far as the outright nationalization of critical industries. Again, the actual roles of trade unions, political parties, and legislative assemblies today give small support to the old Marxist charge that they are instruments for the preservation of the privileges of a narrow ruling class.

Capitalism and democracy are far different philosophies and systems in the 1960's than they were in Marx's day—a fact to which many Marxists are strangely blind. Despite such changes, however, in the realm of political values and organization, Communism and democracy remain far apart in both theory and practice. Despite the shedding of many of the political and economic ideas of the nineteenth century, democracies today still cling to their old political values of individual freedom, of argument and persuasion rather than indoctrination and force, and of gradual change based on broad acceptance and consent rather than that arbitrarily imposed by the few upon the many. These are values widely shared by the citizens of most democratic systems. They are part of the "ideology" of democracies and condition their political actions and performance.

This question remains, however: Which type of political system, the democratic or authoritarian, will prevail in world-wide competition? Particularly in Asia and the underdeveloped parts of the world is this competition intense and undecided. These societies can still choose institutions and practices that will gradually build toward democratic practices, or they can choose the false simplicities of the authoritarian, perhaps even the totalitarian, way. This is a problem of performance that will engage our attention in both volumes of this series. Which system, the democratic or the authoritarian, is more apt to meet the needs of contemporary societies in both Asia and Europe? The answer cannot be given in terms of individual preferences or value commitments. It must be given in terms of the categories of analysis we have spelled out.

So much, then, for the manner in which we visualize our task in the two volumes of this series. We have defined a political system as a mechanism for the identification and posing of problems and the making and administering of decisions in the realm of public affairs. We have established certain broad categories of analysis for such systems: political foundations, political dynamics, and the formal decision-making organs of government on the input side of the process, and governmental efficiency and performance considered over both the short and the long run, on the output side. In the chapters that follow, an attempt will be made to apply these categories in such a way as to illuminate the functioning and performance of a number of quite different political systems. Marked variations in the natures of these systems and in the extent and reliability of our information about them preclude the discussion of all of these systems in identical format, but in all cases an attempt has been made to apply these general categories and to answer the principal questions posed by them.

SAMUEL E. FINER

Great Britain

Introduction

I

Britain is a tiny country. It takes up a mere 0.2 per cent of the earth's land area and ranks seventy-fifth in area among nations. Despite its smallness, however, Britain is a major world power. With a population of 53 million, she stands ninth in total population and fourth in density of population. She imports one-fifth of the world's output of raw materials and, in return, exports one-fifth of the world's manufactured goods that are shipped in international trade. She is the second largest trading nation in the world. Her people are comparatively rich: they enjoy an annual per capita income of about $1,340, as compared with $2,790 for the United States, $1,200 for France, $1,170 for Germany, and only $69 for India. Economically, therefore, Britain is a considerable nation. Militarily, her capacities are dwarfed by those of the United States and the Soviet Union, but she is nevertheless the only country besides these to possess operational H-bombs.

Up to 1939, Britain ruled a world-girdling Empire of some 15 million square miles. Today, the majority of the former dependencies have become self-governing states, and most of the remainder are soon to follow; almost all of them, however, have chosen to remain linked with the United Kingdom as members of the British Commonwealth. Britain's cultural achievements at least equal those of any of her European neighbors. A French poet has celebrated France as the "mother of the arts, of arms and of the laws," but Britain fills the description just as well. Newton and Faraday bear witness to her scientific achievements, Chaucer and Shakespeare and Milton to her literature, Wren and Gainsborough to her role among the arts, Locke, Berkeley, and Hume to her contributions to philosophy.

In the long perspective of history, however, Britain's pre-eminent contribution to civilization may well come to be listed as the common law and the invention of parliamentary democracy. Except possibly in Sweden, every such system in the world today has been modeled directly or indirectly on the British pattern. This even includes the American presidential system, which was derived from the British constitution as it was understood in the eighteenth century.

Britain began her rapid economic ascent after the political "Settlement" of 1689, which established parliamentary supremacy and secured the position of the mercantile interests and later of the industrial middle class. Cheap credit, maritime enterprise, and a vigorous trade, themselves the reflection of secure internal conditions and a benevolent government, began to enrich the country. A century later came the quick succession of agricultural advances, improved internal communications, and mechanical inventions that go under the name of the Industrial Revolution. Between 1815 and 1911, Britain's population leaped from 11 to 45 million. Between 1832 and 1913, her exports soared from £36 million ($117,000,000) to £525 million ($1,400,000,-000),[1] her iron production from 0.7 million to 10 million tons, her coal production from 26 million to 287 million tons. And the country became increasingly urbanized; in 1851, 1 male in every 6 still worked on the land, but by 1911 the ratio was 1 male in every 20.

The acme of British industrial supremacy came between 1815 and 1870. Britain was then the most highly industrialized power in the world. After this period, although she became richer and more urbanized with every decade, other countries began to catch up. In 1880, she still produced more coal than all the rest of the world put together; by 1900, the United States had equaled her in coal output and has since forged ahead. In pig-iron production, by 1900 the United States equaled Britain's output and Germany almost did, but now both have surpassed her. And the same is true in steel. As Britain slipped in relative production, however, she turned to the export of capital and became the greatest investor in the world. Today, Britain is economically comparable with West Germany, while the United States and the Soviet Union have far outstripped her in gross industrial production and population. But she is still a formidable industrial and commercial power and, in terms

[1] From 1939–49, the English pound was worth about $4.00; in 1949, it was devalued to $2.80, its present rate.

of gross national product and per capita income, she is richer than ever before.

Britain's political and military power paralleled her economic ascent. Although threatened by the larger and more populous powers of France and Spain in the sixteenth and seventeenth centuries, Britain was easily able to preserve her independence. As her economic power waxed in the eighteenth century, she became a major European power and intervened in Continental affairs whenever any single state seemed likely to dominate Europe. She made up for her lack of military manpower by the gold she used to finance her allies. After the defeat of Napoleon in 1815, the *pax Britannica* settled over the globe until about 1870. The only world rival to Britain's power was Imperial Russia, and the nineteenth century was essentially a conflict between Russia, the great land power pressing down to the Balkans, to the Persian Gulf, the Indian Ocean, and the Yellow Sea, and the great British sea power pressing up to meet the challenge wherever shore and water touched. Britain was so strong that she lived in "glorious isolation," and had no need for permanent alliances.

This phase, like her industrial supremacy, also began to pass away after 1870. By her triumph over France in that year, Germany became the dominant power on the European mainland, and Britain was gradually forced into ententes with Germany's enemies, France and Russia. By 1914, then, Britain had to share her power with several other European nations. Today, following two devastating world wars, Britain's relative strength has declined even further, although she is still one of the world's major powers.

The British Empire and Commonwealth

Britain's rise to imperial status was both the cause and effect of her economic and military advances. Always a maritime nation, she challenged the Spanish and then the Dutch claims to empire in the Americas and in the East Indies, but her aim was to trade with these territories, not to acquire them. She colonized North America herself, and the first British Empire consisted of the American colonies, then the areas won in battle from the French (Canada and India) and, later, Australia, New Zealand, and a foothold in South Africa. After 1782, in the period of the so-called "Second British Empire," she exported millions of settlers to Canada, Australia, New Zealand, and South Africa, endowing these countries with representative institutions; at the same time, she consolidated her hold on India, which she governed efficiently but autocratically. The third great wave of expansion, into Africa and Southeast Asia, occurred after 1870. By 1914, the British Empire comprised 14½ million square miles of the earth's surface, and by 1919, it was even larger, as "mandated territories" were entrusted to the British government by the League of Nations.

This vast Empire has today been transformed largely into a free association of sovereign states. (The basic law that defined the terms of this independence was the 1931 Statute of Westminster.) The Commonwealth now includes the United Kingdom, Canada, Australia, New Zealand, Ceylon, Nigeria, the Central African Federation, the Federation of Malaya, Sierra Leone, Tanganyika, Trinidad-and-Tobago, Jamaica, Uganda, and the republics of India, Pakistan, Ghana, and Cyprus. The Commonwealth is not an empty form. With one exception (Canada), all its members are inside the sterling area and keep their balances with the Bank of England. Their products enter Britain duty free; they take some 38 per cent of Britain's exports and supply her, in return, with 38 per cent of her total imports. Each year a tide of about 80,000 people enters Britain from the Commonwealth, and some 80,000 British people move out to the Commonwealth. The cultural ties are very strong; for example, the universities of the Commonwealth are federated, and a member of one can take up a post in another without, for instance, forfeiting his pension rights. Between the Commonwealth countries, there is a veritable free trade in doctors, lawyers, professors, engineers, and the like.

The political institutions of the Commonwealth are very flexible. All Commonwealth countries recognize the Queen as the Head of the Commonwealth; she is the Queen of some countries (Canada, Australia, and New Zealand), while to the republics (e.g., India, Pakistan, and Ghana) and to the Federation of Malaya, she is "the symbol of their free association and as such, Head of the Commonwealth." And all Commonwealth countries draw some legal distinction between each others' citizens and aliens or foreigners, although the force of the legal distinction varies widely from one country to another. The chief operative institutions of the Commonwealth, however, are the periodic meetings of its Defense and Finance Ministers and, most importantly, of its Prime Ministers. There is extensive day-to-day communication between all the countries that is channeled, in London, through the Commonwealth Relations Office. The importance of these contacts cannot be overrated, for this system of communication and consultation is today the chief distinguishing mark of the Commonwealth as a political entity, an entity that is composed of wholly free and equal sovereign states. The members have no duty to accept Britain's lead nor to agree or concert measures together.

It should be emphasized that the "independent members" of the Commonwealth are entirely different from the "non-self-governing territories," or "dependencies" administered by Britain. These are the responsibility of Parliament, and are run through the Colonial Office. A colony is usually governed by a British Governor-General, assisted by an executive council and some form of legislative council. The number of these dependencies is shrinking rapidly as, year by year, they receive independence and elect to join or not to join the Commonwealth.

Thus economically, militarily, and territorially, Britain is still a world power of great importance. Her past preponderance and her present power are one reason why her institutions have spread throughout the world. Another is the very clear success of these institutions. After Britain's European triumph in 1814 and her subsequent world pre-eminence, foreign countries copied the institutions to which, in part, they attributed her success. These institutions had also already been transplanted to her colonies (including America), and when these areas achieved their independence, it was natural that they should continue, in some form, the political institutions already established. And it has proved equally natural for the newly independent ex-colonies of the post-1945 era—India, Ghana, Nigeria, and the others—to adopt the constitution of their former imperial masters.

The Evolution
of the United Kingdom

Three factors have contributed to making Britain one of the most successful democracies of the world: geography, history, and industrialization (the latter will be discussed in the next chapter).

Geography

Geographically, Britain [2] is a group of islands, cut off from the Continent at the nearest point by 22 miles of sea—the English Channel. The last foreign occupation of British soil was the Norman invasion of 1066. Since then, the British have successfully staved off would-be European conquerors—the Spanish Armada of Philip II in 1588, Napoleon in 1804, Hitler in 1940. Britain is the only nation of Europe that has been unconquered for so many centuries. Her institutions

[2] "Britain" is the popular name for what is officially "The United Kingdom of Great Britain and Northern Ireland." "Great Britain" itself is an official expression: it means the Union (1706) of Scotland and England-and-Wales.

have been developed over nine hundred years by her own peoples behind the ocean moat.

Being a set of islands, Britain has not, till recent years, required a large standing army. Her monarchs were thus deprived of the instrument by which the despots of the Continent were able to centralize administrative machinery and crush political opposition. The absence of an army also prevented political dissidents from taking it over and subverting the country by violence. The only British experience of military revolution and despotism occurred during the Great Rebellion (1642–60) and the dictatorship of Oliver Cromwell. This encounter with military rule proved so odious it created a prejudice against standing armies that endured as a live factor in politics almost to the present day.

The sea not only closed the enemy out, but shut the various nationalities of the United Kingdom *in*. The Kings of England, the most wealthy and populous of its four nations (Wales, Ireland, Scotland, and England), were able to extend their dominion throughout all the British Isles. Wales was conquered by the fourteenth century. Scotland united with England-and-Wales in 1706 to form "Great Britain," through a freely negotiated treaty by which both states agreed to be represented in a single Parliament.

The Scots, as citizens of a former sovereign state, retained, as they do to this day, their own legal system, their own educational and local government systems, and, above all, their own national church—the Presbyterian Church of Scotland. Significantly, for the sea lay between, Ireland was never culturally absorbed. Conquered, colonized, and (in 1800) annexed to the political structure of Great Britain, she remained partly alien. (Here the fact that the bulk of the population is Catholic, while most of the population of England, Wales, and Scotland is Protestant was of great significance.) The rulers of Great Britain could never decide whether Ireland was the farthest bit of Britain or her nearest colony. Although incorporated into the United Kingdom, Ireland was never assimilated. The

BRITAIN

SHETLAND IS.

Miles
0 20 40 60 80 100 120 140

North

ORKNEY IS.

OUTER HEBRIDES

Inverness

Aberdeen

Scotland

Perth

NORTH

Glasgow

Clyde

Edinburgh

Tweed

SEA

Newcastle

Northern
Ireland

Carlisle

Tyne

Belfast

Swale

ISLE OF MAN

Irish   Sea

Leeds

Hull

EIRE

Dublin

Liverpool

Ouse

Manchester

Trent

Nottingham

Wales

Leicester

Yarmouth

Birmingham

Coventry

St. George's Channel

Severn

ENGLAND

Gloucester

London

Cardiff

Bristol

Thames

Dover

Strait of Dover

Belgium

Southampton

Portsmouth

France

Plymouth

English   Channel

break came with the rebellion of 1919 and the subsequent secession of the southern counties to form the Irish Free State in 1922.

History

Long united under the English crown, the four nations of Britain gradually adjusted to one another. The fact that Henry VII, the founder of the Tudor dynasty, was himself a Welshman played a large part in reconciling the Welsh people to becoming a mere region in a unitary state. Scotland remained a separate kingdom even after she was united with England and Wales, in the person of her own King, James VI, who became, in 1603, the king of both countries. She retained her laws and her church even after the union of 1706. Not till the nineteenth century was cultural assimilation advanced. Up to the end of the eighteenth century, the English thought slightingly of the Scots. By the middle of the nineteenth century, thanks to Sir Walter Scott, the reputation of Scotland's universities, royal interest in Scottish custom, and Queen Victoria's Scottish residence at Balmoral, the Scots rose in English eyes. Only the Irish Catholics remained outside the British "community" that developed in the nineteenth century, although the Protestant Ulstermen of Northern Ireland were always and still are an integral part of it.

Time has likewise bound up the wounds of religious intolerance. Henry VIII's break with Rome, in 1534, cast the Catholic faithful into a persecuted minority. The national church (the Anglican Communion) established by Henry VIII and his successors, however, proved too Roman for the more thoroughgoing Protestant sects. These religious differences added bitterness to the fierce political struggles of the Great Rebellion of 1642–60 and the "Glorious Revolution" of 1688–89 that put an end to the King's absolutism and that established parliamentary supremacy. In the eight-

eenth century, therefore, both Catholics and nonconformist Protestants (that is, those who did not accept the Established Church of England) were discriminated against politically as well as socially. The nineteenth century saw the successive removals of restrictions on religious freedom. The chief political disabilities imposed on the nonconformist religious minorities were removed in 1828 and those on Catholics in 1829. In the nineteenth century, there occurred a great revival of Roman Catholicism, as well as a revival of Protestant dissident groups, which was accompanied by an increasing measure of religious tolerance.

The British Constitution

The British constitution is a democratic one, but poured into an antique medieval mold. It is still full of officials, terminology, and procedures that originated in the Middle Ages. The government is called the Queen's government; ministers are the Ministers of the Crown; the armed forces are the armed forces of the Crown; and officers in any branch hold their rank by virtue of a Royal Commission. The courts and the judges are Her Majesty's Courts and Her Majesty's Judges. High officials still bear titles like Lord Chancellor, Lord Privy Seal, and Chancellor of the Exchequer, which all go back over six hundred years.

The importance of this tradition is that it has preserved not only the medieval form, but the medieval *essence,* which in sum, said: the King governs—but conditionally, not absolutely. At the heart of the British political system, there has always been a group of officials who formulated policy and saw that it was carried out. Except during the rule of the Long Parliament (1640–49), the opponents of the government have never sought to destroy this group, only to *control* it. British constitutional history is, simply, the story of the struggle for the control of this administrative machinery. Originally, it was the King and his officials versus the barons in the Great Council or Magnum Consilium. Today, it is the Cabinet on one side and the Commons (or, more realistically, the Opposition party) on the other. The form of an Act of Parliament links the present to the remote past and attests to the underlying continuity of the medieval conception of government. An Act always begins with these words: "Be it enacted by the Queen's Most Excellent Majesty, by and with the consent of the Lords Spiritual and Temporal and Commons in this present Parliament assembled and by authority of the same. . . ." In present-day Britain, it is the Queen's Ministers, the Cabinet, that really enact, but "by and with the consent" of the Commons.

The evolution of the constitution took place in two stages. First came the long and persistent effort of the more powerful of the King's subjects to control and direct his officers, and thus his policy. In the "Settlement" of 1689 and 1701, the age-old power of the Monarch to govern on his own responsibility was terminated. Henceforward, he could act only through an official who could be impeached or dismissed by the Parliament and who could not plead the royal command as an excuse for his actions. The second stage, which began with the loss of the American War of Independence and has continued through the years ever since, has been the struggle to democratize the Parliament, which in 1689 had emerged triumphant from its contest with the Crown.

The "Settlement" of 1689 determined that in the supreme body of the land (the King-in-Parliament) Parliament and not the King would be pre-eminent. But Parliament at that time was not a very democratic institution. The House of Lords, by definition, was composed of the great landlords. The House of Commons consisted largely of the nominees of these great lords, or of wealthy men who had bought themselves a seat, or of Members who sat owing to the Ministers' manipulation of the votes (although there were always a great number of independents sitting also). The great landmark in the development of the British system toward democracy was the Reform Act of 1832. It increased the electorate from half a million to some three-quarters of

a million people, allowed many of the members of the growing middle class to vote, eliminated many of the so-called rotten boroughs (boroughs entitled to send one or two members to Parliament despite the fact that in the course of the years their population had been drastically reduced), and created additional electoral districts in the new urban centers. This weakened the hold of the nobility and the landed gentry over Parliament and paved the way to the representation of the new industrial centers from which the country was beginning to derive most of its wealth.

After 1832, the extension of the franchise to wider sections of the population continued. The 1832 Act enfranchised 7 per cent of the population over 20 years of age. The 1867 Act, enfranchising chiefly the artisans of the towns, extended the vote to 16 per cent of the population over 20 years old. The Third Reform Act, in 1884, extended the franchise to the rural workers, enabling 28 per cent of the population to vote. In 1918, the Representation of the People Act extended male suffrage still further and gave the vote to women aged 30 and above. With this, 70 per cent of the population over 20 was entitled to vote. Finally, in 1928, the voting age for women was reduced to 21, the same as for men, and the electorate now comprises about 97 per cent of the population over 20 years of age.

This century-long movement to expand the franchise changed the constitution in three important ways. First, it caused the political parties, particularly after 1885, to adopt the structure they have today, i.e., organized bodies with central headquarters and local branches. Secondly, it enabled the Commons to become pre-eminent over the House of Lords. In 1911, the power of the Lords to veto a bill passed by Commons was terminated; the Lords can now only delay the passage of such a bill. Thirdly, the Monarch was divested of all real power. The Queen retains certain residual personal prerogatives, but since the early nineteenth century, the power of the Crown has been diminished until it is true to say that today the Queen reigns but does not govern.

The Salient Features of the Modern British Constitution

The modern British constitution is characterized by six features.

1. It is unwritten. There is no single document in Britain, as there is in France, Germany, and the United States, which purports to prescribe all the most important rules relating to the government. To find out the constitutional position on any particular point in Britain, one must consult all or any of five particular sources. First, there are Acts of Parliament, such as the Parliament Act of 1911 which limits the life of any one Parliament to five years. Next there are the decisions of the courts of law. Thirdly, there are certain principles of the common law; for instance, the basic freedoms—e.g., of speech or of association—are derived from the common law. Fourthly, there is the law and custom of Parliament (*lex et consuetudo Parliamenti*); among other things, this prescribes the special privileges attaching to Parliament and to an individual Member. Finally, there is an entirely unwritten element, the *conventions* of the constitution.

The conventions are rules of practice. The constitution depends very largely upon the conventions. Examples of some of the more important of them are: (1) Parliament must meet at least once a year; (2) the Monarch does not attend Cabinet meetings; (3) Ministers who lose the support of the Commons on a major policy issue must either resign or seek to reverse the opinion of the Commons by advising the Monarch to dissolve Parliament and so permit a General Election in which the electorate can be called upon to make a decision, and (4) the Cabinet is *collectively* responsible to Parliament on matters of policy.

Conventions are *not* laws. They could be broken without incurring a legal penalty. Sometimes they are, but this is most infrequent. The conventions are one of the most conservatively regarded elements of the constitution.

2. It is flexible. No greater sanctity attaches to a law of constitutional significance than to any other law. Laws altering the succession to the Crown or the status of political parties would be passed in exactly the same manner as a Wild Birds Protection Act.

3. Britain is a unitary, not a federal state. Parliament is supreme over the whole of the United Kingdom. No localities exist whose governments have co-equal legal status with that of Parliament. Local authorities such as County Councils or Borough Councils can be altered or abolished altogether by an Act of Parliament.

4. Parliament is sovereign. The Law courts recognize that Parliament's Acts are law and that they therefore must apply it as such. The Parliament is therefore the supreme organ of authority. No authority in the kingdom is competent to override it or to set it aside, but Parliament can override or set aside any other authority in the kingdom. It can legislate on any matter it chooses. It can repeal or amend any Act of any former Parliament. It can pass Acts of Attainder and *ex post facto* laws. It can legalize past illegalities. It can illegalize past legalities.

5. The separation of powers. In the American sense, this principle does *not* operate in Britain. Parliament unites the executive and legislature and it itself is the "High Court" of Parliament. In another sense, the principle does operate; the legislature does not interfere with the day-to-day workings of either the judiciary or of the civil servants. And only Ministers, not the civil servants in the Ministries, are responsible to the Houses of Parliament. The tenure of judges is guaranteed during "good behavior," and the Crown (effectively, the government) can remove them only on a joint address from both Houses. In practice, this has guaranteed them immunity from political pressure. In addition, the judges enjoy considerable judicial immunities for the things they say or do in their official capacity.

6. *A Cabinet system.* The late L. S. Amery has said that the constitution still consists, as in medieval days, of "a continuous parley or conference in Parliament between the Crown, i.e., the directing and energizing element, and the representatives of the nation." Today, the *essential* parley or conference occurs between the Cabinet on the one side and the Commons on the other. This forms the subject of Chapter V and will be discussed there in more detail.

The Foundations of British Politics

II

one can participate in running the country without standing for public office, simply because a large part of the administration of the country is left to private and not official bodies.

British democracy is characteristically an amalgamation of the public and the private sectors; the public bodies, controlled by elected members, draw into their work the private bodies, who are also controlled by elected members. Two ways of participating in public affairs other than through politics, therefore, are open to the citizen. The first is participation in a private association, e.g., the British Medical Association, the National Council of Social Service, or the Transport and General Workers' Union, helping to carry out their functions of public concern. The second is by being either (1) co-opted to, (2) associated with, or (3) consulted by, the public authorities.

The *third* way of political participation is open to the citizen through election to local councils and, above all, to the House of Commons. Public participation in local elections is low, by General Election standards, for the average turnout is not more than 50 per cent. By contrast, the turnout in the British General Elections since World War II has been: 75 per cent in 1945; 84 per cent in 1950; 82.5 per cent in 1951; 77 per cent in 1955; and, in the last election, in 1959, nearly 79 per cent. But these figures underestimate the extent of participation, since deaths and removals account for about 10 per cent of the voters on the regis-

Public Participation in Government

The quality of British democracy is not revealed by election statistics alone. For one thing, elections are infrequent and the number of elective officers a mere fraction of those in the United States. The only public elections are the General Elections (every four years on the average) and the local-authority elections (generally once a year in the urban areas and once every three years in the rural areas). The only public elective offices are those of Member of Parliament (630) and those for the local authorities (about 30,000 in number).

Much of what passes as the responsibility of public authority in other lands is in Britain a matter for private bodies. In Britain, then,

ter. Of the *effective* voters, therefore, figures about 8 per cent higher would give a truer picture. Thus voting has ranged between about 85 and 92 per cent of the effective electorate.

The British, by the way, take their elections very soberly. Just before the last election, a Labour M.P. said to the author: "You know, the politicians think the public go mad at a General Election. They don't. The only people who go mad are the politicians."

The Climate of British Politics

Pluralism

Underlying British political behavior is the concept of pluralism, the assumption that many different viewpoints are reflected in the community and that each has a right to exist and to be heard. These various sections of the community, as long as they are not breaking the law, or planning to do so, have the common law rights of all British subjects to speak, publish, and associate freely, even if their cause is considered odious by the majority of the public. Democracy is seen as a set of procedures to get things done, not to get *particular* things done.

British politics is emphatically not the politics of all or nothing; it is the politics of *less* or *more*. Few wish to exterminate the capitalist class, but many wish to see more public ownership or control of industry, heavier taxation on high incomes, a capital gains tax, and the like. Few wish to destroy the trade-union movement, but many would like to see restrictions imposed on its power to strike in vital industries. In the last decade, politics has even become a matter of a *little* less and a *little* more: Should a greater or a lesser share of the national income go to the workers, the middle classes, or old-age pensioners? Should there be a greater or a lesser pace in the emancipation of the colonies, and so forth?

This pragmatic attitude toward political issues is reflected in a third feature of British politics: the virtual absence of effectual ideological conflict. Ideologists are in evidence in the country, as is attested by the popularity of the Left-wing weeklies, the *New Statesman* and *Tribune,* and by the emergence of the group of young men and women who publish the *New Left Review,* but the existence of these factions merely highlights the empirical viewpoint of the Labour Party as a whole. On the Right, there are hoodlums of the fascist or Nazi type, but they have neither a mass following nor do they make any ideological contributions. The Right is, in Britain, the powerful Conservative Party, which is even more pragmatic and empirical in its attitude than the Labour Party. In short then, there are no serious ideological cleavages to sunder the nation into pro-capitalist and anti-capitalist factions or into pro-Church and anti-Church groups, as there are in so many other countries.

Politics of this sort still leaves plenty of room for passionate dispute. There is bitter disagreement over the distribution of the national income; the Labour Party and the Trades Unions press for a larger share for the manual wage earners at the expense of other sections of the community, while the Conservatives argue that the claims of the other sections are equally worthy. Disagreement has smoldered over the pace and extent of the liquidation of the Colonial Empire, although the second Macmillan Cabinet (1959–   ) has proceeded so fast and so far in this matter that the margin of disagreement between the parties has been almost eliminated. In foreign policy, there have been times, especially when Britain and France forcibly intervened in the Suez Canal zone during the fighting between Israel and Egypt (1956), when the country was most bitterly divided; then, a slow return to a bipartisan foreign policy took place, until October, 1962, when all seemed set for a mighty clash between the pro-Common Market Liberals and Conservatives, and the anti-Common Market Labour Party.

The Symbols of British Unity

The unity of the people of a state can be sensed from the national symbols they revere. In Britain, as in other countries, the appeal to national sentiment, as typified in its flag, the Union Jack, is a common one. Yet the British, unlike the Americans, have no "cult" of the flag. There are no flag-raising ceremonies at its schools.

The unique symbol of unity and community in England, is the Monarchy. What do the British people experience in the Monarchy? Although it is impossible to detail what individual participants derive from a cult, which is what the Monarchy has become in Britain, the Queen's subjects experience through her a sense of oneness with the other subjects of the realm and a feeling of uniqueness among the peoples of the earth.

No serious anti-monarchical sentiment exists in Britain. Although a scattering of Left-wing ideologues are critical of the Monarchy, they feel much more strongly about such matters as the colonies or capitalism than they do about monarchy. The real point in dispute—if dispute it be—is not whether the Monarchy should remain, but whether it ought not to become "more democratic," to evolve in some elusive way into "a classless Court." This view represents the limit of critical feeling about the Monarchy. As the Monarch's power to influence events has waned, her role as a symbol of national unity has vastly increased.

The Legacy of Industrialism

The Industrial Revolution of the eighteenth and nineteenth centuries opened a new and very deep class cleavage in Britain that still remains. A new class, the industrial workers, emerged and increased in numbers while those employed in agriculture steadily decreased.

Trades Unions were legalized in 1824 and 1825. In 1871 it was established that they might not be declared illegal simply because their activities were in restraint of trade. In 1875 peaceful picketing was legalized. In 1906 the unions were made immune from legal proceedings against them in respect of any civil wrongs (torts) they committed in the contemplation or pursuance of a trade dispute. For instance, employers could not sue them for damages incurred through a strike, or because they had induced employees to break their contracts of employment. In 1913 Parliament recognized the unions' right to spend money for political purposes, such as the financing of candidates for election to Parliament.

The early unions were numerous and small and largely confined to artisans and skilled workmen. The movement to organize the laborers and semi-skilled only began in the late 1880's, but it gained ground rapidly, and large unions emerged through federation and amalgamation, until today over half the total membership is concentrated in seven unions (out of a total of 657). Significantly, one of these unions is that of shop assistants, i.e., a "white-collar" union. The growth of such white-collar unions has been a marked feature of recent Trades Union history; teachers, civil servants, and local government officers are now largely unionized.

Most large unions are affiliated with the Trades Union Congress, founded in 1868. However, in 1958, one and a half million Trades Unionists out of nine and a half million were not so affiliated, chiefly teachers and public servants, both local and national. Table 2-1 (on page 29) lists only the numbers affiliated with the Trades Union Congress, but it does indicate the massive increase of membership.

The Trades Unions represent only the economic aspect of the labor movement. During the last century and a half, a definite rhythm has occurred between the economic and political demands of the workers. When their economic needs were frustrated, they increased their political activity, and if this proved a failure, they concentrated again on economic

TABLE 2-1   *Trades Unionists*
Represented at the Trades Union
Congress, 1868–1961

1868	118,867
1888	816,944
1908	1,777,000
1928	3,874,842
1948	7,791,470
1958	8,176,252
1961	8,299,393

TABLE 2-2   *National Income*
per Capita, 1960 [a]

India	$ 69.90
Japan	383.00
France	1,200.00
U.K.	1,340.00
U.S.	2,790.00

[a] Source: See Appendix.

TABLE 2-3   *Urbanization in the*
United Kingdom Compared with
That in Other Countries [a]

Country	Percentage of population living in towns of over 100,000 inhabitants
U.K.	51.0%
Germany	30.7
U.S.	28.4
U.S.S.R.	23.5
France	16.8
Turkey	12.1
India	8.6

[a] Source: See Appendix.

demands. In the 1880's, their political activity began to take the form of socialism. A Marxist organization, the Social Democratic Federation, was formed in 1881, but was not successful in winning over the rank and file Trades Unionists. More attractive was the Independent Labour Party, a non-Marxist body, founded by Keir Hardie in 1893. After a seven-year struggle, the leaders of the Independent Labour Party were able to persuade some unions to join them in setting up a Labour Representation Committee in an effort to return workingmen to Parliament; before this, the unions had tended to work through the machinery of the Liberal Party. In 1906, the Labour Representation Committee contested the General Election as an independent force, gained 29 seats (out of 50 candidates), and changed its name to the Labour Party. Since then, the Trades Unions have been the backbone of the Labour Party, and the Trades Unions and the Labour Party are commonly referred to, respectively, as the economic and the political wings of the "Labour movement."

The Industrial Revolution began in Britain and, as we have seen, had a profound impact on the nation. In the first place, it made Britain very wealthy and this in turn made it easier to close the gap between extreme wealth and poverty by equalizing income through taxation, by extending social services, and by putting amenities within the reach of the masses. Although the British standard of living falls woefully short of that of the United States, it is a rich country by European standards and a fabulously wealthy one by Asian or Latin American standards, as Table 2-2 shows.

Secondly, industrialization has changed the British into a nation of town dwellers and town workers, thus greatly consolidating social attitudes and narrowing the kinds of social problems the government must face. Britain is, indeed, the most urbanized country in the world. Table 2-3 takes on added significance when we realize that six urban centers, accounting for less than 4 per cent of the total area of the country, contain 40 per cent of the entire population.

Current Factors in British Politics

Homogeneity and Difference

In England, regional differences are slight. After a recent questionnaire survey, Geoffrey Gorer has concluded that

In the three years during which I have been occupied with the data on which my study has

The Foundations of British Politics

been founded, I have been increasingly more impressed with the basic unity of the people of England. The upper-middle and lower working classes, the mother-centered North-West and father-centered North-East and North depart to a somewhat marked extent from the habits and attitudes of the rest of the country; but in the main, the English are a truly unified people, more unified, I would hazard, than at any previous period of their history.[1]

When we are considering the United Kingdom as a whole, however, we must take into account that Northern Ireland, Wales, and Scotland are ethnically and culturally very different from England and that these differences do manifest themselves politically. Northern Ireland is perhaps the least politically restive of the three, because it has its own local Parliament. But particularism is very marked in Scotland and Wales; both countries have a vital sense of nationhood. The historical fact that Scotland joined England as an independent state, coupled with the retention of her own indigenous legal, educational, and, above all, religious institutions, forms the basis for Scottish nationalism; historical tradition, a rich literary tradition, and the survival of the Welsh tongue provide the Welsh basis. In Scotland, there is a Scottish Nationalist Party whose goal is to create an independent Scottish state and also the "Covenant" movement aiming at "home rule" for Scotland. In Wales, *Plaid Cymru* (the Welsh Party) advocates Dominion status (i.e., effective independence) for Wales.

Religious Differences

Religion no longer drives divisive wedges into British society, nor does it emphasize political differences as it did up to the First World War. In the last fifty years, the coincidence of party allegiance and religious affiliation has continually declined. Estimates

[1] Geoffrey Gorer, *Exploring English Character* (London: Cresset Press, 1952).

of the number of religious denominations differ, but this is probably an accurate count of the memberships of the largest ones: the Church of England, the Church of Wales, and the Church of Ireland (twenty-six million); the Roman Catholic Church (five million baptized members); Presbyterians (two million); Methodists (one million full members); Congregationalists and Baptists (each with about a quarter of a million). About one-fifth of the adult population belongs to a religious association of some kind. Evidence indicates that, with the exception of the Roman Catholics, there has been a decline in church-going over the last half century. Of the 346,903 marriages celebrated in England and Wales in 1957, some 50 per cent were in the Anglican communion, 22 per cent in churches and chapels of other denominations, and 28 per cent were civil marriages in a Registry Office. In Scotland, the proportions were: Presbyterian, 56 per cent; Roman Catholic, 17 per cent; other churches, 9 per cent; Registry Office, 18 per cent.

The Mass Media

Local, regional, and religious differences, such as they are, are increasingly eroded by the mass media, notably the press, radio, and television. Despite regional editions of newspapers, a flourishing provincial press, and regional radio and television broadcasts that emphasize the interests of Scotland, Ireland, and Wales (including many Welsh language items), the effect of the mass media is overwhelmingly to standardize tastes, outlooks, and even accents—and accents, whether lilting Scots, sing-song Welsh, nasal Cockney, or broad Midlands, are the most obvious way, in Britain, of distinguishing between natives of one region and another.

THE PRESS. The salient facts about the British press are (1) that the country has more newspapers per head (573 copies for every 1,000 people) than any other country in the world and (2) that circulation is dominated by the great national newspapers. They all purvey a type of national, as opposed to regional, news, but they differ in character from "popular" or "tabloid" to "quality" papers, and they also differ politically. The *Daily Herald* is Labour, and the *Daily Telegraph* is the unofficial spokesman of the Conservative Party. But the other newspapers take sides, too. Table 2-4 lists them, with the most recent circulation figures (1961), according to their political attitudes. (The Liberal *News Chronicle* disappeared, in 1960, by absorption into the Conservative *Daily Mail*.)

TABLE 2-4   *Circulations and Political Affinities of the National Dailies, 1961*

Labour and independent Labour		Conservative and independent Conservative		Liberal		Independent	
Daily Herald	1,419,000	Daily Telegraph	1,251,000	The Guardian	235,000	The Times	260,000
Daily Mirror	4,593,000	Daily Express	4,313,000				
		Daily Mail	2,687,000				
		Daily Sketch	1,000,000				
Total	6,012,000		9,251,000		235,000		260,000

The Sunday newspapers range from the tabloid *News of the World* to quality papers such as the *Observer* and the *Sunday Times*. The popular ones reach fantastic circulations; that of the *News of the World,* at six and a half million, constitutes the world record. Like the dailies, these newspapers also have their political affinities, but are, roughly, evenly balanced.

RADIO. Radio is organized quite differently from the way it is in the United States. One single corporation (the British Broadcasting Corporation) is responsible for all sound broadcasting, although extensive provision is made for regional variations in programs. The B.B.C. is a public corporation, whose directors are nominated by the government, and its charter stipulates that it must use its services to disseminate information, education, and entertainment. It is forbidden to accept commercial advertisements, must refrain from expressing any editorial opinion, and is expected to be impartial in presenting current affairs and politics. From time to time, each political party is given facilities for a "Party Political Broadcast," the proportion accorded to each party being decided after consultation between them. Politically and socially, the effect of the B.B.C. is prodigious, especially since it is a monopoly and is neutral, for practically every household has a receiving set.

TELEVISION. Until 1954, the B.B.C. enjoyed a monopoly of television as well as of radio broadcasting. Since then, it has had to share the field with a second body, the Independent Television Authority (I.T.A.). The I.T.A. owns and operates television stations for programs which are provided by outside companies. The programs are not sponsored, as in the United States, but the program companies sell time for spot announcements at intervals throughout their broadcasts. The I.T.A. is responsible for regulating the system and for securing proper standards in the programs. It must see, for example, that the companies are impartial in presenting matters of political controversy and accurate in news reporting. Political advertising is forbidden, and the I.T.A. has been extremely strict in interpreting this provision. For instance, it refused to sanction an advertisement for the Communist *Daily Worker* on the ground that it was a political rather than a commercial advertisement.

Today, over two-thirds of the families in Britain own television sets. Special provision is made for regional variations of programs, notably for Scotland, Wales, and Northern

The Foundations of British Politics

Ireland. Yet the main effect of television is to emphasize and to create uniformities. It brings national leaders rather than local ones into the home. By excellent documentary features such as "Tonight" and "Panorama" (both B.B.C.), it focuses wide attention on national issues. Independent (i.e., commercial) television creates an additional set of uniformities through its effect on consumer tastes—by the products which it advertises throughout the country. In all these ways, television is the most compelling instrument of "nationalization" in British society. While the mass media are "nationalizing" attitudes and eliminating regional and religious difference, forces are also at work flattening out social inequalities.

THE REDISTRIBUTION OF THE NATIONAL INCOME. The national income has grown from nearly £5 billion in 1938 to some £21 billion in 1959 (Table 2-5). Even after the necessary adjustment for the inflation of prices, this represents a leap from £13.5 billion to £21 billion at 1959 prices. Between 1948 and 1959, the percentage increase in real terms was 33 per cent. The labor force, only 19 million at the census of 1931, had risen to 24 million by the end of 1960.

Together with these developments have gone various leveling factors. For one thing, a greater share of the national income now goes to those who are employed and a lesser share to those collecting rents, dividends, and

interest; the former took 60 per cent of the total in 1938, but 70 per cent in 1959, while the latter, which took 22.5 per cent in 1938, took only 11.5 per cent twenty years later. Secondly, and particularly since the war, the wages and salaries of the less well-paid have risen proportionately more than those of the better paid and more than professional earnings. These two factors are reflected in Table 2-6. It shows the proportion of the national

TABLE 2-6   *Distribution of Personal Income before Taxes, 1938 and 1955* [a]

Population, in order of income	Percentage of total national income before taxes	
	1938	1955
First 100,000	11.7%	5.3%
First 500,000	21.5	12.3
First 1,000,000	27.8	17.4
First 5,000,000	51.6	42.6
Remainder	48.4	57.4

[a] Source: Carr-Saunders, Jones, and Moser, *Social Conditions in England and Wales* (London: Oxford University Press, 1958), p. 181.

income taken by various classes of persons, in 1938 as compared with 1955. As you can see, the richer have become less rich, the poor have become better off. For example, the top 100,000 persons in income in 1938 received 11.7 per cent of the nation's income, but in 1955 they only received 5.3 per cent.

Note that these proportions are of income *before* taxes. Taxation has become more progressive since the war. Thus there were 405,000 *gross* incomes of over £2,000; after taxation, there were only 195,000.

THE TRANSFORMATION OF THE LABOR FORCE. The 1951 census showed that less than a third of the male work force and less than a quarter of the female work force were employed in manual occupations in mining and manufacturing. This reflects a long-term trend away from manual labor in favor of organizational, clerical, or distributive occupations—and from wage-earning to salary-earning. Since 1900, agricultural employment has steadily declined and so has employment in mining and tex-

TABLE 2-5   *Gross National Product* [a]

	Pounds (in millions)	Dollars (in millions)	Population (in millions)	Dollars per capita
1945	8,750	24,500	43.7	561
1946	8,787	24,604	46.8	526
1950	11,695	32,746	50.2	652
1955	16,936	47,421	51.0	932
1959	20,882	58,470	52.0	1,127
1960 (est.)	22,100	61,880	52.4	1,340

[a] £1 = $2.80.

tiles: On the other hand, employment has steadily increased in the chemical, metal, engineering, and automobile industries. Private domestic employment, mostly of women, declined by almost one million between 1901 and 1951, while administrative and clerical work, and jobs in the distributive trades, all employing large numbers of women, have greatly expanded.

These trends continue. From 1939 to 1959, the numbers employed in professional, financial, and miscellaneous services (i.e., in tertiary employment) and in local government rose by an estimated 300,000, while the number of "staff" (as against "operative") employees in manufacturing rose by 400,000. Allowing for similar changes in transport, distribution, etc., it appears that salaried workers rose by one million. During the same period, the number of manual workers fell by half a million. It is estimated that by 1959 the number of salaried workers had risen from 30 per cent to 34 per cent of the population.

In short, the British labor force is more "white collar" and perhaps "middle class" than at any time in the past, and appears to be becoming more so. The redistribution of incomes in favor of the poor and these occupational shifts are beginning to blur the sharp class divisions that the Industrial Revolution created. British society is becoming somewhat more equal and is being transformed in that direction by still another factor—the changes in the educational system.

SOCIAL MOBILITY AND EDUCATION.   In Britain, one of the principal hallmarks of "class" is occupation. The 1951 census divides the population into five main classes (Table 2-7). Class I explains itself. Class II consists largely of lesser professional, administrative, and managerial occupations, and of farmers, shopkeepers, and small employers. Class III consists of skilled manual workers, shop assistants, typists, foremen, and the like. The last two classes comprise, for the most part, the operatives and workmen in field, factory, and workshop—the "manual working class" proper.

In 1950, Professor D. V. Glass and his associates completed an extensive survey into

TABLE 2-7   *Census Classification of Males by Occupation, 1951*

	Social Class	Percentage
I	Professional occupations	3%
II	Intermediate occupations	15
III	Skilled occupations	53
IV	Partly skilled occupations	16
V	Unskilled occupations	13
		100%

the degree of social mobility in Britain. He used a scale based on the census, but with seven divisions instead of five. His investigations showed that in the two top classes 54 per cent stayed in the same class as their parents, and 46 per cent fell to a lower class. In the two bottom classes, 53 per cent rose and 47 per cent stayed in their parents' class. Thus there was extensive mobility, but it produced a similar structure, since the movements largely balanced one another. The principal cause of this mobility is less likely to be individual aggressiveness or laziness than alterations in the occupational structures discussed above: for since the beginning of the century, the number of middle-prestige (Class III) occupations has grown.

Since education greatly affects occupation and occupation is one of the chief determinants of social class, the educational system is obviously a crucial element in the class structure. In England, the so-called "public" schools are, in fact, entirely private establishments, and mostly boarding schools. The greatest of them, Eton, Harrow, Winchester, etc., offer a much better education than does the typical state school. Since they are expensive, their pupils are drawn from a narrow social group. They inculcate an intensive group loyalty among their pupils, so that the "old-school tie" or "old-boy network" proves to be a significant factor in a pupil's career. To the egalitarians in British society, the public schools are "islands of privilege."

The Foundations of British Politics

33

The state school system consists of a small number of "direct-grant" schools and a greater number of "maintained" schools. Direct-grant schools are day-schools of the public-school type, but they receive public funds, which are granted directly from the Ministry of Education and not through the local education authority. The maintained schools are run by the local authorities and are divided into primary and secondary levels. The secondary schools are either of the "Technical," "Modern," or the "Grammar" type. Modern Schools are designed for children who (on the strength of a competition or a school record adjudged at 11 years) are regarded as suitable for a practical and non-literary education. The Grammar Schools offer their students literary and scientific training designed to prepare them for colleges of technology and universities and eventual professional work. Until 1944, secondary education was not free, but bright pupils from poor homes could qualify to have their fees remitted. It was, however, possible and usual for parents to place a child by paying the fee. The Education Act of 1944 abolished this and threw all places open to merit.

Up to the outbreak of World War II, it was not easy for poor pupils to go to a university. Nearly all students had to pay their own fees and maintain themselves, for scholarships were neither lavish nor plentiful. Since 1945, however, it is broadly true that any student who is accepted by a university can apply to his local authority for a scholarship and is not likely to be refused. Thus since 1944 the opportunities for poor children have greatly expanded. Today, 27 per cent of the university population comes from working-class homes, whereas in the 1930's the proportion was less than half of this. In the 1930's, about one-third of the university population came from the secondary Grammar Schools, while today, in a university population that has doubled in size, two-thirds of

the students come from such schools. Thus, very roughly, those who go to a university from the well-to-do homes are, in absolute numbers, about the same as before the war; but those who come from the poorer homes are four times as numerous.

At the most, 3–5 per cent of the school population goes to the "public" (i.e., private) schools; the remainder go through the state system. Table 2-8 compares the educational situation in 1921 with that in 1951. (The years 1921 and 1951 were chosen because in both years the census asked the relevant questions.)

TABLE 2-8 *Proportion of the Population Attending Educational Establishments Full-time in England and Wales, 1921 and 1951* [a]

	Number per 1,000 in each age group	
	1921	1951
Age 10–14 (roughly, elementary)	809	984
Age 15–19 (roughly, secondary)	62	148
Age 20–24 (roughly, university)	10	26

[a] Adapted from Carr-Saunders, *et al., Social Conditions in England and Wales,* p. 58.

The number of university students, which rose from 83,000 in 1951 to 110,000 in 1959, is expected to be 170,000 in 1970. This expanding population of secondary-school and university graduates will have a further modifying effect on social mobility, and on class structure. Table 2-9 shows the clear relationship between education and occupation.

For a variety of reasons—economics is not the sole one—children of manual workers tend to leave school earlier than children of parents in non-manual occupations, and, of course, a great deal of native ability is thus wasted. This pattern is changing today, however; more are staying on at school and more therefore can be expected to proceed to a university.

Among the pupils of the secondary Grammar Schools, the occupations that pupils take up are closely related to their parents' occu-

TABLE 2-9 *Occupation of School Graduates by Type of School* [a]

	Grammar and Technical School		Modern School	
	Boys	Girls	Boys	Girls
Further education and professional work	24%	30%	—	—
Other non-manual work	22	62	13%	53%
Skilled manual work	25		50	
		4 [b]		39 [b]
Unskilled manual work	4		28	
Armed forces	24	N.A.	5	N.A.

[a] Source: *15 to 18*, Vol. II (London: Her Majesty's Stationery Office, 1960), p. 35.
[b] Skilled and unskilled figures combined.
N.A. = not available.

pations. Those that continue their education (primarily to the universities) come mostly (26 per cent) from the sons of professional and managerial parents, and only 8 per cent from fathers in the unskilled manual-laboring class. Although 28 per cent of the sons of skilled manual workers and 36 per cent of those whose fathers are unskilled go on to do skilled manual work, only 15 per cent of the sons of professional-managerial workers and 18 per cent of those of other non-manual workers enter into this kind of work. These striking examples of occupational continuity, however, are not all due to the pressure of economic circumstances. The highest proportion of school graduates (14 per cent) to record that they took a job because "they had no choice" or "only suitable job available" was from among those taking up clerical posts; the next highest (12 per cent) was from those taking up semi-skilled and unskilled manual work. Yet on the average, only *one in ten* gave this answer.

These changes that are already evident in education, then, will increasingly enable worker-sons to enter professional or managerial occupations, and the resultant occupational mobility will continue to erode the old nineteenth-century class structure.

AFFLUENCE AND THE REACCEPTANCE OF CAPITALISM. When the Second World War ended, in 1945, many people in Britain were disillusioned with capitalism and considered it wasteful, inefficient, and inhuman. The critics of capitalism charged that it was incapable of fully utilizing either the human or the productive forces of industry and that, by its nature, it must alternately boom and bust. Riding the crest of this feeling, the Labour Party swept to victory in 1945 (to the surprise of most of the citizens of the United States). The Labour Party honored its pledge to intensify the planning of the economy by nationalizing the key fuel and power, transport, and steel industries and by extensively regulating and controlling what remained of the private economy. The Conservatives, on their return to power in 1951, reversed the trend to public ownership.

The standard of living, almost stationary between 1945 and 1951, rose by over 2 per cent per year from 1951 to 1959. The eight-year increase was as much as for the entire 1918–39 period, and, as we have seen, the income was more evenly distributed than it was in the interim between the World Wars. The relaxation of consumer credit controls permitted working people to spend their swollen earnings on consumer durables: washing machines, television sets, cars, and houses. Between 1956 and 1959, the more prosperous half of the working class (one-third of the electorate or some 12 million adults) doubled its ownership of such goods. By 1959, 83 per cent of these households owned a television set, 44 per cent a washing machine, 44 per cent a lawnmower, 32 per cent a car, 16 per cent a refrigerator, and 35 per cent either owned or were buying a house.[2]

Britain today, like the United States, has been called an "affluent society," and the nation's new wealth has brought an enormous prestige to business and the businessman. Informed observers are wondering whether the

[2] Mark Abrams, "New Roots of Working Class Conservatism," *Encounter* (May, 1961), 57–59.

The Foundations of British Politics

capitalism of the nineteenth century, the capitalism that divided Britain into "two nations," rich and poor, still exists or whether it has not, in fact, so transformed itself as to be something else, which has not yet received a name. Perhaps, they submit, the present phase in British society ought to be termed "post-capitalist." The very fact that such a question can be raised is another sign that the legacy of the Industrial Revolution—the sharp cleavage of British society into the wealthy and the indigent, owners and industrial proletariat—is beginning to disappear and is no longer even what it was twenty years ago.

SOCIAL CLASS. Thus far we have talked about wealth, education, and occupation, but these are all related to a fourth factor, social class. The essence of social class lies in the notion of superiority-inferiority, in the idea that some people are considered to rank (by some criterion or other) higher or lower than other people. There are two elements in establishing the rank-ordering of social class. The first is the *objective* element; granted that certain people are more esteemed than others, by what external characteristics (wealth, dress, speech, etc.) are they recognized as such? The second is the *subjective* element; given that certain people are, say, wealthier or pursue a certain type of occupation, how does society rank them?

A survey carried out by Dr. Mark Abrams in 1956 showed that:

1. British society recognizes some occupations as solid middle class, others as lower middle class and others as upper working class or lower working class.
2. British society uniformly tends to assign a given occupation to the same rank. The labels attached to any particular occupation were the same irrespective of the wealth, age, or sex of the persons questioned.
3. British society not only distinguishes be-

tween these four groups. It ranks them in order of prestige, with solid middle class at the top and lower working class at the bottom.

Dr. Abrams computed (from the census) the numbers of each occupation contained in the four classes and then determined the proportion of the population falling into each class (Table 2-10).

TABLE 2-10   *Social Classes in Britain, 1956* [a]

Class	Occupation	Percentage of all heads of households
1. Solid middle class	Doctors, company directors, senior university teachers, research scientists, factory managers, headmasters, technicians with professional qualifications, etc.	15%
2. Lower middle class	Schoolteachers, junior civil servants, small shopkeepers, skilled clerical workers, medical auxiliaries, etc.	20
3. Upper working class	Firemen, skilled workmen, shop assistants, etc.	30
4. Lower working class	Unskilled laborers, agricultural workers, railway porters, cleaners, etc.	35

[a] Source: Mark Abrams, "Class Distinctions in Britain," in *The Future of the Welfare State* (London: Conservative Political Centre, 1958), p. 67.

Dr. Abrams found that these classes differ in other respects than just occupation, however.

WEALTH. Net assets varied from about £10,000 in the solid middle class to £2,000 in the lower middle class to about £700 in the upper working class and £300 in the lower working class. Thus among the 15 per cent of the solid middle class, the average wealth was perhaps thirty times that of the lower working-class families. *Wealth is much more unequally distributed in Britain than in-*

come, despite death-duties of great severity for the larger estates.

INCOME. The solid middle-class earners tended to make over £1,000 per annum and most of them made over £1,500. The lower middle-class range was £750–£1,000. The upper working-class range was £500–£750 and the lower working-class range below £500.

DURABLE CONSUMER GOODS. In 1956, Dr. Abrams noted that the higher the class the more durable consumer goods (except for television sets) its members owned. But this is no longer as true in 1960, owing to the huge rise in working-class expenditures on consumer durables in the last few years.

EDUCATION. Despite the extended facilities under the 1944 Education Act and the figures already quoted, it was still true in 1956 that although 60 per cent of the children of solid middle-class families stayed at school beyond the age of fifteen, only 5 per cent of those of the lower working class remained at school after that age.

There are, however, important similarities between the various classes.

EDUCATION. The educational difference stated above should not be over-stressed. Looking at the educational statistics another way, we see that 40 per cent of the solid middle class and 68 per cent of the lower middle class had a similar educational experience to that of the working class; i.e., they, too, left school at age fifteen.

POPULAR ENJOYMENTS AND TASTES. To a large extent, the middle class and the working class share the same taste for newspapers, films, and television shows. "In at least one sense," writes Richard Hoggart, "we are becoming classless—that is the great majority of us are being merged into one class. We are becoming culturally classless." [3]

Although the British people as a whole agree on the existence of social classes and on which occupations "belong" to which class, individuals differ considerably when asked to what class they assign *themselves.* When members of the public are asked to assign themselves to a class, the procedure is called *self-rating.* Dr. Abrams discovered that the numbers in the classes as *self-rated* differ importantly from the numbers as rated *objectively* by the sociologist, as listed in Table 2-7.

For example, according to Dr. Abrams, the middle classes (solid and lower) must be regarded as comprising 35 per cent of the population and the working classes (upper and lower) 65 per cent. Yet the British Institute of Public Opinion (Gallup Poll) shows that the self-rating of individuals is different from this. In 1955, only 53 per cent of the respondents assigned themselves to the working class; in March, 1959, only 49 per cent; in September, 1959 (with the election imminent), only 52 per cent. These figures are not inconsistent with the findings of Dr. Abrams' post-election survey of 1956; he found that of the persons he assigned to the working class, 30 per cent assigned *themselves* to the middle class.

It should be stressed that in her long history Britain has experienced nearly all the catastrophic social cleavages that make democracy so precarious in the emergent nations of today. The fusion of Scots, Welsh, Irish, and English into one peaceful political community was neither natural nor inevitable, nor did it occur peacefully and all at once. Scotland and England were at war for some 500 years before they joined together in the Treaty of Union. The peoples of the islands were killing one another for the sake of religion not much more than three hundred years ago. English did not become the majority language in Wales and the common tongue of Ireland until the nineteenth century. Tribe, nationality, religion—all have struggled against one another; yet today, none of these is politically significant.

The Foundations of British Politics

---

[3] Richard Hoggart, *The Uses of Literacy* (London: Pelican, 1961), p. 284.

These "lateral" divisions that tend to split society into a number of watertight compartments have all but been erased. Today the only cleavage of political significance is the "horizontal" division into social and economic classes. Perhaps that is the reason why British academics and intellectuals, not to speak of visiting Americans, are so obsessed by "class." In an otherwise homogeneous society, this one difference sticks out like a sore thumb.

British society is still unequal. The top 1 per cent of the population draw 5 per cent (after taxes) of the national income, and the top 20 per cent draw 38 per cent (after taxes). Wealth is much more unequally distributed than income, and those who possess it are able to add to it by capital gains, which are very lightly taxed in Britain. Since the public schools charge fairly stiff fees, the wealthy buy a better education, and one with more prestige, for their children than does the rest of the community. Educational opportunities are therefore still unequal, and education is the key to occupation, which, in turn, is the key to social and economic class. Consequently, the higher ranks of industry and commerce, of the Civil Service, and of the armed forces are still disproportionately manned by the products of the public schools. At the other end of the social scale, certain manual occupations such as the dockers and miners are so fiercely aloof from the rest of society that they are almost tribal in their occupational loyalty. In between these two poles, we find the new social phenomenon of the "rising working class," the manual wage earners who regard themselves as moving up the social scale into the middle class and who have been tending (so the surveys show) to follow the Conservative Party as the party of "ambitious, forward-looking people." Shifts in occupation and the equalization of wealth and educational opportunity have produced this group, and its emergence indicates that a more equal and less hierarchical society is evolving in Britain.

Social Foundations

Dr. Mark Abrams, whose essay on "Class-Distinctions in Britain" we have cited before, has made the estimates of voting behavior that appear in Table 3-1, based on the 1945, 1950, 1951, and 1955 General Elections.

TABLE 3-1 *Parliamentary Voting by Social Class*

	Solid middle class	Lower middle class	Upper working class	Lower working class
Percentage of total electorate	*(15%)*	*(20%)*	*(30%)*	*(35%)*
Conservative	85%	70%	35%	30%
Labour	10	25	60	65
Liberal, and others	5	5	5	5

Religion and the Roman Catholic Church play an important part in French and Italian politics. Nationalities play an important role in Canadian politics. The region—the South, for instance—is very significant in American politics. But in Britain, as we have seen, religious, racial, and regional groupings are no longer central to British politics. Are other social elements or groups important? And is any single element or group preponderant?

The Political Role of Social Class

Social class is an important factor in British political behavior. The class to which a voter assigns *himself* is a significant indicator of the way he is going to vote. Sociologists have also found that the class to which *they* assign a person (as determined by his occupation or his income) is closely related to his voting habits.

The Gallup Poll has also compiled estimates from which we can compare voting behavior in 1955 and 1959. Gallup's "classes" are different from Dr. Abrams', for they are based on income, not on occupation. But both findings tell the same story: the higher up the social scale, the greater the tendency to vote Conservative; the lower down the scale, the greater the tendency to vote Labour.

Thus from Table 3-2 we see that 57 per cent of the Conservative strength, totaling

TABLE 3-2 *Class Composition of Party Support, 1959* [a]

	Conservative		Labour		Liberal	
Well-to-do	1,240,000	9%	—	—	81,000	5%
Middle class	4,670,000	34	970,000	8%	465,000	28
Lower middle class and working class	7,180,000	52	9,269,000	76	930,000	56
Poor	690,000	5	1,950,000	16	180,000	11
	13,780,000	100%	12,189,000	100%	1,656,000	100%

[a] Based on Gallup Political Index, No. 2, February, 1960, Table 9. Percentages are rounded off to the nearest digit, so that there is a slight discrepancy between the totals of votes cast for each of the parties as shown here and the *official* totals which are given below in Table 4-1.

nearly 8 million votes, came from the lower middle class, the working class, and the poor, but from these sources the Labour Party drew 92 per cent of its strength—almost the whole—totaling some 11 million votes. From this we can conclude (1) that the Labour Party appeals almost exclusively to the two lower classes, while the Conservatives appeal to all classes except the poor and (2) that over half the Conservative strength comes from the two lower classes. Class is thus an important factor in voting behavior, although a very qualified one.

Public-School Men and the "Power Elite"

We have already mentioned the "public" schools, the independent schools that educate between 3 and 5 per cent of the school population, almost entirely on a fee-paying basis. No discussion of British politics and public life would be complete without mention of these schools, or, as their critics call them, these "islands of privilege." In 1955, about half the entrants to Oxford and Cambridge came from such schools. In 1958, an official committee, inquiring into the recruitment of officers to the armed forces, regretted that the candidates came from so few schools other than these. All the High Court judges but one, all the Bishops but one, about three-quarters of the Conservative M.P.'s and about one-fifth of the Labour M.P.'s attended these schools. The explanation behind these statistics derives from the social character of the public schools. Most of them are boarding schools. They are socially selective. Their teaching, which in the best of them is very good indeed, lays stress on character building, on leadership, and on tradition. The relative over-abundance of public-school men in the top ranks of industry and the Civil Service and in the House of Commons is not the result of a diabolical plot. Industry fills its ranks by open recruitment, the Civil Service by publicly formulated rules of competition, and the House of Commons by popular elections. Thus three entirely different methods of selection produce a similar result.

Although public-school men are found in substantial numbers in Parliament, in the higher Civil Service, and in the top ranks of industry, this by no means implies that they form a corporate body. They do not act identically nor do they have identical interests, for all their similar school backgrounds. They are important in the British political system for three main reasons. In the first place, their common school experience does tend to create a set of shared values that assists in producing a mutual understanding between Civil Service, industry, commerce, and, to some extent, Parliament. Secondly, this seemingly tight-knit group causes many to conclude that the top decision-making levels rest *exclusively* in the hands of a narrow social stratum, a view that generates egalitarian resentment. Thirdly, it makes British public life seem much more exclusive and static than in fact it is.

For the public schools inculcate in their pupils the "gentlemanly ideal," the old chivalric tradition of a bygone landed aristocracy. Such is the esteem that attaches to this tradition that newcomers to the ruling circles often try to adapt themselves to it and will usually, if sufficiently wealthy, send their children to public schools so that they too, may enjoy the social advantages which this kind of education unquestionably brings. Thus, at any one time, Britain appears to be governed by an exclusive "elite," although, in fact, there is, as we have seen, considerable movement into the higher walks of public life. The social origin changes but the "style" remains. Yet even if such an "elite" group did exist, it could not be said to be *the* ruling body in Britain. For there are many other powerful corporate bodies to offset any group that tries to rule: the Trades Union Congress, the Federation of British Industries, the National Farmers' Union, and many others. These organizations form a system of pressures and counterpressures; all government in Britain must accommodate itself to them.

Pressure Groups

In Britain, as in any democratic society, a plurality of groups represents the disparate views of the nation's citizens. The groups in the United Kingdom fall into two main types, with a hybrid type in between. The *interest groups* are those that have some kind of tangible stake in society, either a status or an economic good to lose or to gain. Groups with a "status" to lose might be, say, the universities or the churches. Groups with an economic stake are cooperatives, trade unions, and so on.

Organizations that have a propagandist aim we call *promotional groups*. They are out to promote a particular cause: pacifism, nuclear disarmament, the abolition of hanging and flogging, the protection of children or of animals, etc. The most important difference between these two types of associations is that the interest group is designed to serve the interests (material or non-material) of its *mem-*

bers, while a promotional organization works for a cause—it has its members carry billboards and *Peace News,* or march from Aldermaston on blistered feet, in an anti-nuclear demonstration.

Certain *hybrid groups* combine the features of both interest and promotional groups. A good example is the Roads Campaign Council, which advocates more and better highways. It is overtly financed by organizations that have a material interest in roads—for instance, the Automobile Association and the Royal Automobile Club—and also by such bodies as the Society of Motor Manufacturers and Traders. It is therefore the propagandist spokesman of certain interest groups. In addition, many interest groups (for instance, the National Union of Teachers) have a promotional side to their activities. The N.U.T. believes that education should be improved, but the group also enhances its own interests by promoting this worthy goal.

The Major Pressure Groups

EMPLOYERS. There are some 2,500 organizations in Britain that serve the many needs of commerce and industry. In a special category is the powerful National Farmers' Union, with 200,000 members, over 90 per cent of all the farmers of England and Wales. Another special association is the Institute of Directors. In mid-1962, its membership was 41,000, over 80 per cent of all the managers in the United Kingdom. Its object is to ease legal and financial restrictions on executives, e.g., to reduce corporate taxes, death duties, etc. It has jokingly described itself as the "bosses' trade union."

Of the major industrial associations, the British Employers' Confederation consists of 270 individual employers' negotiating bodies. It provides for consultation between its members and acts on general matters, but its constitution forbids it to interfere with its members' functions. The Federation of British

Industries (F.B.I.) and the National Union of British Manufacturers (N.U.B.M.), which are rivals, have a dual membership, partly individual firms and partly trade associations. The F.B.I. attracts the large firms, claims to represent six out of seven of the firms employing over eleven workers, and is incomparably the more important of the two. Its membership in 1960 was 8,000 individual firms and 300 trade associations, as opposed to 5,000 firms plus 70 trade associations for the National Union of British Manufacturers.

Whereas the F.B.I. and N.U.B.M. represent manufacturers, we find that merchants, insurance houses, shippers, truckers, etc., are associated locally in Chambers of Commerce, of which there are 100 in the country, and nationally in the Association of the British Chambers of Commerce (A.B.C.C.), which is a very influential body, representing about 60,000 firms.

THE TRADES UNIONS.   Excluding the armed forces, nearly 24 million persons are at work in Britain. Ten million belong to a trade union, and of these, 8,300,000 were affiliated (in 1961) with the Trades Union Congress. Although the constituent unions are autonomous, the Congress has developed an important headquarters staff that draws up policy and acts on mandates received from the Congress. The Congress does *not* negotiate wages. That is the concern of the individual unions.

THE COOPERATIVE MOVEMENT.   In 1957, there were 936 retail distributive societies in Britain, with a total membership of over 12 million people. There were also 4 wholesale societies and 38 productive societies. The sales turnover of the distribution societies amounted, in 1958, to nearly £1 billion. Almost all the societies were affiliated with the Co-operative Union, the principal organization of this movement. The Co-operative Party fights the political battles for the movement; it is supported by 623 of the societies, with 85 per cent of the total membership of the cooperatives.

THE PROFESSIONS.   Another group of interests consists of the professions. Three large organizations are often in the news. The British Medical Association (B.M.A.), the National Union of Teachers, and the National and Local Government Officers' Association (none of these is affiliated with the T.U.C.). Although the B.M.A. is not the only body representing the interests of doctors, it is *the* negotiating body for the profession par excellence, containing as it does some 80 per cent of the practitioners. The National Union of Teachers does not have a monopoly of representation either, but it does include in its membership about 80 per cent of the whole profession.

The National and Local Government Officers' Association, which recently celebrated its fiftieth anniversary, caters to the clerical and administrative grades of the local government service, not the manual workers. It counts in its membership about 180,000 out of some 200,000 such employees.

CIVIC GROUPS.   Among the interests that may be styled civic groups are charities (temperance societies, societies for the prevention of cruelty to children or to animals, family case-work agencies, etc.), various bodies that defend particular groups in government (the Magistrates Association, the Association of Municipal Corporations), and large organizations that advocate specific public policies and aspire to a mass following, of which the most influential at the moment is the Campaign for Nuclear Disarmament (C.N.D.). Founded in 1958, the C.N.D. is trying to persuade the British government to lay down its nuclear weapons "unilaterally," i.e., without waiting for the U.S.S.R. and the United States to disarm. The group also wants Britain to deny bases to the United States for nuclear missiles, aircraft, and submarines and to withdraw from NATO unless this alliance agrees to renounce the use of nuclear weapons. By organizing eye-catching appeals, public marches, and rallies in Trafalgar Square, the C.N.D. has won thousands of supporters to its cause and, in 1960, proved so influential in the trade unions that many of the largest ones declared their support for "unilateralism"; as a result, later in that year the Labour Party Conference rejected the official policy of its leaders and declared for a unilateralist policy. (The decision was reversed in 1961 and 1962, however.) Recently, a group called the "Committee of 100" broke away from the C.N.D. in order to pursue its policy of embarrassing the public authorities by civil disobedience. It organizes rallies and "sit down" demonstrations, and its members offer no resistance when they are carried into the waiting police vans and off to the police station.

Pressure Groups in Action

The groups or associations that habitually work closely with the government or with local authorities can exert pressure simply by breaking off relations, although this recourse is used only rarely. Pressure groups direct their fire at these targets: the executive, the legislature, and the general public.

THE EXECUTIVE LEVEL (GOVERNMENT DEPARTMENTS). Government departments and private associations generally cooperate with one another, since both sides stand to gain through the exchange of information, the sharing of each other's goodwill, etc. If the Ministry of Transport has to prepare emergency plans for maintaining transportation during a rail breakdown, for example, it would need the advice of dozens of trade associations. Between government administrators and private associations, there is an extensive system of both formal and informal contact. The formal arrangements comprise three chief methods.

1. By official inquiry, such as Royal Commissions, departmental inquiries, courts of arbitration, and the like. All interested parties put their views before such bodies.

2. By special advisory committees. Over 500 of these committees are attached to their appropriate Ministries and bring together civil servants and representatives of all the interested associations. They have meetings throughout the year, at which relevant matters are discussed.

3. Finally, there is the method of prior consultation. Ministries sometimes consult associations in advance of action. Bodies such as the Association of Municipal Corporations and the County Councils' Association have become almost official revising bodies for the administrative departments that make rules and orders affecting local government.

The formal contacts, however, are not nearly as important as the extensive informal contacts that continuously take place. Many of the arrangements are like those in a football match, where each player picks a particular man on the other side to attack. The director or secretary of a trade association "works to" certain civil servants in the various departments he frequents over a period of years, and is often on the best of personal terms with them.

Pressure can be and often is generated at the departmental level. To pursue a certain program, a director of a trade association might first go to his "opposite number" in the department and give "advice." If non-controversial, this might be acted on. But if it is not adopted, the association might send a more high-powered delegation, and its "advice" would become open advocacy. If this also failed to move the civil servants or the Minister, the association might decide upon more drastic action. It might sever relations with the governmental department and withdraw cooperation. But this is most abnormal. Its usual alternative would be to go to the top and try to influence Parliament.

THE PARLIAMENTARY LEVEL. Members of Parliament are frequently representatives of special "interests" themselves. They may belong to an outside association, such as the

Social Foundations

Institute of Directors; they may be approached by some interest, e.g., the textile or pottery industry, that is prominent in their constituency; they may be asked by an outside interest to sit on its "Parliamentary Panel," i.e., to act as its spokesman in Parliament.

More importantly, the two great parties themselves incorporate many important interests. As we shall see later, 87 Trades Unions are affiliated with the Labour Party; they provide it with much if not most of its money, they finance individual candidates, and they command an overwhelming majority of votes at the Party Conference. Ninety-two of the Labour Party's 256 seats in the present Parliament are held by Trades Union-sponsored candidates. Similarly, 18 are held by Co-operative-sponsored candidates. No interest groups are affiliated with the Conservatives, although most of the organizations of employers, industry, trade, and commerce must be regarded as being aligned with the Conservative Party. The link is not, as in the Labour Party, by organizations qua organizations; it is a personal linkage. Members of these organizations are often members of, or give support to (by money or assistance), the Conservative Party.

A group that has failed to get satisfaction from the Minister or the civil servants (i.e., the executive) may therefore try to exert pressure by raising the matter in the House of Commons. Pressure of this sort is usually checked by the very firm discipline exerted on each party by the Whips, but sometimes a particular interest may win enough sympathy in Commons, with both the majority party and the Opposition, to force a Minister to change his mind. The legislative influence of pressure groups is often focused on the committee and report stages of bills, when detailed amendments are introduced. It is here, particularly, that little "caves" of Government backbenchers and/or Opposition

members come together and try to secure specific changes.

Some pressure groups, however, dislike having their policy handled in Commons. The leaders of the British Medical Association prefer to negotiate directly with the Ministry of Health rather than have some M.P. state their views in Commons. The National Farmers' Union has acted similarly. If such organizations fail in their attempts, of course, they might get "their" Members to argue their case on the floor of the House.

THE CONSTITUENCY LEVEL. The third and widest area of political pressure is at the level of the constituency. In Britain (unlike in the United States), pressure groups operate comparatively rarely at this level. Such activity is most effective at election time, but in British elections, party candidates stick to the party line laid down by the party headquarters. Individual promises to local groups are discouraged by the central headquarters of both the Labour and the Conservative Parties. It is therefore very difficult for pressure groups to operate at the constituency level to anything like the degree that occurs in America or France, where party structures are so different.

Pressure groups conduct two kinds of publicity campaigns: the selective type and the saturation type. The selective campaign is directed at the individuals who are the "opinion-makers" in their field: local journalists, churchmen, schoolteachers, university teachers, doctors, members of Rotary Clubs, Chambers of Commerce, Trades Councils, etc. The saturation campaign (or "grass roots lobby") is comparatively rare and (apparently) relatively ineffective. Most of the saturation campaigns have been those used by capitalist interests against nationalization, but there is no evidence that these campaigns were successful. One reason may be that one does not get very far in Britain by simply advertising in the press, and, as we have seen, neither radio nor television can be used to transmit political propaganda.

Sometimes a pressure group will operate at

the executive, the parliamentary, *and* the constituency levels simultaneously. For instance, in 1947 commercial interests pressed the Labour government to amend the Transport bill to permit individual firms to continue to carry their own goods in their own vehicles. Their attack was directed to the public, to Parliament, and to the Ministry of Transport. Most pressure groups, however, concentrate on the administrative level, chiefly because the Cabinet is so pre-eminent in Parliament. If the Cabinet is prepared to espouse a policy, it usually is adopted. Even if only an individual Minister or the civil servants favor a program, it is likely to be put into effect.

A second reason for the importance of the administrative level is that the Ministries are in an excellent position to evaluate differing viewpoints. They consult with committees of inquiry, which are set up to enable interested parties to an issue to present their arguments, and with permanent advisory committees, on which civil servants and their opposite numbers in the pressure groups sit together. One of the first things a pressure group tries to do is acquire "consultative status," i.e., to get the Ministry to recognize that it is widely representative of a point of view and therefore worthy to be brought in for "advice and consent." This relationship is eagerly coveted, and organizations work hard to achieve it. It is regarded in Britain as the ideal tie between government departments and outside bodies. An informal code governs this relationship. As the director of one trade association described it:

The recognition which government departments give to any particular association depends primarily on the statesmanlike way with which the association handles its problems and on the confidence inspired by the staff in their dealings with government officials. Under such conditions mutual co-operation and understanding can be established on a basis which is not only satisfactory to both parties but can be very beneficial to the industry: the government officials will trust the staff sufficiently to inform and consult them on matters which are still highly confidential, without prejudice to the ultimate action of either party, but, if there is the slightest suspicion that the associations staff had failed to maintain the confidential nature of the information imparted to it, the government officials will shut up like clams and it will be a very long time before the association's staff is entrusted with inside information. . . .[1]

Not surprisingly, therefore, the most influential pressure groups tend to be the ones that are most silent. The Federation of British Industries or the County Councils Association or the Trades Union Congress usually achieve their results by consultation and discussion with the civil servants and Ministers. Bodies like the C.N.D., however, since they have no "foot in the door," must resort to public clamor. Nearly always, the noisier an interest group, the less effective it is.

The Value of Pressure Groups

In pursuing their own goals, the pressure groups actually perform several vital services in the functioning of British democracy: (1) They provide both Parliament and the administrators with technical information they would ordinarily not possess—for example, the exact dimensions of tires or the permissible width of trucks. Opposing pressure groups challenge inaccurate information. (2) They often challenge the government's policy and, conversely, give the government an idea of what the various groups, and through them the people, will accept in the way of new programs and legislation. The only other way a citizen could contact the government would be through the more restricted channel of approaching his M.P. or his local party organizations. (3) They sometimes provide administrative assistance or facilities to the government Departments.

The fact that the various pressure groups present so many points of view serves as a check and a balance to the power of the

[1] *Industrial Trade Associations* (London: Allen and Unwin, for P.E.P. [Political and Economic Planning], 1957), pp. 75–76.

government. In the absence of pressure groups, new policy presented to Parliament would probably be formulated exclusively by the parties' research departments and the Civil Service, both of which would be grievously handicapped without the information and advice supplied them by the associations.

WELL-ORGANIZED VS. POORLY ORGANIZED GROUPS. Industrial producers are very well organized in Britain, but consumers are not. The Institute for Consumer Research's influence is not equal to that of a railway or dock strike. Generally, organizations that are well organized and mobilized have a clear advantage over those that are not. *Les absents ont toujours tort* ("Those who are absent are always in the wrong"). The larger organizations frequently wield more power than the small ones. Great attention is paid to the big British Medical Association, which can marshal a large following, but not to the diminutive Fellowship for Freedom in Medicine. Those in a position to affect the country by direct action have a clear advantage over those who are not. Railwaymen on strike will inhibit the whole economy; not so a strike in the cosmetics industry. Those who have the power to harm (even though they do not exercise it) are better able to influence the government than those who have no such power at all. The British system of pressure groups does not consist of a set of evenly matched organizations, but of a series of groups of varying strengths, from the very powerful to the weak and innocuous. The system is biased towards industrial producers; it favors capital and labor over the rest of the community.

The pressure groups play a major part in the British political process. Yet, by and large, they are *not* a corrupting influence in British public life; they do *not* result in erratic and grossly inconsistent policy; and they do *not*

lead to the oppression of minorities—or indeed, of majorities. Britain remains the same justly governed country that it is usually represented to be. Without question, pressure groups tend to give a British government a distinctive bias—toward the trade unions when Labour is in power and toward the business and middle-class groups when the Conservatives rule. But this bias is moderated by the factors set out below, and the end result is that British Labour or Conservative governments are, like the renowned Irish judge, "neither partial nor impartial."

The three checks against undue distortion of government policies by pressure groups are (1) certain ancient and revered institutions; (2) well-defined governmental processes; and (3) public beliefs. First among the institutions is the Civil Service. Composed of well-trained and permanent career men, each Department in the course of its long and intimate dealings with the pressure groups has formed some kind of "departmental view" about them, and a pressure group has to have a strong case to win over the Department to its side. Another institutional check on the pressure groups are the political parties themselves. Each party must strike a balance between conflicting interests, and in the process of modifying the extreme positions of the contenders, the parties tend to reduce the warring factions into two more moderately opposed sides. Parliament and the press also help check the excesses of pressure groups. Both turn pitiless publicity on any deal they regard as "shady."

In addition to regulation by the political institutions of Britain, pressure groups must abide by the well-established procedures that govern the way the public interest is conducted. As we shall see when we consider the genesis of a bill and its consideration by Parliament, the whole process is based, from beginning to end, on maximum consultation with the affected interests at every stage. The Political Correspondent of *The Times* has written:

How many Bills get published without the responsible Minister spending cautious months in sounding every organization with any possible vested interest to ensure that the Bill will command broad agreement? Very few, if any; and it ought to surprise nobody that the average Bill should read like the compromise made in advance that it almost certainly is.

The Land Drainage Bill brought forward by the Government this session (1960) is an example. Nine years have passed since the Heneage Committee reported, and much of the interval was spent by successive Ministers of Agriculture in striking bargains with the river board interests, the farming interests, and the local authorities. The Licensing Bill is another case in point. Consistent with doing anything at all to alter licensing law, it is the product of consultations, we may take it, with the brewers, the licensed trade, and any union which represents barmen and barmaids. . . .

Of course the preparation of the ground for government action in this way is no new thing. But the practice has increased and is increasing as the isolated voices of a thousand and one sectional interests have been organized into protection associations and pressure groups to which ministers and governments may with more and more facility apply to smooth their path in carrying out a policy; and the consequence is that today many new Bills are more a form of administration than of government, and positively hundreds of sectional associations with the T.U.C., the N.F.U., and the F.B.I. at the head of the list have a built-in relationship with any government that may happen along in office.[2]

Extreme policies of the pressure groups are modified, finally, by the shared beliefs of the British community. These beliefs (one, for instance, is that it is the duty of government to promote full employment) are broadly held by all sections of the nation, and pressure groups whose claims conflict with these deep-seated views will invariably be thwarted in their goals. No pressure group can afford to argue that its policy is "good for the trade." It must show that it is "good for the country," for most Britons believe there is a "public interest" that must be respected, and feel a sense of outrage when it is not. In his essay, "In England, Your England," George Orwell, that pitiless but discerning critic, pointed out the essence of this characteristic:

Here one comes upon an all-important English trait: the respect for constitutionalism and legal-

[2] *The Times,* November 14, 1960.

ity, the belief in "the law" as something above the State and above the individual, something which is cruel and stupid, of course, but at any rate, *incorruptible.* . . . The totalitarians' notion that there is no such thing as law, there is only power, has never taken root.[3]

Big Business in Politics

Some observers, while agreeing that the producers' organizations are more influential than other groups in Britain, would go on to argue that those representing business are far more influential than those representing labor. This could hardly have been said of the period 1945–50, when a Labour government, closely tied to the Trades Unions, held office with a large majority. It was a very dubious proposition between 1951 and 1957, when the Conservatives were in power, since the Trades Unions were able to frustrate much of the government's economic policy. But since 1957, the power and prestige of the unions have appeared to falter and that of the business groups to have increased. One common complaint is that the business groups claim to be non-political but really do, in fact, enter the arena of political controversy. What about this issue of political participation? Who is "political" and who "non-political" in British public life?

The only bodies that belong organically to a political party and that contribute to its policy-making are those individual Trades Unions that are affiliated with the Labour Party and the cooperative societies that are affiliated with the Co-operative Party. Outside these, no particular groups belong to, or participate formally in, the policy-making of any political party. In this respect, the Federation of British Industries and the Institute of Directors are in exactly the same position as the T.U.C. The T.U.C. is *not* affiliated to the Labour Party and has made it quite

[3] George Orwell, *Selected Essays* (London: Penguin, 1957).

plain in public pronouncements that it does not regard itself as a politically motivated body. Nevertheless, it does discuss matters of public controversy; it undoubtedly espouses the cause of nationalization and social welfare benefits; and it advises its members to vote Labour. Yet, strictly speaking, since it is not party-affiliated, it is in exactly the same position as any kind of business group.

The term "political" can also be used to mean that a particular group is habitually aligned with one party or another. The business groups certainly tend to be aligned, through personal connections, with the Conservative Party. Yet the groups representing the owners or entrepreneurs in a particular industry sometimes make common cause with the Trades Unions representing the workers in that industry. They form a faction by banding together against the rest of the sectors of the economy. The most recent examples of this, having political repercussions, have occurred in the textile industry. Both the employers and the employees urged the government to restrict cheap imports from the East.

A more serious criticism is that "business," through its wealth, has an unfair advantage in industry and politics. Business groups and certain publicity organizations they support (such as the "Aims of Industry" or the "Economic League") do, indisputably, spend much more than labor organizations. But, as we have already seen, the effect of such expenditure is overrated. Certain bodies like the National Union of Teachers have had much success with successive postwar governments, but did little spending to achieve it. The medium open to the capitalist groups is limited to the press, for neither radio nor television is available for political purposes in Britain. Since these latter, more influential media are barred from presenting political advertising, Britain is assured that those with

the longest purse do not invariably win. Although business groups and firms are naturally economically powerful, since employers and managers direct the strategy of industry in the country, labor, too, is influential. It has weapons it can and does use, and, as a last resort, can go on strike. Industrial power, therefore, rests on both sides of the economic fence.

The charge that business is politically powerful takes us back to the power-elite theory with which we started. The capitalist groups are indeed politically significant at the moment, because they are aligned with the Conservative Party, which is in power. *But this is the result, and not the cause, of the popular verdict rendered at the last General Election.* As Left-wing critics tirelessly repeat, there is today a close personal link between the Conservative Party, including the Conservative Ministers who form the government, and outside business interests. But this is not a permanent condition. In 1945–51, when a Labour government was in power, there was an organic bond between the Labour Party, the Labour government, and the Trades Unions and Co-operatives.

Whatever the influence of business on the Conservative government today, it is not absolute but conditional. It is qualified by the voting power of the working class, for the Conservative Party has to keep the support of these seven million voters (including some one and a half million Trades Unionists) in order to stay in power.

Because of the inherent "veto" power of business and labor groups—their power, by non-cooperation, to thwart the government— these groups always exercise *some* influence over the government of the day. Generally speaking, labor has more influence with a Labour government and business with a Conservative government, although neither frame the policy of the government, but only qualify it. Labor and business groups cannot impose policies on the government that would not be tolerated by the electorate. The parties must "sell" their programs to the people, and thus what they can adopt from "their" pressure groups is always qualified by this central feature of British politics.

The influence of business or of labor waxes and wanes according to the complexion of the government, but this is decided by the electorate. If business is influential with a Conservative government, it is so by the verdict of a free election. And it is the parties, not the pressure groups, that mobilize the electors, fight the election, and organize the House of Commons. To these we must now turn.

Political Parties and Elections

IV

The two major parties in Britain are both highly disciplined, and they both enjoy a hard core of electoral support that since 1945 has never sunk much below 40 per cent of the total electoral vote. The candidates of both parties must agree to support their party's platform, and they must be accepted by their party headquarters if they are to enjoy the help of the national party machine at election time—and without it they are most unlikely to win. In the House of Commons, the party members act, for the most part, with iron discipline; abstention from voting with the party is not common, and cross-voting is almost unknown.

The two-party system is the key to understanding the present operation of the British government. This system is responsible for the following factors:

1. The near-certainty that one party or the other will be returned with a clear and working majority in Parliament.

2. The formation of a Cabinet drawn from the majority party.

3. The stability of the Cabinet, since its party majority is disciplined.

4. The assurance that the Cabinet can last out the full term of Parliament's life.

5. The unambiguous responsibility of the Cabinet for all that has happened during its period of office.

6. The presentation to the electorate of a clear choice between the Government party, running on its performance, and the Opposition party, running on its promise.

The importance of the two-party system in British government cannot be over-stressed. British government is government by the Cabinet. The Houses of Parliament act as a checking and controlling force, but the directing and energizing element is the Cabinet, which is *collectively* responsible for its policy to Parliament, and beyond Parliament to the people. This collective responsibility for policy is based on the monolithic nature of the party majority that supports it. In France, until the coming of the Fifth Republic, the Cabinet was never really a collective unity (although the Constitutions of the Third and Fourth Republics said that it had to behave like one), because its parliamentary support fluctuated. If Cabinets in Britain were regularly overthrown by temporary combinations of various parliamentary groups, as indeed they were between 1851 and 1868, the legislature would, in effect, formulate policy. Legislative initiative would prevail and not, as at present, Cabinet initiative. Such was the character of the French parliamentary system under the Third and Fourth Republics. And such was the character of British government in 1923–24 and in 1929–31, when minority Labour Cabinets held office and were liable at any time to be defeated by a combination of their Conservative and Liberal opponents. The short lives of those two Cabinets, compared with the usual duration of some four and a half years, tell their own story.

The History of the Parties

Today the two main parties are the Conservative and Labour Parties. The Liberal Party is a remnant left over from earlier days of power and responsibility. The Communist Party is negligible.

1688–1830: WHIGS AND TORIES. The parties really began just before the Revolution of 1688, although some trace them back past the Restoration of 1660 into the time when the conflict was King versus Parliament (1640–60).

"WHIG" AND "TORY." The whole period, 1688–1830 was dominated by these two factions, or alliances—the Whigs and the Tories. The backbone of the Whigs was the family connection of the great landed magnates, who formed a veritable oligarchy. Their allies among the humbler folk, which gave them a national backing, were the Protestant sects (known as Noncomformists) who were outside of and opposed to the established Church of England, together with the traders, and the commercial interests who had recently backed the newly founded central Bank of England. The Tories were mostly drawn from the lesser landholders (squires) and were closely allied with the Church of England. For some time after 1714, when the Whigs engineered the accession of the German King of Hanover (George I) to the throne instead of the son of the last Stuart King, James II, whom the Tories had tried to bring back, the Tories were tainted with a suspicion of treason to the dynasty. After 1760, George III turned out his Whig Ministers and installed the Tories. With three brief intervals, they governed Britain from 1760–1830.

1830–1846. The Tory majority in the Commons dissolved in 1830, and, amid huge popular excitement, which later turned into agitation and rioting, the Whig aristocracy formed a Cabinet pledged to reform the corrupt electoral system that had permitted the Tories to perpetuate their power between 1760 and 1830. With the Reform Bill of 1832, the modern history of the parties begins, as we have seen. First, the Whigs were in power (1830–41), then the Tories, who began to call themselves Conservatives. The Whigs, supported by the M.P.'s from Ireland and by Left-wing radicals, were the party of non-conformity, of commerce, and the new industry. The Tories stood for the Church of England and for the agricultural interests, but Sir Robert Peel, the Tory Prime Minister in 1841, began to move his party closer to the manufacturers. In 1846, however, his Conservative government split into two factions when he decided to bow to the free-trade views of the manufacturers and repeal the protective duties on corn. One band consisted of his own devoted followers (notably William Gladstone) and the other of a rabble of inarticulate squires led by the young Jewish-born Benjamin Disraeli.

1846–1868. The split ushered in a period of predominantly Whig rule, to which the Peelites after Peel's death in 1851 tended more and more to adhere. The amalgam of Whigs and Peelites gradually became known as the Liberals. The Tories slowly gathered strength and soon abandoned protectionism, but in other respects their devotion to the Anglican Church and to the land remained as before, while the Liberals increasingly depended on non-conformity, industry, and commerce. This was primarily a period of three- or even four-party rule; Whigs, Peelites, Radicals, and the Irish formed a rather loose alliance, with the Conservatives in opposition. The period ended with both main parties espousing a new Reform Act (1867). By enfranchising the artisan class of the towns and expanding the electorate from one to two and one-quarter million people, the Act broke the political deadlock. The parties had to find new and popular issues to attract the new electors, and they also had to organize them. Contemporary party structure may be said to begin from the election of 1868.

1868–1886: LIBERAL AND CONSERVATIVE. This period was the heyday of Gladstone, the Liberal leader, and Disraeli, who led the Conservatives. Governments were stable and long-lived, strengthened as they were by somewhat more disciplined majorities. Of the two parties, the Liberals were the less homogeneous. When Mr. Joseph Chamberlain and his Radicals joined the party on its extreme left, they alienated the old Whig aristocrats and left Mr. Gladstone with the job of healing the breach in the party.

The rise of Irish nationalism, led by Charles Parnell, provoked a catastrophic shift in party alignments. Parnell removed his Irish party from association with the Liberals and made it an independent force. In 1886, Gladstone decided to introduce a Home Rule bill for Ireland, which had the effect of driving both his Left wing (the Chamberlain Radicals) and Right wing (the old Whigs) out of the party, to the other side of the House. This brought his government down and ushered in a period of "Unionist" rule. "Unionist" denoted the supporters of the Act of Union of Ireland and Great Britain (passed in 1800)

who were thus opponents of Home Rule. The group comprised both the original Conservatives *plus* the refugees from the Liberal Party. Gradually these groups merged into the "Conservative and Unionist Party," which is the official title of the Conservative Party today.

1886–1915. The Liberals stood for Irish Home Rule, for free trade, and, increasingly, for the trade unions. The Conservatives became the party of Union with Ireland, of imperialism, and, increasingly, of protection. The Conservatives dominated politics until 1906 when they were badly defeated by the Liberals, who ruled from 1906 to 1915.

Meanwhile, however, the trade unions had begun to break away from their dependence on the Liberal Party. In 1900, some of them formed the Labour Representation Committee with the object of attaining independent working-class representation in the House of Commons. This move succeeded in forcing the Liberals to negotiate a number of electoral deals with the Labour Committee. In 1906, 29 Labour M.P.'s were elected, and the Labour Representation Committee changed its name to the Labour Party. Thus a third party was born. After the 1910 election, the Liberal Party commanded a majority of the House only with the support of Labour and the Irish (who had, since Parnell's death, returned to their alignment with the Liberals).

1915–1922. World War I brought the Liberals and the Conservatives together in an uneasy coalition in 1915. The Coalition fought and won the "khaki" election (1918), but the Liberal Prime Minister, David Lloyd George, in his electoral arrangements with his Conservative allies, decided not to endorse a number of Liberal candidates, among them the former Prime Minister and leader of the Liberal Party, Herbert Asquith. This maneuver split the Liberals in two—one group being led by Lloyd George, the other by Asquith. In 1922, the Conservative backbenchers decided to quit the Coalition and fight the next General Election on their own (Fig. 4-1). Lloyd George, having no majority behind him, re-

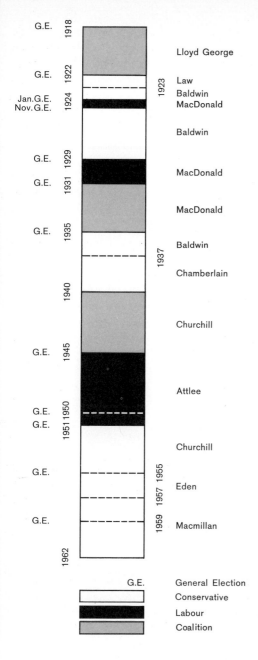

		G.E.	General Election
		Conservative	
		Labour	
		Coalition	

FIGURE 4-1 BRITISH CABINETS SINCE 1918.

the official Opposition. The Conservatives won and formed the new government. In the 1923 election, the Conservatives lost their absolute majority and were defeated in the House. The King called on Labour leader Ramsay MacDonald to form a Cabinet. Since this first Labour government was a minority one that rested on tacit Liberal support, when this support was withdrawn in 1924 the Labour government was defeated in the House, and the Prime Minister, getting the King's consent for a dissolution of Parliament, called for a General Election. The Conservatives were returned with an absolute majority; the Labour Party lost some seats, but the Liberals sank from 159 seats to 40. Its annihilation as a political force dates from 1924.

In 1929, Labour came back as the largest of the three parties and formed the second (minority) Labour government. Caught almost immediately in the great depression, the government foundered in 1931, and another coalition of Conservatives and Liberals, and a few Labour Members, called the National Government, was formed, with Ramsay MacDonald as Prime Minister. Some Labour and half the Liberals left in 1932 when the Conservative-dominated Cabinet decided to introduce protective tariffs. From then on, the so-called National Government was really the Conservative Party, and from 1935, when MacDonald quit the Prime Ministership, the Prime Ministers were Conservatives.

1940–1945. The disastrous handling of the beginning of World War II by Prime Minister Neville Chamberlain led to a hostile vote in the House in 1940 that forced him to resign and make way for Winston Churchill, who presided over a Coalition government of Conservatives, Labour, and Liberals, until the end of the war.

1945–1960. Labour was returned in 1945

signed. Parliament was dissolved, and a General Election took place.

1922–1940. Contesting the election as a divided party, the Liberals lost so heavily that the new Labour Party emerged as the second largest party and supplanted the Liberals as

Political Parties and Elections

53

with an enormous majority (see Table 4-1). In the 1950 election, however, the Conservatives staged a powerful revival, and the Labour Party had an absolute majority of only six seats. Nevertheless, it managed to endure for eighteen months. In the election of 1951, although it polled more popular votes than the Conservatives, it was defeated, and the Con-

TABLE 4-1. *General Elections since 1945*

	Total electorate	Total voting	Percentage voting	Conservative and allied vote	Percentage of votes cast	Labour and allied vote	Percentage of votes cast	Liberal votes	Percentage of votes cast	Other votes	Percentage of votes cast
1945	32,836,419	24,082,612	73.5%	9,577,667	39.8%	11,632,891	48.3%	2,197,191	9.1%	674,863	2.8%
1950	34,269,764	28,769,477	84.0	12,101,983	43.5	13,295,736	46.4	2,621,489	9.1	350,269	1.9
1951	34,645,573	28,595,668	82.5	13,717,538	48.0	13,948,605	48.8	730,556	2.5	198,969	0.7
1955	34,858,263	26,760,493	76.8	13,286,564	49.7	12,404,970	46.4	722,405	2.7	346,554	1.2
1959	35,397,080	27,859,241	78.7	13,749,830	49.4	12,215,538	43.8	1,638,571	5.9	255,302	0.9

servatives ended up with an absolute majority of 16 seats. Despite this slender majority, they maintained office and soon began to gather strength, a development that was much assisted by the division in Labour ranks, between the bulk of the party led by Clement Attlee (the former Prime Minister) and the rebellious Left wing led by the late Aneurin Bevan. In 1955, Churchill resigned the Premiership to Anthony Eden. In the election of 1955, the Conservatives triumphed again, their majority rising to 61, a good working majority. In January, 1957, Eden resigned and Harold Macmillan became Prime Minister in his place. In the election of 1959, the Conservatives did what no party since 1832 had ever done—won three elections in a row. This time they increased their majority to 101.

The Conservative Party

The Conservative Party can trace its pedigree back to the seventeenth century. Deeply conscious of its long heritage, the party regards itself as a national institution, yet it is remarkably skillful in adapting itself to new political conditions. The Whigs' Reform Act of 1832 appeared to have destroyed forever the basis of its electoral support; but within two years a Conservative government was in office again, and within nine years the party had overwhelmingly defeated its Whig rivals at the polls. Shatteringly defeated in 1945 by the Labour Party, it drew almost level by 1950, and has governed the country ever since the General Election of 1951.

It has the advantage of broad support from all classes of society, rich and poor, dustmen and duchesses, and its empirical approach to politics has enabled it to appeal to all these classes at once. Historically, the party is associated with the Crown and the aristocracy, and also (though this is of minor importance today) the Church of England. It was the party of imperial expansion, and still is the party of national self-assertion. It is associated too, with the landed interest, with free enterprise, and at the same time with paternalistic protection of the interests of the working classes. But the Conservatives have been swift to alter the emphasis of this varied tradition to meet the challenges of the day.

At the end of the Second World War, the party's "image" was sadly tarnished. Since it had dominated the governments of the interwar period, it was linked in the public mind with the doleful memory of "the years that the locust had eaten," with high unemployment, harsh conditions for public relief, and the Trades Disputes Act, passed in 1927 to hamper the trade unions after the failure of the General Strike of 1926. It was also blamed for the class-biased society of the pre-war years and for what has been styled "the religion of inequality." Finally, it was charged with appeasing Hitler and Mussolini and with signing the humiliating Munich agreement of 1938.

Not surprisingly, then, the party was swept away at the polls in 1945, but its recovery since then has been very remarkable indeed. Thrown back upon itself, the party reorganized its structure, and re-examined its principles, and came up with a program that creates the impression of a progressive party and appeals particularly to "the rising working class" that is in a hurry to get on in the world.

Ideology

Conservatives profess neither *laissez faire* nor state collectivism. In its long history, the party has veered between both, stressing the points overlooked or opposed by its opponents. In the nineteenth century, it advocated collectivist measures against Liberal *laissez faire*. Today, it argues for limited government and for individual liberties as against the centralization and bureaucracy that accompanied the Labour program in the immediate postwar years.

The Conservatives have a deep reverence for tradition, and when change has to come their first care is to safeguard the continuity of national institutions. The core of their belief is the unity of the nation. For them, social classes are both necessary and natural, given the differing abilities of men, but these classes ought not to be founded on the accidents of wealth or birth, but on ability. To this end, they seek an equal opportunity for all to move forward and upward. The classes, founded on quality, are, in their view, essential *organs* of the nation that transcend all personal differences. Hence they deplore appeals to class warfare, which they consider a wanton attack on national unity, and they challenge the assumption that there is a basic enmity between employer and employed, holding that both are partners in industry. They accuse the Labour Party of favoring one class above all others. They themselves claim that they are the party of all classes, of the whole nation.

For them, the development of character is founded on the individual's freedom to choose. The wider the choice, the greater the development of self-reliance. From their preference for voluntary effort over public assistance stems their insistence on free enterprise in industry, their hostility to nationalization, and their defense of the profit motive. Favoring giving local authorities responsibility wherever they can be substituted for the central government, the Conservatives have also tried to decentralize the nationalized industries and to introduce competition from the outside wherever possible. Their slogan, "a property-owning democracy," reflects their faith that private property is both a safeguard of the individual's independence and an incentive to his personal effort.

This is not to deny the state any part in the conduct of industry. Conservatives would even nationalize an industry if they thought the facts warranted it, e.g., the publicly owned B.B.C. (1927) and the Central Electricity Board (1926) were both Conservative creations. On the whole, however, they maintain that detailed physical controls encumber rather than help the economy. The state ought certainly to prevent monopolies and restrictive practices, to safeguard individuals and firms against calamitous occupational risks, and to act to insure full employment and the proper geographical distribution of industry. Lastly, nothing in the Conservative tradition bars them from providing social welfare services. In the nineteenth century, the Conservatives championed the Factory Acts and workmen's compensation for injuries. However, they believe such services must be a "springboard rather than a sofa," a "ladder rather than a net."

Today, the Conservative Party has fully caught up with the climate of public opinion that has developed since the Second World War. Abroad, it conducts its diplomacy through the United Nations, but regards the world body as ancillary to, not a substitute for, a policy of national strength, military preparedness, and defensive alliances. Although the party is the traditional party of Empire and imperialist expansion, it has conceded independence to the former colonies as fast as, if not faster, than the Labour Government of 1945–51. Indeed, in one respect it has gone further; in 1961, it opened negotiations to join the European Common Market, although this seems bound to weaken Commonwealth ties. Such a remarkable decision well illustrates the shrewd empiricism of the party.

At home, the Conservatives accept the state's duty to provide full employment and to exercise a general regulation of the economy in the public interest. They have accepted the duty to provide social services, also, but differ with the Labour Party over the mode of administering them. These services are still based on the Labour reorganization of 1945–51 and provide for a flat rate of benefit for each recipient. Conservatives regard this as wasteful of the limited resources available and would prefer to vary the payments to each individual by some test of personal need.

In industry, the Conservatives have abolished physical controls on prices and output, have denationalized the steel and trucking industries, and have encouraged competitors to enter against the remaining nationalized industries wherever possible—e.g., in television and air transportation. Also, they passed the important Restrictive Practices Act (1956) to break up price-fixing in industry, a bill that is consistent with their policy of incentive and opportunity. This attitude is also uppermost in their educational policy. They favor the present system of segregating children by an examination at the age of 11, and sending the brighter ones to the secondary Grammar Schools. To them, this appears to be rewarding ability and letting it make its way in the world instead of holding it back to the pace of the slowest. The Labour Party, on the other hand, deplores the social stratification that results from this policy. They would prefer to have all children sent to a single "comprehensive" school, inside which they could be classified according to their ability and educated accordingly. These rival policies point up the differences between the two parties on the question of "equality" and help illustrate what Conservatives mean when they talk of the "opportunity state."

Structure

The paper organization of the Conservative Party is so chaotic that one is led to exclaim, "How on earth does it work?" Its structure, however, is far more tight than a superficial look would suggest. The party is composed of three different organizations (Fig. 4-2). The first is the *National Union of Conservative and Unionist Associations*. A federation of the constituency parties, it was established in 1867 and was re-shaped between 1884 and 1886. The second component is the party in the Houses of Parliament, the *Parliamentary Party*, an autonomous body. The third is the *Central Office*, which was formed in 1870 as the secretariat of the Leader of the party, a role it has retained.

The National Union, as the name suggests, is a union of the constituency associations—there is one association for every constituency (electoral district). Its governing body, the Central Council, consists of 3,600 persons and meets once a year, in a sort of annual semi-conference. This Central Council has an Executive Committee of 150 persons, which meets every two months, but is so unwieldy that the General Purposes Committee of 56 persons, which meets frequently, makes most of the executive decisions. The most important duty of the General Purposes Committee, perhaps, is to compile the agenda for the annual meeting of the Central Council of the Conference and of the National Union.

But it would be naive to think that the Union is run just by its Council or its Executive Committee or its General Purposes Committee, for a number of advisory committees help the Union chart policy: the Women's, the Young Conservatives', the Trade Union-

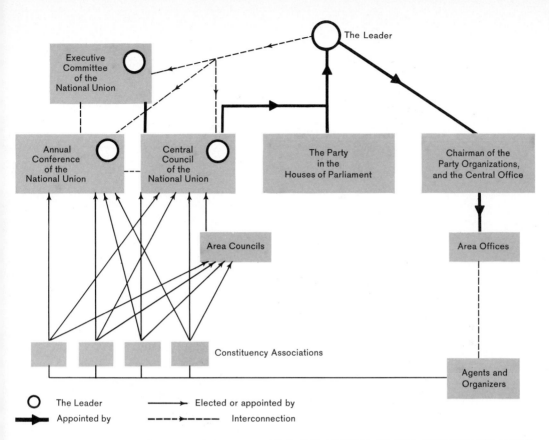

FIGURE 4-2   THE ORGANIZATION OF THE CONSERVATIVE PARTY.

ists', the Local Government, and the Political Education and Publicity Committees. Among the Advisory bodies that are not responsible to the Union, the most important are the Advisory Committee on Policy, the Central Board of Finance, and the Advisory Committee on Candidates. In theory, no candidate may be endorsed by a constituency association until this Committee is satisfied as to the candidate's personal character, party loyalty, past record and experience, political knowledge, speaking ability, and financial integrity. It also maintains a list of approved candidates that is available to the constituency organizations. Actually, however, the effective decisions on candidates are largely in the hands of one of the Vice Chairmen of the party organization, who reports to this Committee. This Vice Chairman is especially responsible, in the Central Office, for the candidates' file. He is appointed by and responsible to the Leader, but by tradition is a respected backbencher of the Parliamentary Party.

THE CONSTITUENCY ASSOCIATIONS.   In both the Conservative and the Labour Parties, these associations are a vital element and, indeed, play a significant role in the political life of the country. The functions laid down for them in the Conservative Party's Model Rules show why: The associations are expected to provide an efficient organization for the Conservative Party in each constituency; to spread knowledge of the party's principles and policy; to promote the interests of the party in the constituency; to support, in local government elections, those candidates for the council

Political Parties and Elections

chosen by the party; and to watch over the revision of the constituency register of voters.

The constituency party also has the important function of choosing the parliamentary candidate. The executive committee of the constituency association appoints a selection committee. Before a candidate is recommended for adoption, his name must be submitted to the National Union Standing Advisory Committee on Candidates. The constituency thus proposes, but the central headquarters may dispose. As a result, the people who are permitted to stand as candidates (and this is true also in the Labour Party) are "seeded," that is, they have already pledged themselves to support the party's policy and its election manifesto.

Since 1950, the constituency's selection committee is forbidden to ask intending candidates for financial contributions, and a maximum scale for these is laid down. The most a candidate may contribute to the general running expenses of the association is £25 per year and the most to the association's election-fighting fund also £25; so £50 in all. When contesting the seat, however, he may also be asked to contribute £100 for "personal expenses." Nevertheless, the local associations have been just as keen as before to pick their candidates from the higher professions and from business rather than from the working class, and have continued to prefer candidates with a public-school and Oxford or Cambridge education. The most marked effect of the reform has been its encouragement to young men to come forward in much larger numbers than before.

THE LEADER AND THE CENTRAL OFFICE. The Leader of the party is, in effect, the nominee of the Parliamentary Party and, once chosen, falls heir to the Central Office. He appoints the Chairman of the party organization, its two vice-chairmen, and the treasurers, chairman, and vice-chairman of the Policy Committee. The Central Office, which is virtually his personal secretariat, consists of several sections, which handle constituency organization and finance, publicity and propaganda, and speakers. Outside the Central Office is the Conservative Political Centre—a propaganda and education organization—and the Research Department. The Central Office appoints the regional officials of the party, and these—the Regional Agent, the Regional Women's Organizer, and so forth—represent the Central Office in the constituencies. Constituency associations appoint their own election agents and officials, who are Central Office trained, and they have direct access to headquarters in London, but they are encouraged to deal with the regional staff as much as possible.

The Central Office must therefore be regarded as a national organization of highly skilled professional partisans. Their duty is to assist the party leadership in the formulation of policy, to carry out decisions, and to act as an intelligence network, advising the constituency associations on the views of the leadership, and in turn advising the leadership on the outlook, morale, and preparedness of the voluntary workers in the constituencies. This party machine is kept at a high pitch of readiness at all times. Local elections and constant by-elections keep it on the alert, and every defeat provokes a reassessment of the party's preparedness for the object of the entire enterprise—to fight and win the next General Election.

THE CONFERENCE. The National Union and its associated organs and the Leader and his headquarters meet together at the Annual Conference. Each constituency association is entitled to send seven persons, irrespective of its size (unlike the Labour Party, where representation is proportionate to membership). Furthermore, the persons sent are representatives, not (as in the Labour Party), mandated delegates. In addition, the Parliamentary Party, the official candidates, election agents, and certain members of the Central Office also attend. About 6,000 are entitled to attend, but only about 4,500 turn up—still too many for effective policy-making. This group is by no means the supreme policy-making body of the party; in its advisory capacity, it can pass resolutions, but they are not binding. They are "conveyed" to the Leader (as the phrase goes) and if he does not want to adopt them, he need not, for the party's rules clearly state that policy is the responsibility of the Leader. This is the reason the Leader is not present *during* the Conference, but comes *after* the Conference has concluded its discussions, his speech being its closing feature. He may thus be saved from many embarrassing situations. At best a sounding-board, the Conference is usually listened to by the Leader, for it would be very unwise of him to ignore its views altogether.

THE PARLIAMENTARY PARTY. Now let us turn to the truer policy-making mechanism of the Conservative Party, the Parliamentary Party, consisting of the Conservative Members of Parliament. In choosing a leader of the Parliamentary Party, who becomes the Leader of the Party in the country, the Conservatives, who do not care to create ill feelings through open elections, arrange the choice by discussion and by "taking the sense" of the Parliamentary Party.

The Leader is appointed for an indefinite period. There is no annual election of the Leader, as in the Labour Party, but the Leader does not automatically serve for the rest of his life. He has to live with his party and give it good—i.e., successful—service. If he does not, he is liable to face intolerable pressures that will force him to resign. The Conservative Party can be very tough on its Leaders and has, in the past, removed many of them. It got rid of Arthur Balfour before the First World War and dismissed Austen Chamberlain immediately after it.

The Leader has, nonetheless, formidable powers. If he is Prime Minister he, of course, selects his Cabinet. In Opposition, unlike his Labour counterpart, he selects his own "shadow cabinet," those men who would serve as Ministers if the party were to form a government. He appoints his Chief Whip and the Junior Whips, who serve as his right-hand men in the House of Commons. And it is the Leader who ultimately fixes policy. These powers give him a much stronger constitutional position vis-à-vis the members of the Parliamentary Party, the backbenchers, than is possessed by the Leader of the Labour Party. Yet this authority is by no means absolute. It is qualified by the other party Members of Parliament, who are highly organized. A full meeting of the backbenchers, called the "1922 Committee," convenes every Thursday for about an hour or more. The Chief Whip is always present and reports the results of the meeting directly to the Prime Minister (or Leader). Ministers are not normally present, but the Committee may call in a Minister or even the Leader to hear his point of view if the party is going through some crisis.

In addition to the 1922 Committee, there are several specialized committees, about 30 in number. They have their honorary officers and any Member may attend, but, when the party is in power, Ministers are not members. In Opposition, these bodies play an important role, for attached to each of them is a special Secretary who is a member of the Conservative Research Department. The Research Department prepares briefs (sometimes from information supplied by outside bodies) and passes them on to the appropriate backbenchers' committee. This is the way the Conservative Opposition organized itself between 1945 and 1951. When the party is in power, a different kind of situation tends to occur. It is then that, for instance, a Minister (say the Minister of Agriculture or the Minister of Fuel and Power) tends to encounter backbencher opposition on a particular bill. The appropriate backbencher committee might then invite him to explain to them his position. The Minister might have to decide to moderate his policy or he might be able to persuade the backbenchers to his viewpoint.

Crucial in the organization and work of the Parliamentary Party are the Whips. The Whips' office is the party's nervous system.

Through the Whips, the Leader knows just what the mood of the party is, and he can transmit back through them his own reactions. He must rely on the Whips' techniques of cajolery and persuasion to keep the party loyal to him.

Do not suppose that the backbenchers on the Conservative side are a pack of sheep, for they can be very tough and very fractious and need careful handling. While Sir Anthony Eden was Prime Minister (1955–57), for instance, whirlpools of dissension churned up the backbenchers, and the Government was forced to give way to them on such matters as the ban on heroin, the white-fish subsidy, and the Education Superannuation Bill. Recently, backbench dissidence has arisen concerning nationalized industries, government spending, the Rent Act of 1957, and, most dramatically, the future of Northern Rhodesia. In December, 1961, the Government decided to meet a UN request for 1,000-lb. bombs for its forces in Katanga, but was forced to reverse its decision owing to a flare-up of backbench intransigence.

POLITICAL ATTITUDES IN THE PARLIAMENTARY PARTY. The candidates of the Conservative Party fall into three main groups: professional men, members of miscellaneous occupations, and businessmen. Of those actually elected to the House of Commons, professional men and businessmen predominate. In 1955–59, 22 per cent of the party were from the professions, 9 per cent were members of miscellaneous occupations, and 61 per cent were businessmen. In addition, the party draws very largely from the more exclusive public schools. In 1959, no less than 102 of the 365 Conservative Members came from Eton, Harrow, and Winchester, and 263 came from some kind of public school. Well over half the Parliamentary Party had been to Oxford and Cambridge. In short, the party is composed of businessmen and professional

people, with almost no representation from the working class.

One recent study of the Parliamentary Party discovered a close relationship between the backgrounds of M.P.'s and the attitudes they assume. The age of the candidate and the year he entered Parliament appear to be decisive factors in his attitude toward Europe and the Commonwealth. The younger the member and the more recently he entered Parliament, the less disposed he is to put the needs of the Commonwealth before those of Europe. Again, the younger the candidate and the more recent his election, the more humane he is likely to be on penal matters.

*Problems of
the Conservative Party*

The Conservative Party faces three primary problems. First, it must reconcile the broad and often conflicting interests of those who put it into office. The supporters of the Conservative Party are much more heterogeneous than those of the Labour Party, which gets about nine-tenths of its vote from the working class. Over half of the Conservative vote is supplied by the working class, but the remainder comes from the middle class, and, of course, it has the almost unanimous support of big business. The task of reconciling these three groups is none too easy. The party's tight credit policy has been much disliked by the banks and the finance companies; its refusal to set up quotas to protect the home textile industry against Hong Kong cottons resulted from the party's adherence to the principle of Commonwealth preference. Its working-class supporters expect it to spend more on the social services; its middle-class supporters expect it to reduce personal taxation. Therefore, the party rarely pursues a preconceived detailed program as the Labour Party did when in office, but tacks about, and steers a rather devious course.

The party's second great problem also relates to home affairs. Its successes since 1951 have been chiefly due to its ability to convince about one-third of the manual working class that it offers them opportunities for material self-advancement. It can only continue to satisfy the working class if it·is able to keep the economy buoyant. In the 1959 General Election, the only two regions to swing away from the Conservatives were Lancashire and Scotland, both of which were suffering from more than average unemployment; and in 1961–62, while the government was maintaining a "pay pause" that held back wage advances throughout the whole economy, the Gallup polls and by-elections showed a dramatic drop in the popularity of the Conservative Party. Conservative electoral success, therefore, depends on economic expansion. Here, however, it stands a chance of becoming the prisoner of its own ideology. Against the Labour Party's program of control and public ownership of industry, it has preached that "Conservative freedom works." But it is becoming apparent that its reliance on purely financial and fiscal measures to guide the economy is not sufficient. In the fall of 1961, the party was already beginning to talk of the need for "planning." These inconsistencies must be resolved and the economy put on a course of steady expansion if the party is to retain the allegiance of the "rising working class."

The party's third problem comes from the chauvinistic and imperialistic elements of its Right wing. These exist both in the Parliamentary Party and in the constituency associations. They are vocal, and their views have a seductive appeal for the rank and file. The Conservative Right has still to be convinced that the transformation of the former Empire into a Commonwealth of independent nations is a necessity; that in matters of diplomacy Britain's first and possibly last line of defense must be the American alliance; that Britain cannot "go it alone"; that the "Headship of the Commonwealth" is no substitute for national diplomacy or a system of defensive alliances. None of these views is palatable to the Right-wingers. To a large extent, the claim that the Empire is being freely transmuted into a Commonwealth makes the policy of imperial retreat less objectionable. Yet there are limits to what this formula will cover. The Right wing is particularly recalcitrant if this policy means—as it seems to mean—the abandonment of the British settlers in such countries as Kenya and the Rhodesias.

This group is also disturbed by the government's bold decision to negotiate entry into the European Common Market, a policy that seems inconsistent with the Conservative tradition that has for decades "put the Empire (latterly, 'the Commonwealth') first" in its foreign dealings. Again, the need for British diplomacy to march side by side with the United States rankles since the Suez intervention of 1956. Most British Conservatives regard the actions of the United States in that crisis (which exercised strong pressure on Britain to withdraw) as unworthy of Britain's closest ally. At the height of the crisis, one-third of the Conservative backbenchers went on public record to condemn American policy. Such anti-Americanism must somehow or other be mastered. The Conservative Party thus faces a difficult future with its triple challenge of educating its followers in the realities of the modern world, of securing continued economic expansion, and of reconciling the competing interests of its supporters.

The Labour Party

Although the Labour Party was founded, officially, in 1900, it had antecedents in such organizations as the Independent Labour Party (founded in 1893), the Fabian Society (founded in 1883), the Social Democratic Federation (founded in 1881); in the ideals of the Trades Unions, whose history goes back still further into the nineteenth century; in the Co-operative movement, founded in 1844; and in the working-class political tradition spanning the years of Owenism in the 1830's and Chartism in the forties to the mass strikes and the new trade unionism of the 1880's. The party of 1900 was a mere beginning. It was not avowedly socialist, but merely an amalgam of socialist and trade-union elements; it was not a unitary body, but a federation of societies and Trades Unions which individuals could join only through membership in one of the component organizations. There was no doctrine except the goal of establishing a distinct Labour group in the House of Commons.

The Labour Representation Committee (as it called itself until 1906) was transformed into a socialist party in 1918, with the adoption of a constitution that is still in effect today. Individual members were allowed to join directly, and the party headquarters organized constituency Labour Parties that systematically covered the whole country. The new constitution declared that the object of the party was to "secure for the producers by hand or by brain the full fruits of their industry and the most equitable distribution thereof that may be possible upon the basis of the common ownership of the means of production and the best obtainable system of popular administration and control of each industry and service. . . ." [1] This statement is from the famous "Clause 4" of the party's objectives, about which we shall have much to say later.

The Labour Party is, today, the second great party of Britain. Its voting support rose steadily from 1906 (except in the special circumstances of 1931) to 1951, and it still commended massive support in 1959 (see Table 4-2). Its membership, too, has increased vastly (see Table 4-3).

TABLE 4-2   *Votes Cast
for Labour, 1906–1959*

1906	323,195	1931	6,648,023
1910 (Jan.)	450,969	1935	8,510,566
1910 (Dec.)	370,802	1945	12,149,605
1918	2,370,240	1950	13,266,592
1922	4,251,011	1951	13,948,605
1923	4,508,504	1955	12,404,970
1924	5,483,088	1959	12,215,538
1929	8,389,512		

[1] Later on, in 1927, the words "distributions and exchange" were added.

Ideology

Although its program is basically socialistic, the Labour Party has never been the prisoner of an all-embracing Marxist ideology like some of the Socialist Parties of Continental Europe. Many elements have shaped its viewpoint. At an early stage, Hyndman's Social Democratic Federation introduced Marxist ideas but these were not influential. The Independent Labour Party was a much more important component, and its philosophy derived largely from the religious nonconformity of the working classes, embodying a disgust for the class injustices of a competitive society and a plea for a more just and humane society based on fellowship and cooperation. Another ingredient was introduced by the small but extremely influential Fabian Society, which favored gradualism. The Fabians wanted to bring industry under public ownership and control and to redistribute the nation's wealth so as to provide all citizens with the minimum requirements for a decent and civilized life. Syndicalism (called, in its British form, Guild Socialism) espoused workers' control of their employers' industries. At different periods in the party's history, different views have been uppermost. In the 1920's, for instance, it was the idealistic desire for fellowship and cooperative living; in the thirties, there was a stronger flavor of Marxism; and throughout the forties, the party laid its main stress on the need for economic planning, of which nationalization of the basic industries was an essential part.

Just as the Conservative Party still contains Right-wing elements who believe in British imperial supremacy, so the Labour Party contains a Left-wing group that maintains an unsystematic, inconsistent kind of Marxism. This group believes in the class struggle of the workers against the capitalists. It wants to remove the capitalistic order altogether by placing the whole economy under public ownership, and in foreign affairs it advocates the unilateral renunciation of nuclear weapons and a neutralist foreign policy for Britain. Such views are held by only a tiny handful of Labour voters and are not those of the bulk

TABLE 4-3 *Labour Party Membership, 1900–1960*

	Total	Individual membership [a]	Trade-union membership	Socialist societies
1900	375,931	—	353,070	2,286
1905	921,280	—	904,496	16,784
1910	1,430,539	—	1,394,402	31,377
1913	2,093,365	—	2,053,735	32,828
1920	4,359,807	—	4,317,537	42,270
1925	3,373,870	—	3,337,635	36,235
1930	2,346,908	—	2,011,484	58,213
1935	2,377,515	419,311	1,912,924	45,280
1940	2,571,163	304,224	2,226,575	40,464
1945	3,038,697	730,224	2,510,369	41,281
1950	5,920,172	908,161	4,971,911	40,100
1955	6,483,994	843,356	5,605,988	34,650
1958	6,542,186	888,955	5,627,690	25,541
1959	6,436,986	847,526	5,564,010	25,450
1960	6,328,330	790,192	5,512,688	25,450

[a] In addition to trade-union members listed as individual members.

of the party militants in the constituencies and certainly not those of the Labour M.P.'s.

The essential philosophy of the Labour Party springs from a belief that man is inherently good and that institutions and society are mostly to blame for making him behave badly and live miserably. Economic institutions are particularly guilty because of the enormous influence they exert over the size of the national income, over the way its rewards are distributed, and over the social priorities that are established as the economy's goal. Democracy must therefore be extended from politics into economic affairs. Using the processes of parliamentary and local democracy—in which the party fervently believes—the electorate should bring firms and enterprises under the ownership or control of the people. The object is to create a cooperative fellowship in place of the scramble for private competitive gain.

In home affairs, therefore, the party has four major objectives. First, it wishes to "democratize" the economy, to give the people a say in the running of the economy instead of leaving this to groups of private individuals. It demands the nationalization of key industries and public control of the private sector of the economy. Secondly, it favors a more equal distribution of wealth, by means of death duties, taxation of unearned incomes, and sharply progressive income taxes on earned incomes.

Thirdly, it believes in comprehensive social welfare services and is prepared to spend proportionately much more of the national income on these than is the Conservative Party. Finally, it wants to make Britain less class-ridden. It sees the public schools as a privilege of the wealthy. It deplores the segregation of children, at the age of 11, into the brighter pupils who go to the secondary Grammar Schools and the less bright who go to the secondary Modern Schools. It argues that this creates social snobbery from the classroom onwards. It would prefer that all children go to large comprehensive schools where they could meet and play together, and where they could be separated on the basis of ability and taught accordingly.

Carrying its idealistic concern for fellowship and cooperation into the field of foreign affairs, the Labour Party would like to see collective cooperation among the nations replace national sovereignty and self-interest. To this end, it is far warmer toward the United Nations than is the Conservative Party. Also, its members have a pronounced aversion to the threat or use of force in world affairs, unless employed to support the UN. The Labour

Party opposed the Conservative government's landings in the Suez Canal zone in 1956 and the British air-drop in Jordan in 1958, but supported the UN action in Korea and, later, in the Congo.

The advent of nuclear weapons has caused a sharp conflict of conscience inside the Labour Party. Since 1955, when the British government first contemplated making an H-bomb, a minority in the party has protested against the manufacture, then the testing, and finally the stockpiling of British nuclear weapons. Since then the party has broken into two factions. The "multilateralists" are only prepared to renounce the use of nuclear weapons as a part of a general agreement with the United States and the U.S.S.R. The "unilateralists" wish to renounce the manufacture and use of nuclear weapons without waiting for such an agreement; in addition, they would deny the United States any British bases for the employment of nuclear weapons, and if necessary withdraw from NATO, unless this alliance also agreed to renounce the use of nuclear weapons.

Finally, the Labour Party is strenuously anti-colonialist. It supports the speediest emancipation for the colonies, and also believes it is the duty of the richer and more powerful nations like Britain to give material assistance to the weaker and underdeveloped countries.

Structure

Basic to the structure of the Labour Party is the difference between *individual party members,* who are organized in the constituency Labour parties (the C.L.P.'s) and the *affiliated members,* mostly trade unionists from the unions that have affiliated with the party (Fig. 4-3). These unions collect a political levy, part of which goes into the party's coffers. Both types of membership are represented at the Annual Conference. The trade unions and local constituency Labour parties

both send one delegate for every 5,000 members. Also entitled to be present, ex officio, are the National Executive Committee, the whole of the Parliamentary Party, and all the candidates. But these ex officio members have no votes. Usually some 1,000 or 1,200 persons attend. Resolutions are introduced by the delegates and then are debated and voted on by the Conference. Since inevitably too many resolutions are presented for the Conference to discuss adequately, the party headquarters tries to have them boiled down into "composite" motions. Of some 30 possible resolutions about the H-bomb, for instance, three might reach the Conference: one Right-wing, one middle of the road, and one Left-wing.

The next function of the Conference is to elect the National Executive Committee. In addition to acting as the keeper of the party's conscience, the N.E.C. runs the party between the annual meetings of the Conference. To prevent the 5½ million trade-union affiliated members from overriding the less than a million individual members and choosing their own men for the N.E.C., the latter is divided into four groups. (1) Twelve members of the Committee are nominated by the trade unions and are voted on by them only. (2) Seven members are nominated and elected by just the constituency parties. (3) The third group consists of 5 women only. Since they are not elected solely by the women (as one might expect) but by the whole Conference, they must, clearly, secure the backing of the trade unions. (4) The fourth group consists of only one member, who is elected by the Socialist and the Co-operative Societies represented at the Conference. To these 25 members are added the Leader of the Parliamentary Party and the Deputy Leader, who are ex officio members, and the Treasurer, who is elected by the whole Conference, for a total of 28 in all. With the Parliamentary Labour Party, whose Leader is ex officio a member of the National Executive Committee, the formal Labour Party structure is complete.

How is policy decided in the Labour Party and who is most influential in formulating it? We shall discuss this under three headings: (1) the role of the Conference vis-à-vis the

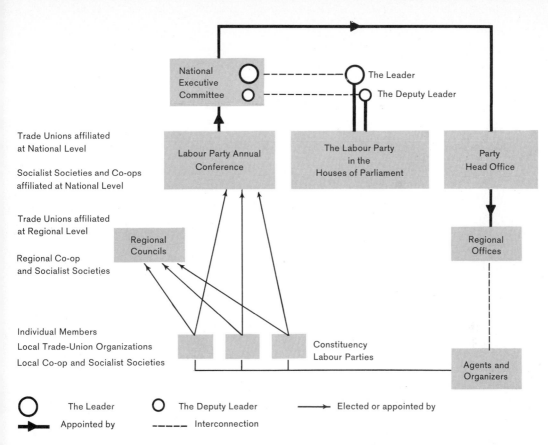

Trade Unions affiliated
at National Level

Socialist Societies and Co-ops
affiliated at National Level

Trade Unions affiliated
at Regional Level

Regional Co-op
and Socialist Societies

Individual Members
Local Trade-Union Organizations
Local Co-op and Socialist Societies

National Executive Committee · Labour Party Annual Conference · The Leader · The Deputy Leader · The Labour Party in the Houses of Parliament · Party Head Office · Regional Councils · Regional Offices · Constituency Labour Parties · Agents and Organizers

○ The Leader   ○ The Deputy Leader   ⟶ Elected or appointed by
▶ Appointed by   ----- Interconnection

FIGURE 4-3   THE ORGANIZATION OF THE LABOUR PARTY.

Parliamentary Labour Party; (2) the role inside the party of the constituency parties and of the trade unions; and (3) the Parliamentary Labour Party itself.

THE CONFERENCE AND THE PARLIAMENTARY LABOUR PARTY. The Conference and the Parliamentary Party are supposedly independent of one another, yet both are responsible for establishing the policy of the party. Before 1952, the Parliamentary Party dominated the National Executive Committee because (1) many of the leaders of the Parliamentary Party belonged to the Committee and (2) the Committee was able to rely on the vote of the largest trade unions. In addition, since the Labour Party was in power, from 1945–51, the leaders of the Parliamentary Party, who formed the Cabinet, enjoyed a high prestige. But after the defeat of 1951, the constituency parties represented in the

Conference revolted against the leadership of the Parliamentary Party and began to elect to the National Executive Committee an increasing number of leftist M.P.'s, the so-called "Bevanites," named after the late Aneurin Bevan, the fiery Welshman who strove to infuse the party with its old radical zeal. Later there was a shift to the Left in the largest of the trade unions, the Transport and General Workers Union, which disposes of one-sixth of the votes in the Conference. This further weakened the hold of the leaders of the Parliamentary Party in the Executive Committee and the Conference.

In 1960, a serious cleavage sundered the party. Early in that year, the National Execu-

Political Parties and Elections

tive Committee and the Trades Union Congress issued a joint statement on defense policy. It called for a general disarmament agreement between nations, and (until this was negotiated) the maintenance of nuclear arms by Britain, the granting of bases for nuclear-arms-carrying aircraft and submarines of the United States, and continued reliance on NATO. The Annual Conference, however, rejected the official policy by the slim margin of 297,000 votes out of a total of nearly 6½ million.

Another resolution, which seemed to imply that Britain must leave NATO (it demanded "a complete rejection of any defense policy based on the threat of the use of strategic or tactical nuclear weapons"), was passed by 43,000 votes. Hugh Gaitskell, the Leader of the Party, refused to change his own standpoint, and stated that the Parliamentary Party was not constitutionally obliged to do so either. When Parliament reconvened, the Parliamentary Party re-elected Mr. Gaitskell as its leader by a 2 to 1 majority and elected a parliamentary committee of anti-unilateralists, thus also indicating that it intended to go its own way.

Mr. Morgan Phillips, the party's General Secretary, had summed up the constitutional question in this way: the National Executive of the party and the Parliamentary Labour Party are two autonomous bodies, the first responsible to the Conference, the second to the electorate; neither is superior to the other, and both touch only at certain points laid down by the constitution. More specifically, he pointed out:

1. The Annual Conference does *not* instruct the Parliamentary Party. It can instruct only the National Executive Committee.
2. The Parliamentary Labour Party is unquestionably an autonomous political body, owing ultimate responsibility only to the electorate.
3. The Parliamentary Labour Party cannot maintain its position in the country if it can be demonstrated that it is at any time and in any

way subject to dictation from an outside body, which, however representative of the *party,* could not be regarded as representative of the *country.*

For some months after the Conference, the struggle between the two factions was envenomed. A special committee was set up to draft a new statement on defense. Mr. Gaitskell stuck to his point of view, and the approved final draft made no substantial concessions to unilateralism. Meanwhile, the multilateralists took the fight to the membership. By Easter, 1961 (Easter is when most of the trade-union conferences begin to meet), it became clear that their campaign was having an effect. One by one, unilateralist unions (but not the giant Transport and General Workers Union) changed their minds and voted for the official multilateralist policy. When the party Conference met again in October, 1961, Mr. Gaitskell's multilateralist policy was carried by a huge majority. Thus, after an embittered period of strife between the Conference and the Parliamentary Party, unity was restored—on the Parliamentary Party's terms and its view was reaffirmed in the Conference of 1962.

THE CONSTITUENCY LABOUR PARTIES AND THE TRADE UNIONS. The role of the unions in the Labour Party is enormously important in respect to (1) money, (2) votes, (3) the National Executive Committee, and (4) the sponsorship of candidates.

Financing. The unions contributed £325,-000 to the Labour Party's 1959 Election Fund. In 1955, the sum was £100,000. Since 1945, they have never contributed less than 80 per cent of the General Election Fund. Of the current annual revenue of the party organization of about £300,000, £245,000 comes from the trade unions and only about £36,000 from the constituency parties.

Voting. At the Conference, there are some five and a half million trade-union votes to three-quarters of a million constituency party votes. Furthermore, the "big six" trade unions control two-thirds of that huge trade-union vote, and it is the practice of each trade-union delegation to vote as a single bloc. (In 1960, for example, the Executive Committee of the

National Union of Railwaymen decided, by *one* vote, to support the unilateral renunciation of nuclear weapons; at the Labour Party Conference in October, the *whole* of the union's 294,000 votes was cast for this resolution.)

The National Executive Committee. As we have seen, the Committee has 12 trade-union members and 5 women and a Treasurer elected by a majority of the whole Conference. Thus as many as 18 out of the 28 places can be held by people who are either trade unionists or favorable to them.

Sponsoring candidates. Certain trade unions have "panels" of candidates, and when any of these candidates is adopted by a constituency, the trade union is prepared to contribute to that candidate's election expenses and also to make a certain annual contribution to the running of his constituency party. How much they actually give depends on the circumstances and on the individual union. A union may pay up to £350 or half a full-time agent's salary (whichever is the larger) to a borough constituency and £420 per year or half the salary of a full-time agent (whichever is the larger) to a county constituency. These figures must be contrasted with the very small sums a Conservative candidate is permitted to contribute to his constituency association.

In addition, unions pay a sizable proportion of the election expenses for their own candidates when they are adopted: the maximum is 80 per cent and the average sum paid out is £550. This has increased the gulf between the constituencies that adopt ordinary candidates and those that are tempted by the allure of a trade-union candidate or a candidate sponsored by the Co-operative Party (who also will bring money with him). Since 1950, the proportion of trade-union sponsored candidates elected to the total elected has been 35 per cent, a slight rise from 1945, when it was 30 per cent. The trade unions tend to adopt candidates for the safer seats. This explains why the proportion of trade-union sponsored candidates has risen as the party's total number of seats has declined.

Militants in the constituency parties have tried to demonstrate that the constituency parties raise and spend more money than the trade unions contribute. An independent scholar, however, estimated the income as follows for 1957: [2]

Autonomous central and regional income	£ 10,000
Autonomous constituency income	275,000
Co-operative donation to Labour Party	30,000
Trade-union donation to Labour Party	370,000
Total	£685,000

These figures show that the unions contributed at least half of the money, and, counting their expenditures on administration and other party activities, their contribution is nearer £490,000 or 70 per cent of the party's total.

THE PARLIAMENTARY LABOUR PARTY. In Opposition, the Parliamentary Labour Party is, in certain important respects, organized in ways widely different from those of the Conservative Party. The Labour Party's traditional passion for equality and for democratic leadership has handicapped the Parliamentary Party. The Leader is annually elected and then is saddled with a group of people (known as the Parliamentary Committee), who may be personally obnoxious to him, by a vote of the whole Parliamentary Party. The Leader does have the right (and this gives him some patronage) to choose which area of policy he will assign to each man.

Like the Conservatives, the party organizes itself into a number of committees, but instead of the more casual Conservative weekly meeting, the Labour M.P.'s convene each week and discuss a formal agenda, often containing very important business. What is decided in this meeting is *binding* on the whole Parliamentary Party (under Standing Or-

[2] Martin Harrison, *Trade Unions and the Labour Party since 1945* (Detroit: Wayne State Univ. Press, 1960), pp. 99–100.

Political Parties and Elections

ders). Ministers or ex-Ministers are members of this meeting.

STANDING ORDERS. After the Labour Party was defeated in 1951 and the dissident Bevanites were challenging a number of the party's policies (on such vital matters as German rearmament, for instance), the party meetings would often get out of the control of the Leader. Although the Bevanites numbered only 55 or 60 (about a fifth of the Parliamentary Party), often as many as half the members would support their right to differ, and the rebel group would sometimes refuse to argue a motion or would introduce a motion opposed to that of the party leadership. To eliminate the harassment, the party's Standing Orders were reimposed in 1952. They required that a member vote along with the party unless on a matter of conscience, in which case he might abstain. If he broke this rule, he could be summoned to the Parliamentary Committee to explain his reasons. If his reasons were not satisfactory and he continued to disobey, he might be expelled from the Parliamentary Labour Party and thus become an independent M.P. As a result, he would not be likely to receive the National Executive's endorsement at an election and might consequently lose his seat.

Following the 1959 defeat, the party voted, 59 to 24, to abandon its Standing Orders. They were replaced by what was officially called the Chairman's Statement. Although the intention was the same as before, the *formal* power of the Parliamentary Committee was eroded. In March, 1961, however, five particularly recalcitrant Labour M.P.'s were summoned before the party for breaches of discipline, and, despite the formal absence of Standing Orders, were expelled from the Parliamentary Party. In parliamentary terms, they were "refused the party Whip." Then, following Mr. Gaitskell's triumph at the Blackpool Conference in 1961, the Parliamentary Party

reimposed the Standing Orders. These harsh measures to insure party discipline should be contrasted with the practice in the Conservative Party, which has no Standing Orders and which has withdrawn the Whip from a rebel Member only once since the First World War.

The Parliamentary Party, therefore, is organized on a democratic basis. The majority decides the policy, for it selects the Leader, elects his colleagues on the Opposition front bench, and chooses the Chief Whip. It also makes policy in the full party meetings and this is binding on the minority.

*Social Composition
and Political Attitudes*

As we have seen, the Labour vote comes overwhelmingly from the working class, but the Labour candidates elected are largely from the middle class. In an analysis made by the author of the 1955 Parliament, the occupational, educational, and sponsorship breakdown of the Parliamentary Party was found to be similar to that of the 1959 Parliament. Of the manual workers, who formed 33 per cent of the Parliamentary Party in 1955–59, four out of five had not gone beyond elementary school, and four-fifths of them were trade-union sponsored. Of the professional men, who made up 31 per cent of the party (mostly lawyers and teachers, plus a few doctors), 86 per cent had had a university education, and almost the same proportion were non-sponsored constituency party candidates. The miscellaneous occupations who formed 26 per cent of the party were roughly one-third from the elementary schools, one-third from secondary schools, and one-third from universities; three-quarters of them were non-sponsored constituency party candidates, and less than one in ten was trade-union sponsored.

Thus there were three "cultures" inside the party—a working-class, a professional, and a miscellaneous "culture." Although we might imagine that the most frequent clash would occur between the elementary-school-educated manual workers of the trade unions and the university-educated teachers, lawyers, and doctors, this is not, in fact, what happened. On material issues, such as social welfare benefits and services, the keenest advocates in the party were the manual workers and the least interested the professional men and the miscellaneous group. But on the ideological issues—unilateral nuclear disarmament, support for Red China and for India, anti-colonialism, and humane penal legislation—members from the miscellaneous occupations were the most enthusiastic and the workers the least. The university-educated professional class steered, on the whole, a middle course. On unilateral disarmament, they stood with the manual workers against the miscellaneous occupations, and, on anti-colonialism, with the miscellaneous occupations against the manual workers.

Nor are these attitudes altogether surprising. "The working class member," it has been said, "has tended to be concerned with immediate objectives, with immediate if small improvements in the living standards of his fellow workers. . . . Hence, for fear that the Party might be diverted from immediate needs, he suspected middle class members, who, less conscious of hardships in their own surroundings, tried to widen the Party's horizons." [3] This helps explain why the trade-union members from the working class are more interested in social welfare services and benefits than are the professions and the miscellaneous occupations and also why they are the most resistant section of the party on the ideological issues. What remains to be explained is why the miscellaneous occupations tend to be to the left of the professions on these ideological matters.

The type of occupation listed under "miscellaneous occupations" goes far toward answering this question. One-third of the people were, so to speak, from minor professions: welfare workers, local government officers, insurance agents, and the like. The remainder fell into a variety of groups. Five were full-time professional journalists. Seven were Labour Party publicists and journalists. Fourteen were part-time journalists. Fourteen were "speakers" or "lecturers," party organizers, and research workers. In short, many of this group

were ideologists who used their careers merely as steppingstones to Parliament.

The Parliamentary Labour Party likes to boast that it is more widely representative of the nation than is the Conservative Parliamentary Party. It is, and for this reason it is much more socially and occupationally heterogeneous, which also accounts for its internal schisms and convulsions.

Problems of the Labour Party

The Labour Party has lost three elections in eight years. Its individual membership is declining. It is losing the support of youth. Since 1959, it has shown little sign of benefiting from any temporary decreases in the Conservative government's popularity—not even during the catastrophic drop in that government's fortunes during the by-elections of 1962.

The Labour Party was established to represent the working classes in Parliament; it was a federation of labor organizations to which individual membership was grafted on only in 1918; and it developed a program for the transference of the major industries of the country to public ownership and control. Are these features and policies relevant today? Whatever the answer, they are still sentimentally revered; they have presented the party with three great areas of ambiguity and have produced profound dilemmas with which the party is desperately grappling today. The Labour Party—the party of social change—is a prisoner of its past.

THE AMBIGUITY OVER PARLIAMENTARY PARTY FREEDOM. One of the things the Labour Party was unquestionably founded to achieve was the election of workingmen to Parliament. The party was conceived as a democratic movement, with the Annual Conference that represents all the members acting as the supreme policy-making organ. But should this Conference be able to bind the

[3] J. P. W. Mallalieue, "The Trade Union M.P.," *New Statesman* (November 28, 1959).

Labour M.P.'s, who have been elected by the general public, to policies that the Conference itself establishes? Should M.P.'s be delegates of a special-interest group rather than represent the people as a whole, as the constitution requires? It would be improper for any government to be instructed or directed by a body other than Parliament, which, as we have seen, is legally supreme.

As early as 1907, the party recognized this conflict, and the Annual Conference that year proclaimed that "Resolutions instructing the Parliamentary Party as to their actions in the House of Commons be taken as the opinions of the Conference on the understanding that the time and method of giving effect to these instructions be left to the House in conjunction with the National Executive." [4] In the 1945 election, Mr. Attlee affirmed that *"within the program* adopted by the National Conference, the Parliamentary Party had complete discretion in the conduct of Parliamentary business and the attitude which it would adopt to legislation tabled by other parties."

As we have seen, however, in 1960 the issue became intensely practical, because it was a central item in Labour's civil war. At Scarborough, the Labour Conference voted that Britain should, unilaterally, abandon her nuclear armament and her nuclear allies, a view opposed by the great majority of Labour M.P.'s. The Parliamentary Party stood on what it regarded as its strict constitutional right to differ from the Conference. Many of its members, to say nothing of the thwarted delegates who had triumphed in the Conference, disputed its interpretation of the party constitution. The conflict was resolved at Blackpool, in 1961, when the Conference reversed its position of the previous year and brought itself into line with the Parliamentary Party; but this was an act of power, the result

[4] Quoted in R. T. McKenzie, *Political Parties* (London, 1955), p. 393.

of a vote, not an authoritative constitutional verdict—and the Conference may re-reverse itself in the future. Thus the rights and duties of the Parliamentary Party vis-à-vis the Conference are still obscure.

THE AMBIGUITY OVER MEMBERSHIP. As we have seen, originally one became a member of the Labour Party only by being a member of another organization (mostly trade unions) affiliated to the party. Individual membership was not initiated until 1918. As Table 4-3 showed, the trade-union affiliated members still vastly outnumber the individual members, a situation that inflicts the party with at least three acute problems. First, there has always been tension at the Conference between the constituency parties, in which members are very militant, and the trade-union blocs, much of whose membership is tepid. It is possible to be both an individual member and a trade-union member, and the party constitution encourages this, but many individuals do not belong to a union, and most trade unionists decline to become individual members of a constituency party.

Second, some of the trade-union affiliated members are only nominally members. They become "members" by paying the "political levy" that the affiliated unions are, by law, entitled to collect. Since they may refuse to pay if they wish, "not to refuse" is, therefore, a way of becoming a member, but a way that indicates that the "member" is unlikely to be more than lukewarm in his attachment to the party. A recent study of this matter found that the number of trade unionists who have become party members in this fashion is at least 2 million—one-third of the trade-union affiliated membership.

Third, when the Trades Unions decide on their policy before the party Conference, *all* their members may (depending on their individual rules) decide the stand to be taken by their union's delegates at the Conference, not just the Labour Party affiliated members. But at least one-sixth of the Trades Unionists are Conservatives, and some of the leaders are Communists. All these non-Labour members and leaders thus help to shape the policy which their union will later put forward at the Labour Conference!

THE AMBIGUITY OVER POLICY. The third area of ambiguity is that of the aims and policies of the party. The great 1945 program of public ownership and control of the economy, redistributive taxation, and extension of the social services had been mapped out in the thirties. When Labour lost control of the government in 1951, the program had been largely put into practice, and the party was left wondering what to do next. Labour prophecies that the Conservatives would bring back unemployment and dismantle the welfare services if they returned to power turned out to be groundless, so the party could not campaign on these issues. The charge that the Conservatives would denationalize certain industries proved largely true, but very popular. Meanwhile, the prosperity of the 1950's, which we have already discussed, tended to undermine the party's class appeal. The old spirit of class solidarity was melted away by the new opportunities that opened up for personal advancement. The party's claim to be able to conquer depressions and unemployment by economic planning had become out of date, while public ownership of industries was actively unpopular. In the 1959 election, the only sector of the electorate with whom the party increased its appeal was the old-age pensioners. They were attracted by Labour's flat promise to raise the old-age pension by £10 a week immediately. The party used to be able to rely on a majority of the younger voters, those casting their first vote. Today, polls suggest that new electors tend to favor the Conservatives in at least equal proportions to Labour.

Since the 1959 election defeat, three schools of thought have emerged in the party. One school, widely associated with the late Mr. Gaitskell, argues that the party should recognize the social changes that have taken place and realize, in particular, that the old policy of nationalization is not merely out of place, but so misunderstood as to give the party a bad name. Another group argues that the "affluence" of British society is temporary, that sooner or later a depression will come and sweep the party back into power and that in the meantime the party must continue to stand "Simon pure" by its first principles. A third group claims that the electoral defeats occurred, not because the Labour program was too radical as compared to that of the Conservatives, but because it was not nearly radical enough. The electorate, so this argument runs, found little difference between the two programs, and therefore, naturally enough, voted for the party that had had experience in office; the remedy is thus to adopt a radically socialistic program with nationalization in the forefront.

The controversy came to a head in the 1960 debate within the Labour Party over the notorious Clause 4 of the party's "Objects," as it appeared in the party's 1918 constitution. This clause is the only explicit statement of intention in the whole document, and it makes particular reference to "the common ownership of the means of production, distribution and exchange." Mr. Gaitskell argued that the party had many other, equally worthy objectives—social welfare, greater equality, colonial emancipation, world peace—and that these, too, should be explicitly recognized. In addition, he pointed out that Clause 4 as it stood gave the misleading impression that the party wished to put even small shops and garages under public ownership, which it really had no intention of doing. He therefore suggested that Clause 4 should be both revised and expanded. The leftists in the party immediately challenged his view and were joined by many others, including trade unionists, for whom Clause 4 had a sentimental and traditional appeal. Mr. Gaitskell and his fellow revisionists were forced to accept defeat. The National Executive Committee decided not to press for revision but instead to commend a "Statement of Aims" to the Conference that would recognize that "both public and private ownership have a place in the economy."

Political Parties and Elections

71

This Statement was adopted by the Conference in October, 1960. Thus there are now *two* official versions of the party's aims, and they contradict each other.

Elections

The object of political parties is to win elections, and we must now discuss the election procedure in Britain that decides which party will govern the country. The Parliament Act of 1911 limits the life of a Parliament to five years. A Prime Minister, however, for a number of reasons, sometimes calls an election before the time limit expires. He may seek a mandate from the electorate to make some radical change in the program on which his party was originally elected; perhaps he has just succeeded to the office and wishes to win an election in his own name; or he may judge that he can improve his party's position in the House of Commons through a new election.

Parliament can only be dissolved by the Queen, but on the request of the Prime Minister. It is a disputed point whether the Queen has the constitutional right to refuse the request. In practice in recent years, no Prime Minister has ever been refused a dissolution.

To vote, in Britain, one must be over 21, be a British subject or a citizen of the Republic of Ireland, and have his name inscribed in the voting Register. Excluded from the franchise are aliens, peers, lunatics (unless they have lucid intervals), felons, and persons convicted of past election offences. The Register (voting lists) is made up once a year. A form is sent to every house in the nation by the Returning Officer (usually the Town Clerk), and householders must state who is living at the residence, their ages, and whether they are British citizens. After the rolls are compiled by the Returning Officer, an announcement appears that the Register is being prepared and all

are invited to check if their names are on it.

Elections in Britain are short affairs compared to those in the United States. The first step in the procedure is an announcement by the Prime Minister that on a certain date—usually in about ten days' time—the Queen will dissolve Parliament. As soon as she has done so, a Royal Proclamation is published, summoning a new Parliament, and the elections, by law, must be held within three weeks of the Proclamation. Thus from the time of the Prime Minister's announcement to the election itself, only about four and a half weeks elapse.

Writs are issued to all the constituencies commanding them to return a representative to Parliament. The very next day, the Local Returning Officer (the Town or County Clerk) must put up an announcement that there is to be an election; and within eight days of the summons to the new Parliament, the nominations of candidates must be complete. Parliamentary candidates require nomination by two voters and support by another eight. Also, the candidate must put down a deposit of £150. This provision, dating from the 1918 election, was introduced to discourage freak and frivolous candidates. Candidates get their deposit back if they poll more than one-eighth of the total votes cast; otherwise it goes to the state to help pay the election expenses.

Nine days after the last day for nominations, the polling takes place, from 7:00 a.m., to 9:00 p.m., usually on a Thursday. About a week before the poll, the voter will have received a "poll card," which bears the voter's "number" assigned by the Electoral Register. It also tells him where he should vote. Only the names of the candidates appear on the ballot, not the parties they represent, for, in theory, the vote is for the individual not the party. This is important because it means that much party effort has to be spent during the election connecting the candidate with his party, through posters and signs such as "Berrington = Conservative," "Blondel = Labour," and the parties seem to do this quite effectively. At 9:00 p.m., the ballot boxes are sealed. The votes are counted at one central point in the presence of the candidates and party officials. By about 2:00 a.m., unless an election is very close (as it was in 1950), one usually knows how the election has gone.

Between 1945 and 1955, elections in Britain cost the candidates an average of £1 million. Party expenditure is limited by law; the Conservatives spent an average of 88 per cent of the legal maximum, the Labour Party 73 per cent, the Liberals 50 per cent, and all others 46 per cent. There was not a great deal of difference, therefore, between Labour and Conservative expenditures—15 per cent. In the 1959 election, the total spent was £1,051,217, or an average of £684 per candidate, some £43 more than in 1955. Candidates spent (on the average) 80 per cent of the permitted maximum.

The Electoral System

Each constituency elects one M.P. (and is thus known as a single-member constituency). Voters cast one ballot only. The candidate with the most votes wins, which means that in a field of more than two candidates, the winner might have captured less than half the total vote. This system produces a discrepancy between the number of votes cast for a party in the country and the number of seats it wins in the House of Commons. On strict proportionality in 1959, the Conservatives (who won 365 seats) would have won only 311, the Labour Party (which won 265) would have had 270, and the Liberals (who won only 6) would have had 37. "Others" who won 1 would have about 7 seats. And with strict proportionality, *no* parties in *any* of the postwar elections would have had a clear parliamentary majority. It may be argued, however, that if there were a formal proportional representation system, the voters would not vote in the way they do at present.

The British electoral system has two important consequences. It strengthens the predominant two parties against smaller parties, and it keeps the parties united. The weakest of the three main parties could poll up to one-third of the national vote and still run third to the two other parties in *all* the constituencies. Once a party tends to fall to third

place, the electors desert it to vote for one of the two predominant parties, rather than "waste their vote" on a candidate who appears to stand no chance of success. This reduces the weak party's vote still further and drives even more of its supporters to vote for one of the two major parties. In this way, a new party finds it hard to challenge the old established ones, and weak parties become weaker and are eventually "squeezed out."

Only in special circumstances have third parties been able to maintain themselves in Britain. If its vote is heavily concentrated in certain constituencies, it can win seats there. In the nineteenth and early twentieth centuries, the Irish Nationalist Party had a very small proportion of the total vote, but it was almost entirely concentrated in Ireland, where it was, therefore, able to win most of the seats. A third party may make electoral arrangements with one of the two major parties. Thus in 1906 the newly founded Labour Party concluded agreements with the Liberals by which the Liberals supported the Labour candidates in certain constituencies, and Labour did the same for the Liberals in others, so that the anti-Conservative vote would not be split.

But where a weak third party stands aloof from the other major parties and its vote is evenly distributed over the whole country, it will have to poll about one-third of the vote to win a sizable number of seats. This is the Liberal quandary today. The Liberal Party won 6 per cent of the vote in the 1959 election but won only 1 per cent of the seats. In some by-elections since 1959, however, the Liberal Party has as often as not unseated the Labour Party from second place in constituencies held by Conservatives. If this trend continues, electors might come to believe that the Liberal and not the Labour candidate stands the better chance of beating the Conservative. In that case, Labour supporters might regard a vote for Labour as "wasted" and transfer their support to the Liberal. This would further worsen Labour's performance and induce even more voters to desert it for the Liberals. In other, Labour-held constituencies, the Liberals have been ousting *Conservatives* from second place, and the same argument may apply. As of now, however, the electoral system confirms the advantage held by the two major parties, and it is principally for this reason, no doubt, that neither the Conservative nor the Labour Party favors proportional representation, which is strongly advocated by the Liberals.

The electoral system also unifies the parties, because it imposes a heavy electoral handicap on parties that break up. This can be seen from a simple example. Suppose a constituency has split its vote 60 per cent Labour and 40 per cent Conservative. If the Labour Party divided into two roughly equal factions, one supporting unilateralism and the other multilateralism, the result of the next election might well be: Unilateralist-Labour 30 per cent, Multilateralist-Labour 30 per cent, Conservative 40 per cent. Since the Conservative candidate comes at the top of the poll, he would gain the seat from Labour. Parties are deeply conscious of the need to contest the elections as one single body. In the past, the parties that have split—the Conservatives in 1846, the Liberals in 1886, the Liberals in 1922 and 1932, and the Labour Party in 1931—have always lost at the ensuing election. This would not happen under a system of proportional representation, where each half of the divided party would win seats proportionate to its share of the poll. Under the British electoral system, however, even if the two halves of the divided party poll, together, even more than they did as a united party at the previous election, they are still almost certain to win far fewer seats than their united opponent.

"SWING." The lack of proportion between the seats won and the votes cast does not mean that the results of an election are un-predictable. On election night in 1959, an electric computer was able to say, on the basis of the first hour's results, that the Conservative majority would be about 100 to 106 seats (it was actually 100), indicating that there must be some kind of mathematical relationship between votes cast and seats won in the House of Commons. This brings us to the phenomenon known as "swing."

If in 1955, say, the votes in a constituency were divided 51 per cent Conservative and 49 per cent Labour and in 1959 they changed to Conservative 52 per cent, Labour 48 per cent, we say there was a "swing" of 1 per cent. The result is as though 1 per cent of the voters had transferred their allegiance or "swung" over from Labour to Conservative. In a normal constituency (which has between 50,000 and 60,000 voters) and given the normal turnout of about 80 per cent of the electorate, a 1 per cent swing represents about 500 votes, which we subtract from the Labour candidate and add to the Conservative candidate.

Projected onto the national stage, a small percentage swing will shift a disproportionate number of seats in the House of Commons from one party to the other. In the 1959 election, for example, a swing of 1 per cent to the Conservatives would have brought them an additional 19 seats, a 2 per cent swing 10 *more* seats, and a 3 per cent swing yet another 21 seats. There was actually a 1 per cent swing to the Conservatives in 1959, and it was sufficient to push the Tory majority from 54 to a clear 100 seats. But if there had been a 2 per cent swing *against* the Conservatives—that is, if a mere thousand voters had transferred their allegiance in each constituency—the Conservative majority would have been wiped out, and a 3 per cent swing, representing a switch of only 3 in every 100 voters, would have put the Labour Party in power! Clearly, then, any government is based on a knife-edge margin of popular support.

The Election Campaign

The parties employ three main techniques to increase their mass support: political gatherings, propaganda campaigns, and (at elections) drives to get out the vote. Such mobilization and propaganda campaigns go on all the time, for the parties must keep alert between elections. All this effort is for one purpose, to "get out the vote" and see that it votes for the proper candidate. To this end, both parties utilize their complete organizations. The constituencies are the front-line groups. Behind them stand regional organizations; the country is divided into regions, each managed by regional party organizers, and each central headquarters has a staff ready to give financial and legal assistance and political advice to the constituency parties. There are never as many professionals on hand as either party would like, although the Conservative Party has more full-time workers than does the Labour Party.

In a study of the organization of the Labour Party in 1955 (the year of its defeat), published in the 1956 Report of the Annual Conference as the *Wilson Report,* these facts were revealed. The Labour Party was losing the battle for Britain's youth, since "the Tories are able to mobilize far more young people in active work at Election time." As for the effect of large expenditures by the Conservatives, "It is an exaggeration to stress the role of Tory money and large local subscriptions. . . . It is dangerously misleading to think exclusively in terms of Tory money and ignore the efficiency of their voluntary organization which explains a great deal of their success." In addition, in practically all their constituencies, the Conservatives had a full-time "agent," while the Labour Party had only 244 (in about 40 per cent of the constituencies). The Report attributed most of the Conservatives' success to their adoption of a "permanent marked register" of electors, i.e., a card-indexing system listing the electors in the constituency as Conservative, Labour, or doubtful, and the dates at which they had been followed up.

As a result of the Wilson Committee's recommendations, the Labour Party reorganized between 1955 and 1959. For the young voters, it created a new group known as the Young Socialists, with its own organization. To strengthen the party organization, the full-time agents were concentrated in the 50-odd marginal constituencies, and in the 1959 elec-

tion, Labour's pre-canvassing was equal to that of the Conservatives, which it certainly had not been in 1955. And the subscriptions of the constituency parties to central headquarters were increased.

Who Votes and Why?

Hitherto, most voting has been habitual. When the 1959 *Daily Telegraph* poll asked, "What did you vote last time?" and "Do you intend to vote the same way again this time?" it found that 92 per cent of the Conservative sympathizers and 91 per cent of the Labour sympathizers replied they were going to vote for the same party again.

Voting was also largely predetermined. To the question, "When did you make up your mind the way you were going to vote in this Election?" another poll collected these responses:

	1955	1959	
"A few days ago"	3%	4%	
"Two to three weeks ago"	5	8	
	8%	12%	(voters swayed by the actual campaign)
"Months ago"	12%	20%	
"Years ago"	30	27	
"Always have"	50	41	

Note that more people made up their minds to vote at the last minute in 1959 than in 1955.

"Swing" occurs by indirection. A fairly small proportion of the electors actually changes sides in a General Election. The "swing" results mainly from two factors: (1) from more people abstaining on one side than on the other, thus giving the impression of a turnover of votes between the parties, and (2) from the votes of those people (a) who didn't vote last time but are going to this time, (b) who were too young to vote last time and are now casting their first ballot, (c) who had a Liberal candidate last time and have none

Political Parties and Elections

75

this time, (d) who did not have a Liberal candidate last time but have one this time.

What makes people vote the way they do? Although it is often assumed that voters are rational, that they read the party manifestos, make cool appraisals, and vote for the best interests of the country or, possibly, of themselves—in short, that they vote after a rational consideration of issues—in fact, most people vote for what Graham Wallas (writing in 1908) called the "party image."

The "image" of a party may be such as to cause the voter to identify himself with that party. If, for instance, the public image of the Labour Party were the "party of the working class," voters who thought of themselves as "working class" would identify it as *their* party and would tend to vote for it, particularly if the image of the Conservative Party were the party of the rich.

VOTER IDENTIFICATION IN 1951. In his book, *The Middle Class Vote*,[5] John Bonham analyzed Gallup Polls and found that, in 1951, 87 per cent of the Labour sympathizers saw the Labour Party as the party of the working class, of the underdog, of social welfare services, and that 76 per cent of them saw the Conservatives as the party of privilege, big business, and vested interests. On the other side, 22 per cent of the Conservative sympathizers saw the Labour Party as the party of the working class, but 30 per cent saw their own party as "fair to all classes." Another 30 per cent considered the Labour Party incompetent, while 20 per cent thought of their own party as efficient. Again, about 30 per cent of them conceived of the Labour Party as the party of nationalization and overweening bureaucracy, but viewed the Conservatives as the party of individual initiative and free enterprise. Thus on the Labour side, sympathy with the Labour Party and antipathy to

[5] John Bonham, *The Middle Class Vote* (London: Faber, 1954).

the Conservatives was almost entirely a matter of identification with the working class and animosity against privileged interests. For the Conservatives, identification with the Conservative Party and antipathy to the Labour Party was based partly on class feeling, partly on relative efficiency, and partly on dislike of nationalization and bureaucracy. Finally, only 20 per cent of the persons interviewed thought that it mattered "little or not at all" which party was in power; four out of every five were convinced partisans of one party or the other.

VOTER IDENTIFICATION IN 1959. By 1959, working-class self-identification with the Labour Party had diminished. For example, 38 per cent of those interviewed said it mattered little or not at all which party was elected—double the proportion of 1951! Although 80 per cent of the Conservatives recognized major differences between the parties, only 60 per cent of the Labour sympathizers did so; even more significantly, only 29 per cent of the undecided did so. Thus the pro-Conservative voters largely continued to identify themselves with their party, but the Labour sympathizers' bonds to the Labour Party had weakened. This attitude was reflected in a greater determination to vote on the part of Conservative sympathizers relative to Labour supporters (Table 4-4).

TABLE 4-4 *Intensity of Voting Intention, 1959*[a]

	Conservative sympathizers	Labour sympathizers
What is the likelihood of your going to the polls:		
(a) If it is a fine day?		
Definitely yes	88%	77%
(b) If it is wet and cold?		
Definitely yes	84	70
(c) If it means missing a favorite television program?		
Definitely yes	85	71

[a] Source: Gallup Poll, *Political Index Report* (No. 1, January, 1960).

A post-election survey by Dr. Abrams gave even more positive evidence of the falling-off of working-class identification with the Labour

Party. He discovered that many Labour supporters' views could be summed up about like this: "The Labour Party stands for policy X and the people of type Y, but I don't care very much for policy X and I am not a person of type Y!" Dr. Abrams also found that in the eyes of these supporters the outstanding features of the Labour Party were that "it stands mainly for the working class" (89 per cent of the sample maintained this); that "it is out to help the underdog" (75 per cent); that it "would extend the welfare services" (64 per cent); that it "would raise the standard of living of ordinary people" (62 per cent); that it "would try to abolish class differences" (55 per cent).

But when asked to rate which four out of the sixteen given attributes they regarded as "most important for a good political party," only 11 per cent gave one of their four votes to "helping the underdog," only 15 per cent to "abolishing class difference," and only 23 per cent to "extending the welfare services"! In short, as the Russian proverb says: "It's a beautiful country, but no one wants to go there."

Conversely, on three issues the respondents saw little to choose between either party: (1) "really work to prevent nuclear war" together with "would do most for world peace"; (2) "fair treatment for all races"; and (3) "would make the country more prosperous." Yet these were the three issues they rated as "the most important for a good political party"! In short, the matters these Labour respondents regarded as peculiarly the concern of the Labour Party were matters they themselves were relatively unconcerned about; the matters that did concern them were, in their view, as safe with the Conservatives as with the Labour Party.

Nor was that all. Eighty-nine per cent of the respondents stated that the Labour Party stood "mainly for the working class." The investigators then interviewed the working-class Labour supporters (i.e., those rated by the investigators as "skilled working class" and "laboring working class") and asked them to which class they assigned *themselves*. One-third of these Labour supporters who, objec-

tively, were rated by the survey team as working class, rated *themselves* as middle class! They believed the Labour Party favored the working class, but they did not regard themselves as such.

These surveys point to one conclusion: those who, by objective standards, are "working class" had weakened in their emotional self-identification with the Labour Party. And the Labour image no longer evoked as much allegiance from Labour sympathizers and working-class men and women as it did eight years before. In those circumstances, issues became more important in the 1959 election than in either the 1955 or 1951 elections. The Gallup Poll question, "What is the best Party for *yourself?*" was, in 1955, a more accurate guide to the final voting figures than it was in 1959. In 1959, on the other hand, the question, "Which Party is the best one on the most important issues?" gave a more accurate indication of the actual results.[6]

Compared with 1955, Labour lost support among voters under thirty, but gained votes among the old-age pensioner groups. These appear in Table 4-5 as the "65 and over" group, but also as the "poor" (mostly, today, those dependent on National Assistance, pensions, and casual earnings). These votes were unquestionably attracted by Labour's election campaign promise to increase immediately the old-age pension and to devise a more generous superannuation scheme than the Conservative one. Finally, Labour lost support in the richer groups. These backsliders did not vote Conservative; they either voted Liberal or abstained.

The Liberal Revival

There is now much talk of a "Liberal revival" in Britain. The Liberals polled better

[6] Gallup Poll, *Political Index Report* (No. 1, January, 1960).

TABLE 4-5 *Voting in 1955 and 1959* [a]

	1955					1959				
	Conserva-tive	Labour	Liberal	Other	Non-voters	Conserva-tive	Labour	Liberal	Other	Non-voters
SEX										
Men	39%	43%	2%	2%	14%	39%	41%	6%	1%	13%
Women	44	34	2	—	19	43	36	5	—	16
AGE										
21–29	33	42	2	1	22	35	36	5	—	24
30–49	42	41	2	1	14	42	41	5	—	12
50–64	48	36	2	1	13	46	35	6	1	12
65 and over [b]	40	33	1	1	25	35	40	4	—	20
CLASS										
Well-to-do	84	8	2	1	5	79	5	6	1	9
Middle class	66	18	2	1	13	66	14	7	1	12
Lower middle and working class	34	47	2	1	16	34	46	5	—	15
Poor	31	38	2	1	28	19	51	5	—	25

[a] Source: Gallup Poll, *Political Index Report* (No. 2, February, 1960).
[b] Pensionable age.

at the 1959 General Election than in previous elections, and, since then, at by-elections they have dramatically increased their vote at the expense of the other two parties, although sufficiently well to win only one seat. Their representation in the House of Commons stands at the insignificant figure of seven. But the increasing restiveness of the electorate with the two major parties is attested by a rise of Liberal support, as adjudged by the Gallup poll, from 7½ per cent in January, 1960, to over 24 per cent in the summer of 1962. Even more significantly, when respondents were asked whether or not they would like to see the Liberal and Labour Parties join together to oppose the Conservatives, no less than 48 per cent of the Labour supporters answered "Yes," pointing to a considerable decline in Labour morale, if nothing else.

As we saw in our sketch of the history of the parties, the Liberal Party, an offspring of the former Whig party, has a long tradition, as long as that of the Tory-Conservative Party. Throughout the nineteenth century, it was

the natural alternative to the Conservatives, and government alternated between these two until 1915, when the wartime Coalition was formed. From that date to this, the party has been in decline.

In the nineteenth century, the Liberal Party was the party of free trade, of individualism, of radical attack on the landed aristocracy. In the later years of the century, it took the nascent working-class movement into a sort of junior partnership, and in its great administration of 1906 became the champion of wide-sweeping social reforms and social welfare services. In foreign affairs, its attitude was less consistently expansionist than was that of the Conservatives; indeed, its Left wing was militantly anti-colonial. It favored self-government (Home Rule) for the constituent nations of the United Kingdom, notably for Ireland, and it was over Home Rule for Ireland that the Liberal Party split in 1886. In 1912–14, it embarked on a ferocious battle with the Conservatives that might have led to civil war in Ireland.

The Liberal Party has stuck to its principles down to the present, but has adapted them to changed circumstances. It sees the Labour Party as preaching an obsolete doctrine and thinks Labour is too closely tied to the trade unions to be capable of independence. It sees the Conservatives as a reactionary party, with strong associations with big business. The Liberal Party sees itself as independent of any vested interests, and it strives to present itself as a fearless radical alternative to the Labour Party and as the opponent of conservatism.

The party favors free trade and is committed to entering the European Common Market. It is hostile to all forms of monopoly or price-fixing; unlike the other parties, it does not except the restrictive practices and privileged legal position of the trade unions. It stresses individualism more unrestrainedly than do the Conservatives. In the economic order, it opposes nationalization and public control of private enterprises, and, in the political order, it champions civil liberties. It supports the welfare state, although with reservations about present methods of administering it, and is particularly keen on extending educational opportunities, which it believes are the guarantee of social mobility. It opposes colonialism and supports the colonial independence movements. On defense, the Liberal Party, many years ago, took the view that Britain could not and should not compete in the nuclear race with the United States and the U.S.S.R. It recommended that Britain abandon its own H-bombs, rely on American nuclear support or on a common NATO deterrent, and concentrate on developing its conventional arms as part of the Western alliance.

Many of its views have now become fashionable. When the Liberals pressed for free trade in 1945, they were considered completely out of date. Not so today. The Liberals were the first party to advocate British entry into the European Common Market. The Liberal opposition to the British H-bomb was very unpopular when first announced; today, a number of responsible military thinkers concur with this policy.

The Liberal Party often raises issues that the two major parties tacitly combine to suppress. For example, the Liberals do not hesitate to state that the British farmer is over-subsidized ("feather bedded," in the British terminology); the Labour and Conservative Parties are too politically committed to the agricultural vote to take this line, and they are like-wise too dependent on the trade unionists to advocate the control of trade-union restrictive practices. In their denouncement of the British H-bomb, the Liberals have long said what Labour has only just adopted as its policy and what a number of Conservative back-bench critics say or think. The Liberals' support for entrance into the European Common Market is unequivocal, but both the Labour and Conservative Parties are self-divided on this matter. By raising issues that the two other parties avoid or repress, the Liberal Party has been able to create the impression that it is a radical and forward-looking party, different from the other two, and not simply a "middle of the road party" between them.

But their strength is also their weakness. Liberals can afford to tilt at vested interests because they draw no financial or voting support from them. By the same token, the party is poorly organized in the constituencies and cannot rely on electoral support from many segments of British society. The party does much better in by-elections, when it receives free publicity and can concentrate its meager resources on a few candidates; in General Elections, it is drowned out by the clamor of the two larger parties and outstripped by their professional organizations. The Liberal Party is badly hurt by the British electoral system, which squeezes out a small third party unless its votes are geographically concentrated or unless it enters into an electoral alliance with one of the large parties. Since the party's support is thinly and evenly spread over the whole country, it would require a national vote of something like 30 per cent of the electorate for it to capture an appreciable number of parliamentary seats.

Nevertheless, its performance in 1959 and in the by-elections of 1962 show that the party is being taken more seriously now than at any time since 1945. The Liberal vote rose from 2.7 per cent in 1955 to 5.9 per cent—the only party in the 1959 election to increase its share of the vote. True, much of the increase was due to the fact that the number of its candidates had doubled, but this was not the whole story. The average Liberal vote rose from 15.1 per cent to 16.9 per cent, and the number of seats in which it lost its deposit (i.e., in which it polled less than one-eighth of the total vote) fell from the 1955 figure of 60 out of 109 to the 1959 figure of 55 out of 217.

Since 1959, the Liberal record in the numerous by-elections has been impressive. In a large number of cases, the party has topped the Labour or the Conservative vote, which helps its claim to be the true alternative to Conservatism. In many more, it has taken as much as *half* of the previous Conservative vote! Previously, both Labour and Conservatives told the electors that a vote for a Liberal was a vote wasted, because only the Labour and Conservative candidates stood a chance of being elected. Now the Liberals are able to say that a vote for either candidate is a vote wasted, since it is the Liberal candidate who stands a better chance of beating the Conservative or the Labour candidate to first place depending on the constituency.

Parliament and the Crown

V

Following a General Election, the new Parliament assembles, the parties "organize" the House of Commons (which today contains 630 members), the Queen appoints the leader of the majority party as her Prime Minister, and the Prime Minister sets about appointing his colleagues to what is collectively known as "the Government," or (a more old-fashioned term) "the Administration." About seventeen to twenty-two of the Ministers are appointed by him to the inner and policy-directing circle, known as the Cabinet. The Cabinet *is* the government of Britain, and British government is best described as "Cabinet government."

The Cabinet

The Cabinet is responsible for:

1. The final determination of the policy to be submitted to Parliament.
2. The supreme control of the national executive in accordance with that policy as regulated, modified, and consented to by Parliament.
3. The continuous coordination and delimitation of the activities of the various Departments of the government.

The Cabinet, therefore, is the powerhouse of the entire British constitutional system. It enjoys this unique authority because its members combine in themselves three kinds of status. Like the American Cabinet, the British Cabinet constitutes the executive branch of the government because its members are Ministers, i.e., the heads of government Departments. But, unlike the American Cabinet, it is also the steering committee of the legislature; with two or three peers as exceptions, all its members are M.P.'s. Finally—again unlike the American Cabinet—it is a committee of the majority party, since it is composed for the most part of the trusted and tried party chiefs. The executive is thus a committee of the legislature and enacts by and with its consent; it gains such consent precisely because it is a party committee of the party that controls the House of Commons. Thus the peculiarly dominating role of the Cabinet is an outcome of its party's solidarity. As long as the

Cabinet and its party hang together, they will never hang separately.

Unlike the American Cabinet, the British Cabinet is no mere aggregation of Ministers. It is a corporate unity. Each Minister is personally responsible to the Commons for the day-to-day administration of his duties, and it is the Minister who stands up in the House of Commons to explain, justify, and answer awkward questions about the way he has carried out these duties. In practice, of course, nearly all the things done in his name are performed by civil servants; but he, not they, must take the responsibility for acts of omission or commission carried out in his·name. If he fails to give a convincing explanation, M.P.'s may demand his resignation. Most commonly, the Cabinet regards an attack on a Minister as directed against itself and expects its party to support it. But occasionally Ministers *are* forced to resign—when their fault is so grave that even their own backbenchers feel too uneasy to support them. In 1954, a Conservative Minister of Agriculture, Sir Thomas Dugdale, was compelled to resign. He had failed to control the activities of some of his civil servants in the disposal of an estate called Crichel Down, which had come into the Ministry's hands after being taken from its owners during the war for military purposes. The case revealed such muddle and sharp practice in his Ministry that the Minister, morally responsible for what had happened, offered his resignation.

But although each Minister is personally responsible to Parliament for the good conduct of his Department, on matters of *general policy* all members of the Cabinet (and indeed of the whole ministerial group, i.e., "the Government") take equal responsibility and stand or fall together. Every member of the Cabinet is deemed to have acquiesced in the policy of his colleagues. If he disagrees with his colleagues, his proper course is to resign. He is then entitled, by convention, to make a speech

to Parliament explaining his reasons for resignation. Lord Salisbury, a most influential Conservative peer, resigned from Mr. Macmillan's first Cabinet because he disagreed with its policy of independence for Cyprus. In 1958, the Chancellor of the Exchequer (Mr. Thorneycroft) and his two Parliamentary Secretaries—i.e., the whole Treasury team—resigned simultaneously because they thought their colleagues' economic policy was too mild.

On policy matters, the Cabinet, in effect, tells the Commons: "You take us and our policy as a whole. You may not pick or choose your policy, approving this and rejecting that. You must take a 'package deal.' " The Cabinet maintains that it is uniquely responsible. "Who is responsible for executive current administration, the Government or Parliament?" asked Mr. Herbert Morrison (now Lord Morrison), the former Labour Deputy Prime Minister, in 1946. "I say it is the Government that is responsible. . . . Parliament's business is to check the Government, throw it out if it wants to, go for it, attack it, criticize it by all means, for Parliament is not a body which is organized for current administration—not in this country." [1]

The Cabinet and the Cabinet alone, then, is answerable to Parliament and beyond it to the country for all acts of policy during its term of office. How does it maintain its position in the House of Commons? It does so only as it retains the support of a united party. How then does it retain this support? Most of the common explanations are misleading. (1) It is said that the Cabinet can expel rebel M.P.'s from the Parliamentary Party. This could only be effective if the rebels were few in number. Movements of backbench protest numbering forty or more M.P.'s—such as are quite common—could not be disciplined in this way without breaking the party up. In any case, rebel M.P.'s are not frequently disciplined. (2) It is argued that since the Prime Minister can get the Queen to dissolve Parliament and plunge his party into a General Election, this makes his backbenchers more compliant, since they do not care to face

[1] *Third Report,* Select Committee on Procedure (Her Majesty's Stationery Office, 1946), Q.3260.

more election campaigns than are necessary. But for a Prime Minister to seek a General Election at a time when his party was divided would be to court disaster—for, as we have seen, the electoral system works heavily against a disunited party.

In practice, the Cabinet controls its supporters for three main reasons: (1) The Government as a whole (including the junior Ministers) includes almost all of the party leadership. Its Members are particularly influential party men. (2) There is constant consultation between the Government and its supporters, and both make concessions to one another. (3) On many things, the backbenchers are content to let the Ministers run things their own way, for under the British Cabinet system, Cabinet and its party supporters are elected on the same platform and believe in the same principles. The party's successes at the next election are entirely bound up with the success of its Cabinet.

The main threats to the Cabinet are the Opposition, which is constantly trying to defeat it or at least to embarrass it, and the next election, which the Government must win by convincing the electorate that it is best qualified to run the country for another five years.

The House of Commons

The primary function of the House of Commons is to sustain or oppose a Government. The physical shape of the House reflects this division between the Government and the Opposition. Unlike the semicircular arrangement of most legislatures, the Commons is a rectangular room. On the long benches to the right of the Presiding Officer, the Speaker, sit the Members of the Government, with the front benches occupied by the Ministers, and on the Speaker's left sits the Opposition, with its leaders on the front bench.

The role of the House of Commons is threefold: (1) it debates general principles and passes laws; (2) it criticizes administration; and (3) it controls finance. Standing Orders set aside certain special occasions (Supply Days) when the Opposition chooses the topics for debate, but apart from this the timetable is largely in the Government's hands. Its decisions, however, are tempered by three factors: (1) by the convention that the Opposition has a special status in the constitution and must have fair play; (2) by its own discretion, and anticipation of what Members of Parliament will support; and (3) by the possibility—still a real one—that if it does not consult the House and take it into its confidence, the Opposition will manage effectively to obstruct the moves of the Government.

It should be emphasized that the detailed arrangements for the Common's business are, for the most part, arranged amicably between the Whips of both sides, "behind the Speaker's Chair." Such arrangements are known, in Parliament, as "the usual channels." Whenever, as sometimes happens, the Opposition contests the Government's arrangements for a debate, or decides to keep a debate going all night, or otherwise obstructs business, the observer can be sure that the Whips of both sides have failed to agree.

The Government has at its disposal three weapons for shortening debate. The first and oldest of these is "closure." Any Member can move for closure, but the Speaker has the right not to put the motion to the vote unless he is satisfied that the debate has run long enough and that all points of view have had a fair hearing. If he accepts the motion and it is carried by the prescribed majority, the Speaker stops the debate. Closure is often moved by the Government's Whips at a time prearranged between them and the Opposition Whips. Sometimes, however, the Opposition wants the debate to go on, and the Government's closure motion is greeted with anger.

The second parliamentary weapon is the hated "guillotine," formally known as the "Allocation of Time Order." It lays down in detail when and for how long the various parts of the bill shall be debated. The Order is put to the House, debated and passed. At the end of each of the stages specified in the Order, the "guillotine" comes down and ends the discussion. Any clauses contained in that stage and still not debated are put to the vote, notwithstanding. For these reasons, the "guillotine" is sometimes also described as "closure by compartments."

Since the time to be spent on each batch of clauses is also laid down in detail, the "guillotine" forces the Opposition to debate only those clauses which it thinks are particularly blameworthy. The "guillotine" is a reserve weapon for the Government which it can invoke when the Opposition obstructs the use of simple closure.

Finally, we come to the "kangaroo." If a great many Members introduce amendments to clauses in a bill, as is their right, the House would never get through the bill at all. It has therefore been left to the Speaker to select the amendments he regards as the most representative of a particular class of amendment, which means that he will leap from one amendment to another, like a kangaroo.

What about the parliamentary rights of the Opposition? Standing Orders guarantee time to the Opposition for discussing matters it thinks are important. This time comprises the set of debates on the Queen's Speech (opening the session), during the 26 Supply Days, and on numerous adjournments. The Opposition also, of course, debates the bills brought forth by the Cabinet. Of the 158 days the House was in session in 1959, the Government had the floor 47 per cent of the time, the Opposition 25 per cent, and miscellaneous business (including debates on national taxation) took up 28 per cent of the session.

The Composition
and Organization of the House

"HONORABLE MEMBERS." Several kinds of citizens are disqualified from sitting in the House of Commons. They include peers, certain types of clergy (those of the Church of England, the Church of Scotland, the Church of Ireland, and the Roman Catholic Church), minors, lunatics, bankrupts, felons, etc. Once duly elected and sworn in, the Member remains a Member for the term of the Parliament. He can be expelled only by the House itself. (One Member was expelled in October, 1947, after the House found him guilty of gross contempt; in 1954, a Member was expelled after he had been convicted of a criminal offense and sentenced to imprisonment.) An M.P.'s membership cannot be canceled by any outside body, including even his own constituency.

To maintain independence from outside pressures, Members are protected by the hallowed "privileges" of Parliament. The three most important of these are:

Freedom from arrest. This does not protect Members in criminal cases, nor from detention under Defense Acts in time of war. It applies to civil actions only (excepting bankruptcy proceedings). In fact, since imprisonment for debt has been largely abolished, this privilege has lost its one-time significance.

Freedom of speech. No action can succeed against any Member for words spoken in the course of parliamentary proceedings, or for publication among M.P.'s by order of the House or in the course of parliamentary business.

Freedom from molestation. No one may "obstruct and insult the Members of [the] House in the coming to, the going from the House [or] endeavour to compel Members by force to declare themselves in favour or against any proposition then depending or expected to be brought before the House." (Resolution, June 6, 1780). The offer of a bribe to a Member is included under "molestation." So, too, is the intimidation of Members—for instance (as happened in 1946), publishing a poster to the effect that M.P.'s voting in a certain way would have their names published as "enemies of the people." The threat to inflict pecuniary loss on a Member because of his conduct in Parliament is also an act of molestation.

Although he enjoys ancient privileges, an M.P. is poorly paid by contemporary standards. His annual salary is £1,750. This is roughly equivalent to $6,000, but in purchasing power is equal to a United States salary of some $10,000. It is very low by any British professional standards. Out of this he must pay for postage, stationery, and secretarial help, as well as a considerable sum for travel. And all of it is subject to income tax.

THE SPEAKER OF THE HOUSE. The principal officer of the House of Commons, the Speaker, has a status of such dignity that in the Order of Precedence in England he ranks only two places behind the Prime Minister. (The Lord President of the Council ranks second.) He is elected by the Members from among themselves at the beginning of every new Parliament; if he is returned at the next election, it is customary to re-elect him. Usually the Government and Opposition try to agree on a candidate and elect him unanimously, but this does not always succeed. There were contested elections in 1951 and 1959. Once elected, he sheds all party ties. His functions are (1) to represent the House in its relations with the Sovereign, the House of Lords, and all external bodies, and (2) to preside over the deliberations of the House. Here, unlike the American Speaker, he is expected to be completely impartial. He never votes except to break a tie, and then he is expected to vote for the existing situation. He takes no part in debates. As presiding officer, he regulates debate, enforces the rules governing its conduct, selects the speakers at his own discretion, and decides points of order and procedure, giving rulings (which cannot be questioned) where required. He does all this by reference to the custom and law of the House, whether this hinders the Government or not. Since, physically, he cannot always preside, there is a Deputy Speaker who is authorized to take his place when necessary. The Deputy Speaker is chosen from the Government side of the House of Commons, but he, too, is expected to preside with complete impartiality.

COMMITTEES OF THE HOUSE. There are three main types of committee in the House of Commons.

Select Committees of the House. Some of these are sessional, i.e., created at the beginning of each session, and others are appointed *ad hoc* as the occasion arises. They usually (but not always) consist of 15 Members, drawn proportionately from both sides of the House. By tradition, they are not supposed to operate on party lines; indeed, they may not even produce a minority report. A single report is issued which is adopted by the whole committee. Select committees are convened to consider such matters as the disqualification of a Member or the procedure of the House. Sometimes, but not often, they may be asked to discuss a bill.

Committee of the Whole House. The House of Commons as such and a Committee of the Whole House both consist of exactly the same Members (except for the Speaker), but the procedure for each is different. In order to symbolize the fact that the House is in Committee, the Speaker is "moved" out of the Chair, and the Deputy Speaker takes his place. All matters involving finance *must* be begun in the Committee of the Whole House and never in the House of Commons as such. In addition, one of the stages of every bill is the Committee stage, and it is open to the Government to take this stage in the Committee of the Whole House ("on the floor of the House") or in one of the standing committees ("upstairs").

STANDING COMMITTEES. These committees are symbolized by the letters of the alphabet— A, B, C, etc. One, however, is called the Scottish Committee because it contains all the Scottish Members and deals with all Scottish business, the only standing committee that is in any sense specialized. The others each consist of up to 50 Members, drawn proportionately from the parties in the House, and empaneled by the Speaker assisted by his Committee of Selection. These committees meet in rooms which are small replicas of the House itself—the opposing Members range themselves on each side, with the Chairman presiding on a cross bench at the top. The party Whips are always present on each side of the Committee.

These committees play an entirely different part from that played by the committees of the United States Congress or, indeed, by the committtees in the various legislatures of continental Europe. First, they are unspecialized; they are allocated bills as soon as they are free to consider them. Secondly, they never conduct hearings from outside witnesses, nor from civil servants; they do nothing but discuss the bill in front of them according to strict committee procedures. Thirdly, their proceedings are printed in an official record which is placed on sale. Fourthly, it is not their function to report to the House their views about the policy of the bills, nor is there any way in which they can suppress bills or hold them up indefinitely. The House of Commons, in its Second Reading of a bill, is the body that pronounces on whether its policy is good or bad, not the committee. The Cabinet decides whether to hold back or expedite a bill, not the committee. The function of the standing committee is to take the bill after the House of Commons has approved its policy in a Second Reading and to work through it in detail. The committee considers the bill word by word and line by line, considering new clauses and amendments as it does so.

These standing committees act in the same way as the Committee of the Whole House does when it is taking the committee stage of a bill. They are established simply to save time. While a Committee of the Whole House is considering merely the one bill before it, five standing committees can be considering five bills.

Law-Making
in the House of Commons

PUBLIC ACTS. Although some laws, known as Private Members' Bills, usually concerning minor matters, are made on the initiative of private Members, the chief legislative work of the House of Commons consists of Government Bills, which are put forward by the Cabinet. In legislating, the Government derives its policy from three sources, separately or together: (1) the policy of the Government party, i.e., an election promise or a program devised by the Cabinet; (2) the desire of the Civil Service to introduce or amend legislation; (3) the wishes of outside interest groups.

Technically, a bill may be initiated in either the House of Lords or the House of Commons, but in practice the great majority of Government bills originate in the Commons. In either case, a bill must receive three readings in the initiating House before going on to the other. The first step for a bill in the Commons is taken when the Order Paper states that the bill is about to receive a First Reading. This is usually just a formality, for only the title of the bill is read by the Clerk of the House, from a printed sheet called a "dummy bill," which is then laid on the desk of the House. Publication follows soon after. Usually some two or three weeks elapse between the First Reading and the Second Reading, allowing time for the Opposition to decide its line of attack, and for outside interests to make their views known.

The Second Reading ordinarily lasts a day or two (an unusually long three days will be allocated for very important bills like the Transport Bill of 1946–47), and it is at this time that the general principles of the bill are debated between the Government Ministers who are in charge of the bill and the Opposition "Shadow Ministers" who are "marking" them. The Ministers open the debate; then follow the backbenchers, who often speak to a nearly empty House. As the evening wears on, the Ministers reappear and the frontbenchers on both sides re-enter the debate. Finally, normally at about 10:00 p.m., debate ends and a division (a vote) takes place.

Next comes the Committee stage of the bill. The task of the appointed committee is to examine the bill very carefully and to consider amendments. This is the great opportunity for outside interest to influence the bill. Working through their friends on the committee, they often greatly change legislation through the amendments they submit that are accepted. When a bill comes out of committee, it enters the Report stage: the bill "as amended in committee" is circulated to all Members and then debated in the House. If additional clauses are found to be necessary, they are added, and further amendments can also be considered at this time. These are not the same amendments that were discussed in committee and rejected, but substantially new amendments; the Speaker, under his powers of "kangaroo," selects the amendments he regards as meeting this criterion.

One other important feature of the Report stage must be noted. During the Committee stage, the Minister may tell a Member (either one of his own backbenchers or an Opposition Member) that although he cannot promise to accept the Member's amendment, he will consider it. The Report stage gives the Minister the opportunity to bring forward amendments he wanted time to consider during the Committee stage.

When the Report stage is over, the bill goes forward for its Third (and final) Reading, which is, once more, a general debate, this time on the final version of the bill. Third Readings do not last more than a day. If a majority of the Members vote for the bill, it has passed the House of Commons. But it is still not a law, for it must then be voted by the House of Lords. If approved by the Lords, the Royal assent is then given and the bill has become a law.

Although few bills come out of the House of Commons just as they went in, by and large the Government's general policy is upheld. A bill is often altered in one or two important particulars and usually greatly changed in its details. And sometimes a bill receives such a hostile reception that it is dropped altogether.

PRIVATE BILLS. When private individuals or corporations seek particular powers and benefits not granted by the ordinary law of the land, bills to embody such powers and benefits are Private Bills. Ordinarily introduced by local authorities and other statutory bodies such as public corporations, Private Bills rarely meet any opposition, since objections are usually warded off by compromises before the petition is framed. If, however, the bill is opposed, it runs a double hazard: it may have to stand up to a grueling examination in specially constituted committees, each consisting of four M.P.'s, and, even if approved by the committee, it may face a debate on the floor of the House of Commons or the House of Lords. In most cases, however, any changes are made in the Committee stage, and the House accepts them.

SUBORDINATE LEGISLATION. Yet another type of legislation is known as "delegated" or "subordinate" legislation. This legislation is made by a public (or, much more rarely, a private) body under the authority of an Act of Parliament, which is called the "parent" Act. There is an enormous amount of this kind of legislation. In 1952, for instance, the public Acts of Parliament numbered 64, but the number of "Instruments," i.e., the delegated legislation made under Acts of Parliament, totaled 2,312. There are five reasons for the growth of delegated legislation: the pressure on parliamentary time; the technical nature of many Acts; the likelihood of unforeseen contingencies arising during the administration of a complicated Act; the need for legislative flexibility; and the occasional development of emergency conditions that require speedy action. The need for delegated legislation is generally conceded today, but the adequacy of control over it is more widely disputed.

Parliament and the Crown

Since Instruments are so numerous and technical, for every one that a Member detects as objectionable, scores probably escape his notice. Consequently, in 1944 the House created the Select Committee on Statutory Instruments, usually known as the Scrutiny Committee, consisting of eleven Members with an Opposition Member as its Chairman, to bring to the attention of the House any statutory Instrument it thinks should be reviewed by Parliament.

The Committee may not consider or report on the merits or the policy of any of the Instruments. Its duty is to draw the attention of the House to whether it imposes a tax, excludes challenge by the courts, purports without authority of the parent Act to have retroactive effect, or whether there has been unjustifiable delay in publication or laying before Parliament, or, more generally still, whether its language should be clarified, or whether it seems to make some unusual or unexpected use of the powers conferred by the parent Act. The Committee makes no comment to the House beyond listing the heading under which it is reporting the Instrument. The Committee must have consulted the Department that promulgated the Instrument, and the Department's reply is printed along with the Committee's report. Between 1944 and 1952, the Committee examined 6,900 Instruments and reported 93 of these to the House.

Financial Legislation and Control

THE CONSTITUTIONAL PRINCIPLES. In matters of finance, the House of Commons is supreme, according to the Parliament Act of 1911. A bill that the Speaker of the House of Commons certifies to be a money bill cannot be amended by the Lords nor does it need to receive the assent of the Lords to become law. If the House of Lords refuses assent, the bill is merely delayed a month.

A motion to expend public revenue can only come from a Minister of the Crown. This rule was established in Standing Order 63, one of the oldest of the Standing Orders, dating from the reign of Queen Anne. The Opposition, therefore, cannot suggest *increases* in expenditure. In order to combat the Government, it is forced to move for reductions— even if it favors increases; this is its paradoxical way of drawing attention to the inadequacy of the grant. There are two financial committees of the Whole House. One, the Committee of Supply, appropriates money to the various services that need it; the other, the Committee of Ways and Means, raises money. Both are Committees of the Whole House.

THE TAXATION CYCLE. A Budget is introduced every year early in April, which is the beginning of the financial year. The House then, on certain days from April through July, goes into the Committee of Ways and Means and discusses what are known as Budget Resolutions. When all the Resolutions have been debated, they are collected together into a bill which when passed is known as the Finance Act. It embodies the Government's taxation program for the year.

"SUPPLY." Parliament must also "supply" the Government with money, i.e., grant it the right to spend for certain approved purposes. The Treasury collects and revises the Estimates presented to it by the different Departments, and these are introduced in the Commons before April, which is the beginning of the financial year. The House then discusses these Estimates over the next four months, after which, in July, they will be incorporated in a bill called the Appropriation Bill. This Bill when passed, as the Appropriation Act, permits the various Departments to spend on the purposes detailed in the Estimates and on *nothing else*.

Two points must be noticed. First, the House has little control over the details of the Estimates. The days on which these are discussed are called the Supply Days. There are twenty-six of them. On the last day, all the Estimates that have not been debated are simply put to the vote without discussion. Furthermore, the choice of which Estimates are to be debated lies with the Opposition. Finally, the Opposition does not use the occasion to probe the details of the Estimates but for a general debate on the broad policy of the Department whose Estimate is up for discussion.

On the other hand, the House exercises minute control over the spending of the money granted, to make sure that it has been spent only as Parliament has authorized and in no other way, save in very exceptional and justifiable cases. It does this through its officer, the Comptroller and Auditor General, and its Select Committee, known as the Public Accounts Committee. The Comptroller and Auditor General audits the accounts of every Department and presents a report to the Public Accounts Committee, which draws attention to divergencies between what Parliament authorized and what the Department actually spent its money on; to cases of unwise or wasteful administration of the sums granted; and to other irregularities. The Committee summons the Accounting Officers of the Departments to its hearings to justify any departures mentioned in the Report.

THE COMMONS' CONTROL OVER FINANCE. Thus the Commons can partly affect the course of taxation, but has little control over expenditures. It relies on the Treasury and the Cabinet for the formulation of the Estimates and has neither the time nor the machinery to control them in detail. As long ago as 1912, the Commons set up a Select Committee on Estimates, but both this Committee and the Public Accounts Committee can, at best, examine the detail *after* the Estimates have been voted and the money is spent.

Meanwhile, the Government gets exactly what sums it asks for and for the purposes it has approved. Furthermore, it knows in advance that it will do so. It is therefore impossible for any Department to rely on its friends in Parliament to get its Estimate altered or improved. Three important results

follow. First, all Departments are strictly subordinated to the Cabinet's general financial plan. Secondly, the Budget is a coherent document representing the financial aspect of the Government's policy. Thirdly, lobbyist pressures are kept in firm check.

Commons' Control of the Executive

The Commons largely controls the Government through its ability to debate and resist its bills and its financial measures, but it has other special devices at its disposal which enable it to keep a running check on all the Government's activities. Short-range issues—for instance, the decision to deport an alien—are ordinarily taken up during the parliamentary question period and the adjournment debates; long-range issues—e.g., the Government's policy in respect to higher education—are taken up in the "set-piece" debates—the Queen's Speech debates, the Supply Days, and occasional Votes of Censure. Yet sometimes all these occasions may be used to control both matters of detail and matters of policy. This is a matter of tactics—not of usage or convention.

We must also distinguish between the actions of individual Members and the collective action of one of the parties. Questions and adjournment motions are the weapons of the individual Member, the set debate of the whole party. But questions and adjournment debates may also be used by a Member as a preliminary to a general assault.

PARLIAMENTARY QUESTIONS. The parliamentary question addressed to a Minister, to elicit information or to register criticism, and the daily Question Time are distinctive and vital features of the parliamentary system in Britain. Every Member has the right to ask questions of a Minister. He may, however, star his question for an *oral* answer; he must give at least two days' notice for such an answer, and he may not request more than two such questions for any one day. The chief reason for demanding an oral answer is that it entitles the Member, *and other Members, too,* to ask supplementary questions, and these are used to entrap the Minister into damaging admissions.

Question Time runs from 2:45 p.m. to 3:30 p.m. every day except Friday (the Prime Minister can only be questioned on Tuesdays and Thursdays). The turn of each Ministry comes up at intervals of about ten days. It is up to the Clerks to decide which Minister is constitutionally responsible, and they will, if necessary, transfer the question from the Minister queried by a Member to the constitutionally appropriate one. Not all questions are admissible; of the twenty-nine grounds for admissibility, these are some of the most important: the purpose must be to gain information or press for action and not be just an excuse to make a speech; the Government must, in some way, be responsible for the matter questioned; questions to which answers have been refused cannot be repeated.

The questions are numbered and printed on the Order Paper. At Question Time, the Member rises and—addressing the Speaker—says "No. 63, Sir," upon which he resumes his seat while the Minister rises and reads the reply. (He has been known to read the wrong reply with side-splitting results.) On answering, the Minister may expect a veritable drumfire of supplementary questions, not merely from the Member who asked the original question but from other Members. Where the issue is controversial, the process turns into a cross-examination of the Minister by all the House. And sometimes the question or answer may be dynamite.

Question Time is important because it enables the Opposition to probe weak points in the Government's handling of affairs, because it permits this immediately, and because this probing occurs by cross-examination in the presence of the House (which is always crowded for Question Time). When, in 1957, the Opposition asked if it were true that American bombers were flying patrols carrying H-bombs from British bases, the Government was forced to answer in the affirmative and disclose a state of affairs that proved most alarming. Again in December, 1961, the Government first acceded to a UN request to supply 1,000-lb. bombs for use against Katanga and then reversed its decision; the Government was forced into the dilemma of answering questions from the Opposition, who wanted the bombs delivered, and from the Government's own supporters, who did not.

The questions always range over an enormously wide area. For instance, the Minister of Defense in one afternoon can be asked to provide information on a long list of topics, from how many Scottish miners aged 18–30 joined the armed forces, to the Government's policy on cooperation with Germany on armament production. As soon as a question is received in a Minister's Department, it is given priority over all other business. Many Departments have a special parliamentary branch, part of whose business is to take responsibility for getting the question answered. A single sheet of text is prepared for the Minister, embodying the answer, background data, and suggested answers to possible supplementaries. A well-briefed Minister can often defend himself even if he has a bad case. It is much more likely that his weak position will be exposed. The House may not always discover the truth, but it infallibly recognizes a cheat.

ADJOURNMENT MOTIONS. An adjournment motion enables a Member to start a debate unrelated to the motion itself. Adjournment motions take place at the end of every day and also when the House disbands for a vacation or holiday. Members who are dissatisfied with a Minister's reply to their questions can seek to raise the matter again "on the adjournment." If successful, they can force the Minister into an additional half-hour debate on the issue. Although no vote is taken on such debates, they can be a useful check on ministerial action. For instance, a Conservative M.P. recently raised at Question Time a complaint from a constituent who charged that the local police had beaten his son. Failing to get a satisfactory reply, the M.P. raised the matter on the adjournment. His case raised such wide sympathy from both sides of the House that the Government had to institute a public inquiry.

THE "URGENCY" ADJOURNMENT MOTION. For business that brooks no delay, Standing Orders provide for an "urgency" adjournment motion, under which a debate can take place at 7:00 p.m. that very night, usually amid great excitement. Confidence in the Government is often at stake, and since the Whips on both sides have to take crash action, by telephone, telegram, and runners, to collect their scattered Members, the occasion is generally one of high drama.

When Ministers have to speak with only a few hours coaching on a question, all sides are tense with anticipation. The Savidge Case of 1928 arose from an "unsatisfactory" answer to a question put in the Question period. It was concerned with the activities of the police in investigating a Miss Savidge. The debate was held that very evening. The police actions that formed its subject were found to be highly discreditable, and the matter was closed only by the Government promising to set up an inquiry into the whole matter of police investigations. When in 1946 the Foreign Secretary, Ernest Bevin, stated that the Labour Government proposed to evacuate the Suez Canal zone, Winston Churchill, Leader of the Opposition, moved the adjournment and the Speaker accepted the motion. A more recent example, in 1958, relates to a Spanish fugitive from the Franco regime who had arrived in Britain as a stowaway. In Question Time, it was learned that the Home Secretary was about to deport him immediately. Members argued that to deport him back to Spain was tantamount to a death sentence since he had already spent prison terms there for his opposition to the government. A Member moved the adjournment which the Speaker accepted, and the matter was debated that evening. The

Home Secretary did deport him, not to Spain but to a friendly country willing to take him. But such occasions are rare because the issue has to be one of "immediate, urgent and public importance," and Speakers interpret each of these three separate words—i.e., what is "urgent," what is "public," and what is "immediate"—very conservatively. Since 1945, only eight of seventy-three requests for the adjournment were successful.

QUEEN'S SPEECH DEBATES. Every session of Parliament is opened by the Speech from the Throne, which is either read by the Queen in person or by her commissioner, in a ceremony of antique grandeur and dignity; but the speech has actually been drafted by the Cabinet, and it sets out the Government's legislative program for the session. Six days of debate follow, and the Opposition usually mounts a sustained attack on the Government, ranging over foreign affairs, defense, colonial affairs, the state of the economy, and any other matters of strong interest to the Opposition.

THE SUPPLY DAYS. As we have already seen, the 26 days allocated by Standing Orders for voting on the Estimates are, in fact, used by the Opposition to criticize the Government's handling of particular affairs. Since the Opposition has the right to select the topics, it can take up matters previously raised during Question Hour or the adjournment debates and thus initiate a full debate on them.

VOTES OF CENSURE. In addition to the debate on the Queen's Address and on the Estimates, the Opposition can persuade the Government to "give" it days to debate certain urgent topics. But the Government, naturally enough, is miserly of its time, since it has a program of its own to get through and is reluctant to turn the floor over to the Opposition.

The Opposition, however, always has a

weapon in reserve. It can call for a discussion of a motion expressing lack of confidence in the Government—a vote of censure, as it is called. Strictly an emergency move, it must be used with discretion, and by convention the Government never fails to accede to a demand from the Leader of the Opposition for a vote of confidence. This convention is based on the fact that the Leaders of the Opposition are responsible Members who form a potential alternative government—a position that guarantees the legitimacy of such an interruption of the normal course of business. For their part, the Government ordinarily has everything to gain by meeting such a direct challenge to its authority at the earliest possible moment.

In a study made in 1955, it was found that the time of a session of Parliament was divided up as shown in the table below. The table compares the pre-war breakdown with that of the postwar years; note that the main change has been the drop in time devoted to miscellaneous business.

	Private Members		Opposition		Government		Remainder		Total
Pre-war period	25 days	18%	34 days	23%	69 days	46%	21 days	14%	149 days
Postwar period	29 days	18%	41 days	26%	75 days	48%	13 days	8%	158 days

Is the House of Commons Important?

"Parliament in Danger"; "The Passing of Parliament"; "Parliament in Decline"—these are some of the titles of books and articles that have appeared in Britain recently, and they show that many British critics feel the Commons is losing its powers to the executive, that is, to the Cabinet and the Civil Service. Foreign observers, and particularly some Americans, consider the Cabinet to be all-important and the Commons to be little more than a rubber stamp. At first sight, there appears to be much truth in what these critics say. As we have seen, the power of the Commons is undercut by several factors. (1) It is not a law-initiating assembly. Private Members' Bills do not usually deal with important matters and only reach the Statute book if the Cabinet is neutral or favorable. On other matters, the Cabinet initiates legislation, controls the parliamentary timetable, and receives exactly the appropriations it requests. (2) The parties vote on predetermined lines, with almost no cross-voting and very rare abstentions on either side. If the Cabinet forces a vote of confidence on any issue, it is certain to get a majority vote. (3) Governments have tended more and more to make all issues matters of confidence—i.e., they will resign on a defeat, unless it is the defeat of some clause in committee (which they can always get the House to reverse in the Report stage if they think it important enough), or if it is obviously the result of some hasty vote, which, again, can be rectified at a later sitting. But to argue from this that the House is a rubber stamp or that it is no longer of importance would be to misunderstand its role completely.

The outward show of a Cabinet triumphing all along the line and never being overturned by a hostile vote of the Commons is deceptive. The mechanics of control are much more subtle. Cabinets are not overturned, because they take steps to meet the mood of the House, which means taking into account first their own backbenchers and secondly the Opposition. The results manifest themselves in three ways. (1) The Cabinet trims and tailors its policies and proposals to anticipate the criticisms that will arise in the House of Commons. Since this is done behind the scenes, it is not immediately obvious to the outside observer. (2) A Cabinet that has miscalculated the extent or the kind of criticisms that will develop in the House will accept amendments to its measures or even withdraw them altogether. (3) If the Cabinet still remains obstinately out of tune with the mood of the House, the Members will not ordinarily react by an adverse vote, but in other ways, including abstentions from the vote. If these warning signs are sufficiently serious, the Government will either modify its policy or, in a very grave crisis, make way for a new Government, though this might be drawn from the same party (witness the resignation of Neville Chamberlain in favor of Winston Churchill in May, 1940).

THE ROLE OF THE GOVERNMENT'S BACK-BENCHERS. We have already seen that both Parliamentary Parties organize themselves into committees. The influence of such committees on the Ministers is hard to measure, because they are private meetings and great care is taken to see that the proceedings do not leak out. But there is no doubt that Ministers "put themselves right" with restive supporters in the committee rooms. In one week in June, 1960, for instance, the Fuel and Power Committee attacked a Minister for appointing a Labour M.P. to the chairmanship of the National Coal Board, and, more significantly, the Foreign Affairs Committee considered the Government's approach to the Common Market as too cautious; the Committee's officers went to the length of putting a motion on the Order paper calling for the Government to draw up proposals for negotiations with the six Common Market countries. The Cabinet is always uneasy when the Whips report that the members of a specialist committee have taken the bit between their teeth, and it is in these meetings that the arts of party management are brought into play, that the compromises in policy are arranged, and that the rank and file make their strength felt.

An example will illustrate this. It relates to the Cabinet's proposals over the Northern Rhodesian franchise in 1961. Essentially, the question was whether the Africans should be given enough votes to constitute a majority immediately or given only parity with the whites. The Colonial Secretary, Ian Macleod, devised an elaborate franchise scheme that might possibly result in African preponderance. The Colonial Committee of the Con-servative Party asked Mr. Macleod to attend. About 50 backbenchers were present. The Minister was received politely rather than warmly. Of those who spoke, only one seems to have supported the Minister. The remainder voiced concern about the likelihood of this policy creating an African majority. After the meeting, they expressed their disquiet by passing a motion which soon received the support of over 80 backbenchers (about one in three of the total). Ten days later, Mr. Macleod attended yet another meeting of the Committee. This time about 180 Members were there to hear him, some two out of every three backbenchers. For the first time, Mr. Macleod made some headway against his critics; but even then he was made to realize that 40 or more backbenchers were still unreconciled to his policy.

The Role of the Opposition

All constitutional governments must somehow reconcile the rights of opposing interests with the necessity for the government to continue functioning. Some systems—the American presidential system is one—seek to achieve this by dividing authority among a number of constitutionally equal and independent bodies. The decision-makers are thus checked and balanced by *exterior* organs. In contrast, the ultimately supreme power in the British system, the House of Commons, contains an *internal* check and balance, in the form of the Opposition Party.

The notion of a neat pyramid by which the Cabinet commands the Commons, the Commons the Parliament, and the Parliament the nation is inadequate and misleading. It omits the major characteristics of the system— the integral status of the Opposition. The parliamentary Opposition has five characteristics and four functions. Its characteristics are:

1. It is *organized*. It presents a united challenge to the Government on all issues it

chooses to contest. We have already noted its organization—its leadership, its nervous system (the Whips), its intelligence system (the backbenchers' committees).

2. It is *permanent*. It does not band and disband but is a permanent feature.

3. It is *representative*. It is the leader of a group of dedicated party-followers throughout the country, with whom it is organically connected.

4. It is the *alternative*. If the Government falls, the Opposition succeeds it. If the Government is beaten in an election, the Opposition takes over. This possibility forces the Opposition to be more moderate in what it condemns and what it promises.

5. It is a *participant*. It helps the Government shape the program of the House and participates in the decisions made in each session.

The functions of the Opposition are:

1. To participate in the deliberations of the House of Commons.

2. To oppose objectionable policies by its voice and vote.

3. To compel the Government, by all acceptable methods, to modify its policy.

4. To create by its voice and vote a public revulsion against the Government and public sympathy for itself, as the pre-condition for winning the next election. Since, as we have already seen, a relatively small swing of votes in any election can mean the difference between victory and defeat, this is not as difficult as it sounds.

5. To pose an alternative program. Perhaps this is the most important of all the Opposition's functions. The mere fact that the Opposition makes promises toward, say, the old-age pensioners or the farmers, and advocates a particular view about the draft or the H-bomb forces the Government party to counter or outbid such promises. Students who

compare the manifestos of the two main parties will find a surprisingly large measure of agreement. The reason is that both parties are out to attract the votes of relatively uncommitted groups. A long time ago Benjamin Disraeli, the future Conservative Prime Minister, talked of the Conservatives as "catching the Whigs bathing and running off with their clothes." He also characterized the conservatism of Sir Robert Peel as being "Tory men and Whig Measures." Both the major parties play this game of borrowing their opponent's most popular measures and adapting them to their own use. In the early 1950's, when R. A. Butler was the Conservative Chancellor of the Exchequer, the public could detect so little difference between his policies and those of his Labour predecessor, Hugh Gaitskell, that it coined the name "Mr. Butskell."

Today, surface appearances show that the Cabinet is in complete control of policy, finance, and the House of Commons' timetable. To detect whether the Cabinet is weak or strong, whether it is really dominating the Commons or is being pressured by it requires much more detailed and subtle inspection. The observer would first look for the warning telltale signs of unrest among Government supports: awkward parliamentary questions directed at their own Ministers; critical motions on the Order paper supported by key names such as the officers of the backbench committees; critical speeches in debates; and possibly abstentions from voting. The Government is in constant communion with its members. This communion has been well illustrated in Professor H. H. Wilson's recent book, *Pressure Group*,[2] which tells how a small group of Conservative backbenchers advocating commercial television was able by degrees to win substantial support in the Conservative Party, to negotiate with the Cabinet, and ultimately to induce it to introduce a commercial television network.

The Cabinet, then, must placate its own supporters, but it must do so in the face of unrelenting attacks by the Opposition. The last

[2] H. H. Wilson, *Pressure Group* (London: Secker and Warburg, 1961).

time a Government which had a nominal majority over all parties in the House was overthrown by an adverse vote was in 1895. The Opposition cannot hope to repeat this performance today. The most it can count on is to be able to shame so many of the Government's supporters into abstention that the Government's stand is morally condemned in the eyes of the nation. This is what the Labour and Liberal Opposition parties did in the famous debate over the Narvik campaign of May 7 and May 8, 1940, in northern Norway. Only a few weeks before, Prime Minister Neville Chamberlain had told the Conservative Central Council that Hitler had ."missed the bus." Then Hitler seized Norway in a lightning sweep and had just defeated the woefully ill-equipped and badly handled British expedition. The Commons debated the failure of the campaign on a motion for the adjournment. At the beginning of the second day's debate, the Labour Party announced that it would force a vote at the end. In the voting, the Chamberlain Government had a comfortable majority of 81, but its full majority should have been more than *double* that figure! Over 30 Conservatives voted with Labour (some in tears) and 60 more abstained. "There was no doubt," wrote Sir Winston Churchill, "that in effect, though not in form, the Debate and the Division were a violent manifestation of want of confidence in Mr. Chamberlain and his administration." Chamberlain resigned, and the King called on Winston Churchill to form a new Cabinet, which became the wartime Coalition Cabinet.

Such a dramatic success for the Opposition is almost as unprecedented as is its defeat of the Government in a straight vote. Although the Opposition does not entertain the hope of overturning the Government, it can and does wring concessions from the Government and exposes the weaknesses or unfairness of Government policies. In 1960, when the questioning showed that American spy flights over Russia were being made from British airdromes, the Opposition challenged the Government and could justly claim credit for the Prime Minister's subsequent redefinition of the Anglo-U.S. agreements on the use of bomber bases. Again, when the Government announced in 1960 that it had decided to abandon its costly attempt to build a British ballistic missile (the Blue Streak), the Opposition moved a vote of censure and succeeded in creating wide public uneasiness over Government defense policy. The Opposition focuses attention on important matters that might not otherwise have been heard of, and its pressure has led to a large number of influential committees of inquiry. For instance, a committee wes set up to inquire into the disturbances in Nyasaland in which some 58 natives had been killed by the police. The report was not flattering to the Nyasaland Government, the British Colonial Secretary, or to the Cabinet.

The Opposition knows that it can bring tears but can never overturn a Government. But though it cannot overturn the Government, it can capture votes outside the Commons. It is to the electorate above all that its criticism is directed. The Cabinet has power, but only contingent power. It faces a dedicated enemy which is armed with procedural privileges and commands an organized national following. And all the Government says or does is staked on the hazard of the few votes—3 in 100—that will turn it out.

The House of Lords

In the beginning, government lay with the King in his Great Council, which was the forerunner of the present House of Lords. The House of Lords still consists, overwhelmingly, of hereditary peers. But it is a mere adjunct of the Commons. Today neither the Crown nor the House of Lords can stand out against the expressed will of the House of Commons. The Crown never tries, and the House of Lords can easily be overborne should it try to do so.

The existence of the House of Lords shows

the British custom of preserving antique institutions as long as they can be made to play some useful role. It also dramatically illustrates a unique feature of British democracy—the continued existence of a vigorous aristocracy, playing a full part in public affairs. In this respect, Britain differs sharply from France, Italy, Germany, and, indeed, from almost every other modern democracy in the world. The fact that the majority of these noblemen are recent creations who have come up from middle-class origins (as we shall see below) offers one reason why the British nobility, and the House of Lords in which they sit, still have a political role to perform.

Of the 900-odd members of the House of Lords, some 840 are hereditary peers; in addition, there are 16 "representative peers" of Scotland (chosen from their own numbers to represent the Scottish aristocracy as it existed before the union of England and Scotland in 1707); the princes of the royal blood; the nine Law Lords; and twenty-six Spiritual Lords (i.e., the Archbishops and Bishops). Since 1958, there sit an increasing number of Life Peers, and Peeresses, under the Life Peerages Act of 1958. These are eminent persons who are created peers to enable them to sit and act in the House of Lords, but whose titles die with them. Most of the hereditary peerages are recent creations. As of 1957, over half had been created in the present century. Over one-fifth were the first holders of the title, and another fifth were but the second holders of the title. Table 5-1 shows that the "aristocracy" does not derive from noble blood but from success in politics, commerce, industry, and public life generally.

TABLE 5-1   *Background of Peers Created between 1916 and 1956* [a]

	M.P.'s	Labour Party workers	Commerce and industry	Military, etc.	Other public servants	Lawyers, etc. (except Lords)	Others	Total
1911–1919	32	—	14	9	2	—	3	60
1920–1929	46	—	26	1	5	6	3	87
1929–1931 [b]	9	2	—	1	1	2	4	19
1932–1939	37	2	23	3	8	—	7	80
1940–1944	18	2	3	4	3	5	2	37
1945–1951 [b]	24	10	—	16	—	—	10	60
1951–1956	27	—	4	—	2	2	2	37
	193	16	70	34	21	15	31	380

[a] Source: P. A. Bromhead, *The House of Lords and Contemporary Politics, 1911–1957* (London: Hillary House, 1958).
[b] Periods of Labour rule.

The Judicial Function of the House of Lords

The highest court of appeal in the United Kingdom is the House of Lords, but in practice (1) no *lay* peers ever sit with the court and (2) no appeal may be heard unless at least three qualified legal personages are present. Such personages are the nine Lords of Appeal and the Lord Chancellor; should an insufficient number of these be available, any other of the legally qualified peers may be invited to sit.

The Powers of the House of Lords

Until 1911, each House of Parliament had a full veto over the legislation sponsored by the other. The Parliament Act of 1911 made three great changes.

1. A bill, certified by the Speaker of the House of Commons as a money bill and

passed by the Commons and sent to the Lords at least one month before the end of the session, would become law even if the House of Lords refused its consent. Thus the Commons' pre-eminence in finance matters ceased to be a convention and was made statutory.

2. Any other bill (other than a Private Bill), if passed by the House of Commons in three successive sessions inside a two-year period or more and sent up to the Lords at least one month before the end of the third session, would become a law even if the Lords rejected it in each of those three sessions. Since a Government can easily split the life of Parliament into sessions, the real limitation was the two years' delay. The Lords' right to veto had been cut down to a right to delay.

3. The life of a Parliament, hitherto seven years, was cut down to five years, i.e., since the Lords had lost their veto, there were to be more frequent appeals to the people in General Elections.

Even the two years' delay was irksome to any radical government contemplating far-reaching legislation. Accordingly, in 1947, the Labour government introduced a new Parliament bill and passed it over the opposition of the House of Lords. Thus, the Parliament Act of 1949 requires that a bill be passed in only *two* successive sessions within a period of *one* year. The Lords, therefore, can nowadays delay Commons' legislation by one year at the most.

Although there are some 900 members of the Lords, only about 60 attend sessions regularly; the average number voting is about 80, and the average daily attendance is about 100. The Lords are organized into parties, each with its Whips. Among the total membership, Conservatives preponderate overwhelmingly; of the active 60 or so, two-thirds are Conservatives and one-third are Labour peers. A Conservative government can always rely on support in the Lords; a Labour government must always expect opposition.

DELAY. In the past, the House of Lords tended to act against Liberal and Labour governments and not against Conservative ones. In recent times, its great chance to act as a "barrier to hasty legislation" was during the period of Labour rule, 1945–51. In fact, it passed almost all the Labour measures. It contested the Parliament bill which was designed to cut its delaying power down from two years to one, but this was to be expected. It also rejected a Labour bill providing for the abolition of capital punishment. In addition, it used the threat of delay to exact a compromise from the Labour government over the timing of the Iron and Steel Nationalization Bill. The government got the Bill in the form it demanded, but the Bill's effective date was postponed until after a General Election. Thus, on the whole, the Lords used their delaying power with great moderation.

REVISION. With much more time at its disposal than the Commons and containing a nucleus of highly eminent lawyers and other professional people, the House of Lords is a valuable revising chamber. The author has analyzed the Labour Government's Transport Act of 1947 in some detail. The Lords discussed 450 amendments and passed 210. Of these, 177 were substantive amendments; 86 were introduced by the Government, of which 53 were designed to meet points raised by the Opposition in the Commons; and 91 were introduced by the Conservative Opposition in the House of Lords itself. The Lords do not use their revising powers only against Labour Governments. Many Conservative peers opposed the Conservative government's Television Bill in 1953, and although the Government got its way, it had to make substantial concessions.

INITIATION. Governments introduce many bills in the Lords so as to relieve pressure on the Commons. In fact, between 1947–55 over a quarter of all Government bills were initiated in the Lords. Most are largely non-partisan and technical bills, like the Companies Bill of 1948 and the Copyright Bill of 1955–56.

AS A DEBATING CHAMBER. It is argued that the House of Lords provides debates of a high order by many eminent men and women, and that this helps to form and inform public opinion. Opinions differ as to what constitutes a good debate. The speeches, which are better read than heard, are reproduced only in the "quality" papers. The influence of the House of Lords would be crippled if its delaying and revising powers were abolished, but it would not suffer at all if all its debates were held behind closed doors.

REFORM OF THE HOUSE OF LORDS? The reform of the House of Lords is not a lively issue. The Conservatives do not want to democratize its composition, but would like to strengthen its powers. The Labour Party does not want to strengthen its powers, but would like to democratize its composition. Hence nothing has been done. Meanwhile, the Lords give good service; they save the Commons time, give bills an excellent legal scrutiny, and use their delaying power with moderation—just sufficiently to get themselves taken seriously and to take themselves seriously.

The Crown

The Royal Title is: Elizabeth II, "by the grace of God of the United Kingdom of Great Britain and Northern Ireland and of Her other Realms and Territories Queen,

Head of the Commonwealth, Defender of the Faith." This form of title is varied for those other nations of the Commonwealth that owe allegiance to the Crown. In those countries, the Queen is represented by a Governor General. (Though the Queen's representative, he is entirely independent of the British government and is often a national of the country in which he holds office.)

The Crown is passed down according to the stipulations of the Act of Settlement of 1701, which provided that the succession "should remain and continue to the said Most Excellent Princess Sophia and the heirs of her body being Protestants." The rules of descent provide that the sons of the Sovereign succeed to the throne in order of their seniority; if there are no sons, then the daughters succeed in order of seniority. When a daughter succeeds, she becomes the Queen Regnant and holds all the powers of the Crown as fully as though she were a King. The "King never dies." There is no interregnum between the death of the Sovereign and the accession of his successor. The successor is immediately proclaimed King (or Queen) at an Accession Council. This is the meaning of the phrase "The King (Queen) is dead, long live the King (Queen)."

The Prerogatives of the Crown

Every act of government is carried out in the Queen's name. The Queen's personal discretion is very limited indeed, however. In law, she has the right to dismiss her Ministers at her own discretion; but this right was last exercised in 1834, and even then with the acquiescence of the Prime Minister. Again, she has the legal right to veto a bill passed by both houses of Parliament; but the last time this was exercised was when Queen Anne vetoed the Scotch Militia Bill in 1707. Again, the Queen convenes and dissolves Parliament. May she, at her personal discretion, withhold her consent to a dissolution of Parliament when this is asked for by her Prime Minister? For more than a century, no Sovereign has rejected such advice to dissolve (though examples have occurred in other countries of the Commonwealth).

Whether the Queen can refuse today is still a contested question.

Those personal prerogatives of the Crown which the Sovereign still exercises at her own discretion today are two. In the first place, she has the right to "be consulted, the right to encourage and the right to warn" her Ministers. She has the right to see all Cabinet papers and to receive the Cabinet Agenda in advance, to receive copies of all the important Foreign Office telegrams, and receive the reports of the Cabinet's Defense Committee and its important sub-committees. In constant touch with what is happening, she becomes increasingly well informed as her reign lengthens. This may well make her influential; but this influence is advisory only. If her Cabinet insists, she must give way.

Secondly, in certain circumstances the Sovereign may have a discretion as to the choice of Prime Minister. Usually, one party has a clear majority and a recognized leader. In such circumstances, the Leader of that party must be sent for; there is no alternative.

It has happened, however, that no one party has an absolute majority in the House of Commons. Here the Sovereign may be able to exercise a personal discretion. The rule is that when the Prime Minister's party has been defeated, the Queen offers the chance of forming a government to the Opposition. In 1923, the Conservative government was defeated at the polls but still remained the largest party in the Commons, with the Labour Party second and the Liberals third. The Prime Minister met the new House of Commons, was defeated in a vote and resigned. A new Prime Minister had to be chosen. For whom should the sovereign send? In the event, Mr. Baldwin made it clear that he would not form a coalition with the Liberals, and the Liberals themselves told the King that he ought to send for the Leader of the Labour Party. This he decided to do, with the result that Ramsay MacDonald became Prime Minister and formed a (minority) Labour Cabinet.

What happens when there is a clear majority of one party in the House of Commons but the party lacks a recognized leader? In 1923, when the Conservatives were in a majority, the Prime Minister, Bonar Law, was dying and a successor had to be chosen. The rule in such matters seems to be that the Monarch takes advice where he can find it. In this instance, the King received advice from some to appoint Lord Curzon and from others to appoint Mr. Baldwin. In the end, the King appointed the latter.

A similar example occurred in early 1957, when Anthony Eden, the Conservative Prime Minister with a majority in the House of Commons resigned owing to ill health. Clearly, the Conservatives as the majority party could alone form a stable government, and hence a successor to Sir Anthony had to come from their ranks. The Queen is said to have taken advice from Lord Salisbury and Sir Winston Churchill. What they told her is not known, but she subsequently invited Harold Macmillan to form the new government. Some Labour politicians objected to the propriety of this. They thought that the Conservatives should have elected their Leader to succeed Sir Anthony, and thus leave the Queen with no other choice but to appoint him. But the Conservative Party has always held that the Sovereign should have a choice of Prime Minister when the office falls vacant while the party has a majority in the House of Commons, and that the party should *then* elect as Leader the person so selected as Prime Minister by the Queen.

The Importance of the Monarchy

The Monarchy makes a unique contribution to the British constitution, for the Sovereign is two things in one—a tradition and a person—and the two things reinforce each other. When the Queen opens Parliament, none can fail to note the poignant contrast between the splendid and solemn ritual that recalls the nation's long panoply of history, and the pale, fragile human being, stiff in brocades and wearing her crown, moving in its center. When, in contrast, the Queen takes a cup of tea with an old-age pensioner, none could fail to remember that this visitor is the embodiment of the whole nation in her person. The "magic of Monarchy" lies just in this. Other countries have their flags, their constitutions, and their schoolbook histories, but these are all abstractions. The uniqueness of the British Monarchy is that all these are, so to speak, "made flesh." They are embodied in the activities of a Sovereign who is remote, splendid, and legendary, and yet, at the same time, a very human person. The public's attitude to the Queen is made up of reverence, awe, curiosity, and warmth. This is a unique relationship, and in Britain a good Sovereign is one who succeeds in inspiring it.

The Queen, then, is the visible focus of British patriotism. She is also the embodiment of the permanency of the state, outside and above the strife of parties and of social and political change. Her authority does not stem from the people. It is recognized by them as springing from a remoter, more awe-inspiring source. In all these aspects, the Queen is outside the common run of humanity.

What does the Monarchy contribute? First, the Queen is today the only tangible link between the countries of the Commonwealth. There is no Commonwealth flag, religion, or language. But all the countries of the Commonwealth—even the republics—recognize the Queen as the Head of the Commonwealth. This gives them a feeling of common identity. And this feeling is reinforced by the many Commonwealth tours made by the Queen. Her tumultuous welcome in such countries as India or Ghana—which have by no means seen eye to eye on international problems with the British government—smoothed Commonwealth relationships and made all member nations conscious of a continuing link.

The Royal presence makes abrupt changes, in both domestic and foreign affairs, more tolerable. When the first Labour government took office in 1924, the fears of the wealthy were allayed by the fact that the King had seen fit (as constitutionally he was bound to do, of course) to send for the Labour Party's Leader to be his Prime Minister. The loosened ties of the Commonwealth, indeed the very dissolution of Empire, are made to appear less revolutionary because the Queen still presides over it.

The Queen's presence invests occasions and institutions with a national significance. Parliament is in reality the scene of a continuous and not always very elevating struggle for power between the rival parties. When the Queen opens it, she brings home the other and equally true fact that this is the supreme institution of government in the realm, and all the pageantry, solemnity, and majesty that she brings to the ceremony is transferred to the institution itself. When the Queen reads the Speech from the Throne, this speech, although it is put into her mouth by Ministers and is shortly to be savagely attacked by the Opposition, nevertheless acquires the flavor of a policy for the nation, written by a party that is acting for the nation. Its partisan character is, for the moment, subdued. One has only to suppose how changed its reception would be if it were read, not by the Queen, but by the Prime Minister.

Finally, the Monarchy serves to ennoble important aspects of public life that would be humdrum at best and sordid at worst. Since the Queen is the "fount of honor," all national honors and awards are made in her name, and the more important of them are invested by her personally. Britain is the only democracy in which an aristocracy still plays an important political part. The reason is not that the ancient landed aristocracy has maintained its privileges but that newcomers who have distinguished themselves in public or political service or in their chosen professions have been turned into "aristocrats" by the Royal grant of an honor or title. In this way, the old chivalric idea of public service has been perpetuated in Britain, and the result is that hundreds of persons pursue their vocations up and down the country, not for self or personal power, but for the unsubstantial but signal honor of being brought into this circle of aristocracy of which the Queen is the head.

Honors and awards are not limited just to the grand figures in their professions. Every year thousands of humble citizens are honored by the award of some Order—e.g., the Order of the British Empire (O.B.E.), and thus thousands who have persevered in voluntary or public service find that their good work has been recognized publicly. The Queen is the patron of many learned societies; she is always on hand to open a new hospital, inspect a factory, launch a ship, and in all these ways, her presence makes the people involved feel appreciated and important.

In brief, the Queen brings home to all men and women, in all parts of the country, their common partnership in the national community; she personifies the continuing identity of the nation, irrespective of party discords, changes of government, and alterations in Britain's place in the world. Although an hereditary Monarch is not indispensable to the working of the constitution, it wonderfully humanizes it and smooths its often difficult path.

The Cabinet and the Central Administration

VI

Today the powers of the Queen, with the exception of her remaining discretionary prerogatives, are carried out by her Ministers. All these are chosen by the Prime Minister. The Cabinet is composed of an unspecified number of Ministers, most of whom head up specific government Departments. Outside the Cabinet, there are a number of non-Cabinet Ministers who also are in charge of Departments; in addition, most Departments have at least one junior Minister appointed by the Prime Minister. Such junior Ministers act as deputies to the Minister and usually have the title of Parliamentary Secretary. All the Ministers collectively are known as "the Ministry," "the Administration," or, most usually, "the Government." None of these three terms has any precise legal meaning, however.

The essential difference between the Cabinet Ministers and those not in the Cabinet lies in the fact that the former have the right (possibly the obligation?) to attend every Cabinet meeting and to receive in full all the memoranda and minutes circulated by the Cabinet Secretariat, while the non-Cabinet Ministers are summoned to attend Cabinet meetings only when business affecting them is being transacted. In October, 1962, there were 21 Cabinet Ministers, including the Prime Minister; in June, 1960, 19; and there have been as few as 16 in the postwar cabinets. The Cabinet, as an institution, almost never appears in British constitutional law, being recognized indirectly only in the Ministers of the Crown Act of 1937 (an Act principally concerned with regulating ministerial salaries).

In forming his Cabinet, his intimate team, the Prime Minister must be guided by four considerations: (1) the members' personal compatability with himself and possibly with one another; (2) the need to satisfy the various and often conflicting wings of his party (in Labour Cabinets, for instance, it is always necessary to balance the Trades Unionists against the non-Trades Unionists, and to give at least one post to the Co-operators); (3) the need to have three or four Cabinet Ministers in the House of Lords to look after government business there; (4) the special qualifications required by certain specific Departments.

Since 1946, the holders of the following offices have always been members of the Cabinet: (non-departmental members)—the Prime Minister, Lord President of the Council, Lord Chancellor, Lord Privy-Seal; (departmental members)—the Chancellor of the Exchequer, Minister of Defense, Secretary of State for Foreign Affairs, Secretary of State for Home Affairs, Secretary of State for Scotland, President of the Board of Trade, Minister of Labour and National Service. These number only 13, and Cabinets since 1945 have varied between 16 and 22 in number. The additional three to nine offices are included in the Cabinet or not, depending on the importance of an office at a particular period or the importance of a particular officeholder to the Prime Minister.

The Primacy
of the Prime Minister

The office of Prime Minister is also virtually unmentioned in British constitutional law. The Ministers of the Crown Act of 1937 lists the office in order to regulate the Prime Minister's salary—and that is all! Yet this man, even more than his Cabinet, unites in his person three positions of tremendous political power. He is the Leader of his party, the ultimate leader of the House of Commons (true, since 1942 Prime Ministers have delegated their duties in this respect to another Minister, but the crucial decisions are made by the Prime Minister), and the Chairman of the Cabinet and thus the coordinator of policy.

Since the time of William Pitt (1783–1806), Prime Ministers have usually taken the post of First Lord of the Treasury, a position that has no departmental duties but does carry certain departmental privileges. (The working head of the Treasury is the Second Lord, known as the Chancellor of the Exchequer.) It is as First Lord that the Prime Minister receives his £10,000 salary per year.

The Powers
of the Prime Minister

OVER PERSONNEL. The Prime Minister appoints Ministers in the government and in the Cabinet, and promotes them from one post to another when he sees fit. He can remove Ministers when he pleases. And it is up to him to decide when to ask the Queen to dissolve Parliament. For this, he does not need to consult the Cabinet, and in recent years he has not done so.

The resignation or death of the Prime Minister requires the resignation of the whole Ministry. Thus the Prime Minister wields the power of political life and death over his government collectively and its members individually. In addition, as First Lord of the Treasury, the Prime Minister's assent is required for the appointment of the permanent (i.e., non-political) heads of Departments and their deputies and principal officers, which gives him extensive control over promotions to the higher Civil Service.

OVER CONTACT WITH THE QUEEN AND THE COMMONWEALTH. Although individual Ministers can communicate with the Queen on matters affecting their Departments, the Prime Minister is the channel of communication between his Cabinet and the Queen on general policy matters. The Prime Minister is also in direct contact with the other Commonwealth Prime Ministers and presides at the important annual Commonwealth Prime Ministers' Conference. He sometimes receives foreign ambassadors and increasingly represents Great Britain at international conferences.

OVER DEFENSE AND FOREIGN AFFAIRS. The Prime Minister keeps in particularly close touch with the Foreign Office, and most recent Prime Ministers have played a very active role in foreign affairs. Since the end of

The Cabinet and the Central Administration

the First World War, only two Foreign Secretaries have clearly predominated over their Prime Ministers in Foreign Office matters—Austen Chamberlain (1924–29) and Ernest Bevin (1945–50). And at least four Prime Ministers have clearly overshadowed their Foreign Secretaries: Neville Chamberlain (1937–40), Winston Churchill (1940–45 and 1951–55), Anthony Eden (1955–57), and Harold Macmillan (1957–   ). One reason for the Prime Minister's involvement in foreign affairs is his heavy responsibility for defense. He is the Chairman of the Cabinet's vital Defense Committee, and the Minister of Defense is responsible to him for the execution of military operations.

OVER THE BUSINESS OF THE CABINET. All the Ministers usually consult the Prime Minister on major problems. The Prime Minister is the authority for settling interdepartmental disputes, and he also controls the business of the Cabinet through its Agenda. The Cabinet meets regularly twice a week, and the Prime Minister can summon additional meetings; the Secretary to the Cabinet prepares the draft Agenda for the Prime Minister, and departmental Ministers who wish to put an item on the Agenda must consult the Prime Minister first.

OVER PARLIAMENT. With this wealth of patronage, responsibility, and power behind him, the Prime Minister is the center of attention in the House of Commons. Ultimately, he decides on its business. He speaks in the most important policy debates. He is responsible for answering questions and making statements on general policy. He personifies the Cabinet, and, as the Leader of his own party, he attracts to himself the unrelenting attacks of the Opposition.

Nevertheless, the constitutional position of a British Prime Minister is not that of the American President. As Earl Attlee, an ex-

Prime Minister of much experience has said:

The essential principle of our British system is that of collective responsibility. Ministers are not mere creatures of the Prime Minister but for the most part elected representatives, Ministers responsible to the Crown, Parliament, and the electorate. In the American system, on the other hand, the President is the sole executive. His Cabinet is only a collection of Departmental Heads chosen by and responsible to him. Their authority is only derivative. . . . A second feature of our system is that on any given subject there is a Minister responsible to Parliament. He cannot shelter behind his officials or his colleagues. . . . The Prime Minister is not responsible for general policy in the same way as the American President. *The opposite number of the President is the Cabinet.* Neither the Prime Minister nor the Foreign Secretary has a policy distinct from that of the Government of which he is a member.

The Cabinet at Work

As the supreme formulator of policy and the supreme executive, the Cabinet faces three problems. First, how are twenty-odd ambitious and able men, constitutionally equals, each with a departmental view to press, to reach a collective decision? They must achieve this through discussion, yet how can they do it in the limited time available? Secondly, with the amount of Cabinet work continually multiplying, how can the members of the Cabinet address themselves to all the issues they must consider? Thirdly, how are all these men, meeting twice a week for a two-hour meeting, to maintain consistency between one meeting and another in what they decide?

These three problems have been attacked by three institutions: (1) the Cabinet Secretariat, which acts as a collective memory; (2) the Agenda, which sieves out the less important matters, and (3) the committee system, which also weeds out the less crucial matters but also reduces the time needed for the Cabinet's collective discussions.

THE SECRETARIAT. Established under the stress of wartime conditions in 1916, the Secretariat has become increasingly useful as

a recording agency. It takes the minutes of all Cabinet discussions and all Cabinet committee meetings and circulates them to the Cabinet members. It also sends appropriate extracts to the non-Cabinet Ministers daily; thus each member of the government is acquainted with the work of the entire membership and is notified of any action for which he is responsible. Since all these records are on file, the Secretariat serves as the memory of the Cabinet and thereby provides for its self-consistency.

THE AGENDA. Much of the Cabinet business, like that of any well-run committee, is based on the advance circulation of papers. Before a Department can put an item on the Agenda, for example, it must first send a draft paper around to all interested Departments, for their comments.

THE COMMITTEES. The Cabinet Agenda is relatively formal, for most of the preliminary work will already have been done by committees. The development of a committee system serviced by a Secretariat is one of the most important changes in Cabinet procedure in the last quarter century. There are two kinds of committees, the temporary *ad hoc* ones that study particular problems, and the standing committees. We know little of these committees, because the Cabinet is a secret body, with no "organization chart." Its members take the Privy Councillors' oath of secrecy on all official matters. This secrecy is a necessary condition for their collective responsibility for policy, since no rumors, let alone information, must leak out of any differences of opinion.

Consequently, all we know of these committees is derived from the memoirs and analyses of ex-Ministers, such as Lord Morrison's *Government and Parliament* (the most revealing book on the subject), which are inevitably out of date, and from incidental disclosures of the work being done by the various committees. It is impossible to name or number the *ad hoc* committees. Between the World Wars, there were perhaps as many as 20 at any one time; between 1945 and 1950 as many as 30. Each comprises only three or four men. The standing committees known to exist today are the Future Legislation Committee, the Legislation Committee, and the Defense Committee, which, with the assistance of the Chiefs of Staff, advises the Minister of Defense (who is one of its Members) and the service Ministries (of each armed service). The Cabinet thus stands at the intersection of three powerful institutions: the majority party, Parliament, and the Civil Service, and it draws strength from all three. It is the policy-making body of Britain. The other organs of government act as checks and controls on it.

In the Cabinet, the Prime Minister overshadows his colleagues. The wars and many crises of the twentieth century have inevitably enhanced the position of the Prime Minister, who stands out as the leader of the nation. And where a Prime Minister is greatly senior in age and experience to his Cabinet members, he will be apt to dominate it. Today, certain tendencies in British politics give him even greater prominence than before: he is increasingly thought by the electorate to personify his party, and the discipline of the Parliamentary Parties spotlights the Prime Minister and the Leader of the Opposition as opposing gladiators. In the Cabinet, the Prime Minister carries heavier responsibilities and wields more influence than his colleagues. But it would be quite wrong to say that the Prime Minister enjoys the same formal authority as the American President. He does not. He is the leader of a team that collectively shares responsibilities for the policies it formulates.

The Executive

We have seen how the Cabinet stands at the intersection of Party, Parliament, and the Civil Service. We have discussed the Cabinet's relationship with the parties and Parliament but not its relationship with the Civil Service. In Britain, the senior ranks of the Civil Service play an influential role in shaping government policies. We should mention in passing that besides the Civil Service there are two other types of administrative organs that are responsible for executing the policies set by the Cabinet and Parliament and that thus play some part in determining government policies: the public corporations (such as the B.B.C. and the nationalized industries) and the elected councils that constitute the local governments of the country. Neither of these is regarded as part of the "Executive," although they are certainly administrative agencies. But the spinal column of the whole administrative system is undoubtedly the Departments of the central government which are manned by the Civil Service, and we shall devote most of our time to them.

The Central Executive

The so-called Executive in Britain consists of the important government Departments, with their associated boards, and other powerful public agencies. At the head of each Department is a political appointee, the Minister, who is assisted by a varying number of junior Ministers (also political appointees). The civil servants in each Department are answerable to Parliament only through their Minister, who, for his part, is answerable to Parliament for the actions of his civil servants. It is this relationship that produces "the individual responsibility of Ministers for their Departments" which we have already discussed.

The Executive is much more influential in shaping policy nowadays than it used to be. This is due first to its inherent characteristic as a permanent body of officials, but secondly to the vast growth of the duties of government in the last half century. The Civil Service consists of trained and skilled specialists who remain in their posts while Cabinets and parties come and go. This permanency and

special skill is the source of their influence. It counterbalances the popular and elective element in the policy-making processes. The Minister, the political head of the Department, is temporary; he is an amateur, the source of his strength is the popular mandate, and his view is highly colored by immediate political needs. The Civil Service, on the other hand, is a skilled, permanent, and dispassionate (since it is not elected) body of public servants that keeps its eye on the future, since it will be left with the consequences of a Minister's policies long after he has departed. As the duties of government have increased, much work that used to be done by Ministers and Parliament has been delegated to the Civil Service. Today, Acts of Parliament do not usually aim at doing more than laying down the essential principles of the law, leaving the details to be filled in by Statutory Rules, Orders, and Regulations, which are drawn up by the Civil Service, with the knowledge of the Minister, who has the final say. These regulations vastly exceed the Acts of Parliament both in number and in bulk. Many Acts now establish special arrangements for adjudicating breaches of these Statutory Rules and Orders through administrative tribunals, and in many cases the jurisdiction of the ordinary courts is excluded. In addition to these two relatively new functions of the Civil Service, its ancient one of giving assistance and advice to the Minister has enormously expanded. The work of a Department is so complex today that on all but the most vital or politically controversial subjects the Minister is bound to lean heavily on his Civil Servants to execute his policy.

STRUCTURE. The central Executive has three main characteristics: (1) it is organized into a number of Departments and their dependent boards and agencies; (2) it is more highly integrated than in, say, the United States; (3) the senior ranks of the Civil Service that make up these Departments are highly influential in the shaping of policy.

The organization of a typical government Department is shown in the diagram at the top of the next page.

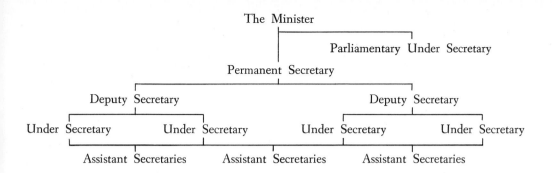

In striking contrast to the typical American governmental Department, in Britain an entire Department is the responsibility of a single civil servant, the Permanent Secretary (except in the Treasury, which now has three Permanent Secretaries). Although the Permanent Secretary concentrates on particular aspects of the Department, he is charged with overseeing all the operations of the Department and is assisted in this by one or more Deputy Secretaries. Under this central direction come the Under Secretaries, each in charge of a Section, and, below them, the Assistant Secretaries who head up the lower-echelon divisions of the Department. Within these divisions, smaller units are administered by Principals and Assistant Principals.

The lower-echelon divisions correspond roughly to the "bureaus" in an American Department. Two very important differences from American practice must be noted here. First, the ranks between the equivalent of "bureau chief" and the political head of the Department are in Britain filled by permanent career men who have spent a lifetime in the service. In the United States, the equivalent ranks are usually filled by political appointments who may change rapidly. The chief advice given to the incoming political head of a British Department thus comes from the tried and trusted top civil servant of the Department, not from the party appointees who are brought in together with him. Nor do British incoming Ministers follow the French practice of bringing with them their own "cabinet" of advisers.

Secondly, the fact that the higher ranks consist of career men who have usually spent many years in that particular Department helps to make the Department a real unity instead of a collection of separate bureaus. All controversies between the different divisions of the Department gradually work their way to the top, where they can receive a final decision from the Permanent Secretary if necessary.

Attached to most of the Departments are several boards or commissions for which the departmental Minister takes Parliamentary responsibility, but which have structures of their own—for instance, the Civil Service Commission, the Board of Customs and Excise, the Board of Inland Revenue, and so forth. Against the 24 Departments that existed in 1960, there were about 100 boards or commissions of this kind.

Coordination within the Executive

How are the competing policies of so many Departments and agencies brought together into a coherent whole? The institution of the Cabinet is one answer. Since it consists of the heads of Departments, any disputes can be and are cleared at that level. We have already seen, for instance, how a Department must consult all other interested departments, especially the Treasury and the Law Officers, before bringing the draft of a bill to the Cabinet.

But if all the minor differences of policy were to be brought to the Cabinet to be ironed out, it would have to sit continuously and even then would have no time left to consider major policy. In practice, only the most serious of

The Cabinet and the Central Administration

departmental collisions are brought up to the Cabinet. Below the Cabinet level, the Treasury establishes many of the administrative procedures and minor policies common to all the Departments, and there is also a network of consultation and cooperation among Departments that buffers any very serious collisions between them.

THE TREASURY. The British Treasury is often known as "the Department of Departments." Its pre-eminence is recognized by the other Departments. As its name suggests, it is concerned (like the United States Treasury) with all the financial transactions of government; but in Britain it does much more besides. It is charged with the responsibility for economic planning, and this gives it a degree of control over what the Departments concerned with industry and commerce are doing. And it is responsible for negotiating all pay, recruitment, promotion, and training policies in the Civil Service. Finally, it is responsible for the Estimates of the various Departments. This control of the staffing and the finances of the other Departments gives it a unique insight into their outlook and into the policies they are pursuing and wish to pursue.

The Treasury certainly never tells Departments what their policy must be. A Department's policy, as we know, is in the hands of its Ministers, who must answer for it to the House of Commons. But the Treasury can and does influence to some degree the policies of the other Departments. It has the right to say "No" to a Department's Estimates. The Minister of the Department may fight the decision up to the Cabinet, but at least the result will be clearly understood by all and not cloaked in secrecy or subject to breaking out suddenly in full view. Although the Treasury can say "No," it cannot and does not seek to tell other Departments how they ought to spend their money. Actually, the great bulk of spending today follows automatically from some pre-vious policy decision—e.g., the decision to raise the school-leaving age to 15—and all that the Treasury can do is to process the Estimates accordingly. The Treasury reviews and challenges the financial and staff arrangements of the other Departments rather than controls them, and even if in some cases it really does succeed in controlling them it never directs them.

But in the course of the Treasury's review of Departments' spending and staffing, it is in the unique position of knowing in what directions their policies are moving. It is, therefore, able to detect divergencies from the government's policies at an early stage and can point these out to the Departments themselves or, if the issues are too serious for the Departments to settle, to the Ministers in charge. In getting the Departments to work together, it has a very strong position. It is bound to be represented on every important, interdepartmental committee. It is a "high prestige" Department and thus tends to get the very best of the new recruits to the Civil Service. It has the right and the duty to make difficulties over finance and staff. And, since one of its permanent heads is the Prime Minister's adviser on all top-flight promotions throughout the Departments, it can see that like-minded officials are in charge of them, men who will work together and cooperate with the Treasury.

INTERDEPARTMENTAL CONSULTATION. Most governmental disputes and frictions occur in the actual carrying out of government policy, i.e., at the departmental level rather than at the Treasury or, still more rarely, Cabinet level. The principal interest of one Department tends to be a secondary interest of other Departments—for instance, housing conditions are a principal interest of the Ministry of Housing, but a secondary interest of the Ministry of Health.

The Departments try to hammer out a coherent policy between themselves as far as possible. They succeed largely because of the habit of mind of the highest class of the Civil Service, the Administrative Class, which we shall discuss later. This class, which consists of no more than 2,500 civil servants, is drawn from a wider social class than ever before but still derives much of its strength from the fee-paying "public" schools and comes preponderantly from Oxford and Cambridge. This common educational background is reinforced by the nature of recruitment, which is by a general not a technical examination, thus heavily emphasizing the humanities. The slow turnover of civil servants brings in recruits in such small doses that they become absorbed into the traditions of the Civil Service. Many if not most of the members of the Administrative Class belong to the same half-dozen men's clubs in and around Whitehall and so regularly meet one another informally. The long-term effect of this informal collaboration—telephoning one's opposite number, chatting at lunch, "dropping in to see" a colleague in his office—is very far reaching.

Formal methods of collaboration are also essential, of course. The most common and the most influential method is the interdepartmental committee or conference. The whole Administrative Class is continuously involved in transient interdepartmental committees that arise in the course of executing policy. Many are not established by any regular process but are created on the initiative of a particular civil servant with a specific problem to solve. Lord Franks, who went into the Civil Service from an academic post during the war, has explained how the system works:

Every official . . . had to take some executive responsibility for the policies he devised or received from his superiors. Once he was clear about what in general was desirable he would normally go on to find out, through inquiry, consultations, and meetings with experts, what was practicable in the circumstances, establishing the main heads of a workable scheme and identifying the agents whether members of the Civil Service or of the public who must carry out the several parts of the scheme. He would then call a meeting of all these people and go through the plans.

The interdepartmental committees are veritable forges of policy. If a Department already has a policy, it will, of course, try to stick to it. But many interdepartmental committees are convened at an earlier stage, when the Departments have not so much policies as views. The committee will consist of representatives of the Departments, trained in committee work and anxious to find a solution. In the end, somehow, a policy is arrived at, which, if important enough, will be considered by a top-level official committee, by a committee of Ministers, or even by the Cabinet where the matter is most grave. But most of the matters discussed will never go that far. Thus policy—some might prefer to call it sub-policy—is being made all the time. Within limits set by the party and the Ministers, the interdepartmental committees make the bulk of governmental policy; and it is in these committees that the presence of the Treasury representative is at its most influential.

In brief, it is misleading to think of the Cabinet as the origin of all policy, as the top of a pyramid that transmits its orders down to the lowest postman or clerk. Major policy is indeed hammered out at the Cabinet level. But the details of such policies, and the whole mass of their practical consequences—what we might call sub-policy—are not settled at that level. These decisions originate with the middle and junior ranks of the Administrative Class and then filter upwards, being sifted as they go; the important items reach the permanent heads of the Departments, the still more important ones the Ministers, and only the vital or the politically controversial matters reach the Cabinet itself.

The Administrative Class

There are at present about 670,000 non-industrial civil servants in Britain. (Industrial civil servants are such persons as postal engineers or Admiralty dockyard workers). Following are the main characteristics of the non-industrial Civil Service.

1. It is made up entirely of "career" personnel. Once a civil servant has passed his probationary period, he holds a permanent appointment and will not be discharged except

in the very rare cases of personal misbehavior or dishonesty. Resignations are infrequent and the turnover is extremely small.

2. It is recruited by open competitive examinations (or, in the appropriate cases, open competitive interview). Examinations for other than technical, scientific, and professional staff test for general aptitude and not special skills; they are similar to the school-leaving examinations or university examinations, according to the class of civil servant involved.

3. For purposes of pay, working conditions, and promotion, the Civil Service is treated (by the Treasury, which is responsible for these matters) as one service. Apart from the professional, scientific, and technical classes that are found in several Departments and specialized classes found in a few Departments, the Civil Service is divided into three main classes. Starting from the bottom, the Clerical Class (about 120,000 in number) carries out general clerical duties. The Executive Class (67,000) is concerned with the details of governmental operations and contains most of the highly trained semi-professional staff such as auditors. At the top is the Administrative Class (about 2,500) to be discussed below.

4. It is politically neutral. Neither appointment nor dismissal takes place for political reasons. The senior civil servants may not take part in any partisan activities. The lower ranks are freer, and members of them may even become candidates for election providing their Departments approve.

5. The Civil Service is almost totally free from corruption, and in the senior ranks is completely so.

The Administrative Class is partly recruited from the Executive Class by special examinations, but comes mostly from the outside, from young men and women between 21 and 28 years of age. There are two kinds of examination, one written followed by an interview,

the other a competitive interview, provided the candidate has obtained First- or Second-Class Honors at his university. In fact, both methods of examination presuppose similar standards of academic ability. The candidate may choose subjects he wants to be examined on from a very wide range. In any case, both the examination and the interview test for general knowledge and for intelligence, not for technical qualifications.

The work and outlook of the Administrative Class are all geared to the prime fact that the Minister is the head of his Department and that the Minister takes responsibility before Parliament for everything the civil servant does or does not do. Civil servants rarely have to work directly with Parliament. They only deal with M.P.'s when summoned before the Public Accounts Committee or the Estimates Committee or some other select committee, where they appear as witnesses to explain details of administration, not to expound policy. Apart from this, the only contact between legislature and civil servant is through a Minister. The Minister is the civil servant's chief, and the civil servant must serve him, not merely with political neutrality, but with loyalty and enthusiasm. His first task, therefore, is to keep his Minister out of trouble with Parliament and, more widely, with public opinion. Consequently, all decisions in the Department are made in the knowledge that the Minister may be called on to defend them in Parliament, either at Question Time or in the course of a debate.

For his part, the Minister, who often changes more than once in the lifetime of a single Cabinet, inevitably turns to his senior civil servants, the officials from the rank of Permanent Secretary down to the Assistant Secretaries, for advice and help in running the Department and developing its policies. Obviously, one of the first requirements of the civil servant is a thorough grasp of the way the whole machinery of government works and of the problems and difficulties his Minister is likely to encounter with Parliament, the press, pressure groups, and the public generally. The Minister brings, or should bring, to his Department his own special political skills: his knowledge of party and Cabinet policy, his keen scent for what will be popular and what the public will not stand for, a sense of urgency, and his own conception of what should be the Department's policy. The senior civil servant in turn impresses on the Minister what may be called "the departmental view." Most Departments, out of their own past relationships with their clients and their own internal workings have evolved a collective view of their own responsibilities and have developed certain rules of thumb to guide them. Ideally, then, the policy that emerges from a Department should blend the enthusiasm, will, and sense of urgency of the professional politician with the craft, dispassionateness, and concern for the future of the permanent Civil Service. Where Ministers are strong personalities with clear heads, this is likely to happen. Where Ministers are weak, they are apt to rely on their senior officials and be little more than the mouthpiece of the "departmental view."

The Administrative Class and particularly the higher Civil Service are not simply agents carrying out the policies set by Parliament and Cabinet. They are part of the policy-making process, and, although Parliament and the Cabinet necessarily have the last word, the civil servants very often—indeed, usually—have the first one.

The responsibility of a civil servant of the Administrative Class is:

1. To oversee the day-to-day work of his particular branch of the Department. He must settle difficult cases brought up to him by the junior staff, and know when to take a particularly serious problem higher up. On a given matter, he will have to confer with his fellow civil servants in his own Department and in the others which have an interest in the matter, with local authorities, and with outside interests and pressure groups of all kinds and sizes.

2. To put forward his own views for advancement of the Department's policy. In addition to forecasting accurately the costs in terms of money, manpower, and materials, he must assess the likely reactions of Parliament, the press, and the interested pressure groups. It is here that the friendly relations developed between the civil servants and their "opposite numbers" in the pressure groups are so valuable.

3. To help prepare legislation. From time to time, he will have to work out the details of a bill for his Minister and to draft the Cabinet memoranda and the Heads of the Bill from which the government lawyers will prepare the draft bill. And he may have to prepare departmental rules, orders, and regulations to give effect to clauses in an Act of Parliament for whose operation his Department is responsible.

4. To brief his Minister for discussions in the House and in committee. He may actually attend the debate, to prepare and pass up notes to his Minister.

5. To prepare parliamentary answers for his Minister and to supply him with material for speeches, committees, and the like.

It is in these ways that the higher civil servants enter the policy-making process. Their constitutional position and their duty to see that the departmental decisions can withstand parliamentary attack tend to make them critical rather than enthusiastic, cautious rather than adventurous. Critics sometimes disparage them for these qualities. The criticism is unfair. It is the Minister's task, not that of the civil servants, to bring enthusiasm and imaginativeness to the Department, for he is its head and alone takes credit for the policies that issue from it. The job of civil servants is, precisely, to bring all their critical acumen and foresight to bear on their Minister's policy, so that the immediate demands of political expediency or popularity are measured against the administrative problems involved and the long-range consequences that are lately to ensue.

The Cabinet and the Central Administration

The Public Corporations

In Britain, the government has long participated in the economic activities of the nation. This intervention into the economy did not begin with the Labour government of 1945–51, for the Conservatives, by 1939, had set up six government corporations while they were in power: the Central Electricity Board, which nationalized the generation of electric power in 1926; the British Broadcasting Corporation, in 1927; the Electricity Board for Northern Ireland, in 1931; the London Passenger Transport Board, which operates the entire Metropolitan Transport system, in 1933; the Northern Ireland Road Transport Board, in 1935; and the British Overseas Airways Corporation, in 1939.

All of these were run by government-appointed boards and subject to little or no parliamentary control. The Labour Party at the time was much influenced by these models, notably by the London Passenger Transport Board, the brain-child of Herbert (now Lord) Morrison. As early as the mid-1930's, the party had decided to nationalize key industries into public corporations when it had the opportunity to form a government. Elected to power in 1945, the Labour Party proceeded to nationalize the Bank of England (1946), the coal mines (1946), civil aviation (1946), inland transport (1947), electricity supply and distribution (1947), and gas supply and distribution (1948), as well as iron and steel (1949), which were subsequently denationalized in 1952.

The public corporation has five characteristics:

1. Parliament may not inquire into its day-to-day management. Ministers are empowered to give general directions to the corporations on matters affecting the national interest; they appoint the directors of the corporation; they control the corporation's investment plans; and they can set specific goals for each individual industry. In addition, most of the corporations are required to report on their activities annually to Parliament, and the report is subject to debate. To the extent that a Minister establishes the policies for a corporation, he is answerable to Parliament for what these policies are. But he need not answer questions on the details of a corporation's operations. This system has caused considerable dissatisfaction in both parties in the House of Commons. The notion that the work of these corporations could somehow be insulated from the Commons would make sense only if the policy of nationalization had been non-political—or if, by its success, it had been removed from the reach of criticism. Neither condition prevails. Nationalization is one of the issues that still distinguishes the two parties, and the success of the nationalization program is still a moot issue in Britain. Two of the largest nationalized industries, transport and the coal mines, have piled up large deficits and have suffered from severe labor disputes; the railways have been badly managed. The Commons has been attempting to learn more about these industries and to exert greater control over them. Recently, it established a Select Committee on the Nationalized Industries to provide it with more information.

2. The personnel of the public corporations are not civil servants and so neither the Treasury, the Civil Service Commission, nor even Parliament can regulate their remuneration or conditions of service.

3. Their funds are not derived from public taxation. The corporations raise most of their own money on the market, or the Treasury raises it for them.

4. The directors and the chairman of a corporation are appointed by the appropriate Minister for a fixed term; thus they do not enjoy the permanent status of a civil servant.

Electricity supply and distribution may serve as an example of the way a nationalized industry works. The generation of electricity was nationalized as long ago as 1927, by a Conservative government. The principal reason was the technical desirability of providing one national "grid" to supply the whole nation. Distribution was nationalized in 1947, with the government taking over the private and municipal concerns. Today, the control of the industry vests in two central bodies, the Electricity Council and the Electricity Generating Board. The Council is the central body of the whole industry. Consisting of a number of directors appointed by the Minister of Fuel and Power, together with the chairmen of 12 Area Boards, it is responsible for general policy and, more specifically, for capital financing and research. The Electricity Generating Board, consisting of a chairman and other directors, also appointed by the Minister, has the technical duty of generating the electricity and supplying it to the Area Boards, which distribute and sell the electricity. Each Area Board is composed of a chairman, a deputy chairman, and a number of part-time directors—all appointed by the Minister. In each area, Area Consultative Councils represent the interests of consumers. Each Council consists of from twenty to thirty members, about half of whom are appointed by the Minister from lists nominated by the local authorities. The Minister's responsibilities in all this are to appoint the directors, to approve the capital development plans of each Area Board and of the research program, and to approve the boards' borrowing arrangements. He also has the power to issue general directions in the general interest where he thinks it necessary. Under the 1957 Electricity Act, each Area board, not just the industry as a whole, must pay its own way taking one year with another. The industry has been prosperous. Up to and including the year 1958–59, its surpluses amounted to over £125 million.

The Government and the Economy

Taking a hand in domestic industry was long a major concern of the state on the continent of Europe. Britain did not experiment in planning the nation's economy on a wide scale until the Labour Party came to power in 1945. The Labour government, which, like its Conservative partner of the wartime coalition, was committed to insuring full employment for the working population, then initiated the two-pronged economic policy it had formulated in the 1930's. (1) It greatly expanded the "public sector" of the economy, by nationalizing coal, steel, railways, canals, long-distance trucking, gas and electricity, and civil aviation. By accelerating or retarding capital development in these industries, it hoped to affect the development of the whole economy. (2) It increased governmental control over the "private sector" of the economy, by rationing consumer goods, by licensing and rationing raw materials, by controlling imports and exports, and by regulating the rate of capital investment in industry. It tried to influence labor mobility and the wage level through its close ties with the trade-union movement, but was not very successful. Finally, it established in the Treasury embryonic planning machinery, which, however, largely confined itself to economic forecasting.

In its efforts, the Labour government was both assisted and bedeviled by the fact that it had come to power in the aftermath of a tremendously destructive war, which had dislocated the economy and impoverished the people. Because of the shortages of goods, licensing and rationing had to be imposed; this was easily accomplished by simply continuing the wartime regulations. But the shortages were resented by the war-weary population, and they bit by bit came to be identified as the "fruits of socialism," whereas they were, in fact, the fruits of war.

When the Conservatives were voted into office in 1951, they, too, were committed to maintaining full employment (since they achieved power, in fact, the unemployment rate has usually ranged between 1 and 2 per cent of the total labor force). Under their more laissez-faire philosophy, they quickly denationalized the steel and long-distance trucking industries and abolished all the direct controls over the private sector of the economy.

In addition to nationalization, the government has numerous other ways it can regulate the economy. (1) By means of its fiscal policy (this is the chosen weapon of the Conservatives), it can vary the rate of taxation, manipulate the bank rate, and alter the rates of the purchase-tax and the conditions for instalment buying. (2) The government has extensive control over capital investment; it can, for instance, advance or retard the railway electrification program, the hospital building program, etc. (3) By the practice of "sponsorship," which continues a wartime innovation, a particular government Department establishes advisory committees with the major industries in its field. The Board of Trade is the principal "sponsoring" Department and looks after industry as a whole, except where others take responsibility for specific cases, e.g., the Ministry of Aviation for aircraft and electronics and the Ministry of Agriculture for farming, horticulture, fisheries, and agricultural machinery. The Ministry of Agriculture also prepares elaborate advisory and specialist services for farmers and determines the price supports that British farmers receive. (4) To insure freer competition between firms, the Monopolies Commission, established by the Labour government in 1948, and the Restrictive Practices Court, set up by the Conservatives under the Restrictive Trade Practices Act of 1956, decide whether business agreements are in the public interest. If they are adjudged not to be, a case handled by the courts is dealt with by court order; in a case handled by the Monopolies Commission, the "sponsoring" Departments take the required action under the circumstances, subject to Parliament's approval. (5) The government has both negative and positive powers over the location of industry. The Board of Trade must approve the location of all factories of over 5,000 square feet, and the Board can also designate "development" districts, in areas of heavy unemployment, and build factories there or make capital grants to firms that will construct plants there.

Are these powers adequate? And are they well-used? The Labour and the Conservative Parties differ in their answers. The Labour Party wants, for instance, to renationalize steel and long-distance trucking, to rely more on direct controls of the economy, through rationing and licensing, and to have stronger powers over the location of industry. The Conservatives resist all these proposals.

The Social Services

The citizens of the United Kingdom are covered by an extensive system of social services, administered by a number of different Ministries. These services fall into four categories: the educational system; the health services; the services, such as housing and slum clearance (discussed above), that attempt to control the physical environment; and, finally, social security.

THE EDUCATIONAL SYSTEM. Schooling is free and compulsory from ages 5 to 15, but pupils may remain in school until age 18. The schools and their teachers are a local responsibility, although these authorities come under the supervision of the Ministry of Education. Teacher-training, the school-meals service, and the school medical service are also local responsibilities, similarly supervised by the Ministry. For administrative convenience, the school medical service is tied in with the local authorities' maternity and child welfare clinics (supervised by the Ministry of Health), which are maintained by the local authorities to provide a free service for expectant mothers and for children up to school age.

Universities are a different story. A university is an independent corporation with legal rights and privileges granted it by Royal Charter. It is subject to no supervision and control of any outside body whatsoever. A university establishes its own faculties and its own curricula, appoints its own staff, and determines its own scale of tuition fees. It is the sole judge of whom to admit or refuse, and sets up its own standards for admissions and examinations.

Universities derive their income partly from the tuition paid by students, partly from endowments and money given by local authorities, but mostly (about three-quarters on the average) from the central government. The rapid expansion of the university population in Britain is causing particularly heavy demands for money for new buildings, further increasing the universities' dependence on the government. How, then, is independence maintained? By a remarkable piece of academic "syndicalism." The responsibility for the amount of money disbursed to universities rests ultimately with the Chancellor of the Exchequer (i.e., the Treasury), but he generally follows the advice of an independent commission known as the University Grants Committee, or U.G.C. This body, which has a permanent chairman (a distinguished scholar), is almost wholly composed of university teachers. Grants are made for a five-year period so that universities can plan in advance. At the end of this period, each university submits its estimates for the next five years, including increases for proposed developments, and it is from these estimates that the U.G.C. makes up its total budget for Treasury approval. And it is the U.G.C., not the Treasury, which allocates the approved sum among the universities.

There are twenty-six universities or university colleges in Britain, and the student population is now about 110,000. Over three-quarters of these receive financial assistance from the central or local authorities. The payments per student are governed by a test of need, but every student admitted by a university can count, if necessary, on the full cost of his fees, his board while at college, and about £1 a week for pocket money during vacations.

THE NATIONAL HEALTH SERVICE. The National Health Service provides free medical advice, drugs, and treatment for every person

resident in the United Kingdom; it also provides free hospital care and treatment by specialists; and it carries on a wide range of miscellaneous activities, called the personal health services—child clinics, the ambulance service, and the midwife and health visitor service, to mention just a few. These personal health services are the responsibility of the local authorities, under the supervision of the Ministry of Health, but the hospitals, under the National Health Service Act of 1946, are a national responsibility. They are grouped together under fifteen Regional Hospital Boards, which are composed of doctors, local government authorities, and members of the general public, all appointed by the Minister of Health. Finally, the General Practitioner Service is left in the hands of the medical and allied professions themselves, under the control of the Minister of Health. They work from their own premises. The administration is in the hands of 138 Medical Executive Councils, each consisting of doctors, dentists, and pharmacists, all appointed by the Minister.

From the patient's point of view, the system could hardly be simpler. He chooses the general practitioner he wants and has his name put on that doctor's list. (He can change if he wants to.) From then on, he and his family go to that doctor, who treats them or summons the other services—ambulance, health visitor, specialist, midwife, hospital—as and when he decides they are required. Many criticisms may be leveled at the National Health Service, as at any administrative agency, but the charge, often made in the United States, that the patient is regimented is totally without basis.

An example will show the flexibility of the system. A professional writer, on holiday, experiences a mild pain in his chest. Because he is far from his home doctor, he consults a local general practitioner, who treats him (and collects from the Ministry for so doing) as a "temporary" patient. The doctor thinks the pain is due to heart trouble. He suggests that the patient should consult the cardiologist at the local hospital, and offers to arrange this. The patient agrees. That very morning the doctor telephones to say the appointment has been fixed for that afternoon. (Consultations are by no means always as speedy as this, particularly if they involve minor ailments, but in this case the specialist thinks the symptoms point to the earliest stages of coronary trouble, where immediate attention may be required.) The specialist at the hospital carries out a full examination. He affirms that the pain is certainly due to heart trouble. He suggests that the patient stay in the hospital to undergo treatment for the next five weeks.

The writer is in anguish. He has a book to finish. He can now do one of two things: agree to go into one of the general wards or (to get on with his writing) pay for a private room in the hospital. The private room will be expensive—the Ministry says the patient must be charged the full costs of the room, in this case some £30 or about $90 a week. For this the patient will have his own room, special meals, and visitors can enter at all times. He will be able to write there. This particular writer has been prudent and has insurance that covers 50 per cent of the cost of his room. He therefore decides to take a private room and get on with his writing. Had he decided to go into the public ward, however, he would have had to pay nothing, and would have received identical medical treatment with what he receives in the private room.

On the patient's discharge from the hospital, the specialist writes a full report to the patient's general practitioner, and prescribes that the patient is to continue taking anticoagulant pills. On receiving the report, the general practitioner writes out a prescription for the pills. The patient pays two shillings (about 28 cents) for a supply of these expensive drugs. When he runs out, the doctor

will prescribe them again, for another two-shilling fee. Thus the whole treatment has cost the patient simply the price of the private room. Had he elected to go into the public ward, it would have cost him nothing at all.

SOCIAL SECURITY. This service consists of two parts: compulsory insurance, handled by the Ministry of National Insurance and Pensions, and the "national assistance" program, administered by the National Assistance Board, which is a kind of "safety-net" for those who are inadequately covered by regular insurance programs. The system works in this way. All employed and self-employed persons over the age of 16 *must* contribute to a national insurance fund. The payments vary according to one's age; the employer also contributes an amount for each employee. The government provides a third contribution. Wives are insured with their husbands, unless they work themselves and choose to be insured separately. This system of compulsory insurance entitles the insured and his family to benefits for sickness and consequent absence from work, and for unemployment and industrial injury. Wives receive a maternity grant upon the birth of a child, and a widow a benefit upon the death of her husband. If both husband and wife survive, he to the age of 65 and she to the age of 60, they receive an old-age pension. A death grant is also payable for the death of any adult or child.

Many persons, for one reason or another, fail to pay up their insurance, or are in such circumstances that the insurance benefits are inadequate to maintain their families, or are not covered by the insurance plan, or are overtaken by events such as fire and flood that are not covered by the insurance. In a hardship case of this sort, a citizen can seek the help of the National Assistance Board, which is responsible for relieving instances of extraordinary distress and for supplementing, where necessary, the benefits due under the National Insurance scheme. The difference between the two systems is this: National Insurance benefits are paid according to a fixed rate, irrespective of need; National Assistance is paid at variable rates, dependent on need.

Great Britain Today ... and Tomorrow

VII

The last time politics became envenomed in Britain was at the end of 1956, when the Conservative government launched an ill-fated expedition into the Suez Canal zone. The public took sides ferociously, and emotions were more deeply engaged than they were (so reliable witnesses attest) even over the disputes about the future of Ireland which nearly led to civil war in 1914. Yet by the end of the summer of 1959, when the people were saturated with sun and with a burst of unexampled prosperity (largely based on the relaxation of credit controls), the Suez invasion was not even an issue in the General Election campaign. The mood which Left-wing critics bitterly stigmatize as "apathy" had once again set in. This mood of disinterest has settled on all but a few issues and these are mostly domestic ones. The state of the economy, the rights and wrongs of employers and trade unions, the European Common Market, dissatisfaction with the two major parties and curiosity about the chances of the rising Liberals—these are among the hottest topics of discussion in British politics. Yet behind all public discussion looms the threat of nuclear attack, against which Britain cannot protect herself.

Britain's problems do not go to the root of the country's political system, as they do in France, for instance. Although the system may seem at times to be a bit worse for wear, it is not a burning issue, and public criticism of it is marginal. Britain's most pressing problems arise from two sources. Internally, the social structure is not only changing, but is seen to be changing. Externally, Britain's place in the world has altered dramatically since 1945. She has declined as an economic, military, and colonial power, and this has created a host of difficulties for the nation and the Commonwealth.

Questions about
Some Political Institutions

Parliament

Parliament is now criticized for just the opposite reasons to those put forward before World War II. The complaint then was that it talked too much and did too little, now that it talks too little and lets the Cabinet do too much. The rigid party discipline on the floor of the Commons is one of the chief matters of censure. The demand for greater freedom to vote in the House often comes from those who want to see the House become a legislature similar to the United States Congress and not the sounding-board for the Cabinet, which at present it largely is. Although the Liberal Party strongly favors some procedural reform, most Labour and Conservative M.P.'s do not advocate a sweeping change; many of them, however, would like to see rigid party lines on two issues disappear: the control of expenditure and the control of nationalized industries.

For nearly a century, votes on government Estimates have been equivalent to votes of confidence, and a defeat on such an Estimate entails the government's resignation. The last time a government was overthrown on such an issue was in 1895. With government expenditure increasing from year to year and showing no signs of abating, a large number of Conservative M.P.'s have openly criticized the procedure of the House for not giving them enough opportunity to effect any changes in the Estimates. Some new procedural rules made in 1960 go a little way, but not very far, toward increasing the Commons' control over the Estimates.

Regulation of the nationalized industries has become an almost intractable problem. Here again the challenge comes from a wing of the Conservative Party that thinks the nationalized industries are expensive and inefficient white elephants. Until these industries become, like the General Post Office, a non-partisan issue, they will be used as a political football between the contending parties. Their enemies in the Commons will fight to hobble them at every turn, while their friends on the Labour benches will bitterly resist such moves.

A second cause of concern is the alleged "low esteem" of Members of Parliament. It is argued that Parliament is ceasing to attract men of the highest quality and that those who do serve are rapidly disillusioned and quit Parliament for outside professions and industry. The cause is alleged to lie partly in the "muzzling" of M.P.'s that we have just discussed, but also partly in the low salaries paid the M.P.'s. A number of Conservative Ministers have resigned because the rewards of office were too low and have gone back to their professions and businesses. The effect of the low salaries and the depressing prospect of being in opposition for a long time to come are also wreaking losses on the Labour benches, which have recently lost many of their best men.

The parliamentary salary of £1,750 is unquestionably low, and it is, of course, very embarrassing for the M.P.'s to have to advocate raising their own salaries. Many M.P.'s, particularly on the Labour side, suffer real hardship in having to live on their salary, of which all but £1,000 is likely to be spent on postage, telephone calls, etc., on behalf of constituents. The usual counter-argument is that if the salaries are raised, candidates will run for Parliament for the financial reward alone, but this view can only be held by people for whom any four-figure salary still represents a level of great affluence, as it did in 1939. Unhappily, the Labour Party, which has most to lose from the present meager parliamentary salary and which has repeatedly pressed for increases, has many of its own supporters to blame for perpetuating this old-fashioned attitude towards professional salaries.

The Political Parties

There is much speculation about the future of the present political parties in Britain, and rightly so. The central question is whether the country is destined to have to choose between just the Labour and the Conservative Parties for the foreseeable future, or whether any third party is going to become strong enough to challenge them. At the moment, the only possible contender seems to be the reviving Liberal Party. In 1945, many Labour men confidently predicted that the Conservative Party was finished forever. And just before the General Election of 1959, the Chairman of the Conservative Party, Lord Hailsham, predicted that if the Labour Party were defeated again, for the third time in a row, it would disappear as a decisive political force in Britain. The first prophecy was manifestly untrue, and the second seems likely to be no less so.

Signs increasingly indicate that a growing proportion of the population would like a wider electoral choice. This is shown by the steady increase of voters who tell the Gallup Poll that they would vote Liberal at the next election; from 7½ per cent in January, 1960, the proportion more than trebled to over 24 per cent in the summer of 1961. Not all these respondents will actually vote Liberal at the next election, of course; but their answers do reveal that some 24 per cent of the population has become dissatisfied with both of the two large parties. The Liberals might need to gain between 25 and 30 per cent of the electorate before the party could hope to capture any appreciable number of seats in a General Election. So far it seems most unlikely that its support will develop to this extent in the next few years, despite the dramatic Liberal victory in the Orpington by-election in March, 1962, where the Liberals turned a Conservative majority of 15,000 into a Liberal majority of 8,000—the Labour candidate coming last with less than one-eighth of the total vote—and despite their equally dramatic showing in the by-elections of 1962 when they cut the Conservative vote in half.

The Conservative Party is looking decidedly ragged at the edges. After more than ten years in power, its leaders appear tired. Although it created an excellent impression at the Annual Conference in 1961, when huge majorities opposed tougher punishment for criminals, supported the entrance of Britain into the European Common Market, and approved early independence for the remaining colonies—all were issues the critics thought would divide the party and weaken its leadership—the party dissipated its advantage during the first few weeks of the 1961–62 session of Parliament. The government fumbled its legislative program, raised dangerous Right-wing revolts against its European and African policies, and, above all, seemed unable to surmount one of the typical balance-of-payments crises that have beset all governments since 1945. Furthermore, recruitment of new party members faltered. The party sets great store on winning young people to its cause, largely through the Young Conservative Movement, whose 1½ million members are claimed to form the largest political youth movement in the free world. But a recruiting drive in 1960 failed to win many new members for the Young Conservatives and, in fact, barely enabled the movement to hold its own in membership.

Yet all these misfortunes, over the long haul, may prove only to be "little local difficulties," to quote the phrase used by Mr. Macmillan when all his Ministers at the Treasury simultaneously resigned in 1958. For the party has shown itself to be extremely resilient, quick to adapt itself to new public moods, eager to use all its facilities to make a public impact, and, most importantly, possessed by a drive to win that, somehow, its Labour opponents lack. The Conservative Party has one great psychological advantage over the Labour Party—it thinks of itself as the natural government of Britain. The Labour Party contains far too many members and M.P.'s who consider themselves rebels. This "opposition" mentality often leads such members to prefer the purity of their principles to the potentialities of power.

The Labour Party, however, will certainly stay alive for a number of years yet. In fact, according to the Gallup Polls in 1962, the Labour Party was well ahead of the Conservatives in popularity. But no observer can fail to notice the manifold signs of confusion, disillusion, and despair issuing from within the Labour Party, and the widespread disaffection for it among the public. The party's ignominious showing in the Orpington by-election of March, 1962, already noted, highlighted these symptoms. The bright hopes of 1945 have

Great Britain Today . . . and Tomorrow

turned sour, and many members admit that nationalization has not met the purposes it was designed to serve. Why not? What future is there for nationalization? Indeed, is it necessary to socialism? Again, the welfare state, in retrospect, turns out to have been far less important for the British worker than the maintenance of full employment. The increased educational opportunities for the working class seem merely to have produced an exodus of the working class into the lower middle class. When the sons of workers graduate from the universities and the technical colleges into white-collar jobs, they tend to identify themselves with the interests of their new colleagues at work and in their home neighborhoods and forget the Labour and trade-union movements that won for them Grammar School scholarships and university grants. As one Labour intellectual recently put it, "We misread the banner under which we marched on that sunny July morning in 1945. We thought it bore the device, 'Let us face the future.' In fact it read 'Let us solve the problems of the past.'"

Today, the public image of the Labour Party is coming increasingly to be that of a humorless and aging party of zealots and puritans, clinging to old-fashioned homespun virtues, and more and more given over to nostalgia for the epics of its past—from the solidarity of the General Strike of 1926 to the sunburst of power and splendor of 1945–50. None of this makes much of an impression on the present youth of Britain. Those of radical or liberal temperament are more attracted to anti-nuclear street demonstrations, and those of conservative temperament naturally to the Young Conservatives; and those who wish to demonstrate against the government do so by voting Liberal in by-elections, not Labour. Nor have those few but highly vocal leaders of the Labour movement who disdain the new-found prosperity of the working people helped Labour's cause. Those

who call this prosperity "affluence"—as though it were a dirty word—and call television the new "opium of the people" and washing machines "status symbols" do not realize that television is a handier and cheaper means of entertainment than the movies or that washing machines are increasingly necessary when such a high proportion of working-class wives work to augment the family income. Of course, not all members of the Labour movement are this unrealistic, but there are enough to make those rising into the middle class feel that the Conservatives, not the Labour Party, are more likely to help them get on in the world.

The "Establishment"

Many in Britain today, usually those of more radical persuasion, decry the "apathy" they claim has settled on the British public, particularly for the causes that excite them—anti-colonialism, disarmament, neutralism, and the like. But "apathy" is not quite the word to denote the British mood at the present. The Gallup Polls show that an ever-increasing number of people believe there are no important differences between the two main parties. As we said at the very outset of this essay, politics in Britain has changed from the politics of less or more (not of all or nothing) to the politics of a little less and a little more. The operation of the party system guarantees that as soon as one party has a bright and vote-catching idea, the other one grabs for it, too. At the end of 1959, after the scandals of the Nyasaland disturbances and the deaths of native prisoners in the Hola camp in Kenya, the Labour Party proclaimed that 1960 would be its "Africa Year." It was not, simply because Prime Minister Macmillan adroitly took the initiative. He warned the Union of South African Parliament that "a wind of change" was sweeping Africa and that the Union was not adapting itself to it, and the speed of the Conservative Party's accommodation to this "wind" was such that it left the Labour Party becalmed.

Thus, to the young men in a hurry (and to the old men in a hurry, too—the Bertrand Russells), the more British society changes the more it appears to be the same. Those who feel powerless in the face of Britain's ancient traditions, attitudes, and institutions often castigate what they call the "Establishment" and blame it for their frustrated condition. Invented by a Conservative journalist, Henry Fairlie, the term has now become a household word. No precise meaning attaches to the expression. It denotes those who without formal authority nevertheless determine British policy and attitudes by their prestige and their personal connections. The term is broad and loose enough to encompass conventionality, "stuffed shirts," conservatism, and fuddi-duddiness. At various times, it has been applied to the B.B.C., the Archbishop of Canterbury, the London *Times,* the editor of the *Times,* the senior Civil Service, the House of Lords, and many other worthy institutions. Unmistakably a term of abuse, the "Establishment" serves the important psychological function of enabling the frustrated in society to sublimate their emotions by venting their rage on symbolical objects. This device is not a new one in British public life. Today, it is the "Establishment," but William Cobbett, a century and a half ago, lumped the more unattractive elements of British society under the label of the "Thing."

Internal Problems

The political system itself, then, is not under serious attack. The problems that perplex British society are substantive, not procedural, and rise from internal developments and from Britain's changed position in the world. British society has seen three highly significant developments in the last twenty years: the maintenance of full employment, the coming of the welfare state, and increases in educational opportunity.

Full Employment

In 1944, the wartime coalition government (composed of Conservative as well as Labour members) produced a White Paper pledging, as a matter of principle, all future governments to the maintenance of full employment. In light of the persistent and heavy mass unemployment of the 1920's and 1930's, this seemed a bold and indeed revolutionary step, for if it could be carried out, it would give to the workingman what socialists had demanded in vain for a century or more—the so-called "right to work." When the Labour government came into power in 1945, full employment was indeed maintained. Although in the elections of 1950 and 1951, the Labour Party warned the electorate that the Conservatives would reintroduce unemployment if they were returned to power, they have not done so. In fact, employment has run at record high levels.

It has become more obvious that full employment, not the welfare services or redistributive taxation, has been the principal cause of increased working-class prosperity since the war. Recent researches show that taxation does not redistribute income much more drastically today than it did before the war, and that the undoubtedly increased share of the national product which now goes to the manual and salaried workers is mostly due to full employment, i.e., to the fact that labor, once the cheapest of commodities, has now become the most scarce and is thus able, by collective action, to bid up its price against the other claimants—farmers, white-collar workers, property owners, and those living on investment incomes.

Full employment is the central social phenomenon of postwar Britain and has brought two other important benefits in its wake. First, it has made the theoretical right to social mobility a genuine right. The legal opportunities in education that the postwar epoch opened up to the children of working-class parents only became real when these parents could afford to send their children to school for a longer period instead of requiring them to help out with the family income. The second consequence, discussed in more detail below, has been the enhanced individual status of ordinary men and women. A steady job, like the possession of property, safeguards the individual's liberty and his independence of action and thought.

The Welfare State

Although it is not generally realized, most of the services of what later became known as the welfare state existed before World War II in Britain. There was a national health service scheme, limited, however, to those earning below £5 per week—the equivalent of £15 today. Bright pupils could still earn scholarship places at the Grammar Schools. There were state unemployment and sickness benefits, even for those who had failed to join the state insurance plans or had overdrawn the amount to which they were entitled. There were provisions for free hospital service for the poor. The Labour Party, therefore, did not invent the welfare state; it spent more on it and also extended services to a much larger segment of the population. The postwar welfare state in Britain was based largely on two major documents: the wartime coalition White Paper, *A National Health Service* (to which the Conservatives also subscribed), and the *Beveridge Report* of 1942, an exhaustive survey of the administration of the social services, carried out under the chairmanship of the distinguished sociologist, Sir William (now Lord) Beveridge. While the Conservatives had some reservations about many provisions of this report, the Labour Party accepted it and worked—successfully—to translate it into practice.

The welfare services in Britain are thus still stamped with the pattern that Labour gave them in the 1940's, and this pattern, as is now increasingly clear, was designed to meet the conditions of the thirties, with their heavy unemployment, rather than those which attended, so unexpectedly, the almost effortless achievement of full employment after 1945.

Doubts over the "Beveridge principle" are

nowadays to be found among Labour thinkers as well as Conservatives.

Were the achievements of 1945–8 as remarkable as so many people suppose? Future historians will, I think, pick out the uncritical acceptance of the Beveridge recommendations as one of the most significant phenomena of domestic politics from 1942 to 1946. Here was a set of proposals for social security which caught the imagination of the public. Central to them was the idea that benefits should be enough without other resources for subsistence; yet this idea was never scrutinized. Beveridge took over the kind of measure used by those who had carried out surveys of poverty before the war. It looked bogus, was bogus, yet right up to 1954 successive governments stuck to it bravely and pretended they were trying to live up to it. The subsistence standard, even as Beveridge worked it out, has never, by a good many calories and proteins, been attained. How many know that the unemployment and sickness benefits for a man in 1958 form a much smaller percentage of the average wage than they did in 1938 or indeed in 1912? Full employment and not social insurance has been responsible for the reduction in poverty since the war.[1]

Besides the "subsistence" basis, the other principle of the Beveridge Plan was the principle of the *flat rate* of benefit for everyone—for all cases of unemployment and retirement, and for all types of sickness. Today, both the subsistence basis and the flat-rate basis are under attack.

The two principles are linked. The Labour Party makes two radical criticisms of the way the Conservatives have handled the social services since 1951. They say the application of the subsistence and flat-rate principles to retirement pensions at the age of 65 (for men) results in both inadequate and unequally distributed incomes for these old-age pensioners. It is inadequate because the pension itself is not enough to live on, which forces pensioners in increasing numbers to turn to the National Assistance Board, where they have to show, by a *means test,* that they require supplementation. The N.A.B. rates are based on subsistence levels, and the old-age pension no longer is. The Labour argument is that the pension

[1] P. Townsend, "A Society for People," in N. Mackenzie, ed., *Conviction* (London: MacGibbon & Kee, 1958), p. 100.

should be granted as a right and not depend on the means of the applicant. A means test is held to be degrading, and since many pensioners feel this to be so, they do not claim their right.

The second objection, that the flat-rate principle creates inequality among the old-age pensioners, rests on the fact that more and more employees, particularly among the salaried, are members of private superannuation schemes run by their employers. Hence, the unlucky worker has little but his old-age pension to fall back on, while the lucky one has his superannuation as well. For this reason, the Labour Party introduced proposals for national superannuation in 1958 just before the election. (The Conservatives followed suit with a much less ambitious one, and this plan is in operation today.)

In short, the Labour criticism was that a superannuation scheme should supplement the basic Beveridge flat-rate subsistence principle and that the basic rates of pensions and of sickness and unemployment benefits should be increased. Labour's most widely quoted argument is that out of roughly five million old-age pensioners, over one million go to the National Assistance Board for supplementation to bring their pensions up to the subsistence level and that, therefore, over a million people in the welfare state are living below a subsistence level for this reason alone.

So far, the Conservative Party has let matters stand. But in its ranks are many who feel that the flat-rate principle should be abandoned. They argue that it is wasteful, since it gives too much to those who do not need it and not enough to those who do. If, these critics argue, one in every five old-age pensioners finds the pension insufficient, what is the point of raising the old-age pension to the subsistence level? This would simply mean raising it for all—for both those who are below the subsistence level and for the four out of five who are *above* it! Would it not be wiser, they suggest, to suit the old-age allowance to the means of the recipient? In this way, many people who are entitled to the old-age pension but do not need it would not draw it, and the money thus saved could go to the

people who do need it. Labour critics resist this plan, since it would require a means test. So far, the Conservative Party has not dared to put this idea into practice. Instead, despite several increases in the old-age pension, they have watched over the steady erosion of pensions by inflation, which sends an ever-increasing proportion of elderly persons to the National Assistance Board to show their need for supplementation.

The Labour Party wants to spend more money on the social services, to increase the provisions and benefits made by the various programs discussed above, and also to extend their coverage. But some voices in Britain have recently been asking whether the welfare services of the government should not be actually curtailed in view of the nation's prosperous condition. Why, they ask, should not individuals themselves bear the cost of health (as they do in the United States) and of education? Arguments for privately financed education have been very muted, and the suggestion has received an official reprimand from the Chairman of the Conservative Party. There is more support for the idea that individuals should insure themselves by programs like the Blue Cross plans in the United States and that the present Health Service should be dismantled. It is very unlikely that this will happen at present. Those who advocate such proposals seem to have overrated the affluence of the British worker. He is richer than he was, but not all that rich, and by American standards not rich at all. Furthermore, the National Health Service is extremely popular in Britain, as Gallup Polls attest.

Education

After full employment, the new educational opportunities have proved the chief dissolvent of the pre-war social pattern. We have already seen why. An increasing number of the children of the manual workers are remaining at school and proceeding from there to universities. The same number of public-school boys as before the war apparently go on to universities, and at Oxford and Cambridge they greatly preponderate; but the number of boys and girls from Grammar Schools attending universities has increased fourfold since 1939 and should rise even more sharply in the near future.

Eighty-three per cent of the students in full-time attendance at universities receive some public help, and under the more generous terms recently laid down, the proportion is likely to reach 90 per cent. In Britain, undergraduates are supposed to be full-time students, and they are not expected to "work their way through college" or borrow money against future earnings, as is common in the United States and on the Continent. And the assistance paid to students is far more generous than in, say, France or Germany and is likely to rise even higher.

The New Mobility

From the despair of the 1930's, when attention was focused on mass unemployment and efforts to restrict production, Britain has blossomed with optimism in the postwar period which has been characterized by a drastic change of mood that has instilled the working class with the desire and the means to improve their lot. Before the war, it seemed that the only way for the workingman to improve his prospects was as a part of his class. He had no hope of rising out of his class and therefore had to rise or fall with it. He had to demand collective effort to promote his class interests in order to change society. But postwar full employment has brought with it a number of freedoms unhoped for in the drab pre-World War II period. Workers are free to change jobs and free to choose between a higher income and more leisure (i.e., free to work overtime or not). Housewives can keep house or go to work. There is hope for the

children, too; it has long been the ambition of working people to see their children graduate from a university. This is not only possible today, it happens with increasing frequency. For the first time, the working class can look forward to *individual* self-advancement. Not surprisingly, this opportunity has sapped the old tradition of collective action, and it is this new individualism that the Conservative Party has appealed to with such success.

Britain and the World

British society has meanwhile been subjected to strains arising from external conditions. Britain's position in the world has declined and is still declining.

The Decline of British Economic Power

The British national income, both absolutely and per capita, is now much greater than before the war. Britain is growing richer, not poorer. In one sense, then, it is quite false to think of her as a declining economic power, but she does face serious problems, of which these three are perhaps the most pressing: (1) industrial production has not expanded as rapidly nor as smoothly as that of most of her competitors—chiefly Germany, France, Italy, and Japan; (2) the balance between her imports and exports is always precarious since she must import nearly all her raw materials except iron and coal and half her food; and (3) inflation threatens to price her out of the world market if it continues unchecked, and to destroy her position as the banking center of the sterling area if it is permitted to cause the devaluation of the pound sterling.

The problems of the export surplus and of inflation are closely linked. The export problem has dogged Britain since 1945, when she was devastated by the war. When, as has happened many times since the war, the country imports more than it is able to pay for from its exports and from the services it provides countries overseas, the balance must be paid in gold, which diminishes the reserves not only of Britain but of all the sterling area.

Sometimes the drain occurs because Britain has a deficit with the rest of the world, although the rest of the countries of the sterling area are earning a surplus. Sometimes it is the reverse; one of the Commonwealth countries may go on a spending spree while Britain herself has a surplus. The Labour government met the balance-of-payments crises by imposing import cuts, by placing limitations on capital investment at home, and, in 1949, by a devaluation of sterling accompanied by a wage freeze. The Conservative governments have met them by raising the bank rate, slicing domestic consumption, and—as at the moment —imposing some kind of a pay "pause."

Neither Labour nor the Conservatives has yet been able to solve the basic problem of the recurring deficit, largely because Britain has tried since the war to do much more than simply balance her internal and external accounts. She has attempted to improve her home standard of living; to maintain a very costly armament program; to keep troops abroad; and to export capital to the Commonwealth countries and to underdeveloped countries generally. Other countries—for instance, Germany—have no troops abroad, spend proportionately less on armaments, and have not till recently exported capital to the outside world.

Unfortunately, Conservative efforts to dampen demand at home have tended to slow down *all* industrial production. Economists differ sharply in their diagnosis of Britain's economic ills. One school sees the root of the problem in costs and advises that they be lowered through increased foreign competition and a check on wage rises (unless they are matched by an increase in productivity). This policy clashes head-on with the trade unions, who argue that if there is to be a competitive free-for-all, they want to be free to bargain for higher wages.

For a brief period of some eighteen months in 1949–50, the Labour government, with Sir Stafford Cripps as the Chancellor of the Exchequer, persuaded the trade unions to exercise a voluntary restraint over wage claims. But the Conservative government's efforts to get tough with the unions generally failed

until the latter part of 1958, when there was a brief period of stability. During 1961–62 also, the Conservatives managed to impose a partial pay "pause" on the unions, but only for a short time and at the price of creating a serious quarrel between the government and the unions, and a quite disastrous withdrawal of voting support. The unions have insisted they will not accept any voluntary wage restraint unless profits and dividends are limited, too, a demand that no Conservative Chancellor of the Exchequer is likely to accept. In any case, the experience of the Labour government in 1949–50, when dividend restraint was accepted by industry, gives no reason to suppose that, even if this policy were again adopted, the trade unions could keep their side of the bargain. The Trades Union Congress has no authority over individual unions, and if one union were to secure a wage increase for its members, others would press their own claims, especially if a Conservative government were in power.

Another school of economists believes that the basic cause of trade deficits is the reluctance of the government to impose controls on the parts of the economy that need restraining in a balance-of-payments crisis. These economists, mostly from the political Left, advocate national supervision and control of corporations' investment and expansion programs (a national investment policy) and the threat of nationalization against inefficient industries to remedy such crises.

The problem of Britain's economic growth and the problem of her export surplus are directly connected with the nature of British relations with the Commonwealth and with the Continent. The Commonwealth is, in large part, a free-trade area. Commonwealth goods enter Britain duty free or get a preferential tariff and British goods get preference in Commonwealth markets. But for some time now, the proportion of British total trade to the Commonwealth has steadily declined (though it still makes up 38 per cent of her total) while that to Europe has increased. British manufacturers see much more chance of selling their products—chemicals, cars, woolens, airplanes, machine tools, etc.—to the booming markets of an expanding Europe than to the countries of the Commonwealth, which are either, like Canada, trying to develop their own industry and therefore imposing high tariffs against British goods, or, like Ghana or Nigeria, are primary producers that cannot afford to import as much as the European countries. Furthermore, the Conservative government favors entry into the Common Market because it would expose both management and trade unions to a keen blast of competition. Left to themselves behind a tariff wall, there is every inducement in some industries for both labor and management complacently to tolerate poor management on one side and restrictive union practices on the other, and to seek government help whenever they get into difficulties.

Whether Britain should join the European Economic Community (the Common Market) raises questions that go far beyond economics. Broadly speaking, the lineup for and against joining is as follows: In favor of the move are the bankers—the big national banks and also the merchant banks for which the City of London is famous—because with their acknowledged banking skill they feel confident that their importance will be vastly increased as part of this powerful economic bloc. In addition, all the dynamic sectors of British industry—automobiles, engineering, chemicals, and the like—favor entry because they are convinced they are highly competitive and will do well in the huge new markets open to them. Against entry is, first and foremost, the National Farmers Union. The farmers are highly subsidized in Britain today and do not wish to see certain Continental products (vegetables, flowers) compete with the highly protected British producers. The method of

paying subsidies will clearly have to be altered to conform to the practice on the continent of Europe, and this has given rise to fears that the farmers' net income will be reduced as a result of entry. The farmers are joined in their opposition by some of the more heavily protected and less efficient branches of British industry. Labor, as represented by the Trades Union Congress, has so far adopted a neutral wait-and-see attitude. In general, the line taken by individual unions tends to follow that taken by the employers. Members of unions in industries which are likely to gain from entry tend to favor entrance; those in heavily protected or declining industries fear and oppose it.

But the principal opposition is political, and a very confusing pattern is beginning to emerge, which cuts across the two main parties. The Labour Party is divided. Its Left wing bitterly opposes entry. Its motives are mixed. Some leftists see the Common Market as simply an extension and consolidation of NATO and the cold war. They oppose entry in the name of their own neutralism. Others find the prospect of linking British destinies with Right-wing leaders like de Gaulle and Adenauer inconsistent with their principles. Still others fear that entry into the Common Market would prohibit future Labour governments from "planning" British industry according to socialist principles. All these groups unite, therefore, in opposing the Common Market on the grounds that it infringes on British sovereignty. In this they are joined by certain trade unionists and intellectuals who are usually on the Right of the Labour Party spectrum.

These elements in the Labour Party find allies in the extreme Right wing of the Conservative Party, which has always had an "imperialist" group that has harbored the will-o'-the-wisp notion of forming a Commonwealth "common market." These Conservative extremists are joined by others who fear, with some justice, that the Common Market will obliterate the specialized patterns of trade which at the moment bind Britain and the Commonwealth countries very close together, and that one inevitable result of this must be the fading away of the Commonwealth as an entity. Still others resent the erosion of British sovereignty. The Conservative opponents, therefore, resist entry into the Common Market on the grounds that it will impair British sovereignty and the political structure of the Commonwealth. They have drawn considerable strength from the fact that some of the members of the Commonwealth—notably Canada, Australia, and New Zealand—have themselves protested vigorously against British entrance into the Common Market. The economies of these countries are very largely geared to the British market. Indeed, about 90 per cent of New Zealand's trade goes to Britain. These countries naturally fear a disruption of these trade ties and a possible dislocation of their economies.

Until September, 1962, public opinion was very fluid, and neither party was officially committed either for or against entry into the Common Market. Then, dramatically, opinions crystallized. In July, the Government had obtained a fairly clear idea of the economic terms for entering the Market. In September, the Conference of Commonwealth Prime Ministers took place in London. Almost with ostentation, they one after the other—with few exceptions—complained that the terms so far negotiated would damage their interests. There followed a television appearance by the Prime Minister in which he put the Government's case for entry into the Common Market. The very next day he was answered in another telecast by Mr. Gaitskell, the Leader of the Labour Opposition; Mr. Gaitskell made it clear that he was against entry on the terms so far negotiated. Indeed, he went further; by raising the bogey of European Federation, he pictured Britain brought down to the status of Texas, and spoke of "the end of one thousand years of British history."

When a Labour Party statement on the terms of entry was issued, the pro-market members of Labour's National Executive protested at its one-sidedness, and Mr. Gaitskell agreed to re-word it; but the published result did not in substance differ from the original draft. At the Labour Conference, Mr. Gaitskell, in a speech of nearly an hour and a half, disclosed his personal hostility to the entry on the terms so far negotiated in language that was far more passionate and one-sided even than that in the policy document. Despite the speeches of "pro-marketeers," the Conference overwhelmingly supported his stand. The Labour Party is not committed to unconditional opposition, but it does threaten fierce dissent unless certain terms are met— and by general consent these terms are unattainable.

The stage was now set for the Conservative Conference. Would the very vocal "anti-marketeers" of the Right manage to split the party? On the eve of the Conference, Mr. Macmillan published a short pamphlet setting out his reasons for British entry, and then the Conservative Central Office distributed pamphlets and leaflets in favor of entry to the assembled delegates. When the Conference debated the issue, the case for entry had overwhelming support from the floor, and when the Prime Minister, who by custom addresses the delegates at the end of the Conference, made the Common Market the central feature of a moving speech, he was rewarded with an ovation.

On January 28, 1963 what appeared to be a highly controversial issue with regard to British domestic politics became a serious international one and left the British in a serious predicament. France vetoed Britain's entry into the Common Market. General de Gaulle alleged British insularity, her special economic ties with the Commonwealth and her unwillingness to cooperate fully in the past or to accept the terms of the Rome Treaty. Britain's efforts to maintain its influence in Europe and to keep its special relations with the United States endangered de Gaulle's dream of continental supremacy. Thus after a full year of agonizing debates Britain's future course seemed uncertain.

Great Britain Today . . . and Tomorrow

The Decline
of British Military Power

Britain today is but a medium-sized power. This should have been obvious in 1945, at the close of the war, but it has penetrated to most of the British people only since 1956 (the date of the Suez expedition), or, perhaps, 1957, the year of Sputnik. Up till then, circumstances concealed the extent of the decline. When the war ended, Britain was one of the "big three" victorious powers, and both Russia and the rest of Europe were badly crippled from wartime losses. But Europe and Russia recovered very fast. Now that their recovery is achieved, the British decline in power seems more rapid than it really was.

Contemporary Britain is a victim of both her geography and her economics. A few well-placed Russian H-bombs could wipe out life in the Islands. Although Britain has developed H-bombs of her own, she can only deter the Russians from attacking, not protect herself. Pursuing her deterrence policy against Russian attack, Britain for a while concentrated on her own intermediate-range missile, the Blue Streak. This had to be fired from fixed sites and by the time it was ready to go into production, the Russians had shown that they could zero their rockets to hit fixed bases. To be able to retaliate, then, Britain had to develop mobile sites—either airplanes or ships at sea. Geography and expense make this difficult. The British answer has been to order Skybolt missiles from the United States that can be launched from British V-type jet bombers, and to continue to grant the United States bases for its missiles, bombers, and Polaris submarines.

In these circumstances, there are three courses open to Britain. The first is to continue to make its own H-bombs, and the long-range bombers to deliver them. The drawback here is that it must rely on an American weapon, the Skybolt missile, to complete its delivery system. This prevents Britain from achieving its primary objective—to make it independent of any other military power.

The second alternative, which has been strongly pressed by the Liberals (and now, belatedly, by the official Labour Opposition), is that Britain should abandon her costly deterrent system and rely on the United States for nuclear protection. Britain, according to this view, should concentrate on strengthening her armed forces to make them better able to fight a conventional war and thus bolster the non-nuclear power of NATO.

The third alternative is that Britain should not only abandon her nuclear weapons, but also any alliance that uses or threatens to make use of them, including NATO if necessary. This view is espoused by the Communists, of course, and by sincere pacifists. But it is also held by neutralists—those who think that Britain can opt out of the nuclear world by simply standing alone, or with the so-called uncommitted countries. Many of the neutralists, like many of the pacifists, argue that if Britain were to announce that she were laying down her nuclear arms, she could break the "nuclear deadlock" between the United States and Russia. The moral gesture would so influence opinion in both these countries, they feel, that both would be compelled to lay down their arms also. In addition, the moral gesture would prevent other countries, like France, from developing their own nuclear deterrent systems.

This "moral gesture" is the rallying cry of the Campaign for Nuclear Disarmament, which unites many disparate factions—Communists, pacifists, neutralists, and old-fashioned moralists—to the cause. Cool reason may suggest that such a renunciation by Britain is unlikely to have any further effect than to make other foreign offices think that Britain at last is out of the race, and that she is abandoning her weapons out of necessity not out of good will. The nuclear disarmers simply choose to believe that Britain has a tremendous moral stature in the world, an hallucination that the extreme Left in Britain shares with the extreme Right. But the hallucination produces an extraordinary moral fervor among those who believe in it. The controversy has also aroused a storm in the political parties. Whether Britain should unilaterally renounce her nuclear weapons and withdraw from NATO has already divided the Labour Party into two bitterly antagonistic groups. Now some Conservative backbenchers are beginning to ask whether Britain would not do better to rely more on conventional weapons than on a nuclear arsenal.

The Decline of Imperial Power

To the outside world, nothing seems to symbolize more the changed position of Britain than its retreat from Empire. No less than 600 million persons received their independence between 1947 and 1962, and soon the only territories still dependent on the British government are likely to be "fortress" areas like Gibraltar. This huge transformation, surprisingly enough, has had little effect on Britain's economic fortunes, or on British public opinion. Its most notable consequence has been a military one. When Britain had full command of the Empire, one military base supported another. Thus the possession of India secured Britain's hold over the Persian Gulf area, and the occupation of the Suez Canal zone greatly strengthened Britain's influence in the Middle East. As the various territories become independent, the bases they previously supported are often given up, too, and Britain's military hold over adjacent areas is weakened. For instance, when Iraq threatened the independence of Kuwait in 1961, British troops were moved there from Mombasa, in Kenya. But when Kenya attains her independence, which will be as soon as her rival parties stop contending among themselves, it seems unlikely that the Kenyans will permit Britain to retain the Mombasa Base. As a result, Britain's power to move into the Persian Gulf will be much reduced. Such developments have spurred a reappraisal of the value of almost all British overseas bases.

The economic value of the Empire was always questionable. If it ever brought a net return to Britain (i.e., over and above the cost of the military preparations required to defend it), the surplus could not have been large. The transition to independence is certainly not responsible for Britain's economic difficulties since the war.

Surprisingly, there has been little public outcry at the granting of independence to the colonies. When one thinks of how the Conservative Party was the great champion of the Empire before the war, this is especially noteworthy. But since 1951, the Conservatives have pursued the same policy toward the colonies as did the Labour Party when it was in power and, more recently, at a speed that even the Labour Party probably could not have surpassed. Both main parties (and the Liberals) are now committed to complete independence for the remaining colonies. Indeed, the Conservative government almost seems to have decided that in the present state of the world, the colonies, to use Disraeli's old phrase, are "damned millstones round our necks." It appears that the Conservatives want to set the colonies free as soon as possible, so as to be dubbed an anti-colonial power in a world increasingly obsessed by colonialist issues.

Recently, however, resistance to the independence program has increased within the Conservative ranks. There has always been a faction, led by the clamorous Beaverbrook-owned *Daily Express,* that hoped to fashion the Commonwealth into a self-contained economic and, conceivably, political bloc, and this group is the government's fiercest critic over its decision to negotiate with the European Common Market. But another Conservative faction that also expresses alarm is concerned with the problem of the white minorities that will exist in several colonies after they become independent. Most of the colonies in Asia and Africa were simply administered by the British, not populated by them. To concede independence to these meant simply to withdraw soldiers and administrators. But in Kenya and the Rhodesias, there are sizable British populations. What is to be done for them? Are they to be left to make the best terms they can with the native populations, which vastly outnumber them? Can any constitutional guarantees be arranged before independence is granted, and, if so, are these likely to be effective? In these colonies, the white settlers are apprehensive, and with good reason. This uneasiness has been communicated to members of the Conservative Party—and is no doubt shared by the government, too.

Paradoxically, while problems of this sort are enhancing the sympathies of many Right-wing members of the Conservative Party for what remains of the colonies, other Conservatives are becoming disenchanted with the Commonwealth. It was all very well to cheer for the Commonwealth when it consisted of the so-called "white" dominions and a chain of dependent territories. It is quite another thing to laud it when the majority of Commonwealth members are Africans and Asians who pursue, often with ostentation, policies that are exceedingly distasteful to the British public. The flirtation of such countries as Ghana with the Communist powers, their suppression of civil liberties, their constant sniping at Britain, all these have tended to disillusion many Conservatives with the Commonwealth and caused them to turn with a receptive attitude to the European Common Market.

In sum, resistance to the emancipation of the remaining colonies is only marginal. It is focused on those colonies with sizable British minorities and, in any case, runs deep only in a relatively small, albeit very vocal, section of the Conservative Party. This group has impeded the Conservative government's actions and has unquestionably made the move toward complete independence slower and more tortuous than it otherwise would have been. But in the last analysis, it can only modify the policy of emancipation, not prevent it. The bulk of organized British opinion supports the policy of withdrawal from the Empire.

This passing of the British Empire, without leaving more than a superficial scar upon the political attitudes and public consciousness of Britain is, of all Britain's political accomplishments of the postwar period, surely the most momentous and the most praiseworthy. The Netherlands gave up its Empire only after a protracted and bloody war in Indonesia. The loss of Indochina and of Algeria has produced a national trauma in France. In Britain, there have been brief whirlpools of dissension—over Palestine in 1948, over Cyprus in 1955–58, and now over the Rhodesias—but these have been transitory. The British public has accepted emancipation, certainly not with fervor, but not with hate, not even with nostalgia or regret—but rather with a calm resignation.

American newspapers often give a misleading account of British politics. They frequently write about Britain's frustration over its "comedown in the world," but however rapid the British change of status may have been, the great majority of Britons by no means mourn for past glories and power to anything like the extent that many American newsmen assume. Having learned that the world has grown smaller and more dangerous, Britons look to security, not in the English Channel, but in military alliances with other Western powers. The higher rates of economic growth of the countries on the Continent do not panic them (although they probably should worry more about the discrepancy than they do), for most Britons compare their new wealth and social mobility with the dismal days of stagnation and unemployment of the inter-war years. Finally, the whole nation, except for the far Right of the Conservative Party, accepts the move away from Empire.

Toward the Next General Election

When the Party Conferences of October, 1962, revealed that the Common Market would become a great issue in British politics, Britons suddenly became aware that another General Election was not far away and might even be imminent. Indeed, only this possibility explains the newly found solidarity of the Labour and the Conservative Parties, which have hitherto been self-divided on the Common Market issue. Legally, the latest date at which a General Election may be held is October, 1964. Yet, if trends seem favorable, the Prime Minister, faced by a Labour Opposition that is likely to become increasingly severe, may feel strong enough to appeal to the country and win an election soon after the final terms of entry have become known—say, in May, 1963. On the other hand, if the tide is running against his government, he may be forced to call an election if the Labour Party threatens to repudiate any accession to the Common Market if and when it is returned to power.

The election, however, will not be fought on the Common Market issue alone. The issues will range over all of the government's policies, including its poor domestic record. In any event, the result is problematical. It is made even more so by the recent Liberal revival. The Liberals agree with the Conservatives in favoring entry into the Common Market, and it is to their party that defecting Conservatives have turned at the by-elections. If the Liberals, at the General Election, continue to do what they have done in the 1962 by-elections, that is, if they take two or three Conservative votes for every single Labour vote they pick up, the anti-Common Market vote may be split, and a Labour Parliament may be elected by a minority of the popular vote.

The election, therefore, promises to be one of the most fateful British elections of this century, for it might well decide whether Britain is to join in closer unity with her neighbors in Europe, or whether she is to remain an island of 53 million people in a world of four super powers—the U.S.S.R., China, the United States, and Western Europe.

The great debate has now opened. No reader should fail to notice how the debate is carried on within the framework of the great features of the British constitution: the parties have the primary role of shaping and mobilizing political attitudes; the right of the parties to alternate in power is unquestioned; the opportunity for free debate is accepted up and down the land; and, whatever the outcome of the election, the new government that emerges will be regarded as the rightful government and will be obeyed. It is fitting, therefore, to close with General de Gaulle's remarks about the British constitution, delivered on his state visit to Britain in May, 1960. Before the assembled members of both Houses of Parliament, the General spoke these words:

But, in this achievement of yours, for how much also has counted the value of your institutions! At the worst moments, whoever contested the authority or the legitimacy of the State? Today, at Westminster, allow me to testify to what is due to Britain in this respect as in others.

Sure of yourselves, almost without seeming so, you put into practice in freedom, a well founded and stable political system. With you in the political field, tradition, loyalty and the rules of the game are so strong that your Government is quite naturally endowed with cohesion and endurance; that your Parliament has, for the duration of each legislature, an assured majority; that the Government and this majority are always in tune; in brief it is in a sense in the nature of things that your executive and your legislative powers are balanced and cooperate. Although since 1940 you have undergone the most severe vicissitudes in your history, only four statesmen, my friends Sir Winston Churchill, Lord Attlee, Sir Anthony Eden and Mr. Harold Macmillan, have conducted your affairs during these 20 extraordinary years. Thus, without closely correlated constitutional texts but by virtue of undeniable general consent, you find the means of assuring always the best results from democracy.

Bibliography

Chapter I

An excellent geography of the United Kingdom is S. H. Beaver and L. D. Stamp, *The British Isles* (Longmans, 1954).[1] The history of the country may be followed in G. M. Trevelyan, *History of England* (Longmans, 1944). The constitutional history is covered by Chrimes, *English Constitutional History* (Oxford, 1947), which is a brief introduction; and by C. Stephenson and F. G. Marcham, *Sources of English Constitutional History* (Harper, 1937). For recent economic and social history, see G. D. H. Cole and R. Postgate, *The Common People, 1745–1945* (Methuen, 1961); and C. L. Mowat, *Britain between the Wars, 1918–1940* (Chicago: University of Chicago Press, 1955). General introductions to the British constitution are W. Harrison, *The Government of Great Britain* (Hutchinson, 1948) and Sir Ivor Jennings, *The British Constitution* (Cambridge, 1950). However, much is to be learned from a great classic on British government: W. Bagehot, *The English Constitution*, first published in 1867 and reprinted in numerous editions.

Chapter II

This chapter deals with a variety of topics, and so the bibliography tends to range widely. The essential statistics are to be found in *Whitakers Almanac, 1961; Britain—An Official Handbook* (Her Majesty's Stationery Office [H.M.S.O.], 1961); Carr-Saunders, Caradog Jones, and Moser, *A Survey of Social Conditions in England and Wales* (Oxford, 1958); *The Annual Abstract of Statistics* (H.M.S.O.); and *National Income and Expenditure* (H.M.S.O., 1960).

General impressions of British life and character are to be found in D. W. Brogan, *The English People* (1942) and, more recently, in D. Middleton, *The British* (Secker and Warburg, 1957). Left-wing criticisms of the existing order are to be found in N. Mackenzie, ed., *Conviction* (MacGibbon and Kee, 1958); and E. P. Thompson, ed., *Out of Apathy* (Stevens, 1960)—the last being a product of the so-called "New Left." In addition, one may con-

[1] All titles listed in this bibliography were published in England unless otherwise noted.

sult G. Gorer, *Exploring English Character* (Cresset, 1958) for the findings of a nationwide survey into English attitudes; T. N. Pear, *English Social Differences* (Allen and Unwin, 1955); and Nancy Mitford, *Noblesse Oblige* (Penguin, 1959). The last contains the famous (and rather funny) essay on the distinction between upper ("U") and lower ("non-U") vocabularies in current speech. For the educational system generally, see L. Smith, *Education in Great Britain* (Oxford, 1958). For the press, see A. P. Robbins, *Newspapers Today* (Oxford, 1956). For sound and television broadcasting, see B. Paulu, *British Broadcasting* (Minneapolis: University of Minnesota Press, 1956); and Lord Simon of Wythenshawe, *The B.B.C. from Within* (Gollancz, 1953).

Chapter III

The relationship between voting and social class can be followed in J. Bonham, *The Middle Class Vote* (Faber, 1954); and in M. Abrams and R. Rose, *Must Labour Lose?* (Penguin, 1960). The topic is also dealt with in the final chapter of Sir Ivor Jennings, *Party Politics; Vol. I, Appeal to the People* (Cambridge University Press, 1960), which is a history of electioneering and voting patterns up to the present day. The notion of the "power elite" is outlined by P. Shore, "In the Room at the Top," in N. Mackenzie (ed.), *Conviction* (MacGibbon and Kee, 1958). On pressure groups, consult S. E. Finer, *Anonymous Empire* (Pall Mall Press, 1958); and A. Potter, *Organized Groups in British National Politics* (Faber, 1961). Much has been written about the trade unions. E. L. Wigham, *Trade Unions* (Oxford, 1956) is a brief introduction to the subject. J. Goldstein, *The Government of British Trade Unions* (Allen and Unwin, 1952) is a detailed study of a branch of the T.G.W.U. V. L. Allen, *Trade Unions and the Government* (Longmans, 1960) contains much useful information but is disappointing. There are now several full-length studies of British pressure groups. H. Eckstein, *Pressure Group Politics* (Allen and Unwin, 1960) is a study of the British Medical Association; P. Self and H. Storing, *The State and the Farmer* (Allen and Unwin, 1962) is a study of the National Farmers' Union; J. B. Christoph, *Capital Punishment and British Politics* (Faber, 1962) is a case study of the effort to abolish capital punishment and of the work of the Howard League for Penal Reform in trying to bring this about; H. H. Wilson, *Pressure Group* (Secker and Warburg, 1961) is a case study of the campaign which succeeded in getting the Conservative government to adopt commercial television.

Chapter IV

For the parties in general, see first, R. T. Mc-Kenzie, *British Political Parties* (Heineman, 1955); and I. Bulmer-Thomas, *The Party System in Great Britain* (Phoenix, 1953); also, Sir Ivor Jennings, *Party Politics: Vol. I, Appeal to the People* (Cambridge, 1960); and its sequel, *Vol. II, The Growth of the Parties* (Cambridge, 1961). There is no full-length study of the Conservative Party. Its doctrines may be partly gleaned from Lord Hailsham, *The Conservative Case* (Penguin, 1959); and from its *Campaign Guide* (Conservative Party Publication, 1959), which is a mine of information and quotation. The Liberal Party's attitude can be followed in R. Fulford, *The Liberal Case* (Penguin, 1959) and that of (rather Right-wing) Labour in R. Jenkin, *The Labour Case* (Penguin, 1959).

Considerably more has been written about the Labour Party. G. D. H. Cole has left his *Working Class Politics, 1832–1914* (Routledge, 1942) and his *History of the Labour Party from 1914* (Routledge, 1948). Three books throw light on current difficulties: A. C. Crosland, *The Future of Socialism* (Cape, 1956), a penetrating and scholarly work representing the Right-wing Labour attitude; the special Labour Party edition of the *Political Quarterly* (Stevens, July–Sept., 1960), which canvasses current difficulties, again from a Right-wing point of view; L. Hunter, *The Road to Brighton Pier* (Barker, 1959), a journalist's account of the "Bevanite" movement between 1950 and 1956. For the Communist Party, see H. M. Pelling, *History of the Communist Party of Great Britain* (Black, 1958). A truly excellent study of the role of the trade unions in the Labour Party is M. Harrison, *Trade Unions and the Labour Party since 1945* (Allen and Unwin, 1960).

The general electoral system and its consequences are analyzed, statistically and otherwise, in a brilliant volume: D. S. Butler, *The Electoral System in Britain* (Oxford, 1953). The course of all the elections since 1945 can be followed in the "Nuffield" election series: McCallum and Readman, *The British General Election of 1945* (Oxford, 1946) and the subsequent studies, with the same general title, by H. G. Nicholas for the election of 1950, D. S. Butler for the elections of 1951, 1955, and 1959 (all published by Macmillan). All contain valuable statistical analyses of the results, as well as descriptions of campaign issues, techniques, and so forth.

Chapter V

The procedure of Parliament finds its classic exposition in "Erskine May," the colloquial description of the great manual called *Treatise on the Law, Privileges, Proceedings and Usage of Parliament* (Butterworth, 1957), first produced by Sir Thomas Erskine May in 1844, and subsequently revised by successive clerks to the House of Commons. Lord Campion's Introduction to the *Procedure of the House of Commons* (Macmillan, 1958) is an abbreviated manual by the former Clerk to the House; and E. Taylor, *The House of Commons at Work*

(Pelican Books, 1951) is a first-class elementary introduction. The place of Parliament in the British system of government is systematically treated in Sir Ivor Jennings' second classic, *Parliament,* 3rd ed. (Cambridge, 1957). This not only describes its practice and procedure, but also treats of the M.P.'s, the Parliamentary Parties, the Whigs, and the sources of legislation. Lord Campion, ed., *Parliament: A Survey* (Allen and Unwin, 1952), is a series of essays on selected topics, of variable quality. A. H. Hanson and H. V. Wiseman have produced a case book of examples in *Parliament at Work* (Stevens, 1962). R. Young, *The British Parliament* (Faber, 1962) is a very perceptive study of Parliament, with certain key cases being analyzed in detail.

There are many works on particular aspects of Parliament. The House of Lords is dealt with in a symposium: S. D. Bailey, ed., *The Future of the House of Lords* (Hansard Society, 1954). A much more systematic and rigorous study is that of P. A. Bromhead, *The House of Lords and Contemporary Politics, 1911–1957* (Routledge, 1958). In his *Elections and Electors* (Eyre and Spottiswoode, 1955), J. F. S. Ross has explored the backgrounds of M.P.'s in respect to their age, education, occupation, and the like. S. E. Finer, H. B. Berrington, and D. Bartholomew, in their *Backbench Opinion in the House of Commons, 1955–1959* (Pergamon, 1961), have pioneered the technique of examining backbenchers' signatures on the motions on the Order Paper in order to discover backbench opinions on matters of political concern and to relate these to the social background of the M.P.'s who have signed such motions. The role of the backbencher has recently been explored in P. G. Richards, *Honourable Members* (Faber, 1959). An interesting and provoking book, describing the relationship of the Member to his constituents and to the Parliamentary Party, is Nigel Nicolson, *People and Parliament* (Weidenfeld and Nicolson, 1958). Nigel Nicolson was the Conservative Member for the safe seat of Bournemouth East and Christchurch. His hostility to the Suez intervention, as well as his attitude to capital punishment, led his local constituency party to refuse to readopt him as its candidate; Nicolson's book was written at the height of the controversy this decision aroused. Finally, D. N. Chester and N. Bowring's *Questions in Parliament* (Oxford, 1962) is a full-length and definitive study of the parliamentary question and its effects on the Civil Service and Parliament.

The working of the Monarchy can be followed in D. Laird, *How the Queen Reigns* (Hodder, 1959); and D. Morrah, *The Work of the Queen* (Kimber, 1958). It is necessary to supplement these by biographies such as H. Nicolson's classic, *George V* (Constable, 1952); and J. W. Wheeler-Bennett, *George VI* (Macmillan, 1958). For the mystique of the Monarchy, see the critical volume, Lord Altrincham, ed., *Is the Monarchy Perfect?* (Calder, 1958).

Bibliography

133

Chapter VI

The classic work on the Cabinet is Sir Ivor Jennings, *Cabinet Government* (Cambridge, 1959); but see also A. B. Keith, *The British Cabinet System* (Macmillan, 1952). An indispensable text is H. Morrison, *Government and Parliament* (Oxford, 1960), which gives an inside view by a former Leader of the House of Commons. Reference may also be made to Byrum E. Carter, *The Office of Prime Minister* (Princeton: Princeton University Press, 1956). Reference should certainly be made to the new history of the Cabinet, J. P. Mackintosh, *The British Cabinet* (Stevens, 1962), which contains a good account of its workings today.

For a general introduction to the British administration, consult S. E. Finer, *A Primer of Public Administration* (Mullers, 1957); and for a comprehensive text, W. J. M. Mackenzie and J. W. Grove, *Central Administration in Great Britain* (Longmans, 1957). The Civil Service is described in W. A. Robson, ed., *The Civil Service in Britain and France* (Allen and Unwin, 1956); and F. Dunnill, *The Civil Service* (Allen and Unwin, 1956). The individual Departments are described in the New Whitehall Series, published by Allen and Unwin, as follows:

Sir C. J. Jeffries, *The Colonial Office* (1956); Lord Strang, *The Foreign Office* (1955); Sir Frank Newman, *The Home Office* (1954); Sir Geoffrey King, *The Ministry of Pensions and National Insurance* (1958); Sir Gilmor Jenkins, *The Ministry of Transport and Civil Aviation* (1959); Sir Harold Emmerson, *The Ministry of Works* (1956); Sir David Milne, *The Scottish Office* (1957). The important and unique position of the Treasury is described in S. H. Beer, *Treasury Control* (Oxford, 1957). On nationalized industries, R. Kelf-Cohen, *Nationalization in Britain* (Macmillan, 1958) is up-to-date but tendentious; see also A. H. Hanson, *Parliament and Public Ownership* (Cassell, 1961). The most complete treatment, however, is in W. A. Robson, *Nationalized Industry and Public Ownership* (Allen and Unwin, 1960).

The most complete general introduction to the services is P. Hall, *The Social Services of Modern England* (Routledge, 1959). For a critical appraisal, see R. Titmuss, *Essays on the Welfare State* (Allen and Unwin, 1958). B. S. Shenfield, *Social Policies for Old Age* (Routledge, 1957), H. Eckstein, *The English Health Service* (Cambridge: Harvard University Press, 1959), Sir P. Abercrombie, *Town and Country Planning* (Oxford, 1960) are the titles of some works on particular aspects of the welfare services.

ROY C. MACRIDIS

France

Introduction

I

France is a relatively small country—smaller than Texas. It has approximately forty-seven million inhabitants. Despite certain backward sectors in her economy, France is a highly industrialized and prosperous nation. The average Frenchman enjoys an individual income that ranks him seventh in wealth in the world. Progress made since World War II in the production of energy, chemicals, aeronautics, aluminum, and automobiles place France in the same industrial rank with England and West Germany, second only to the United States and the Soviet Union.

Located in the western part of Europe on the Atlantic Ocean and, to the south, on the Mediterranean Sea, France has been both a continental and a maritime power. Until very recently, she had the second largest colonial Empire, stretching into the heart of Africa, the Middle East, and the Far East. More than one hundred million people lived under the French flag, and the great majority still remain linked to France by economic and cultural ties.

France has long been considered the crucible of what we loosely call "Western civiliza-tion." Her name carries a special, even if not always the same, message to every educated person in the world. She is the "oldest daughter" of the Catholic Church, and her missionaries and religious orders worked to restore the unity of the Church against the Reformation and later helped to diffuse the teaching of the Church. It is the land where Monarchy became associated with national greatness; the land of the Revolution of 1789, in which all privileges were swept aside in the name of popular sovereignty, freedom, and equality; the land from which Napoleon spread the doctrine of the Revolution and established his dominion over the greater part of Europe. It is a land of people who have constantly experimented with ideas, who take nothing for granted, especially in politics. No other nation has radiated its influence for so long a period and so profoundly affected the world's thoughts and ways of life.

It is precisely the richness and the diversity of the French past that accounts for one of the most characteristic features of the French political system—instability. Without any ethnic minorities to speak of (only after the turn of the century and more particularly since World War I has there been an appreciable immigration of Italian, Spanish, and Polish workers and more recently of Algerians); without any significant religious minorities; with a strong feeling of national unity forged by a thousand years of national existence, the French have been unable to come to terms with any political system.

Since the Revolution of 1789 that overthrew the Monarchy (the *Ancien Régime*) and proclaimed a Republic, France has had sixteen different constitutions that have created many forms of government. The Revolution led to a Constitutional Monarchy (1789–91), which became a Republic (1792–95), which in turn gave place to the Directorate and the Consulate (1799), with Napoleon as the First Consul. In 1804 France was transformed into an "Empire," and Napoleon became the "Emperor," governing by proclamations and executive orders. In 1814 the Empire was brought down by an alliance of most of the major countries of Europe, and the Bourbon kings were restored. But they gave way after the Revolution of 1830 to the "July Monarchy," the Orleanist branch of the Bourbon dynasty that ruled until 1848. The Revolution of 1848 again discarded the Monarchy in favor of a new Republic (the Second) based on universal male suffrage and a presidential system containing checks and balances between the legislature and the presidency. The President, Louis Napoleon, abolished the Republic in 1851, however, to introduce the "Second Empire," in which he governed (as Napoleon III), as his uncle had done, by executive proclamations, although he did seek popular support through plebiscites.

The defeat of Napoleon III in the Franco-Prussian War (1870) spawned another crisis, and a new republican constitution (the Third Republic) was introduced in 1875. It was destined to have the longest life in French political history. It weathered many crises, including World War I, which ravaged the economy and decimated France's population, but col-

lapsed when France was overrun by the Nazi armies at the beginning of World War II (1940). The unoccupied part of France was then ruled by the so-called "Vichy Régime" (1940–1944), in which all powers were concentrated in one man, Marshal Pétain, who was granted broad authority by the constitutional convention that met on July 10, 1940, in the wake of the French defeat. After the Liberation, France returned to a republican form of government—the Fourth Republic—whose Constitution was approved by the people in a special referendum on October 21, 1946. It lasted for only 12 years and was radically overhauled in the summer of 1958. On September 28, 1958, the French voted overwhelmingly in favor of a new republican constitution—the Fifth Republic—in which substantial powers are invested in the President.

This turnover of political regimes was not capricious. To understand these fluctuations, we must keep in mind that whenever compromise between conflicting social groups is not possible, the dominant one will impose its views, often by force. Thus political changes frequently reflect, as Aristotle pointed out, profound shifts in the balance between various social forces. The Revolution of 1789 struck a heavy blow at the landed aristocracy and the Monarchy. It also affected adversely the rights of the higher clergy and thus the overall position of the Catholic Church. From then on, throughout the whole of the nineteenth century, the nobility and the Church looked for revenge at every opportunity. They conspired against all Republics. The restoration of a Monarchy in 1814 meant their return to power and influence. They were opposed by the middle and lower middle classes, many of the farmers, and, after the first half of the nineteenth century, by the workers.

"Bonapartism" is a more difficult phenomenon to define. It borrowed both from the Revolution of 1789—it extolled equality and maintained the symbols of the Revolution—and from the *Ancien Régime*—it re-introduced titles of nobility, was in essence a one-man rule, relied on the Army and the bureaucracy, and found it convenient to come to terms with the Church. Bonapartism secured the support of the middle class, and its appeal to national unity and greatness found a ready ear among all groups of the population including even the workers. Napoleon tried to forge national unity and eliminate the various social conflicts, but in vain. By the middle of the nineteenth century, the working class began to grow in numbers and to develop political consciousness. This class sought political participation, but twice found itself—in 1848 and in 1870—rejected or suppressed. The universal suffrage granted in 1848 became a mockery under the dictatorship of Louis Napoleon, and the Third Republic was inaugurated in the wake of an uprising of the workers of Paris—the Paris Commune—and a bloody repression in which more than 10,000 workers were killed. It was not that the French ruling classes were by disposition hostile to the workers, but rather that the prevailing climate of opinion made compromise difficult. The workers themselves were unwilling to accept the ways of democracy and use the ballot to further their claims. They favored violent and revolutionary schemes that promised them control of the machinery of the state.

At the turn of the century, the appeal of the Monarchy showed unmistakable signs of decline, while the Republic was clearly on the ascendancy. Bonapartism, however, characterized by an appeal to personal government and leadership, continued to be a part of the French political tradition. It emerged twice in the twentieth century when the Republic, and especially the parliamentary institutions, appeared hopelessly deadlocked over the issues confronting the nation, and when disaster threatened from abroad—after France's defeat in 1940 and more particularly during the repeated setbacks in the colonial wars between 1945 to 1958.

Every constitutional change in France since 1789, therefore, has resulted from a change in the equilibrium of social forces, from a shift in the alliances between workers, farmers, the lower and middle classes, business, and the professions. Important social and interest groups like the Church, the Army, the bureaucracy, business, the trade unions, intellectuals, and often students and teachers frequently became deeply involved in these power struggles. It is not accidental, for instance, that three out of the four Republics that preceded the Fifth were toppled by a combination of a military setback and a military coup and that in all cases they were replaced by a political regime, which whatever its form, was headed by a general.

The French since the Revolution of 1789 have not agreed on the political system they want. They have alternated between a Monarchy, a Republic, and a third type that for lack of a better term we call Bonapartism, in which broad powers are delegated to one man (Table 1-1). France thus has experienced a continuous "crisis of legitimacy." It has experimented with many forms of government, but none of them developed the respect and deference that the British pay their parliamentary system and their Monarch. At the most, the various governments in France have known only a low degree of legitimacy. Many have been overthrown by violence; uprisings and even revolutions are an integral part of French history. Without knowing these past cleavages, one can hardly understand the present French society or governments. Past divisions continue to be registered among the French today, coloring their emotions and actions and shaping their political goals.

A different and better-known form of instability has been Cabinet instability—the high turnover rate of the Cabinets under both the Third and Fourth Republics. When France seemed to have become reconciled, even if reluctantly, to the republican regime and had adopted a parliamentary system, the Prime Minister and his Cabinet were unable to stay in office for long. Under the Third Republic (1870–1940), there were more than 100 Cabinets. Under the Fourth Republic (1946–58), there were 20 Cabinets and 17 Prime Ministers. Thus, while in England the life of the Cabinet, which is in charge of the

TABLE 1-1 *The Instability of French Political Systems*

Republics	Monarchy	Bonapartism
	The *Ancien Régime* (to 1789) (ended by revolution)	
The First Republic (1792–1799) (ended by military coup)	The Bourbon Restoration (1814–1830) (ended by revolution)	Napoleonic dictatorship (1799–1814) (ended by military defeat)
The Second Republic (1848–1851) (ended by military coup)	The Orleanist "July Monarchy" (1830–1848) (ended by revolution)	The Second Empire: Napoleon III (1852–1870) (ended by military defeat and revolution)
The Third Republic (1870–1940) (ended by military defeat)		
The Fourth Republic (1946–1958) (ended by military uprising)		The Vichy Regime: Marshall Petain (1940–1944) (ended by military defeat of the Axis powers)
The Fifth Republic (1958–) ⟵————————————⟶		The Fifth Republic (1958–)

most important activities of government, averaged about four years, that of the French Cabinet has been seven to eight months. This instability, whose causes we shall discuss in detail later, illustrates that within the framework of republican institutions the French have been unable to provide themselves with long-range, dynamic, and positive leadership. French society under the Third and Fourth Republics seemed to be caught inextricably in the contradictions of conflicting groups and parties and could not resolve them; in the end they reached a standstill—*immobilisme,* as some French commentators put it.

The relevance of France to our comparative study is therefore great. Long a world power and still one of the ranking nations, France exhibits more clearly than any other Western political system the characteristics of constant crisis in constitutional legitimacy and governmental stability. The very function of government—the translation of conflict into accepted decisions—is continuously imperiled. The French remain locked in bitter conflicts they cannot resolve. Why is this? It will be our task to search for the reasons behind the unique workings of the French political system.

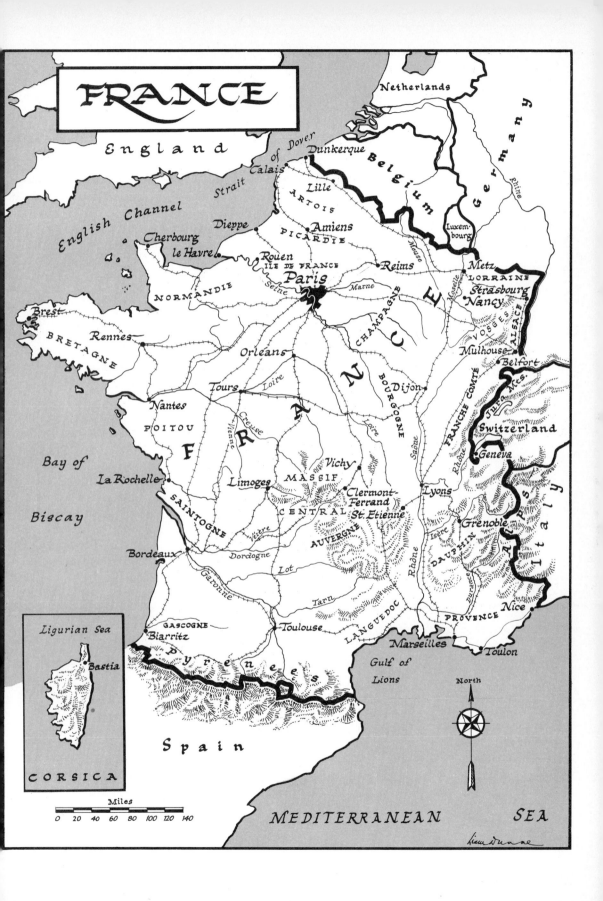

The Foundations of French Politics

II

As we have pointed out, a political system operates within a context of many factors; it is bounded by its own peculiar territory—history, ideas, economy, resources, social structure—and its place in the international community. These forces we lump together and call the foundations of the politics of a particular country.

Historical Foundations

The history of a nation, Aldous Huxley once remarked, is very much like the history of a family. It keeps alive traditions and symbols that give its members a sense of unity and continuity and provides a vocabulary with which they can communicate clearly and rapidly. The Declaration of Independence, the Boston Tea Party, Lincoln's refusal

to consider that the Union might be destroyed, the western frontier, the World Series—these are all rich with meaning for Americans. They symbolize common efforts and evoke common memories.

But every country does not have a national memory that serves to unify its peoples. For some nations, the past is a source of discord that divides rather than unites. Traditions and symbols are differently shared by different groups. To evoke the past is to raise clouds that cast shadows across the present and the future. New differences are added to old ones, piling up obstacles to reconciliation and common action. This is the case with France; understanding this is the key to understanding its political system. But the job is just as difficult as comprehending the personal and sometimes very subtle quarrels that divide a family.

France became a national state under the Monarchy. It was one of the first countries in Europe to overcome the various regional and personal loyalties of feudalism and develop a sense of national unity, which was enhanced by the growth of a strong central political organization. France rose to its peak of monarchical power during the reigns of Louis XIII and Louis XIV in the seventeenth century, under the direction of the great Cardinals Richelieu and Mazarin, who presided over the King's Councils. By the time the long reign of Louis XIV came to an end in 1715, foreign enemies—particularly Spain and Austria—had been neutralized, a strong Army had been mobilized, a network of highways had been constructed, the nobility and religious minorities —especially the Huguenots—had been brought under control, and even more important to the future of the Nation, a well-organized and efficient central administrative service had been established.

The subsequent overthrow of the Monarchy by the Revolution of 1789 did not affect one of the vital pillars of national unity—the administrative departments, which continued to collect taxes, provide services, raise armies, and quell dissidence throughout the nation. Napoleon perfected the administrative system that had been built up during the *Ancien Régime,* and the Republic inherited and made full use of it. Thus the *Ancien Régime* left one legacy—the memory of the King as a symbol of national unity—and Napoleon firmly established one permanent institution—a central administration, an elite corps of men who where rigorously trained- and who preserved the interests of the state. The conception and institutions of an administrative state remained side by side with the republican regimes, ushered in by the Revolution of 1789.

The republican tradition of the Revolution of 1789 stressed the claims of the citizens for representation in the government. The state, it was proclaimed, was a creature of the people, vested with no powers other than those delegated to it. The sovereignty of the people resided in the elected representative assemblies. All orders and privileges were abolished; equality and individualism were emphasized. This democratic conception, stemming from Rousseau's idea of the general will (interpreted to mean national will), clashed with all the privileged orders of the *Ancien Régime*— particularly the nobility and the clergy—and with the tradition of the administrative state. The contradiction was never resolved. The proponents of the Republic used the power of the state and its central bureaucracy to crush the privileged orders, while Napoleon used it to buttress the rule of equality and to advance his military designs. The republican theory of popular representation and sovereignty of the people conflicted with the idea of a one-man government and a centralized administration that had been developed under the Monarchy and perfected by Napoleon.

During the nineteenth century, many new forces came to divide the community. Representative institutions never took root, and the people often resorted to civil disobedience and revolution. In 1830, in 1848, and again in 1870 the people of Paris, joined sometimes by those of the provinces, overthrew the government. The privileged orders, on the other hand—the Church, the nobility, and very often the Army and the administration—advocated the restoration of the Monarchy or the restoration of Bonapartism.

In the latter part of the nineteenth century, these divisions were further intensified. The first President of the Third Republic, Marshal MacMahon, was suspected of trying to institute a constitutional monarchy, and, indeed, there is evidence that he worked for the restoration of a king. But the Republic survived. Within two decades, republican leaders launched a direct attack against the Catholic schools and religious orders. Many of the schools were closed, the orders were disbanded, their property confiscated. The conflict between the Church and the Republic flared anew, and the old wounds of the Revolution of 1789 were reopened.

After the repression of the workers' government—the Paris Commune—in 1870 the workers formed militant trade unions that advocated the overthrow of capitalism, thus frightening the middle class, who began to waver in their attachment to the Republic. Having persecuted the clergy, disappointed the conservatives by failing to restore a king, lost the loyalty of many in the middle class, and alienated the workers, the Republic began to weaken.

The wave of nationalism accompanying World War I (1914–18) brought the feuding groups together, but after the final victory, which was attained at tremendous cost, the differences broke into the open even more sharply than before. The Church claimed subsidies for its schools; the workers demanded social reforms and many joined the newly formed Communist Party; the farmers asked for increased protection and price supports; the proponents of the administrative tradition wished to curtail the powers of the representative assembly; while many conservatives and, later, "fascists" urged the establishment of a one-man government. Caught in these contradictory interests, the representative assemblies were unable to make policy decisions, and the Civil Service performed only the routine functions of government. A weak state and a divided nation were unable to withstand the German attack in 1940.

Defeat in World War II brought about the expected reaction against the Third Republic in the form of the Vichy government, in which all powers were concentrated in the hands of Marshal Pétain, who governed with the support of the Army, the Civil Service, and conservative Catholics. But their rule was short-lived. After the Liberation, the Fourth Republic, very similar to the Third, returned the republican forces to power. But it was as divided as before.

A serious rift developed between the advocates of a strong state and the proponents of the representative tradition. The former did not reject the Republic but wished to greatly increase the power of the executive, the President or the Prime Minister, to give him, for instance, the right to dissolve the representative assembly and call for elections, to prepare the budget, and to control the agenda of the legislative assemblies. The defenders of representative government remained steadfastly in favor of legislative supremacy and wanted to keep the President and Prime Minister and his Cabinet subservient to the legislature. The quarrel about constitutional reform was in a subtle sense the old quarrel of the two political

traditions—the monarchists and Bonapartists versus the republicans.[1]

The historical foundations of the French political system are thus constructed on a base of shifting sand. National unity is undermined by the existence of many conflicting conceptions of government and authority. Catholics still remember the years of repression under the Third Republic; the workers retain a revolutionary posture, even though they have long had the right to vote and to organize; monarchists and authoritarians bide their time to scuttle the Republic at the slightest provocation. History has dealt France a series of blows that have become part of the living memory that divides the French and impedes the creation of an integrated political community and a smoothly functioning government.

The Ideological Foundations

To the extent that historical events live in the minds of a people, they are more than "history"—they become ideas that fashion beliefs and shape conduct. And ideas, as a French writer has said, "are politics." Ideas that impregnate groups and motivate them to action are political ideologies. They are both the lenses through which people look at their society and the world at large and a set of beliefs that makes them act in one way or another. There are numerous political ideologies in France today, and many of them trace their origin back to the French Revolution, to the regime of Napoleon Bonaparte, and to the restoration of the Bourbon kings, when, in the words of the poet, France hovered "between two worlds, one dead, the other powerless to be born. . . ."

One French author, writing in 1932, identified six "ideological families" in France: traditionalism, liberalism, Christian democracy, industrialism, socialism, and radicalism. To these we can add two more: Communism, which has emerged as a distinct ideology, and

[1] For a fuller discussion, see Macridis and Brown, *The de Gaulle Republic: Quest for Unity*, Part II (Homewood, Ill.: Dorsey, 1960).

"Gaullism," which has revived the old Bonapartist idea of a one-man government.

Traditionalism is characterized by a marked respect for the past, more specifically, for the traditions of the Monarchy and the Church, and also for the privileged groups and the instruments of order in the society—the Army, the Civil Service, the propertied groups. *Liberalism* favors limitations upon the state, advocates a laissez-faire economy and extreme political freedoms, and remains attached to parliamentary democracy. *Christian democracy* accepts the separation between Church and state (although it favors public subsidies to Catholic schools), but encourages the active participation of lay Catholics and priests in solving concrete social and economic problems. It urges social welfare programs, economic controls, and the equitable distribution of income.

Industrialism takes its cue from the early nineteenth-century utopian writer, the Comte de St. Simon, and extols the application of rational techniques to questions of economic production and distribution. It defers to the expert and the administrator and often favors authoritarian solutions. *Socialism* has traditionally advocated the control of the means of production by the state, but has espoused the Republic and its representative institutions, while *Communism* continues to pronounce its intent to overthrow the government and forcefully expropriate private property. *Radicalism* claims to be the proper heir of the Revolution. It retains a deep faith in government by the people and their representatives and is suspicious of all vested interests. Like liberalism, it distrusts the state and all its instrumentalities, notably the Civil Service and the executive, is anti-clerical, and invariably supports the supremacy of the legislature.

Finally, *Gaullism* is not basically different from Bonapartism. It is the belief that one man can break through the contradictions of the political system and solve the nation's problems. Based on loyalty to one individual, it rejects the properly constituted republican organs in favor of personal rule by a strong leader, namely, Charles de Gaulle. Since the end of World War II, de Gaulle has claimed, very much as Napoleon I and Napoleon III did before him, to incarnate the nation in his person. As we shall see, the institutions of the Fifth Republic are dominated by this element of personal fealty to one man.

The Left and the Right

Another way to look at the ideological families in France is to divide them into two large groups, the Left and the Right (Fig. 2-1). The Left, which has traditionally included the radical ideology, has been joined by the Socialists, Communists, and, on a number of issues, by Christian democrats. The Right, on the other hand, consists of the traditionalists, the advocates of "industrialism"—the technocrats—many of the "liberals" who advocate economic freedoms, the Gaullists, the outright authoritarians, and a few monarchists.

"Left" and "Right" have had different political connotations in French history. The location of the line between them depends on the criteria used to distinguish them, whether it be the attitude to the Church, to private property, to business or the privileged groups, to the Republic or constitutional reforms, to foreign policy, to atomic rearmament, etc. The line of division, in fact, has become so blurred that many argue that the distinction between Left and Right has only a historical symbolism and does not correspond to reality. But they forget that this is true for so many other aspects of the political system in France. Whatever the utility of the distinction, it does demonstrate that one of the prime characteristics of the French ideological tradition is its fragmentation. Within the Left and the Right are subdivisions, and within each subdivision even more subtle differentiations.

The multiplicity of ideologies has a profound effect on the French political system. In the first place, most of the ideologies listed above are *intensely held* by the citizens. They are taken very seriously and are more than mere political slogans. This intensity often makes the *ideological differences irreconcilable.* People tend to agree more readily on conflicts over material interests than on clashes between deeply felt principles. Those who think that the *curé* is an enemy will never willingly agree to allow their tax money to be used to support parochial schools, while, on the other hand, a compromise can usually be reached between those who believe in a two per cent sales tax and those who oppose any sales tax.

The multiple and contradictory ideologies of France naturally result in a *weak state.* The government is immobilized by the divisions that split the nation, and the various factions work to perpetuate an ineffectual government, for each group fears that opposing forces will prevail if the state is allowed strong control over the country. This paralysis of government in turn produces another important trait in French citizens, a *negative opinion* toward the state and the government. The French characteristically refer to the government as "they"—something alien, remote, and perhaps hostile. Their attitude is apolitical not because they do not care or think strongly about politics but because, being so much at odds with each other, they finish by rejecting politics as an activity that can solve national problems through common effort.

The end result of this condition is an extreme form of individualism. Having denied to the nation the means of effective action and having splintered the state into many irreconcilable divisions, the French finally come to reject collective programs and to rely only on individual action. In the words of Voltaire in *Candide,* they demand to be left alone to cultivate their own gardens! The ideological foundation of the French system, then, like

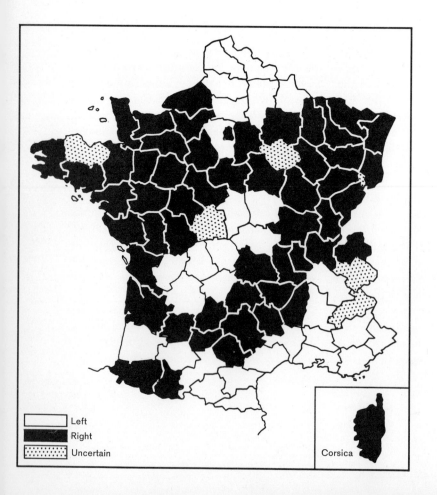

Left

Right

Uncertain

Corsica

FIGURE 2-1 RIGHT VERSUS LEFT (TRADITIONAL REGIONAL DIVISIONS). *Adapted from François Goguel,* Géographie des Élections Françaises, de 1870 à 1951 *(with the kind permission of the Fondation Nationale des Sciences Politiques and the Librairie Armand Colin). Paris: Armand Colin, 1952.*

the historical tradition, is a fragmented one that provides an uncertain base for the erection of a responsible and effective government.

The Social Foundations

Since the *Ancien Régime,* French society has undergone vast changes. The nobility has virtually disappeared, although traces can be found among the big landowners, especially in the North and Northwest. The middle class, the merchants, businessmen, professional men, and smaller manufacturers, who were the most influential groups in the nineteenth century, continue to exert strong political influence today. The farmers were the pillars of the political regimes of the nineteenth century. They allied with the middle class to support Napoleon and later to usher in the Third Republic. Before the end of the nineteenth century, the workers appeared in numbers and in strength —the inevitable result of industrialization—and they began to assert themselves in politics. Their emergence as a powerful force tended to polarize society—with the workers pitted against the upper middle class, headed by the big industrial and business groups, who often joined with the farmers to stave off social and economic reforms. On some issues, the workers were able to win over to their side the lower middle class, the professions, part of the intellectuals—particularly teachers—and even a number of farmers.

One striking phenomenon of the French social structure, as Professor John E. Sawyer has pointed out in a very illuminating essay,[2] is the existence of overlapping social orders. The first is the *traditional order,* which is prevalent in the villages and in many social groups imbued with the spirit of authority; the second is the *liberal order,* represented by the middle class—merchants, artisans, small entrepreneurs—which is essentially egalitarian and individualistic; and the third is the *indus-*

trial order, which borrows some of the elements of liberalism—individualism, equality, mobility—but emphasizes mass production, social discipline, and social organization.

In France, the traditional and liberal orders clashed all through the nineteenth century, largely in the struggle between the nobility, the Army, and the Church, on one hand, and the Republic, on the other. Just when these two "orders" were learning to live side by side, during the best years of the Third Republic, between 1905 and 1914, the impact of industrialization was being strongly felt in some regions of France. The "traditional order" survives in some rural areas and among conservative Catholic groups. The "liberal order" is still very much alive among the merchants, artisans, lawyers, shopkeepers, and small entrepreneurs, while the "industrial order," until recently restricted largely to Paris and the North, is gaining ground.

The French attachment to individualism, the stubborn survival of small firms and family-controlled enterprises, the characteristic enthusiasm for smallness, for a sense of balance, and for craftsmanship reflect the heritage of the liberal nineteenth-century tradition and have tended to slow down industrialization. The workers themselves have been influenced by the liberal tradition in both their ideological and economic thinking. Many factories continue to employ only a few workers, making it difficult for them to organize. The workers, exhibiting the individualistic traits associated with the middle class and even the peasants, often reject the discipline and organization required by industrialization. Romantic ideas favoring the destruction of industrial capitalism through the general strike and revolution permeate their ranks. But the industrial order has also been deeply influenced by the liberal order. Industrial managers frequently shy away from modernization and mass production in order to stay small and secure and avoid risks.

[2] John E. Sawyer, "Strains in the Social Structure of Modern France," in Edward M. Earle, ed., *Modern France,* (Princeton: Princeton University Press, 1951), pp. 293–312.

The Foundations of French Politics

Until 1940, the economy remained "retarded" simply because none of the three social orders was able to win out. France remained a land of moderation and balance, with a few highly developed industries and many artisans and small craftsmen; with a few efficient large farms and many small plots, some still cultivated with a wooden plow; with one of the world's most cosmopolitan urban centers, Paris, in a land of antiquated villages; with some 40 per cent of its inhabitants living without electricity and running water; with a few chain stores competing with thousands of ubiquitous and disgruntled shopkeepers.

As in the case of ideology, the French social structure contributed to sharp and often irreconcilable divisions. Industrialization did not advance as rapidly as it did in Great Britain and Germany, and such development as there was was hampered by the existence of backward groups in agriculture, trade, and even manufacturing. To make matters worse, the Republic gave in to marginal units by subsidizing them and protecting them by favorable legislation. France was called *la république investie*—"the besieged Republic."

✗ Economic Foundations [3]

Until a few years ago, the dominant characteristic of the French economy was stagnation. While industrialization rapidly advanced in the last hundred years in England, Germany, Japan, the United States, and, more recently, in the Soviet Union, France's econ-

[3] In preparing the various tables and estimates of the French economy, a certain degree of simplification was unavoidable. The following sources were used: (1) *United Nations Economic Survey for Europe in 1960*; (2) *Tableaux de l'Économie Française, 1958 and 1960*; (3) *Mouvement Économique en France de 1944 à 1957*; and (4) *L'Espace Économique Français* (1955). The three last publications were prepared under the auspices of the official *Institut National de la Statistique et des Etudes Économiques*.

omy grew at a relatively slower pace. In some decades it did not grow at all. Yet France began with a marked advantage over *all* the other countries. During the Napoleonic era and on through till the middle of the nineteenth century, France was one of the more developed nations of the world. From then on, however, despite her wealth of resources (though lack of coal and energy was an important deficit) and skilled labor, her economy declined in comparison with almost all the countries of Western Europe. Her national income between 1870 and 1940 rose by about 80 per cent, while that of Germany increased five times and that of Great Britain three and a half times. After a rise in economic production and investment between 1924–1931, net investment declined in the 30's to a point below zero—that is, France was living on her capital, using her factories and equipment without replacing them in full. She was going through a period of disinvestment. The destruction of World War II, estimated at approximately 50 billion dollars, was an additional blow. With her industrial equipment destroyed or dilapidated and her transportation network paralyzed, the French economy was in a state of collapse at the end of the war.

What were the major factors behind France's long economic stagnation? First, the slow growth rate of population; second, a backward agriculture; third, the protectionist policies of the state; and, finally, the attitude of business groups.

POPULATION. In 1800, France had a larger population than any other country in Europe or the Americas, with the exception of Russia. The Napoleonic armies were recruited and supported from among 26 million French citizens; England at the time had only 11 million people, the United States 5½ million, and Germany, including Austria, about 23 million. France maintained her population advantage until around 1860, when she numbered 38 million inhabitants. After that, the population level remained virtually static, despite a sharp decline in birth rate (Table 2-1). In 1940, for instance, her population was almost exactly 40 million, while the United States numbered

TABLE 2-1 *Growth of French Population in the Twentieth Century*	
Year	Population (in millions)
1900	38.9
1913	39.8
1929	42.0
1949	41.4
1962	47.0
1970 [a]	49.0 [b]

[a] Projected.
[b] Estimated rate of growth between 1960 and 1970: approximately 250,000 per year.

TABLE 2-2 *Number of Hired Farm Workers per Farm, 1940*	
Number of workers	Number of farms
0	1,855,000
1	214,000
2	64,000
3–4	32,000
5–9	12,000
10–19	3,000
20 or more	800

close to 150 million, Great Britain 50 million, and Germany (but without Austria) 65 million. Between 1930 and 1940, the French population actually declined. Some of the Italian and Spanish immigrants returned to their homes, and there was an excess of deaths over births. The two World Wars took their heaviest toll from among the young and most economically productive, leaving a disproportionate number of older people, which contributed to the economic stagnation.

AGRICULTURE. A quick review of France's agriculture between 1870 and 1940 reveals that she had a high percentage of farmers—35–40 per cent—that the productivity of French farmers was low, and that the many small marginal farms were divided and subdivided into minute parcels that were unsuitable for mechanization and new techniques (Table 2-2); until 1940, France used only a small amount of chemical fertilizers, and the number of tractors on the farms was insignificant.

PROTECTIONISM. Unfortunately, the unproductive farms were encouraged by the tariff policies of the state. Agricultural interests, and also manufacturing groups, formed powerful lobbies that demanded and got high protectionist tariffs, special subsidies, and guaranteed price supports, all of which sheltered French business and agriculture from foreign competition. The state was thus helping to perpetuate the antiquated economic system.

BUSINESS ATTITUDES. Industrialists and businessmen in France did not show in many cases the initiative and willingness to take risks that we generally associate with a capitalist system. Many business affairs were family enterprises. Managers tended to keep production geared to a limited demand instead of seeking new markets, and profits were often "saved" instead of being reinvested in the business.

The system of distribution was particularly faulty, although there were some large chain stores. The economy was encumbered with too many small merchants and shopkeepers who eked out livings through limited volumes of trade. As a result, costs remained high because efficient techniques of distribution were not developed. Retail prices were at a much higher level than wholesale prices, and the small profits extracted by the numerous middlemen who handled the products unduly inflated the price to the consumer. Although a relatively unproductive segment in the economy, the middlemen were organized into strong pressure groups who demanded and received protection, and, to top it off, the sturdy virtues of the storekeepers were extolled as much as the diligence and stamina of the farmers.

The Beginning of Rapid Economic Modernization

The task facing the country immediately after the Liberation in 1944, when industrial production was not even 40 per cent of the level in 1938, was twofold: to replace the industrial equipment that had been damaged or destroyed in the war and to eliminate the

The Foundations of French Politics

weak elements in the economy. This was the objective of the first "Monnet Plan" for 1947–50 (but actually extended to 1952), named after Jean Monnet, who was its architect in economic planning and modernization.

This plan, known as the "plan for modernization and equipment," had the following goals:

1. To assure a rapid rise in the living conditions of the population, and particularly an improvement in their diet.

2. To modernize and re-equip the basic industries—coal mining, electric power, iron, cement, farm machinery, and transportation.

3. To bring agricultural methods and machinery up to date.

4. To devote the maximum resources possible to reconstruction, keeping in mind the needs of the basic industries, and to modernize the construction-material trades, the building trades, and public works.

5. To modernize and develop the export industries to assure equilibrium in the balance of payments by 1950.

These targets were set for the year 1950: the production of 65 million tons of coal; the generation of 25 billion kilowatt hours of electricity; the production of about 12 million tons of steel; the production of 50 thousand tractors. Many of these targets were not achieved by 1950 (see Table 2-3), partly because they were too ambitious, partly because the plan often lacked vigorous administration, and partly because of social unrest and strikes. But a beginning had been made. Two more "plans" ensued, and their cumulative impact

TABLE 2-3 *Industrial Production in the Twentieth Century* (Annual averages)

	1892–1902	1909–1913	1925–1929	1934–1938	1948–1952	1955–1959
Steel (millions of tons)	1.5	4.6	9.7	6.2	9.1	15.2
Aluminum (thousands of tons)	1.0	13.5	29.1	50.8	74.6	217.5
Automobiles (in thousands)	2	45	254	227	286	1,283
Tractors	—	—	—	1,750	17,290	77,940
Iron (millions of tons)	5.4	29	50	33	31	61
Bauxite (thousands of tons)	59	309	666	649	767	1,746
Merchant Marine (thousands of tons)	1,597	2,319	3,303	2,881	2,710	4,461
Electricity (billions of KW per hour)	—	—	15.6	20.8	40.6	70.0+

began to be felt by 1955–56. Despite the weaknesses of the Fourth Republic and the vacillations of the various governments, business and public investment in the economy soared, and the rate of growth began to accelerate.

Several key economic activities were nationalized immediately after the Liberation. The political leaders of the Left and even

some in the Center believed that public ownership of certain industries was superior to private enterprise. Nationalization had been advocated by many resistance groups and endorsed by the National Council of the Resistance. In many speeches General de Gaulle had implied the need for state control and planning. Sometimes nationalization was urged as a punitive measure against companies that had collaborated with the Germans, sometimes as a necessary step to curb the monopolies, sometimes as an indispensable instrument for intelligent state planning, and almost always as a way to insure social justice and improve the living conditions of the poor, particularly of the workers.

In 1946, electricity, gas, and some automobile plants, notably the Renault Automobile Co., were nationalized, and the Bank of France and Air France, the most important airline, came under state direction. These nationalizations greatly increased the scope of public ownership, which already had included rail transportation and the production and sale of cigarettes and matches. A sizable part of the economic activity of France thus came under state direction. Massive subsidies, both for state-controlled activities and for private enterprises, were necessary after the war.

Contrary to popular opinion about the French not paying their taxes, taxation—both direct and indirect—reached high levels in the postwar period. The total tax receipts in France in 1952–53, for instance, amounted to over 30 per cent of the gross national product, as compared to only 25 per cent for the United States. And they have continued to increase. It is true that indirect taxation accounts for about 60 per cent of the total, but this is because so much of the economy is still composed of small entrepreneurs and individual workers, for whom tax collection is more difficult and evasion easier, rather than because the French are more reluctant than the citizens of other countries to pay their taxes.

An extensive program of social legislation has been adopted. It includes old-age insurance, accident and unemployment compensation, maternity benefits, medical care (a very large part of the patient's expenses for medical treatment, hospitalization, and drugs comes from the national insurance fund), and family allowances that provide supplementary income to families with two children or more.

By 1956–57, the impact of the expanded economic activity became clearly discernible. In 1957, France's economy (except in housing) was growing at a rate that compared favorably with that of Germany in the years 1952–56. The decline in the total volume of coal was fully compensated for by the increased use of gas and electricity. By 1958, agricultural production was 30–35 per cent

higher than in 1949. Chemical fertilizers were finally beginning to be widely used, and the annual production of tractors increased from about 2,000 a year before 1940 to over 75,000 in 1959. The pre-war national income almost doubled and the population began to grow. France today, therefore, is quite similar to other industrialized nations (Table 2-4). Of

TABLE 2-4   *National Income and Industrial Production*

(Base: 1938 = 100)

	National income	Industrial production
1900	65	72
1910	76	97
1920	71	67
1930	118	133
1939	107	100
1949	113	122
1955	151	172
1960	175	227

her labor force of over 19,000,000 people, about 26 per cent work in agriculture, 36 per cent in industry, and about 38 per cent are engaged in so-called "tertiary employment," as merchants, teachers, members of the professions, in services, etc. (Table 2-5).

Both the agricultural and the industrial sectors, however, exhibit certain peculiarities. The concentration of industry is not as marked as it is in Great Britain, West Germany, or the United States, for 96 per cent of the industrial firms employ less than fifty workers and 83 per cent employ less than five. There are 1¼ million self-employed (*patrons*) in industry and commerce. Fifty-three per cent of the firms are privately owned, and only a small percentage are incorporated. But, again the larger part of production is in the hands of corporations and firms that employ thousands of workers. In commerce, however, the predominance of individual units continues to be high, and the number of persons em-

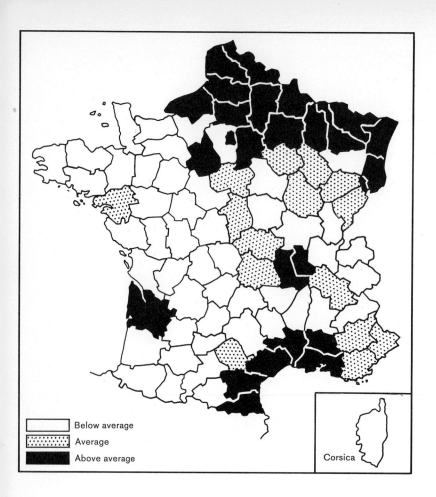

FIGURE 2-2 ECONOMIC MAP OF PER CAPITA PRODUCTION ("DYNAMIC" AND "STATIC" FRANCE). *Adapted from François Goguel, Géographie des Élections Françaises de 1870 à 1951 (with the kind permission of the Fondation Nationale des Sciences Politiques and the Librairie Armand Colin). Paris: Armand Colin, 1952.*

ployed in agriculture is inordinately large compared to that in Great Britain, where about 5 per cent of the work force is on farms, and in the United States, where the figure is 9 per cent. The agricultural population, however, is decreasing. The process of urbanization has been slower in France than elsewhere. With the exception of Paris, which has about 5 million inhabitants, there are only six cities in France with over a quarter of a million people. More than one-third live in small hamlets of less than 2,000 population.

The distribution of income is somewhat uneven. The wages of the industrial workers have usually lagged behind the income of other groups, partly because of inflation but also because of their inability to unite in a common front against employers. Now that tax favors and social benefits, particularly family allowances, add, in effect, about 50 per cent to the average worker's wages, the standard of living of the working class today, compares favorably with that of workers in Great Britain and West Germany. Pockets of underdevelopment persist in France. Housing construction fell far behind that in England and West Germany, and only in the last five years has France been able to build as many as 300,000 units a year. The lag in agriculture is being diminished by the increased use of fertilizers and tractors. The number of self-employed workers is also decreasing.

Not all of the various regions of the country share equally in her wealth. Until recently, France was traditionally divided into two areas: a "static" region, composed of some 64 Departments, accounting for less than the na-

TABLE 2-5 *Gainfully Employed by Socio-Economic Categories* [a]
(Based on last census of 1954)

Category	Total	Self-employed	Family "help"	Private sector	Public sector	Unemployed
Farmers	3,983,840	1,919,960	2,063,880	—	—	—
Agricultural workers	1,151,520	—	—	1,125,380	11,460	14,680
Businessmen, industrialists, shopkeepers, etc.	2,295,840	1,848,140	447,700	—	—	—
Professions, higher Civil Service	554,240	115,420	7,400	210,880	216,580	3,960
Middle echelon (teachers, services)	1,139,540	26,980	940	608,640	487,460	15,520
Salaried employees	2,078,480	—	—	1,233,300	787,460	57,720
Workers	6,465,100	—	—	5,266,560	999,620	198,920
Domestics	983,780	23,820	500	861,040	65,940	32,480
Others	499,040	169,980	440	29,000	295,500	4,120
Total	19,151,380	4,104,300	2,520,860	9,334,800	2,864,020	327,400

[a] From *Tableaux de l'Économie Française* (Paris: Institut National de la Statistique et des Études Économiques, 1960, hereafter referred to as I.N.S.E.E.), pp. 136–137.

tional average in economic production, and a "dynamic" region (26 Departments, mostly in the Paris region, the North, along the Mediterranean coast, and around the cities of Lyon and Bordeaux), in which production was above the average. But even this has been changing. The areas of the Southwest are being modernized rapidly, thanks to the discovery of natural gas, and the areas of the Southeast and South are benefiting from the construction of dams and the production of electric energy. Some industries—oil refineries, aircraft and aluminum factories, and atomic energy plants—have been shifting to the "static" regions, bringing them welcome prosperity.

The increasing number of radio and television sets and the increasingly widespread ownership of automobiles and perhaps more particularly of scooters and motorcycles have brought the farms closer to the towns and broken through the old parochial barriers of the village that were so well described in books such as Laurence Wylie's *Village in the Vaucluse* a few years ago. Although there are rural Departments in which individual income remains abominably low and in which life is not much different from what it was at the end of the nineteenth century, the number of people living under pre-industrial condi-

tions is becoming progressively smaller. The poorer sections of France are certainly no worse off than the rural areas of Mississippi or the depressed mining areas of West Virginia and of South Wales in England.

Two long-range trends should help boost France's economy tremendously: the increase in population and the decrease in protectionism. The European Common Market, by progressively eliminating the tariffs between France and West Germany, Italy, Luxembourg, Belgium, and Holland—it is expected that they should be reduced to nearly zero by 1970—will greatly stimulate the flow of goods, labor, and capital among the participating countries. Thus all sectors of the French economy, including agriculture, will be forced to step up modernization in order to meet the competition and the demands of her rising population. What will be the impact of modernization? How will it affect the political attitudes and actions of the average Frenchman? To these crucial questions we shall return at the end of our discussion.

The Foundations of French Politics

Social Foundations

III

Social Groups

The political analyst ordinarily classifies individual citizens of a country into groups with similar interests or backgrounds. These social groups—workers, farmers, intellectuals, businessmen, the Church, the Army, and so on—vie with each other for positions of political influence. In many countries, these groups are relatively homogeneous blocs that tend to operate as a unit. Not so in France, where these groups are splintered internally along political and ideological lines. The workers are divided into many political attitudes; so are the Catholics, the intellectuals, the farmers, and the veterans. The failure of the French to create a political system that is an instrument of compromise perpetuates, and even tends to exacerbate, the deep divisions that sunder these social groups into quarreling factions.

The Workers

Out of some 19,000,000 gainfully employed persons in France, 7,000,000 are considered to be workers. Although it is difficult to generalize about such a large group of people, they do have certain common traits that put them in an identifiable socio-economic category. In the first place, the worker is relatively poor, and his standard of living improve little even in years of prosperity. As of 1950, for instance, the real wage of the industrial worker remained somewhat below the 1938 figure. The average income of an unskilled or semiskilled worker ranges from 45 to 65 cents an hour and from about 85 to 130 dollars a month, to which a varying percentage should be added for married workers with children. Other social benefits account for an additional 40–50 per cent of the average wage. The worker's opportunity for education is limited. Few go beyond what corresponds to the first grades of junior high school, and, as a result, their social mobility is restricted. The sons of workers who go into higher education and the university are few.

More important than the economic conditions of the workers in characterizing them as a social group are their ideology and attitudes. About two-thirds of the workers vote Communist or Socialist; one out of five believes, in a romantic sort of way, that "revolution" rather than reform will better his condition. In the areas of the country where the workers live together in the same residential sections—as in the Paris area, in the North, and in other industrialized centers—there is a sharp division between the workers and other groups—the middle class, members of professions, and even the lower middle class. Differences in manners, dress, entertainment, education, income, housing, summer camps, and vacations separate the workers from these other classes.

The workers' trade unions are divided into a number of organizations: the CGT (General Confederation of Labor), which is controlled by the Communist Party, the Force Ouvrière (CGT-FO), which seceded from the CGT in 1947 and is associated with the Socialists, and the CFTC (French Confederation of Christian Trade Unions). There are, in addition, a number of "independent" trade unions. The CGT has about 1,750,000 members, the FO less than 500,000, and the CFTC less than 1,000,000. This total of around 3,500,000 represents a considerable drop in trade-union membership since the Liberation. The unions have become weakened through political division, and workers seem unable to pursue a united front to improve their conditions.

The workers have been handicapped by their belief that the eventual solution to their problems will come through the destruction of the social order, enabling them to take over the reins of production; many of them remain convinced that the class struggle calls for an assault upon the state for the purpose of expropriating the property owners and establishing socialism. Thus the myth of class warfare, which is shrewdly exploited by the Communist Party, is kept alive and the separation of the workers from the political community becomes a self-fulfilling prophecy. The more they maintain their class consciousness, the more isolated they become and the harder it is for them to extract the proper concessions from industry and the state.

In the last ten years, the lot of the workers has improved, and this has tended to mitigate their revolutionary spirit. Real wages have risen; there is full employment; specialized industries have grown up that attract workers with ability and give them the chance to attend technical schools and improve their earnings rapidly (a specialized worker may earn more than three times the wages of an unskilled or semiskilled one); opportunities for promotion have increased. Internal mobility within a class or sometimes even mobility between status groups is on the rise. Better wages and living conditions have started to eliminate the sharp difference of dress, habits, and manners. Those workers with higher wages can move to better housing facilities and can buy a scooter or even a small car.

But many of the French workers remain attached to old habits and ideas. Real wages for many of them, perhaps as many as half, are not much higher than during the best years of economic prosperity in the 1920's. The feeling of exploitation and separateness persists. Workers continue to consider themselves inferior and dream of a revolution that will square accounts with history. This attitude makes the workers an unstable element in French society and a constant danger to a democratic society.

The Farmers

There are some five million "farmers" in France (individual owners, tenant farmers, and agricultural workers), and they comprise approximately 26 per cent of those gainfully employed. A little over one million are agricultural workers, who earn less than $80 a month. The rest own their land or lease it. The larger farms account for a disproportionate area of the land cultivated and amount of crops produced (Table 3-1).

More than one million farmers own such small holdings that they are unable to utilize modern techniques for increasing their productivity. As a result, the productivity of French farmers remained until very recently low compared to that of American, British, or Danish farmers. The authors of the Monnet

TABLE 3-1 *Landholdings of Farmers, 1956–1959*

Acreage (approx.)	Number of farms	Percentage of cultivated land
Less than 5 acres	379,200	16.8%
5– 13 acres	411,265	18.2
13– 25 acres	470,763	20.8
25– 50 acres	530,048	23.5
50–125 acres	373,810	16.5
Above 125 acres	84,000	4.2

Plan complained immediately after the Liberation that a French farmer produced only enough to feed three persons, while an American farmer could feed sixteen, a British farmer seven, and a Danish nine.

Foreign observers have described French farmers as a homogeneous group, characterized by their courage against adversity, their moderate political outlook, their sacrifices and patriotism, their labor and wisdom. French authors also have extolled the rural virtues of stoicism and courage, patience and moderation. These impressions were accurate to a great extent for the nineteenth century and the time before World War I. The farmers provided two of the nation's most precious commodities, in addition to their agricultural produce—their sons for the Army and their savings. But the devastation of World War I brought to the fore the farmers' sense of individualism and their suspicion of the state. This spirit, coupled with the increasingly antiquated machinery and procedures used on the farm, and the constant fragmentation of the land, has resulted in open defiance in a number of regions against agents of the central government.

The ideologies that have had the most appeal for the farmers are *radicalism* and *Catholicism*. The elements of radicalism—individualism and anti-state philosophy—are rooted in the thinking of many farmers. Catholicism, on the other hand, accounts for much of the conservative attitude of farmers. But after

World War II, the farmers and their organizations adopted views all across the political spectrum, which increased the political instability of the country. For instance, if we take for purposes of illustration five Departments of France with the greatest percentage of farmers—Creuse (85 per cent of the population), Côtes du Nord (81.5 per cent), Gers (80 per cent), Vendée (80 per cent), and Haute-Savoie (80 per cent)—we find that in the elections of 1951 in Creuse the Communists received 40 per cent of the votes, in Côtes du Nord the liberal Catholics (MRP) and center groups received 38 per cent, Gers gave to the Socialists and the center groups 47 per cent, while the Vendée and Haute-Savoie gave a very high percentage of their votes to the Gaullists and the MRP.[1]

The political orientation of a farm region largely depends on its types of agriculture, on its level of income, its historical experience, and the intensity of religious practices. Wherever landholdings are small and the Church weak, the general political orientation is to the Left, ranging from radicalism to Communism. In areas where there are small landholdings and where religious practices are prevalent, the farmers usually vote conservative and sometimes for the liberal Catholics. Where farms range from medium to large in size, the crucial determining factor is religion. In the areas where religious practices are strong, the farmers tend to vote conservative or moderate; where religious practices are weak, they vote for the Center or the Left.

Catholicism is thus, generally speaking, a conservative force in French politics. But the fact that a farmer owns property, particularly in some of the Southern and Southeastern regions, does not guarantee that he will not adopt radical ideas. In fact, in one Department like Creuse, where private ownership is both widespread and widely parceled, the Communist Party is particularly strong. The average parcel of land is so small, however, that poverty drives the farmer to the Communist Party.

[1] From an article by Jacques Fauvet in *Partis Politiques et Classes Sociales en France* (Paris: Armand Colin, 1958).

The Middle Class

The "middle class" instigated the Revolution of 1789 against the nobility and the Crown. Its economic power had increased greatly in the eighteenth century, and it was anxious to augment its political power by establishing a representative government. After the Revolution, it was generally the champion of the Republic against the nobility, the Church, and the Army. Thanks to it, the doctrine of the separation of Church and state became well established, the Army came under the control of the state, the representative institutions became supreme, and vested interests have been subordinated to the legislature.

The term "middle class," however, covers many heterogeneous elements. Do we define it according to occupation, income, or status? One French political scientist uses these three basic criteria for categorizing French citizens as members of the middle class: (a) the nature of their jobs, (b) their way of life and the manner in which they spend their income, and (c) common status with reference to their income tax. On the basis of these criteria, the French middle class consists of the following groups. Among the salaried are engineers, office personnel, the bulk of the civil servants, judges, teachers, professors, and noncommissioned officers (sous-officiers) in the armed services. Among the non-salaried are members of the professions, small merchants, small businessmen, small entrepreneurs, and artisans. They are roughly estimated to total seven and a half million people, or approximately 37 per cent of those gainfully employed. This large figure is what many authors have in mind when they refer to France as a "bourgeois"—middle-class—country, a land of small entrepreneurs, independent artisans, small family enterprises, and small shops where the nineteenth century values of individualism and quality, moderation and balance, reign.

From the natural affinities that exist within the middle class, you might guess that the group would exhibit a unified and constant attitude in matters of politics. But this is hardly the case in France, where the middle class has often changed its political orientation and is today split into many different viewpoints.

HISTORICAL SHIFTS. Until about the end of the nineteenth century, the middle class was generally anticlerical and pro-republican. Since the turn of the century, however, the middle class has slowly turned back to the Church and toward a more conservative political attitude. Their distrust of the state, very much like the emphasis on states' rights in the United States, often led them to block social and economic reforms, while the advocacy of socialism by the emerging working class put them increasingly on the defensive. One segment of the middle class, the so-called Radicals, continue to pay lip service to anticlericalism and reform, but they are not very strong about them in practice and end up oscillating between the Left and the Right.

The lower middle class, the artisans and shopkeepers, retained their attachment to the Republic until the end of World War II. Since 1945, the "small man" has begun to rise against the income tax and the financial burdens imposed upon him by the state. Conscious that the tide of history is sweeping France toward greater industrialization and is eroding his very existence (the chain stores are driving out the small shopkeeper, the big factories are eliminating the artisan, mechanized farms are squeezing out the small independent farmer, etc.), the "small men" are attempting to arrest this development. Through powerful lobbies, they pressure Parliament for increasing protection and subsidies. In the 1950's, they began to repudiate the republican parliamentary system they had supported for so long and to join extreme Right-wing nationalist groups.

DIVERSITY AND FRAGMENTATION. In the last twenty years, the middle class has become divided in its political views among all political parties. Regional, historical, religious, and economic factors account for this wide dispersion of political orientation. In a number of instances, middle-class groups have even supported the Communists. It has been estimated, for instance, that 8 per cent of the salaried employees, 5 per cent of the civil servants, 5 per cent of the merchants, 3 per cent of those belonging to the professions, and 3 per cent of the pensioners vote Communist. Perhaps as many as 750,000 to 1,000,000 of the Communist Party votes have come from the middle class. A greater percentage of middle-class votes, however, goes to other parties: to the Socialists, particularly the votes of salaried groups, teachers, and the civil servants; to the MRP, especially the votes of practicing Catholics; to the Radicals, supported by the merchants and shopkeepers; and to various conservative parties and notably the Gaullists. All political parties in turn make a concerted effort to appeal to the various segments of the middle class and to organize them into a number of professional front associations.

The diversity in political outlook divides and weakens the middle class and hampers it in formulating concrete programs that would promote its own economic interests. As a group, it is susceptible to the unifying appeal of a "strong" man, and has succumbed at different times to Bonapartism. During the Second Empire (1852–1870), with Marshal Pétain in 1940, and, finally, with General de Gaulle, the middle class has opted for what amounts to a one-man government. Generally, however, the middle class has supported the Republic as the best instrument for accommodating its desires. It has often saved the Republic from disintegration, but in time of crisis it has been its gravedigger. It has not displayed in the realm of politics the moderation and tolerance that Aristotle and later John Stuart Mill associated with it.

The Church

France is a predominantly Catholic nation. There are only a little more than a million Protestants and Jews and three to four hundred thousand resident Algerian Moslems in France. Yet of the forty-five million Catholics, not more than about 25 per cent, a maximum of around ten million, can be classed as practicing believers. The great majority are "indifferent"; they observe only the basic sacraments prescribed by the Church—baptism, communion, marriage, and extreme unction— and perhaps conform outwardly to some of the most important religious ceremonies and rites. A minority, maybe seven or eight million, is strongly anticlerical and even antireligious. Many densely populated urban centers are virtually "de-Christianized," without churches, priests, or practicing Catholics. Much of the urban population, especially in the working-class districts, is militantly atheistic. In some areas, even burial is a civil affair. A close correlation exists between conservatism and attachment to the Church, and between Communism and socialism and hostility to the Church. The Right, generally speaking, is religious; the Left is overtly anticlerical and very often atheistic.

The degree of religious participation in the various parts of France is largely the result of historical factors. There is both *more* and *less* religious practice in the rural areas. For instance, in the regions of the Northwest (Brittany and Normandy), about 80 per cent of the population are devout Catholics, while in some thirty departments of Central and Southern France, the figure drops to about 20 per cent (Fig. 3-1). In the towns, generally only about half the population is religious, and in urban centers like Paris, Marseille, Lyon, Toulouse, and Grenoble, the number is even less. In some of the suburban centers of the larger towns, areas dense with working-class settlements, religious practices are almost nonexistent. In the Paris working-class districts, not more than 2 per cent of the people "practice."

History has produced strange things on the religious map of France. The American Catholic tourist who decides to drive from, say, Luçon to Bayeux in Normandy will find that to his left the churches are usually well kept, regular services are held, and priests are readily available, for some 85 per cent of the people to his left "practice." Only a few miles away to his right, however, the situation is exactly the reverse. Only about 20 per cent of the people practice, and priests are difficult to find. Often the tourist will discover a rivulet that divides a village in two, with one part intensely Catholic and the other intensely anticlerical and nonreligious!

The correlation between social groups and religion is fairly precise, but, as with any generalization, there are exceptions. Many farmers, especially in the Northwest and Northeast, the upper middle class, the bigger landowners, and part of the middle class itself have a higher proportion of practicing believers. The workers, many of the farmers of the South, teachers, intellectuals, and some of the lower middle class show a low percentage of practice.

ORGANIZATION. The Catholic Church in France is technically separated from the state. Until recently, this separation has also applied to education. The Church receives no subsidies and its schools—grammar schools, nurseries, and technical and high schools—are strictly "private." [2] Only the diplomas given by the public schools and universities are recognized. Matters of religious dogma and practical administration are decided by a loose organization headed by the Assembly of Cardinals and Archbishops. The country is divided into dioceses that correspond to the Departments, and these in turn are subdivided into parishes. A total of some forty thousand priests and about one hundred thousand auxiliaries be-

[2] Except for Alsace-Lorraine, where the Church and Catholic schools have been subsidized since 1918.

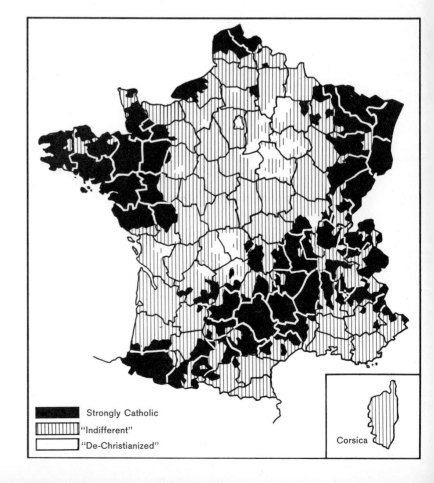

FIGURE 3-1 RELIGIOUS PRACTICE IN FRANCE. *Adapted from François Goguel,* Géographie des Élections Françaises, de 1870 à 1951 *(with the kind permission of the Fondation Nationale des Sciences Politiques and the Librairie Armand Colin). Paris: Armand Colin, 1952.*

Strongly Catholic
"Indifferent"
"De-Christianized"

Corsica

longing to various religious orders perform the services and administer the many activities of the Church—charity, education, relief, hospitals, and so forth. The state intervenes only when a bishop is nominated by the Pope, for it must approve the choice for the appointment to be valid.

What is the political orientation of the practicing Catholics? As with other groups we have examined, there is great diversity in the political behavior of Catholics. Some follow the Church's dogma and believe the state to be subordinate to the Church. Many remain extremely conservative. In the thirties, this group was represented by a militant antirepublican organization, the National Federation of Catholics. On the other end of the spectrum, the "progressive" Catholics are actively concerned with social and economic reform and are more interested in social action than in proselytizing and maintaining the dogma. This group, since the Liberation, has been moving toward the Left and has been responsible for establishing new reformist Catholic groups, parties, and trade unions. Between the Left and the Right are the majority of believers, who generally vote for the center parties.

In the last decades, many Catholic youth organizations composed of lay believers have been particularly active in social, economic, and political matters. The most significant among them have been the J.A.C. (*Jeunesse Agricole Catholique*—Catholic Agricultural Youth), the J.O.C. (*Jeunesse Ouvière Catholique*—Catholic Workers' Youth), and the J.E.C. (*Jeunesse Étudiante Chrétienne*—Christian Student Youth). They have to spread a new progressive philosophy among the workers and farmers. Often looked upon with suspicion by the Catholic hierarchy and frequently in sharp disagreement with other parareligious organizations of the Church, these groups have been quite successful in organizing Catholic workers, farmers, and students,

and in bringing about progressive reforms. They have not been able to reduce appreciably Communist influence, but they have succeeded in reaching those who might otherwise have succumbed to it.

In 1944, Catholic Action organizations spurred the creation of a large liberal Catholic party, the Republican Popular Movement (MRP); in the fifties, they successfully rebuilt the Christian trade union, the French Confederation of Christian Workers (CFTC). Today they are trying to penetrate the countryside, by sparking a desire for reform among the farmers and villagers, by encouraging economic and technical reforms that are so much needed in French agriculture, and by supporting enlightened candidates at the local level for the offices of mayor, municipal councilor, and, more recently, senators and deputies.

The Army

As in England and in all European countries, the French Army, except in the relatively brief period during the Revolution and during the reign of Napoleon and since World War II, has been composed of officers of aristocratic and upper middle class background. Seldom could young officers of low birth move up through the ranks. After the Bourbon Restoration of 1814, the officer corps became almost a caste—hierarchically organized, anti-republican and, until the turn of the century, predominantly royalist. The young officers received their "high school" training in exclusive Jesuit schools where they faced rigorous examinations and then were sent to the few select military schools, later to be assigned to regimental or divisional commands or to the various staff organizations in Paris. Family, social, religious, and school ties made them a well-knit group, whose autonomy was assured by the frequent appointment of a general as Minister of War. Time after time, the Army imposed virtually a veto on the regularly constituted governmental authorities. When the Third Republic was introduced, Army officers attempted on two occasions to subvert it in favor of the Monarchy. It was the Dreyfus Affair in 1894—a landmark in the political history of France—that broke the political autonomy of the Army and changed its social composition.

The real issue in the Dreyfus Affair (1894–1906) was whether the Army could continue to be a state within a state, immune from political scrutiny and able to impose its own will upon the civil government. The Army court-martialed Alfred Dreyfus, a Jewish captain, for treason and, when challenged that the documents used to convict Dreyfus had actually been forged by another officer of the General Staff, the Army claimed that any interference with its own jurisdiction and rules would destroy its morale and ultimately undermine the unity of the nation. A wave of nationalism, anti-Semitism and antirepublicanism swept across the country when Émile Zola and others charged that Dreyfus was innocent and demanded a new trial for him. After some ten years of unremitting social and political strife, the republican forces won; civil control over the Army was asserted, and the hold of the Church and the aristocracy on the Army was broken.

The end of the Dreyfus Affair virtually coincided with the establishment of separation of Church and state in France and the dissolution of a number of religious congregations and the confiscation of their property. These developments marked, in a real sense, the culmination of the Revolution of 1789: they weakened the ultraconservative elements of the Church, virtually wiped out the influence of the aristocracy, and paved the way for the democratic reorganization of the Army under the supremacy of the republican government.

From the turn of the century until 1940, the bulk of the Army officers adopted an attitude of political neutrality. It was referred to as the *"grande muette,"* the "great deaf and dumb." It did not interfere in politics. However, few high-ranking officers were genuinely republican. The Army was not attuned to the world of politics, to the need for give and take, negotiation and compromise, and it thus tended to stand aloof from the arena of political bargaining.

The defeat of the French armies in World War II shook the Army to its foundations. It weakened the Army's loyalty to the state, shattered the Army's internal discipline and cohesiveness, and radically changed its social composition; it also led the Army to search for a scapegoat to blame for the disaster. When the Armistice was signed between the French and the Germans in 1940, the Republic was set aside and one man, Marshal Pétain, established an authoritarian system. He was supported by the bulk of the Army. Following the Army's tradition of political neutrality, virtually all the officers commanding colonial garrisons obeyed Pétain. In Senegal, Madagascar, Morocco, and Algeria, discipline held. But one general, de Gaulle, did not obey. With a small group of followers, he decided to reject the legitimacy of Marshal Pétain's government and continue the war. De Gaulle's rebelliousness was not a unique phenomenon, but it was remarkable that he was able to win over more and more officers and colonial garrisons and eventually to march into liberated France as the country's legitimate representative and spokesman. The logic of the situation carried dangerous seeds for the future. If one general could do it, why not another? The dissidence split the ranks of the Army. Some officers had sided with de Gaulle, others with Pétain. "Pétainists" and "Gaullists" became expressions conveying two political tendencies and two orientations in the Army. Even if the passage of time could temper the hostility between the two blocs, mutual suspicion was inevitable. The hierarchy and discipline of the Army was therefore rudely shaken.

Defeat makes any army unpopular. It took a long time, for instance, for the German Army to recover from the debacle of World War I. Disgraced, useless, and frustrated, the defeated soldiers, and especially the officers, realize that they are something of a pariah in a country that only shortly before had heaped glory and distinction upon them. With the

French officer corps, the situation was even more discouraging. The collapse of 1940 was followed by a series of colonial wars in which the French Army continuously had to withdraw. The war in Indochina that lasted from 1946 to 1954 took a heavy toll among the officers, while few at home seemed to care what was going on halfway around the globe. In 1956 France pulled out of Morocco and Tunisia; in 1954 the Algerian rebellion erupted and raged intermittently for almost eight years.

Years of defeat and neglect have embittered the French Army, and the officers no longer have wealth or social position to help siphon off their frustration. The French Army in the 1950's contained only a few hundred wealthy officers, compared to some 30,000 in the latter part of the nineteenth century. The twentieth-century officers were mostly from the lower middle class, and many rose from the ranks. Their parents were frequently military officers or civil servants, members of the professions, small landowners. The officers shared the anxieties and fears of the lower middle class, who were frightened of a world that was changing too rapidly and of a future that carried unknown threats to their security. They thus considered that status and prestige were inordinately important, but found themselves ignored, underpaid, and criticized for losing battles the country itself did not seem to want to win. The officers found their scapegoat in the Republic, which they believed had badly let them, and France, down. They formed dissident organizations and sought allies among Right-wing, antirepublican forces in an attempt to impose their view on the Fourth Republic. The Army thus re-entered politics in a rebellious mood.

Algeria was the breaking point. Some half a million recruits and their officers were confronted with a far-from-orthodox war. It was a battle involving ambushes, street fighting, and terrorist attacks. The rebels had the sup-

port of the overwhelming Moslem majority, who surrounded the French settlers and the Army at every turn. There could be no retreat. Yet victory in the traditional military sense was impossible, since the enemy consisted of elusive bands of guerrillas. In an attempt to "win," the Army embarked on a broad-scale campaign that ranged far beyond just firing weapons. They utilized censorship, propaganda, coercion, and torture. They were given the power to censor newspapers, to control the schools, to administer new schools for the Moslems, to set up "resettlement camps" in which Algerians were screened and indoctrinated, and to move hundreds of thousands of Algerians into barracks and new villages where they could be closely watched. But back in Paris, political leaders criticized the war and urged negotiations with the rebels. The Army was prevented from "solving" the problem in its customary way—by victory. More and more Army leaders came to see that the only way out was to assume political control and eliminate the Republic.

Thus the Army had come full circle since the Dreyfus Affair. Before 1890, it could, in effect, veto actions of the government, but after the Dreyfus case and the victory of World War I, it was assimilated into the Republic. It adopted a neutral stand in politics, but not for long. In the late thirties, it began to question the weak and vacillating policies of the Republic, and in 1940 most of the officers supported the authoritarian system that emerged from the Armistice. General de Gaulle's call emboldened many officers to set their own goals ahead of those of the legally constituted government. All pretense to neutrality was abandoned. At the same time, the Army's social character had changed. The Army began to recruit its officers extensively from the middle class and the lower middle class. Slowly the insecurities and anxieties of this class crept into the ranks, especially into the officer corps. Algeria spurred the officers, fired by years of isolation and defeat, to become the spokesmen of a new nationalism, and a political regime that would support them. Hoping de Gaulle would do this, they backed him in May 1958.

Intellectuals

Intellectuals are people who work with ideas and manipulate symbols and words. Broadly speaking, we can include in this category teachers, lawyers, doctors, higher civil servants, writers, artists, editors, radio commentators, newspaper columnists. If we apply this very general definition of the term, there are about one million intellectuals in France, but, for purposes of political analysis, we need a more limited, a more functional definition of intellectual. Here, then, we will consider an intellectual to be a person of some education and sophistication who, by using his medium of communication, consciously attempts to influence the course of events.

To understand the intellectual's role in politics, we must go back again to the Dreyfus Affair. The trial of Captain Dreyfus not only brought sharp conflict over the fate of the officer, but generated more profound discussions about the nature of justice, the power of the state, and the rights of the individual. Émile Zola's famous article, "I Accuse," in which he levied a bitter attack against the Army and its officers for framing a fellow officer in the name of the rights of the state, crystallized the deeper issues in the case and awakened in the intellectuals a desire to enter the arena of political dispute. Intellectuals thus became "engaged" in politics, but, like the other groups we have examined, they have been fragmented into many ideological camps that support Catholics, anticlerics, nationalists, republicans, Communists, militarists, antimilitarists, etc. They began to reflect the divisions of the society.

Instead of objectively analyzing and clarifying issues, therefore, the intellectuals became protagonists of political causes. The Jesuit schools produced, until the end of the nineteenth century, intellectuals for the Army and the bureaucracy, while the Teachers' Schools (Écoles Normales) graduated teachers and intellectuals deeply committed to a lay republic and to the separation of Church and state. The "League of the French Fatherland" (Ligue de la Patrie Française) consisted of conservative, nationalist pro-Army intellectuals, while the "League of the Rights of Man" (Ligue des Droits de l'Homme) included those who were attached to the Republic, to individual rights, and to the separation of Church and state. Numerous groups in the thirties took an overtly pro-royalist and authoritarian stance. The sympathy of some university professors with Communism provoked, in turn, many conservative intellectuals to favor peace with Germany and later to support Pétain's authoritarian regime. After the Liberation, a sharp debate erupted between those who were sympathetic to the Soviet Union and the cause of socialism and those who opposed the totalitarian means the Soviets imposed to accomplish their goal of socialism. The old question of whether the end justifies the means split the intellectuals into bitterly opposed pro-Soviet and anti-Soviet camps.

The intellectuals speak through organizations that constitute important pressure groups, but they speak with so many different voices that they tend to cancel one another out. By often exaggerating and distorting their arguments, the intellectuals end up by aggravating the differences that divide the community. The lively discussions of ideas that continuously take place in France are one of the glories of French culture. But they put a great strain on the nation's political system, and, by mounting ideas as weapons in political battles, make the compromises necessary for effective political action even more difficult to achieve.

Interest Groups

Economic, social, intellectual, and religious interests are solidly organized in France. For every conceivable interest group, there seems to be an association or a spokesman: war widows and orphans, invalids, private distillers, parents and teachers of private (i.e., Catholic) schools, fruit growers, mothers of illegitimate children, owners of private hotels, wheat growers, mayors, country priests and city priests, refugees from Morocco and Tunisia, university professors, professors of technical schools, civil servants, doctors, artisans, students, members of agricultural cooperatives, retailers, meat packers, meat distributors and butchers, gas-station owners, motel owners, white-collar workers, architects, restaurant owners, tobacco vendors and liquor retailers, graduates of St. Cyr, of the Institute of Political Studies, of the School of National Administration, non-commissioned officers, comedians who fought in the Resistance, Music Hall artists who are veterans of World War II, hospital interns, former prisoners of war, holders of war decorations, producers of *apéritifs*, "Christian" workers, grocers, toymakers, newspaper distributors, fishmongers, graduates of colleges and lycées, bakers, stenographers, typists, etc., etc.—all have their official associations. If we look at the Paris telephone directory under "association" or "union" or "syndicat," we shall quickly realize that there is no possible interest that does not have an office or organization in France. What is more, for each single interest there are *many* different associations. We cannot hope to discuss all the interest groups in France, but we will try to examine their general characteristics and study the mode of action of the more important ones.

Types of Interest Groups

At the risk of oversimplification, the interest groups can be divided into three broad categories. First are the *representative groups,* organizations that speak for the most important activities and interests at a national level. Their voice is that of a great number of members and often a large number of affiliated groups and subgroups. Most important among them are: the CNPF, *Conseil National du Patronat Français* (The National Council of French Employers), which represents a great

assortment of business enterprises and roughly corresponds to our National Association of Manufacturers and Chambers of Commerce combined; the CNPME, *Conseil National des Petits et Moyens Entreprises* (The National Council of Small and Medium-Sized Business), which is affiliated with the National Council of Employers, and represents a vast number of smaller-sized enterprises; the FNSEA, *Fédération Nationale des Syndicats des Exploitants Agricoles* (The National Federation of Farmers), speaking for farmers; the three major trade union organizations—CGT, FO, and CGTC; the FEN, *Fédération de l'Éducation Nationale* (Federation of National Education), an "independent" union representing most of the grade school, high school, college, and technical school teachers, the UNEF, *Union Nationale des Étudiants de France* (National Student Union), representing the university students. All these affiliations are nationally organized. They have branches all over France. Their members usually, but not always, agree on a particular means of action, so that their leaders can speak on any given issue with considerable authority and weight.

Second, there are organizations that have a *distinctly economic and corporative character.* Some of them act independently, although most belong to the organizations mentioned under the first category. Some have such a mass membership that their effectiveness is primarily "electoral," that is, they urge their members to vote for or against a particular party or a candidate. Here is just a partial listing of this type of group: high school teachers, Catholic families who receive subsidies for the education of their children in Catholic schools, the organizations that belong to the so-called "highway lobby"—motel owners, gas-station owners, car producers, truck and moving companies, gas producers, oil companies, etc., tavern and bistro owners backed by the powerful alcohol lobby, some two million private distillers who each produce up to two and a half gallons of alcohol every year free of tax, veterans, with their various organizations, war widows, invalids, etc. Other groups occupy critical areas in the country's economy whose temporary suspension may paralyze a good part of the nation: mailmen, electrical workers, railroad employees, miners, dockworkers.

Finally, the third and perhaps least powerful category consists of *particular interests*. These are "lobbies" in the classic sense of the term that try to influence the political system and the economy to their advantage.

CHARACTERISTICS. The most significant characteristic of all these interest groups is their diverse and fragmented nature. We have already noted their diversity. Even when groups and interests are represented in associations like the National Council of French Employers, or the National Council of Small and Medium-Sized Business, or the National Federation of Education, they maintain their individual autonomy and often act in their own behalf against the wishes of the national organization with which they are affiliated. Even associations that claim to represent one social group like the workers, farmers, the Catholic Church, businessmen, civil servants, or intellectuals are usually divided into different ideological and political units that are often connected directly or indirectly with the various political parties.

MEANS OF ACTION. In general, French lobbies are quite similar in their methods of action to American lobbies. They give financial support to candidates; they place their spokesmen in the legislature and in the Civil Service; they have their own journals and hand out news releases in an attempt to sway public opinion to their point of view; they often exact pledges from the candidates they support and sponsor "study committees" in the legislature to promote their own interests.

French lobbies are also directly active in the legislative process. Through their spokesmen, they introduce bills and see to it that the proper amendments are inserted in pending legislation or that prejudicial amendments are blocked. Their influence even spills over into the executive branch. When a bill is passed, the interested lobby tries to prevent the release of any executive order that might be prejudicial to their interest or, conversely, attempts to see that the proper executive orders will be issued. To do this, spokesmen are often planted in certain crucial administrative services—the Ministries of Public Works, Agriculture, Veterans, Finance, and Industrial Production. With the growing participation of the state in economic matters, lobbying at the ministerial level has greatly increased. Every interest attempts to "colonize" the government in a number of ways—by influencing administrators, by offering them important jobs in their own organizations, by presenting them with facts and figures that appear to be convincing.

In conclusion, one characteristic of French pressure groups should be mentioned, a characteristic that both gives the lobbies strength and that denies them the ultimate effectiveness enjoyed by pressure groups in other countries. The French pressure groups have easily been able to secure favors in the form of legislation, tax benefits, subsidies, tariff protection, insurance against risk, price supports, and the like because of two reasons: (1) the governments have been too unstable to be able to say "no" to anyone, and (2) real governmental power has been diffused among many agencies. Under the Fourth Republic, the following seats of power competed with the National Assembly, which was pre-eminent but far from omnipotent: parliamentary committees (just as powerful as our congressional committees); parliamentary party *groups*, some twelve or fifteen of them; the Civil Service, which was already in part colonized and receptive to pressure-group influence; the Minister, whose tenure was always precarious; the Cabinet and Prime Minister, whose political life averaged about seven months. In such a system, pressure groups, through backstairs maneuvering, could exploit every advantage opened up by party disagreements, or the contradictions arising from coalition cabinets. But this system also worked against the lobbies. Since *all* pres-

Social Foundations

sure groups succeeded to some extent, it was impossible for *any* of them to produce radical changes of policy. The various groups could thus check each other.

The greatest weakness of the lobbies lay, however, in their political fragmentation. The splits among the important groups, like the workers and farmers, were so deep that they could not act in unison. In Great Britain, lobbies are effective because they are able to adopt a common action in favor of specific policies. In France, on the other hand, the interest groups are so divided that they often fail to generate a common strategy and action.

The Articulation of Interest

Each of the major social groups we have discussed is represented by several associations.

LABOR INTEREST GROUPS. The working class is represented by at least five organizations. The General Confederation of Labor (CGT), the largest of all, includes craft unions and industrial unions, i.e., those with members from an entire industry: steel workers, construction workers, automobile workers, etc. Its directive organ is the National Confederation Committee, which is elected by the delegates to the annual National Congress. The leaders are Communists and have been since World War II, and they often use the union for political purposes. They have called strikes to protest the establishment of the North Atlantic Treaty Organization, the European Defense Community, and the continuation of the wars in Indochina and Algeria, and they generally pursue the political objectives of the Communist Party.

The CFTC, the French Confederation of Christian Workers, is organized very much like the CGT. Half its members are salaried workers, and it is committed to social reform and to increasing the standard of living and wages of the workers. It, too, has gone on strike—

often in collaboration with the CGT—but it is usually unwilling to strike for political purposes.

The CGT-FO, General Confederation of Labor-Force Ouvrière (Workers' Force) split off from the CGT in 1947 when its predominantly Socialist membership would not accept the pro-Soviet political directives of the Communist-controlled CGT. They seceded to form their own group, primarily composed of low-ranking civil servants and workers in nationalized industries. It, too, says its goals are "apolitical," but in practice it has followed the policies of the Socialist Party.

There is a small anarchist union, the CNT (National Confederation of Labor), which consists of unions not affiliated with any of the three larger unions. Non-affiliated unions serve the needs of other employees. The National Federation of Education, for instance, has a membership of more than a quarter of a million grade school, high school, technical school, and university teachers. Although claiming to be apolitical, it has consistently taken political positions on a number of issues. The Socialists and Communists have vied for its control, and the resolutions of the members often reflect sharp political divisions.

FARM INTEREST GROUPS. About 700,000 farmers belong to the National Federation of Farmers. Nationwide in scope, it includes farmers who deal in such products as wheat, wine, beets, milk, and poultry. Although the avowed purpose of the organization is to "represent and defend on the national plane the interests of the agricultural profession in the economic, social, moral, and legislative domain," the Federation represents only a small percentage of farmers and is generally dominated by the wealthier ones, notably the beet growers, the so-called alcohol lobby, the dairy interests, and meat producers. The smaller landholders benefit, to be sure, from the Federation's activities, but they are not often happy with the group's program.

Almost all the political parties have tried to woo the farmers by setting up their own farm organization or by demonstrating favorable actions within the National Federation of Farmers. The Socialists established the General Confederation of Agriculture, which was quite powerful right after the Liberation; the Communists ran the General Confederation of Farm Workers, which is influential in central France and in the Southwest, where the farms are parceled into small private holdings; the Catholics and the MRP work through various agricultural Catholic Action groups, particularly the Catholic youth farm organizations; the Right-wing has a number of farm associations; and the Radical Socialist Party has become the spokesman for middle-income farmers in a number of areas. Thus extreme diversity and fragmentation have been the rule with farm organizations, which is clearly reflected by the voting behavior of farmers.

When political-action and pressure-group methods have failed to achieve the farmers' goals, they have borrowed the tactics of the working class and staged demonstrations and strikes, complete with road blocks and acts of violence. This form of direct action has, of course, precedents that go back to the farmers' uprisings under the *Ancien Régime,* especially in the South; but even as recently as the thirties, farmers were organized into a rural fascist militia known as the "Green Shirts." The postwar infiltration into farm groups of both the extreme Left (the Communists) and the extreme Right (the Poujadists) intensified the farmers' rebelliousness.

The political unrest of the farmers has been exacerbated by economic developments. Since the end of World War II, modernization has increased farm productivity to such an extent that prices of agricultural products have sagged. Although the costs of goods that the farmer buys have dropped, the decrease has not been enough to prevent a decline in farm income and a consequent exodus from the farm to the city. Every year about 50,000 people move from agricultural areas to the larger towns. The farmers have demanded and received increased aid in the form of subsidies, tax exemptions, and price supports. Help of a sort has also come from those who preach that the farmer is the backbone of the nation's moral character. In 1959, for instance, the Minister of Industrial Production and former Professor of Economics, J. M. Jeanneney, wrote that agriculture has a "civilizing mission" and that the stability of a people derives from a sufficient number of farmers.[3]

But the process of modernization cannot be easily arrested. In most mature societies, people are moving off the farms into towns, from agriculture into industry, leaving in their wake severe dislocations in the life of the countryside, especially in France, where intense resentments and political divisions already existed. Efforts to ameliorate the French farmer's condition, to teach him new techniques, to provide him with fertilizers and tractors, to develop cooperatives, and to show him what and how to plant, have been undertaken by the state and a number of voluntary associations. The farmers' situation is on the upswing.

MIDDLE-CLASS INTEREST GROUPS. As we have seen, the middle class is badly divided politically. However, one large organization, the National Council of Small and Middle-Sized Business, claims to include some 3,000 associations representing a total of 800,000 firms, the great majority of members being shopkeepers and merchants. Dedicated to preserving the interests of the "small" and "medium-sized" firm and store, it has spokesmen in the legislature who influence legislation on tariffs, subsidies, prices, taxation, and means of modernizing the distribution of goods. The Council gives financial support to political candidates and has occasionally run its own men in national elections. But the "unity" of the small and middle-sized businessmen is a myth. Their loyalties are divided among all political parties. The Communists, for instance, have set up a number of "front" organizations in commerce and industry—among grocers, artisans, holders of liquor licenses,

[3] *Forces et Faiblesses de l'Économie Française* (Paris: Armand Colin, 1957), p. 65.

and small businessmen—and pose as the protector of the "small man" against the big corporations.

The discontent of the lower middle class came to a head in 1954 when Pierre Poujade organized the Union for the Defense of the Merchants and Artisans, dedicated primarily to protecting small businessmen against what it claimed was an intolerable burden of taxation. The organization grew like wildfire and was transformed into a political party, the UFF (Union and French Fraternity), which clearly had an antiparliamentary and antirepublican orientation. It cut sharply into the strength of the National Council of Small and Middle-Sized Business and forced the Council to become more politically active. When Poujadism collapsed in 1957–58, the lower middle class continued to be restive.

THE ARMY AND VETERANS. Like any professional organization, the Army has a number of associations closely tied to it. The officers, noncommissioned officers, and graduates of the different military schools all have their own organizations. In addition, France's veterans are organized into several groups that concentrate largely on obtaining pensions and other economic privileges for their members. These veterans' associations are affiliated with various political organizations. The National Union of Veterans supports the moderate political groups of the Center; the Republican Association of Veterans is linked with the Communists, the National Federation of Republican Veterans with the Radicals, the Federation of Worker and Peasant Veterans with the Socialists. There are also specialized veterans' groups: veterans of the Algerian war and the Indochinese war and veterans of specific military branches and divisions.

An effort to unite all these associations into one apolitical organization that would speak on behalf of the veterans' common economic interests and thus become an effective pressure group resulted in the formation right after World War II of the French Union of the Associations of Veterans and War Victims. It was a powerful organization, probably representing more than five million members. However, disagreement over the colonial policy of the government and the war in Algeria led to the inevitable fragmentation of the group. By 1956, a special committee was established to support the continuation of the war in Algeria and to assure that France would never allow independence for Algeria. By attracting very nationalistic and often extremely antirepublican support, this committee caused the estrangement of more liberal members of the Union and the formation of rival factions.

INTEREST GROUPS OF INTELLECTUALS. The only genuine professional association among what we may call the "intellectuals" is the Confederation of Intellectual Workers of France. A very loose organization of some 400,000 members representing about eighty associations, it includes painters, writers, members of professions, and many others. Although it professes to represent the material interests of the intellectuals, this claim of unity around economic themes is illusory. The intellectuals, as we have seen, are divided into all the political families of the nation, and are deeply "engaged" in the political issues of the day.

Among the political organizations of the intellectuals, the League of the Rights of Man has been one of the most powerful. Founded at the time of the Dreyfus Affair, it grew in the thirties to a membership of over 200,000. Since then it has been on the decline, but continues to represent the forces of the Left and champions such causes as individual and political freedom and freedom of the press, and opposes all forms of authoritarianism. It considers itself the guardian of the rights secured by the French Revolution and is a stanch believer in the separation of Church and state. Its support comes from all the elements of the Left, including civil servants, teachers, university professors, and, at times, even the liberal Catholics.

Students should perhaps also be listed under the category of "intellectuals." They are specifically concerned with advancing their own status and well-being, in the form of scholarships, living quarters, loans, etc., but, as is the case with all the groups we have discussed, it is impossible for students to maintain an apolitical posture. Their organization, the UNEF (National Student Union), has branches at all the universities in France and includes in its membership around half the total number of registered university students—about 100,000. It is a very active lobby, constantly sending letters to deputies and parliamentary leaders, either supporting or criticizing government projects.

BUSINESS INTEREST GROUPS. Probably the most solidly organized professional group in France is that of the businessmen: industrialists, corporation managers, bankers, and merchants. Their strongest organization is the CNPF, Conseil National du Patronat Français (National Council of French Employers). Founded after World War I, it includes, according to its own statement, almost a million firms, which employ about six million wage earners and salaried personnel. Besides individual firms, it also includes other business associations, of which the National Council of Small and Middle-Sized Businessmen is one, together with organizations representing particular industries, such as the chemical, aeronautical, steel, and shipbuilding industries.

The functions of the CNPF are (a) to establish a liaison between industry and commerce, (b) to represent business firms before the public authorities, (c) to undertake studies for the purpose of improving the economic and social conditions of the country, and (d) to provide information for its members. The Council thus speaks on behalf of many powerful interests. Its "representative" character and its huge size render it somewhat inflexible and immobile, and its highly diversified membership makes it difficult to arrive at a common attitude on particular issues. On the other hand, the Council is more effective than most other interest groups. It is prudent in its lobbying tactics, for fear of antagonizing the many groups that are traditionally hostile to

business. Most of its pressures are exercised secretly, through a network of personal contacts, particularly between the "businessmen" and the legislators and administrators. Whenever it takes a position on specific policies that are of direct interest to the business world, on, say, the Common Market, plant and equipment modernization, or fiscal policies, it does so more discreetly than the other interest groups. By successfully avoiding direct identification with political causes, the Council has been able to maintain its cohesiveness and prevent the splintering that has plagued other groups. Consequently, it has been strong enough to resist attack and to block policies that are prejudicial to the interests of its members.

But even within the business community, fragmentation cannot be completely avoided. Catholic business groups have set up their own organization, the French Center of Christian Businessmen, which is dedicated to the establishment of "a Christian social order," and, as we noted before, the Communists, the Socialists, and the Poujadists have tried to win over the small businessmen.

THE STUDENTS: A BRIEF CASE STUDY. Nothing illustrates better the advantages of unity and the disadvantages of fragmentation than the recent history of students' organizations. Founded in 1907, the National Union of the General Association of Students, later the UNEF (National Union of French Students), became active immediately after World War I as an organization dedicated to the advancement of the interests of students. It managed to accomplish a number of its objectives: a sanatorium was built for sick students, a student travel service was initiated, a special sports center was constructed, preferential housing provisions for students were enacted, and cheap meals were provided for students. In its congress held at Grenoble right after the Liberation, in 1946, it pledged itself to stay out of politics and to limit its activities to protecting the interests of the students. It was able to bring the students under the social security laws and to obtain a number of special dispensations for them and continued to work for special "student salary" and additional scholarships.

But it was impossible for the students to stay neutral in politics. During the war in Indochina and especially during the war in Algeria, the students were torn between their professional interests, which required a unified organization for the greatest advancement, and their political ideologies, which, if projected forcefully within the organization, would produce disunity. In 1955, they agreed in a compromise resolution "not to engage in politics" without, however, going so far as to require that they "become disinterested in the subject." Particularly thorny was the relationship between the French and the Moslem students, the latter affiliated with the UGEMA (General Union of Moslem Algerian Stu-

dents) which favored Algerian independence. A new resolution was passed in 1958 that called for an apolitical attitude while allowing the students to engage in politics on their own! It was clear, however, that the proponents of political neutrality were mostly conservatives who were unwilling to allow the students to support a negotiated settlement of the war in Algeria. Whenever students did advocate such a settlement, the conservatives threatened to secede from the National Union.

In 1959, the UNEF abandoned neutrality, re-established contact with the UGEMA, and staged demonstrations in favor of peace in Algeria and negotiations with the rebels. Many of the more conservative subgroups within the Union promptly seceded. Whatever the merits of the political action of the students, the unity they needed for the betterment of their interests was destroyed—another example of how political and ideological conflict undermine the organization of interest groups.

Political Parties under the Fourth Republic

IV

In our discussion of Great Britain, we have seen an example of a two-party system, in which the parties are disciplined and formulate policies on the basis of the general pledges they make during elections. In France, the party system is vastly different from that in Great Britain. France has a multi-party system. Without counting the small regional and factional groups that often go under the names of parties, there have been from eight to ten political parties since the introduction of the Third Republic.

Compounding the multi-party system is the fact that most of the parties are internally divided. After national elections, the elected representatives of a party often form small groups and thereafter act independently of the party under whose label they ran. Under the Fourth Republic, any fourteen deputies could organize one of these "parliamentary groups" in the National Assembly, and it was not uncommon for fifteen of more of these groups to exist at one time. When individual parliamentarians "seceded" from their party to form a minuscule group with a new name,

they often elected a president and were granted representation under their new banner in the various parliamentary committees and given a voice in organizing the business of the legislature.

Fragmentation results from weak party discipline. France has been plagued by this disease for generations, and it is easy to point out the factors that account for it. First, it was very difficult for the Prime Minister or the President under the Third and Fourth Republics to dissolve the legislature and call for elections. A representative, once elected, was secure in his seat—no matter how he voted and acted—for the length of the legislative term. He could oppose the Cabinet with virtual impunity, even when the Prime Minister happened to be from his own party, a procedure, as we know, that is rarely permitted in Great Britain.

Secondly, most of the French deputies are, like many United States senators, strongly entrenched in their local constituency—they are often mayors of important or strategically located cites and towns and are frequently spokesmen for the lobbies that are prominent in their constituency.

Thirdly, with the exception of the parties of the Left, particularly the Communists and the Socialists, the parties are, in effect, loose affiliation of notables, political bosses and leaders. The party organization, in other words, both reflects and encourages lack of discipline. The nomination of a candidate is mostly a local matter; the control of funds is highly decentralized so that the candidate, once elected, owes little to the party, and the central organization cannot penalize him for his actions.

Fourthly, the multi-party system made it difficult, under the Fourth Republic, for national political leaders to emerge. Many parties, for instance, have no recognized leader who can speak on behalf of the party with assurance that he will be followed. French parties are, in fact, quite often like small detachments composed only of generals. When by chance, as it occasionally happened under the Third and Fourth Republics, a man of great quality attempted to speak directly to the nation about pressing problems and suggest solutions, the various party leaders united against him to thwart his efforts. No leadership was allowed to develop or centralized party machinery to grow that would enforce discipline and initiate collective action. Lack of leadership thus has been both the result and the cause of undisciplined political parties.

Finally, the underlying social and historical factors we have already discussed—the multiplicity of ideologies and their incompatibility—not only accounts for multi-partyism but also for the internal fragmentation of parties and for their lack of discipline and central organization. The religious conflicts about parochial schools, the division between the proponents of a welfare state and of economic individualism, the perennial problem of constitutional and electoral reform, and the quarrels over the many pressing issues of the day—such as foreign policy, European integration, colonial disengagement, and Algeria—have merged with uncompromising ideological attitudes to splinter the parties. Virtually every one of the

issues that confronted the Fourth Republic was fought *within the parties, not between them.*

It is often argued that French political parties are too ideological and issue-oriented to compromise their differences. This is not quite true. Parties, other than the Communists and the Socialists, are very much like American parties in that they have no precise position on issues or ideology. The ideological fights take place *within* the parties. The parties in France have never become common denominators of agreement on policies. Although a party focuses broadly on certain ideas and attitudes, which are mostly historically derived, these are largely matters of style and mood that in no way reflect a common ideological position. French political parties are thus characterized by internal heterogeneity and fragmentation.

Because of their multiplicity and internal divisions, the parties in France have not performed two vital functions that parties in other countries ordinarily provide. First, they have not been able to debate and clarify issues for the public. Members of the same party (excepting the Communists and possibly the Socialists) often advocate different things in different parts of the country, and in their party congresses their differences cannot be resolved. In a congress of the Radical-Socialist Party, for instance, one speaker argued for extensive nationalization and social legislation and another favored the return of the Post Office to private hands. Yet they both were Radicals!

Secondly, the parties could not, under the Fourth Republic, provide for a stable government that was committed to certain policy objectives. Unlike elections in Britain and the United States, an election in France does not determine the national government. The electorate votes for the members of the lower house of the legislature—the Chamber of Deputies under the Third Republic and the National Assembly under the Fourth and the Fifth—which in turn endorses a Prime Minister and supports his Cabinet. It is impossible to tell what combinations among parliamentary groups may provide temporary support for a

Prime Minister and what new combinations will bring about his downfall and subsequently that of his successors. The purpose of the referendum of October 28, 1962, was precisely to alter this situation and enable the French to elect their President directly in a national election, as we do in the United States.

The structure of the parties under the Fourth Republic was responsible for another unfortunate development: the widening gap that grew up between the people and the government. To survive, the government had to rely on the support of a coalition of groups that was called the "government majority." But since this coalition was the creature of the party leaders in Parliament and was never in itself approved by the electorate, the public became increasingly alienated from a system that did not give it an opportunity to select its government and hold it accountable. Again, the referendum of October 28, 1962 allows the people to participate in the selection of their national leader—the President.

The Communist Party

One of the most remarkable phenomena in the political history of France has been the strength of the Communist Party, especially since the end of World War II. The country that has been portrayed as a haven of individualism has had, as its largest party, a totalitarian and authoritarian one. Since the Liberation, with the exception of 1958 and 1962, more than five million French men and women (25 per cent or more of the electorate) have voted Communist.

History

The French Communist Party was founded in 1920, when almost three-fourths of the delegates to the Socialist Congress of Tours decided to split off from the Socialists and follow the Bolshevik leadership from Moscow. The Communists took over the Socialist newspaper, but not the bulk of the trade unions, which remained faithful to the Socialists. The new party joined the Third International, accepted Soviet leadership, endorsed the revolutionary philosophy of Lenin, and openly advocated the overthrow of French capitalism. It organized the Confederation General des Travailleurs Unitaire (CGTU) in an appeal for broad working-class support. Its membership, however, did not exceed 100,000, its voters did not number more than one million until 1934, and its parliamentary representation was small (10 to 26 members).

In 1934–35, the Party greatly increased its popularity and strength by cooperating with the Socialists and the democratic parties of the Center in a Popular Front, a broad political alliance directed against the Right-wing forces. In the election of 1936, the CGT (under Socialist control) and the CGTU (under Communist control) joined the alliance between the Socialists, Communists, and Radicals. Thanks to this alliance, the Communists received a million and a half votes, and their representation in the legislature jumped to 72 deputies, a sixfold increase. A Socialist government was formed with the participation of the Radicals and the support of the Communist Party, which had soft-pedaled its revolutionary posture in order to cooperate with the democratic parties.

When the Nazi-Soviet military pact was signed in 1939, the French Communist Party did an about-face overnight. It declared that the war against Nazi Germany was unnecessary, reasserted its support of Russia, the fatherland of revolutionary Socialism, and called for a world revolution of workers to take the place of the "imperialist" war against the Axis. The government could not accept this reversal of policy, outlawed the Communist Party, and imprisoned many of its leaders. Stunned by the Soviet pact with Hitler, many Communists dropped out of the party, and its membership fell off sharply. The shock of 1939 lasted only until the Nazis attacked the Soviet Union in 1941. For the French Communists, the war then became a holy war against fascism. They joined the underground to harass the occupying Germans, organized guerrillas in many areas, collaborated with all anti-Nazi groups, and generally were the most effective leaders of the wartime Resistance movement. During the Occupation, their membership grew, and their efforts earned them the respect and the support of the people. Capitalizing on their strength, the Communists captured control of the trade unions from the Socialists. By 1945 they emerged as the strongest party of postwar France. They supported General de Gaulle and cooperated with him from 1944 to 1945.

As soon as the cold war opened a rift between the Soviet Union and the United States, the Communists took the Soviet side. They refused to collaborate with any French government, led the workers into long and crippling strikes against American aid, the Marshall Plan, and NATO, and intensified their attacks in Parliament against every Cabinet, thus contributing, for reasons we will soon explain, to Cabinet instability and the weakness of the French state.

Organization

The organization of the French Communist Party resembles that of the Communist Party of the Soviet Union. It is like a pyramid, in which the base represents the rank-and-file members and the apex the leaders. The image of a pyramid also conveys the principle on which the party is founded: "democratic centralism." By democratic centralism, the Communists mean that the superior organs of the party make the decisions, after discussions among all the members, but that once a course of action is set by the majority, it is binding upon the minority. There can be no dissension within the Communist Party, even in France. Open opposition usually brings swift reprisals, and frequently expulsion from the party.

The lowest echelon of the Communist Party is the *cell*, which consists of 15–20 party

members, including a secretary, and is the most significant innovation of the Communists in the development of their party because it seeks membership at the place of work. There are three types of cells: *factory cells,* composed of members working in the same plant, *rural cells,* composed of farmers from the same farm or village, and *local cells,* composed of people living in the same neighborhood. In 1958, 21 per cent of the cells were factory cells, 32 per cent were rural cells, and the remaining 47 per cent local cells, indicating that the party was not doing as well as it desired in the factories and on the farms.

Above the cells are the *sections,* consisting of the elected delegates of the cells. They, too, have a secretariat or a governing committee—a *bureau.* Like the cells, they are primarily agencies of information, propaganda, and action. The *federation* is composed of delegates chosen by the sections. There is one federation for each French Department, totaling ninety in all. They are ultimately responsible for the party's activities and electioneering tactics at the departmental level. Their bureaus and secretariats are in the hands of loyal party members who are often on their way to higher positions. The cells, sections, and federations are the local or functional organs of the party and all are under the control of the national organs: the National Congress, the Central Committee, the Politbureau, and the Secretary General.

The *National Congress* is composed of delegates from the membership at large. It meets once every two years—a rule that has not always been respected—and passes on all resolutions and policy reports submitted by the party leaders. Although, in theory, debates are free and open, the members rarely question the proposals that come from above. The slate of candidates submitted by the leaders is always re-elected. The Congress elects the *Central Committee,* a body composed of 40–70 members, with mostly deliberative functions, which in turn elects a small group of ten members to the *Politbureau,* which selects the *Secretary General.* The Politbureau and the Secretary General are the true powers of the party. They decide what the party will do in

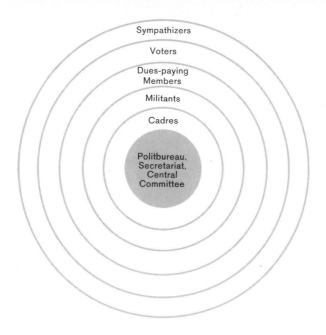

FIGURE 4-1   THE WEB OF THE FRENCH COMMUNIST PARTY.

Parliament, among the workers, in the trade unions, during elections, and on whatever other issues that come up. Over the last twenty years, this well-knit body has been under the virtual domination of the same two or three men, who have thus far been able to avert or repress serious internal strifes and dissensions.

Strength

While the organization of the French Communist Party can be viewed as a pyramid in which control and membership flow from top to bottom, the "strength" of the party is better studied in terms of a series of concentric circles (Fig. 4-1). The very center is the leadership, while the wider circles represent diminishing degrees of support. The first two circles are the cadres and militants, a hard core of organizers and believers; the outer circles are, respectively, members, voters, and sympathizers.

MEMBERS AND MILITANTS. In the last twenty years, the membership of the party has fluctuated considerably. From the early thirties, when there were not more than 50,000

members, the membership rose in the years of the Popular Front (1936–38) to over 300,000. After the decline following the Nazi-Soviet Pact, the party enjoyed a phenomenal growth during the Nazi Occupation. In 1946–47, membership exceeded one million, the highest point it has ever reached. Since then, it has been sinking. In 1960, the figure given officially by the party was 407,000, but there is good reason to believe that it was less than that. Forty per cent of the members are workers, 30 per cent farmers, 15 per cent salaried employees, 10 per cent civil servants, and 5 per cent belong to other groups. The distinction between members and militants is largely based on the degree of commitment to the party. Members simply pay their dues and perhaps participate in party meetings, while militants actively work for the party and often aspire to rise through the party hierarchy. Of the present membership of some 400,000, not more than 25 per cent are militants. The

Political Parties under the Fourth Republic

militants who have jobs as administrators, secretaries, members of the bureaus, editors of Communist newspapers, and leaders of trade unions are called *cadres*. Forming a small core of about 15,000 men and women at the most, they are the nervous system of the party.

VOTERS. Far more Frenchmen vote Communist than carry party membership cards. Since the Liberation, with the exception of 1958, one out of four French voters has cast his ballot for the Communists. But less than one out of ten is a party member. These Frenchmen vote Communist for a number of reasons: they dislike the government; they dislike the Republic; they think the Communist Party will defend their economic interests; or they are dissatisfied with certain policies of the government. A majority of the Communist Party "voters" do not believe in revolution or in the program of the Communist Party. Their vote is more in the form of a protest vote, and the party leadership has to woo them back into the fold when, as often happens, they vote for non-Communist candidates and causes.

The last circle consists of *sympathizers*. Mostly intellectuals, students, artisans, and farmers, some veterans and housewives, they frequently belong to organizations that are dedicated to certain ideals and actions that coincide with those of the Communist Party, and thus they can often be exploited effectively by the Communists.

SOCIAL COMPOSITION AND CHARACTERISTICS. Although the Communist Party continues to be essentially a working-class party, many middle-class members and intellectuals have gained positions of power as cadres. Of all Communist voters, perhaps around 45 per cent are industrial workers, some 9 per cent are agricultural workers, another 9 per cent are salaried employees, 5 per cent are civil servants, 5 per cent are farmers, and the rest are

members of the middle class and the professions, intellectuals, teachers, artisans, merchants, etc. Only a little over one-third of all French workers vote for the Communist Party. More than half of its electoral support comes from non-working-class groups. Communist strength in the rural sections of the country should particularly be noted. In two Departments that are predominantly agrarian, Corrèze and Dordogne, the Communists received over 35 and 38 per cent of the votes in 1956. They received over 30 per cent in another agrarian Department—Creuse. More than two million Communist votes come from the rural Departments.

In age distribution, more than 40 per cent of the Communist voters are below thirty-five, indicating that the party remains active and strong among the young. Although the party does not fare particularly well among women voters, it has made a consistent effort to win them over. More than in any other party, women are used to disseminate party propaganda and are given positions of responsibility. While trying to keep a firm grip on its working-class support and to maintain its appeal for the younger voters, the French Communist Party has made a serious bid to attract other groups of the population: the farmers, civil servants, white-collar workers, artisans, and small shopkeepers.

Ideology

The ideology that binds the party to the mass of its supporters is difficult to define. The party faithfully accepts Marxism-Leninism and thus believes in the inherent evils of capitalism and in the inevitability of its overthrow or demise. It is dedicated to ushering in a new socialist world founded on equality and social justice in which the economy will be harnessed to collective goals. It borrows from the vocabulary of the French Revolution in emphasizing equality and individualism and in echoing the old anticlericalism of the nineteenth century. It also portrays itself as the champion of the ordinary person—small farmers, artisans, widows, and veterans—against the inequities of the social order. While wholeheartedly endorsing the republican form of government, it has invariably criticized the parliamentary institutions. By exploiting many of the historical myths of the French Revolution—anticlericalism, republicanism, and equality—it has given the revolutionary tradition of the nineteenth century a new Marxist twist.

Perhaps we can best explain the strength of the party if we dissociate the two roles it plays. For some, it is still a revolutionary party dedicated to the cause of Communism. These avid supporters have never found themselves at home with democratic institutions and principles. For them, the working class is the midwife of the revolution that will bring about utopia, and the party is something like a Church that demands unqualified loyalty and support. We must quickly point out, however, that the number of such Communists in France today is small, being limited to the cadres and the militants. They have their own schools, their own vacation resorts, their own holidays, their own social life, their own newspapers. They live in a political world that is separated from the rest of the community. But their number does not exceed 100,000.

The second role of the party is to provide an outlet for the expression of protest on the part of French voters. The party's program has become broad enough to encompass many different and, seemingly, some inconsistent views. It is both a revolutionary and a reformist party in the eyes of the voters. It advocates economic modernization but also supports many of the marginal groups that impede it; it is for the socialization of basic industries but favors the retention of individual private property. It is the party of the "Revolution" in terms that satisfy both the past (the Revolution of 1789) and the future (the Communist Revolution). It encourages the national goal of emphasizing the greatness and the civilizing mission of France, and, at the same time, it advances the international ideology of Communism. It is proletarian but also the stanchest supporter of the small farmer in the South; it is against the curé but usually stands ready to cooperate with Liberal Catholics. With an uncanny perception of the basic historical predispositions of the French voter, it has used effective themes and slogans to direct those inclinations to the interests of the party. This accounts for both the wide support it receives among so many socioeconomic groups (a fact that continues to baffle all observers) and for the remarkable strength it commands in regions that appear to be so different—in both industrialized and rural France.

But by trying to appeal to such a broad spectrum of the electorate, who have many and often contradictory interests, the party is slowly becoming a captive of the diverse forces whose support it has cultivated. It has compromised on so many issues that it can now hardly move in any direction without serious electoral, and perhaps organizational and ideological, dislocations. The party is becoming progressively embedded in the social and ideological structure of France and, as a result, is beginning to reflect within itself the very contradictions of the French society. The past is beginning to weigh more heavily than the future, to which the party is in theory dedicated.

The Socialist Party (SFIO)

History

The French Socialist Party was founded before the turn of the century, but did not succeed in unifying its internal factions until 1905, just in time to ride the mounting wave of socialism that swept Europe in the early part of the twentieth century. It and the German Social Democratic Party were the two most powerful national parties associated with the Workers' Second International, which was organized in 1889 and was committed to socialism. Technically, the name of the party remains SFIO (*Section Française de l'Internationale Ouvrière*), and it is officially dedicated to the Marxist principle of the revolutionary overthrow of capitalism by the working class.

While continuing, in its early days, to pay lip service to Marxist slogans, the party became more and more inclined to accept parliamentary democracy as a means of implementing its program. In 1914, the party received a million votes and had one hundred members in Parliament, but its support of France's war effort in World War I alienated many of its more radical followers, who later seceded from the party and joined the Communists. The Socialists lost the majority of their members, although they managed to retain their hold over the trade unions.

Three conflicting views prevalent in the French labor movement have vied with each other for the allegiance of French Socialists. The first is syndicalism, which advocates strong unions and strikes rather than political action as the best way to achieve social justice. The second is Marxism, which encourages political action but only as a subsidiary tool in the revolutionary struggle of the workers against the capitalistic class. The third is the "reformism" inspired by French and German intellectual socialists. It endorses political action in parliament and elsewhere as a legitimate means in the struggle to nationalize the means of production and establish a welfare state.

Right after World War I, the Socialist leader, Léon Blum, followed the reformist tradition and, after overcoming a number of internal quarrels and splits, attempted to adapt socialism to the multi-party system that characterized French democracy. Since it was impossible, reasoned Blum, for the Socialist Party to secure a majority, it should cooperate with other parties to form a government. In the elections of 1936, after the Communists finally agreed to join a Popular Front, the Communists, Socialists, and Radicals won a majority in Parliament. The Socialists re-

ceived 19 per cent of the electoral vote (approximately two million votes), captured 149 seats in the legislature, and proceeded to form a coalition Cabinet. But the victory was short-lived. Attacked from the left by the Communists and abandoned on the right by the Radicals, the Socialist Prime Minister resigned.

The onset of World War II found the Socialists divided and demoralized. Some 80 of their deputies voted to invest Marshal Pétain with absolute powers in 1940, and during the Occupation they were unable to match the leadership provided by the Communists, who succeeded in wresting control of the Socialists' last bastion of strength, the General Confederation of Labor.

Immediately after the Liberation, the Socialists cooperated with the Communists and the MRP. The Communists, however, soon moved into the opposition, and the Socialists then became the pivot of a centrist coalition called the "Third Force." But constant participation in the government created such serious internal dissension in the party that in 1951 the Socialists decided to abandon the "exercise of power," at least temporarily, and take what they called the "cure of opposition," by refusing to participate in any government. The attraction of power and the need to support the Center democratic forces, however, forced the Socialists, in 1954, into an alliance with other Center parties. In the elections of 1956, they improved their electoral strength slightly, and a coalition cabinet under a Socialist Prime Minister governed from January, 1956, until June, 1957, only to give place to more conservative parties and ultimately to the return of General de Gaulle to power.

Organization

Two principles characterize the organization of the Socialist Party. Like the Communist Party, it purports to be a *mass party,* and it also emphasizes internal discipline, both for members of the party and its parliamentarians. This discipline, however, is tempered by a democratic system within the party that tolerates "tendencies." This makes it often impossible for the leaders to enforce party discipline. As a result, the Socialist Party is frequently prey to sharp divisions and dissensions.

The basic unit of the party is the *section,* a group of party members from a given city, town, or village. In each Department there is a *federation,* composed of sections, with a secretary who is its spokesman and executive. The federations control the departmental finances and make decisions about political action not only in local matters but often in national elections. They enjoy considerable autonomy. It is not unusual, for instance, for one federation to make an electoral agreement with a party at the departmental level and for another federation to attack bitterly the same party in a different Department. This is particularly the case whenever electoral alliances with the Communists or the MRP are involved.

The supreme organ of the party is the *National Congress,* composed of delegates chosen by the party federations. It meets regularly once a year and more frequently in extraordinary congresses. Delegates are selected by proportional representation, so that the various "tendencies" within the party are represented. Each delegate has a "mandate-vote" representing from ten to fifty members.

Every three months there is a meeting of the *National Council* of the Socialist Party, a miniature congress that consists of the secretaries of the departmental federations. It makes decisions between congresses on policy and parliamentary tactics and takes disciplinary measures. The Congress elects a *Directing Committee* of forty-five members (though the number has varied), which must include a maximum of twenty parliamentarians and twenty-five members drawn from the cadres or leaders who are not members of Parliament. Generally, a 2:1 ratio in favor of non-parliamentarians is considered a safe margin for party control of the action of its parliamentarians. The Directing Committee elects a *Bureau* composed of ten members: the General Secretary, the Assistant General Secretary, the Treasurer, and seven others. A body comparable to the National Executive of the British Labour Party, it makes all the interim decisions on policy, propaganda, parliamentary tactics, discipline, and sanctions.

Strength

As with the Communist Party, the "strength" of the Socialists must be studied with reference to voters and members.

VOTERS. The Socialist Party has experienced a marked decline since the Liberation. In 1945, it received 23 per cent of the total vote; in 1946, 21 per cent; in the second election of 1946 (November), 18 per cent; in 1951, 14.5 per cent; and in 1956 and 1958, the vote seems to have stabilized around 15 per cent.

Many of the strongholds of the Socialists have been lost to the Communists. This is notably the case among the urban centers and the highly industrialized Departments in the north, with the exception of the coal-mining areas. The character of Socialist support has undergone a considerable transformation. The working-class vote has diminished, but there has been a gain among the salaried group: white-collar workers, members of the lower middle class, civil servants, school teachers, and pensioners. It has been estimated that among the Socialist voters 33 per cent are civil servants (particularly school teachers), a little over 15 per cent are workers, 11 per cent are salaried, and the rest come from lower middle-class groups: artisans, merchants, pensioners, shopkeepers, and others. The Socialist Party is also becoming a party of older people. Two-thirds of its voters are 35 years of age or over. The average age of its parliamentarians has been the highest in the National Assembly.

MEMBERSHIP. The membership of the party has decreased sharply since World War II. In 1946, it boasted 354,000 members. In 1952, the figure was down to 90,000, and it may well be smaller today. What is more, the recruitment of new members has virtually come to a standstill; the party is thought to lose members every year. The aging of the party's voters is duplicated in the aging of its members. More than 70 per cent are above the age of forty. Seniority rules give preference for party administrative positions to those with long service and discourage the young from joining. As for the social composition of the membership, 25 per cent are civil servants, about 25 per cent are workers, 25 per cent are artisans, white-collar workers, small-town lawyers, teachers, and pensioners, and the rest come from diverse groups.

As in the Communist Party, a special group, the *cadres,* hold administrative positions in the various echelons of the party. The majority are over forty years old, and they consist mainly of salaried groups, professional men, and civil servants. Militancy is at a low ebb, and the propaganda organs of the party, including many of its newspapers, have virtually disappeared.

Program

The Socialist program is hard to define. The party continues to use Marxist vocabulary and slogans; it accepts the "class struggle" and favors the socialization of the means of production; yet both its internal composition and its policy pronouncements in the last twenty years reveal it to be a moderately progressive party, dedicated to social legislation and welfare measures. It has been opposed, but with considerable qualifications, to colonial wars. Its progressive attitude, however, has been tempered by its readiness to modify its program whenever it has participated in a coalition cabinet.

The most significant ideological positions of the party do not derive from Marxism but from French political history. One of the strongest of the party's traditions is its anticlericalism, and the Socialists remain unalterably opposed to state subsidies to Catholic schools. The party generally supports parliamentary supremacy and is hostile to personal government, yet it supported General de Gaulle's return to power! It steadfastly refuses to cooperate with the Communist Party. Memories of past conflicts with the "brother party" to the left, in which the Communists invariably secured advantages, makes reconciliation difficult. All overtures of the Communists to revive the Popular Front have been turned down until 1962.

In the last few years, the Socialist Party has increasingly reflected the nationalism that has been so much in evidence in France and that accounted to a great degree to the overthrow of the Fourth Republic. The party has become more and more opportunistic in trying to stave off electoral defeat by aligning itself with the prevailing nationalist current of opinion.

The root of the SFIO's postwar decline has been its inability either to adopt an effective pragmatic approach to problems or to retain a coherent ideology of socialism. In form, it has remained a "class party," a section of the Second International dedicated, according to its charter, to "the conquest of the means of production and exchange," in order to "transform the capitalist society into a collectivist or communist one." Its saints are still Marx and Engels and some of the canonized martyrs of French Socialism—Jaurès, Guesde, and Blum. Its ritual dates back to the militant years of European socialism, everybody is still a "comrade," and at the conclusion of all party meetings the "Internationale" is sung and the clenched fist is raised. But the substance has been at great variance with the form. The Socialist Party in actuality has been a parliamentary bloc of political leaders and notables, who play the parliamentary game with consummate skill and infinite patience, are involved in everlasting compromises and "deals," and cater to all groups in their efforts to win votes. The results have been devastating. The party has progressively lost those for whom socialism is a living ideal, but it has failed to attract new groups who believe that utilizing the machinery of the state to solve concrete problems is more important than ideology.

The difficulties of the SFIO have been heightened by the postwar maneuvering of the other French political parties. The Socialists have been challenged from both the Left and the Right. The Communists to the Left adopted everything the Second International stood for and more: they led the forces of anticlericalism and republicanism, became champions of reform, and gathered wide support on the basis of their record during the Resistance. To the Right, the progressive Catholic movement, spearheaded by the Popular Republicans (MRP), provided, at least immediately after the Liberation, a judicious balance between social and economic reform and Catholicism, while actively working for "limited internationalism," toward cooperating if not actually integrating with Western Europe. Caught between the two, the SFIO was forced to become eclectic, even opportunistic. Moreover, parliamentary considerations made Socialist participation in the governments of the Fourth Republic imperative. The party became the bastion of the centrist Third Force and later the pivot of the Cabinets that led the Fourth Republic to its demise. Confronted with the uprising of May 13, 1958, in Algeria, the Socialist leaders chose the only possible alternative—the return of General de Gaulle. They supported the rising wave of nationalism, hoping to capitalize on it. A small but growing minority refused to follow them and for the first time since the Congress of Tours, the party experienced, in 1958, a serious split when the Unified Socialist Party was organized to its left.

The Radical Socialists and "Allied" Center Formations

The Radical Socialist Party (the exact name is Republican Radical and Radical Socialist Party—*Parti Républicain Radical et Radical Socialiste*) symbolizes best the history and the predicament of the Center groups. It is a party without a program, without an organization, without leadership, and without any membership to speak of. Yet this "party," under different labels and thanks to many

shifting alliances, played a controlling role in the formation and life of virtually all the governments under the Third and Fourth Republics. It participated in Right-wing electoral alliances only to abandon them and move to the Left, but more frequently it managed to do exactly the reverse. Its internal instability both reflected and caused the instability of the Cabinet and the divisions of the Republic. It has had its own Left, closely anchored to the Socialists and even to the Communists, its own Center, and its own Right, which has often been affiliated with extreme Right-wing groups—Poujadists, Gaullists, and others.

History

As a distinct political formation, the Radical Socialists date from 1901, the year the party was officially founded. But its heritage goes far back, perhaps to the years of the French Revolution. Its roots have grown out of the traditions of anticlericalism, individualism, economic liberalism, and republicanism. In 1869, the so-called Program of Belleville was drafted by a number of Radical leaders and became the political charter of every self-respecting Radical. It advocated public education, separation between Church and state, democratization of the military service, and modification of the tax structure in favor of a progressive income tax, a program that had great appeal to the middle class, farmers, artisans, storekeepers, teachers, and above all to the professional men of the small towns—lawyers, public notaries, doctors, engineers. It expressed the interests of groups that were still striving to dislodge the Church, the Army, and the remnants of the aristocracy from political power.

To win elections, the Radicals soon found that they needed some sort of organization, and Radical committees were established in most Departments. Since they were allowed considerable autonomy, diversity among the local formations developed. Until 1910 and perhaps through World War I, the party was no more than a powerful electoral organization. In 1906, it gained an unprecedented—for any political party before or since—victory. Two hundred and sixty Radical deputies were returned to Parliament. But with the end of World War I, the party became increasingly divided when confronted with the economic and social problems that the Industrial Revolution was belatedly thrusting upon the country. The agitation of the workers and the gains of the Socialists and the Communists began to attract some of its members and to force many of its remaining candidates and voters toward a more conservative point of view. The hearts of the Radicals, it has been said, remain always with the Left but their pocketbooks tightly sewn to the Right. With most of the demands of the Belleville program realized by the end of World War I, their ideology and electoral program was becoming exhausted.

In 1940, almost all the Radicals turned their backs on the Republic and voted to delegate full powers to Marshal Pétain. As a result, the Liberation found them seriously weakened. In 1945, they managed to have 25 deputies in the Constituent Assembly. In 1946, their strength rose to 50 seats in the National Assembly—70 if one were to count allied groups. In the elections of 1951 and 1956, they held to an average of about 70 deputies, a far cry from their former strength but a remarkable political comeback nonetheless.

In a divided legislature, however, strength does not lie in numbers only. After 1951, the Radicals became a pivotal party. One of their members became Speaker (President) of the National Assembly and another President of the Senate, and the party participated in all the Cabinets. Radicals assumed the office of the Prime Minister more often than did the leaders of any other political party.

But today the party is badly divided, and it may never again play the same important political role./

Organization

In contrast to the Communists and the Socialists, the Radicals have no mass organization. It is a party of "notables"—of influential men and political bosses. They have formed local committees, departmental federations, a congress, and a number of national executive organs, but the heart of their organization continues to be the local and departmental committees that operate under the leadership of influential political leaders, intellectuals, and newspaper editors. Many have been mayors of large cities like Lyon, Bordeaux, Marseille, and Toulouse. Party leadership, as a result, is highly personal and decentralized.

The members of the party are technically the men and women who are affiliated with a local committee and pay dues. But the directors of Radical newspapers, ex-parliamentarians, and the secretaries and often ex-secretaries of departmental federations are ex officio members. Since the departmental federation is solely responsible for keeping the membership rolls (on the basis of which voting strength in the national meetings is estimated), nobody has ever been able to tell exactly what the membership of the party is.

The major national organ of the party is its *Annual Congress,* to which one delegate for every hundred members is sent. Every departmental federation has an interest in padding its membership figures, and verifying the credentials of the delegates is often a hot issue on the opening day of many congresses. In addition to the delegates that represent real or putative members, all parliamentarians and ex-parliamentarians, committeemen, and newspaper owners claim the right to attend and vote. The annual Congress hears and debates motions, passes resolutions, and elects the top body of the party, the *Executive Commission* or *Bureau,* composed of some sixty-five members, of whom forty are, as a rule, non-parliamentarians. This is in theory the top decision-making body.

Strength

The strength of the Radical Socialist Party has been primarily electoral—that is, it should be gaged in terms of the votes it receives and the number of its representatives that are elected. According to even the most optimistic accounts, its membership has never exceeded 200,000. Today it is doubtful if there are more than 25,000 members.

Since the Liberation, the party's voting strength has ranged from two million to about two and a half million. Where do these votes come from? The party has strong support from some specific regions. The town of Lyon, the Department of Vaucluse, and the Southwest part of France have sent a great number of Radical deputies to Parliament. The party's main strength lies in the small towns and rural sections. The "urban radicalism" of the nineteenth century is being replaced by a "rural radicalism," largely supported by small-town doctors and lawyers, artisans, and some teachers and civil servants. In the larger urban centers, the Radicals can count on some middle-class vote from merchants and small industrialists, but very few workers vote for the party. The supporters of the party come, therefore, mostly from the groups and classes that were in the ascendancy in the nineteenth century but that have definitely declined since 1918. They believe in a liberal individualistic order and have not quite reconciled themselves to industrialization.

It is no wonder, then, that the party has gone through a period of severe conflicts in the last ten years that may end in its permanent disintegration. A minority of its members, led by the young and dynamic Pierre Mendès-France, argued in the 1950's for a renovated radicalism, for a strong and disciplined party dedicated to economic expansion and welfare, with a program that would appeal to many groups: white-collar workers, engineers, civil servants, intellectuals, and workers. Others, however, contended that the strength of the party lay in its "pluralism" (another name for its internal divisions). According to them, the party was not a mass party with a program and discipline but a government party that thrived on electoral alliances, deals, and coalitions which gave it a power disproportionate to its actual numerical strength.

The issue was squarely joined in the years after 1955 and has never been resolved. The proponents of a disciplined mass party favoring welfare measures and economic and social renovation, led by Mendès-France, won a Pyrrhic victory when two opposition groups were either expelled or seceded from the party. From some 64 deputies in the National Assembly, their number shrank to about 34. But even within this group, it was impossible to enforce discipline in the voting on crucial issues like Algeria. A third internal split occurred when 20 or so members claimed to be the true heirs of the "orthodox" radicals and refused to accept the leadership of Mendès-France, who was forced to resign as leader of the party. These dissidents participated in the last three Cabinets of the Fourth Republic and had the dubious privilege of heading two of them.

Program

The Radical Socialist Party has no coherent program. The Belleville manifesto has long since passed into history. On the crucial issues that have confronted and confront the nation—how to accelerate industrialization and economic expansion, how to formulate a responsible colonial policy of retrenchment and gradual emancipation, how to end the Algerian war, and how to construct a foreign policy within or without the various European organizations and Atlantic alliances—the Radicals remained in hopeless disagreement. Many are nostalgic for the past greatness of France and have argued in favor of the Empire and the war in Algeria. Some remain stanch economic individualists; others agree with the Socialists on the need for reform. Some advocate European integration; for others, the Common Market and NATO trespass on the sacred sovereignty of France. Some favor sub-

Political Parties under the Fourth Republic

sidies to Catholic schools, while others believe strongly in a lay Republic. The party has reflected all the divisions and quarrels of the society at large, and there is no prospect of unity.

The MRP
(Popular Republican Movement)

To understand the character and program of the MRP (Mouvement Républicain Populaire), we must remember that Catholicism does not coincide with any single political philosophy in France. There is both a conservative and a liberal Catholic tradition. The first favors a paternalistic, authoritarian government and a hierarchically organized social order. It often stands in defense of the *status quo* and property rights and is sympathetic to privileged social groups. The liberal Catholic movement, on the other hand, is inspired by a genuine concern for human rights, equality, and the welfare state. It does not shrink from advocating economic planning and even the nationalization of key industries. It urges its members to political action in order to bring about a more just and equitable society.

History

The MRP is the heir of the liberal tradition of Catholicism. Although that tradition goes back to the nineteenth century, the party was not founded until 1944. It was able to draw on a venerable and rich past populated with eminent Catholic figures who believed in working within the Republic to effect social and political reforms. These liberal Catholics are thus strongly attached to the republican form of government.

Prior to World War II, there was a strong tradition of social action on the part of Catholics, and a number of small Catholic political formations had existed. As we have seen, a Catholic syndicalist movement and a number

of liberal groups, such as Catholic Youth Action, had long been active politically. In the thirties, the Popular Democratic Party, a Catholic group, advocated social legislation and was firmly attached to the League of Nations.

These groups were just waiting for an opportunity to unite into a larger political formation, and the impetus was provided by the German Occupation and the Resistance. Since the old moderate and conservative political parties appeared to have been irremediably weakened by the fall of France, many of the intellectual leaders among the progressive Catholics wanted to demonstrate the attachment of Catholics to the Republic and to the nation and so decided to establish a Movement in 1943 and a party in 1944. Thus a long-standing dream of one of the oldest spiritual families in France seemed to be moving resolutely toward political realization.

Two additional factors contributed to their success. The first was the immense popularity of General de Gaulle, who was a devout Catholic with a paternalistic view of government and who, as the leader of the Free French Forces, incarnated national unity. The MRP became associated in the minds of the public with de Gaulle and thus benefited from his great prestige. The second reason was the resurgence of Marxism and the Communist Party. Much of the middle class and many of the conservatives were frightened enough to throw their support to the MRP. The youngest party in France became, in one national election, also the strongest party. In 1945, the MRP polled 23.9 per cent of the popular vote, and in June, 1946, it polled 28.2 per cent, thus for once dislodging the Communists from the number one position.

Since the war, however, the MRP has run into stiffened opposition. When de Gaulle criticized the new Constitution of the Fourth Republic and when he formed his own political party in 1947, the RPF (Rally of the French People), the MRP had to dissociate itself completely from the General. In fact, it joined forces with the Socialists and the Center formations when it appeared that de

Gaulle's movement was gaining momentum. But the MRP soon clashed with the Socialists over the issue of state subsidies to Catholic schools. It continued to urge European unity while many Center groups dragged their feet, and it stoutly favored continuing the war in Indochina, which for many Socialists and the Communists was a "dirty war." Having lost many conservative voters to de Gaulle and having alienated many liberal voters with its pro-war and Catholic school subsidy stand, the electoral strength of the MRP dropped sharply.

Organization

As a party, the MRP attempts to reconcile the principle of internal democracy and respect for minorities with political discipline and unity. It gives considerable weight to the parliamentarians of the party. Like the Socialist Party, it has *sections* and *departmental federations*. Ten members constitute a section and five sections with a minimum of one hundred members a departmental federation. At the national level, the annual *National Congress* debates and votes resolutions and elects the executive organs—the *National Committee* and the *Executive Commission*. All members are represented by delegates at the National Congress, and the various federations are allowed one "mandate-vote" for every fifty members for the first two hundred members, an additional "mandate-vote" for every hundred members up to a membership of five hundred members, and one "mandate-vote" for every additional two hundred members. Thus it is more difficult for the larger federations to control and dominate the Congress than it is in the Socialist Party. The Congress elects, by majority vote, the President of the party, who is re-eligible only twice —a rule designed to avoid personal control of the party and its organization.

The National Committee, which is responsible for important interim decisions, is composed of some two hundred people. One-third are selected by the MRP parliamentarians, and the rest are chosen by the party members. The majority is in the hands of the parliamen-tarians who control nominations. The 54 members of the Executive Commission are elected by the National Committee. The Commission charts the general policy of the party, subject to the ratification of the National Committee and ultimately by the National Congress. In the party are a number of "specialized teams": the various Catholic Action groups, associations of the families of children that go to parochial schools, delegates to several international organizations, and special technical and educational bodies.

The most serious problem in the organization of the MRP is the gap that exists between the party's leaders and its members. The leaders are mostly parliamentarians, who are naturally preoccupied with parliamentary tactics and electoral strategy. The members, on the other hand, are in closer touch with the voters and the social groups whose support the party solicits. They tend to be more liberal, especially in matters of social legislation and foreign policy, while the leaders are usually cautious and often conservative. Fearing the ascendancy of the liberal militant members, the leaders strive to copy the Radicals and keep the party in the hands of the "notables" and influential politicians. Most of the militants want to appeal more to the masses, particularly the workers, and implement the old dream of progressive Catholicism—Christian Socialism.

Strength

The strength of the MRP in terms of members and voters is difficult to determine. Of all the political parties in the post-Liberation period, it has experienced the most drastic ups and downs. In 1946, the party was extremely strong in the East and the West—the two predominantly Catholic regions of the country. In addition, it received the bulk of the votes that would have normally gone to the conservatives or moderate groups. By capturing a number of urban centers that had traditionally gone to the Left, the party managed to work part of both sides of the street, as well as the middle.

In 1951, many of the MRP supporters turned to de Gaulle and his party—the RPF— or to the revived moderate and conservative parties, or to more compatible Left-wing parties. It has kept its strength in the East and the West, and some observers fear it is becoming a "regional party," for in the elections of 1956, despite the collapse of the Gaullist movement, the party failed to attract either the conservative or leftist votes that it had received in 1946. Its voting strength seemed stabilized to about two and a quarter million or around 12 per cent of the voters.

VOTERS. Among the electorate, the party continues to be popular with the salaried groups, and it seems to have maintained relatively strong support among the working class —19 per cent of its voters are workers—and among the farmers in the sections where religious practice is widespread. In the cities, it appeals to some of the professional men and well-to-do groups of the middle class, especially among devout Catholics. It is also quite successful among women. Sixty out of every hundred of its voters belong to the weaker sex, more than half of whom are over forty years old. These are generally women who are more tradition-bound and more religious than the men in the same age bracket.

MEMBERSHIP. From over 200,000 in 1946, MRP membership has dropped to not more than 60,000, although the most active members—the militants—are young. In fact, of the total membership, it has the youngest average age of any party in France, which accentuates the conflict between the members and the older leaders. Being primarily young men and women who belong to the specialized teams and to the various Catholic Action groups, the members have intensified their efforts to

liberalize the political contents of the Church doctrine. In the factory and on the farm, they represent perhaps the most dynamic leadership in France today, and it will not be surprising if the MRP soon experiences a revival. Since at least 20 per cent of its members are workers, the party hopes to neutralize the impact of the Communists by stepping up its program among the working class. At the same time, many of its Youth Action groups have strengthened their influence among the farmers.

Independents and Moderates

The terms "Independents," "Peasants," and "Moderates" do not technically apply to a political party. They refer rather to a number of political formations that have, under both the Third and the Fourth Republics, corresponded to what might be called the "conservative" forces in France. These formations have been led by influential local leaders and have been regularly supported by powerful economic interests. They constitute the bulk of the French "Right."

History

The French Right may be divided into at least two categories: (1) the first consists of groups that have never accepted the Republic. An increasingly small number prefer a return to Monarchy; others aspire to a strong one-man government similar to that of the two Napoleons, thus embodying what we have earlier called the Bonapartist tradition; while still a third small but active group favors an authoritarian one-party system. (2) The second consists of groups that accept the Republic and its institutions, but that wish to move it far to the Right of its present position. One such party, the Republican Alliance or Republican Federation participated in coalition governments before World War II, but their support of Marshal Pétain discredited them after the Liberation.

The Independents have prospered since the war. After the Communists went into opposition in 1947, and the Gaullist surge in 1951 gave the General's party 117 deputies in the

National Assembly, many Right-wing groups played an increasingly important role in supporting a centrist coalition government to defend the Republic against the extremes of Left and Right. In 1952–53, they succeeded in splitting the Gaullist formation in Parliament and attracted some 30 of the Gaullist deputies to their own ranks. In 1956, the Independents emerged as the second strongest political formation in the National Assembly.

Organization

Being a group rather than a party, the Independents do not depend on cohesiveness or discipline for acquiring or keeping members, but instead rely on their national committees and known personalities and notables. In fact, they do not seek mass membership. In 1948, however, the first step toward establishing some kind of organization was made with the founding of the National Center of Independents, a committee composed of top political leaders. In 1951, the Independents were joined by the Peasants—some twenty-five deputies—and later by a number of Gaullists.

The *National Center* makes all important decisions. It appoints the leaders of the local committees, finances various candidates, endorses names of candidates, and strives to provide some unity and leadership. Its most important organ is the *Executive Committee,* composed of some thirty members. In 1954, a congress consisting of the most prominent local and departmental leaders met and passed a resolution calling for the imposition of voting discipline on the Independents in the National Assembly. With the help of the Secretary General of the party, who was very active in promoting the establishment of departmental federations, more than fifty such federations were formed and have lasted down to today. Speaking in 1956, the Secretary General revived the old dream of the French Right: the formation of a conservative party like the one in Britain—a dream often evoked but never realized.

Strength

In assessing the power of the Independents, we must look to their electoral strength and not their membership, of which they have very little. Regionally, they are strong in the East, West, and the Massif Central and have captured some of the Radical votes in the rural Departments and among the lower middle class, which has provided them with a broad electoral base they lacked in the past. Much of their support comes from voters with above-average incomes, and powerful economic groups, notably the industrialists, contribute heavily to the relatively wealthy National Center.

A peculiar mix is this convergence of industrialists and bankers from the upper middle class and small businessmen, artisans, farmers, and shopkeepers from the lower middle class. Had it not been for the emergence of a new party—the Poujadists—in the elections of 1956 and later on the return of General de Gaulle to the political scene in 1958, this combination of lower and upper middle-class voters might have made the Independents the largest party in the country. As it was, they received over 15 per cent of the national vote in the election of January 2, 1956, and returned some 90 deputies.

Program

The program of the Independents, as proclaimed during the elections of January 2, 1956, was as follows: (a) nationalism, (b) anti-parliamentarism, (c) anti-Communism, (d) subsidies to Catholic schools, (e) constitutional reform, (f) maintenance of French rule in Algeria, and (g) opposition to welfare measures. Suited to the wealthy, the program also appealed to those who were disenchanted with the Republic, while it promised to maintain the *status quo* for the lower middle class. Nationalism has provided the cement that has bound the party's supporters together. Extolling French authority in Algeria evoked the support of the more reactionary forces there and in France. The 1956 demand for constitutional reform was aimed at strengthening the executive (which has been largely carried out in the Fifth Republic), but many saw in this the old anti-republicanism of the Right. Finally, the Independents favor the outlawing of the Communists, and they have bid for Catholic support by ardently proposing subsidies for Catholic schools.

The Rally
of the French People (RPF)

Since the French Revolution, strong political leaders—frequently Army generals—have occasionally assumed personal rule. The latest one is General de Gaulle, a career officer who in 1940 refused to accept defeat at the hands of the German Army and led a small core of followers to London to proclaim from there his determination to continue the war in the name of France. Since then, de Gaulle's towering personal stature has overshadowed the course of public events, even when he was in political retirement.

History

In 1944, de Gaulle returned to France at the head of a Provisional Government and a small well-equipped Army. He favored a strong presidential government, the overhaul of the nation's stagnant economy, and broad social welfare measures. Within eighteen months, on January 20, 1946, he resigned, after it became clear that the Communists and Socialists who had a majority in the First Constituent Assembly were preparing a new constitution that established the supremacy of Parliament.

De Gaulle saw in the Constitution of the Fourth Republic the same defects that had been inherent in the Constitution of the Third: a weak executive, a legislature divided into many groups unable to generate policy, Cabinet instability, lack of leadership. To counter these weaknesses, he formed the Rally

of the French People (RPF) and in his Strasbourg speech of April, 1947, outlined his program: a new constitution embodying strong executive leadership; stern measures against the Communists, whom he called "separatists"; the reassertion of French independence from both the Soviet Union and the United States; the dissolution of the National Assembly; new elections.

The movement grew rapidly. By the end of 1947, it reportedly had some 800,000 members, and it won municipal elections of October, 1947, in what amounted to a landslide. More than 40 per cent of the voters in towns of over 9,000 inhabitants went for de Gaulle and the RPF. In the election for the Senate (elected indirectly by the municipal councils), the RPF won 120 seats, almost a third of the total. Sensing political victory, de Gaulle pressed for a dissolution of the legislature and for new elections.

The Gaullist victory helped the Center parties bury their differences. A Third Force composed of Socialists, Radicals, the MRP, and Independents was formed to stave off the Gaullists. It succeeded. It prevented the dissolution of the legislature, and the new elections were not held until the expiration of its term in 1951, when the wave of Gaullism had subsided. The General refused to avail himself of the "alliances" that the electoral law permitted, and his party ran in splendid isolation. All the other parties, except the Communists, improved their position through alliances and barred the RPF, which won 22 per cent of the popular vote (second only to the Communists) and returned 117 deputies, from forming a government.

Between 1951–56, the Parliament was deadlocked between six evenly divided political formations. The RPF began to disintegrate. Its members were asked to oppose all governments and measures. Time after time the RPF and the Communists voted on the same side—together they controlled 220 members out of the total of 617—and thus created "negative majorities" that destroyed governments without providing for any alternatives. RPF deputies became increasingly restive, and in 1952 27 of them voted to endorse a coalition

Cabinet headed by a leader of the Independents, Antoine Pinay. These maverick deputies entered more fully into the parliamentary game and some of them joined the Cabinet. De Gaulle withdrew his leadership; the Gaullist ranks dissolved; and de Gaulle retired formally from the political scene and returned to his village to write his war memoirs. But even in retirement, he remained very much in the thoughts of most Frenchmen—of foes and friends alike.

In the elections of 1956, the poor showing of one of the RPF factions that remained loyal to de Gaulle, the Social Republicans, indicated that there could be no Gaullist party without de Gaulle. The Social Republicans won only 4 per cent of the popular vote and only 21 seats in the National Assembly.

Organization

The RPF was not supposed to be a party. It called itself a "movement." It had no congress but "assizes," no members but "compagnons," no program but "objectives." Yet there were similarities between its organization and those of other political parties. It had communal and departmental sections and federations, national meetings, and national organs, and, in order to combat the Communists, it developed "factory teams" (analogous to the Communist cells) in industrial plants, and "professional organizations" among farmers, intellectuals, teachers, and merchants. In this way, it hoped to penetrate quickly to the people and gain the support of a broad range of social groups.

The most significant trait of the structure of the RPF was its centralization. The various local and departmental units had only consultative powers. Authority was in the hands of a delegate appointed by the central organization, and within the central organization, the *President*, General de Gaulle, and a *Directing Committee*, whose members were appointed by the President, made all decisions. A *National Council*, composed of some 150 members, a majority of whom were appointed by the Directing Committee, debated policy issues. The parliamentary group was only an adjunct to the party and was expected to vote as the Directing Committee prescribed.

The party was definitely authoritarian, which is not surprising, since it was created to do the bidding of one man.

Strength

The electoral strength of the RPF came mainly from the more industrialized northern part of the country. More urban than rural, the RPF received support from the traditional strongholds of both the Right—the West and East—and the Left and extreme Left—notably in the proletarian centers of the North, in the Paris region, and in the Lyon area. The RPF received more working-class votes than did the Socialists—16 per cent versus 15 per cent for the Socialists. It appealed also to women voters and conservative Catholics, thus cutting into the strength of the MRP.

From 800,000 members in 1947, the party dropped to a little over 400,000 in 1949 and to no more than a quarter of a million in 1951. The greater part (some 40 per cent) were workers, including white-collar workers and technicians; 20 per cent came from the middle class; 15 per cent were farmers; and the rest came from various other groups, including a good number from the professions. Although anti-parliamentarian, nationalist, and authoritarian in character, the RPF was not anti-republican. Avowedly anti-Communist, it favored a drastic overhaul of the Constitution to allow stronger executive government. But its philosophy had distinctly personal overtones. Loyalty to de Gaulle was the very essence of the movement, and his return to power was the party's major objective.

The old appeal of Bonapartism arouses sleeping passions in both conservative and leftist voters in France. Bonapartism, as we have seen, is a latent force in French political history and when it erupts in troubled times, many workers reject the advice of their party leaders and give their vote to one man. The upwelling of support from the mass of the people that swept de Gaulle to power in 1958 and that ratified his new Constitution had already been presaged in 1951. The only difference was that in 1958 the times were more troubled and Parliament could not agree on a government and could not maintain its authority over the Army.

The "Poujadists" (UFF)

History

By the time the Gaullist Party had disintegrated, in 1954, a curious political movement emerged among groups that had been traditionally most loyal to the Republic and to parliamentary government—the shopkeepers, artisans, small farmers, and local and provincial political leaders. They became known as Poujadists, after the name of the movement's leader, Pierre Poujade. Beginning as a powerful pressure bloc called the UDCA (Union for the Defense of Merchants and Artisans), whose aim was to lighten the allegedly heavy tax burden on small businessmen, the movement later became a party, the Union and French Fraternity (UFF). It demanded the complete overhaul of political institutions; Parliament was to be closed down, the Estates-General convoked (last convened in 1789 and composed then of the aristocracy, the clergy, and the bourgeoisie—the three social orders that existed in the *Ancien Régime*), leaders of the Fourth Republic tried before a "High Court." By 1955, Poujade was able to organize local and departmental federations in most of the Departments. His slogan was "throw out the rascals" (the "rascals" being the deputies of the National Assembly). In the national elections of January 2, 1956, Poujade nominated candidates in many Departments, refused to ally himself with any other political formations, and called for a massive vote for his movement. He received two and a half million votes, 12.5 per cent of the total, and 52 seats in the National Assembly—some of which were contested and lost to the party.

This phenomenal success was followed by an equally remarkable collapse. No subsequent by-election ever gave Poujade or his candidates more than 7 per cent of the vote. In most cases, they received less. With the return of de Gaulle in 1958, the Poujadist movement literally disappeared.

Organization

The members of the movement came very largely from the groups it was designed to protect—the small merchants and artisans. They provided the funds for the party and even used their trucks to transport members to meetings and demonstrations. Whenever Poujade came to talk in a large city such as Paris, Lyon, or Grenoble, the rally transformed the city into what looked like a makeshift open air market.

Although Poujade himself dominated the movement, it did have a formal organization, consisting of a *National Bureau,* with ten members, a *National Council* composed of delegates and propaganda agents mostly appointed by Poujade, and a *Congress* of delegates chosen by local and departmental organizations. In addition, there were a great number of "front" or "parallel" organizations—the Union for the Defense of the French Workers, the Union for the Defense of Intellectual Professions, the Union of "Producers," the Union of Civil Servants, etc. Most of these bodies existed only on paper, but Poujade used them to give his party the flavor of a genuine national and interprofessional movement. In 1955, many dues-paying members contributed two dollars apiece to the party's coffers, but it is difficult to tell exactly how many there were. Poujade himself claimed the figure was 800,000.

Strength

The Poujadists had a spectacular but short-lived success. Why? Essentially it was because Poujadism was strong in "static" France, mainly in the South, but failed in the economically advanced Departments of the North and East and in the urban areas. Besides the artisans, shopkeepers, and small farmers and those in the backward Departments plagued by a declining per capita income, Poujade's clever evocation of the "little man"—crushed by taxes, by a big Civil Service, by large industrial corporations, and by parliamentarians corrupted by wealth and the pressures of big lobbies—uncovered smoldering frustrations embedded in the history of France: distrust of the state, contempt for the politician (a man who does no honest work), disenchantment with Parliament and the Republic, fierce pride in the individual and his rights. The only thing new in all this was the fact that the very groups that had supported the Republic and the Parliament in the past now followed him. His nationalism and his anti-Jewish and anti-Communist stance captured the emotions of many Frenchmen. Poujadism was the lower middle class revolt against the Republic.

The reasons for the dissatisfaction of this group must be sought in the economic and social developments we discussed earlier. Threatened by industry, by the exodus from the farm to the city, by the drop in agricultural income, by the supermarket, by the highway and the automobile that were dislocating village life, the lower middle class rose in a body to defend their way of life. The word "defense" is crucial in understanding Poujadism, for its members reacted like an individual who wishes to protect himself against change.

There was something pathetic and incongruous in a movement that wanted to pull France backward into a world of small enterprises and of little or no taxes, a world that would somehow still enable her to become a militarily strong nation that could stand by herself if necessary. The revolt of the shopkeepers was romantic in its futility, but it demonstrated that whenever social groups feel threatened, they will react violently and often preach revolution in the process.

The Fourth Republic: 1946-1958

V

The Fourth Republic, established by the referendum of October, 1946, was set aside by the new Constitution of October 5, 1958. It was in many respects so representative of the republican tradition of France that many of its features and institutions are bound to influence political and institutional developments now and in the future. Since the present Constitution—that of the Fifth Republic—is so intimately dependent on the leadership of General de Gaulle, it can probably be viewed as a transitional system. Many commentators are beginning to talk already of a Sixth Republic, and they claim that it will resemble the Fourth! As is so often the case with France, it is the study of the past, in this case the Fourth Republic, that may give the student a good understanding of how the French political system may evolve in the future.

The Electoral System

In an attempt to end the internal divisions of political parties, the Fourth Republic established a system of proportional representation. Each of the 90 administrative Departments became an electoral district and was assigned three, four, or more seats in the National Assembly, depending on the size of the population. A list of candidates was made up for each party, and the number elected from each party was determined by the number of votes cast for the party. Each party, then, would receive a number of seats in the National Assembly roughly proportional to the total number of votes it received in the country as a whole. In defense of the system, it was argued that it was more equitable than a majority system like that used in the United States and Britain and that it would strengthen the control of the national committees of the parties over their candidates, thus increasing party discipline and unity.

In 1951, this system was modified. The parties were allowed to join together to form common lists (known as *apparentments* or alliances) to present a united front in the various electoral districts. If an "alliance" list received over 50 per cent of the ballots in a particular district, it would win *all* the seats, which would then be divided among the allied parties in proportion to the votes cast for each of them. This modification was designed to isolate the Communists on the Left, with whom nobody wanted to make an alliance, and the RPF on the Right, which did not want to make alliances with anybody. The system, therefore, favored the Center groups, the so-called Third Force whose overt purpose, as we have seen, was to stave off threats from both extremes.

This is how the system worked. Assume that the total number of votes cast in one constituency was 220,000 and that the number of seats allotted was 3. Assume also that there are five party lists, A, B, C, D, and E, and that parties B, C, and D have concluded an alliance.

First possibility. One list, E, obtains an absolute majority of the votes cast.

A	25,000	
B	55,000	
C	20,000	80,000
D	5,000	
E	115,000	

Party List E thus obtains all 3 seats.

Second possibility. The group of allied lists, B, C, and D, receives an absolute majority.

A	20,000	
B	50,000	
C	45,000	120,000
D	25,000	
E	80,000	

The 3 seats are won by the alliance and distributed among the parties B, C, and D.

Third possibility. If no list or alliance obtains an absolute majority, the proportional representation rule is applied, and the seats are proportionally distributed among the parties.

Neither the proportional representation system nor its modification, the alliance system, accomplished its purpose—ending the fragmentation of political parties in France. In the elections of 1946, three parties—the Communists, Socialists, and MRP—obtained 71 per cent of the total national vote and 448 out of 579 seats in the National Assembly, but they could not cooperate. In 1951, with the emergence of the RPF, and in 1956 with the political resurgence of the Independents and the Poujadists, the electoral vote was split up, and several parties gained substantial parliamentary representation. In 1951, the National Assembly was "hexagonal," that is, political strength was about evenly divided among six blocs (Fig. 5-1). In 1956, the decline of the Gaullists was compensated for in part by the strength of the Independents and the Poujadists, and the Assembly continued to be badly divided. Many observers began to criticize the electoral system: it led to fragmentation, it stifled political leadership, and it undermined the healthy and intimate relations between a deputy and his electoral district. These critics asked for a return to the system of the Third Republic, with smaller electoral districts and the election of a candidate by absolute majority on the first ballot and, whenever no absolute majority was obtained, by relative majority on a second runoff ballot.

Throughout the last years of the Fourth Republic, electoral reform was constantly debated but no decision was reached, for many of the parties felt that a change would jeopardize their strength. The Communists argued for straight proportional representation, fearing, rightly, that any other system would encourage the Center-Left and Center-Right groups (Socialists, MRP, Radicals, Independents) to join against them. The MRP, on the other hand, was afraid that a majority system would lead to its extinction by forcing it to participate in an electoral alliance with the Center.

Electoral Trends and Shifts

The Fourth Republic, in contrast to the Third, was not only characterized by multipartism but also by large electoral shifts—usually of 15–20 per cent of the vote—in every

The Fourth Republic: 1946–1958

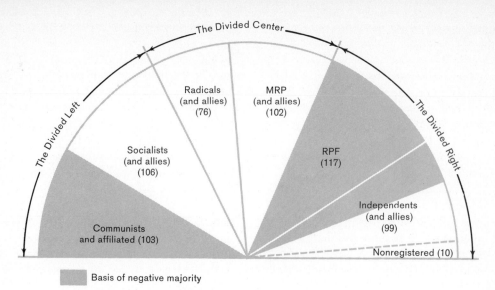

The Divided Center

The Divided Left

The Divided Right

Radicals
(and allies)
(76)

MRP
(and allies)
(102)

Socialists
(and allies)
(106)

RPF
(117)

Communists
and affiliated (103)

Independents
(and allies)
(99)

Nonregistered (10)

Basis of negative majority

FIGURE 5-1   MAJOR PARTIES AND PARLIAMENTARY GROUPS IN THE SECOND
LEGISLATURE: FOURTH REPUBLIC, 1951–1956, "THE HEXAGONAL ASSEMBLY."

national election. In 1946, a *new* political party—the MRP—won over five million votes, the first important shift (see Table 5-1). In 1951, another new political party—the RPF—won over 4,000,000 votes, many of which came directly from the MRP, a second radical shift. A third switch occurred in 1956; the RPF collapsed but many of its votes were captured by the Poujadists, who received almost two and a half million votes. In another changeover in the same election, almost 2 million votes went to an electoral alliance—the Republican Front, formed between the Radicals and the Socialists. A fifth shift took place, as we shall soon see, in 1958, in favor of the UNR—the new Gaullist party. Postwar elections were thus characterized by a "floating vote" of from one to three million votes, which shifted from the MRP to the Gaullists, from the Gaullists to the Poujadists or the Republican Front, and to the Gaullists again in 1958. These shifts did not, of course, all come from the same voters, but in each election they were roughly of the same size.

Was this floating vote a protest vote? Or

simply a personal vote for de Gaulle, Poujade, or, to a lesser extent, for Mendès-France, the leader of the Republican Front? Was it directed against parliamentary immobility, or perhaps even against the Republic? Did it grow out of the profound social and economic changes sweeping France, particularly economic modernization? These are difficult questions to answer. But the conclusion is inescapable. New forces were troubling the political life of France throughout the period of the Fourth Republic. And they are still operative in the Fifth Republic.

The Governmental Machinery

The Constitution of October, 1946, that ushered in the Fourth Republic was, like the electoral system, sharply criticized throughout its short life, even by those who helped create it. Known as "the system," the governmental machinery of the Fourth Republic was portrayed as being dominated by lobbies, incapable of making needed decisions, and unresponsive to its leaders, who, by and large, were not commanding figures. The Constitution vested supreme power in Parliament—notably in the lower house, the National Assembly. The Prime Minister and His Cabi-

TABLE 5-1 *Legislative Election Results in the Fourth Republic and in 1958*

	1946	1951	1956	1958
Communists and Progressives	5,489,288	5,057,305	5,514,403	3,882,204
Socialists	3,431,954	2,744,842	3,247,431	3,167,354
Radical Socialists and allied groups	2,831,834	1,887,583	2,834,265	2,695,287
MRP	5,058,307	2,369,778	2,366,321	2,378,788
Gaullists: RPF, 1951; Social Republicans, 1956; UNR, 1958		4,125,492	842,351	3,605,958
Independents and Moderates	2,565,526	2,656,995	3,257,782	4,092,600
Poujadists			2,483,813	669,518
Extreme Right			260,749	
Other parties	63,976	87,346	98,600	
Votes cast	19,203,070	19,129,064	21,298,934	20,489,709
Number of registered voters	25,052,233	24,530,523	26,774,899	27,236,491

net governed as long as they had majority support in the National Assembly. The President of the Republic was elected by Parliament and, like the British Monarch, was only the titular head of state. Prime Ministers came and went with disturbing frequency as the majorities shifted back and forth in the Assembly. The twelve years of the Fourth Republic saw twenty Cabinets form and dissolve, an average of one every seven months (Fig. 5-2).

This Cabinet instability was fundamentally the result of multi-partism. But the Cabinets' difficulties were aggravated by the fact that the Prime Minister could not dissolve the National Assembly unless two consecutive Cabinet crises had occurred within a period of eighteen months. A Cabinet "crisis" was constitutionally defined as the overthrow of the Cabinet by an *absolute majority* on certain solemn occasions—when the Prime Minister asked for a vote of confidence, as the British Prime Minister can do, or when the Assembly voted a motion of censure. These conditions for dissolution were not respected. Cabinets suffered defeat after defeat by *relative majorities* and were forced to withdraw without being allowed to retaliate by dissolving and calling for a new election. Only five governments under the Fourth Republic fell by absolute majority on the question of confidence and only once were the conditions for dissolution fulfilled and the right exercised—in December, 1955.

Other procedural devices further subordi-

nated the Cabinet to the Assembly. The legislative committees in the National Assembly were miniature Parliaments with sweeping prerogatives similar to those of congressional committees in the United States (whose powers, however, in the American system are offset by a stable and powerful Presidency). They could pigeonhole bills, amend them at will, or rewrite them. It was their version of a bill (not that of the government) that came on the floor for debate. The agenda of the National Assembly was prepared by the presidents of the various parliamentary groups, not by the Prime Minister and his Cabinet. These powerful parliamentarians established the legislative calendar by sidetracking important governmental measures with which they disagreed. Wrangles over the "order of business" became sharp political conflicts, and the Cabinet was reduced to appealing to the National Assembly to restore some of its own items on the agenda. Often it had to risk a vote of confidence on this purely procedural question.

When a budget was submitted to the National Assembly by the government, it was often overhauled by the legislature and particularly by the Committee of Finance. During financial debates, amendments could be introduced from the floor which, contrary to the prevailing practice in England and other

The Fourth Republic: 1946–1958

parliamentary systems, provided for diminution of credits or increased expenditures. Only in the last years of the Fourth Republic were certain procedural safeguards introduced providing for expenditure ceilings beyond which no amendments could be entertained. Continuous parliamentary debate constantly endangered the position of the Cabinet, which frequently had to resort to a vote of confidence on even minor issues. A Cabinet's margin of support usually underwent a progressive decrease until it either had to resign or fall on a question of confidence—such was the history of every Cabinet in the Fourth Republic.

Parties and Parliamentary Groups

We have already noted that there was no direct association between the political parties and the parliamentary groups and that any fourteen deputies could form a parliamentary group in the National Assembly. This is not to say that all parliamentary groups were different from the political parties. Generally, the Communist and Socialist members of the National Assembly and the Communist and Socialist parliamentary groups coincided. But the Center and Right parties tended to split up and form independent parliamentary groups, and many parliamentary groups broke up into even smaller units.

Cabinet Crises

Since there was no majority party at any time during the Fourth Republic, all Cabinets were coalition Cabinets, composed of the leaders of many parliamentary groups and parties. Divisions in the Assembly were so sharp that forming a Cabinet was like trying to sign a treaty among warring nations, and, indeed, the formation of the Cabinet became known as the "contract of the majority." When a Cabinet fell, the President of the Republic asked a political leader to scan the political horizon (*tour d'horizon* or *tour de piste*) to determine the willingness of the various political leaders to participate in a new Cabinet and the conditions under which they would join it. If his report were encouraging, he would probably be asked to form a Cabinet. He would then appear before the National Assembly to deliver his "investiture speech," which would spell out what he proposed to do and quite frequently, in order to placate certain groups, what he proposed not to do. If he were "invested"—that is, if he received majority approval—he would become the Prime Minister, presiding over a coalition Cabinet. If he failed to receive the approval of a majority, the whole process would have to be repeated.

In a prolonged crisis, the President of the Republic would call a solemn gathering of all former Prime Ministers and all the presidents of the various parliamentary groups. At this "round table" conference, the leaders would seek to reach enough agreement to form a Cabinet. If the crises lengthened, these meetings would be held more frequently until some consensus was established and a new Cabinet created. Within a matter of months, if not weeks, after the formation of a Cabinet, small

FIGURE 5-2   FROM DE GAULLE TO DE GAULLE, CABINET INSTABILITY IN THE FOURTH REPUBLIC.

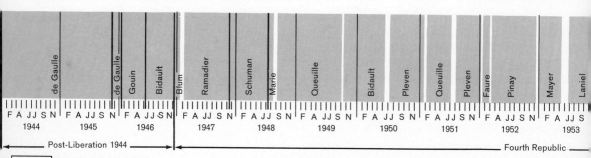

parliamentary groups would usually detach themselves from the government majority. It was estimated that the defection of forty or so members of the National Assembly was ordinarily sufficient to bring down the Cabinets of the Fourth Republic. Since a small group of parliamentarians constituted a powerful veto bloc, they were able—because the life of the government depended on them—to exact concessions from the Cabinet and impose conditions far disproportionate to their numerical strength.

Cabinet instability, however, had certain positive aspects in a system where party and ideological divisions were so deeply embedded. First, it provided access to positions of political power for many ambitious politicians, thus moderating the intensity of the conflict between parties. A political leader had but to wait his turn for a high post. Among the some 600 deputies, over 120 were known as *ministrables,* persons who were likely to be picked as Cabinet members. During the Fourth Republic, about 200 members of the National Assembly held ministerial posts at least once. The Cabinet "crises" allowed many men peacefully to come and go in the Cabinet without necessitating an appreciable change in policy. Occasionally, however, a crisis did spawn a genuine shift in policy. This was notably the case when Joseph Laniel's Cabinet fell in 1954 and Pierre Mendès-France was invested after he pledged to seek an immediate end to the Indochinese war. Even though the war was soon terminated, his Cabinet was unable to retain its majority and collapsed within a short time.

The "Immobilisme" of the Fourth Republic

The French political system under the Fourth Republic was, in a word, paralyzed. The numerous parties prevented any one of them from gaining a majority, and the legislature so hobbled the executive branch that leadership was virtually impossible. The Cabinet itself was almost always divided and lacked the prerogatives possessed by the Cabinet in England, notably the right of dissolution and the control of the business of the legislature. The system plainly failed even the most relaxed test of good government, in its inability to arbitrate the many claims of opposing interest groups, to settle political and social conflicts, and to meet new challenges. The divisions of French society as expressed through the multi-party system and coalition Cabinets reduced the effectiveness of the government sometimes to almost zero. To see how immobilized the governments of the Fourth Republic were we shall investigate some of the specific problems that arose in the years following World War II.

The Alienation of the Communists

Out of the 627 seats in the National Assembly during the Fourth Republic, the Communists had 183 in 1946, 103 in 1951, and 149 in 1956. From 1947 until roughly 1954, they were in a permanent state of opposition. They voted against all governments, and, with the exception of some tactical votes, against most

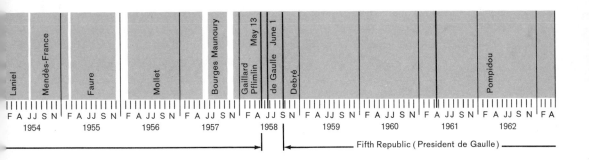

policy measures. After 1954, they began to urge the formation of alliances and to vote for the endorsement of Prime Ministers; no Prime Minister and Cabinet, however, were willing to govern if they had to count on Communist support. Hence the *true* number of deputies from which a majority had to be found to counter the Communist vote ranged from 400 to a maximum of 475.

The "Third Force"

If all the non-Communist parties had been in agreement, the Communist strength could easily have been neutralized. But they were not. The parties of the Center and the Right cooperated to form the so-called Third Force, which lasted from May, 1947, to the middle of 1952. It was composed of the Socialists, the MRP, the Radicals, and some of the Independents and Moderates. The Socialists and the MRP both favored price controls, social welfare legislation, increased governmental investments, economic modernization, and wage increases, while the Moderates and the Independents and a number of the Radicals were opposed to many of these measures. The MRP favored subsidies to Catholic schools and was supported in this by the Independents, but the Socialists would rather vote with the Communists than vote to help Catholic schools. The Third Force disintegrated every time this question came up.

On the question of continuing the war in Indochina and restoring complete French sovereignty there, the Socialists favored negotiations and a liberal policy, but the MRP became increasingly clamorous for a stepped-up military effort, and it was joined by many Radicals and Independents. In foreign policy, the MRP advocated European integration and the establishment of European super-national organizations, including a European military force. The Socialists, the Radicals, and the Independents were internally divided on this issue.

On colonial policy—notably the attitude toward Algeria, Morocco, Tunisia, Madagascar, and French West and Equatorial Africa—parties took various positions. The Socialists argued for a liberal policy leading to autonomy for these areas and in most cases, with the exception of Algeria, favored their independence. The Radicals were divided. Most of the MRP leaders, but not all of its deputies, supported the *status quo* and, at most, urged a gradual policy leading ultimately to internal autonomy. Some Radicals and most of the Independents voted against measures they considered as undermining French rule and sovereignty in these overseas territories.

When the Third Force came to an end in 1952, these disagreements became public debates, further paralyzing the Center parties. The Communist strength was reduced to about 100 deputies, but the RPF emerged to the Right with almost 120 members. Since the combined Gaullist-Communist group totaled at least 220 deputies, as long as the RPF and the Communists voted together against all Cabinets, the Assembly was literally ungovernable, faced as it was with a classic case of a "negative majority"—a majority *against* but never *for*. No stable majority could be formed from among the some 370 deputies of the other parliamentary groups to counter the combined Communist-Gaullist opposition.

When some of the RPF members split off from the party and began to vote *for* certain Cabinets and later to participate in Cabinets, the Center groups—the Socialists, Radicals, MRP, Independents, and the dissident members of the RPF—again became strong enough to form Cabinets. But these groups were hard put to agree on very many issues. First came the "clerical question": whether to grant subsidies to the schools. When the RPF introduced a measure providing for small subsidies, which passed by a small majority, the MRP-Socialist cooperation quickly broke up over the clerical issue. The Socialists began to move into the opposition, and Cabinet majorities consequently shifted to the Right, being composed of Radicals and members of the MRP, RPF, and Independent parties.

Sharp divisions also cut across party lines.

One prime example of this will serve as an illustration. A French Minister had suggested in 1950 the formation of a European Defense Community (EDC) composed of the five western European states plus West Germany, which had not become fully independent at the time and did not have an Army. The units from the various countries were to be genuinely integrated into the common Army, which would have a supra-national organization and command. When the proposal came up for a vote, the Socialists, Radicals, and Independents were split right down the middle. These political parties, then, especially in the crucial years 1952, 1953, and 1954, were divided internally into two groups: pro-EDC and anti-EDC. The MRP was united in favor of EDC while most of the members of the RPF were against it. On two occasions, a Prime Minister was endorsed on the explicit promise that he would not force a vote on this question. A third received majority support only when he promised that his Cabinet would not take sides. In all three cases, the coalition Cabinets included both strong pro-EDC and anti-EDC leaders—the best possible guarantee of inaction.

Since the EDC question overshadowed all others, action on almost all issues became difficult. Pressing economic and social problems, the war in Indochina, the decline of French prestige and strength, which forced the United States to encourage the rearmament of Germany—these, and many other challenges remained unmet. The MRP and the RPF drifted increasingly apart, while the divisions within the Socialist and the Radical parties prevented a realignment of forces and destroyed any chance for the formation of a Cabinet capable of acting.

The Search
for Strong Personal Leadership

Since the parties were so stalemated on so many vital issues, the Assembly began to search for strong political leaders to solve particular problems. In 1952, Antoine Pinay, a popular parliamentary leader in the Independent Party, was invested as Prime Minister with authority to launch a new economic policy. In 1954, another popular Radical leader, Pierre Mendès-France, was approved as Prime Minister on his pledge to end the war in Indochina in a month's time, to undertake extensive economic and social reforms, and to cope with the North African uprisings in Morocco, Tunisia, and, after November, 1954, in Algeria. When fighting in Indochina did cease within the month, Mendès-France received an overwhelming vote of confidence from all the parties, from the Communists to the RPF. But when he began to initiate economic reforms, he found his majority dwindling, and when he promised "internal sovereignty" to Tunisia, the Independents, the Radicals, and some of the RPF turned against him. When he allowed the National Assembly to shelve the European Defense Community, he incurred the hostility of the Communists (because he compromised by approving the rearmament of Germany within NATO) and of the MRP (because he did not press hard enough for EDC). Thus, in the end, the Radicals, Independents, Communists, MRP, and RPF—a negative majority—joined to bring the Cabinet down.

In December, 1955, the National Assembly was dissolved, and the ensuing elections, on January 2, 1956, ushered in the third, and what proved to be the last, legislature of the Fourth Republic. The Socialists and the Radicals agreed to an alliance under the banner of the "Republican Front," and made an impressive showing in the election, capturing some 170 out of the 596 seats in the Assembly (Fig. 5-3). The Independents received about 95 seats, the MRP 70, the Poujadists 52 (later reduced to about 42). The Communists and the Poujadists controlled one-third of the "negative" votes. With Communist support (150 seats), a Left-wing Popular Front alliance could have been revived, but the Communists remained excluded. In the National Assembly, then, the Republican Front—and notably the Socialists—could govern only with

The Fourth Republic: 1946–1958

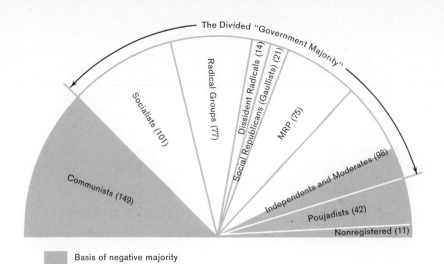

The Divided "Government Majority"

Socialists (101)

Radical Groups (77)

Dissident Radicals (14)

Social Republicans (Gaullists) (21)

MRP (75)

Communists (149)

Independents and Moderates (98)

Poujadists (42)

Nonregistered (11)

Basis of negative majority

FIGURE 5-3   PARTIES AND PARLIAMENTARY GROUPS IN 1958 PRIOR TO THE
RETURN OF GENERAL DE GAULLE.

the support of the Independents; the Independents, in turn, could form a Cabinet only with the support of the Socialists. No government from other groups could survive for any length of time without the combined support of the Independents and the Socialists.

The Independents and the Socialists, however, were at odds on economic and social legislation and on the question of subsidies to Catholic schools. Their mutual distrust had been aggravated by the many pronouncements made against the Independents by the leader of the Socialists, Guy Mollet, who, during the electoral campaign, had called the French Right (alluding to the Independents) the most stupid in the world.

Surprisingly enough, this parliamentary situation produced a coalition Cabinet led by Mollet with the participation of Gaullist, MRP, and Radical members that lasted for a record seventeen months. The rebellion in Algeria spurred a wave of nationalism in the country that seemed to enable the French to compromise some of their differences. Mollet shied away from negotiations with the Al-

gerian rebels and intensified the repressive policies of the French Army in that strife-torn country. The Army also received increasingly broad powers to govern in Algeria. Under Mollet, the independence of Morocco and Tunisia, already pledged, was proclaimed, and generous legislation providing for internal autonomy of the African territories (they became semi-independent republics with freedom to manage their own internal affairs) was passed. As long as the Socialist-led government followed an intransigent attitude in Algeria, the Independents were content, provided no drastic social legislation or higher taxes to meet the military effort were contemplated. Above all the political life in France, Algeria hung like a black and ominous cloud.

Algeria

Algeria was conquered by France in 1830 and administered as a French Department—as a part of France. There were until 1962 roughly one million Europeans (all of whom were French citizens) in Algeria and some nine million Algerian Moslems. The Europeans, often called *colons*, had much higher incomes than did the Moslems and dominated them. Thanks to the tight grip they held over the administration and economic life of the region. The two communities had little to do with each other socially. No representation was granted to the Algerians for over a hundred years, and when they were allowed to elect local assemblies and deputies in the French National Assembly (after 1945), the elections were manipulated by French officials and Army officers.

After World War II, many Algerian leaders demanded political emancipation and full political and economic integration with Metropolitan France. This was rejected. Only after 1952 did they begin to demand independence, and, in 1954, small rebel bands began to harass French detachments and commit acts of terrorism. The threat of losing Algeria, considered by Frenchmen to be an integral part of their country, provoked strong reaction in France. Troops were dispatched across the Mediterranean, and by 1957 more than 400,-000 soldiers were combatting the rebellion. Many Army officers developed close ties with the French settlers in Algeria; together they formed a dedicated group favoring repression and vehemently opposed to any moves in the direction of political autonomy. To avert the possibility of the independence of Algeria, the French settlers and officers advocated, in 1955, the full political and administrative integration of Algeria into France. This offer came too late, however. It was quickly rejected by the rebels.

The shock of the rebellion quickly stirred up heated debate in Paris. The Poujadists, the Independents, many of the MRP leaders, many of the Radicals, and the small Gaullist groups in Parliament demanded integration and the maintenance of French sovereignty in Algeria. The Socialists favored negotiations. The Communists wanted to start negotiations toward independence, but dared not pronounce the word, such was the wave of nationalism sweeping the country. From all over the nation, the clamor for a strong government that would put an end to the vacillations of the Republic increased. Right-wing organizations, fascist groups, the Poujadists, and many veterans' associations were ready to defy any government that threatened to relax French rule in Algeria. The Army itself became deeply involved. Many officers began to participate directly in politics and sought to impose its will on the government, and went so far as to refuse to obey some of the instructions issued in Paris. As the cleavage in the political system became deeper and more widespread, the government became more helpless, and the public more prone to accept the return of the hero of the war years—General de Gaulle.

In the last year of the Fourth Republic, the power of the government was further weakened by the insubordination of colonial administrators in Algeria, who began acting on their own, thwarting the policies of the Paris government. Supported by the colonial administration, the Army and the *colons* became a powerful political lobby that could exercise a veto power and hold the government at its mercy. The Socialist government gave the Army sweeping powers of administration in Algeria, which the Army used to indoctrinate and punish the Algerians and to establish concentration camps, in an attempt to stamp out the rebellion. As the military leaders in Algeria became more powerful, of course, the greater was their challenge to the government and the Republic. They soon became a state within the state.

The Last Crisis

Using some minor issue of social and economic reform as a pretext, the Independents withdrew their support of the Socialist-led Cabinet. From June, 1957, until May, 1958, the rivalry of the Independents and the Socialists made the formation of another Cabinet virtually impossible. The Radicals—but without Mendès-France—moved to fill the gap by forming two short-lived coalition Cabinets. Supported by powerful patriotic and Right-wing organizations, the Army and the *colons* refused to obey the last government of the Fourth Republic, formed by Prime Minister Pierre Pflimlin on May 13, 1958. They called for a government of "public safety." Army units in Algeria and elsewhere were alerted and prepared for a show of strength against Metropolitan France, involving, if necessary, a military invasion. The Gaullist groups, fearing a military coup, called for the return of General de Gaulle, who emerged from his long silence to declare his readiness to assume the government of the Republic. Pflimlin's Cabinet resigned two weeks after it was formed. On June 1, the National Assembly endorsed General de Gaulle and his Cabinet and the next day amended the Constitution to empower de Gaulle to draft a new one. A military coup had been narrowly averted. With the support of the majority of the Army, de Gaulle, like Marshal Pétain in 1940, was granted full powers to govern and to prepare a new Constitution. The breakdown of parliamentary government, the military stalemate in Algeria, the rebellious attitude of the Army, the economic difficulties at home—all eventually led the French to return to the tradition of Bonapartism, the personal leadership of one man to solve their problems.

A Premature Obituary

May 13th has now become the day that symbolizes the end of the Fourth Republic. On that day, the Army and the French settlers rose in Algeria against the parliamentarians and the "system," thus triggering a chain reaction that brought to power General de Gaulle with a mandate to draft a new Constitution, aimed at correcting the basic evils of the Fourth Republic—Cabinet instability, immobility, political apathy, and lack of leadership and central direction. With de Gaulle back, Gaullists and the new political leaders were naturally ready to write off the Fourth Republic as a failure. For us, however, the question remains: Why were the institutions of the Fourth Republic what they were?

The answer is that they corresponded to and reflected the basic realities of the French society that we outlined in the earlier chapters

of this book. The Cabinets came and went because there was no agreement on many issues; political parties were many and a majority difficult to find simply because many ideological currents were stirring the country. Compromise was difficult. Occasionally however, compromises were made and basic decisions taken. For instance, after protracted disagreement the war in Indochina was put to an end; a liberal colonial policy was endorsed by the French National Assembly and paved the way to France's colonial disengagement; the Monnet Plan, which we discussed earlier, was generally accepted by many political leaders, and massive social and economic investments were voted by the National Assembly, thus starting France on the road to today's prosperity. That many of these decisions were made "too late," and that many of the measures designed to implement them were ambiguous and hastily drawn is true. In some cases, no decisions were made. But the "weakness" stemmed directly from the social and ideological conflicts within the society and not from the governmental institutions alone.

The truth of the matter is that, barring critical upheavals caused by war and national setbacks, the institutions of the Fourth Republic fitted best the social and political needs of the country. They produced a government that governed little, a Parliament in which the most important social and economic and ideological forces were represented, and a mechanism by which decisions were made slowly, after long and open bargaining. These same forces continue to exist, and it is difficult to see how they can be eliminated from the French political scene in a matter of a few years. They are, as we have argued, deeply embedded in the history and the political tradition of France, especially if we remember that the Fourth Republic was in essence a rather faithful reproduction of the Third. The republican political tradition in France, in other words, is almost one hundred years old. It would be rash to say that the system today, even though shaped and manipulated by the towering personality of a great national hero, will prevent these same forces from returning.

The French Administration:
A Countervailing Force?

Cabinet instability in the Third and Fourth Republics resulted in ever-shifting and ever-changing government coalitions. Very often lengthy periods of time would elapse between the fall of a Cabinet and the formation of another; during this period, the incumbent Cabinet would have only caretaker functions or there would be no Cabinet at all. But the government would keep on functioning, thanks to the skilled efforts of experienced civil servants, who had a tradition of administrative discipline and stability that stretched all the way back to the days of Napoleon Bonaparte, the one who brought the French Civil Service to an extremely high level of competency.

The Chain of Command:
From Central Government
to Local Mayors

The key to understanding the French administrative organization is the realization that France is a unitary state and that decision-making is centralized and tightly controlled by the national government. Almost all important governmental decisions are made in Paris, and these decisions are enforced by a network of agents throughout the country. The three principal organs in this network are the Minister of the Interior, the Prefects, and the mayors.

THE MINISTRY OF THE INTERIOR. The Ministry is responsible for the execution of all the decisions of the central government and for administering departmental and local units throughout the country. Staffed primarily by permanent civil servants—and assisted by a number of civil servants "loaned" to it from the Council of State—the Ministry supervises all national services. It is responsible for the enforcement of the law, for which it has broad police functions and sweeping powers in time of national emergency.

PREFECTS. The most important instruments of the Ministry are the Prefects, who are in charge of the Departments of France. They are civil servants responsible for the execution and enforcement of laws and executive orders in each Department, and they have supervisory functions over all the local units within the Department as well. Assisted by elected departmental councils and by a number of sub-Prefects, they are the true spinal cord of the administrative machinery and serve as a highly centralized and disciplined extension of the central government.

MAYORS. Below the Prefect and his sub-Prefects are the mayors and the municipal councils. Both are elected. But once elected, the mayor assumes a double role—he represents both the state and his municipality. For certain matters the mayor is the representative of the national authority, and must account for his actions to the Prefect and perform a number of functions required by the national government. In many instances—notably in matters concerning the local budget and local taxation—his decisions have to be endorsed by the Prefect before they come into force. In other instances, the Prefect can command him to perform certain acts and failure to do so may result in his suspension from office for a period of time or, in extreme cases, his dismissal by an executive order of the Minister. Thus local government—more than 36,000 small communes with their municipal councils and mayors—is controlled from Paris. The mayor operates under what French lawyers call the "tutellage" (*tutelle*) of the Prefects and the central authority. Uniformity is the rule.

In the last few years, the Departments—established in the years of the Revolution and Napoleon—seem to have shrunk in size and importance, in this day when virtually the whole of France can be traveled by car in a matter of 24 hours and when the telephone

The Fourth Republic: 1946–1958

and the radio have brought every part of the country so close to Paris. As a result, an effort is being made to establish *super-Prefects,* with authority over many Departments. Municipalities are allowed to make agreements with surrounding areas for the joint administration of services that can be rendered more efficiently and economically on a regional basis—electricity, water supply, etc. Subsidies are provided to spur rather than control local effort. The central government has already taken firm steps to "decongest" the Paris region by giving special incentives and subsidies to industries so they can establish themselves outside of Paris, thus helping to inject new economic strength into many backward Departments.

The Central Government

In Paris, a stable bureaucracy is at the disposal of the Cabinet. The basic unit, as in England, is the Ministry, which is responsible for the execution, enforcement, and, at times, policy-formulation of matters under its immediate jurisdiction. The Ministries, again as in England, are divided into bureaus, and the French civil servants, like their English counterparts, form a permanent body of administrators, the top members of which are in close contact with the Ministers and, therefore, with policy-making. As with the British Treasury, the Ministry of Finance plays a predominant role, since it prepares the budget, formulates the estimates, collects taxes, and, to a lesser degree, controls expenditures.

Who are the French civil servants? If we include manual workers and teachers of grade schools and high schools, their total comes to about one million persons (Table 5-2). The vast majority are engaged in subordinate tasks. Only a small group of about six to eight thousand persons forms the top echelon, which participates in the formulation and execution of policy. The top echelon are selected on the basis of competitive examinations and, as in

Great Britain, the majority come from certain schools (open to all on the basis of merit):

TABLE 5-2   *Civil Servants in 1956*[a]

Ministry	Number
Ministry of Foreign Affairs	3,900
Ministry of Agriculture	18,000
Ministry of Veterans	9,200
Ministry of National Education	313,000
Ministry of Finance	132,000
Ministry of Overseas France	1,500
Ministry of Industry and Commerce	3,800
Ministry of Interior	73,000
Ministry of Justice	15,000
Prime Minister's Office	2,900
Ministry of Radio and Post Office	213,000
Ministry of Reconstruction	13,500
Ministry of Health and Population	6,300
Ministry of Labor and Social Security	8,700
Ministry of Public Works and Merchant Marine	83,600
Total	897,700
National Defense (civilians)	146,000
Grand total	1,043,700

[a] From *Tableaux de l'Économie Française,* 1960, I.N.S.E.E.

the law schools, the École National d'Administration, the École Polytechnique and a few others. Most of the candidates come from the middle and upper middle class.

Since the beginning of the Fourth Republic, the government has attempted to give all prospective candidates for the Civil Service a common education. In 1946 a special school, the National School of Administration, was established for this purpose. The school is open to candidates on the basis of merit and not only is free but the student is paid a stipend by the government for a period of three years as a trainee civil servant. Common training makes rotation from one job to another and from one Ministry to another easier. The prestige of the National School of Administration has to some degree overshadowed the law schools (although most prospective civil servants continue to study law) and the other specialized schools.

The factors that account for the cohesiveness of the Civil Service and for its ability to govern the country when political leadership is weak and Cabinets change are stability, permanence in tenure, discipline, and hierarchical organization. In times of emergency, the Service becomes a well-knit group that performs rapidly and efficiently. The trains run; the postman brings the mail; the sick or unemployed receive medical care, pensions, and social insurance benefits; the Army is trained and equipped; the taxes are collected; students throughout the country are taught to decline their Latin verbs. But can the Civil Service do more than just keep things operating?

The French "administrative tradition"[1] is primarily a state of mind rather than an efficient decision-making organization. It cannot be considered as a countervailing force against the internal divisions of the Republic; it has not been in the past and is most unlikely to be in the future. The Civil Service has been trained to be politically neutral and its goal ordinarily is efficiency and stability. Many of the civil servants have a predilection for a highly centralized government and have generally supported the Fifth Republic. And many admire what they call *technocratie* (rule by the expert). But in practice, the bureaucracy is shot through with divisions and incompatibilities. It cannot generate policy or develop a common point of view; it cannot even become a veto group. It performs the routine tasks of government but it cannot lead the country when leadership is lacking. The members of the Civil Service, like those of other institutions in the country under the Fourth Republic, were fragmented into groups with many different political loyalties. They were also very sensitive to pressure groups. The lack of central leadership and direction made them even more susceptible to the pressure from the various interests. Some of the Ministries—especially the Ministries of Agriculture, Veterans, and those concerned with economic affairs—were virtually "colonized" by the interests the Ministries are supposed to oversee. Despite de Gaulle's assertions of leadership, many of the internal weaknesses of the Civil Service persist.

Ministerial Cabinets

One factor in particular that has weakened the Civil Service is the Ministerial cabinet, an institution unknown in England. As we have seen, in England there is a parliamentary undersecretary to help the Minister. The rest of the Minister's staff comes exclusively from permanent civil servants. In France, in addition to parliamentary undersecretaries, every incoming Minister appoints his personal staff, his own personal cabinet, consisting of six, eight, and sometimes even ten officials to assist him in running the Ministry. This cabinet comes in and leaves with the Minister. Its members are drawn usually, but not always, from a rostrum of civil servants. Many of them naturally put their interests above those of the Service. Without any permanent position in the Ministry, they are prone to look out for their own political and administrative careers—at times even for their own personal advantage. Since the life of their Minister was and often continues to be short—even in the Fifth Republic—they naturally hope to exploit their brief stay in the Ministry. The Ministerial cabinet is an element of instability at the very heart of the administrative machinery. As Ministers and their cabinets shift, administrative stability, and with it the alleged integrity and neutrality of the Service as a whole, suffers.

The Council of State
(*Conseil d'État*)

One of the most remarkable institutions in the government of France is the Council of State, whose parallel cannot be found in England or the United States, but which has been widely copied in most of the Continental countries. Founded by Napoleon, it originally consisted of top-ranking civil servants who screened executive orders and decrees and be-

[1] See the analysis of Nicholas Wahl in Beer and Ulams, *Patterns of Government* (New York: Random House, 1962).

The Fourth Republic: 1946–1958

205

came the "watchdog" of the administration. All litigation involving civil servants or the state would be heard by it. Today, the Council of State continues to perform important advisory and deliberative functions. A number of government executive orders require its approval before they go into force. It is reputed to consist of the best lawyers in France. Once admitted, the *"conseiller* of state" achieves, by custom, permanent tenure in the Civil Service. Until the Fifth Republic, no *conseiller* had ever been arbitrarily dismissed by the government.

The Council of State has, however, emerged primarily as a court. It hears cases involving acts of civil servants in their official capacity and cases arising between an individual and the state. Instead of being the watchdog over government administration, the Council has today become the defender of individual rights —both property and civil rights—against the state. This change has been the result of a jurisprudence developed over the years by the Council. It has declared executive orders or acts of the government to be illegal if they are not consistent with the "parent law": if they are *ultra vires* (i.e., beyond the powers authorized by law); or if the reasons for which an executive order is issued are not clearly set forth. It has obliged the state to pay damages to private individuals whenever negligence on the part of civil servants could be proved. Finally, in some decisions it has held that the government is obligated to compensate the plaintiff even when no negligence has been proven. In each of the following cases, a public officer and, through him, the state were declared liable even though negligence was absent: a Prefect suspended the publication of a newspaper; a mayor refused to allow a peaceful religious ceremony to be held; munitions ex ploded in a state depot.

Thus the Council of State has attempted to curb the arbitrary actions that are inherent in any powerful and centralized administrative system and to protect the individual in all the cases where he has no redress before the civil courts. As a result, its jurisprudence has been one of the most progressive in the world.

The Constitution of the Fifth Republic

VI

The Constitution of the Fifth Republic * originated in the enabling act of June 3, 1958, in which the National Assembly provided, by the requisite majority of three-fifths, that "the Constitution will be revised by the government formed on June 1, 1958," that is, General de Gaulle's government. A small group of Ministers and experts, headed by the Minister of Justice and later Prime Minister, Michel Debré, prepared the new Constitution in two months. A special consultative committee, composed of 39 members (two-thirds elected by Parliament and one-third nominated by General de Gaulle), endorsed the proposed new text after suggesting only minor modifications. Submitted to the people in a referendum held on September 28, 1958, it was ratified by an overwhelming majority of 79.25 per cent of the voters.

Although the new Constitution (Fig. 6-1)

was written in a short period of time under the stresses and strains of the Algerian war with which the institutions of the Republic could not cope, it institutionalized a number of revisionist ideas that had been uttered by General de Gaulle and many political leaders throughout the period of the Third and Fourth Republics. Without entering into the details of the various schemes and ideas of constitutional reform, we ought to single out two major themes that dominated the thinking of the framers. First, the reconstitution of the authority of the state under the leadership of a strong Presidency. Second, the establishment of what came to be known as a "rationalized" Parliament—a Parliament with limited political and legislative powers. The new Constitution was to establish a "parliamentary system," but one in which Parliament was no longer in a position to dominate the executive as it did in the period of the preceding Republics.

Both General de Gaulle and his close associate and later Prime Minister, Michel Debré, expressed clearly in a number of their pronouncements the purpose of the projected constitutional reform. The most important landmark was the speech made by General de Gaulle at Bayeux on June 16, 1946, where he

* For a more detailed discussion of the Constitution, see Roy Macridis and Bernard Brown, *The de Gaulle Republic: Quest for Unity* (Homewood, Ill.: The Dorsey Press, 1960), Chapter X. Portions of that chapter are reproduced here in a modified form with the permission of the publisher.

SENATORIAL AND PRESIDENTIAL ELECTORS
(Municipal councilors and general councilors: 81,000–110,000)

UNIVERSAL SUFFRAGE

Legislative

NATIONAL ASSEMBLY

552 members (Algeria plus Sahara, 71 delegates)

Mandate: 5 years. Elected directly by equal and universal suffrage.

Limited Legislative Powers: Legislates on civil rights, nationality, status and legal competence of persons, penal law and procedure, taxation, electoral system, organization of national defense, administration of local government units, education, employment, unions, social security, and economic programs. Authorizes declaration of war. Can initiate constitutional revision. Can delegate above powers to Cabinet—votes organic laws. (All other matters fall within rule-making power.) Can question Cabinet one day a week. Meets in regular sessions for a total that does not exceed 6 months. Votes budget submitted by government. If budget is not decided with Senate within 70 days, may be issued by decree.

SENATE

306 members (Algeria, 31; Sahara, 2)

Mandate: 9 years. Renewable by thirds every 3 years.

Elected indirectly by municipal and general councilors and members of National Assembly. Approximate size of electoral college, 110,000. Majority system, but PR for 7 Departments with largest population.

Functions: Full legislative powers jointly with Assembly. Bills must be approved in identical terms by both houses unless Prime Minister, in case of discord, asks lower house to vote "definitive" text. Otherwise Senate has full veto powers.

Executive

PRESIDENT OF THE REPUBLIC

Elected for 7-year term by members of Parliament, departmental councils, municipal councils, and towns of over 30,000 at rate of 1 for each 1,000 in excess of 30,000, and assemblies and municipal representatives of member states of Community. Total electoral college for election of de Gaulle, Dec., 1958, 81,671.

Personal Powers: Nominates Prime Minister; dissolves Assembly; refers bills to Constitutional Council for examination of constitutionality; calls referendum; issues decrees with force of law; nominates 3 of 9 members to Constitutional Council; can send messages to legislature; invokes state of emergency and rules by decree; not responsible to Parliament.

PRIME MINISTER AND CABINET

Prime Minister proposes Cabinet members to President for nomination; "guides policies of nation"; directs actions of government and is responsible for national defense; presides over Cabinet meetings; proposes referendum; has law-initiating power. Prime Minister is responsible before Assembly.

THE ECONOMIC AND SOCIAL COUNCIL

Elected by professional organizations. Designated by government for 5 years as specified by "organic law."

Composed of representatives of professional groups (205 members for French Republic and overseas Departments and territories, 24 members represent Community).

Gives "opinion" on bills referred to it by government. "Consulted" on over-all government economic plans.

Judiciary

CONSTITUTIONAL COUNCIL

Composed of 9 justices and all ex-Presidents of Republic. Three justices each appointed by Presidents of Republic, Senate, and Assembly.

Functions: Supervises presidential elections and declares returns. Supervises referendums and proclaims results. Examines and decides on contested legislative elections. On request of Prime Minister or Presidents of Republic, Assembly, or Senate examines and decides on constitutionality of pending bills, treaties, and legislative competence of Assembly.

HIGH COURT OF JUSTICE

HIGH COUNCIL OF THE JUDICIARY

REFERENDUM

Called on specific matters by President of Republic.

FIGURE 6-1   MAJOR FEATURES OF THE CONSTITUTION OF THE FIFTH REPUBLIC. *Since July 5, 1962, the deputies and senators from Algeria and Sahara have been deprived of their seats by Presidential ordinance. Thus the National Assembly and the Senate consist of 482 and 273 members, respectively. The amendment of October 28, 1962 provides that the President is to be elected by direct popular vote.*

outlined the ideas that were to serve as the foundations of the new Constitution.

The rivalry of the parties takes, in our country, a fundamental character, which leaves everything in doubt and which very often wrecks its superior interests. This is an obvious fact that . . . our institutions must take into consideration in order to preserve our respect for laws, the cohesion of governments, the efficiency of the administration and the prestige and authority of the State. The difficulties of the State result in the inevitable alienation of the citizen from his institutions. . . . All that is needed then is an occasion for the appearance of the menace of dictatorship.

To avoid this menace, de Gaulle outlined the following institutional arrangements:

1. The legislature, executive, and judiciary must be clearly separated and balanced.
2. Over and above political contingencies there must be a national "mediation" (*arbitrage*).
3. The voting of the laws and the budget belongs to an assembly elected by direct and universal suffrage.
4. A second assembly, elected in a different manner, is needed to examine carefully the decisions taken by the first, to suggest amendments and propose bills.
5. The executive power should not emanate from the Parliament. Otherwise the cohesion and authority of the government would suffer, the balance between the two powers vitiated, and the members of the executive would be merely agents of the political parties.
6. A President of the Republic (*Chef d'État*), embodying the executive power above political parties, should be elected by a college, which includes the Parliament but is much broader than Parliament . . . to direct the work and the policy of the government; promulgate the laws and issue decrees; preside over the meetings of the Council of Ministers; serve as mediator above the political contingencies; invite the country to express its sovereign decisions in an election; be the custodian of national independence and the treaties made by France, and appoint a Prime Minister in accord with the political orientation of Parliament and the national interest.[1]

Michel Debré himself pointed out that the object of constitutional reform was to "reconstruct state power."[2] He advocated a rationalized Parliament that involved shorter ses-

sions, a division between legislation and rule-making, the right of the executive to legislate by decree, and reorganization of the legislative and the budgetary procedure in a manner to give the government a controlling position. Certain rules that normally were part of the standing orders of the Parliament were also put into the Constitution: the personal vote of the deputies, the length of time for which the presidents of the National Assembly and the Senate were elected, the preparation of the order of business of the National Assembly, and so on. But why all these detailed provisions? Debré's answer underlined the perennial dilemma of the French body politic. He insisted that all these provisions were necessary because there was no majority in France and because multi-partyism made effective government impossible.

Ah, if only we had the possibility of seeing tomorrow a constant and clear majority, it would not have been necessary to establish an upper chamber whose role it is to support the government against an Assembly which attempts, because it is so divided, to invade its sphere of action. . . . There would be no attempt to establish order and stability by cutting the ties that united the parties with the government. . . . It would not be necessary to regulate so carefully the motion of censure.[3]

Thus the crucial task was to create a strong and stable government to succeed a parliamentary system that could not produce stable majorities.

The new Constitution, however, respects the French republican tradition. The Preamble solemnly affirms the attachment of the French people to the Declaration of the Rights of Man of 1789 and to individual and social rights that were affirmed, after France's Liberation, by the Constitution of 1946. Article 1 proclaims that "France is a Republic, indivisible, secular, democratic, and social." It insures the rights of all citizens and respect for

[3] *Ibid.*

[1] The text of the Bayeux speech in de Gaulle, *Discours et Messages* (Paris, 1946) pp. 721–727.
[2] Michel Debré, *La Novelle Constitution* (Tours, 1958).

The Constitution of the Fifth Republic

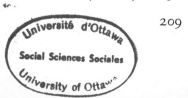

all beliefs. Article 2 affirms that "all sovereignty stems from the people." But this sovereignty is not to be exercised solely through the representatives of the people but also through a referendum. Respect for the freedom of the political parties is reiterated in Article 4, where, however, it is stated that the parties "must respect the principles of national sovereignty and democracy"—a provision that many thought was aimed at the powerful Communist Party.

The Constitution establishes the familiar organs of a parliamentary system: a bicameral legislature; a politically irresponsible chief of state; a Cabinet and a Prime Minister in charge of the direction of the policies of the government and responsible to the lower chamber; the right of the lower chamber to censure and overthrow the Prime Minister and the Cabinet. But, in contrast to the Fourth Republic, it delegates broad powers to the chief of state (the President) and places serious limitations on the legislature. There is a new principle—that of the incompatibility between a parliamentary seat and a Ministerial portfolio, requiring a member of Parliament who agrees to become a Minister to resign his seat. Otherwise, the Constitution reproduces many of the time-hallowed provisions of a democratic government—tenure of judges, immunity of parliamentarians from arrest and prosecution without prior permission of the chamber to which they belong, freedom of speech and press, freedom of association, protection against the arbitrary detention of an individual. Finally, a long section (Section 12) organizes the relations between France and the former colonies that had become semi-independent Republics. They are all grouped into the "French Community," a loosely federated organization in which important powers are lodged in the hands of the President of the Community who is also the President of the French Republic. This structure was abandoned after

1960 in favor of complete independence for all the former colonies. The only ties that bind them to France are individual treaties and agreements that can be renegotiated or revoked in the future. The real novelty of the Constitution lies, then, in the establishment of a strong executive and a limited Parliament.

The President of the Republic

In 1958, the framers wished to give to the President the prestige and prerogatives that would enable him to provide for the continuity of the state, to cement the bonds between France and the former colonies of the French Union, and to supervise the functioning of the Constitution. The President is the "keystone of the arch" of the new Republic—he is both the symbol and the instrument of reinforced executive authority. To accomplish this, the framers modified the manner in which he is elected and strengthened his powers.

The President was at first elected by an electoral college, which, in addition to the members of the Parliament, includes the municipal councillors, the general councillors, and the members of the assemblies and the municipalities of the overseas territories and Republics. It was a restricted electoral college favoring rural municipalities and small towns and discriminating against the large urban centers. As a result it was widely criticized at the time it was introduced by many political leaders and constitutional lawyers who saw in it the perpetuation of the old political forces of the Fourth Republic.

In the middle of September and again early in October, President de Gaulle proposed to modify the manner in which the election of the President was to take place. He suggested that after the end of his own term (early in 1966) or in the event of his death in office, the President be elected by direct popular vote. In a message to Parliament on October 2, 1962, he put the matter very succinctly: "When my seven years term is completed or if something happens that makes it impossible for me to continue my functions, I am convinced that a popular vote will be necessary in order to give . . . to those who will succeed me the possibility and the duty to assume the supreme task. . . ." On October 28 in a referendum the people endorsed de Gaulle's proposal, but not before the first government crisis had erupted endangering his own position and bringing about the dissolution of the National Assembly and new legislative elections. The system adopted provides for the election of the candidate for the Presidency by absolute majority of the popular vote. Failing this, there is to be a second run-off election two weeks later limited to only two candidates. It is expected that they will be the two who received the highest number of votes, but the adopted reform does not exclude the withdrawal of the first or second most successful candidates in favor of others. The heart of the proposal is that the run-off election will be limited to two candidates, thus forcing the parties to combine for or against the two and enabling the people to make a clear-cut choice between the candidates.

Under the Third and Fourth Republics, the President as the chief of state was irresponsible. His only personal act was the designation of the Prime Minister. But even this was carefully circumscribed by parliamentary tradition. All his other acts had to be countersigned by a responsible Minister or the Prime Minister. The Constitution of the Fifth Republic maintains the political irresponsibility of the President but at the same time gives him personal powers that he can exercise solely at his discretion.

1. The President designates the Prime Minister. Although the President presumably makes the designation with an eye to the relative strengths of the various parties in the National Assembly, it is a personal political act.

2. The President can dissolve the Assembly at any time, on any issue, and for any reason solely at his discretion. There is only one limitation—he cannot dissolve it twice within

the same year—and one formality—he must "consult" with the Prime Minister and the Presidents of the two legislative assemblies.

3. When the institutions of the Republic, the independence of the nation, the integrity of its territory, or the execution of international engagements are menaced in a grave and immediate manner and the regular functioning of the public powers is interrupted, the President may take whatever measures are required by the circumstances (Article 16). Again, this is a personal and discretionary act. The President needs only to inform the nation by a message and to "consult" the Constitutional Council. The National Assembly, however, reconvenes automatically and cannot be dissolved during the emergency period.

4. Finally, the President can bring certain issues before the people in a referendum:

The President of the Republic on the proposal of the government . . . or on joint resolution by the two legislative assemblies . . . *may* submit to a referendum any bill dealing with the organization of the public powers, the approval of an agreement of the Community or the authorization to ratify a treaty, that without being contrary to the Constitution would affect the functioning of existing institutions [Article 11].

The calling of a referendum is, however, a personal act of the President of the Republic. He may elicit or refuse it depending on the circumstances. Constitutional provisions to the contrary notwithstanding, the President claimed in October, 1962, that this article empowered him to submit directly to the people amendments to the Constitution. The proposal providing for the direct popular election of the President was thus submitted directly to the people by the President in the referendum of October 28, 1962.

The Constitution also vests explicitly in the President other powers that he can exercise at his discretion. He has the nominating power for all civil and military posts, and, unless it is otherwise provided by an organic law (a law passed by absolute majority of the legislative branches), he signs all decrees and ordinances prepared by the Council of Ministers. He can raise questions of unconstitutionality on a bill or on a law before a new special constitutional court—the Constitutional Council.

The President continues to enjoy the prerogatives that were vested in the office in the past. He presides over the meetings of the Council of Ministers, receives ambassadors, and sends messages to Parliament. He may ask for the re-examination of a bill or some of its articles, which cannot be refused; he promulgates laws within fifteen days after their enactment; he negotiates and ratifies treaties and is kept informed of all negotiations leading to the conclusion of international agreements; and he is commander-in-chief of the armed services and presides over the Committee of National Defense.

The President
as Mediator (Arbitre)

The Constitution explicitly charges the President to guarantee the functioning of the institutions of the government:

The President of the Republic shall see that the Constitution is respected. He shall ensure, by his arbitration, the regular functioning of the governmental authorities, as well as the continuance of the State.
He shall be the guarantor of national independence, of the integrity of the territory, and of respect for Community agreements and treaties [Article 5].

Mediation is a personal act involving the exercise of judgment. As a result, the President is given an implicit veto power on almost every conceivable aspect of policy. He becomes an integral part of policy-making and policy-execution, despite the fact that he is politically irresponsible.

The list of Presidential prerogotives is thus

an impressive one. In matters of war, foreign policy, the preservation of internal peace, and the functioning of governmental institutions, his powers are overriding. He is deeply involved in politics and can no longer be considered as an "irresponsible head of the state" like the British Crown.

De Gaulle as President

There was little doubt that General de Gaulle would assume the office that had been tailored for him. All political parties, with the exception of the Communists and some splinter Left-wing groups, favored de Gaulle. The election held on December 21, 1958, was a formality, with de Gaulle getting 78.5 per cent of the vote of the electoral college. There was no electoral campaign and no debate between the candidates on the manner in which they intended to use the enormous powers of the office.

Speaking one week after his election, de Gaulle reaffirmed his conception of the office and his own personal role: "The national task that I have assumed for the past eighteen years is confirmed. Guide of France and chief of the republican state, I exercise supreme power to the full extent allowed and in accord with the new spirit to which I owe it." This view of the office stems directly from French monarchical traditions. De Gaulle is the custodian of a national unity that has been forged through some thousand years of history —a unity that is "real" and therefore assumed by him to be perceived by every French man and woman, despite the vicissitudes and squabbles of the republican regimes. He is "invested" by history and is responsible to the people only in a vague fashion. He stands above the everyday party conflicts and quarrels, intervening in order to lead and to "arbitrate."

De Gaulle seems to divide the task of government into two not very clearly distinguished categories. The first, la Politique, concerns France's position in the world and thus involves matters of defense, foreign policy, and relations with the former colonies and Algeria. In this area, de Gaulle alone apparently initiates policy and makes decisions.

He may demand a full-dress debate in the Cabinet or he may ask the advice of his Ministers, notably the Minister of Foreign Affairs. But the final decision is his own.

The second category of responsibility consists of economic and social matters, the means for the realization of over-all national objectives. Problems in this area are delegated to "subordinate" organs—the Prime Minister, the Cabinet, and Parliament. It is for them to make appropriate decisions, subject, of course, in the case of conflicts among Ministers or between the Cabinet and Parliament, to the President's "arbitration." Thus far—on two occasions, during the preparation of the budgets of 1959 and 1960—de Gaulle has had to resort to such "arbitration."

Because a sense of unity is one of the first requirements of a strong nation, de Gaulle has been anxious to impart his view of France's historical mission to the people (which was also one of his prime concerns right after the Liberation). He has sought to renew his contact with the people, by frequent tours through the country, in order to create a common national purpose. Thus, General de Gaulle has given to the Fifth Republic a strong personal orientation. He has controlled and shaped French foreign policy, with the aid of his Foreign Minister. He has been solely responsible for all decisions concerning colonial policy; he has been the sole spokesman for the policies pursued in Algeria. He has been the architect of the new organization for defense and the modernization of the armed forces. The office of the Presidency is no longer a mere symbol; it has become the prime seat of political power in France.

The Cabinet

In the language of the Constitution, the Cabinet, composed of the Prime Minister and his Ministers, "determines and conducts the policy of the nation" and is "responsible before the Parliament." Special recognition is accorded to the Prime Minister. He "directs" the action of the government and is "responsible" for national defense. He "as-

sures the execution of the laws and exercises the rule-making power"—but on condition that all decrees and ordinances are signed by the President of the Republic (Articles 20 and 21). He determines the composition of his Cabinet, presides over its meetings, and directs the administrative services. He defends his policy before the Parliament, answers questions addressed to him by the members of Parliament, states the over-all program of the government in special declarations, and puts the question of confidence before the Assembly. Thus the Constitution establishes a parliamentary government side by side with a strong Presidency.

After his election, President de Gaulle asked Michel Debré to become Prime Minister. Debré picked his Cabinet and went before the National Assembly with a proposed program. The National Assembly adopted his general program and thus "invested" the Cabinet by a vote of 453 against 56. Only the Communists and the Socialists voted against the government, while some 29 deputies from the Center and from the Independents abstained. In the new Cabinet, the ratio between non-parliamentarians and parliamentarians (who must resign from the Assembly) has increased in favor of the non-parliamentarians, who occupy half of the Cabinet posts and hold the most important positions. The most significant areas of la Politique were entrusted to technicians who are presumably able to implement the policies of the President of the Republic.

The meetings of the Council of Ministers under President de Gaulle are frequent and prolonged. Reports prepared by the Ministers or their aides are debated, but generally the discussion revolves around the suggestions and directives of the President. In contrast, the Cabinet meetings under the Prime Minister are becoming rare. Instead, several small interministerial committees have been set up to implement the decisions reached in the Council of Ministers by President de Gaulle. The Cabinet has become a mere instrument for the execution of policy and in some matters—especially defense and foreign policy—is simply by-passed. For instance, when on September 16, 1959, President de Gaulle announced his policy of self-determination for Algeria, the Prime Minister and his Cabinet were taken by surprise. Again, on December 13, 1959, de Gaulle surprised everybody when he announced that Senegal and Sudan (grouped in the Federation of Mali) would be given their independence. As one commentator put it: "Those who imagined conflicts between the two heads of the executive may be reassured; there is but one head"—meaning President de Gaulle.

The Legislature

The Parliament of the Fifth Republic is, as in the past, bicameral, consisting of a National Assembly and a Senate. The Assembly, elected for five years by universal suffrage, was composed of 552 deputies (465 from Metropolitan France, 67 from Algeria, 4 from the Sahara region, 10 from the overseas Departments, and 6 from the overseas territories). The Senate, elected for nine years, was composed of 306 members (255 from Metropolitan France, 31 from Algeria, 2 from the Sahara region, 7 from the overseas Departments, 6 from French citizens living abroad, and 5 from the overseas territories). The representatives from Algeria and Sahara were deprived of their seats, however, on July 5, 1962, following the declaration of Algerian independence. The corresponding figures as a result are 482 for the National Assembly and 273 for the Senate. The Senate is elected indirectly by the municipal councillors, the departmental councillors, and the members of the National Assembly. One-third of its membership is renewed every three years.

The two chambers have equal powers except in two respects—the traditional prerogative of the lower chamber to examine the budget first is maintained, and the Senate cannot introduce a motion of censure. The Cabinet is responsible only before the National Assembly. Article 45 specifies that every bill "is examined successively in the two assemblies with a view to the adoption of an identical text." But if there is continuing disagreement on the text of a bill after two readings by each assembly, the Prime Minister can convene a joint conference committee, consisting of an equal number of members of the two chambers, and ask it to propose a compromise text, which is then submitted by the government for the approval of the two assemblies. In case of a persistent discord between the two assemblies, the Prime Minister *may* ask the National Assembly to rule "definitively." Thus, the National Assembly has the last word and the Senate a veto power. If the government and the Senate are in accord, the senatorial veto is ironclad. The Senate can be overruled only if there is an agreement between the government and the National Assembly, something which has occurred frequently during the first legislature of the Fifth Republic between January, 1959, and October, 1962.

A "Rationalized" Parliament

The new Constitution establishes a "rationalized" Parliament—a Parliament with limited powers.

1. Only two sessions of the two assemblies are allowed—one lasting from the beginning of October to the middle of December and the other from the last Tuesday of April to the end of July. Extraordinary sessions may take place at the request of the Prime Minister or of a majority of the members of the National Assembly "on a specific agenda." They are convened and closed by a decree of the President of the Republic, who, it appears now, seems also to have the last word on whether to convene an extraordinary session or not, despite the terms of the Constitution.

2. The Parliament can legislate *only on*

matters defined in the Constitution. The government can legislate on all other matters by simple decree.

3. The government now fixes the order of business.

4. The President of the National Assembly is elected for the whole legislative term, thus avoiding the annual elections that in the past placed him at the mercy of the various parliamentary groups. The Senate elects its president every three years.

5. The Parliament is no longer free to establish its own standing orders. Such orders must be found to be in accord with the Constitution by the Constitutional Council before they become effective.

6. The number of parliamentary committees is reduced (only six are allowed), and their functions are carefully circumscribed.

7. The government bill, not the committees' amendments and counterproposals as under the Fourth Republic, come before the floor.

8. The government has the right to reject all amendments and to demand a vote on its own text.

All these provisions are directed against "Assembly government." By putting rules into the Constitution that are essentially of a procedural character, the framers hoped to limit Parliament to the performance of its proper function of deliberation and to protect the executive from legislative encroachments. Many of the new rules reflect a genuine desire to correct some of the more flagrant abuses of the past and are consistent with the strengthening of the executives in modern democracies. Others, however, are designed to weaken Parliament.

Relations between Parliament and the Government

Four major provisions in the Constitution determine the nature of the relations between Parliament and the government; they concern (1) the incompatibility between a parliamentary mandate and a Cabinet post, (2) the manner in which the responsibility of the Cabinet before the Parliament comes into play, (3) the distinction between "legisla-

tion" and "rule-making," and (4) the introduction of the "executive budget."

THE RULE OF INCOMPATIBILITY. Article 23 of the Constitution is explicit: "The 'office' of a member of government is incompatible with the exercise of any parliamentary mandate." Thus, a member of Parliament who joins the Cabinet must resign his seat for the balance of the legislative term. He is replaced in Parliament by the person whose name appeared together with his on the electoral ballot —the *suppléant.* Despite the rule of incompatibility, however, Cabinet members are allowed to sit in Parliament and defend their measures. They are not allowed, of course, to vote.

The purpose of the rule was to introduce a genuine separation of powers and to discourage parliamentarians from trying to become Ministers, which was one of the major causes for the high rate of Cabinet turnovers under the Fourth Republic. It was also the intention of the framers to establish a government that would be better able to resist pressures emanating from parliamentary groups and thus be in a position to give its undivided attention to its duties.

RESPONSIBILITY OF THE CABINET BEFORE THE LEGISLATURE. The responsibility of the Cabinet to the legislature comes into play in a specific and limited manner. After the Prime Minister has been nominated by the President of the Republic, he presents his program before the National Assembly and, through a Minister, before the Senate. If this program is accepted by the Assembly, the Cabinet is "invested"; if defeated, the Prime Minister must submit his resignation to the President of the Republic.

The Parliament can bring down the Cabinet in the following manner: The National Assembly (but not the Senate) has the right to introduce a motion of censure, which must be signed by one-tenth of the members of the National Assembly. The vote on the motion is lost unless it receives an absolute majority of the members composing the National Assembly. In other words, blank ballots and abstentions count for the government. If the motion is carried, the government must resign; if the motion is lost, then its signatories cannot move another one in the course of the same legislative session.

The Prime Minister may also, after consultation with the Cabinet, stake the life of his government on any general issue of policy or on any given legislative bill. Although the Constitution does not use the term, this is equivalent to putting the "question of confidence." A declaration of general policy is presumed to be accepted unless there is a motion of censure voted under the conditions mentioned previously. A specific bill becomes law unless a motion of censure is introduced and voted according to the same conditions, but with one difference: the same signatories may introduce a motion of censure as many times as the Prime Minister stakes his government's responsibility. If the motion is carried by an *absolute* majority, the bill does not become law and the government resigns. If, however, the motion of censure is lost, and it is lost even if carried by a *relative* majority, then the text becomes law and the government stays in office. Thus bills may become laws even if there is no majority for them.

"LAW" AND "RULE-MAKING." The Constitution provides that "law is voted by Parliament." Members of Parliament and of the government can introduce bills and amendments. The scope of Parliament's law-making ability, however, is limited. It is defined in the Constitution (Article 34) to include:

. . . the *regulations* concerning:
civil rights and the fundamental guarantees granted to the citizens for the exercise of their public liberties; . . .

nationality, status and legal capacity of persons, marriage contracts, inheritance and gifts;
determination of crimes and misdemeanors as well as the penalties imposed therefor; criminal procedure; . . .
the basis, the rate and the methods of collecting taxes of all types; the issuance of currency; . . .
the electoral system of the Parliamentary assemblies and the local assemblies; . . .
the nationalization of enterprises and the transfer of the property of enterprises from the public to the private sector; . . .
[and the] fundamental *principles* of:
the general organization of national defense;
the free administration of local communities, the extent of their jurisdiction and their resources;
education;
property rights, civil and commercial obligations;
legislation pertaining to employment, unions and social security.

This enumeration of legislative power cannot be enlarged except by an organic law (a law passed by an absolute majority of the members of both houses). Article 37 makes this point clear. "All other matters," it states, "than those which are in the domain of law fall within the rule-making sphere." It goes even further: "Legislative texts pertaining to such matters may be modified by decree." Thus, laws made under the Fourth Republic dealing with matters that are declared by the new Constitution to be beyond the powers of the legislature can be modified by simple decree. They are "delegalized."

The Constitution also allows Parliament to delegate law-making power to the executive. "The government may for the execution of its program ask Parliament to authorize it to take by ordinances, within a limited period of time, measures which are normally reserved to the domain of law" (Article 38). Such ordinances come into force as soon as they are promulgated, but they are null and void if a bill for their ratification is not submitted by the government before Parliament within a prescribed time, or if the ratification of the bill is rejected.

THE BUDGET. The Constitution consecrates the "executive budget." The budget is submitted by the government to Parliament. Proposals stemming from members of Parliament "are not receivable if their adoption entails either a diminution of public resources or an increase in public expenditures" (Article 47). No bill entailing diminution of resources or additional expenditures is receivable at any time. If "Parliament has not decided within seventy days" after the introduction of the budget, then "the budget bill can be promulgated and put into effect by simple ordinance" (Article 47, par. 2 and 3). Thus the government may be able to by-pass Parliament in case the latter has failed to reach an agreement.

These, then, are the major principles of the Constitution: a bicameral Parliament that gives the Senate a genuine veto if it has the support of the government; a division between law-making and rule-making that in effect gives legislative powers to the executive; the provision that bills can become law unless there is an absolute majority against the Cabinet; the delegation of law-making power to the executive; the priority of government bills over private members' bills before Parliament; a mechanism restricting the use of the motion of censure; the ever-present threat of dissolution; numerous devices in the hands of the President of the Republic and the Prime Minister that enable them to suspend legislation by appealing to the Constitutional Council; and, finally, the possibility of a referendum on certain matters. The only concession made to Parliament is the provision for a question period with debate on one day a week in which deputies and senators can question the Cabinet members.

Other Constitutional Organs and Principles

The new Constitution re-establishes an Economic and Social Council. Representing the most important professional interests in France, it has consultative and advisory powers to give advice on proposed economic and social legislation, and particularly on measures related to economic planning. As

under the Fourth Republic, a High Court of Justice, whose members are elected by the National Assembly and the Senate, may try the President of the Republic for high treason and the members of the government for criminal offenses committed in the exercise of their functions. A High Council of the Judiciary, presided over by the President of the Republic, nominates judges to the higher judicial posts, is consulted about pardons by the President, and rules on disciplinary matters involving the judiciary. The same section of the Constitution (Article 66) provides what purports to be a writ of habeas corpus clause: "No one may be arbitrarily detained. The judicial authority, guardian of individual liberty, assures the respect of this principle under conditions provided by law."

A most striking innovation is a Constitutional Council, composed of nine members who serve for a period of nine years. Three are nominated by the President of the Republic, three by the President of the National Assembly, and three by the President of the Senate. They are renewed by a third every three years. In addition, all former Presidents of the Republic are members *ex officio*. A variety of powers has devolved on the Constitutional Council. It supervises the presidential elections and the referendums and proclaims the results; it judges the validity of all contested legislative elections, thus avoiding bitter and long controversies in the legislative assemblies. It is the ultimate court of appeal on the interpretation of the Constitution on a specified number of matters. All bills, including treaties, may be referred to it, before their promulgation, by the President of the Republic, the Prime Minister, or one of the presidents of the two assemblies. A declaration of unconstitutionality suspends the promulgation of the bill or the application of the treaty. The Council determines the constitutionality of the standing orders of the National Assembly and the Senate which go before it automatically. It is, finally, the guardian of legislative-executive relations; it decides on all claims made by the government whether the legislature exceeds its legislative competence.

The constitutional review provided by the Constitution of the Fifth Republic differs from the American practice in two important respects. First, it is almost exclusively limited to certain specified categories of cases involving the relationship between the legislature and the executive, and, second, it is brought into play *only* upon the request of four officers of the Fifth Republic—the President of the Republic; the Prime Minister, and the two presidents of the legislative assemblies. Review applies only to pending bills. A law cannot be attacked for "unconstitutionality" except under the specific and very restrictive terms of Article 37—that is, only when it is claimed by the government that the legislature exceeded its competence in enacting it. In contrast to the American practice, the Constitutional Council cannot hear cases brought to it by individuals and is not competent to judge matters where individual rights are violated.

The Constitution provides two ways to amend the Constitution. An amendment proposed by the two legislative assemblies by simple majorities becomes effective only after it is approved in a referendum. A proposal stemming from the President of the Republic and approved by the two chambers by simple majorities may go, at the President's discretion, either before the two chambers, meeting jointly in a Congress (in which case a three-fifths majority is required), or to the people in a referendum. Thus amendments that emanate from the government may either go before the Congress or the people, while a proposal stemming from Parliament must always be submitted to the people in a referendum. As we have seen, President de Gaulle has claimed, by invoking Article 11, that an amendment can also be submitted directly by the President to the people in a referendum—thus by-passing Parliament.

The Evolution of Political Forces
under the Fifth Republic

VII

Since General de Gaulle returned to office and subsequently to the Presidency, there have been eight occasions on which the French people were consulted in one form or another; the referendum of September 28, 1958, on the new Constitution; elections for the National Assembly (November 23 and 30, 1958); the election of the President, December 21, 1958; the municipal and senatorial elections in the spring of 1959; and the second and third referendums on January 8, 1961, and April 8, 1962, on the future status of Algeria. On October 28, 1962, a fourth referendum was held on a proposal to elect the President of the Republic by direct popular vote. It was followed in November by legislative elections for the National Assembly.

The First Referendum

The result of the referendum of September 28, 1958, was an overwhelming en-

dorsement of the new Constitution.[1] In Metropolitan France, out of 26,606,948 registered voters, 22,595,703 cast their ballots—an unprecedented 84.8 per cent participation—with "Yes" ballots totaling 17,666,828 against 4,624,475 "No" ballots, 79.25 per cent against 20.75 per cent. In the French Union (the African Autonomous Republics and Madagascar), the "Yes" vote was equally overwhelming, with the exception of Guinea, which voted "No." In Algeria, of the total number of votes cast, the percentage of "No" votes was negligible.

The vote reflected a transformation in the electoral map of France. Traditional bastions of Left-wing republicanism—the South, the Paris "red belt," some of the Departments in Central and Southeast France—were swept by the pro-Gaullist current. Only in the Departments of Corrèze and Haute-Vienne, strongholds of the Communists, did the "No" vote total as much as 34 per cent. In eleven Departments, including some of the most industrialized areas, the "No" votes amounted to no more than between 25 and 30 per cent. On

[1] For a detailed account, see Macridis and Brown, *The de Gaulle Republic: Quest for Unity.*

the other hand, some 21 Departments returned a "Yes" vote of 85 per cent and more. They included the regions of French conservatism—the West, the East, and the region south of the central plains.

The Communist Party, virtually the only important party to campaign vigorously against the adoption of the new Constitution, went down to defeat. If one were to assume—which is unwarranted—that every "No" vote was a Communist vote, even then the Communists had lost heavily. The percentage of "No's" was only 20.75—below the average electoral strength of the Communist Party. Thus the Communist Party found itself abandoned by many of its voters. The losses came from both industrialized and non-industrialized Departments, from proletarian and agricultural strongholds alike.

Even more convincing were the returns from Paris and its southern and eastern proletarian suburbs—the pro-Communist "red belt." While in Paris proper the "Yes" vote totaled 77.6 per cent, in the suburbs it amounted to 68.1 per cent. The "No" vote was everywhere well below the vote of the Communist Party in 1956, and in a number of the personal fiefs of the party leaders, the Communist vote dropped substantially.

The First Legislative Elections

The first legislative election took place in the wake of the referendum, in November, 1958. It was a relatively apathetic campaign compared to the three general elections that had preceded it under the Fourth Republic, and the public seemed to view the elections as part of the process of investing General de Gaulle with the powers of the Republic.

THE "NEW" ELECTORAL LAW. The government decided to adopt the single-member district system with run-offs, which had been used during the greater part of the Third Republic. The election took place in two stages: on the *first ballot,* the candidate was elected only if he received an absolute majority of the votes cast; failing this, a *second ballot* took place a week later in which the candidate with the greatest number of votes was elected. In the week between ballots, the various candidates had an opportunity to drop out in favor of a better-placed rival, or simply to retire.

Seats were allocated to each district on the basis of one deputy for every 93,000 inhabitants, with a minimum of two deputies for each Department. The district lines within the Departments were drawn by the Ministry of the Interior and the Office of the Prime Minister on the basis of reports submitted by the Prefects. The boundaries were carefully traced, and, despite certain discrepancies, there was no gerrymandering.

THE RESULTS. As was the case with the referendum, the results of the two ballots held on November 23 and November 30 at first glance appeared to have transformed the configuration of the political forces. The new Gaullist party—the Union for the New Republic (UNR)—won 189 out of the 465 seats at stake in Metropolitan France. The Communists, having lost 95 per cent of their seats, were reduced to 10 deputies (compared to 150 in 1956); the Socialists retained only 40 seats (as against 88 in 1956); the various factions of the Radical party held 37 seats (compared to 74 in 1956); the MRP, together with the dissident Christian Democrats, did better than anticipated, retaining 57 of their 71 seats. The Independents emerged as the second largest political group in the Assembly, with 120 deputies (a gain of 24).

The popular vote, however, revealed greater stability on the part of the electorate. The main features of the first ballot in terms of the popular vote were the relative success of the UNR (17.6 per cent of the vote), the decline of the Communist Party (which lost 1,650,000 votes, going from 25.7 per cent in 1956 to 18.9 per cent in 1958), the weakening of the Radicals, the eclipse of the Poujadists, and the relatively high number of abstentions. Abstentions amounted to 22.9 per cent, compared to 15 per cent in the referendum and 17.3 per cent in the elections of January, 1956. Over four million voters, or 20 per cent of the total (1,650,000 former Communists, half a million Radicals, and two million Poujadists) switched to other parties or into abstention as compared with the elections of 1956.

The Socialists and MRP maintained their popular strength. There were, therefore, two big winners compared to 1956: the Independents and associated Moderates, who gained one million votes (from 14.5 per cent to 19.9 per cent of the total), and the UNR. The UNR received 3,604,000 votes on the first ballot compared to 4,266,000 for the RPF in 1951. With half a million votes fewer than the RPF, the UNR spread its strength a little more evenly throughout the nation. Like the RPF, the UNR was strong in the East, West, and Paris region, but weaker in traditionally conservative Departments. On the other hand, the UNR penetrated south of the Loire more successfully than did the RPF, particularly along the east coast of the Mediter-

ranean, and in the Pyrenees and the Toulouse regions. In twenty-five Departments (mainly in the Center, South, and West), the Poujadists had rolled up over 12 per cent of the vote in 1956. In six of these Departments, the UNR vote improved noticeably over that achieved in 1951 by the RPF.

THE SECOND BALLOT. Only a few candidates won on the first ballot by absolute majority. The composition of the National Assembly was decided, therefore, on the second ballot. The UNR victory became nation-wide. It won all the seats in five Departments, 33 out of 55 seats in Seine, 8 out of 10 in Gironde, and 12 out of 23 in Nord. In spite of the UNR success, the Independents maintained their position surprisingly well. The losers were the Radicals and, above all, the Communists and Socialists. The isolation of the Communists worked invariably to their disadvantage when the field narrowed on the second ballot. The massing of non-Communist votes behind UNR candidates is illustrated by the results in three election districts in Paris (Table 7-1).

TABLE 7-I *First and Second Ballot Results in Three Election Districts in Paris, 1958*

13th District		36th District		45th District	
First Ballot		**First Ballot**		**First Ballot**	
Garaudy, Communist	12,030	L'Huillier, Communist	17,773	Duclos, Communist	21,049
Sanson, UNR	7,309	Devaud, UNR	14,139	Profichet, UNR	18,218
Independent	5,748	Republican Center	7,897	Socialist	10,416
Socialist	3,460	Socialist	4,071	Diverse	2,538
Diverse	7,700	Diverse	7,700		
Second Ballot		**Second Ballot**		**Second Ballot**	
Sanson	22,181	Devaud	29,315	Profichet	29,662
Garaudy	13,767	L'Huillier	21,383	Duclos	21,252

The run-off system precipitated an evolution of public opinion by compelling a choice from a restricted range of candidates. In most cases, the UNR was preferred over the Independents by those who had voted for non-Communist parties on the Left on the first ballot.

The National Assembly

Elected at the height of the pro-Gaullist enthusiasm that followed the referendum, the National Assembly reflected in its composition the deep popular distrust of the former parliamentarians and Ministers. The electors belatedly heeded Poujade's old battle cry and "threw out the rascals" (including, however,

The Evolution of Political Forces

the Poujadists). Out of 552 members (including the deputies elected in Algeria and some overseas Departments), only 131 had served in the previous Assembly; among the rest, only a small number had parliamentary experience either in the second legislature (1951–56) or in the Council of the Republic. The new men were about evenly divided among the political parties. A 75 per cent turnover was experienced not only by the UNR, which had some forty former parliamentarians in its ranks, but also by the MRP and the Independents. Only on the Left could one see many familiar faces. Never before had an election in France accounted for such a drastic reshuffling of deputies, apart from the election of the first Constituent Assembly in 1945.

SEATING ARRANGEMENTS. Tradition in politics calls for a distinction between Left, Center, and Right, and it was precisely this distinction that the UNR did not wish to accept, for fear it might be placed to the Right. After a long debate, a compromise was reached. As Fig. 7-1 shows, the UNR was seated in a Left-Center position at the expense of the Independents, who found themselves on the extreme Right. Both because of its size and its position, the UNR straddles the Left and Center and physically dominates the Assembly.

The standing orders stipulate that a minimum of thirty members is required to form a parliamentary group. The Communists were therefore unable to form a group, while the various Radical groups managed to compromise their differences and form the *Entente Démocratique*. Die-hard nationalists dedicated to the cause of French Algeria formed a parliamentary group called the Unity of the Republic with some 37 members—mostly French deputies elected in Algeria and Right-wing members who seceded from the UNR. It lost, however, more than two-thirds of its members when de Gaulle on July 5, 1962, deprived all

deputies from Algeria of their seats (Fig. 7-2); as a result, it ceased to be a parliamentary group.

COMMITTEES. The Assembly decided that the composition of the members of the six standing committees should correspond to the numerical strength of the parliamentary groups. Selections from among those who did not have enough members to constitute a parliamentary group were to be made by a majority vote. Each committee was to consist of at least 60 and not more than 120 deputies. The following committees were formed: Foreign Affairs; Finance and Economic Planning; National Defense and Armed Forces; Constitutional Laws, Legislation, and General Administration of the Republic; Production and Trade; and Cultural, Social, and Family Matters.

Election of the Republican Senate

The 255 senators from Metropolitan France were chosen by a senatorial electoral college. All Departments were to have run-off ballots except the seven Departments that were assigned more than four senatorial seats. These seven Departments elected their senators—60 in all—by proportional representation. The Algerian Departments elected 31 senators, who also lost their seats after the proclamation of Algerian Independence.

The electors in Metropolitan France were the municipal councillors. Cities with more than 30,000 inhabitants received one extra elector for each additional thousand inhabitants. Despite this provision, the small towns and villages continued to play a dominant role. Those with less than 1,500 inhabitants have a majority in the senatorial electoral college. They represent only 33 per cent of the population but 53 per cent of the senatorial electors. The larger towns, those with more than 10,000 inhabitants, which represent more than 40 per cent of the population, have only 21.5 per cent of the senatorial electors.

The senatorial election returned a Senate that was almost the exact replica of the old one under the Fourth Republic. The Gaullist wave in the referendum and the legislative

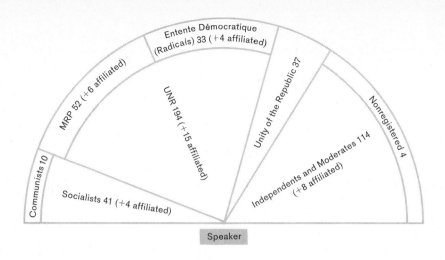

FIGURE 7-1   THE NATIONAL ASSEMBLY BEFORE THE PROCLAMATION OF ALGERIAN INDEPENDENCE, JULY 3, 1962. (*Approximate strength of groups and seating arrangements.*)

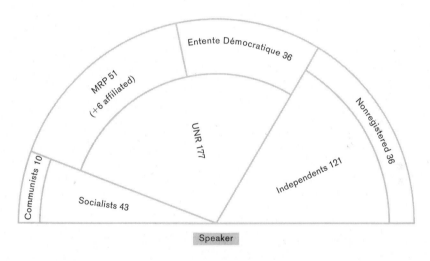

FIGURE 7-2   THE NATIONAL ASSEMBLY AFTER PROCLAMATION OF ALGERIAN INDEPENDENCE. (*Approximate strength of groups and seating arrangements.*)

elections appeared spent. Of the 255 senators elected in France proper, only 85 were new; and among those, 35 were formerly members of the National Assembly. Eighty-four per cent of the incumbent senators were re-elected. In 35 Departments, there was no change at all. In 17 Departments, despite changes of individual senators, the party position and strength remained unchanged.

As for the over-all results, the Communists lost two seats and the Socialists five. The vari-

ous Radical groups that traditionally coalesce in the Senate under the name of "Democratic Left" gained three seats, another proof that the Radical families continued to be strong among the local notables and bosses. The UNR had two seats less than the old Gaullist

The Evolution of Political Forces

party—the RPF—an indication of its inability to establish local roots, while the MRP and the Independents gained eight and five seats, respectively. The two traditional political formations, Independents and Radicals, together with the MRP, held a majority in the new Senate. The forces of the Fourth Republic continued to be alive!

On September 24, 1962, one-third of the Senate was renewed. The election again revealed the stability of the senatorial electoral college after four years of Gaullist rule. There was virtually no change in party strength; the MRP gained one seat and the Socialists two, and the UNR and the Independents lost one and two seats, respectively. Out of a total of 89 seats at stake, only three seats changed party labels.

The New Political Forces

The referendum and the legislative and senatorial elections provide us with adequate data to assess the evolution of the political forces in France.

The Union
for the New Republic (UNR)

The UNR was joined by some other deputies in the National Assembly and its strength soon increased to about 210. The Prime Minister, the President of the National Assembly, and five Ministers came from the UNR. As a "new" party, it capitalized on the general reaction against the "men of the system," a feeling that accounted for the very large turnover in the personnel of the National Assembly. Yet 40 of its 189 members had been deputies or senators either in the previous legislature or in 1951. The professional composition of its representation was not very different from that of the National Assembly as a whole.

The UNR deputies took an oath of fidelity to General de Gaulle:

Elected Deputy of the UNR I confirm in a solemn manner my adherence to the Union for the New Republic and to its parliamentary group. Respectful of the mandate which was given to me by the electors I will abstain during the period of the legislature from participating in or becoming a member of any other group. I take the following engagement: to remain faithful to the objective of the UNR, to support in Parliament and in my electoral district the action of General de Gaulle, to accept the discipline of voting as decided by the majority of the group for all the important questions relating to the life of the nation and of the French community, in order to maintain the cohesion of our group and the general spirit of our movement.

After the election, the UNR had a rudimentary organization, few members, and no program. Some of its leaders believed that the UNR ought to become a "mass party" like the RPF and create a vast network of well-disciplined militants, obedient to the leadership and in touch with public opinion. But de Gaulle repudiated the notion of a mass party. Such a party with a program would inevitably make his role of "arbitrator" on national issues difficult and would seriously limit presidential discretion on matters on which he wishes to have the last word—i.e., on Algeria, foreign policy, and defense. The party has remained thus far what de Gaulle wished it to be: a parliamentary *masse de manoeuvre* without policy and doctrine, without mass membership and organization, ostensibly ready to follow the President of the Republic wherever he might lead them.

The Communist Party

The Communist defeat on the referendum and in the elections was not as damaging as it first appeared. The vote for de Gaulle was in the nature of a protest vote, which the Communists had captured in the past (such a personal vote has not been uncommon in French history). This modern form of Bonapartism received considerable support from the workers and the lower middle class. Even in defeat, the Communists derived some solace. They were still the most popular party in the country and continued to control a major part of the unionized workers. Despite some internal conflicts, they had the largest membership of any party, and their organization remained solid.

Less than two years after their defeat, the Communists found themselves in a better tactical position. They had led the opposition to de Gaulle's return and, together with some splinter formations and individual leaders, are taking a firm stand against the Fifth Republic. It was with a note of optimism, therefore, that the party held its Fifteenth Congress in Ivry late in June, 1959. Maurice Thorez presented the report of the party.

Since our fourteenth congress (in 1956) we have witnessed the destruction of the democratic institutions and the establishment of personal power. Our party has been the principal force to resist the reaction. . . . The Communist party predicted the fascist danger but the leaders of the Socialist party continued to divide the working class.

In his lengthy report, Thorez proceeded to identify every factor (real or imaginary) that was likely to get him popular support and hence strengthen the party: the alleged slump of the economy, the growth of big monopolies, the drop in the real wages of the workers, the fall in farm income, the "proletarization" of the artisans, the intrusion of the Army into politics and the creation of a "military bureaucracy," the continuation of the war in Algeria for which the party advocated negotiations, and de Gaulle's "adventurous" foreign policy based on military strength. The Communists resented personal government and the weakening of the powers of Parliament and above all objected to the electoral law that decimated their strength in the National Assembly. The party made a bid for the creation of a new Popular Front—a comprehensive union of all the republican forces (Socialist rank and file, liberal Catholics, Radical Socialists, trade unions, and intellectuals). The party morale was good, he asserted, and membership was on the increase. The task of the party, Thorez concluded, was to create a vast reservoir of good will, in order to attract millions of prospective sympathizers. Again in 1961 and in 1962, the party, through its congress or Central Committee, reiterated its stand. It

accused de Gaulle of being the spokesman of the big monopolies and of establishing a personal dictatorship and asked for a constitutional reform that would do away with the limitations the Fifth Republic had opposed upon Parliament. The Communists pleaded for direct democracy and a weak President of the Republic. Above all, claiming that their membership was on the increase, they made every effort to organize a Popular Front in which the Socialists, the Radicals, the Left-wing Socialists, and perhaps even the MRP were to be included.

These declarations on the part of the Communist leaders should not be taken lightly. In the by-elections and municipal elections held since the end of 1958, the party appears to have recovered its former strength. It continued to receive 25 per cent of the votes, and on certain occasions it received even higher percentages. Its discipline and leadership remains unshaken and its appeal to the masses continues to be powerful. While the party is likely to lose whenever it opposes single-handedly de Gaulle's policy in a referendum, there is every reason to expect that its mass of voters will remain loyal in elections. It is this strength that forced many parties to heed its appeals, if not for a Popular Front at least for electoral alliances in which the Communist voters supported the candidates from other parties in some electoral districts on condition that these parties support Communists in others.

The Socialists

Following the elections, in which the Socialist Party suffered no decrease in its electoral strength—3,167,354 as compared to 3,180,656 in 1956—but in which its parliamentary strength was reduced to forty-one deputies, the position of the party appeared to be extremely difficult. To the Right, the UNR and the Independents took over the nationalist policy that the Socialists had previously pursued when in power. To the Left, the Communists and other groups were raising the battle cries of social reform, republicanism, and peace in Algeria. The party was demoralized by the initial position of its leader, Guy Mollet, in supporting de Gaulle while providing "constructive opposition" to the Cabinet in the National Assembly. A number of its members and federations were beginning to look to the Unified Socialist Party—a dissident Socialist party group—and to entertain thoughts of cooperating even with the Communists.

While supporting de Gaulle's policy of self-determination in Algeria, the Socialist party gradually became increasingly impatient with the slow progress made with negotiations and overtly hostile not only to the Prime Minister and his Cabinet but also to the President of the Republic. They objected to his economic and social policies at home, alleging that national wealth was not being equitably divided and that the working class was being discriminated against; they opposed de Gaulle's personal government and disputed on a number of points the interpretation he was giving to the Constitution of the Fifth Republic; they took strong exception to the practice of referendums that overshadowed Parliament and reinforced personal government; they promised to abrogate the legislation giving subsidies to the Catholic schools and pledged to work for a genuine European unity. All motions of censure were introduced in the National Assembly by a coalition of Socialists and Radicals, with the Socialists taking more and more upon themselves the leadership of the opposition to the government.

However, there was a certain futility in this opposition. The Socialist Party was getting progressively weaker. Its membership continued to decline, and in 1962 even its official newspaper could no longer appear daily. The Christian and Communist trade unions continued to make inroads into Socialist trade-

union strength, except into the ranks of civil servants and the teachers. Above all, the position of the party in regard to the other Left-wing groups remained tenuous. It continued to refuse any alliance with the Communists, but its deteriorating relations with the Left-wing Socialists (who envisaged cooperation with the Communists) and with the MRP (which favored subsidies with Catholic schools) dimmed the prospects of alliance with them.

The MRP

After its surprisingly good showing in the elections, the MRP seemed to enter a new period of vitality thanks to the support of the dynamic French Confederation of Christian Workers, of Catholic Action groups, and of liberal rural leaders primarily drawn from the Catholic organizations. In the senatorial elections, the party managed to improve its position by increasing its number of senators from twenty-one to twenty-nine—the largest net gain registered by any party. The MRP joined the "majority" in the Assembly and several Ministers were drawn from its ranks. But the liberal Catholic Youth Formations, the white-collar workers, and the more liberal rural elements forced the party progressively to oppose de Gaulle's regime on social and economic questions in both the Senate and the National Assembly. The MRP parliamentarians thus voted against many of the financial measures of the government and became restive over de Gaulle's foreign policy.

Gradually, the party began to express its hostility both to the government and to General de Gaulle. There were three reasons for this. First, the party began to be apprehensive about the government's economic and social policies for reasons similar to those advanced by the Socialists. Second, it began to take exception to de Gaulle's personal rule and to the denigration of Parliament. Finally, it came out openly against de Gaulle's foreign policy, both with regard to the development of an independent atomic striking force and, more particularly, with regard to de Gaulle's unwillingness to consider seriously measures of genuine European political integration. Many MRP members decided to abstain from voting for the new Cabinet of Georges Pompidou when the latter refused to promise a full-dress debate with a vote on de Gaulle's foreign policy. On May 16, 1962, all five of the MRP Ministers withdrew from the Cabinet at the express request of the party as a protest against de Gaulle's opposition to European integration. It was the first time that the government did not include any MRP Ministers. A few weeks later, the MRP parliamentary group signed a resolution favoring European political integration and almost half the group voted to censure the new Prime Minister. Yet the MRP was reluctant to move into permanent opposition. In their party congress held in June, 1962, they promised to vote for or against governmental measures on the merits of the issues involved.

As with the Socialists, the future of the MRP depends to a large measure on the ability of the party to appeal to the younger and more dynamic forces of the country. In its last congress, it decided to include in its top executive councils members from professional and agricultural associations—a concession to the dynamic groups that have come from the Catholic professional, rural, and youth associations. It is doubtful that this will be enough. It will take more drastic reforms to make a mass party out of the MRP. There is also the constant dilemma of electoral alliances. The UNR has made repeated overtures for an alliance. Such an alliance, however, no matter how attractive to the leadership of the party, is strongly opposed by the Catholic workers' unions, the intellectuals, and the progressive professional and youth groups. An alliance with the Socialists, on the other hand, will raise again the "clerical question," at least with regard to subsidies to the Catholic schools.

The Radicals

The various Radical families lost votes on the first ballot of the November, 1958 election (from 15.3 per cent in 1956 to 12.9 per cent in 1958), but it was their failure to unite on the second ballot that seriously reduced their representation in the National Assembly. In order to qualify as a group under the new standing orders of the National Assembly (requiring a minimum membership of thirty), various Radical formations managed to create an *Entente Démocratique,* which has a fluctuating membership of 35. In the municipal election, the Radicals recovered lost ground and improved their position in the Senate by electing 51 senators, as compared to 47 in the Senate of the Fourth Republic. The loss of their most dynamic leader, Pierre Mendès-France, was felt to be an advantage by those who remained in the party. Yet the party had lost its following among the youth, and remains apprehensive about the future. As in 1945, it expressed nostalgia for the institutions of the previous regime. The old anti-clerical Radical battle cry finds little response among the delegates. Nor is the suggestion of cooperation with the Socialists warmly received.

Like the Socialists and the MRP, the Radicals moved gradually into the opposition. They voted against many of the government's social and economic measures. More particularly, they have been hostile to de Gaulle's personal government, to his interpretation of the Constitution, and to the decline of Parliament, to whose supremacy they have been traditionally attached. They have allied themselves with the Socialists in the introduction of virtually every motion of censure and have sided with the MRP and the Socialists in their opposition to de Gaulle's foreign policy. They have also voted against an independent atomic striking force for France. Many Radicals abstained in the vote for Pompidou's Cabinet, in which, for the first time in many years, there are no Radical Ministers. A majority of their members voted for the motion of censure against Pompidou. It is very likely that the Radicals will continue their traditional electoral attitude, forming alliances with Independents, Socialists, Communists, and the UNR, as the occasion arises, to strengthen their parliamentary representation. But, like the other parties, they, too, need a new platform that will appeal to the voters in terms of concrete issues rather than out-dated slogans.

The Independents

The Independents welcomed the Fifth Republic with great complacency. The party did remarkably well in the elections of 1958. It gained about a million votes and at least 20 deputies, to bring its strength in the National Assembly to 120. Without mass membership or a coherent program, it exploited the wave of nationalism for its own electoral ends. The Independents became the conservative party in the National Assembly in matters of economic and social reform, and in regard to Algeria. They joined the UNR in the Cabinet, and one of their leaders, former Prime Minister Antoine Pinay, became Minister of Finance and was responsible for the formulation of financial and economic policy. The Independents did well in the municipal and senatorial elections, in the Senate gaining 5 seats (85 as compared to 80) to emerge as the largest group in the second chamber.

Complacency, however, was transformed into feverish political activity when it became clear that President de Gaulle threatened both the policies and the future electoral chances of the Independents. In the first week of 1960, Antoine Pinay, the Minister of Finance, was unceremoniously dismissed by the President of the Republic. The policy of self-determination for Algeria began to divide the Independents, while the presidential style of government undermined seriously their role in Parliament. They began to move increasingly into the opposition as more than half their members began to vote against the government on a number of issues. A majority of their members abstained during the vote for the investiture of the Pompidou government and voted to censure him.

In its last party congress, held in June, 1962, the party criticized sharply de Gaulle's Algerian policy and came out openly in favor of European integration. It attacked government by referendum and urged the respect of the Constitution.

Activist Formations

Virtually without supporters and without organization, Poujade continued after the electoral setback of November, 1958, to speak in favor of French Algeria, to issue appeals to various military leaders to "take over," and to demand a drastic overhaul of the Fifth Republic. Most of the other Right-wing groups limited themselves to specific objectives. Many of the veterans' organizations agitated in favor of the "integration" of Algeria and against de Gaulle's policy of self-determination. Other formations were reconstituted under new names and reacted vehemently to de Gaulle's promise of self-determination. The Unity of the Republic continued to agitate for the maintenance of French rule in Algeria, until July 5, 1962, when the deputies from Algeria were deprived of their seats. They were joined by a motley of deputies from among the Independents and some others to become the "nationalist" opposition to General de Gaulle's government, voting frequently with the Communists and the Socialists against the government for diametrically opposed reasons.

Between the middle of 1961 and July, 1962, a secret organization—the O.A.S. (*Organisation de l'Armée Secrète*), the Secret Organization of the Army—took over the leadership of the activist groups. It indulged in indiscriminate acts of terrorism and assassination in which many innocent victims perished both in Algeria and France. It conspired to assassinate de Gaulle and proclaimed its determination to keep Algeria French. The Organization seemed to have the support and sympathy of many influential and political leaders, and it appeared for some time that it might be able to block de Gaulle's policy of self-determination. It was only after January, 1962, that intensive police efforts led to the arrest of many of its leaders, including the two top generals, Jouhaud and Salan, and to the dismantling of the Organization in France. With the declaration of Algerian independence, its strength seems to have been spent.

The massive exodus of the French from Algeria into France in the summer and early fall of 1962 led many to fear that the Organization would recruit from among them. Violence seems to have come to an end, and although the reappearance of activist groups cannot be ruled out, their threat to the Gaullist regime is no longer as serious as it was in the past.

As the first legislature of the Fifth Republic entered its last year, most of the party formations had moved into opposition both to de Gaulle's Cabinet and to his own personal rule. The only exception remained the UNR, which, true to its pledge, has been the party of fidelity. The prospect that it would win the next legislative elections as the "party of de Gaulle" naturally cemented the bonds of loyalty to de Gaulle.

Were the political parties in a position to provide a constructive and effective opposition to de Gaulle? Could they mobilize public opinion against him and his government? In case of a new election, would the floating vote return to the traditional parties or would it remain loyal to the UNR and to de Gaulle? Until October, 1962, none of these questions could have been answered. In the first week of October, however, three spectacular developments were to test the very foundations of the new political system and with it the strength of the political parties and the popularity of President de Gaulle. In the middle of September, 1962, de Gaulle announced, as we have seen, his intention of by-passing the Parliament and organizing a referendum in which he proposed and strongly favored the election of the future President of the Republic by direct popular vote. Sharply stung by de Gaulle's intention to amend the Constitution without consulting it first, the National Assembly for the first time in four years voted to censure the Prime Minister and his Cabinet (since it could not censure the President who, as we noted, is politically irresponsible), thus forcing their resignation. De Gaulle retorted by pronouncing the dissolution of the National Assembly, by reiterating his intention to hold the referendum on October 28, and by ordering new legislative elections for November 18 and 25, 1962. The issue between all the parties (excepting the UNR, which remained faithful to de Gaulle) and de Gaulle was to be joined for the first time since his return to power. Many commentators remembered that when de Gaulle had confronted all the political parties in 1946 he had lost. Was history to repeat itself?

Government and Parliament

The Cabinet of Michel Debré, formed in January, 1959, was endorsed by the National Assembly with an overwhelming vote of 453 to 56 (the latter mostly Socialists and Communists). In the last two motions of censure introduced against the Cabinet (there were six in all), in November, 1960, and December, 1961, the opposition grew. On the motion of censure introduced against the government military budget providing for nuclear weapons and an independent striking force, 210 deputies voted against the Cabinet—out of the absolute majority of 277 votes needed to bring the Cabinet down (Table 8-2). In the second motion of censure, introduced against the government's general policies, 199 deputies voted against the Cabinet.

A number of reasons, as we have seen, accounted for the weakening of parliamentary support. The Communists remained opposed from the beginning. They were joined by the Socialists, who also dislike de Gaulle's personal government (though they had earlier supported his Constitution) and oppose the government's social, military, and foreign policy. But the crucial factor that produced the shift against the government was the opposition of the Right (the Independents) and the extreme Right and the beginning of wavering of the Center groups—notably the MRP and the Radicals. Immediately after the announcement of the policy of self-determination for

The Evolution of Political Forces

TABLE 7-2   *The Last Two Votes of Censure against the Cabinet of Michel Debré*

November 22, 1960. Breakdown of the 210 votes against the Cabinet (the vote was on the budget's credits for atomic striking force).

December 18, 1961. Breakdown of the 199 votes against the Cabinet (the vote was on the government's general policies).

9 Communists (out of 10)	10 Communists
45 Socialists (out of 45)	44 Socialists (out of 45)
17 Radicals (out of 18)	23 Entente Démocratique (out of 36)
8 Entente Démocratique (out of 19)	23 MRP (out of 57)
21 MRP (out of 59)	42 Independents (out of 121)
69 Independents (out of 122)	36 Unity of the Republic (out of 38)
22 Unity of the Republic (out of 32)	1 UNR (out of 208)
19 Nonregistered (out of 36)	20 Nonregistered (out of 36)
210	199

Algeria, many of the deputies elected from Algeria formed a group called the Unity of the Republic, which was opposed to self-determination and favored integration. They began to vote regularly against the government. Many of the Independents, perhaps 50 out of 120, who had favored a nationalist policy and the maintenance of French rule in Algeria also began to vote against the government. A small group of Radicals followed them. The MRP, while favoring the policy of self-determination, became increasingly restive with de Gaulle's social and economic policy and, above all, with his military policy and his unwillingness to accept military and political integration of Western Europe. Many parliamentary groups began to be hostile to the government and to de Gaulle himself for different and often opposed reasons. Communists and die-hard Right-wing activists then joined hands with Socialists, Independents, Radicals, and even MRP members against the government.

This opposition became even more pronounced after the resignation of Michel Debré, on April 14, 1962. This first "crisis" under the Fifth Republic was apparently caused by the reluctance of President de Gaulle to accept his Prime Minister's advice and dissolve the National Assembly and call for a new election. Debré reasoned that, as in

1958, the momentum of a referendum and the popularity of the achievement of peace in Algeria would insure a strong majority to his own Party—the UNR—whose record had been one of fidelity to General de Gaulle. He believed de Gaulle's coat tails might help the UNR win a major electoral victory. De Gaulle, however, refused to dissolve the National Assembly. As we saw earlier, he is reluctant to assume the leadership of a political party but at the same time fearful that a strong party in the National Assembly might develop a will and a policy of its own and thus prove to be an obstacle to his own policies. The crisis, if it were one, involved the first conflict between the President and one of his stanchest supporters. But the conflict never broke into view, since Michel Debré stepped down from office.

The new Prime Minister, Georges Pompidou, had served General de Gaulle in many capacities in the past. He had been a close personal adviser, had served for a short time on the Constitutional Council, and later became the Director of the Rothschild Bank. He had never sat in Parliament and had never been a political leader. He was the "President's man." Loyal to the conception of strong presidential power, he outlined before the National Assembly a governmental policy dealing almost exclusively with domestic, social, and economic problems and formed a Cabinet that differed little in its political composition and its membership from the preceding one.

The National Assembly expressed its discontent by giving to Pompidou only a very slim endorsement. He received 259 votes against 128, with about 155 members abstaining. Among those abstaining or voting against the government were 88 Independents, 21 MRP, and 20 Radicals. Speaking in the National Assembly, the veteran political leader, Paul Reynaud, expressed the sentiments of many deputies and underlined the personal character of the institutions of the Fifth Republic when he confronted Pompidou with the same challenge that a deputy raised against a Prime Minister named by King Louis-Philippe: "The proof that we do not live under a parliamentary regime is that you are here." Pompidou, Reynaud claimed, was a political unknown; as with Louis-Philippe's Prime Minister, he had only the "King's" confidence!

Soon the first motion of censure against the new Cabinet was introduced; 205 delegates out of 480 voted against the Pompidou government—the highest percentage of negative votes ever cast on a motion of censure.[4] In addition to 10 Communists and 43 Socialists, 25 Entente Démocratique (Radicals), 33 MRP, 69 Independents, and 26 "Nonregistered" voted for the motion against the government. The MRP moved increasingly into opposition as the foreign policy of President de Gaulle came under mounting criticism. An absolute majority of deputies—293—signed a resolution in favor of a politically integrated Europe to which the President is opposed. With the granting of Algerian independence, it seemed inevitable that de Gaulle and his Cabinet would meet stiffening parliamentary opposition.

Crisis and Gaullist Victory

The restiveness of the National Assembly and the political parties came to a

[4] As we have seen, the first step taken by de Gaulle after the declaration of Algerian independence was to deprive all deputies and senators elected in November, 1958, in Algeria and Sahara of their seats. Thus the total membership of the National Assembly fell from 554 to 482. This did not seriously affect the balance of forces in the National Assembly, as can be seen from Fig. 7-2.

head in a rather explosive manner when de Gaulle proposed a referendum to modify the manner in which the President of the Republic was to be elected. It was not so much the substance of the reform—direct popular election of the President—but the manner in which de Gaulle proposed to modify the Constitution that united the political parties and their leaders against him and his Prime Minister. The Constitution provides (Article 89) that no bill amending the Constitution can be submitted directly to the people in a referendum without being adopted first by the National Assembly and the Senate. At the same time, Article 11 allows the President, at the request of the Cabinet, to submit to the people in a referendum any bill related to the "organization of the public powers." De Gaulle claimed that Article 11 gave him the required authority, but the Parliament and the greatest majority of lawyers, including the Council of State and apparently even some of the members of the Constitutional Council, were of a different opinion. De Gaulle went ahead and submitted his reform directly to the people on October 28, 1962.

On October 5, the National Assembly, in order to express its hostility to the manner in which de Gaulle proposed to amend the Constitution, introduced a motion of censure. It was the eighth motion introduced in the National Assembly and it was destined to be the last: "The National Assembly . . . . Considering that democracy presupposes the respect of law and above all the respect of the supreme law—the Constitution; . . . Considering that the Constitution prepared by General de Gaulle and approved by the French people provides formally that a revision must be voted by the Parliament . . . ; Considering that by bypassing the vote of the two houses the President of the Republic is violating the Constitution of which he is the guardian; Considering that the President of the Republic cannot act except on the proposal of the government, hereby censures the government . . ." This was a stinging indictment of General de Gaulle's action. The censure motion against the government was the only way open to the National Assembly to express its disapproval of the President of the Republic.

The Government Crisis

All the political parties with the exception of the UNR voted in favor of the motion and against the government and de Gaulle. The vote for the motion (against the government) was as follows:

```
     10  Communists
     43  Socialists
     33  Entente Démocratique (out of 37)
     50  MRP (out of 57)
    109  Independents (out of 121)
      3  UNR (out of 176)
     32  (Non-registered)
```

Total 280

Thus 280 members voted for the motion and against the government. Of the 173 UNR, 6 MRP, 4 Entente Démocratique and 4 non-registered deputies who did not vote, virtually all of them by so doing were rejecting the motion and thus voting for the government. For the first time, the requisite absolute majority voted censure, and the government, five months after its formation, had no alternative according to the strict letter of the Constitution but to submit its resignation. Acting in accordance with the Constitution, de Gaulle dissolved the National Assembly, asked the same Prime Minister, Georges Pompidou, and his Cabinet to stay in office until the elections, and in addition to the referendum called for new legislative elections for the National Assembly for November 18 and November 25, 1962. The first governmental crisis had been opened and it was to lead to a crucial referendum, which pitted de Gaulle against the political parties, and to new elections, which were to test the strength of the parties that had dared openly challenge de Gaulle and his government.

The Referendum of October 28, 1962

Opposition to de Gaulle's reform and to his government came from all sides and parties: from the extreme Left, the Center, and the extreme Right. Communists and Socialists stood with the Independents and with some of the extreme Right-wing deputies that had belonged to the Unity of the Republic faction. It was a classic case of a negative coalition of forces, for it was unlikely that these parties and groups could unite either to provide an alternative to de Gaulle or to form a harmonious coalition in the legislative elections. This was the first (and some expected the last) revolt of the "old parties" against de Gaulle. But the opposition to de Gaulle was massive. All parties, except for the UNR and minor groups of defectors in the other parties, were set against the President. The "280," as those who voted for the motion and against de Gaulle came to be called, solidly represented the party leadership; they controlled their party organizations as well as influential newspapers and considerable funds, but television and radio remained in the hands of the government. In the legislative elections of 1958, all these parties together had received more than 75 per cent of the national vote. They now seemed determined and active to carry their fight to the people.

The arguments of the opposition revolved around the following three points: (1) de Gaulle, in submitting a constitutional amendment by referendum to the people without consulting Parliament, had violated the Constitution; (2) the substance of the reform itself would increase greatly the powers of his successor without providing for any checks and would thus lead to a plebiscitary one-man government—some, including the influential and respected Speaker of the Senate, Gaston Monnerville, claimed that this was a return to Bonapartism; (3) de Gaulle's view that the Presidency is a policy-making post, overriding all other organs, constituted a radical departure from parliamentary government and was a gross violation of the Constitution that was written by de Gaulle and his associates. These arguments were cogent enough, but the parties were not in complete agreement. Only the Communists accepted all of them. Many of the MRP and the Independents and some of the Socialists were not opposed to a strong executive nor were they inimical to the popular election of the President. Some of the MRP leaders, in fact, wavered at the last moment and suggested to their followers to vote as they pleased. None of the parties, except the Communists, were anxious to see the return of the parliamentary institutions and practices as they had developed under the Fourth Republic. They favored executive leadership and were willing to allow the rules of a "rationalized Parliament" to continue to exist, but they remained attached to the basic prerogatives of Parliament—control of the government and enactment of legislation. They reasoned that a parliamentary government implied above all things a government that was responsible to the elected representatives of the people. An all powerful President, armed with a seven-year popular mandate and free to appeal directly to the public through referendums and to manipulate public opinion might, as it had happened before in France, destroy republican liberties.

There is no doubt that the challenge of the political parties was both effective and powerful. Communists, Socialists, Radicals, Independents, the MRP, and many Right-wingers actively campaigned for a "no" vote. Despite some of the equivocations of the MRP leaders and some second thoughts on the part of the Independents, this was the most powerful combination of forces ever arrayed against de Gaulle since his return to power. It was strengthened by the resolutions and activities of many other associations—of trade unions, students, progressive Catholic organizations, and, on the Right, the European refugees from Algeria, the Poujadists, and other extremist groups.

De Gaulle had no alternative but to throw his immense popularity onto the scales. He appeared four times on national television to urge a "yes" vote. He attacked the political factions that were agitating against him and reminded the French of the record of his regime as compared with that of the Fourth Republic. He asked for unity—and when the Cuban crisis erupted the week before the referendum, he raised a question that was to carry special weight: were the French prepared to vote against him in a time of world crisis? He left no doubt that if the majority of "yes" was "small and uncertain" he would withdraw for good from politics. In other words, de Gaulle had transformed the referendum into a vote of confidence for or against himself. "For me," he declared, "each 'yes' vote given to me by each one of you . . . will be the direct proof of his or her confidence and encouragement. Believe me, I am in need of this for what I may still do, just as I needed it in the past, for what I have already done. It is therefore your answer which, on October 28, will tell me if I can and if I should pursue my task in the service of France." Thus the referendum on a constitutional question became a plebiscite. The political parties found out that they had to fight against de Gaulle, not against his proposed reform. They were forced into a position of asking the French people by voting "no" to vote de Gaulle out of office. In so doing, they were challenging everything that the people were associating rightly or wrongly with de Gaulle—prosperity, peace in Algeria, full employment, continuing progressive social legislation, and national strength. When the Cuban crisis darkened the shadows across a world in conflict, de Gaulle's chances of victory became good, despite the opposition of the political parties.

THE RESULTS. About 62 per cent of the voters voted "yes" and 38 per cent "no" to the following question.

The Text of the Referendum of October 28, 1962. Do you approve of the bill submitted to

TABLE 7-3 *The Four Referendums, 1958–1962*

Date	Registered voters	Abstentions		Voters	Nullified
		Number	Percent-age		
Sept. 28, 1958	26,603,464	4,006,614	15.06%	22,596,850	303,549
Jan. 8, 1961	27,184,408	6,393,162	23.51	20,791,246	594,699
April 8, 1962	26,991,743	6,589,837	24.41	20,401,906	1,098,238
Oct. 28, 1962	27,579,424	6,273,301	22.75	21,306,123	565,474

the French people by the President of the Republic concerning the election of the President of the Republic by universal suffrage?

Principal Parts of the Text of the Submitted Bill. Article 6: The President of the Republic shall be elected for seven years by direct universal suffrage. Article 7: The President of the Republic shall be elected by an absolute majority of the votes cast. If this is not obtained on the first ballot, there shall be a second ballot on the second Sunday following. Only the two candidates who have received the greatest number of votes on the first ballot shall present themselves, taking into account the possible withdrawal of more favored candidates.

Out of some 27,500,000 registered voters, 12,808,600 voted "yes" and some 8,000,000 "no," while over 6 million abstained. The "yes" vote represented only about 46.5 per cent of the registered voters. Although in 1958 de Gaulle's Constitution had been endorsed by almost 80 per cent of the actual voters and 66.5 per cent of the registered voters, his reform was endorsed by only 62 per cent of the actual voters and by only 46.5 per cent of the registered voters in 1962. (See Table 7-3.) The number of "no" voters, in other words—to the Constitution and to de Gaule—had increased appreciably—from 17.3 per cent of the registered voters in 1958 to 28.7 per cent in 1962 and from 20.7 per cent of the actual voters in 1958 to a little over 38 per cent in 1962. De Gaulle was unable for the first time to clearly defeat the political parties and to hold on to his national constituency as he had done so successfully in 1958 and again in the referendum of Jan-

uary 8, 1961. A little less than four out of ten voters had rejected his appeal, while a fraction of those who abstained did so because they failed to heed it. After four years, de Gaulle's popularity seemed to be in peril and the Gaullist regime in crisis. Was this a portent of the outcome of the new elections? Would the parties that urged a "no" vote—both from the Right and the Left—be able to unite? Could they at least form tactical electoral alliances and isolate the Gaullist party—the UNR?

The Legislative Elections of November, 1962

Long before Sunday, November 18, 1962, the parties got busy for the legislative elections. Their mood was greatly changed when compared with the legislative elections of November, 1958. With the Algerian war settled and with a taste of victory after the overthrow of the Cabinet, the "280" and the political parties they represented, instead of being in a defensive state of mind, now took the offensive. There was no feeling of the inevitability of defeat and helplessness of 1958. In a prosperous and secure France, the indispensability of one man did not loom as large as it did in 1958. It was also the turn of the parties to challenge de Gaulle's policies instead of allowing him to continue to pass sentence on their record in the period of the Fourth Republic. De Gaulle's policy with regard to Europe, his anti-NATO stand, his large military budget for the building of a French atomic force, his unwillingness to proceed faster with social and economic reforms, his personal government—all came under sharp review. De Gaulle had been able to attack quite convincingly the

TABLE 7-3 (cont.)

Date	Valid ballots	"Yes"	"No"	Percentage of registered voters		Percentage of actual voters	
				"Yes"	"No"	"Yes"	"No"
Sept. 28, 1958	22,291,301	17,668,790	4,624,790	66.41%	17.38%	79.25%	20.74%
Jan. 8, 1961	20,196,547	15,200,547	4,999,474	55.91	18.37	75.26	24.73
April 8, 1962	19,303,668	17,508,607	1,795,060	64.86	6.65	90.70	9.29
Oct. 28, 1962	20,740,649	12,808,196	7,932,453	46.44	28.76	61.75	38.25

record of the Fourth Republic. The party leaders were now in a position to retaliate by attacking his own record. But how convincing their arguments would prove to be remained to be seen.

The first weakness of the opposition to de Gaulle lay in the fact that it was divided. Communists, Socialists, MRP, Radicals, and Independents, despite the equivocation of some of them, seemed united in an effort to block the UNR and to return a "republican majority." Yet there was no unity among these parties. The Communists had been isolated for too long and remained suspect in the eyes of the other parties; the Socialists and the Independents had followed different programs and different approaches to the Algerian conflict; the MRP was at odds with both Communists and Socialists on the question of the subsidies to Catholic schools; the Radicals had little to offer that was new. It was unlikely that these parties could cooperate. "Anti-Gaullism," therefore, did not embody any specific program that could be translated into action. This was made abundantly clear in the early efforts to make alliances and to agree on a common candidate to run against the Gaullists. Agreement with the Communists on the first ballot was avoided almost everywhere. But agreements even among the four genuinely republican parties—Socialists, MRP, Radicals, and Independents—proved to be equally difficult. Only in some isolated Departments were such agreements reached. Independents, MRP, Radicals, and Socialists ran against each other and against the Communists and the Gaullists. The contrast with the apparent unity of the Gaullists was obvious. An Association for the Support of the Fifth

Republic was formed on October 17, 1962, under the direction of the Secretary of State for Cultural Affairs, André Malraux. It managed to split the ranks of the Independents and, to some extent, of the MRP. Some thirty Independents and fifteen MRP ran as Gaullists under the label of the "Association for the Fifth Republic." The program of the Gaullists was unambiguous: support of General de Gaulle, the maintenance of the institutions of the Fifth Republic, and the continuation of de Gaulle's policies.

On November 7, General de Gaulle himself did for the first time what no other President of the Republic had done since the very beginning of the Third Republic in 1877, when President MacMahon appealed directly to the people to vote for his candidates. In a televised address, de Gaulle asked the French voters to vote for those who supported him. De Gaulle contrasted the stand taken by the parties with the results of the referendum of October 28, 1962, and concluded that the "old parties" no longer represented the nation. He accused them of slipping back into the old practices and habits and expressed the firm belief that the nation would reject them in the elections as it did in the referendum. If the Parliament "which holds the legislative power and controls the government" is to be dominated again by the "fractions" of yesterday, de Gaulle charged, then it would be unable to govern; the country would once more be confronted with political chaos and paralysis: "Men and women of France. . . . You sealed the condemnation of the disastrous regime of the political parties on October 28, 1962, and expressed your will to see the new Republic continue its task of progress, development and reconstruction. But on November 18 and 25 you will choose the deputies. Ah! I hope you will do it in such a manner that this second vote will not go against the first. In spite of local habits and particular considerations I hope you will now confirm by the choice of men the choice of our destiny you made by voting yes." The electoral contest became once more transformed into a plebiscite, and de Gaulle's immense popularity was again thrown into the balance. In the days preceding the election, his role became even more prominent since many of his closest followers hinted that if the election should return a majority of the "old parties," President de Gaulle might resign.

THE ELECTION. For the election of the National Assembly, the same electoral districts as in 1958 were used. Four hundred and sixty-five seats were at stake for Metropolitan France, with another seventeen from the overseas Departments—bringing the total to 482. More than 2,000 candidates ran, averaging a little over four candidates for each seat. The UNR and the Communist Party ran or supported candidates in virtually every district. The Socialists, Independents, SFIO, and Radicals were represented in at least three-fourths of the districts. As in the past, radio and television time was equally distributed. All political parties presenting more than 75 candidates were given seven minutes on TV and seven minutes on radio each. Between October 29, when the electoral campaign was opened officially, and election day the candidates canvassed their districts, spoke in innumerable meetings, and solicited the vote of the people. Hardly any nation-wide meetings were held and, except for the confrontation between de Gaulle and his UNR followers and the "old

parties," as he derisively called them, there was no overriding national issue at stake. In some areas, where a modicum of agreement had been reached among the republican parties, there appeared to be an anti-Gaullist platform favoring: a constitutional reform to give more powers to the Assembly and to curtail the powers of the President; European integration; and a European, rather than an exclusively French, atomic force. The Gaullists remained identified with a French nuclear force, a loose European association, and a strong presidential system. For the rest, the candidates talked about local and technical issues and discussed their record of fidelity or opposition to de Gaulle. As in the past, the Communists appeared to be better organized and able to mobilize larger audiences than the other parties.

THE RESULTS. The first ballot of November 18 demonstrated once more de Gaulle's overwhelming impact on the French political scene. The election was in essence a second referendum. The UNR won an unprecedented 31.9 per cent of the vote, and all the other parties, with the notable exception of the Communists, lost. As Table 7-4 indicates, only the Communist Party improved its relative and absolute strength compared with that in 1958, yet it failed to recover the strength it had in the earlier postwar years.

The highest percentage of abstention in the French legislative history of the twentieth century was recorded. Of 27,535,019 registered voters, only 18,931,733 (68.75 per cent) went to the polls, and 8,603,286 (31.25 per cent of the registered voters) abstained. The UNR almost doubled its strength throughout the country. The Communists gained votes virtually everywhere. Socialists, MRP, Radicals, and especially the Independents lost, the former heavily and the latter decisively. The extreme right-wing groups were eliminated from the political scene. On the first ballot, however, despite the UNR strength, only 96 deputies received the requisite absolute majorities and were elected. Forty-six were from the UNR, 9 from the Communist Party, 13 from the MRP and 15 from among the Inde-

TABLE 7-4 *First Ballot, 1962, Compared to 1958*

Party	1962	Percentage	1958	Percentage
Communist Party	3,999,431	21.78%	3,870,184	18.9%
Left-wing Socialists and others	449,743	2.45	356,081	1.8
SFIO	2,319,662	12.65	3,176,557	15.5
Radicals and allied groups	1,384,998	7.56	1,710,710	8.3
UNR	5,847,405	31.9	3,589,362	17.5
MRP	1,635,452	8.92	2,408,370	11.8
Independents and Moderates	2,458,988	13.42	4,112,191	20.1
Republican Center	81,627	0.45	604,088	3.0
Extreme Right	159,682	0.87	664,008	3.2

pendents. Only one Socialist managed to win on the first ballot. Therefore, 369 seats remained to be decided on the second ballot of November 25.

The "old parties" singled out for de Gaulle's scorn had received a serious setback on the first ballot. Yet Communists and dissident Socialists (PSU), together with the Socialists and the Radicals, accounted for 44.44 per cent of the vote as compared to 44.5 per cent in 1958. The Left-wing forces had held their own. The UNR increased its strength by some 2,300,000 votes, while the Independents and the MRP, together with the extreme Right, lost some 3,500,000 votes. As in previous elections, a new "shift" of votes occurred. Part of them went to the UNR, and a smaller part into abstention. The vote for the anti-Gaullist parties exceeded by far the "no" to de Gaulle cast in the referendum of October. While only 38 per cent voted "no," Communists, Left-wing Socialists, and Socialists received between them a little over 36 per cent. Counting the votes cast for the Radicals and for the MRP and the Independents who had campaigned for a "no," the vote for the anti-Gaullist parties was much greater than the vote cast against de Gaulle's reform in the referendum—about 60%.

The Communist Party showed remarkable strength in the Paris region—perhaps the most modernized and richest area of France—capturing 31 per cent of the vote as opposed to 26 per cent in 1958. In the suburbs of Paris, the Communists received over 38 per cent of the vote as opposed to 32 per cent in 1958—in some cases managing to surpass in absolute and relative terms the strength they had shown in the period of the Fourth Republic. Thus, after France had experienced five years of economic modernization and unprecedented prosperity, the Communists—one of the oldest and, according to many commentators, most anachronistic of parties—not only held their own in the agricultural areas and in many of the provincial towns but improved considerably their position in the Paris region.

THE SECOND BALLOT. The aphorism about elections in France, "on the first ballot we choose; on the second ballot we eliminate," could hardly apply in this election. As we have seen, only 96 candidates were elected on the first ballot and 369 were to be chosen on the second. The first ballot had revealed the over-all trends of public opinion and party strength. Sunday, November 25 was the day of choice.

Between the first and second ballot of a French election, political activity as a rule becomes feverish. The party leaders try to discipline their candidates and decide who will run again and who will withdraw; local and departmental leaders agree to withdraw some of their candidates and throw the support of their voters behind the candidates of another party, preferably the one that promises to reciprocate in another district; disgruntled candidates often refuse to accept the instructions of their party and decide on their own whether to remain or withdraw their names.

The Evolution of Political Forces

The UNR hoped to capitalize on its first-ballot strength and urged alliances with other parties against the Communists. (See Tables 7-6 to 7-13 at the end of this chapter for the alliances that were formed and the votes that were received by various candidates in several specific districts.) This tactic had paid off well in 1958. In 1962, the reverse occurred. Alliances and agreements were made in the majority of cases against the UNR. Virtually all parties, sensing that unless they united against the Gaullists they faced extinction, decided to combine their strength by withdrawing the least likely candidate and supporting the most likely one from among their own. The Communists were shrewd in their tactics. They withdrew their candidates in favor of Socialist, Radical, MRP, and even Independent candidates. Sometimes they did so even when they headed the list of candidates on the first ballot. Communist voters followed the instructions of their party with remarkable discipline and voted for the candidate they were asked to support in the place of their own man. In return, Communist candidates received the open, but more often the tacit, support of the Socialists and benefited also from the withdrawal of Radicals and MRP candidates. But Socialist voters did not transfer their votes to a Communist candidate from the first to the second ballot. Communist transfers helped elect a number of Socialists, including the leader of the Socialist Party, Guy Mollet. The MRP and Independents played a less important role on the second ballot. Often they withdrew their candidate without any indication of whom they favored, and not infrequently they remained on the second ballot despite heavy odds against them.

In some districts, the Gaullist candidates followed the tactics of the Communists and withdrew to throw their support behind anti-Communist candidates. In return, when they faced Communists in straight fights they benefited to a considerable degree not only from

Independent but also from Radical and MRP and sometimes even Socialist votes. The Radicals, true to their past history and tradition, did remarkably well. Supported both by the Communists and the Socialists in certain districts *against* a UNR candidate, they were also supported in other districts by the UNR, the Independents, and often the MRP *against* a Communist. Thus, with only 8.3 per cent of the popular vote and 7 per cent of the vote cast on the second ballot, they managed to return 42 deputies to the National Assembly.

On the day of the second balloting, the electoral picture had assumed an unprecedented pattern. For the 369 seats that remained to be filled, there were only 889 candidates. In 227 districts, a straight fight involved only two candidates; in 130 districts, a triangular election involved three candidates; and finally in only eleven districts were four candidates facing one another. The UNR was engaged in about 195 straight fights: 100 with the Communists, 2 with the Left-wing Socialists (PSU), 58 with the Socialists, 18 with the Radicals, 13 with the Independents and 6 with the MRP. The other straight fights brought into face-to face-conflict Socialists and Communists, Communists and Radicals, Communists and MRP, Radicals and MRP, Independents and Communists or MRP, and Radicals and Independents. In the triangular fights, UNR, Communists, Independents, Radicals, Socialists, and MRP were mixed in various combinations that reflected no discernible political pattern. Yet the second ballot simplified the choice of the voters by limiting the number of candidates to two or three. In fact, the second ballot resembled, at least for the majority of the undecided seats, the national election of England or West Germany.

With the exception of the appearance on television of the Prime Minister—the reputed leader of the UNR, Georges Pompidou—there was no national campaigning. The candidates fought it out among themselves in their electoral districts and were occasionally aided by the appearance of a national leader who came to talk on their behalf. Outside the districts in which important political leaders (such as the leader of the Socialists, Guy Mollet, and

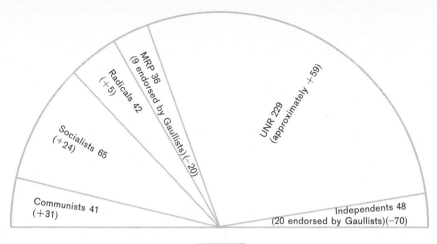

Speaker

FIGURE 7-3   THE NATIONAL ASSEMBLY AFTER THE NOVEMBER, 1962, ELECTIONS.
(Gains and losses are given in parentheses. Figures apply only to the 465 seats for Metropolitan France. The 17 seats for the overseas departments are not included. If we add the 9 MRP and the 20 Independents endorsed by the Gaullists to the 229 UNR, we arrive at a "Gaullist" majority of 258.)

the titular leader of the UNR, Michel Debré) were staking their political future or where there was a close fight involving Communists and the UNR, apathy seemed to prevail and abstentions remained high.

THE RESULTS. As was expected, the UNR transformed the electoral sweep (Table 7-5) into a sizable gain of seats (Fig. 7-3). Of the 369 seats at stake, it captured 183, bringing its total to 223. This was not a majority but when added to the 30 or so Independents and MRP who were pledged to support General de Gaulle, the UNR had what appeared to be a solid and stable backing to form a government. Never before in the political history of France had one party controlled so many seats. The Communists, second in the popular vote, benefited this time from some of the anti-UNR sentiment, the "popular front" arrangements, and the inability of the other political parties to unite against them as they had done in 1958. The party returned 32 candidates, bringing its total to 41. The Socialists became the largest party of the opposition thanks to Communist support. They won 64 seats, bringing their total parliamentary strength to 65.

TABLE 7-5   *The Second Ballot, 1962*

Party	Votes	Per-centage
Communist Party	3,243,041	21.3%
Left-wing Socialists and others	183,844	1.2
SFIO	2,304,330	15.2
Radicals and allied groups	1,068,101	7.0
UNR	6,165,929	40.5
MRP	806,908	5.3
Independents and Moderates	1,367,841	7.4[a]
Republican Center	51,164	0.4

[a] Of which a good percentage went to those receiving Gaullist support.

The Radicals showed remarkable staying power for the reasons alluded to earlier. They won 34 seats, bringing their total to 42. The MRP, Independents, and the extreme Right lost heavily. It is doubtful that the Independents can muster the requisite number of parliamentarians—thirty—to form a parliamentary group of their own. On the other hand, the Communists will have their own parliamen-

The Evolution of Political Forces

239

tary group. Socialists and Communists together have almost twenty-five per cent of the members of the National Assembly, while in 1958 they had less than ten per cent. Together with the Radicals and some of the Independents and the MRP, there are at least 200 deputies out of a total of 482 that may be considered to belong to the opposition.

Many observers believe that the November election will initiate a radical transformation of the French political scene, while others see in it only a proof of de Gaulle's undiminished popularity. The election, in fact, amounted to a second referendum in which the voters reasserted, as they had done a month earlier, their confidence in de Gaulle. It was not so much the UNR that won but the "Gaullist" Party. It was de Gaulle himself who had urged the voters to vote for the men who had supported him. The UNR victory underscored the personal element of the Gaullist regime, this time even at the electoral and party level. This shows again the fragility of the French political system and begs the question about the future of the regime that we shall discuss at the end of this essay.

Although the Gaullists triumphed, the "anti-Gaullists" came out much better than in 1958. In 1958, *all* political parties, with the exception of the Communists, supported General de Gaulle, favored the Constitution of the Fifth Republic, and participated through their leaders in the Gaullist Cabinet. The nation, and with it the electorate, was Gaullist. In November, 1962, however, the anti-Gaullist forces had not only managed to become a political entity—even if defined in negative terms—but had won a majority of the electoral vote. If we add the votes cast for the Independents and the MRP to the Communist-Socialist-Radical strength, which amounted to slightly over 44 per cent of the vote, the total anti-Gaullist vote was about 60 per cent of the voters. The "old parties" had lost an elec-

toral battle. They were neither defeated nor dead.

The high percentage of abstentions also produced an element of instability. About 31 per cent of the registered voters abstained on the first ballot and approximately the same percentage refrained from going to the polls on the second ballot. Thus it appears that about 2,300,000 more registered voters abstained than in 1958. Why did so many voters abstain? One suggested reason was the complacency of the Gaullist supporters. But given the relatively narrow victory of General de Gaulle in the referendum—where abstentions also ran high—this cannot be seriously entertained. Another reason might have been the apathy of the electorate, an apathy born of prosperity and satisfaction. A third and more plausible hypothesis is that a higher percentage of voters stayed home because they could not make up their minds. Caught between conflicting inclinations, interests, ideas, and attachments, they became "paralyzed." They were not apathetic or complacent, but so torn by conflicting sentiments that they were unable to resolve them. Gaullism and the appeal of de Gaulle was not strong enough any more to draw them to the polls.

The victory of the UNR must be weighed carefully. Where did its votes—about 2,300,-000 above the 1958 strength and more than 1,000,000 above even the 1951 vote—come from? It is very hard to give a definitive answer to this crucial question. The best we can do is to relate the increased strength of the UNR with the major shift from the extreme Right and the Independents to the UNR or into abstention. Socialists, Communists, and Radicals just about held their own. But the Independents, the MRP, and the extreme Right lost about 14 per cent of their earlier share of the national vote (the UNR increased its national percentage by about the same figure), and they lost three and a half million votes; the UNR gained more than half of them while the others abstained. Only detailed studies will show who the voters were that swung to the UNR or moved into abstention. Until this is done, the conclusion is inescapable that the bulk of the votes that went to the UNR came from the Independents and the extreme Right and from a fraction of the MRP.

This transfer to the UNR may mean that the UNR benefited from the support of the conservative political forces associated with these parties. It may also mean that these parties were abandoned by the electorate in favor of the UNR because there has been a significant change in the composition and attitudes of the French electorate. Many commentators see in the shift the impact of economic and social modernization and deduce a transformation of French political attitudes and ideologies. According to the first hypothesis, the UNR strength came from the old conservative electoral forces because, with the declaration of Algerian independence and the symbolism of a strong nationalism represented by de Gaulle, these forces found in de Gaulle and the UNR the best expression of their aspirations. According to the second hypothesis, the victory of the UNR represented a profound restructuring of the electorate and reflected the interests and aspirations of new groups: white-collar workers, industrialists, new agricultural groups, and even unionized workers, together with the growing numbers employed in the tertiary sector of the economy. The sweeping victory of the UNR therefore represented the emergence of new social forces and may be considered as the first step in the development of a new electorate and the disappearance of the "old parties." Both these hypotheses should be examined in the light of three other important considerations: the impact of de Gaulle himself on the electorate, the organization of the UNR as a party, and the relative growth of Communist strength and the formation of "popular front" alliances.

The close relationship between de Gaulle and the election can be shown by comparing the returns of the referendum and those of the election. In 21 Departments, the "yes" vote on October 28 amounted to over 70 per cent of the voters. In these Departments, which accounted for 100 seats in the National Assembly, not a single Communist was elected. Only 1 Socialist and 1 Left-wing Socialist (PSU)

squeezed by. The UNR won 70 seats and endorsed 9 victorious Independents, for a total of 79 "Gaullists." The remaining seats went to the MRP (14), the Independents (3), and the Radicals (2). By contrast, in the 12 Departments (accounting for 46 seats) in which there was a majority of "no" votes in the referendum, the Socialists won 24 seats and the Communists 10. The UNR won only 8, with the remaining going to the Radicals (3) and the MRP (1). The Departments that returned a massive "yes" vote and a massive UNR majority generally correspond to the traditional strongholds of French conservatism—the same Departments voted conservative in the past. They voted for the conservative Parliament in the elections of 1919, and supported the MRP, the Independents, and the RPF in the post-World War II period. The Departments that voted "no" and spurned the UNR in favor of Socialists, Communists, and Radicals are the ones traditionally associated with the Left. Whatever the new meaning of party labels, the voting pattern of the French seems to be deeply rooted in past habits and attitudes.

As for the UNR, it is a conglomeration of candidates who, as in 1958, pledged their unequivocal support to General de Gaulle. It is a party whose existence and program depend on the immense popularity and powers of one man. Like the Independents and, to some extent, the Radicals, it continues to have no membership, no regional organizations, and no national organization or leadership. It is a bloc rather than a party.

For the first time since 1936, the Communists moved out of their political isolation and cooperated with the Socialists and the Radicals. In approximately forty out of the ninety Departments, Radicals, Communists, and Socialists (including the Left-wing Socialists) formed open or tacit "popular front" alliances to support each other on the second ballot. In thirty Departments, these alliances accounted

The Evolution of Political Forces

First Ballot		Second Ballot	
FIRST ELECTORAL DISTRICT			
R. Carrié, *UNR*	11,991	R. Carrié	16,630
P. Grasset-Morel, *Independent*	10,044	P. Grasset-Morel	18,805
P. Ville, *Communist*	9,075 ⎫		
E. Ponseillé, *Radical*	6,773 ⎬	E. Poinsellé	18,805
Chaulliac, *Socialist*	5,959 ⎭		
THIRD ELECTORAL DISTRICT			
C. Lurie, *UNR*	12,042	C. Lurie	16,836
M. Calas, *Communist*	13,581 ⎫		
Jules Moch, *Socialist*	11,313 ⎬	Jules Moch	24,281
Thiery, *Independent*	3,026 ⎭		
FOURTH ELECTORAL DISTRICT			
A. Valbrigue, *UNR*	13,004	Valbrigue	20,291
Balmigére, *Communist*	12,298 ⎫	Balmigére	21,747
Crouzet, *Socialist*	6,707 ⎬		
de Seriége, *Independent*	2,839 ⎭		

a Communists, Socialists, and Radicals supported each other in the Hérault Department and won one seat each.

First Ballot		Second Ballot	
Dhotel, *Gaullist*	14,233	Dhotel	21,810
Guy Mollet, *Leader of Socialists*	12,944 ⎫	Guy Mollet	24,375
Coquel, *Communist*	11,362 ⎬		
Pouchrison, *MRP*	5,960 ⎭		
M. Debré, *Leader of UNR*	15,588	Debré	20,712
Berthouin, *Radical*	9,579 ⎫		
Mme. Boutard, *Communist*	7,576 ⎬	Berthouin	23,667
Le Garec (*Left-wing Socialist or PSU*)	2,962 ⎭		
Courteggiani, *Moderate*	1,066		

a The Communists helped elect the leader of the Socialist Party and defeat the leader of the UNR. In a number of districts, the Communists used their strength to elect a potential ally and block key UNR figures. Some ten important political leaders, mostly Socialists and Radicals and one Independent, owe their election to Communist support.

TABLE 7-8 *Many "Popular Front" Alliances Failed*

First Ballot		Second Ballot	
Moulin, *UNR*	12,054	Moulin	17,854
Ulrici, *Communist*	6,829 ⎫	Ulrici	12,358
Courtin, *Socialist*	5,222 ⎬		
Cantimican, *Independent*	1,853		

for the victory of at least one "popular front" candidate. In the remaining ten Departments, the alliances failed to win a seat, and in the majority of electoral districts, no alliances at all were formed. When the candidate was a Radical or, particularly, a Socialist, the "popular front" alliance worked better. When the candidate was a Communist, the "anti-Communist" reflexes of the public tended to decrease the size of the candidate's vote. As is the case with the Gaullist party, the "popular front" alliance does not constitute a party or even an homogeneous bloc. Spurred by an anti-Gaullist attitude, it is also unlikely to survive de Gaulle. Both Gaullism and the "popular front" alliance represent temporary blocs, not the crystallization of political forces into new patterns.

The governmental crisis that was provoked by de Gaulle's referendum was thus resolved with an over-all Gaullist victory. The Constitution was modified in the way de Gaulle

wished, and the new elections returned what seems to be a Gaullist majority. The same Prime Minister who was overthrown on October 5, Georges Pompidou, and who remained in office during the referendum and the election, was asked to form a Cabinet. He made only minor changes in the Cabinet that had been overthrown. The vote of confidence he asked of the new Assembly that convened at the end of 1962 was a mere formality. He and his government were officially endorsed by a vote of 268 to 116, with 81 abstentions. Thus the Fifth Republic under de Gaulle's leadership seemed secure. But a strong minority of Communists, Socialists, and Radicals, together with many of the Independents and the MRP, sits in sullen and overt opposition to de Gaulle and his government. Their tactics will be directed against the Gaullist bloc in an effort to disrupt its unity and voting discipline.

TABLE 7-9 *The UNR Carried All 31 Seats of Paris* (Mostly in Straight Fights with Communists)

First Ballot		Second Ballot	
Ruais, *UNR*	13,238	*Ruais*	16,243
Sibaud, *Communist*	10,200	*Sibaud*	14,084
Ribera, *Independent*	3,000		
Billebaut, *Socialist*	2,136		
Mardi, *PSU*	1,918		

TABLE 7-10 *The Paris Suburbs Voted for Candidates of the Left* [a]

First Ballot		Second Ballot	
THIRTY-SIXTH DISTRICT			
L'Huillier, *Communist*	20,010 ⎤	*L'Huillier*	25,588
Stibbe, *PSU*	2,706 ⎬		
Le Savouzoux, *Socialist*	2,195 ⎦		
Devaud, *UNR*	17,173	*Devaud*	· 21,551
Bideau, *Independent*	4,533		
FIFTIETH DISTRICT			
Maurice Thorez, *Leader*		(Elected on first bal-	
of the Communists	27,703	lot)	
Rochenoir, *UNR*	14,655		
Besse, *MRP*	5,073		

a In the Paris suburbs, the Communists showed their traditional strength, but the UNR won 10 of the 24 seats. Two were won by the Socialists with Communist support and the rest by the Communists.

TABLE 7-11 *Communists Won Many Seats in Triangular Fights* [a]

First Ballot		Second Ballot	
E. Carlier, *Communist*	11,809 ⎱	*Carlier*	19,172
Vincent, *Socialist*	9,014 ⎰		
Dubout, *UNR*	9,878	*Dubout*	13,547
Cassex, *MRP*	9,109	*Cassex*	11,604
Delporte (*Extreme*			
Right wing)	1,608		

a In fact, they won only 10 seats in straight fights. They picked up 22 seats in triangular contests. The division of the UNR and the Independents often helped the Communists, just as the division of the Left helped the UNR.

TABLE 7-12 *The UNR Supported Non-Communists To Defeat Communists*

First Ballot		Second Ballot	
Soury, *Communist*	14,836	Soury	22,450
Valentin, *Independent*			
(*Right wing*)	12,550 ⎱	*Valentin*	24,646
Alloncle, *UNR*	9,313 ⎰		
Perrot, *Radical*	8,916		
Mme. Grappe, *Communist*	10,251	Grappe	14,001
Gauthier, *Radical*	10,116 ⎱	*Gauthier*	20,589
Garcia, *UNR*	8,087 ⎰		
Landu, *Socialist*	4,289		

TABLE 7-13 *Many Run-offs Were Extremely Close* [a]

First Ballot		Second Ballot	
Peron, *Communist*	14,074	Peron	21,592
Guena, *UNR*	12,764	*Guena*	21,608
Rousser, *Radical*	9,830		
Gaille, *Socialist*	6,503		
Moras, *UNR*	18,651	Moras	23,868
Dusarthou, *Socialist*	14,772	*Dusarthou*	24,776
Feugas, *Communist*	7,120		
Defos de Rau, *Independent*	5,179		

a Some 40 of the 465 seats were won by less than a thousand votes. In most cases, the shift of less than one in a hundred votes would have changed the results. Many close contests involved the UNR against the Communists or the Socialists.

Governmental Performance under the Fifth Republic

VIII

An evaluation of the performance of the Fifth Republic may well be premature. In operation since January, 1959, it is more of a government of one man than a political system. De Gaulle symbolizes, as we noted, the Bonapartist tradition in France. It is he who governs and it is he, rather than the Constitution and the governmental institutions we examined in the preceding chapters, who embodies legitimacy. Perhaps the most crucial problem facing the country is: Will the governmental institutions remain the same after de Gaulle? Will the succession to the office of the Presidency be accomplished without serious dissension or will the present governmental machinery, and perhaps the Constitution, be radically transformed? With these troubling questions in mind, we will now attempt to present the balance sheet of the regime and to assess its performance.

Independence for the Former Colonies

During 1956–57, one of the most important steps in French colonial policy was taken when the Parliament of the Fourth Republic endorsed legislation granting the various African territories of France and Madagascar extensive local autonomy. These territories were given the power to legislate their internal affairs and to establish their own responsible governments, while matters concerning finance, defense, foreign policy, higher education, customs, and radio remained under the jurisdiction of the French government.

In 1958, President de Gaulle pledged to all these territories a new political arrangement—the French Community—and at the same time explicitly promised to respect their right to independence, if they opted for it in the referendum of September 28, 1958, by voting "No." All the territories, with the exception of Guinea, voted "Yes" and thus the French Community came into being. The territories became Republics "federated" with France. They were governed, however, by the President of the French Republic who was also President of the Community (de Gaulle), with the assistance of an Executive Council, consisting of a number of French Ministers charged with common Community affairs and the Prime Ministers, or their delegates, of the African Republics and Malagasy (formerly Madagascar). A Community Senate, with mostly consultative powers, was also established, and a Community Arbitration Court was created for the purpose of hearing and passing on controversies among the member states.

In the course of 1959–60, the Community was abandoned. Although it still exists in name, its institutions have been set aside. Speaking in Dakar, Senegal, in December, 1959, de Gaulle promised to grant "international sovereignty," that is, complete independence to all the African territories. Special accords between France and member states were passed and ratified by the French Parliament, providing for diverse modes of cooperation between France and the individual Republics in the domain of economic, social, cultural, and military affairs. All provisions can be renegotiated by new agreements and possibly canceled in the future. All African Republics and Malagasy have become independent and all of them have become members of the United Nations.

France under de Gaulle has thus liquidated her colonial Empire. In doing so, she has improved her position in Africa, where she is now assured of a reservoir of good will. Large subsidies to the African Republics and Malagasy guarantee their economic modernization, which will improve the living standards of the Africans and is eventually bound to increase French trade and investments in Africa.

Algeria

Progress in Algeria, where a powerful French minority and a strong Army were well entrenched, was slow. The action of the government can be divided into two areas: political and socio-economic.

The policy of self-determination, announced in September, 1959, put an end to the expectations of the French settlers to see Algeria become a permanent Department of the French Republic. Instead, de Gaulle offered the Algerians (French settlers and Moslems alike) an opportunity to decide their own future in a special referendum, in which they could choose integration, local autonomy, or independence. This policy provoked an uprising of the settlers early in 1960, and, a year later, when de Gaulle seemed prepared to grant independence, an abortive military putsch. On April 22, 1961, four top generals and a small number of select military units occupied the big Algerian towns in defiance of de Gaulle's authority. The bulk of the Army in Algeria wavered in the face of de Gaulle's determination and of the overwhelming support he received in France, and the putsch collapsed in a matter of four days. It was not until after the military putsch that de Gaulle moved resolutely against the Army insurgents and settlers. Many leaders and officers were arrested and brought to trial and a number of specialized Army formations were disbanded. The civil authority reasserted its claim over the military, and the delegates of the government in Algeria began to assume responsibility and to issue directives to the Army. But open defiance continued to flare up sporadically all over the war-torn region.

In the referendum held in France and Algeria on September 28, 1958, de Gaulle's Constitution was endorsed by a majority of over 95 per cent of the French settlers. Nobody denied that it was a personal vote for de Gaulle rather than for the Constitution. In the second referendum, however, of January 8, 1961, de Gaulle's policy of self-determination for Algeria failed to get a majority vote.[1] Negotiations between the French government, under the direct supervision of President de Gaulle, and the Algerian rebel organization— the Provisional Government of the Algerian Republic—progressed for many years without

[1] Out of 4,470,211 registered voters, 1,749,996 voted "Yes" and 767,546 voted "No."

result. France was unwilling to put the policy of self-determination into effect without firm guarantees for the *colons,* for the safety of the oil installations in the Sahara, and of some of her military bases in Algeria.

The socio-economic policy of the government concerning Algeria was announced by de Gaulle in a speech delivered in Constantine in September, 1958—and it became the basis of the so-called "Constantine Plan." The Algerian economy was to be extensively transformed and modernized, more jobs were to be created for the ever-expanding Algerian population, and steps were to be taken to eventually equalize Moslem and French incomes. The plan provided for: (1) an increase in the wages and salaries paid out in Algeria to bring them to a level comparable to those in France in a period of five years; (2) the distribution of some 670,000 acres of land to Moslem farmers; (3) a five-year plan at the end of which the Sahara oil and gas would be made available to Algerian industries and factories; (4) the development of steel and iron production centers; (5) the construction of housing for about one million people; (6) the construction of roads, ports, and airports. It was hoped that these measures would greatly increase employment opportunities and launch Algeria on the road to economic industrialization.

The 1960, 1961, and 1962 budgets for Algeria earmarked approximately $200,000,000 annually for public investment, which was designed primarily to develop sources of energy, spur industrial production, accelerate the construction of housing and of training centers and schools. The "schooling" of the Algerians became one of the major objectives of the government. In addition, efforts were made, in the form of subsidies and tax rebates, to encourage French businessmen to invest in new industries in Algeria. Thus a major effort to "modernize" Algeria seemed on the way. The wealth of the Saraha oil and gas will sooner or later make itself felt in the industrial and economic life of the region, and the economic effort made by the French, barring serious political upheavals, will inevitably benefit the Algerian people.

Negotiations between the French government and the Algerian revolutionary government were concluded at Evian on March 19, 1962, and the Evian agreements were announced to the public on the same day. They dealt with a great number of technical problems, particularly with regard to the status of the French citizens in Algeria. In substance, concessions were made on both sides; the ground rules were set for Algeria's independence as a state cooperating with France.

The agreements provided for an immediate cease-fire and for the establishment of a provisional caretaker government in Algeria to organize a referendum on self-determination; they gave to the Algerian population an opportunity to express in a referendum a choice between outright independence, independence in cooperation with France, and integration in the French Republic. Since it was presumed that the Algerians would opt for independence in cooperation with France, the Evian agreements provided detailed stipulations on the status of the French citizens. They were to remain French citizens. Even if they opted for Algerian citizenship within a period of 3 years, they could still retain their French citizenship and return to France; their property and freedoms were guaranteed. They were further guaranteed their own schools and publications. Special rights were to be bestowed upon the French who became Algerian citizens; a number of seats in the future Algerian Parliament were to be allotted to them, and they were to be given special representation in the large municipalities.

France maintained her rights to test atomic weapons in Sahara (which became part of Algeria), to maintain the naval base of Mers-El-Kebir for 15 years, to maintain control of three airports for three years, and to maintain the French Army on Algerian soil (but to reduce it progressively in numbers) for a period of three years. Special arrangements guaranteeing the French rights over the

Sahara oil were inserted. In return, France pledged to continue economic assistance to Algeria for at least three years, to maintain Algeria within the franc zone, to allow free transfer of money from and to Algeria (something of capital importance, since there are about 400,000 Algerians working in France), and to continue to provide for cultural and technical aid.

When these accords were ratified by Metropolitan France in a second referendum of April 8, 1962, the way was paved for Algerian independence. On July 1, 1962, the referendum took place in Algeria, and 99 per cent of the voters opted for independence in cooperation with France. On July 3, de Gaulle formally granted Algeria independence and dispatched the first French ambassador to Algeria. On July 5, he abolished the seats of the deputies and senators that were elected in Algeria in the elections of November, 1958. Thus a long, bitter war that lasted seven and a half years at a high cost for France and considerable loss of human life on both sides came to an end. Even more, the political passions that it had unleashed that brought down the Fourth Republic and twice endangered the Fifth were, if not buried, considerably weakened. As it was with the policy of colonial disengagement in Africa, the way was paved for better relations between France and an independent Algeria.

Anxiety about the political orientation of the new Algerian Republic was naturally expressed, and many doubted its ability to establish a tolerant democratic regime and safeguard the rights of the French citizens. Within a month after the declaration of independence, more than 500,000 French settlers had left for France, crowding the French cities in the South and the Southwest and the Paris region. Throughout 1962 the exodus continued. More than four-fifths of the French (about 800,000) had left Algeria for France by the end of the year. Economic life came virtually to a standstill, and the prospects of a Franco-Algerian association seemed endangered by the Left-wing orientation of the Algerian government.

Foreign Policy [2]

On June 1, 1958, when de Gaulle returned to office, the decline of French power in the world was only too obvious. The Suez adventure had swept aside the French cultural, political, and economic influence in the Middle East. In Indochina, the last French soldier had departed long before, leaving a feeling of bitterness and distrust; Morocco and Tunisia had become independent. In Algeria, the rebellion was gaining ground, and a praetorian army was in near revolt against the Republic. In Africa, signs of discontent were becoming ominous. In NATO, France's position was weak, especially when compared with the rising strength of West Germany. As in 1940, de Gaulle considered it his task to weave patiently the fabric of national unity and work for the restoration of French power.

De Gaulle has a vision of a renovated and strong France, with global commitments and world responsibilities. He wants France to weigh heavily in the contemporary balance of forces and to aspire once more to a vocation of world leadership. It is to this task that he has devoted all his energies.

The Memorandum
of September 24, 1958

Immediately after his return to power, de Gaulle asserted that it was not the purpose of France to limit her foreign policy "within the confines of NATO." Four days before the referendum on the Constitution of the Fifth Republic, he addressed a memorandum to President Eisenhower, Prime Minister Macmillan, and Henry Spaak, Secretary General

[2] For a more detailed discussion of French foreign policy, see Roy C. Macridis, ed., *Foreign Policy in World Politics*, 2nd ed. (Englewood Cliffs, N. J.: Prentice-Hall, Inc., 1962), Chapter 3.

of NATO. De Gaulle noted the common responsibilities imposed on the members of the alliance in case of war, but pointed to the inequality in armaments and, what is more, the inequality in the power to make decisions that existed among the allies. He proposed, therefore, the establishment within NATO of a "directorate" of three—England, France, and the United States—with responsibility for elaborating a common military and political strategy for the whole world, for creating allied commands for all theaters of operation, and for jointly deciding on the use of atomic weapons.

Although ostensibly the memorandum was addressed to problems related to NATO, de Gaulle was attempting to raise France to the level of a world power. NATO was to remain a regional organization, but with three of its members—France, England, and the United States—jointly in charge of global strategy. These three great powers were to be in charge, at the NATO level, of Atlantic problems and also jointly in charge of world-wide strategy. De Gaulle reiterated these demands in his press conferences of September 5, 1960, and May 15, 1962, reminding his audience that France had in the meantime become an atomic power.

The Bomb

Since France's allies were unwilling to subject the use of atomic weapons to the control of a "directorate," France proceeded to explode her own atom bomb and develop an ambitious nuclear program. A number of additional reasons were given for this move: the uncertainty about the use of the bomb by the United States; the need for a strictly French deterrent against a possible Russian attack; the desire to inject new pride into an Army that had experienced one frustration after another for over twenty years; and, finally, the need to bolster the world-wide interests of France.

France—Chapter VIII

248

The European Common Market

De Gaulle's enthusiasm for the Common Market has been motivated in part by economic reasons, by his desire for Europe to develop as a "whole." The crucial reason, however, is political. De Gaulle can grant concessions to the British in their bid to join the Common Market in return for British acquiescence to his provisions in the Memorandum of September 24 and also to his views on other issues, notably Berlin and atomic weapons. In repayment for Adenauer's support, he has become a stanch supporter of the Berlin *status quo*. Thus the foundations of a Franco-German *rapprochement* as the basis of a European political force have been laid.

De Gaulle has managed to gather an array of bargaining weapons in order to accomplish what he sought in the years after the Liberation—the achievement of a top rank in the world for France. With a strong Army—once it is moved from Algeria—equipped with atomic weapons, and with an effective striking force, France is an important—perhaps the most important—national force in Western Europe. De Gaulle expects to participate with the United States and England as an equal in all foreign-policy decisions. France, as the leader of a Western European alliance that has become increasingly stronger economically and politically, will achieve, he hopes, a position of world power comparable to that of the United States and the Soviet Union.

Early in 1963 the Franco-German rapprochement was strengthened by a treaty providing for closer cooperation between the two countries. De Gaulle's intransigence and his ambition to assume the leadership of Western Europe became clearer. On January 28, 1963, France vetoed Britain's entry into the Common Market. De Gaulle in a press conference reasserted France's determination to become an atomic power and seemed to seek ways of weakening United States' influence in Western Europe.

The Economy

Four years after de Gaulle's return to power, the economic development of the country continued to show improvement. In 1958, France seemed to be in a difficult financial position. Prices were rising, foreign-exchange reserves were shrinking, and economic growth had slowed down. Only foreign aid, which totaled over $650 million in 1957–58, enabled France to gain a breathing spell.

Foreign Trade

When General de Gaulle took office, the government floated a loan to provide the country with $650 million in currency and the equivalent of $170 million in gold. France's gold and foreign-currency reserves began to rise, and the deficit in France's balance of trade, which had reached $517 million in the first half of 1958, was reduced to $200 million during the second half of that year. By 1959–60, the balance of payments was, for the first time in the post-World War II period, favorable, without the benefit of American aid, which between 1946 and 1956 averaged more than half a billion dollars a year.

The improvement was largely due to measures that had been suggested by a special committee of economic experts. In order to achieve a sounder monetary basis and a better competitive position in foreign markets, the government devalued the franc in December, 1958, by 17.5 per cent and restored the convertibility of the franc, thus enabling foreign companies to invest in France and freely withdraw their profits. Foreign capital began to flow into the country, contributing appreciably to the improvement in the balance of payments.

The new price of the franc also made it possible to liberalize trade and it enabled France to fulfill its commitments to the Common Market. On January 1, 1959, France accepted the provisions of the Common Market Treaty that provided for the beginning of a reduction of customs duties and the liberalization of trade. By 1962, customs within the Common Market had been reduced by half. In May, 1959, for the first time in a long period, France's foreign-trade balance showed a surplus. Exports rose at a rapid rate. By the end of December, 1959, notwithstanding repayments on foreign debts which totaled approximately $1 billion, France's reserves of foreign exchange had reached a level of $844.3 million. They have continued to rise since, and in 1962 they stood at approximately two and a half billion dollars.

Internal Economic Growth

Economic expansion and growth have continued. Public investments in economic modernization, housing, construction, and in the social sector generally, gradually have increased (Table 8-1). Industrial production

TABLE 8-I   *Percentage of GNP for Investment*

Year	Percentage
1949	21.0%
1950	19.5
1951	18.5
1952	19.0
1953	17.5
1954	17.5
1955	18.0
1956	19.0
1957–1962	21.0+

continued its upward trend and has shown an average annual rate of increase of about 6 per cent—one of the highest in the world. Unemployment disappeared. A new four-year economic plan (1961–65) was ratified by Parliament in July, 1962. It envisages a continuing rate of economic growth of 5.5 per cent a year and massive state subsidies and investment in the social sector of the economy—in education, transport, electrification, and urban redevelopment. The number of housing units built—an area where France has lagged for a long period of time—rose from 290,000 in 1958 to 320,000 in 1959. For 1960 and 1961, annual construction averaged about 330,000 units a year. About 90 per cent of this total was built with assistance from public funds (low-income housing credits, subsidies, or loans).

Governmental Performance in Fifth Republic

Persistent Economic Problems

There are four complex and serious problems, however, that confront the French economy.

INFLATION. The first is the persistent problem of inflation. Prices in France spiraled upward after the devaluation of the franc in 1958, then leveled off, but are now on the rise again. The cost of living has been going up by about 5 per cent a year, and governmental controls over prices have either proven ineffective or have provoked outcries from the specific interests that have been affected by particular measures.

REAL WAGES. A related problem is that of the real wages paid workers. Nominal wages have gone up steadily, at times fast enough to compensate for the inflationary trend and to provide the workers with real increases. But generally they have only kept pace with the inflation, and the real income of a sizable minority of French workers remains at a level that is not much higher than that of 1958. In other words, France's industrial development and the growth of its national income have not been equitably distributed to improve the living conditions of its unskilled and semi-skilled workers and its agricultural laborers—at a time when their expectations are growing apace. The result has been a flare-up of strikes on the part of the better-organized trade unions and a generalized social unrest, which takes the form of work stoppages and wildcat strikes.

AGRICULTURE. The agricultural sector of the economy is beginning to be faced with a new problem that is familiar to us in the United States—over-production and falling prices. What is urgently needed is an over-all modernization of the agricultural sector—an improvement in agricultural credit policy, the development of technical agricultural schools,

the fusion of small farms into larger and more efficient units, an extensive rural electrification program, etc. Subsidies by the government simply maintain prices at a level desired by some of the more powerful agricultural interests. They do not help modernize the farm or better the living conditions of the farmer or improve the antiquated system of marketing agricultural products. Intense unrest among the farmers has led them to openly defy the government through strikes, road blocks, and riots, which have resulted in the destruction of property. In 1962, sweeping legislation for the purpose of modernizing agriculture, establishing cooperatives, and reclaiming unused land was introduced, but it will be some time before it is implemented and before we can assess its results.

MILITARY BURDEN. Finally, coming on top of the war in Algeria, France may have undertaken a military program of modernization and development of atomic capabilities that is beyond her resources. About $3.5 billion—that is, around 25 per cent of her budget—is earmarked for defense, a figure above that of Great Britain, Germany, or Italy. How long this burden can be sustained without seriously impairing France's program of economic and social modernization is an open question.

THE REFUGEES FROM ALGERIA. With the massive exodus of the French from Algeria, the burden of their resettlement in France will weigh heavily on the French economy. It has been estimated that the relocation of every refugee will cost about $2,400. Original plans envisaged an exodus averaging 200,000 persons per year. These estimates had to be revised upward. Not only is the exodus much larger than foreseen, but resettlement and relocation will have to be undertaken rapidly if adverse political consequences are to be averted. The total cost until 1965 may well range from $1.5 to $2 billion, which, added to the military expenditures, gives an idea of the effort required of the French economy. Yet given the present prosperity and industrial growth in France and barring an international crisis, the effort needed, even if enormous, is not back-breaking. The economy of West Germany has absorbed a far greater number of refugees from East Germany.

Education

France's growing population, spurred by the increase of births in the years immediately after World War II, has put a great strain on the country's educational system. On top of this, the compulsory school age has been raised to 16. To strengthen the school system, credits have been allocated for the construction of schools and universities, for scholarships and subsidies to students, and for the development of more technical schools to meet the needs of an industrial society. But with the exception of the budget for 1962 and the last four-year plan for economic development, whose goals will not be achieved before 1965, investments in education have lagged behind needs. Although the government has failed to meet the challenge of the skyrocketing enrollments in public schools, it has introduced comprehensive reforms in the relations between state and Catholic schools.

A New Program
for Catholic Schools

The state aid to Private Education Bill was approved on December 31, 1959, by a vote of 437 to 71 in the National Assembly, which was convened in extraordinary session. Before 1951, the Catholic schools—which one French child in five attends—were voluntary, self-supporting schools receiving no aid whatsoever from the state, in accordance with the principle of the separation of Church and state, established in 1905. In 1951, the French Parliament extended the benefit of national student scholarships to students attending Catholic secondary schools and institutions of higher education. In the same year, grants for both public and Catholic elementary school children were provided by the Barangè law. For Catholic school students, this grant was paid to parents' associations and was used to raise the very low salaries of school teachers.

The new 1959 law is based on two considerations. First, school enrollments are rising by several hundred thousand annually, with the result that the Catholic schools are playing an increasingly important subsidiary role in French education. Second, the raising of the school-leaving age from fourteen to sixteen put an additional strain on the resources of the public schools, thus increasing the significance of the Catholic schools.

The new law provided for two different types of contracts between Catholic schools and the state.

(1) *Contracts of Association.* Elementary, secondary, and technical schools, "if they meet an imperative educational need," may conclude with the state a contract of association affecting all or a part of their classes. In the classes covered by the contract, instruction shall be given in accordance with public-school regulations and curricula, and the operating expenses and teachers' salaries shall be borne by the state in the same manner as those of corresponding classes of the public-school system.

(2) *Simple Contract.* Elementary schools may conclude with the state a simple contract, under which approved teachers receive from the state a remuneration based on the degrees they hold. Such contracts may cover an entire school or only part of its educational program and entail financial and pedagogic supervision by the state. In order to qualify for the simple contract, schools must meet certain requirements laid down by decree.

The majority of Catholic schools have signed "simple contracts" with the state and are receiving subsidies. But the law provoked sharp reactions from Left-wing groups, which organized numerous demonstrations against its enactment in 1959. The perennially divisive issue of state-Church relations was thus injected anew into French politics with particular sharpness.

The Political Institutions

The Constitution of the Fifth Republic and the government formed under it are overshadowed by the personality and the popularity of General de Gaulle. He controls the Cabinet; he often appeals to the public over the head of the legislature; he has often been delegated vast powers; he can freely nominate new Ministers, and, although the Constitution does not technically permit it, he can replace at will his Prime Minister; he can refuse to convene the legislature in an extraordinary meeting even when an absolute majority requests it; he can dissolve parliament and can invoke sweeping emergency powers.

Despite the opposition of the extreme Left and the extreme Right and the equivocation of many Socialists, Radicals, and Independents, the referendum of January 8, 1961, on the policy of self-determination in Algeria, amounted to a remarkable popular vote of confidence for de Gaulle. The question on the ballot in the referendum was: "Do you approve the proposal submitted to the French people by the President of the Republic concerning the self-determination of the Algerian population and the organization of the governmental institution in Algeria before self-determination?" The results were as follows:

Registered voters	27,184,408	
Number voting	20,791,246	
Abstentions	6,393,162	
Null and void	594,699	
"Yes"	15,200,073	(75.26 per cent of those voting and 55.91 per cent of registered voters)
"No"	4,996,474	(24.74 per cent of those voting and 18.33 per cent of registered voters)

The Communists (19 per cent of the popular vote in the legislative elections of 1958 and

about 25 per cent in the municipal elections of 1959) and the Socialist Unified Party (about 2 per cent of the popular vote) favored a "No" vote. The Radical Socialist Party (about 12 per cent of the popular vote) and the Independents (about 19 per cent of the vote) also officially favored a "No" vote but also counseled their followers to vote as they pleased. Many of the Right-wing groups and former Poujadists also favored a "No" vote. Thus the combined party strength that favored a "No" vote represented at least 40 per cent of the total electorate. Yet the "No" vote amounted to less than 20 per cent of the registered voters. In other words, the party leaders appear to have been widely disregarded by the electorate. The leadership and the personal appeal of General de Gaulle—except in Algeria—overshadowed the parties.

Even more spectacular was the massive vote for de Gaulle's Evian agreements, which provided for the independence of Algeria, in the referendum of April 8, 1962. In this case, however, virtually all the political parties, including the Communists, favored a "Yes" vote, although some extreme Right wingers like the Poujadists and the Unity of the Republic were joined by some disgruntled Left-wing intellectuals in urging a "No" vote, the rightists because they were opposed to Algerian self-determination and independence, the leftists because they objected to de Gaulle's personal government.

The question on the ballot in the April 8 referendum was: "Do you approve the bill submitted by the President of the Republic concerning the agreements [the Evian agreements] . . . and the measures to be taken with regard to Algeria on the basis of the government declaration of March 19, 1962 [which reproduced the Evian agreements]? The bill appended to this question read as follows:

Article 1. The President of the Republic may conclude all agreements [to be established] in accordance with the government declaration of March 19, 1962, in the event that the Algerian populations after being consulted . . . choose to make Algeria an independent state cooperating with France.

Article 2. Until the institution of the new political organization that will ultimately emerge from the self-determination of the Algerian populations, *the President of the Republic may enact, by ordinance or, as the case may be, by decree taken in the Council of Ministers, all legislative or regulatory measures concerning the application of the government declaration of March 19, 1962* [italics mine].

The results were as follows:

Registered voters	26,983,275	
Number voting	20,402,503	
Abstentions	6,580,772	
Null and void	1,102,477	
"Yes"	17,505,473	(90.7 per cent of those voting and 64.87 per cent of registered voters)
"No"	1,794,553	(9.30 per cent of those voting and 6.65 per cent of registered voters)

It must be noted, however, that many political parties and notably the Communists, the Socialists, and the MRP that favored a "Yes" vote qualified their stand. While favoring Algerian self-determination, they objected strongly to the unlimited delegation of legislative powers to the President of the Republic provided in Article 2.

Special Presidential Powers

To strengthen his position, President de Gaulle has not only relied on his enormous prestige and popularity, which he reinforces through direct contacts with the people, in the form of many public utterances and trips around the country, he also has made full use of the special powers provided by the Constitution. Immediately after the uprising of the Algerian settlers in January, 1960, the Prime Minister and his Cabinet asked and received from the French Parliament broad powers to legislate by decree under the signature of President de Gaulle for a period of one year. Thus the executive assumed full legislative powers, on condition that all measures taken in the course of the year were to be submitted for ratification to Parliament by April 1, 1961, and with the proviso that while the exceptional powers were in force Parliament could not be dissolved.

Hardly had this special delegation of legislative powers come to an end when a new and even broader assumption of powers, this time by the President of the Republic alone, came into force, under Article 16 of the Constitution.[3] Following the military putsch in Algeria on April 22, 1961, President de Gaulle declared: "Beginning today I shall take directly . . . the measures that appear to me necessary by the circumstances." A prolonged state of emergency was declared; a number of persons were arrested or held at their homes without court order; many organizations were dissolved and several publications were forbidden. A number of officers who participated or were associated with the military putsch were expelled from the Army, and special military tribunals were formed to try them and their presumed accomplices, whether military or civilian. Finally, the President of the Republic was allowed to remove civil servants and judges in Algeria from office.

The powers of the President came to an end on September 30, 1961, by virtue of a special presidential declaration, but the application of some of the decisions continued until the summer of 1962. Again by virtue of the referendum of April 8, 1962, the President enjoys, until Algeria has emerged as an independent

[3] Article 16 provides: "When the institutions of the Republic, the independence of the nation, the integrity of its territory or the fulfillment of its international commitments are threatened in a grave and immediate manner and when the regular functioning of the constitutional governmental authorities is interrupted, the President of the Republic shall take the measures commanded by these circumstances, after official consultation with the Premier, the Presidents of the assemblies and the Constitutional Council.

He shall inform the nation of those measures in a message.

These measures must be prompted by the desire to ensure to the constitutional governmental authorities, in the shortest possible time, the means of fulfilling their assigned functions. The Constitutional Council shall be consulted with regard to such measures.

Parliament shall meet by right."

Governmental Performance in Fifth Republic

"political organization," full legislative powers to deal with any matter that relates to the Evian accords. In view of the fact that these accords include a number of stipulations that will remain in force over many years, it is not unlikely that the powers of the President to deal with all such matters may continue even though Algeria is now fully independent and a member of the United Nations.

Since the Fifth Republic came into force, in January, 1959, Parliament has thus delegated its legislative powers to the Cabinet of President de Gaulle for a period of one full year, and special presidential powers have overshadowed all other organs of the government for a period of five months. Since April 8, 1962, the President has had unlimited legislative powers for the purpose of implementing the Evian agreements. It should be quickly pointed out, however, as the President himself has claimed, that the exercise of the "special" emergency powers was indispensable, in view of the military uprising, and that the manner in which his powers have been exercised has not seriously undermined democratic freedoms. But it remains equally true that an important precedent has been established which, under different circumstances and with a different President, could well lead to serious abuse of democratic liberties.

The President as "Guardian of the Constitution"

On three important occasions, President de Gaulle interpreted the Constitution in a way to limit the power of Parliament, and in both cases his decision was accepted. In the first instance, an absolute majority of the deputies (as the Constitution prescribes) demanded the convocation of an extraordinary parliamentary session. It was generally assumed that such a convocation, once the existence of a majority had been ascertained, was automatic. The President, however, claimed that it was only up to him to decide whether it was opportune

or not to convene Parliament. In this case, he refused to convene it.

On the second occasion, the constitutional question was more complex. In the summer of 1961, Article 16, empowering the President to take whatever measures he deemed necessary, was in force, which meant that Parliament was also in session and could not be dissolved. Parliament had adjourned for the summer vacation, but remained technically in session. Given the unrest among the farmers because of falling farm prices, the parliamentarians decided to convene and consider appropriate legislation. Since they were still in session, it was up to the presidents of the two chambers to convene them. Yet President de Gaulle was opposed to this, arguing that the agricultural problems were totally unrelated to the exercise of his powers under Article 16. He could not, in a strict sense, oppose the convening of the Parliament, but he announced that he would not permit Parliament to pass any legislative measures.

When the Parliament did convene, the opposition decided to introduce a motion of censure against the Cabinet. Was such a motion in order? If it were carried, it would, it was argued, lead to a dissolution. But while Article 16 was in force, the National Assembly could not be dissolved! The President of the National Assembly stated that no such motion could be allowed. The President of the Republic, he argued, is the guardian of the Constitution, and if he believes that Parliament could not meet to legislate it follows that it could not introduce a motion of censure that might bring about the fall of the government. Thus, it appeared that while Article 16 was in force the legislative functions of the Parliament were seriously qualified, and its most important power of control—a motion of censure—was denied it.

In the third instance, as we have seen, de Gaulle decided to submit directly to the people, on October 28, 1962, a bill modifying the constitutional provision for the election of the President of the Republic. The overwhelming opinion of the jurists is that a specific bill to be proposed to the people for a constitutional amendment must be submitted and voted first by the Parliament. Again de Gaulle assumed the right to interpret the Constitution in an authoritative and definitive manner.

The President as "Arbitrator" (Arbitre)

Even more sweeping powers are given to the President of the French Republic if we accept the interpretation given by some to his role as "arbitrator." In a strict sense, the word that appears in the Constitution means mediator: a person who reconciles conflicts in an authoritative manner. In case, for instance, the political parties are in conflict on the appointment of a Prime Minister or in case the Ministers themselves are in disagreement, it is the task of the President to seek a compromise between the contending sides. General de Gaulle, however, goes far beyond this interpretation. For him, the act of mediation is not simply one of reconciliation. It is rather that of evolving policy on the basis of the national interest as it is perceived by the President himself. Hence the mediator assumes the task of political initiative and direction. Such a conception of the office of the Presidency is so broad that it overshadows Parliament, the political parties, and the Cabinet and makes the President the ultimate and most authoritative national spokesman. The Presidency overshadows all other governmental organs.

Reserved and Free Powers

To further buttress Presidential leadership and policy-making, an ingenious doctrine has been developed, according to which the scope of governmental action is divided into two broad categories. The first is the "reserved category," which includes defense, foreign policy, and Algerian affairs. Policy on all these matters is "reserved" to the President of the Republic. The advice of the Cabinet may be solicited at the pleasure of the President, but more often the latter will rely on small committees consisting of some Ministers and other officials he designates. The second category consists of matters that come within the purview of Cabinet deliberations and decisions. They are matters generally related to economic and social policy, agriculture, housing, economic planning, education, urban redevelopment, and the like. Thus there is a division between "presidential" and "parliamentary" government. President de Gaulle has stated that the present system can be considered to be both presidential and parliamentary. Such a statement contradicts sharply his earlier assertions in favor of the maintenance of parliamentary government. The President has emerged as the key policy-making organ while the Prime Minister and his Cabinet, which are responsible to Parliament and, according to Article 20 of the Constitution, in charge of determining and directing the policy of the nation, are by-passed.

The Cabinet

The Cabinet of Michel Debré was formed early in January, 1959. It was a coalition Cabinet in which the ministerial posts were distributed among the UNR, the Independents, the MRP, and the Radicals. Some eight posts, including Foreign Affairs and Defense, were in the hands of non-parliamentarians—i.e., civil servants, professors, or military personnel. Three important features of the Cabinet under the Fifth Republic should be mentioned. First, the "longevity" of its Prime Minister: when Michel Debré resigned on April 15, 1962, he had surpassed all records by remaining in office for a total of three years and three months.

Second, the stability of the Cabinet: the Cabinet of Michel Debré as a "collective body" remained in office just as long as did the Prime Minister. The same is not true, however, for the Cabinet members themselves. Instead of the traditional "Cabinet crises," in which the whole Cabinet resigned, the Fifth Republic has produced a new phenomenon that may be called "internal Cabinet crises." The Cabinet was reshuffled seven times (on three occasions seriously) in a period of three years. Out of the 27 original Ministers, 11 withdrew or were dismissed and, of the remaining 16, 7 changed ministerial posts. Important Ministries such as Defense, Finance, Education, Justice, and Interior all changed hands. The stability of the Debré Cabinet, however (January, 1959–April, 1962), contrasts markedly with the fate of the Pompidou Cabinet (April 23, 1962–October 5, 1962), which had to be reshuffled almost as soon as it was formed and was forced out of office less than six months after it was invested.

Third, the Cabinet seems to perform only subsidiary tasks of administration instead of being responsible for the over-all direction of policy as the Constitution prescribes. Important decisions are made by President de Gaulle and debated in the Council of Ministers presided over by de Gaulle. Cabinet meetings or smaller interministerial committee meetings are held under the presidency of the Prime Minister only to implement the policy arrived at by the President himself or by the President in the Council of Ministers.

Very often, policy has been made directly by the President of the Republic without ministerial consultations and deliberations, sometimes even without the prior knowledge of the Prime Minister and the Cabinet. De Gaulle himself, for instance, promised international independence to the former members of the French Community in a speech at Dakar, Senegal, on December 19, 1959; again on September 5, 1961, he declared that Sahara was to be a part of Algeria, a concession that French spokesmen were unwilling to make until then in their negotiations with the Algerian rebels; finally, it is common knowledge that foreign policy is made directly by President de Gaulle—he negotiates directly with the heads of different states. The Prime Minister and the Minister of Foreign Affairs are frequently absent from the talks de Gaulle conducts with President Kennedy, Prime Minister Macmillan, and Chancellor Adenauer. There is every evidence, therefore, that the direction of policy is presidential and that the Cabinet performs primarily the task of implementation.

Parliament

The new institutions of a "rationalized Parliament," a Parliament whose actions are carefully circumscribed, have proven to be effective in expediting legislation and guaranteeing the supremacy of the executive, particularly the ability of the government to control the agenda, to debate its own bills, and to oppose amendments from the floor. The Prime Minister, in contrast to the situation under the Fourth Republic, has rarely had to resort to the "question of confidence." He can use a wide range of procedural devices against Parliament. In many instances, he has asked that all parliamentary amendments to a bill be rejected and that a vote be taken on the government bill. Frequently he has appealed to the Constitutional Council—which almost invariably supports the position of the government—and has either alleged that the matter introduced by Parliament was beyond its legislative competence or that its enactment would call for an increased expenditure and that, therefore, it was against the Constitution. He has allowed questions with debate and occasionally has permitted full-dress debates on crucial issues of policy with or (more frequently) without a vote.

A number of important matters, however, have come before the National Assembly for a debate and a vote. The Algerian problem and the government's policy of self-determination was debated at length twice and received a majority support. The budget and the estimates concerning the various Departments have been carefully discussed, amendments have been introduced and often accepted by the government, and appropriations have been voted within the time limits allotted by the Constitution. Governmental bills have occasionally been rejected, and the government has had to accept compromise solutions. The Fourth Economic Plan was deliberated in the spring and summer of 1962 and was endorsed by a sizable parliamentary majority. Plans for urban redevelopment, agricultural reforms, industrial decentralization, and aid to the refugees from Algeria have come under parliamentary scrutiny. There has been, in other words, an orderly parliamentary process leading to legislative enactments in which, however, the government has continued to have a controlling hand as it never has had in the past. The government has called the tune either by controlling the business agenda of the Assembly or by demanding a vote on the whole of its bill, thus rejecting amendments. In extreme cases, it has put the question of confidence and forced the National Assembly either to accept the bill or to introduce a motion of censure.

The tight control of the government has irked the parliamentarians and the political parties, who have been used to a weak executive and an omnipotent legislature. They have been unwilling to accept the restraints that exist in England and in the Bonn Republic. Some observers claim that the more sensible practices of a "rationalized Parliament" are beginning to bear fruit. Others, however, point out that the government is having its way with Parliament not because of the new procedural devices that limit its role, scope of action, and length of sessions, but because of the overpowering personality of President de Gaulle. They claim, in other words, that executive leadership and governmental stability do not stem from the constitutional rules but from de Gaulle's personal strength and popularity.

Greater opposition has arisen in the Senate, where the UNR is not strong and the "old" parties have a comfortable majority. In some cases, the opposition in the Senate has been overcome only because the government has resorted to the Conference Committee, representing—as in the American system—the two chambers. When agreement has failed, the National Assembly has had the last word and has overridden the Senate. In some instances, however, amendments introduced by the Senate have been accepted by the government, and thus a conflict between it and the government and between the two legislative chambers has been averted. The budget—the perennial graveyard of Cabinets under the Third and Fourth Republics—has been approved without the interminable delays of the past even if the government has had to resort occasionally to the question of confidence.

If the legislative machinery has proved to be more efficient and expeditious than in the past, the Parliament has lost much of its control. The six legislative committees have listened frequently to the Ministers, but since they are large and unwieldy bodies, no serious scrutiny of government policy and measures could be undertaken. The "question period" has not played the role it plays in the British House of Commons. Instead of directing probing questions at the Ministers, the deputies have adopted the habit of making political speeches to which the question appended is rhetorical and often irrelevant. And the Prime Minister and the other Ministers often make declarations of policy that are not to be followed by a debate or a vote, which further reduces the parliamentary criticism that is the essence of parliamentary government.

Executive power is not therefore offset by the healthy legislative scrutiny and ultimate control that exist in other parliamentary systems. The French Parliament cannot easily provoke a debate on policy questions unless it introduces a motion of censure—a rather difficult procedure, as we have seen; questions do not lead to a full-dress debate with a vote as is sometimes the case in England; the government can have its way unless there is an absolute majority against it rather than a majority for its bills; the parliamentary sessions are short and the legislative competence of Parliament limited. With the establishment of executive leadership, Parliament has been belittled and it is very likely that it will seek to regain some of the prerogatives it has lost. The Constitutional amendment providing for the direct election of the President of the Republic by popular vote further enhances his power to the detriment of the legislature. If a new President is effectively elected in such a manner, he will command virtually all the powers of the state, based on his popular mandate. The constitutional amendment of October 28, 1962, makes a President of the French Republic elected for a period of seven years a despot whose powers are qualified only by his own sense of balance and restraint. Such a situation will further aggravate the conflicts between the legislature and the President—whoever he may be—re-injecting in the political life of the country an element of instability that characterized the past.

The Fifth Republic ... and the Future

IX

We have noted the remarkable strides toward economic modernization that were undertaken in France during the Fourth Republic. These advances have continued under de Gaulle. Investments have grown; the construction of housing has been stepped up; trade has expanded; the gross national product has increased by about 6 per cent a year; the move from the farm to the city has continued; the small shopkeeper and the artisan are on the decline. New measures to inject economic life into the provinces have been initiated, and, thanks to the construction of new plants and the discovery of natural gas (particularly in the Southwest), both wealth and employment are spreading to many French regions.

New socio-economic groups have been emerging to replace the old; the white-collar worker, the technician, the executive, the managers of private companies and nationalized industries are growing more numerous and influential in present-day France. The medium-sized farm is replacing the small one, and all farmers are employing more fertilizers and tractors and availing themselves of the credit insurance and

technical assistance opportunities that are now open to them. An extremely competent generation of civil servants—trained by the School of National Administration set up after the Liberation—is gaining access to higher posts in the Administration and is making its weight felt in the deliberations and decisions on economic and social matters. France has entered upon the road of full economic development and modernization. Does this mean that the old political structure—the old institutions, parties, and political ideologies—will be transformed in some way? And if so, how?

To answer the question, we must distinguish between the long-run and short-term effects of modernization and weigh them carefully against the traditions, practices, and institutions of the past. As new socio-economic groups make new claims on the political system and inject their expectations into the system, they will slowly transform it. The members of these socio-economic groups are more practical and pragmatic in their outlook. They demand action and want results—better living conditions and a stable political system. They tend to shed past ideologies. Instead of looking at every issue through the lenses of Communism or socialism, Catholicism or nationalism, they look at them as practical problems to be solved as quickly and efficiently as possible. They tend to consider that a wealthy society should provide better living conditions for the workers and by so doing put an end to the secular conflicts between managers and workers, between the bourgeoisie and the working class. The Catholics among them believe that the task of a good Catholic is to cooperate with others on concrete and specific issues without letting religious differences become divisive.

The trend of modernization is also bound to change the attitude of the workers. They, too, may realize that the traditional arguments about capitalism and socialism are becoming sterile, that a democratic state gives them the opportunity to use their numbers and power in order to satisfy their claims. The more they do so the more pragmatic and practical in their outlook they should become and the more inclined to set aside their ideological quarrels. The British Labour Party (despite its present divisions), the German Social Democratic Party, and, from a different point of view, American trade unionism provide working examples of how the laboring class can organize itself politically to gain a strong voice in determining what share of the country's wealth it will receive.

Many of the social-economic groups associated so closely with the Third and Fourth Republics (the shopkeepers, artisans, and small farmers) threw their support behind Poujade, but are now being squeezed out by the inexorable progress of modernization. Businessmen are beginning to understand that mass production and mass consumption lead to higher profits and are abandoning the protectionist mentality that characterized them for so long. They have accepted the European Common Market, the liberalization of trade, and a policy of cooperation with and investment in the former African colonies. The younger civil servants seem increasingly sympathetic to new rules of fiscal policy and to

state controls over credit, interest, and public investment.

But these developments run head-on into much that has been handed down as the heritage of France. Ancient historical and ideological traditions have shaped the French "political culture," and these traditions are extremely resistant to social and economic changes. They have continued to manifest themselves in French politics—in the long drawn-out war in Algeria, in the ascendancy of the Army as a political force, and in the Bonapartist nature of the Fifth Republic.

While some of the problems facing the country seem to have been settled, new ones have been created that will almost surely affect France's future drastically. The most significant problem of all is France's development as an atomic power and her efforts to develop an atomic striking force. This effort may put a heavy burden on France's industrial and financial capacities and disrupt the present movement toward European economic and political integration. France's insistence on building up a strong national Army with atomic weapons may exacerbate French nationalism and, when de Gaulle has disappeared, may alienate her former allies and upset existing European alliances.

But the basic problem facing France today lies in the inability of her institutions and political parties to adapt themselves to new social and economic conditions. The Constitution of the Fifth Republic is the government of one man—General de Gaulle. It is, therefore, a personal government whose future is clouded by the uncertainty of what happens when the man who created it disappears. It is neither a presidential system nor a parliamentary one. There is a "presidential sector," involving foreign and military policy and Algeria, for which all decisions are made by de Gaulle, and there is a "governmental sector," involving most other matters, for which decisions are made by the Cabinet with the support of the Parliament under the over-all supervision of de Gaulle. The latter governs by virtue of his enormous popularity which overshadows the Cabinet and weakens the healthy parliamentary criticism and debate that is the very essence of democracy.

The political parties themselves have shown no desire to reorganize along lines that stress concrete issues and policies. They continue to fight the old ideological battles. The UNR is not a mass political party. It is a group of men who continue to remain faithful to de Gaulle. But it has no general membership to speak of, no program, and no leadership, since de Gaulle, in whose name the party is run, refuses to consider himself its leader. With de Gaulle's disappearance, the party may well break up into many small groups or dissolve entirely. The Independents continue to be a group of notables who stress local and individual contacts, who are financed by the wealthier elements of French society, and who draw their strength from conservative groups and from many former Poujadist supporters. The MRP has been unable to develop a coherent social policy and continues to be torn between its Left-wing progressive members and the more conservative party leadership. The Radicals are still hopelessly divided; the Socialists are losing strength. The Communists continue to show remarkable stability although they remain committed to the old ideological slogans.

Not a single new party has appeared during the Fifth Republic. The dream of a unified labor party including members of the working class and perhaps of the lower middle class and some of the radical agricultural strongholds remains still a dream. So is the talk of a new conservative party composed of the new Gaullist groups, the Independents, part of the MRP, and some of the Radical Socialist formations. The political system despite the election of November, 1962, continues to be fragmented and splintered.

Now that the fighting in Algeria has stopped, some of the divisive issues and some of the more pronounced ideological conflicts that have long embittered French politics may be tempered by economic progress and prosperity, especially if the national income is more equitably distributed among the various social groups, notably among the workers. France is conceivably about to enter a new era of unity, stability, and prosperity and to bury the ideological divisions of the past.

We must realize that this is a transitional period. Who will succeed de Gaulle and what will follow the Fifth Republic no one can say. We have presented here a profile of the forces that operate and are likely to operate for some time within French society. Whatever the next constitutional arrangement, it is these forces that will determine the functioning and the future of French political society in the Sixth Republic.

After de Gaulle, What?

What will the French political system be like a few years from now? Obviously, such speculation is very tenuous and the most we can do is simply outline, on the basis of existing conditions, a few developments that may possibly take place.

Military Dictatorship

Until the war was ended in Algeria, it was widely believed that in the event of de Gaulle's disappearance the Army might have been inclined or obliged to step in and assume governmental powers. It was the only cohesive force in France; it had been increasingly involved in politics; it had been responsible for the overthrow of the Fourth Republic and had been strong enough to defy at times even de Gaulle's authority.

With the termination of the hostilities in Algeria and the declaration of Algerian independence, a *coup d'état* is extremely unlikely. The Army has been purged of many of the more extremist officers. Two referendums on Algeria showed that the nation as a whole was solidly behind de Gaulle's Algerian policy and perhaps behind de Gaulle's leadership. The extreme Right-wing forces and the deputies—particularly among the Independents—

who advocated the maintenance of French rule in Algeria were, as we saw earlier, literally decimated in the last elections. They failed to receive more than 1 per cent of the total vote, and only a mere handful of nationalist die-hards managed to get themselves re-elected. It is more likely that the Army will return to the role it played before 1940—that of a silent observer of the political world. Only a national crisis—such as a war, a rapid dissolution of the authority of the Republic, or a resurgence of Communist strength—is likely to impel it to step in. Since 1940, the Army has played in one way or another a very active political role. With de Gaulle out of the picture, many of the habits it learned in the last twenty years might return in a time of internal or external stress.

A "Reformed" Fifth Republic

The Fifth Republic is de Gaulle. But a number of institutional arrangements may outlive him. It is possible that the present relationship between government and Parliament may continue, characterized by limited parliamentary sessions, executive leadership, and limited legislative competence. The right of dissolution and the restriction of the censure motion may give the Prime Minister and his Cabinet the control and stability they lacked under the Fourth Republic. But none of these rules can be effective unless there is a majority to support a Prime Minister, or unless there is a powerful President who can use the right of dissolution, can appeal over the heads of the deputies to the people through a referendum, and who, above all, has the popularity that de Gaulle enjoys.

It was precisely the purpose of the constitutional amendment of October 28 providing for the direct popular election of the President to give to de Gaulle's successor a direct popular mandate and thus to strengthen his position. Only after de Gaulle's retirement from the political scene shall we know, however,

whether it will produce the desired effect. The direct election by the people of the President was considered and abandoned in 1958 for three reasons. First, because the President was also at the time President of the French Community. It would be extremely difficult to bring the colonial peoples into the election of what is fundamentally a French President. This reason no longer exists, since the Community has virtually disappeared. Second, the strength of the Communist Party (25 per cent of the voters) made it very unlikely that a President could be elected by absolute majority. This, of course, is compounded by a third reason—multi-partyism. These last two reasons remain but are no longer considered important. The Communist voters, it is pointed out, do not follow the party and do not vote for it when they vote for a person. This was demonstrated both in the referendum of September 28, 1958, and in the referendum of January 8, 1961. In addition, with the choice limited to two candidates only, the parties will have to combine in order to support one or the other, a fact that will tend to favor party coalitions at the expense of multi-partyism. Finally, a direct popular election of the President will give to the French a sense of immediate participation in politics —something which has been lacking in the past. Thus it is hoped that the enacted reform will maintain the strength of the Presidency and will pave the way toward a simplification of the party system.

It should be quickly pointed out that this reform will not approximate the American presidential system. The French President will continue to have the right of dissolution, the power to appeal to the people through a referendum, the use of the emergency powers under Article 16, and many other prerogatives that the American President lacks.

Return to the Fourth Republic

Whether these reforms are effective or not, another hypothesis should be entertained: the gradual return to the institutions and practices of the Fourth Republic, characterized by a weak President and the supremacy of the legislature. The pull in this direction stems from the social, economic, ideological, and political forces we discussed in the early chapters. They can be summed up, perhaps, in one phrase—*there is no political majority in France.* Without a political majority (popular or parliamentary), there can be no strong executive leadership of the American Presidential type or the British Cabinet type. It will be very difficult for the French to elect a President (other than de Gaulle) by a majority that will give him the political strength he needs to govern effectively. If gerrymandering and other political and electoral manipulations make such elections possible, the authority that is rooted in popular political support—the only true cornerstone of a democratic system—will be lacking. Nor will the Prime Minister and the Cabinet fare much better. The Prime Minister will have to seek parliamentary support, which is again the problem of finding a parliamentary majority in a divided country.

It is more than likely, therefore, that the forces that were active under the Fourth Republic will reassert themselves and that a multi-party representative assembly will once more establish practices that will resemble those of the Fourth Republic. The system will again be one of coalition Cabinets, a weak executive. The Fourth Republic moved closer and closer to the practices of the Third, despite the avowed purpose of its framers to reform the Third out of existence. It is just as probable that the Fifth Republic will move closer and closer to the substance and practices of the Fourth Republic.

In all political systems, the government is shaped and fashioned by the existing social and ideological forces. In France, the splintering of ideologies, the sharp divisions between major social groups, the bitterness and distrust between social classes and political traditions have not yet been reconciled. The French political system—outside the transitional Bonapartist form now in effect—has not been able to provide the wide areas of agreement necessary to weld conflicting interests and ideologies together into national parties that are able to produce working political majorities.

Bibliography

Chapter II

Brogan, Denis W., *France Under the Republic* (New York: Harper, 1940).

Bury, J. P. T., *France: 1814–1940* (London: Methuen, 1956).

Duguit, L., H. Monnier, and R. Bonnard, *Les Constitution et les Principales Lois Politiques de la France, Depuis 1789* (VIIIe Ed. par Georges Berlia, Paris, 1952).

Earle, Edward Mead (ed.), *Modern France: Problems of the Third and Fourth Republics* (Princeton: Princeton University Press, 1951).

Halasz, Nicholas, *Captain Dreyfus: The Story of a Mass Hysteria* (New York: Simon and Schuster, 1956).

Hayes, Carlton J. H., *The Historical Evolution of Modern Nationalism* (New York: R. R. Smith, 1931).

Kohn, Hans, *Making of the Modern French Mind* (New York: Van Nostrand, 1955).

Martin, Kingsley, in J. P. Mayer (ed.), *The Rise of the French Liberal Thought: A Study of Political Ideas from Bayle to Condorcet,* 2nd ed. (New York: New York University Press, 1954).

Mayer, Jacob P., *Political Thought in France from Sieyès to Sorel* (London: Faber, 1943).

Morazé, Charles, *The French and the Republic* (Ithaca: Cornell University Press, 1958).

Seignobos, Charles, *The Evolution of the French People* (New York: Knopf, 1932).

Siegfried, André, *France: A Study in Nationality* (New Haven: Yale University Press, 1930).

Soltau, Roger, *French Political Thought in the Nineteenth Century* (New Haven: Yale University Press, 1931).

Thomson, David, *Democracy in France: The Third and Fourth Republics,* 2nd ed. (New York: Oxford University Press, 1952).

Chapter III

Dansette, Adrien, *Destin du Catholicisme Français, 1926–1956* (Paris: Flammacion, 1957).

———, *Histoire Réligieuse de la France Contemporaine sous la IIIième République* (Paris, 1957).

Darbon, Michel, *Le Conflit entre la Droite et la Gauche dans le Catholicisme Français, 1830–1953* (Paris: Toulouse Privat, 1953).

Duveau, Georges, *Les Instituteurs* (Paris: Editions du Seuil, 1957).

Duverger, Maurice, *Partis Politiques et Classes Sociales en France* (Paris: Armand Colin, 1956).

Ehrmann, Henry W., *French Labor from Popular Front to Liberation* (New York: Oxford University Press, 1947).

———, *Organized Business in France* (Princeton: Princeton University Press, 1958).

Fauvet, Jacques, et Henri Mendras, *Les Paysans et la Politique dans la France Contemporaine* (Paris: Armand Colin, 1958).

Fourniére, de la, et F. Borella, *Le Syndicalisme Étudiant* (1958).

Latreille, André, et André Siegfried, *Les Forces Religieuses et la Vie Politique* (Paris, 1957).

LeBourre, R., *Le Syndicalisme Français dans la Viéme République* (Paris: Calmann-Levy, 1959).

Lorwin, Val R., *The French Labor Movement* (Cambridge: Harvard University Press, 1954).

Meynaud, Jean, *Les Groups de Pression en France* (Paris: Armand Colin, 1959).

Micaud, Charles A., *The French Right and Nazi Germany, 1933–1939* (Durham: Duke University Press, 1943).

Monatte, Pierre, *Trois Scissions Syndicales* (Paris: Editions ouvrières, 1958).

Monteil, V., *Les Officiers* (Paris: Edition du Seuil, 1958).

Muret, Charlotte T., *French Royalist Doctrine since the Revolution* (New York: Columbia University Press, 1933).

Planchais, Jean, *Le Malaise de l'Armée* (Paris, 1958).

Rémond, René, *Les Catholiques, le Communism et les Crises, 1929–1959* (Paris: Armand Colin, 1960).

Saposs, David J., *The Labor Movement in Post-War France* (New York: Columbia University Press, 1931).

Williams, Philip, *Politics in Post-War France,* 2nd ed. (London: Longmans, Green, 1959).

Chapter IV

Bardonnet, Daniel, *Evolution de la Structure de Parti Radical* (Paris: Montchretien, 1960).

Blum, Léon, *For All Mankind* (New York: Viking, 1946).

Campbell, Peter, *French Electoral Systems and Elections, 1789–1957* (New York: Praeger, 1958).

Duverger, Maurice (ed.), *Classes Sociales et Partis Politiques* (Paris: Armand Colin, 1956).

Einaudi, Mario, and François Goguel, *Christian Democracy in Italy and France* (South Bend, Ind.: University of Notre Dame Press, 1952).

Godfrey, E. Drexel, Jr., *The Fate of the French Non-Communist Left* (New York: Doubleday, 1955).

Goguel, François, *Géography des Élections Françaises de 1870 à 1951* (Paris: Armand Colin, 1957).

Hoffmann, Stanley, *Le Mouvement Poujade* (Paris: Armand Colin, 1956).

Milhaud, Albert, *Histoire du Radicalisme* (Paris, 1957).

Noland, Aaron, *The Founding of the French Socialist Party, 1893–1905* (Cambridge: Harvard University Press, 1956).

Rossi, Angelo, *A Communist Party in Action: An Account of Its Organization and Operations in France* (New Haven: Yale University Press, 1949).

Soltau, Roger H., *French Parties and Politics, 1871–1930* (New York: Oxford University Press, 1930).

Williams, Philip, *Politics in Post-War France,* 2nd ed. (New York: Longmans, Green, 1958).

Chapter V

Association Française de la Science Politique, *Les Élections du 2 janvier 1956* (Paris: Armand Colin, 1957).

Chapman, Brian, *Introduction to French Local Government* (London: Allen and Unwin, 1953).

———, *The Prefects and Provincial France* (London: Allen and Unwin, 1955).

Duverger, Maurice, *The French Political System* (Chicago: University of Chicago Press, 1958).

Fauvet, Jacques, *La IVième République* (Paris: Arthème Fayard, 1959).

De Gaulle, Charles, *War Memoirs. I: The Call to Honor, 1940–1942; II: Unity, 1942–1944; III: Salvation, 1944–1946* (New York: Simon and Schuster, 1958, 1959, 1960).

Goguel, François, *France under the Fourth Republic* (Ithaca: Cornell University Press, 1952).

Grosser, Alfred, *Le Politique Etrangère sous la IVième République* (Paris: Armand Colin, 1961).

Howard, John E., *Parliament and Foreign Policy in France* (London: Cresset, 1948).

Lidderdale, D. W. S., *The Parliament of France* (London: Hansard, 1951).

Siegfried, André, *De la IVe à la Ve République* (Paris: Grasset, 1958).

Thomson, David, *Two Frenchmen: Pierre Laval and Charles de Gaulle* (London: Cresset, 1951).

Williams, Philip, *Politics in Post-War France: Parties and the Constitution in the Fourth Republic* (New York: Longmans, Green, 1954).

Wright, Gordon, *The Reshaping of French Democracy* (New York: Reynal and Hitchcock, 1948).

Chapter VI

Aron, Raymond, *France Steadfast and Changing* (Cambridge: Harvard University Press, 1960).

Debré, Michel, *La Nouvelle Constitution* (Tours, 1958, pamphlet).

Duverger, Maurice, *La Ve République* (Paris: Presses Universitaire, 1959).

Furniss, Edgar, *France, Troubled Ally* (New York: Harper, 1960).

Hoffmann, Stanley, "La Constitution de la Ve République," *Revue Française de Science Politique*, Vol. IX, No. 1 (March, 1959) p. 211.

Macridis, Roy, and Bernard Brown, *The de Gaulle Republic: Quest for Unity* (Homewood, Ill.: Dorsey, 1960).

Pickles, Dorothy, *The Fifth Republic* (New York: Praeger, 1962).

Williams, Philip, and Martin Harrison, *De Gaulle's Republic* (London: Longmans, Green, 1960).

Chapter VII

Two authoritative studies have been published under the auspices of the French Association of Political Science:

Le Referendum de Septembre et les Elections de Novembre 1958 (Paris: Armand Colin, 1961).

Le Referendum du 8 janvier 1961 (Paris: Armand Colin, 1962).

See also:

Macridis, Roy, and Bernard Brown, *The de Gaulle Republic: Quest for Unity* (Homewood, Ill.: Dorsey, 1960).

Williams, Philip, and Mark Harrison, *De Gaulle's Republic* (London: Longmans, Green, 1960).

Chapter VIII

The greatest number of publications have appeared in article form in various periodicals.

Brown, Bernard, "The Army and Politics in France," *Journal of Politics* (May, 1961).

Clark, Michael, *Algeria in Turmoil: A History of the Rebellion* (New York: Praeger, 1960).

Department of Political Science, University of California, *The Fifth Republic* (collection of essays and papers) (Berkeley: University of California Press, 1961).

Duverger, Maurice, *La VIe République et le Régime Presidentiel* (Paris: Arthème Fayard, 1961).

Furniss, Edgar, *France: Troubled Ally* (New York: Harper, 1960).

Kraft, Joseph, *The Struggle for Algeria* (Garden City, N. Y.: Doubleday, 1960).

Macridis, Roy, "De Gaulle: The Vision and the Record," *The Yale Review* (Winter, 1960).

————, "De Gaulle's Foreign Policy and the Fifth Republic," *The Yale Review* (Winter, 1961).

————, and Bernard Brown, *The de Gaulle Republic: Quest for Unity* (Homewood, Ill.: Dorsey, 1960).

Schneider, Bertrand, *La Ve République et l'Algérie* (Paris: Editions Temoignage Chrétien, 1959).

Tillion, Germain, *Les Enemies Complementaires* (Paris: Les Editions du Minuit, 1960).

KARL W. DEUTSCH
in collaboration with
RUPERT BREITLING

The German
Federal
Republic

Introduction

I

Among the great industrial powers of the world, West Germany—the German Federal Republic—at the beginning of the 1960's seemed very prosperous and stable for the time being, most enigmatic in its long-run future, and crucial for world peace. In the world, it ranked ninth in population (with over 52 million people), fourth in gross national product (about 59 billion dollars), and second in exports (about 11 per cent of the world total). By the end of the 1950's, the exports of the Federal Republic had overtaken those of the United Kingdom. The Federal Republic had achieved and maintained full employment. It had found shelter and work for more than 13 million German expellees and refugees from Eastern Europe and from Communist-ruled East Germany. During much of that decade, its national income grew at almost 8 per cent a year, and it was still growing at about an annual average of 5 per cent in 1961—so rapid a rate that total West German national income by 1960 had outstripped the income of France and was prom-

ising to overtake that of Britain, perhaps by 1963 or 1964, when West Germany would become the third-ranking economic power in the world.[1]

A Picture of Stability

During the 1950's, prosperity in economics had been accompanied by remarkable stability in politics. Parties catering to political extremes elicited next to no response from the voters. Early in the decade, less than 3 per cent of the total vote was cast for the Communists, and less than 5 per cent for the German Reich Party (DRP) and other splinter parties of the extreme Right; when the Federal Constitutional Court outlawed the Communist Party and the DRP in 1953, the decision was accepted with scarcely a ripple of protest by the bulk of the public.

If moderate parties consistently commanded the support of over 90 per cent of the electorate, a single party of moderately conservative leanings, the Christian Democratic Union

[1] From data in United Nations, *Yearbook of National Account Statistics, 1960* (New York, 1961), p. 266; United Nations, *Economic Survey of Europe, 1961* (Geneva, 1962), pp. 1–53; Federal Ministry for Expellees, Refugees and War Victims, *Facts* (Bonn, 1961), Table 6.

(CDU), retained at all times between one-third and more than one-half of the popular vote and the clear preponderance of effective political power. Its main rival, the Social Democratic Party (SPD), concentrated on promoting the interests of labor and policies of social welfare, within the framework of constitutional democracy, and relegated its traditional ideological appeal of socialism and the nationalization of industry to second place. These moderate policies secured for the SPD between one-quarter and one-third of the national vote, a share in the government of several of the states of the Federal Republic, and the control of a number of important municipal governments, including such cities as Hamburg, Bremen, Frankfurt, and others. Between them, the two major parties steadily increased their share of the popular vote, from 60 per cent in 1949 to 72 per cent in 1961, gaining 86 per cent of the seats in the Federal Diet (Bundestag) in the latter year.

No genuine two-party system, however, thus far has emerged. The voting strength of the SPD never was sufficient to carry it into Federal office, and the strategy of the CDU, together with that of the smaller middle-class parties, such as the Free German Party (FDP), effectively barred the Socialists from any coalition government at the national level. West Germany thus has come to be governed by what has been called a "one-and-a-half-party" system, under which the CDU has dominated the Federal executive, but the SPD has made its own substantial contributions in the Federal legislature, and even more at the state and local government level. The result has been a remarkable degree of social peace and political tranquility. Strikes in the 1950's were few, orderly, and relatively easily settled; political riots and violent demonstrations were conspicuous by their absence; and the police has had to worry mainly not about political unrest but about the rapidly swelling automobile traffic.

A Provisional Present

Despite these achievements, the German Federal Republic is still in many respects a provisional structure in law as well as fact. In a sense, it is the youngest of the great powers. A German Federal Government with limited powers was set up in West Germany under the auspices of the Occupying Powers—the United States, Britain and France—only in 1949, after four years of foreign military rule. This Federal Republic was given legal sovereignty in 1955, but had not yet attained full military sovereignty by 1962.

Recent in time, the Federal Republic is also incomplete in space. It includes only two-thirds of the area of present-day Germany, and only three-quarters of its population. One-third of the area and almost 17 million Germans are included in the Communist-ruled "German Democratic Republic" (GDR). A discussion of the institutions and politics of that entity would go far beyond the framework of this section; and they should better be discussed, in any case, among the political institutions of the other Soviet bloc countries, which the government of the GDR now resembles far more than it does those of the German Federal Republic, or of other Western countries.

It is widely believed in the West, and particularly in West Germany, that the Communist-dominated government of the GDR lacks popular support; that it would fall as soon as Soviet Russian military backing were withdrawn from it; and that the territory and population of the GDR would then quickly become reunited with those of the Federal Republic under a single national German government. Accordingly, the government of the Federal Republic—like that of the United States and the other Western allies—denies all formal recognition to the GDR, but by the same token it has officially considered the Federal Republic itself only as the forerunner and trustee of the future reunited German national state.

This reunited national state would then comprise at least 68 million Germans, and it would form by far the strongest power in Europe, and one of the three or four strongest powers in the world. The constitution of that future reunited Germany would have to be drawn up by the representatives of its entire population. Until that time, according to West German political and legal doctrine, the present Federal Republic with all its laws and institutions is in theory provisional, since nothing must take away the right of the future all-German constitutional convention to change the structure of the government.

Not only the frontiers of the Federal Republic, but even those of a reunited Germany, according to West German doctrine, are provisional. The government of the Federal Republic, backed by the United States and other Western allies, has emphatically refused to recognize the eastern frontiers of the GDR—the so-called "Oder-Neisse Line"—and it insists, again in theory, on the full or partial restoration of former German territories east of that frontier, most of which in 1945 were put, with Allied consent, under Polish administration. These lands were then annexed by Poland, with the backing of the USSR, and were settled after 1945 by Polish settlers, following the expulsion of almost all their German inhabitants. In the view of many Poles, these proceedings were justified as the only practical way in which Poland could collect from Germany some reparations for the devastation she had suffered as a result of Hitler's invasion in 1939—and as an essential compensation for the loss of certain eastern Polish territories to the Soviet Union as a result of World War II which Nazi Germany had unleashed. While the Communist-ruled GDR regime has officially accepted the Oder-Neisse frontier as permanent, the West German government, as well as more than 80 per cent of the West German voters, emphatically reject it; and it is thus impossible for anyone in the Federal Republic to say with any authority just where the definite eastern frontiers of a reunited Germany would be.

These problems are not likely to lead to any early political action on the part of the West German government and people. They are likely to persist and to influence political attitudes for some time to come. About ten million expellees, even though successfully resettled in the Federal Republic, cannot help but keep alive, at least for another decade, the memories of their lost homes and territories in the east, as well as the theoretical claim for their return, or else for generous compensation. Many politicians are likely either to share these feelings, or at least to find it expedient to cater to them.

Moreover, between one-quarter and one-half of all West Germans have close relatives or friends in the Soviet-dominated German Democratic Republic, while almost all the inhabitants of the latter, owing to the large-scale exodus from East Germany to West Germany between 1945 and 1960, now have personal friends or relatives in the Federal Republic. Even if the demand for German reunification should remain utopian under the prevailing conditions of international politics, it will thus continue to have a great deal of direct personal relevance for a large part of the German people for a considerable period of time. The Federal Republic is thus considered provisional in its boundaries, as well as in its constitution; and the latter has been called officially since its adoption in 1949 not a "constitution" but "basic law," in order to underscore its temporary character.

The French have a proverb which says that nothing lasts as long as the provisional. When more than a decade had passed since the adoption of the Basic Law in 1949, spokesmen for the ruling CDU party in 1960 suggested in the Bundestag that it was hardly good citizenship for the opposition still to harp on the provisional character of the Federal Republic. Its laws, practices, and institutions, the government spokesmen implied, had been tested by time and had become embodied in the habits of its population. The East German population after reunification, they intimated, would just have to adopt them with few, if any, major changes, for the institutions of the Federal Republic had now acquired a tradition and a past behind them that commanded their retention.

Some of these arguments may represent bargaining positions from which concessions might be made, if reunification should become a possibility in practical politics. In the meantime, however, the German Federal Republic is the only German-speaking state that claims to represent the entire German people, with its history and its traditions. It has backed this claim by a national policy of resettlement and indemnification of German refugees and expellees from Eastern Europe, which has committed the West German taxpayer to come to the financial aid of millions of persons who had not been citizens of the Germany of 1937, or even of 1913, solely on the grounds that they could be considered German in terms of language and culture and of social and political traditions. The implied appeal to German tradition and the past had a strange ring for the ears of some listeners. For, interwoven with the long and proud history of a great nation, there is also a darker German tradition and a less praiseworthy past that stretches for decades and centuries behind the one dozen peaceful and prosperous years of the Federal Republic.

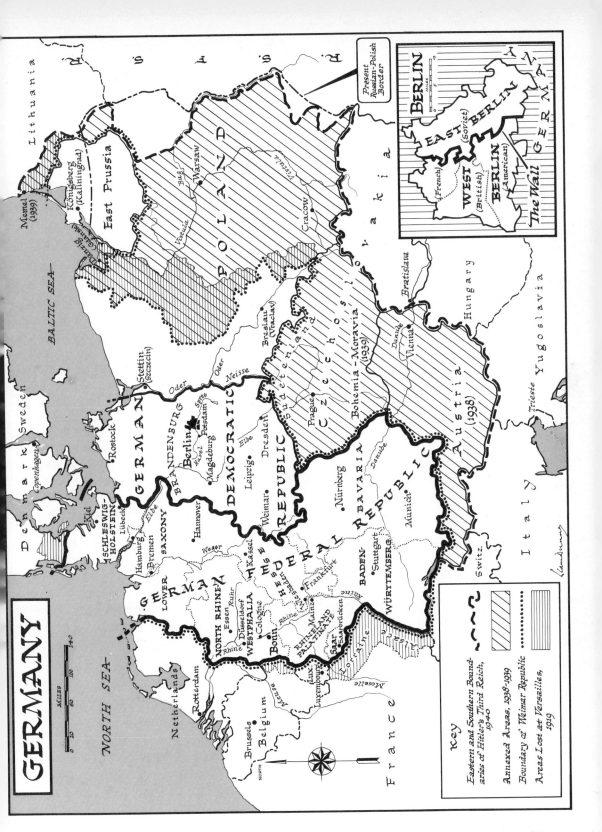

GERMANY

MILES
0 20 60 100 140

Key

Eastern and Southern Boundaries of Hitler's Third Reich, 1940

Annexed Areas, 1938-1939

Boundary of Weimar Republic

Areas Lost at Versailles, 1919

BERLIN

EAST BERLIN (Soviet)

WEST BERLIN
(French) (British) (American)

The Wall

Memel (1939)

Königsberg (Kaliningrad)

East Prussia

Danzig (Gdansk)

POLAND

Warsaw

Cracow

Bratislava

Stettin (Szczecin)

Oder

Neisse

Breslau (Wrocław)

Prague

Bohemia-Moravia (1939)

Vienna

Austria (1938)

Rostock

Lübeck

Hamburg

Bremen

Hannover

GERMAN DEMOCRATIC REPUBLIC

BRANDENBURG

Berlin

Potsdam

Magdeburg

Leipzig

Dresden

Weimar

Nürnberg

BAVARIA

Munich

SAXONY

LOWER SAXONY

NORTH RHINE-WESTPHALIA

Essen

Düsseldorf

Cologne

Bonn

Kassel

FEDERAL REPUBLIC

Frankfurt

RHINELAND-PALATINATE

Mainz

Saarbrücken

SAAR

BADEN-WÜRTTEMBERG

Stuttgart

SCHLESWIG-HOLSTEIN

Kiel

Denmark

Copenhagen

Sweden

Lithuania

BALTIC SEA

NORTH SEA

Netherlands

Rotterdam

Belgium

Brussels

Luxembourg

France

Switz.

Italy

Hungary

Yugoslavia

Trieste

Present Russian-Polish Border

273

The German Political Heritage

II

The German Federal Republic is young among states, but it governs a people that is more than a thousand years old. Words like *theutiscus* for "German," and the tradition of a "German" people go back to the age of Charlemagne. The First German Empire, styled the "Holy Roman Empire of the German Nation," goes back at least to the year 842 A.D., when Charlemagne's heirs divided his empire at Strasbourg into three realms and thus gave rise to the beginnings of modern Germany, France, and a third "realm of Lothar," comprising much of today's Netherlands, Belgium, Alsace, and Lorraine.

Every German school child is taught to see the eleven hundred years of German history since then as a long search for German unity. He is reminded that the German Empire of those early days included a variety of quite different Germanic tribes, speaking distinct dialects, such as the Franks in the Rhineland, the Saxons in northern Germany, the Alemanni or Swabians in the southwest, and the Bavarians in the southeast. Each of these major tribes extended beyond what eventually became modern Germany. Descendants of the Franks also make up most of today's Dutchmen in the Netherlands and Flemings in Belgium, and others have become part of the French people, to whom they have given their tribal name. The Saxon people and their distinctive forms of speech are found also in some districts of the eastern Netherlands and perhaps of southern Denmark, and Saxon tribes contributed the major element in the Germanic settlement of England. The Alemannic tribes also make up the bulk of what is now the German-speaking part of Switzerland, and descendants of the Bavarians also make up most of the population of present-day Austria and of the German-speaking population of South Tyrol, which now forms part of Italy.

Each of these major tribes could have become a separate nation, and to weld the bulk of these and many lesser tribes into a single and cohesive German people took many centuries. The factors that played a part in this long, drawn-out process of integration were many: the centralizing pressure of royal or imperial rule; the rewards of inter-regional trade; the benefits of contacts among the knights, merchants, and artisans of the different "tribal duchies" and regions (all speaking some intelligible variety of German); the unifying educational and administrative influence of the Church, particularly from the ninth to the twelfth century; and the silent but cumulative effects of migration, intermarriage, and, in some cases, resettlement. A major element, however, and the one singled out for emphasis in much of German historiography and education, is the role of a central government with substantial political and military power, and with the will to use that power to compel national unification.

The Middle Ages

For something like the first five hundred years, from the ninth to the fourteenth century, the unification of Germany by some powerful ruler seemed inextricably bound up with the political unification of most of Europe under the same ruler, backed mainly by German military power. German unity and European unification appeared as one and the same task, to be accomplished by a German emperor. During its three centuries of greatness, from the coronation of Otto the Great at Rome in 962 to the beheading of Emperor Konradin at Naples in 1268, the medieval German Empire laid more or less effective claim, as the "Holy Roman Empire," to the dominion of all of Western Christendom.

German empire during those centuries implied the claim to world empire. German government claimed to be, and sometimes was in fact, world government within the Western world; the profound appeal of this idea even for some non-Germans is echoed in Dante Alighieri's famous treatise "On Universal Monarchy" (De Monarchia), in which the poet proposes world government by the German emperor. The image of some world-wide mission, peculiar to one's own nation, has become a familiar trait in the nationalistic movements of the nineteenth and twentieth centuries, but there hardly exists a great country in the world where the image of such a universal national mission is as deeply rooted in the national past and as vividly present in the background of contemporary history and education as it is in Germany.

Despite its glory and appeal, the medieval

German attempt at world empire ended in failure. The German empire of those three centuries lacked the administrative and financial machinery essential for an effective government. What little resources, personnel, and competence in these matters its emperors could command they had to borrow from the Church. What amounts of ready money they could lay their hands on, they largely had to get from the Italian cities, which were then largely governed by their bishops. When, after 1075 A.D., the Church revolted against the political domination and exploitation by the German emperors, the main material and psychological foundations of German imperial power were eventually destroyed. Losing control of Italy and of the Church, the emperors in time lost control of the princes, nobles, and towns of Germany. By the late thirteenth century, Germany was becoming what it was to remain for the next three centuries: a conglomeration of feudal domains and city states, presided over by a nominal emperor with little or no power.

The causes of this collapse of the medieval German empire were not clearly understood at the time. Few, if any, German historians or laymen saw clearly that this empire under the glamorous Hohenstaufen dynasty had lived politically and economically far beyond its means, and that its rulers had attempted the unification of Germany and of Europe in complete and irresponsible disregard of the narrow limits of their actual resources. Rather, the image conveyed by many popular historians and retained in folk memory was one of heroic and glamorous emperors, thwarted by German disunity, by the insubordination of the German princes, and by the devious machinations of foreigners, mostly Italians and Frenchmen, and including notably the Roman popes. If the Germans had only been more united and more disciplined, and if the German clergy had listened more to the German emperors and less to foreign popes, this image

The German Political Heritage

suggested, the medieval German world empire need never have fallen.

The Beginnings
of Political Unity

Even without any strong central government, however, the German people remained predominant in Central Europe during the next 300 years, from the fourteenth to the sixteenth century. German princes, knights, and cities extended their sway deep into eastern Europe. Far beyond these expanding limits of German political rule, German merchants, knights, artisans, and peasant settlers were welcomed by eastern European rulers as valued immigrants and accorded privileged status. No major invasions of Germany took place from the eleventh through the sixteenth century, with the exception of a brief Mongol attack in 1241 which had been stopped by local forces at Liegnitz in Silesia. Without any strong ruler, Germany was safe, while the Hanseatic cities, the Teutonic knights, and the dukes of Austria expanded German power to the north, the east, and the southeast, and German crafts and cities flourished in prosperity.

In the second half of the fifteenth century, however, the foundations of this German prosperity began to crumble, and by the beginning of the seventeenth century Germany was ruined, before the first shots of the Thirty Years War (1618–1648) were fired. Some of the major causes of this economic decline were remote, indirect in operation, difficult to visualize, and yet devastatingly effective. With the fall of Constantinople to the Turks in 1453, the trade of Italy and Germany with the eastern Mediterranean declined, and the subsequent Turkish advance northward across southeastern Europe to the gates of Vienna in 1529 further diminished Italian and German trade with that area. An even more fateful

shift in the routes of world trade away from Central Europe and to the Atlantic coasts occurred after the discovery of America in 1492 and the opening of a sea route to India in 1498. Germany and most of Central Europe became backwaters of international trade; cities stagnated or shrank; and princes found it harder to raise revenues at a time when the costs of warfare and government were rising.

During this same period, more powerful monarchies emerged in Western Europe and changed the scale of politics and warfare. Between 1480 and 1610, Spain, England, France, and Sweden all emerged as vigorous national monarchies, dwarfing the resources of the German petty princes and city states with whom they came in competition for territory, trade, or influence.

The only German dynasty that attained major strength during that period was the house of Habsburg, and it did so mainly by strengthening its non-German connections. In this policy, it was eventually supported by the influence of the Church, which had repudiated in 1462 a religious compromise peace with the Protestant Hussites of Bohemia and was now interested in the rise of a strong Catholic power in Austria, so as to oppose both the Bohemian Protestants and the Turks to the southeast. By a remarkable series of intermarriages, the Habsburgs, between 1477 and 1526, acquired lands and wealth from Burgundy and Spain and eventually the succession to Bohemia and Hungary. The wealth of Spain in particular, derived from the conquest of Mexico and Peru, permitted the Habsburgs to play a major role in German politics—but it was not a role that led to German unity.

After 1517, Germany was shaken by the appeal of Martin Luther's Reformation, which was followed by more than a century of religious warfare. From these conflicts there emerged eventually a standard German language, based in large degree on the central German dialect used by Luther for his translation of the Bible; and there remained a lasting religious division of the German people which by the beginning of our century was composed of about two-thirds Protestants and one-third Catholics, with the latter mostly in the Rhineland, Bavaria, and Silesia.

In Search of Statehood

It was in this period that Germany went through the first stages of political modernization. Between 1500 and 1750, the German principalities passed through the transition to the modern bureaucratic state, which collected taxes in money, paid a standing armed force, and was administered by professional officials. The bureaucrats themselves were paid in money, and they carried on most of their work in writing, and increasingly in accordance with fixed rules of more or less rational procedure. They were organized and disciplined in some hierarchical pattern of command and were effectively subordinated to their immediate superiors, as well as ultimately to the monarch.

Similar developments during the same centuries in England and France were in part counterbalanced in their social and cultural effects by growing economic prosperity, which increased the confidence and power of the merchants and the middle class. It taught them that they could often promote successfully, by their own efforts, their interests as individuals and groups, and that they could often conclude profitable and honorable compromises with other interest groups or individual power holders. Indirectly, commercial and industrial prosperity in France and England increased the values of the lands of many nobles and of the rents derived from them. It also enhanced the opportunities for nobles and gentlemen to take part in profitable business ventures, as in the great companies of English merchants, or to obtain lucrative pensions or payments for nominal offices from the monarch's treasury, without having to perform any serious amounts of administrative work, as in the case of the French court under Louis XIV. The growing bureaucracies of France and England were thus limited by the power of other groups, and the major part of the aristocracies and of the middle classes of those countries did not merge with them.

In the German principalities, economic stagnation in the sixteenth and seventeenth centuries led to the opposite effects. The open pursuit of group interests and the give and take of compromises between groups tended to be less rewarding and less reputable. The middle class stagnated and became more weak and submissive in relation to the growing strength of the bureaucracies and of the petty monarchs who commanded them. The lesser nobles remained impecunious and their sons increasingly took to the service of the state as officers, or as civilian bureaucrats. The higher bureaucracy in the German states thus was less separate as a class, and less independent as a political force, from nobility and monarchy. Just for this reason, however, it gained by this close association a vicarious share in their prestige. The German terms for the new bureaucratic authorities of the period, *Obrigkeit,* and for their subjects, *Untertanen,* appear strikingly in Luther's injunction to his followers: "Be ye subject (*untertan*) to the authority (*Obrigkeit*) that has power over you." These German terms carry far stronger authoritarian and paternalistic connotations than any comparable terms in common use in France, England, or the United States; and in German history they were heavily underscored by Luther's call for the savage repression of the German Peasants' Revolt in 1525.

The churches, too, became allies of and often instruments of princely and bureaucratic authority. After the Religious Peace of Augsburg of 1555, each prince retained the sovereign right to determine the religion of his subjects and to suppress or drive out dissenters. Most of the German principalities, in the course of the sixteenth and seventeenth centuries, became officially identified with a single denomination, Protestant or Catholic, and the theological arguments in favor of the particular ecclesiastical regime established in each state served in effect as a political defense of the state, a safeguard of the reliability of its

The German Political Heritage

clergy, and a religious exhortation to civic obedience and loyalty.

The universities were the chief sources of the juridically trained administrative officials, which all of the modernizing states needed, as well as of the theologians and ministers, which each Protestant prince required in order to give religious backing to his claim of divine right to absolute political power. Between them, the German states, particularly the Protestant ones, maintained a larger number of universities and devoted a higher proportion of resources to them than was usual at the time elsewhere in Europe. The German universities had relatively great importance and prestige with their respective states. Professors, and eventually to a lesser degree all teachers, were viewed as somehow associated with authority, and were respected not only for their learning but also for their association with the authoritarian order of the bureaucratic and aristocratic princely governments. The results of these developments have added in the long run to the strength and glory of German learning and science, but they have also made a large part of the German universities into ready admirers and pliant servants of authority in periods of tyranny or war. For good or ill, the sixteenth and seventeenth century combination of unusually strong universities and bureaucracies with an unusually weak commercial and industrial economy has marked German politics, society, and culture in the centuries thereafter.

In France and England, the growing wealth of the cities made it possible eventually for some one dynasty and region to defeat all its rivals and to establish a strong national state. The contemporary religious conflicts in those countries, bloody as they were, did not prevent this outcome. Rather, they often helped in the end to justify the defeat or expulsion of the losing parties and the confiscation of their property. In Germany during that period, on the contrary, there was not enough solid prosperity to finance the rise of any one prince or region to paramount power and its consolidation. Prosperous France and England won their national unity in the same centuries of religious wars in which stagnating Germany became more deeply divided. Many Germans, however, blame to this day the religious split for the long political division of their country and retain from these memories a longing for stronger national unity.

Economically impoverished and politically divided, Germany early in the seventeenth century became the scene and the victim of the power conflicts among her more effectively consolidated neighbors. In the Thirty Years War (1618–1648), the great and lesser European powers, such as France, Spain, the Habsburg Empire, Sweden, and the Netherlands, fought one another on German soil, with the eager collaboration of the German princes, but with catastrophic consequences for the German people. The war reduced the population of Germany by one-third, and left the country impoverished in comparison to its Western neighbors for perhaps as much as 150 years.

The main responses of the survivors of this catastrophy were increased distrust and fear of foreign nations; increased dependence on the protection of familiar authorities; a greater acceptance of discipline and of sustained habits of hard work; and eventually a greater acceptance of militarism as a means of strengthening their governments and their ability to protect their subjects against the terrors of war and foreign invasion.

Out of these experiences came the German people of the eighteenth century, with a prevailing national character that was different in some ways from that of their predecessors. If Tacitus had described the members of the ancient Germanic tribes as proud, freedom-loving, and lazy, the eighteenth-century Germans were more often submissive and diligent. If some observers in the late seventeenth century judged the Germans to be timid and peculiarly incapable of discipline, from the eighteenth century onward the German people were to impress foreigners increasingly by their discipline and military virtues.

The Prussian State

A major agency in this transformation was the Brandenburg-Prussian monarchy, both through its practices and its example. Bureaucracy, austerity, mercantilism, and militarism were the hallmarks of its policy. Starting out from their holdings in the infertile Brandenburg region—"the sandbox of the empire"—the rulers of the Hohenzollern dynasty soon acquired Prussia, a territory in the northeast, where in earlier days the Knights of the Teutonic Order had imported German settlers, and imposed German speech and culture on the Baltic and Slavic original inhabitants. By the middle of the seventeenth century, the rulers of Brandenburg-Prussia had managed to acquire a collection of widely scattered territories throughout northern Germany, including strategic holdings on the banks of the Rhine, Weser, Elbe, and Oder Rivers.

In the pre-railroad age, these rivers carried a very substantial part of the trade of the various German principalities to the Baltic and North Seas, to the Atlantic Ocean, and generally to the world of expanding overseas trade. If held by a powerful military force, these territories could be used to collect tolls from this river traffic and to impose a variety of tariffs and other economic regulations in accordance with the mercantilist practices of the time, and thus to divert a significant part of the wealth of the other German territories into the coffers of the Brandenburg-Prussian state. By spending most of its income on its army and bureaucracy, that state could maintain more soldiers, gain more territories, collect more tolls, impose more profitable regulations, and spend the proceeds again and again on more soldiers and conquests, in a slowly expanding spiral of power politics.

Under these particular conditions, militarism could be made to pay for itself, provided only that the tax receipts from foreign transit, and from domestic trade, were not squandered on luxury consumption by the monarchs and the nobles of the country. Ostentatious spending on expensive luxuries was widespread during much of the seventeenth and eighteenth centuries at other German courts, as it was throughout Europe at that time, but Prussia formed a conspicuous exception. By comparison with the rest of Europe, court life at Berlin and later at Potsdam sometimes seemed Spartan in its simplicity. Many of the younger sons of nobles had to depend on military or bureaucratic careers for their income; and they had to make greater efforts than nobles in other countries in order to acquire the academic training and the practical knowledge and skills necessary to the performance of their duties.

Even the peasantry followed a life of frugality and ceaseless diligence. From the middle of the seventeenth century to the early years of the nineteenth century, the peasants, and even members of their families, were pressed into compulsory service on the estates of the nobles. During the slack season of the year, between spring planting and harvest, and particularly during the long winters, they had to spin, weave, or perform other duties under the supervision of the landlord and his employees. Similar demands were made on the rural population in other parts of Germany, but in Brandenburg—or, as it was called after 1701, the Kingdom of Prussia—there emerged most clearly a new and disciplined pattern of life. It combined unceasing and diligent labor by the mass of the population with grim frugality on the part of their rulers.

The Prussian state thus functioned as an engine for extracting forced savings from its population. It channeled these savings into an ever-expanding army, and to some degree into the support of industry and education, using all these activities in turn to enhance the future economic resources and political power of the state. A French observer misunderstood the situation when he remarked that other states had armies but that in Prussia the army had a state. For the Prussian army, too, was but one link in this chain of self-expanding

The German Political Heritage

power. Though it received funds more readily than other parts of the government, it, too, had to practice rigorous economies; and a German writer hit closer to the mark when he said that between 1640 and 1780 the state of Brandenburg-Prussia had starved itself into greatness.

The Prussian state won the acceptance, and eventually the loyalty, of many of its inhabitants, for it offered them a better chance of security against foreign attack, of predictable legality and honest administration, some educational opportunity, and long-term economic growth. At the same time, however, the austerity and authoritarian discipline of Prussia repelled many Germans, particularly those outside its borders. They saw it as a vast barracks yard, ruled by a royal drill sergeant. They resented its harsh tariff policies, its ruthless methods of recruiting or impressing young men from other territories into its armies; its unscrupulous policies of territorial expansion and aggression—and they thanked their stars that they were not among its subjects. Yet, when this dreaded and hated Prussian state under Frederick II in 1756 defeated for the first time in several centuries a French army in open battle at Rossbach, many of these same Germans rejoiced. "We all were pro-Fritzian then," Goethe reported of the people of the free city of Frankfurt at that particular time.

The attitude of the Germans in the southern and western parts of what is present-day Germany toward Prussia was a mixture of dislike and admiration. When and where Prussian power seemed unneeded or menacing, dislike would prevail; but where Prussian strength seemed needed against a foreign threat or where Prussian drive and efficiency might promise a way out from pettiness and stagnation, Prussian leadership could seem attractive.

In the meantime, the rest of eighteenth-century Germany remained divided into many weak and sleepy little states. Yet crafts and industries revived, the ravages of the Thirty Years War were slowly healed, and the most gifted and skilled men in many of these petty states came to think of themselves as citizens of a wide and vague "republic of letters," in which their works would be appreciated and in which they themselves might find employment at the courts of hospitable princes, regardless of state boundaries. German composers, scientists, and writers in the eighteenth century did indeed move from one German state court or university to another, or else their works or their pupils did so; and a growing network of German theaters, concert orchestras, publishing houses, and periodicals facilitated the dissemination of their works. Philosophers such as Leibniz and Kant, writers such as Schiller and Goethe, composers such as Bach and Beethoven made Germany one of the major contributors to world civilization. At the same time, however, neither these men, nor indeed most of the educated Germans before the end of the eighteenth century, felt that the unification of the German people into a single national state was at all urgently needed.

With the Napoleonic Wars and the French occupation of Berlin in 1806, this situation changed. Soon a number of German intellectuals became bitterly anti-French and wished for more powerful governments—or even one strong government—for Germany. At the same time, the rulers of Prussia, as well as those of Austria, found it expedient to take advantage of this mood, and to appeal not only to the territorial patriotism but also to the German nationalism of their subjects. In Austria, this policy was again abandoned in 1810, but in Prussia it was strengthened by partial but important reforms and carried through to the immensely popular and ultimately victorious war against France in 1813–15. Victory was followed by a temporary swing back to conservatism, but an important beginning had been made toward linking the aspirations of German intellectuals—and of the German middle class generally—with the military prowess of the Prussian aristocracy and the power interests of the Prussian state.

German Unification in the Nineteenth Century

In 1815, Prussia acquired the Rhineland, including the Ruhr area, and soon became the main industrial power in Germany. Under Prussian leadership, a customs union, the *Zollverein*, united from 1834 onward the territories of all German states with the exception of Austria. In the half-hearted and short-lived revolution of 1848, German liberal leaders tried to unite Germany in a single empire on a constitutional and middle-class basis, but failed to win either the cooperation of the Prussian court and aristocracy or the sustained support of the mass of the population. In the following two decades, however, the growth of German industry and banking, a German railroad network and postal system, and a unified code of commercial law all served to knit the German states more closely together than ever. Through a skillful combination of political and military moves in three wars in 1864, 1866, and 1870–71, the Prussian statesman, Otto von Bismarck, succeeded first in greatly enlarging the territory of Prussia and then in establishing a new unified German empire that preserved and indeed enhanced the power of the Prussian monarchy and aristocracy, while winning at the same time almost solid middle-class consent and widespread popular support.

The Second German Empire, 1871–1918

This new German empire was ruled by the Prussian monarch, who now also became the German Emperor, with sweeping emergency powers at his disposal under the new constitution. The Emperor appointed a Chancellor who was responsible to him rather than to the legislature. The Chancellor, in turn, was in control of the ministers of his cabinet; he, rather than the legislature, could appoint or dismiss them.

The imperial legislature had very little power, and was divided into two chambers. One, the *Bundesrat*, consisted of delegates of the 25 states, with Prussia furnishing 17 out of the total of 58 and usually commanding additional votes from several smaller states. Moreover, since 14 votes sufficed to block any constitutional amendment, Prussia had an effective right of veto on such matters. The Prussian delegates to the *Bundesrat* were appointed by the Prussian government, which was subservient to the Emperor in his role as King of Prussia; and the Prussan legislature was elected by an extremely unequal three-class franchise that insured its effective control by the landowning nobility, and to a lesser extent by the upper middle class of industry and commerce, while virtually disfranchising the rest of the population. In contrast to this extreme form of class franchise for the Prussian legislature, Bismarck's constitution for the empire provided for a second legislative chamber, the *Reichstag* (chosen by popular election), which was designed to attract a greater share of popular interest and, in time, loyalties, to the empire. The *Reichstag*, however, while it made a good sounding-board for speeches and debates, had no real power to decide; even the taxes for the imperial budget could be collected and spent by the imperial government without the *Reichstag's* consent.

The German Emperor thus had vast powers and was subject to no effective constitutional control. The first Emperor, Wilhelm I, accepted Bismarck's personal prestige and influence as Chancellor, so that the system worked not too differently from the way a British Prime Minister and Cabinet might have functioned. From 1888 onward, however, the weaknesses of Bismarck's constitution were becoming visible. A new and erratic Emperor, Wilhelm II, succeeded to the throne; Bismarck himself was soon replaced by a succession of less able but more subservient Chancellors; and German policy began its fateful drift toward diplomatic isolation, the arms race

The German Political Heritage

with Britain, France, and Russia, and the precipice of World War I.

It would be wrong, however, to see the main causes of the German drift into World War I in the personal shortcomings of Wilhelm II, or in the constitutional defects of the "Second Empire." The policies of high protective tariffs for industry and agriculture; of active efforts at colonial expansion; of a frantic search for international prestige; and of ever-increasing expenditures for armaments—all these were backed by the most powerful interest groups and elites of the empire. They were overwhelmingly supported by the German middle class, and had substantial support throughout the population. Germans, during the decades between 1890 and 1914, found themselves in a world of rising tariffs and expanding colonial empires. Coming late upon the scene of colonial expansion, many of them accepted blindly the proposition that was then enunciated by French and British, as well as by German statesmen: that any great industrial country had to win colonies, "living space," and "a place in the sun" for itself, if it was not to lag behind, and eventually to perish, in the struggle for national survival. The old memories of a hostile foreign environment, retained since the days of the Thirty Years War and the Napoleonic invasions, now developed into the notion of a Germany encircled by envious and hostile rivals, and eventually into the widespread belief that war would be inevitable—a belief coupled, as we now know, with almost complete ignorance of what such a war would be like.

World War I proved devastating beyond anyone's expectations. About two million German soldiers lost their lives in it, and almost another million civilian German lives were lost through the hardships of the food blockade imposed by the Allies during the war and prolonged for some time after the Armistice of November 11, 1918. By the end of the war, Germany was thoroughly exhausted and defeated. In the peace that followed, Germany lost all her overseas colonies, and in Europe she had to give up Alsace-Lorraine to France and important territories in the East to a reconstituted Poland. Most of Bismarck's territorial acquisitions thus were lost again. There was left an impoverished and exhausted country, which now turned into a republic but which remained burdened with a large debt of reparations owed to the victorious Allies.

Despite its end in catastrophic defeat, Bismarck's empire lives on in popular memory. Forty-five per cent of German respondents to an opinion poll in 1951 considered the Second Empire (1871–1918) the best period in recent Germany history, and in repeated polls in the 1950's a plurality of respondents named Bismarck as the man who did more for Germany than any other. The stigma of defeat in World War I has been largely transferred in the German popular mind from the empire which actually suffered it to the Republic that emerged in November, 1918, to pick up the pieces.

The Weimar Republic, 1918–1933

The collapse of the empire in 1918 found most German parties and leaders unprepared. About one-quarter of the electorate continued to hold nationalist and militarist views. They would have preferred to see the old empire go on unchanged, with its black, white, and red flag, its Army, and its authoritarian institutions. Most of these nationalist voters came from the middle class and the peasantry. They were represented by the conservative Nationalist Party and by the at first much smaller National Socialists; and they never forgave the new Republic for representing, in their eyes, a betrayal of all the traditions and aspirations of the Army and the empire in World War I. At the other end of the political spectrum, the Left wing of the German Social Democratic Party (SPD) split off and eventually emerged as the German

Communist Party (KPD), which during the next fourteen years often polled between 10 and 15 per cent of the vote. This group, too, rejected the "bourgeois" Republic (although on quite different grounds), as did the conservative Nationalists and the Nazis, and thus the Republic was faced at all times with the open and bitter hostility of more than one-third of its population.

The majority of the Socialists retained the old party name, Social Democratic Party, remained on a more moderate course, and rallied soon to the active support of the Republic. In early 1918, however, most SPD leaders had not thought seriously about anything more radical than a constitutional monarchy, and neither had the leaders and members of the moderate middle-class parties—the liberal German Democratic Party and the Center Party, which represented the particular interests of Roman Catholic voters. Before 1918, none of these groups had advocated a republic for Germany, and when in that year the monarchy suddenly lost so much of its former popular support that only a republic appeared practicable, nobody seemed prepared to draft its constitution or to make it work if practical difficulties should arise.

The Republic thus started out as a make-shift type of government. In order to suppress the challenge from the radical Left, in the tense winter of 1918–19, the SPD and the moderate middle-class parties allied themselves with the German generals and officers who still controlled units of the armies which had returned to Germany after the Armistice in November, 1918. The military indeed supplied the main force to suppress radical leftist uprisings, such as the "Spartacus" revolt of January, 1919, and they received in return a great deal of formal and informal influence over the reduced armed force of the Republic— the *Reichswehr,* whose strength the peace treaties eventually were to fix at 100,000 men. This informal but fateful arrangement came into existence long before the formal Constitution was drafted and ratified, but it was to exercise a crucial influence over the fate of the Republic in later years.

The Constitution was actually drafted in the small town of Weimar, symbolic as the residence of Goethe and Schiller in the classic period of German literature, and safely removed from the labor unrest and political turmoil of Berlin and the other industrial regions of the country. The main provisions of the Constitution showed a marked shift towards democracy, particularly when compared to the imperial constitution of Bismarck's and Wilhelm II's days, but they showed also serious shortcomings and imbalances which revealed the lack of adequate political experience among its authors.

The Constitution of Weimar gave first place to the elected legislature, the Reichstag, and it gave to that body the power to approve and dismiss the Chancellor and his ministers. At the same time, however, it raised a second power to the same level: a popularly elected President was given the power to nominate the Chancellor, to dissolve the Reichstag, and, in case of a broadly defined emergency, to rule by decree. Much of the power of the Republic could thus become concentrated in the hands of two men, or even subservient to the will of one; a strong President with a compliant Chancellor or, more likely, a strong Chancellor with a compliant President, could use the vast emergency powers of government to destroy the constitutional regime —a development that actually took place later in 1932 and 1933.

Compared to this strong centralizing bias, the federal theme was muted. The second legislative chamber, the *Reichsrat,* which included representatives of the state governments, was mentioned last in the Weimar Constitution, and its powers were largely limited to minor matters of administration. In addition to this, the huge state of Prussia was preserved, comprising two-thirds of the total population, so that even state government was far more centralized than would be the case in the United States.

The German Political Heritage

The Record of Weimar

The basic rights of individuals were listed in the Weimar Constitution and protected by it—in contrast to the Second Empire, when they had been left to the various states—but far-reaching emergency provisions could be invoked by the federal government with relative ease to suspend these constitutional protections. This actually happened in the last years of the Weimar Republic, and these sweeping emergency powers, together with the extreme concentrations of power in the hands of the President and the Chancellor, did much to smooth the way to dictatorship in 1933.

This disastrous outcome, however, cannot be attributed only, or primarily, to technical mistakes in constitution-drafting. The Weimar Republic suffered from political and social weaknesses even more dangerous than its legal ones. In the record, four such weaknesses stand out.

First of all, the Weimar Republic was, and remained, illegitimate in the eyes of roughly one-third of its population. Throughout the 1920's, about 20 per cent of the voters on the Right backed the German Nationalist People's Party and similar rightist groups, which longed for the restoration of the monarchy and for a victorious war of revenge for the defeat in World War I, and about 10 per cent on the Left voted for the Communists, who urged the replacement of the "bourgeois" Weimar Republic by a Soviet-style "dictatorship of the proletariat," by which they meant essentially that of the Communist Party. Both the extreme Right and the extreme Left saw the Republic as a regime of treason. To the nationalists, it represented the betrayal of the monarchy and of the supposedly "undefeated" Imperial army in 1918, while to the Communists, the same Weimar Republic represented the betrayal of socialism and of the Russian November Revolution.

Such extremist views, and the intense emotions of hatred and contempt that went with them, were not unusual in European politics between 1918 and 1933, but what was unusual was the large share of the electorate that persisted in these attitudes in Germany through one and a half decades. This hostility of 30 to 40 per cent of the voters in turn produced an unusually great risk of "negative majorities" in the federal legislature, since an adverse vote by only a small part of the deputies from the other parties, when added to this large permanent opposition, was sufficient to produce an anti-government majority—but a majority unable to agree on any positive action. (See Table 7-1 on page 363.)

In the second place, against any violent attempts to overthrow it, the Weimar Republic depended for its defense precisely on some of the groups that were implacably hostile to it. Against the rightist Kapp Putsch of 1920, the Republic had to invoke a general strike of the workers, including the Communists; and against repeated Communist uprisings between 1919 and 1923, the Republic depended on the extremely nationalistic officers and judges who remained its bitter enemies. This dependence on profoundly anti-democratic officers and judges, in fact, undermined the entire security of the Republic. It permitted the assassination of many of its leading statesmen, as well as of many less prominent liberals and leftists, with virtual impunity, and it left the Republic almost paralyzed in the face of the mounting terrorism of the Nazis after 1930.

The third weakness of the Weimar Republic was the relative instability and precariousness of its economic institutions, and the succession of disastrous economic experiences which became associated in the mind of many Germans with the Republic. The first of these experiences was the period of widespread hunger and poverty which followed upon the defeat of Germany in World War I and which was aggravated by the prolongation of the Allied food blockade against Germany in 1919. A second economic disaster was the runaway inflation of 1923, in which the government permitted the value of the mark to drop to less than one-thousandth of a billionth of its value.

When the currency was finally stabilized with United States aid in 1924, one new "Rentenmark" was worth 4,200,000,000 of the old ones. A large part of the savings and pensions of the German middle class were wiped out, and many in this group and their children blamed, not the deferred costs of the war, but the Republic for their ruin.

After a brief period of spectacular recovery, fueled by a stream of private loans from the United States that spurred the technological re-equipment and modernization of German industry, the third disaster struck. After the "Black Friday" of October, 1929, on the New York Stock Exchange, the flow of American credits dwindled, and the German economy suffered particularly heavily from the world-wide depression; by early 1933, about six million workers were registered unemployed—about one-third of the industrial work force of the country. The unemployed, their families, and particularly the young people who graduated from the schools and universities straight into unemployment, blamed the Republic for their misery. The first two of these disasters—the hunger of 1919 and the inflation of 1923— would probably have been tolerated by a majority of voters; in fact, after three years of recovery, the elections of 1928 had strengthened considerably the moderate and pro-democratic parties. The third disaster following hard upon the heels of the preceding ones, however, was too much. From 1930 on, an increasing portion of German voters, and soon a majority, cast their votes for extremist and anti-democratic parties: the Nationalists, the Communists, and the hitherto unimportant National Socialist Party of Adolf Hitler.

In the face of this growing danger, the fourth weakness of the Weimar Republic was to prove fatal: the lack of imagination, competence, and courage in the economic and political policies of its leaders during its last years. In several other industrial countries, such as the United States after 1933, unemployment and depression were eventually controlled to some extent by programs of public works and various measures of credit expansion and government spending. The statesmen of the Weimar Republic, however, whatever their party, remained fearful of inflation, a recent and unhappy memory; they clung to a policy of "sound money," and deflation, which resulted in mounting unemployment, while doing almost nothing for the unemployed except providing some pitifully meager relief payments for those condemned to months or years of involuntary idleness. Even less help was provided for the small middle-class shopkeepers and businessmen who lost their businesses in the depression.

Between 1930 and 1933, as democracy seemed incapable to act, a feeling of desperation spread among many groups—a feeling that something had to be done, regardless of risk or cost. "If you must shoot," the poet Erich Kästner wrote in his *Address to Suicides,* "please do not aim at yourself." Kästner's own sympathies were liberal and humanitarian, but many of the young men whose desperation he echoed were becoming ready to shoot at any target that a plausible leader might point out. At a time when elder statesmen seemed to equate experience with impotence, and when rational discussion seemed to produce only excuses for inaction and frustration, millions from all classes were getting ready to overthrow the restraints of reason and experience, of curiosity and doubt, of kindness and pity, of tradition and religion, in favor of their blind need for security and certainty, for hate and aggression, and above all for action and for power, regardless of the cost in cruelty and suffering to others, and ultimately to themselves as well.

The Hitler Era, 1933–1945

In the politics of the German Federal Republic, the years of Hitler's rule are rarely mentioned, but never forgotten. All Germans over 35 years of age have vivid personal memories of that epoch, and these are the age groups that include practically all political leaders, high-ranking government officials, and military personnel—almost all leaders of interest groups—in short, almost the entire political elite. In order to understand the memories that still shape in one way or another many of their political thoughts and actions, we must look more closely at this unique and crucial period in their past.

Hitler's ideas were basically simple and so was the Nazi ideology derived from them. They offered a primitive but striking explanation for all the troubles of Germany and of the world. The Jews, Hitler asserted, were guilty of everything. They were the rich plutocrats of Wall Street and of all the world's stock exchanges, who were profiting from high interest rates and the misery of debtors and were benefiting from war, inflation, and depression. But the Jews, according to Hitler, were also the agitators for strikes and trade unions, the wirepullers for Communism and subversion. Their conspiracy, as depicted in such pamphlets as the forged but widely disseminated one attributed to Sergei Nilus, *Protocols of the Elders of Zion*, made them the real masters of both Wall Street and the Kremlin, which were the twin arms of a single plot against the world, and first of all, against the German people. Hitler actually seems to have believed these fantasies, but he also shrewdly noted in his book, *Mein Kampf*, that it was part of the art of the successful political propagandist to present several quite different opponents in the guise of a single enemy, and thus as a single target for skillfully aroused and directed popular hatred.

His appeal was aided by the highly visible concentration of Germans of the Jewish faith in journalism, law, and retail trade, including some of the large department stores. As the depression deepened, the law, the established press, and the department stores became more unpopular, particularly among small business-

men to whom Hitler's ranting began to sound more credible. According to some of his biographers, Hitler was a man who needed to hate, perhaps even more than he needed to belong to a group, to feel important, to believe in his own superiority, to be a member of a superior race, to be a great leader, and indeed to be a genius-inspired artist, molding the German people and, if possible, all of Europe and the world into the obedient shape dictated by his visions. A poor, half-educated man of illegitimate birth, he had been marginal even in the provincial middle-class society in the small town of Braunau where he had been born. He had failed to win a scholarship to art school, and as a young man he had been torn between his longing to rise to the level of the social elite and his fear of sinking down into the class of unskilled workers.

Other observers have read Hitler's mind differently. They point to his undoubtedly extraordinary gifts, particularly as a propagandist, and to the lack of adequate opportunities for such a brilliant talent in the rigid social system of pre-1914 Germany. The rage and hate that he so often demonstrated later may have been engendered by the frustration and rejection of his youthful aspirations. Or he may even have found it profitable to display more hate than he actually felt, in a calculated effort to whip up the emotions of his audience.

All observers agree, however, on Hitler's love of the military life and military values. The German Army of World War I had offered him, together with physical danger, the psychological and emotional security of its uniform; and when he stayed in service after 1918, it was the German Army that first sent him as a political intelligence agent into the strong labor meetings of the early Weimar Republic. It was here that Hitler discovered his gifts not only as an orator but as a master propagandist who was later to put down the principles of his craft quite frankly in *Mein Kampf*. Talk to people at meetings in the evening, he wrote, for then they are tired and less apt to resist your suggestions. Crowds are like women, he added; they like to be dominated. The bigger an untruth, he wrote, the more apt are people to believe it, since it seems incredible to them that anyone should lie so much. People who blindly disbelieve all they read in the papers, Hitler noted, are just as easy marks for propaganda as those who believe all that is printed. Above all, he concluded, successful propaganda is based on endless repetition that varies the form of the message so as to keep up the interest of the audience, but that hammers home the same unvarying content with ceaseless persistence.

Hitler did not hesitate to use every device of propaganda or of violence that would serve his purpose. At bottom, he believed, he stood for a great truth—the truth, so he believed, that all life was a pitiless struggle for existence, that nature was the "cruel queen of wisdom," that war as a social institution was eternal, and indeed good, for it subjugated or exterminated the inferior races while elevating the superior peoples and races to mastery. Only superior persons and races, he felt, were truly human, no others deserved consideration. The German people, as he saw it, had no other choice than that between victorious conquest or contemptible suffering. It was his destiny, he was convinced, to lead them; and if they were worth anything, they would eventually follow.

Hitler's hopes and dreams, just as his barely suppressed fears and rages, were those of millions of his countrymen. He represented much of their own feelings and desires, in heightened form. Many of them vibrated to his message because it was their own tune that was being played. At the same time, it copied some of the appeals of Communism—the vision of revolution, the promise of national solidarity and social justice, the emotional security and discipline of a tightly organized party, the heady sense of historical mission. But Hitler's ideology also included many themes borrowed from the ideas and practices of the West. The glorification of colonial empire and of a white master race, the misapplied ideas, borrowed from Robert Malthus and Charles Darwin, about an eternal struggle for survival among human beings,

the rejection of mercy, pity, and the traditions and ideas of the New Testament as unsuited to the real world of eternal struggle—all these ideas had been long propagated by various writers in England, France, and the United States, many decades before Hitler discovered them at second hand and bent them to his purpose.

In a nutshell, National Socialism thus was German nationalism plus a demogogic social promise, and minus moral inhibitions. Its leader, Adolf Hitler, promised to accomplish what many Germans wanted—from high-ranking officers and industrialists all the way down to many lower middle-class clerks and small farmers. He promised to make Germany a very great power, with an empire as large and splendid as the British Empire was believed to be; to make her formidably armed and universally admired and respected; and he promised also to insure for the German people within this greater empire the high level of economic security and living standards that befitted a "master race," comparable to the standards that were supposed to be the rightful due of white men in Africa and Asia.

Even before the coming of the Great Depression, between one-quarter and one-third of the German voters might have approved of some such goal, and an ever larger proportion—including a part of the Communist voters—would have agreed that the world was so largely ruled by naked power, force, and fraud that nothing great could be accomplished in it without extreme ruthlessness.

Like many nationalists and others who confused cynicism with realism, Hitler proclaimed himself a realist, merely because he assumed that the world was inevitably ruled by power and ruthless competition, that the strong and clever were fated to rule, while the weak or gullible were destined to slavery or death, and that in this inexorable struggle, the German people, like all peoples and races, only had the choice to be hammer or anvil, victors

The German Political Heritage

287

or victims—in the last analysis of the struggle for biological survival, to be killers or to be killed.

To be sure, this was an extravagantly over-simplified picture of the world, with no possible room for basic changes in human nature, culture, and society, no room for international cooperation among equals, no common victories of science over nature for the benefit of all. The important point was, however, that at bottom this was the sort of thing that, in somewhat less extreme and consistent terms, many German nationalists had long believed. Hitler thus seemed to them to voice their own beliefs with extraordinary force and fervor, and without introducing any frustrating inhibitions of traditional morality, or any doubts about the adequacy of his knowledge of international politics, economics, and military matters.

Conservative nationalists, however, had long been irked by the coolness of German workers, and generally of the broad masses of the German people, to their programs. Hitler promised to arouse precisely these masses, and to put the hopes and dreams of the poor and the workers behind the drive for a much bigger German empire than that of Bismarck's day. Even though Hitler in fact won far more support among the lower middle classes than he did among the workers, he did seem to offer an alternative to the appeal of organized labor, and it is not surprising that he found at least some sympathy and support throughout most of the 1920's in some military and business circles when his movement was still relatively insignificant and his one attempt at a coup in 1923 had remained a comic-opera affair. After the coming of the Great Depression in late 1929, however, the scale of this support grew very large, just at the time when masses of ordinary Germans became more inclined to listen to his message.

In the electoral campaign of 1930 and there-after, the Nazis had far more money to spend than their competitors—on posters, leaflets, advertisements, political uniforms, a private army of brown-shirted storm troopers and black-shirted "elite guards," on trucks to drive their men to mass meetings, for meeting halls, loudspeakers, spotlights, and all the other machinery of political propaganda. Much, perhaps even most, of this money came from the rank and file of Hitler's followers, for the Nazis were experts at collecting contributions, but much of it also came from prominent leaders of German industry and finance, such as the steel magnate Fritz Thyssen, who saw in the Nazis not only a counterpoise to Communism but also a tool to force down the high costs of trade-union wages and to prevent the welfare state that was being advocated by the Social Democrats.[1]

A much-publicized meeting of many of the best-known names in German heavy industry and in the German high nobility took place in October, 1931, at Bad Harzburg.[2] The meeting demonstrated the alliance of Hitler and his lieutenants with the old-style German nationalists, led by the newspaper publisher and film magnate Alfred Hugenberg, whose newsreels and chain of provincial papers began to transmit to their large unsophisticated audience a favorable image of Hitler and his movement. The Harzburg meeting dramatically underscored this new image of Hitler. Within a few months after the conference, which was featured in words and pictures by the press, Hitler lectured in January, 1932, to the industrial elite of Germany, at the Industrialists' Union at Düsseldorf, and the results of this "breakthrough," according to Hitler's press chief, Otto Dietrich, "became manifest in the following difficult months."[3]

During the last two and three-quarter years

[1] Much later the disappointed Thyssen wrote a book entitled *I Paid Hitler.*

[2] For an outstanding scholarly work, giving a partial list of those present, see Karl Dietrich Bracher, *Die Auflösung der Weimarer Republik* (The Dissolution of the Weimar Republic), 3rd ed. (Villingen: Ring Verlag, 1960), pp. 407–414. An English translation of this work is being published by the Yale University Press.

[3] Cited in Bracher, *op. cit.*, p. 441; see pp. 438–442.

of its existence, the Weimar Republic was governed by political conservatives—President Hindenburg and a succession of right-of-center Chancellors, Heinrich Brüning, Franz von Papen, and Kurt von Schleicher. Their governments were supported mainly by the Roman Catholic Center Party and the Social Democrats (SPD), although these parties—and particularly the SPD—had little influence on the deflationary policies that were becoming ever more unpopular with the electorate. Nevertheless, the two moderate parties lost only a few votes and retained the loyalty particularly of their older voters. The old-style Nationalists also changed little in their voting strength, but a mounting protest vote from millions of former habitual non-voters, including many women, and from young voters, the lower middle classes, and the unemployed, all went to the extremist parties, increasing the Communist vote to a moderate extent but swelling the Nazi ranks by leaps and bounds. At the same time, a number of smaller moderately rightist, nationalist, and conservative parties and groups crumbled, and their members and voters went over to the Nazis. Next to the passivity and political ineptness of the democrats, it was this mounting defection of the German conservatives that paved the way to Hitler's triumph.

Hitler was finally appointed Chancellor of Germany by old President von Hindenburg on January 30, 1933. Hitler thus came to sit at the head of a cabinet in which a few Nazi ministers were greatly outnumbered by Conservatives, including Alfred Hugenberg and Franz von Papen. Elections were called for March 5. Two weeks before that date, the empty building of the Reichstag, the German Parliament, was set on fire and a Nazi rule of terror started. According to the preponderance of such evidence as has survived, the fire was set by the Nazis. There is no doubt that they exploited it to perfection. The Communist Party was blamed for the fire and suppressed at once. In Prussia—which covered two-thirds of Germany—the Nazi storm troopers were deputized as auxiliary police. Everywhere in Germany the press and the meetings of all parties still opposing the Nazis

were drastically curbed; mass arrests, beatings, and acts of torture served to intimidate opponents. Even under these conditions, the Nazis got only 43 per cent of the popular vote. Only together with the Nationalists, who had polled another 8 per cent, could they claim to represent a bare majority of the German electorate.

On March 23, 1933, however, a cowed Parliament, including the Center Party, voted Hitler an Enabling Bill with sweeping powers. Only 94 Social Democratic votes were cast against it. The suppression of the Social Democrats and the major trade unions came in May; the Nationalists dissolved themselves in June; the Center Party—disoriented by a Concordat which Hitler had signed with the Vatican—was obliged to do so in July; and on July 14, 1933, the National Socialists were declared the only political party in Germany. A bloody purge in 1934 eliminated dissident Nazis and some conservatives, and Hitler's power became, for most practical purposes, absolute.

Once entrenched in power, Hitler communicated assurances of moderation to foreign statesmen and promises of extremism to his followers. He talked peace and prepared rapidly for war. At that time, Germany was still largely disarmed. As a result of the restrictions imposed on her by the Peace Treaty of Versailles, her armed forces lacked large trained reserves, any kind of military aircraft, tanks, heavy artillery, submarines, and full-sized battleships. Nor did she have any substantial fortifications in the West. All these deficiencies were overcome step by step, between 1933 and 1939, with the toleration and sometimes the approval of British and French statesmen, whom Hitler soothed with his anti-Communist declarations. Occasionally, he also assured the Soviet government of his peaceful intentions toward them and publicly pledged his friendship to the authoritarian government of Poland.

The German Political Heritage

289

The Nazis in Power

Hitler proclaimed that his empire would last a thousand years. It lasted twelve. The main events are familiar. During the first six years, Hitler achieved full employment and temporary prosperity, through controlled currency inflation and rearmament, which brought profits to industry and took hundreds of thousands of young men off the labor market by putting them into uniform. Added to this was an expanded program of public works—superhighways, new public buildings, and some low-cost housing—and improvements in some social benefits, such as government loans for home repairs and a popular "Strength through Joy" recreation program. As in most dictatorships, bread was supplemented by circuses. There were political and military parades, songs and martial music, and party congresses that became spectacles for millions. A network of press, film, and radio propaganda under the virtuoso direction of Dr. Joseph Goebbels disseminated these spectacles throughout the country and completed the intoxication of the nation.

During the same six years, the persecution of the Jews and the terror against all political opposition were organized into a system. The Jews were driven from all learned or free professions, from journalism, literature, the arts, from finance and industry—where they had been much less prominent than the Nazis had pretended—and finally from practically all kinds of business and employment. They had to wear yellow stars on their clothing, and their children were barred from ordinary schools and universities. Those who did not succeed in emigrating slowly sold their possessions piece by piece in order to live, waiting for a tomorrow that seemed to be becoming ever more bleak. Thousands of Jews were imprisoned and brutally treated in concentration camps, and so was an even larger number of German critics of Hitler; the annual number of concentration camp inmates in the 1930's has been estimated at between 20,000 and 30,000. In these years, the Nazis became masters of the art of concealing from the German people just enough of the crimes committed against their victims in the concentration camps to avoid arousing any widespread disgust or moral revulsion; yet they revealed enough to intimidate thoroughly most of the potential opposition within Germany.

Despite this shadow of fear and terror in the background, Hitler's partial and short-lived but well-publicized benefits made a profound impression: 40 per cent of the respondents to a national opinion poll in 1951 named the Hitler years of 1933–39 as the time when Germany had been best off. An even larger proportion, 45 per cent, named the pre-1914 Hohenzollern empire as Germany's best period, and only 7 per cent were willing to say as much for the Weimar Republic.[4] In a 1948 poll, 41 per cent recalled having approved the Nazi seizure of power in 1933, and 57 per cent agreed with the statement that National Socialism was a good idea which had been badly carried out.[5] Later, in 1956, among a sample of young men, nearly one-half called National Socialism a "good idea," either without qualification (16 per cent) or "in part" (33 per cent), while 29 per cent gave no opinion, and only less than one-quarter called it a "bad idea."[6] This favorable view is fading only slowly. From 1955 to 1956, the number of those who agreed that "Hitler without the war would have been one of the greatest statesmen" shrank from 48 to 42 per cent, while those denying this proposition increased from 36 to 38 per cent. Thus at that time in the Bonn Republic a preponderance of the public were admirers, to some extent at least, of a total nationalistic dictatorship.

The favorable surface image of Hitler's rule in 1933–39 was reinforced by the conspicuous tolerance, if not connivance, of foreign states-

[4] Elisabeth Noelle Neumann and Erich Peter Neumann, *Jahrbuch der öffentlichen Meinung*, I (1947–55), p. 126. (Henceforth cited as *Jahrbuch*, I.)

[5] *Ibid.*, pp. 133, 134.

[6] *Jahrbuch*, II (1957), p. 149; from a sample of 1,000 men born 1929–39.

men before World War II. Between 1934 and 1936 Britain accepted the establishment of a German air force, a limited German program of battleship and submarine construction, the introduction of conscription for a new German mass army, and the remilitarization of the Rhineland—all measures explicitly forbidden under the Treaty of Versailles. Only somewhat more reluctantly, France likewise accepted each of these steps in Hitler's rearmament. In those early years of Nazism, either Britain or France—or, of course, both of them together—could easily have stopped in its beginnings the creation of that German armed force that a few years later was to be used against their countries and peoples. Yet their governments chose to accept passively the creation of these German forces, hoping either that they would not be used, or that they would only be used against some other country.

The most obvious "other" country among the great powers was the Soviet Union, and Hitler's pose as the protector of Western civilization against Communism won him important sympathies outside Germany. These sympathies, no less than the fear of his conspicuously growing military and air power, kept the British and French from contesting his annexation of Austria in March, 1938. At the Conference of Munich in September of that year, Britain and France agreed to the dismemberment of Czechoslovakia and the annexation of the Sudetenland, and they acquiesced in Hitler's occupation of much of the rest of Czechoslovakia in March, 1939. If Hitler's aggression thus seemed to be directed southeastwards, the Soviet government found it to its obvious interest to turn Hitler's ambitions elsewhere.

In August, 1939, Stalin concluded with Hitler one of the most cold-blooded bargains in the history of power politics: a Nazi-Soviet non-aggression pact which left Hitler free to attack Poland and to make war on the West, and assured him of the benevolent neutrality of the Soviet government, which during the preceding four years had loudly called for an international common front against the Nazi menace. Finally, in September, 1939, Hitler took the German people into war against Poland, England, and France. But for the preceding six years, his respectability had been attested at one time or another by diplomatic collaboration, often including formal treaties of friendship, with all the major European powers, and including even Poland and the Vatican.

In the end, Hitler betrayed all the other governments and groups who had trusted his regime, or who had thought to collaborate with him for their own ends. He violated his 1933 Concordat with the Vatican and persecuted the lay organizations, and often the priests, of the Catholic Church. He made war on Poland, France, England, Russia, and many other countries. And between 1939 and 1945, he led the German people into the depths both of degradation and of suffering. His air force started the practice of large-scale bombing of civilian populations, at Warsaw in 1939 and at Rotterdam in 1940. In August, 1941, at the peak of his military triumphs, he gave orders to begin the extermination of the Jews—men, women, and children; he called it "the final solution" of "the Jewish question." Special camps were built with gas chambers and with crematoria for the bodies. From then on, badly needed manpower, building materials, fuel, and transport were diverted from the increasingly hard-pressed German armies to this infamous project of the Nazis. "We could process two thousand head per hour," the Commander of the death camp at Auschwitz, Franz Hoess, later told the International Court at Nürnberg. By the end of the war in 1945, an estimated six million Jews had perished. The shoes of executed children had been sorted into large piles for further disposal; the national bank of Germany had been enriched by a sizable amount of gold melted down from the gold fillings broken from the teeth of the dead; and some thrifty Nazi officials had tried to have some of the corpses used for the manufacture of soap. During the same years, German armies were ground up at the battlefronts while Allied aircraft rained fire and explosives on German cities. In a few nights at Hamburg in 1943, an estimated 200,000 persons lost their lives in a series of Allied air raids that set uncontrollable fire storms raging through whole city blocks, baking countless civilians even in the air raid shelters.

The war became a nightmare, and German defeat ever more certain. Yet the Nazi control of the German people held until the end. No German town or village rose; no German factory crew went on strike; no German troops mutinied, or surrendered without authorization. Thousands of Germans were executed during those years for opposing the government, or for daring to say that the war was lost; but the combination of Nazi propaganda and terror remained effective, since it was backed almost everywhere by the Nazis and Nazi sympathizers among the population, who supplied the secret police with support and information. In addition, the compulsory activities of the Nazis took up so much of the free time of the population that any popular needs for collective political activity became oversaturated, and most of the non-Nazi Germans were left with a mere longing for passivity and privacy—which left the Nazis in control until the end.

A desperate attempt at a *coup d'état* by officers and civilan opponents of the Hitler regime on July 20, 1944, was smashed, and was followed by large-scale executions. In the end, Hitler died under the ruins of Berlin. Germany was occupied by the American, British, and French troops from the west and Soviet forces from the east. The remaining German armed forces surrendered on May 7 and 8, 1945, and the Allied military authorities found themselves in charge of Germany's shattered cities and people.

Germany in Transition

III

Partition and Allied
Military Government, 1945–1949

After the collapse of Hitler's greater German empire, Germany was reduced to a territory smaller than that which had been left her by the Treaty of Versailles. The Nazi annexations of 1939 and 1940 were restored to their original owners. Thus Austria again became independent and the Sudetenland was returned to Czechoslovakia, and Alsace-Lorraine to France. Of the German territories of 1937, those to the east of the river Oder and Neisse (the "Oder-Neisse line")—notably including East Prussia and industry-rich Silesia—were detached from the rest of Germany. Being in fact occupied by Soviet troops, these "Oder-Neisse territories" were administratively separated from Germany with the consent of the Western Powers at the Yalta Conference. The northern half of East Prussia was put under the "administration" of the U.S.S.R.; the southern half, together with Silesia and the rest of the Oder-Neisse terri-

tories, came under the "administration" of Poland.

In theory, the fate of all these territories was to be finally decided only by a future peace treaty of all the Allies, Western and Eastern, with Germany. In fact, no such peace treaty has come into existence—or even seems in prospect. Rather, the governments and the people of both Poland and the Soviet Union consider that the Yalta arrangement was merely a face-saving gesture by the Western powers to mask their actual acceptance of the Polish and Russian annexation of these territories. These areas were quickly incorporated into the Polish and Russian national territories. Their German population—in a tragic and ironic reversal of the earlier population transfers of the Hitler era—was terrorized and expelled into the reduced Germany of 1945, and the territories were resettled by Poles and Russians. Thus the devastated German city of Breslau was gradually rebuilt and resettled as the Polish city of Vroclav, and Königsberg in former East Prussia became Kaliningrad in the U.S.S.R. A similar fate befell the German minorities in the territories that had not belonged to the Germany of 1937 but which Hitler had temporarily elevated to the status of a "master race" among their neighbors, such as the three million Sudeten Germans in

Czechoslovakia, and the smaller minorities of *Volksdeutsche* in Rumania, Yugoslavia, Hungary, and Poland. Almost all of these, too, were expelled into the reduced Germany of 1945.

This remaining Germany was occupied by the victors and divided into four zones of occupation—Soviet, American, British, and French—in accordance with wartime agreements. The city of Berlin, which had been the capital of Germany since 1871 and the capital of Brandenburg-Prussia since the seventeenth century, was similarly divided into four sectors of occupation and put under a separate regime. In theory, Germany was to be governed as an economic unit under an Allied Control Council, and Berlin similarly was to be under an Allied Kommandatura. In practice, although these joint bodies came into existence, the differences between the Soviet Union and the Western Allies proved unbridgeable; each zone was run separately by its controlling power, and the remaining trickle of interzonal trade was carried on much as among different nations.

Within their zones, the Western powers, particularly the United States and Britain, tried to restore gradually some fabric of German administrative effort and political life. After establishing German municipal administration, the Western allies proceeded to set up regional governments, called *Laender* (lands), somewhat analogous to the states in the United States. During the same period, the German press and radio were revived, under personnel screened by the Allies. Political meetings and parties were permitted, and eventually so were elections to representative bodies at the municipal level (January, 1946) and the Land, i.e., regional, level (June, 1946).

From Ex-Enemy to Ally

During 1946, Western policies toward Germany went through a major change. In March of that year, the Allied Control Council, on

which the Western powers predominated, limited the future level of German industrial production to half its 1938 volume, with a future steel capacity set at 7.5 million tons. In September of the same year, the United States Secretary of State, James F. Byrnes, in a speech at Stuttgart, called for a unified German economy and the early creation of a provisional German government, and he treated Germany, by implication, as a potential ally of the West. In the same month, Sir Winston Churchill, speaking at Zurich, called for a united Europe, including Germany, to defend Western values and traditions.

Earlier, in July, 1946, the United States invited economic mergers of their zone with any other zone, and Britain accepted the invitation. Also in July, in the first of several amnesties, the American occupation authorities began· to allow the return of former Nazis into high levels of public and private employment, from whence they had been ousted in large numbers by procedures of "denazification." These amnesties were intended to ease the recruitment of experienced civil servants and other personnel for the task of reconstructing West Germany, and perhaps also to help reorient the more moderate sectors of German nationalist opinion toward an eventual posture of alliance with the West. These policy changes were followed in December, 1946, by the establishment of joint committees of German representatives from the eight Länder comprising the British and American zones, and the Byrnes-Bevin agreement between the United States and Britain merged the economies of their two zones into a "Bizonia."

During 1947, a German Economic Council was created for the Bizone, a revised plan for West German industry set the 1936 level of German production as its aim, and the preparations for the Marshall Plan and the European Recovery Program opened new and increasingly attractive opportunities for German cooperation with the Western family of nations. In 1948, after the Communist takeover of Czechoslovakia alarmed the West, the unification of West Germany and its merger with the Western coalition of powers were accelerated. At the London Conference of February, 1948, the fusion of the three occupation zones of the United States, Britain, and France was clearly envisaged, and so was the early creation of a federal type of German government. In March, 1948, a Soviet walk-out ended the Allied Control Council for Germany, and on June 16, a similar Soviet move put the four-power Allied Kommandatura in Berlin out of operation. Two days later, a carefully prepared currency reform was put into effect in the three Western zones, greatly spurring their economic revival but severing another of the previously agreed-on links between the Western- and the Soviet-occupied parts of Germany.

On the same day, the Soviet Military Government announced its decision to blockade West Berlin from June 19 onward. This was followed quickly by a currency reform for the Soviet zone and East Berlin and, on June 24, by the interruption of railroad traffic to West Berlin. Thus started the Berlin "blockade." A dramatic Allied airlift, using most of the disposable transport aircraft of Britain and the United States, enabled West Berlin to hold out for more than half a year, and the unsuccessful Soviet blockade was lifted on May 12, 1949. By that time, three important precedents had been set. The Soviet government had not attempted to dislodge the Allies from West Berlin by force; the Allies did not attempt to use force to break the blockade; and no Soviet pressure on West Berlin, short of force, had been able to compel the Allies to leave the city or to abondon their plans to establish a united and democratic West German state.

The Formation
of the Federal Republic

Allied steps toward the creation of such a state proceeded throughout the blockade. By August, 1948, travel restrictions were abolished between the French zone and "Bizonia," creating, in effect, a "Trizonia." On September 1, a West German "Parliamentary Council," which was, in fact, a Constituent Assembly, met in Bonn to draft a constitution for Germany—or rather, since Soviet-occupied eastern and central Germany were not represented,

the Council limited itself to drafting a "Basic Law" for the German Federal Republic, until such time as an all-German Constituent Assembly could replace it with a constitution agreed on by the entire German people. By the end of May, 1949, this Basic Law had been drawn up by the Parliamentary Council, adopted by most of the eleven Land Parliaments, and formally promulgated.

After a general election in September, 1949, followed by the choice by the Bundestag—the popularly elected Chamber—of Dr. Theodor Heuss as Federal President and of Dr. Konrad Adenauer as Chancellor—by a majority of one vote—the Western Allies were willing to see the Federal Republic actually launched. The Allies had in the meantime worked out three related instruments: (1) an Occupation Statute, which defined the residual powers of the Allies in the Federal Republic; (2) a Trizonal Fusion Agreement, which set up an Allied High Commission for Germany; and (3) a Charter for this Commission defining its organization and procedure. After the acceptance of these Allied instruments by the President and Chancellor of the German Federal Republic at Petersberg on September 21, 1949, the German Federal Republic came formally into existence.

The formal establishment of the German Federal Republic was followed quickly by the creation, on October 7, 1949, of a Communist-dominated German Democratic Republic (GDR) in the Soviet-occupied zone of Germany. The Government of the Federal Republic as well as the Western Allies, however, refused to concede this rival creation any legal standing whatever. They insisted on considering the Federal Republic as the sole legal representative of the German people, pending its eventual reunification; and the strict maintenance of this position, and of the policies based on it, was still an important preoccupation of West German foreign policy in 1962.

Germany in Transition

A Convalescent Republic, 1949–1955

During the first years of the German Federal Republic, its sovereignty was considerably limited under the Occupation Statute of 1949. Step by step, these limitations were reduced, first by the very nature of the Petersberg Agreement, then by the Contractual Agreement of 1952, and finally by the Paris Agreements of 1955, which made the German Federal Republic in most respects sovereign. It was authorized to form its own national Army, subject only to the major remaining restriction that the Federal Republic renounce certain types of heavy military and naval weapons, and particularly so-called "ABC" weapons—atomic, bacteriological, or chemical. The Republic was prohibited from equipping its own armed forces with such weapons or from producing them for any other country.

Between 1949 and 1955, about 10 million German expellees and refugees from Eastern Europe and East Germany were successfully absorbed by the Federal Republic. West German industry was rapidly reconstructed and the country began to experience prosperity. The 1936 level of aggregate gross national product was surpassed in 1950, and that of the 1936 per capita GNP in 1951. By 1955, the net national income was 179 per cent of that of 1936.[1] A good part—20 to 25 per cent—of this income went into new investments, but per capita consumption, too, by 1953 had reached 114 per cent of the 1936 level. Thus throughout most of the 1950's the population of the Federal Republic was better off economically than it had been before the war.

These conspicuous economic successes had been made possible by massive economic aid from the United States—which pumped an annual average of between 0.5 and 1.0 billion dollars into the Federal Republic—as well as by more modest economic aid from Britain and by the very efficient use made by the West German industries and government of the American aid.

The total amount of this aid up to June, 1956, was given by the Germany ministry of Economic Cooperation as almost $10 billion, of which $6.4 billion had gone to the Federal Republic proper and $3.6 billion to West Berlin.[2] The forms of this aid varied; almost $4 billion were accounted for publicly by the United States government as aid under the Marshall Plan and its several predecessor and successor programs. Some of the rest may have come in the form of commodity surpluses, the spending of American occupation troops, and American payments for the offshore procurement of military supplies, but some of the dollar receipts of Germany in those years, as was the case with the receipts of some other countries, were not publicized and remained in what the United Nations Economic Commission for Europe described as "the twilight zone of quasi-strategic information."[3] There was no doubt, however, about the effectiveness of the American contribution to the "economic miracle" of the Federal Republic: "it was 'dollar therapy,'" said a German official publication, "and the tonic effect of an American blood transfusion. . . . Every Marshall plan dollar spent in Germany has resulted in $10 to $20 worth of goods produced and services rendered."[4]

---

[1] Wolfgang F. Stolper, *Germany between East and West* (Washington, D.C.: National Planning Association, 1960), p. 11, with reference to *Statistisches Jahrbuch für die Bundesrepublik*, 1956 ed., p. 520.

[2] Federal Republic of Germany, Bundesministerium für wirtschaftliche zusammen arbeit, *Der Europäische Wirtschaftsrat* (OEEC Handbuch, 1956), p. 70; see also K. W. Deutsch and L. J. Edinger, *Germany Rejoins the Powers* (Stanford, Calif.: Stanford University Press, 1959), pp. 145–151, with further details and references.

[3] See United Nations Economic Commission for Europe, *Economic Survey of Europe in 1953*, pp. 19–20.

[4] Federal Republic of Germany, *Germany Reports*, 1953, pp. 239–243.

Foreign Policy

Side by side with this rapid economic reconstruction went the gradual recovery of Germany's position in international life. The Federal Republic became a member of the Marshall Plan and the Organization for European Economic Cooperation in 1949, an associate member of the Council of Europe in 1950, and a full member in 1951. In 1951, the Federal Republic also joined the International Labor Organization (ILO), the World Health Organization (WHO), and the United Nations Organization for Educational and Scientific Cooperation (UNESCO). Guided by the prudent and steadfast policy of her government, and aided by the diplomatic support of the United States, the German Federal Republic was regaining for the German people something that many Germans had always deeply desired—a respected and honored place in the family of nations.

At home and abroad, the government of the Federal Republic strove to establish a reputation for reliability, moderation and conservatism—well-suited to the inclinations of its leading statesmen and to the mood of a majority of the electorate. In the pursuit of these policies, however, the government not only strengthened Germany's political credit with its major foreign allies; it also established important precedents for the development of German domestic policies and institutions. From the outset, refugees and expellees who were German by language and culture were accepted on a basis of full political equality, regardless of what citizenship they had held before the war. From the inception of the Federal Republic, Adenauer's CDU/CSU Party has controlled the Federal government and excluded the Social Democrats from national power. From December, 1949, onward— with the endorsement of all major parties— both the Chancellor and the Bundestag have put themselves on record as favoring a German military contribution to Western defense—that is, have favored some form of German rearmament, albeit on a modest scale. After the outbreak of the Korean War in

1950, a contribution to European defense was voted by the Bundestag in 1952, and a force of 500,000 men was promised for 1957.

In contrast to post-1945 developments in Britain, France, and Italy, no significant industries or services were nationalized, and the main emphasis of Federal economic policy favored private enterprise. Here again the exclusion of the Social Democrats from a share in the Federal Cabinet was significant. At the same time, social services by Federal *Land* and local authorities were maintained at a relatively high level; an "equalization of burdens law" (*Lastenausgleich*) further helped to improve the lot of expellees, refugees, and bombed-out families from the Federal Republic; and by 1955, unemployment was down to about 4 per cent of the work force, and dwindled still more in the years that followed.[5] The pattern was thus set for a moderately conservative welfare state in politics, combined with a notable willingness on the part of businessmen, politicans, and government officials to promote investment and innovation in and the re-equipment of industry and commerce—a combination that was to persist with apparent success into the early 1960's.

In foreign policy in the 1949–55 period, Bonn concentrated on maintaining close relations with the United States, and also with France. There was noticeably less emphasis put on ties with Italy, and perhaps still less on those with Britain; and there were no diplomatic relations with the Soviet Union, or any other member of the Soviet bloc.

In contrast to this cold war climate toward the East, Dr. Adenauer proposed as early as March, 1949, a French-German economic union. In 1951, the Federal Republic signed the agreement establishing the European Coal and Steel Community (E.C.S.C.) with

[5] From figures in Arnold J. Heidenheimer, *The Governments of Germany* (New York: Crowell, 1961), p. 36.

Germany in Transition

France, Italy, and the Benelux countries. In the same year, after repeated personal interventions of Chancellor Adenauer in its favor, the German-Israeli Reparations Agreement was signed, pledging to Israel $822 million, in goods, over a twelve-year period. The Agreement was ratified in March, 1953. Already in 1952, steps were taken to outlaw the Communist Party and the extreme nationalistic Socialist Imperial Party (*Sozialistische Reichspartei*, or SRP); the outlawing of the latter party formally took place in the same year, while the legal proceedings against the Communists reached their culmination only in 1956. Germany's old foreign debts were cut in half, from about $7 billion to about $3.4 billion, by the 1953 London Agreements about German Foreign Debts with the Western powers.

In 1954, pursuing the same policy of accommodation with France and close collaboration with the United States, Germany ratified the EDC Agreement which would have created a West European Army. EDC was rejected by the French Parliament, but Germany later in the year signed the Paris Agreement, thus becoming a member of the North Atlantic Treaty Organization (NATO), and signed agreements with France on the Saar territory and on French-German relations. In May, 1955, with the ratification of the Paris Agreement, the German Federal Republic became sovereign, limited only by the few remaining restrictions on nuclear and other special armaments, noted above. Germany slowly built up its national army, which French statesmen had tried to prevent earlier, and it stood ready to get back the Saar territory from France in the near future—an event which was consummated in 1956 when the attraction of West German prosperity had come to reinforce the Saarlander's sense of German national identity. Adenauer's policy of German-French friendship had paid off; and it was going to continue.

Bonn's Return among the Powers, 1955–1962

The years after 1955 brought the rapid return of the German Federal Republic to the rank of such powers as Britain and France. It became not only juridically equal, but increasingly able to diverge from the policies of these European powers and to apply pressure in the pursuit of its own preferred goals. At the same time, the Bonn government showed itself increasingly independent from the day to day policies of its principal ally, the United States, even though the long-term alliance between Bonn and Washington continued.

Thus Chancellor Adenauer's government in September, 1955, opened formal diplomatic relations with the Soviet Union. In 1956, West German public opinion favored Egypt against France and Britain in the Suez crisis, and the Bonn government remained friendly to Egypt. In 1958, Bonn was the first Western power to recognize the new government of Iraq which had been installed by an anti-British revolution.[6]

Again, in December, 1955, the Bonn government yielded readily to pressure from mass opinion and the Bundestag, and cut back the term of military service from 18 months—as demanded by the NATO authorities, as well as by the German military—to a mere 12 months; the 18-month term of service was not restored until early 1962. The target of 500,000 German troops, to be placed at the disposal of NATO, which had first been promised for 1957, and then for 1960, was officially postponed, despite some NATO and United States objections. According to press reports in early 1962, the Bonn government by then expected to reach the target level of 500,000 troops some time in 1963.

Throughout most of the 1950's, West German defense expenditures remained in the neighborhood of 4 per cent of national income, and thus at a proportion similar to

[6] Deutsch and Edinger, *Germany Rejoins the Powers*, pp. 199–200, 226–227.

that of Denmark, and below that of Sweden and Switzerland, which each spent about 5 per cent of their national income on defense, as against 7 to 8 per cent spent in France and Britain, about 12 per cent in the United States, and an estimated 20–25 per cent in the Soviet Union. It was only in 1959 that the defense spending of the Federal Republic approached 5 per cent of its national income. In the 1962 budget, however, this ratio climbed sharply to almost 7 per cent; the $4.1 billion (16.5 billion DM) budgeted for defense amounted to almost one-third the federal budget; and with the attainment of the projected 500,000-man army in 1963, it seemed likely to go appreciably higher in the future.[7]

In sum, the Federal Republic had postponed its scheduled contribution to NATO by about six years, and was able during this time to devote a higher proportion of its manpower and financial resources to its own industrial development than it otherwise could have done. This decision was, in all likelihood, a wise one and in the best interests of both West Germany and her allies. The point here is, however, that it was a decision taken by the executive and legislature of the Federal Republic, and against the advice of the Western powers, and particularly the United States, which for so long had had a major voice in Bonn's decisions.

The Bonn government had been in no hurry to divert a large part of its labor force from industrial development to garrison duties, but its Defense Minister, Franz Joseph Strauss, and a number of its generals began in the late 1950's to press for the eventual equipment of the Federal Army—the *Bundeswehr*—with nuclear weapons, either in the form of a European nuclear force or on a national basis. German soldiers, Strauss argued in June, 1960, ought to be equipped with every kind of weapon that a potential enemy might use against them. This argument sounded moderate enough, but since the "potential enemy" was clearly the U.S.S.R. and since the U.S.S.R. had long been racing the United States in a contest for leadership in rockets and nuclear weapons, the Minister's argument amounted in substance to a demand for qualitative—although not quantitative—German parity with Russia and the United States.

At the same time, the Bonn government expressed officially its willingness to cooperate in the organization of a NATO nuclear deterrent, that is, some form of a joint force within which German soldiers would be trained in the use of nuclear weapons and presumably have a share in their custody. Discussions about such a NATO atomic force were still going on among the Allies in early 1962; if they should fail, the stage was set for the demand for a national German nuclear striking force, somewhat as the failure of E.D.C. in 1954 had set the stage for the creation of a national German army. General de Gaulle's insistence after 1958 upon a national French nuclear striking force furnished a conspicuous precedent for an eventual West German demand for a nuclear force of its own.

The Common Market

By the middle of 1962, however, the main seat of West German power was in the field of economics. The Federal Republic was a party to the European Common Market Treaty of 1957, together with other members of E.C.S.C., who became known as "the Six." Its industries were particularly able to compete in the markets of France, Italy, and the Low Countries, which were opened by the gradual tariff reductions stipulated by the treaty (Table 3-1). Its financial strength enabled the Federal Republic to make a major, and perhaps a crucial, contribution to an agricultural fund under the Common Market. The fund, which was to be used for the support of agriculture, helped to win the consent of French and German farmers and other agricultural

---

[7] From figures for 1962 in *Archiv der Gegenwart* (Bonn), 32:4 (January 21–26, 1962), 9636y; for 1959, *Statistisches jahrbuch für die Bundesrepublik, 1961* (hereafter cited as *SJB, 1961*), p. 426, Table 2; for mid-1950's, UN, *Economic Survey of Europe, 1955*.

TABLE 3-1 *German National Income and Foreign Trade Ratios,*
1870–1960 (In rounded-out billions of marks, at current prices)

State	Years	GNP	National income (Y)	Imports (M)	Exports (E)	Trade (M + E)	Percentage of national income	Percentage of GNP
German Empire	1870–79 [a]	—	14	3.6 [b]	2.5 [b]	6.2	45%	—
	1900–09	—	35	6.7 [b]	5.5 [b]	12.2	35	—
Weimar Republic	1928	—	72	14	12	26	36	—
Hitler's Reich	1938	—	80	6	5.6	11.6	15	—
German Federal Republic	1950 [c]	97	75	11	8	20	27	21%
	1955	178	138	24	26	50	36	28
	1960	276	215	43	48	91	42	33

[a] Source for 1870–1936 figures: K. W. Deutsch and A. Eckstein. "National Industrialization and the Decline of the International Economic Sector, 1890–1959," *World Politics*, 13:2 (January, 1961), 282, with references.
[b] Average imports and exports from 1872–79 and 1900–08, respectively.
[c] Source for 1950–60 figures: German Federal Republic, *Statistisches Jahrbuch für die Bundesrepublik, 1961*, p. 295, Table 1; p. 544, Table 3.

interest groups to the implementation of the Common Market treaty in the field of agriculture.

In 1962, the chief remaining question before the six members of the Common Market was the admission of Great Britain, under conditions lenient enough to permit her to retain some of her special trade relations with the Commonwealth—and particularly with Australia, New Zealand, and Canada—for a long time of transition. Since the French government under President de Gaulle seemed rather unwilling to make any substantial concessions to British interests, much hinged on the attitude of Bonn. Both industrial rivalry and Chancellor Adenauer's policy of close cooperation with France tended to range West Germany against Britain on this issue, while the French policy permitted Bonn to remain inconspicuously in the background of the conflict. Early in 1963 a special treaty providing for greater cooperation between France and West Germany was signed and on January 28, 1963 France vetoed Britain's entry in the Common Market. It was generally believed that the Bonn government had not pressed hard enough for Britain's entry.

The Theat of Soviet Power

American and Russian policies, too, came to feel the newly strengthened influence of Bonn. Since 1958, the Soviet government had been creating an intermittent "Berlin crisis" by threatening to conclude a formal peace treaty with East Germany (the GDR) and to hand over to that state the control of the Allied access routes to West Berlin, forcing the Allies to choose between a new blockade and the necessity of dealing with the authorities of the GDR, which they had thus far so steadfastly refused to recognize. President Kennedy refused to be forced to such a choice. With the consent of American congressional and public opinion, American troops in Germany were demonstratively strengthened.

Even after the building of the wall around West Berlin, American and other Allied access rights were respected; and much of late 1961 and early 1962 were filled with American-Soviet negotiations in search for some agreement that might permit both great powers to retain their essential positions, as well as their prestige, but to trade sufficient concessions in non-essentials to bring about a substantial lessening of the potentially dangerous tension between them. These American-Soviet negotiations, however, were more than once subject to thinly disguised criticism from Bonn. Chancellor Adenauer announced that he expected little if any good to come from them, and his government made clear its objections to most of the Western steps toward a possible accommodation with the Russians that were mentioned as being considered for discussion. Bonn's fears, of course, were directed against any possible American concessions to the Soviets at West Germany's political expense, somewhat as the Ulbricht regime in the GDR feared any possible Soviet concessions to the West that might weaken the grip of dictatorship in the GDR.

President Kennedy, in turn, made evident his displeasure about the manifestly unhelpful attitude of Bonn. The West German government changed its ambassador in Washington, and relations between Bonn and Washington by mid-1962 had become less cordial than they had been for a decade. Nevertheless, Chancellor Adenauer stuck to his main position: no recognition for the GDR and no substantial reduction of Allied and West German anti-Communist activities in West Berlin. On the American side, proposals which came within the limits of what had been indirectly or directly rejected by the Chancellor tended to recede in public discussion. Thirteen years after its founding, owing to the profound engagement of the United States in Berlin, West Germany, and Western Europe, the Bonn Republic had acquired an informal veto over an important range of American policy decisions.

The Problems Ahead

Powerful in diplomacy and economics, powerful even against such victors in World War II as Britain, France, and the United States—such was the international image of the German Federal Republic in 1963, eight years after its attainment of sovereignty under the Paris agreements. Yet how much solid political strength—how much dependable civic consensus—stood behind this impressive international position? How was the political system of the Federal Republic likely to function in the face of major decisions, and how well was it likely to deal with a crisis, political or economic?

At least a part of the international strength of the German Federal Republic came from situations outside its control. It was the rivalry between President de Gaulle's France and the United Kingdom that enabled Bonn to have such a seemingly decisive influence on the fate of Britain's application to join the Common Market, which would have an enormous influence on the future of Britain, of the Commonwealth, and of European integration. It was the long-standing tension between the United States and Russia that made West Germany and her government such key factors in the calculations of both Washington and Moscow. But while Chancellor Adenauer's government was speaking in a more independent tone of voice to its Western Allies, the Federal Republic remained dependent for its defense on the presence of American and British troops on German soil.

Bonn has perhaps given its support to Paris to keep Britain out of the Common Market, but it could not easily afford to have Britain withdraw her troops from the Rhine and have the German taxpayer—and the manpower of West German youth—replace the British contribution. A British refusal to go on supporting the policies of the Federal Republic in regard to West Berlin, or a British recognition, *de facto* or *de jure,* of the GDR—perhaps followed by similar action by other members of the Commonwealth—would mean a crushing diplomatic defeat for the Bonn government. If such an extreme British action seemed almost unthinkable in 1962, it seemed no less unlikely that Bonn could or would continue to use its power to keep Britain out of the Common Market for long, especially in opposition to the United States.

The fundamental dependence of the Federal Republic on the United States remained even greater. Although this dependence was mutual, the need of Bonn for warm relations with the United States remained greater than the need of the United States government for even minimal good relations with Bonn. West

German exports, as well as domestic prosperity, continued to depend in good part on American defense, tax, and tariff policies as well as on the continuing confidence of American investors. An American stock market decline, such as that of "Blue Monday," May 28, 1962, has immediate effects on the economy of the Federal Republic. American taxes on the investments of their nationals abroad, or fears among American and European investors of military or political instability in West Germany, or generally in Western Europe, could change the West German prosperity and balance of payments very rapidly indeed. Under these conditions, the persistent news from Washington that Chancellor Adenauer was being much less frequently consulted by the Kennedy Administration than he had been by its predecessors in the 1950's served as a reminder that Bonn's new power was in fact still a good deal less than it seemed, and that it had best be used with very great caution.

In fact, the international position of the Federal Republic might not always be strong enough to sustain the rigid policies of the 86-year-old Chancellor. Much depends on the solidity of his domestic political support, and on his health, as well as on such matters as the personal and political qualities of whoever might succeed him—a succession which in the nature of things could not much longer be deferred.

In many ways, the end of an era in West German politics seemed to be drawing near by the middle of 1962. Many of the political and economic gains of the preceding thirteen years seemed solid enough. Yet to the careful observer, at least some of the power positions and aspirations of Bonn still seemed built on precarious foundations. The Federal Republic steadily had been getting stronger, but perhaps it still was not nearly as strong as it seemed on the surface.

Under these conditions, much would depend not only on the changing conditions of

world politics, which West Germany for the most part could not control, but also on the underlying political, social, and ideological strength of the German people and on the wisdom of the political elite.

The Continuing Division of Germany

One dark shadow has fallen across the Federal Republic ever since it was established. The Communist-ruled German Democratic Republic (GDR) has continued to exist and to remind West Germans of the persistent division of their country. This rivalry between two states, and two governments, each claiming, in theory, the leadership of the entire German people, did not come into being all at once.[8] The Soviet authorities after 1945 first favored a policy of treating all of Germany as a unit, since they considered their zone of occupation as a potential bridgehead from which to appeal to German national feeling and to extend their influence into the western regions of the country occupied by the Allies.

Political parties in East Germany—the Communists (KPD), Social Democrats (SPD), Liberals (LDP), and Christian Democrats (CCDN)—all were licensed for organization on a nationwide level in 1945, earlier than in the West, where the Allies insisted first on a prolonged stage of local political organizations and activities. Although the Communists were given key positions in the administration, their party limited itself to a relatively moderate policy, promising a multi-party system with free elections and suggesting the possibility of a special German road to socialism. The expropriation of the large factories and the landed estates of the Junkers was justified on grounds of Communist ideology which saw fascism as the creation of landowners and

[8] The following account owes much to the illuminating summaries by Arnold J. Heidenheimer, *The Governments of Germany* (New York: Crowell, 1961), pp. 163–191; and Elmer Plischke, *Contemporary Government of Germany* (Boston: Houghton Mifflin, 1961), pp. 181–211. Both of these should be consulted for further details.

capitalists, as well as on anti-fascist grounds, rather than as part of any overt program of social reform. Large landowners and industrialists, it was said with some truth, had often been friendly to the Nazis; hence their economic power had to be abolished now to prevent a Nazi comeback later, and all parties were expected to support this policy through an anti-fascist bloc that was to assume political monopoly. While some politicians were beginning to withdraw from such Soviet-inspired and directed arrangements, the bulk of the non-Communist leaders, particularly in the SPD, accepted these reforms as, on balance, desirable.

Matters, however, did not stop there. It soon became clear that the Communists had overestimated their chances of becoming popular and that they could not hope to win a free election in the Soviet zone, let alone in West Berlin or in West Germany. By the end of 1945, the Communists began to press the East German Social Democrats to join with the Communist Party, but in the end only a minority, led by the chairman of the Social Democratic Central Committee, Otto Grotewohl, accepted this proposal as a national policy. In West Berlin, only 12.4 per cent of the Social Democratic Party members supported the merger, while 82 per cent opposed it.[9] The pro-merger minority of the Social Democrats did join the Communists, to form a new party called the Sozialistische Einheitspartei Deutschlands (SED) which turned out to be a Communist Party in substance. The SED was refused a license to operate in West Germany by the Allies, so the Communists there had to function under their own name as KPD until their suppression in 1956. The SED became, in effect, the sole ruling party of the Soviet zone, reducing the two remaining middle-class parties—the CDU and the LDP—to the role of powerless appendages.

The Creation of the GDR

Following the creation in West Germany of the German Federal Republic in 1949 and its attainment of substantial sovereignty through the Paris agreements of 1955, a German Democratic Republic (GDR) was set up in the Soviet zone in 1949, and its sovereignty was recognized by a GDR-U.S.S.R. Treaty in September, 1955. Although former Social Democrats have served in a few conspicuous positions—such as Otto Grotewohl as Prime Minister since 1950 and Friedrich Ebert, son of the President of the Weimar Republic, as Mayor of East Berlin—the GDR in 1955–1962 was ruled by a Communist dictatorship, exercised through the SED Party and dominated by a veteran Communist and First Secretary of the SED Politburo, Walter Ulbricht. After 1960, Ulbricht also served as Chairman of the Council of State, the most powerful body of the formal government of the GDR. As we have indicated before, the details of that regime cannot be discussed here. What mattered for the political development of the Federal Republic were the economic, social, and political changes in the GDR that impinged directly and indirectly on the political realities and expectations of the Bonn Republic and its people.

In 1955, the GDR had about 17 million inhabitants, roughly two million more than its territories had had before World War II; despite heavy emigration, it still had in mid-1962 a population of 16 million, or roughly one million above the pre-war level.[10] Its income was beginning to surpass the pre-war level, but it was still much poorer than the Federal Republic. As late as 1957, according to a United States scholar, the gross national product of the GDR "was only 20 per cent above the 1936 level, compared to a 90 per cent increase over the 1936 level recorded by West Germany." [11] Moreover, consumers in the GDR received a much smaller share of the national product than was the case in the Federal Republic. "Output of basic and pro-

[10] See *SJB, 1961*, p. 562.
[11] Stolper, *Germany between East and West*, p. 11.

[9] Heidenheimer, *op. cit.*, p. 168.

duction goods rose to 168 per cent, and of investment goods to 174 per cent of 1936, while consumer goods and food, drink and tobacco reached only a level of 75 per cent and 119 per cent of 1936, respectively." [12] Since the population in 1955 had increased by a million against pre-war times, the survey concludes: "While the total real GNP was in 1957 on a per capita basis about 12 per cent above 1936, consumption was undoubtedly still below it, though probably not very much so.[13]

CONTRAST WITH WEST GERMANY. This striking contrast to West German prosperity is attributed by experts to four major causes.[14] First of all, the Soviet government, during the first years after the war, dismantled and removed substantially more productive equipment from its zone of occupation than the Western powers did from theirs, and the Soviet Union insisted on substantial reparations payments out of the current production in the GDR until at least 1953, amounting, by Western estimates, to about one-quarter of industrial production. While the U.S.S.R.—which had been devastated by the war—was taking wealth out of central and eastern Germany, the United States—whose economy had flourished during World War II—was pouring relief, Marshall Aid, and other forms of economic assistance into West Germany.

In the second place, the Federal Republic had a much larger supply of labor, owing not only to its size and population, but to the 10 million expellees and refugees it had accepted. Therefore, it had both the capital to employ these people and the labor supply to make the best use of its capital. In this way, it was possible in the Federal Republic to increase output, productivity, and real wages very considerably, while at the same time keeping money wages

increasing only moderately, thus avoiding inflation.

The third set of conditions holding back the economy of the GDR centered around its own economic institutions. The division of the estates of the landed aristocracy—the old Junker class—had been carried through for political as much as for economic considerations, but it left the GDR with many inefficient small private farms, which absorbed a relatively large proportion of the labor supply and whose owners often were quite unenthusiastic about economic planning or the prospects of farm collectivization. At the same time, the typical Communist emphasis on heavy industry held back the allocation of capital to agriculture. The GDR in 1955 had only about 34,000 tractors, and this number rose by 1959 to about 42,000, while agriculture in the Federal Republic in the latter year employed about 754,000 tractors—more than eight times as many in proportion to the land used for agriculture in West Germany than was the case in the GDR (Table 3-2). The

TABLE 3-2 *Tractors, 1959* [a]

	Federal Republic	GDR Units	GDR 15 H.P. Equivalent
Agricultural areas (in thousands of hectares)	13,200 [b]	6,400	6,400
Tractors (in thousands, all types)	754	47	63
Tractors per thousand hectares	57	7	10

[a] Source: *SJB, 1961*, pp. 163, 165, 574; *Statistisches Jahrbuch der DDR, 1959*, p. 426, Tables 6 and 7.
[b] Figures for 1960.

greater capital investment in West German agriculture seems evident, even if one allows for the concentration of the GDR on a smaller number of much larger tractors, intended for the sizable fields of its collective farms. These handicaps were combined with the difficulties inherent in large-scale economic planning, the low levels of sophistication in GDR planning methods, and the lack of experience and competence of GDR planning personnel; all these taken together produced a not inconsiderable amount of waste during the 1950's.

[12] *Ibid.*, p. 12.
[13] *Ibid.*
[14] The account that follows here owes much to Stolper, *op. cit.*, pp. 15–17.

The fourth group of conditions hampering economic growth in the GDR was largely international in character. The Federal Republic was quickly integrated into the trading and credit community of the Western countries, which included the richest countries in the world, in a period of business prosperity. The GDR was integrated—much less smoothly—into the Soviet bloc, whose members were on the whole much poorer, and where international economic interchanges were much less well coordinated, although some improvements did start in 1957 and 1958.[15]

Unrest in the GDR

During much of the 1950's life in the GDR for many of its inhabitants was far more harsh and unpleasant than it was in the Federal Republic. The efforts of the Communist-led government to win popular favor by developing the arts, particularly the theater and music, were none too successful, nor did its use of radio and other instruments of propaganda succeed in convincing the population that they were well off now, and would be much better off soon. Since much of this propaganda was so obviously at variance with everyday experience, it tended to infuriate many people rather than to convince them; and since no effective legal expressions of opposition were permitted, those who were dissatisfied felt particularly bitter about the claims of the Communist regime to have "liberated" the working people of the GDR.

Throughout the 1950's, thousands of people expressed their dissatisfaction with their feet. They walked out of the GDR into the Western-occupied parts of Berlin and claimed asylum; then, after having been screened in West Berlin, they were flown to West Germany for further screening and eventual resettlement. The Soviet military authorities, as well as those of the GDR, were powerless to stop this flow, short of cutting off most of the movements of persons between East and West Berlin—a move which the Western powers would have considered illegal, and the Soviets inexpedient. The alternative of cutting off the

movement of persons between East Berlin and the GDR was even less attractive, since such a move would have deprived the GDR of its most important city. The flow thus continued, and the government of the Federal Republic, as well as the Allied authorities in Berlin, in effect did a great deal to encourage it, even though there were also some efforts to urge East Germans to stay in the GDR and hope for eventual reunification. As a result of this migration through West Berlin into the Federal Republic, the GDR suffered from 1950 through 1961 an average net loss of more than 190,000 persons each year, or a total net loss of nearly 2.3 million, which followed the loss of another 0.5 million in 1945–49—more than offsetting her natural growth of population. Some details of the ebb and flow of this migration can be seen from the data in Table 3-3.

These net figures are smaller than the ones publicized by the Bonn government, but they tell a story of a serious—though not fatal—drain on the manpower resources of the GDR. They also show that the peak period of that drain occurred during 1953–55 and that the peak year was 1953, when the net loss to the GDR rose to 320,000, or almost double the seventeen-year average. On June 17, 1953, strikes and riots in East Germany approached the dimensions of revolt, challenging the dictatorial power of the East German government and the tanks of the Soviet forces backing it. The riots, however, were quickly suppressed. Earlier broadcasts from West Berlin, the Federal Republic, and the American stations in Europe had done much, wittingly or unwittingly, to encourage the spirit of revolt in East Berlin and the GDR, and the American station RIAS had been particularly emphatic. At the time of the actual riots, however, the West German broadcasts urged calmness and caution; and the verbal attacks on the Soviet regime in the GDR were not followed by any effective Western action supporting the rebels

15 For details, see Stolper, *Germany between East and West*, p. 17.

Germany in Transition

Year	East to West		West to East		Net shift to Federal Republic	
	Number	Annual average	Number	Annual average	Number	Annual average
1945–61	3,177	187	(388)[a]	(23)	(2,789)	(165)
1950–61[b]	2,612	218	(318)	(27)	(2,294)	(191)
1945–49	565	113	(70)	(14)	(495)	(99)
1950	198		34		164	
1951	166		26		140	
1952	182		15		167	
1950–52	546	182	75	25	471	157
1953	331		11		320	
1954	184		33		151	
1955	253		33		220	
1953–55	768	289	77	26	691	263
1956	279		32		247	
1957	262		38		224	
1958	204		27		177	
1956–58	754	248	97	32	648	216
1959	150		(19)		(131)	
1960	199		(25)		(174)	
1961	204		(25)		(179)	
1959–61	553	184	(69)	(23)	(484)	(161)

[a] Figures in parentheses are estimates, based on the average 8:1 ratio of eastward to westward migration in 1950–58.
[b] Sources of data—for 1950–1960: Alfred Grosser, *Die Bonner Demokratie* (Düsseldorf: Rauch Verlag, 1960), p. 402, with reference to *Frankfurter Rundschau*, January 5, 1960; for 1960 and 1961: *Archiv der Gegenwart* (Bonn), 32:1 (January 6, 1962), 9584A, with references.

by force, because of the risk of local defeat by Soviet troops or the start of a new World War.

In fact, United States policy toward Berlin remained under President Eisenhower in 1953 very much the same as it had been under President Truman during the Berlin blockade in 1948 and 1949. We were pledged to resist any forcible Soviet or East German interference in Allied-held territory, but we refused to use any substantial military force to interfere in territories held by the Soviet Union or its allies. The same policy was followed later by President Eisenhower during the Hungarian uprising against the Communist regime of that country in 1956, and it was again followed by President Kennedy when the East German authorities built a wall between West and East Berlin in 1961. Throughout the period, neither the United States nor the Soviet governments showed any desire to use their armed forces for fear of initiating in Europe a war that might have incalculable consequences in the age of nuclear weapons.

If the unrest of 1953 in East Germany was thus quickly suppressed, it nevertheless was not without results. In the GDR and in East Berlin, it reminded the Communist rulers of the extent to which they had alienated popular feeling; it hastened the ending of reparations payments to the Soviet Union; and it started the transition to a policy of at least some beginning concessions to consumer needs and to creating better living standards.

In the Federal Republic, the East German

uprising of June 17 was taken as a promise of the early collapse of the GDR, and as a confirmation of the wisdom of Bonn's policy of consistent non-recognition of its eastern rival. June 17, thereafter, was celebrated in the Federal Republic as an official holiday—the "Day of German Unity"—but by the early 1960's it seemed that most West Germans were taking it as an occasion for peaceful family outings rather than for attending political rallies and official speeches.

By the beginning of the 1960's, the annual net outflow of refugees from the GDR into the Federal Republic had fallen back to the level of the early 1950's, averaging about 161,-000 per year in 1959–61, as against 151,000 in 1950–52. This flow does not seem, in itself, to have been an intolerable drain on the economy of the GDR, which had borne the much heavier outflow during the mid-1950's. If backed by the Soviet authorities, the East German government could have cut off at any time the movement into West Berlin of persons from the territories it controlled, and it could thus have stopped the westward flow of persons whenever such a step seemed worth its probable political cost.

In August, 1961, the East German regime and its Soviet backers finally exercised their option. A wall was built which completed the existing Communist system of enclosures around West Berlin; crossings were permitted only at a very few heavily controlled checkpoints; and practically no East Berliners or inhabitants of the GDR were permitted to cross to the West. A few desperate individuals still succeeded in making dramatic escapes to the West, but during the first half of 1962 they made up at most a trickle in place of what had been a stream. The United States and its Allies strengthened their troops in West Germany, but held to their policy of refusing as long as their control in the Western-held territories was respected, to interfere by force in the Communist-held territories and thus to risk making Germany a theater of war.

The people of the Federal Republic remained closely connected by ties of family and old friendship, as well as of national sentiment, with the population of the GDR. In the mid-1950's, nearly one-quarter of the population of the Federal Republic were natives of East Germany. Forty-four per cent of the respondents to a poll in 1953 claimed relatives or friends in the Soviet zone of Germany; together with those West Germans who had personal acquaintances there, a majority of West Germans had at least some personal contacts with the population of either the GDR or East Berlin.[16]

Nearly two-fifths of the West Germans, polled in February, 1953, claimed to be writing letters sometimes to the Eastern zone, and nearly one-third had sent Christmas packages there—a claim confirmed by the 24 million packages sent in 1956, which was exceeded by the 30 million packages reported for 1957. In December, 1961, after the building of the wall around West Berlin, the number of Christmas packages increased further, indicating that human relationships were continuing despite political restrictions.[17]

The Future of the GDR

In the face of the political and human desires for unity between the western and eastern parts of Germany, the foreign policy of Bonn in the 1950's had little more to offer than the hope for the eventual collapse of the government of the GDR, or for some drastic loss of power or change of policy on the part of its Soviet backers. None of these hopes of the Bonn government came true in the 1950's, and the outlook in the early 1960's seemed no more promising.

During the 1950's, the planned economy of of the GDR continued to develop, growing at rates not very different from those of West Germany. In the judgment of an expert Western observer:

[16] Deutsch and Edinger, *Germany Rejoins the Powers*, pp. 178–179, with references.
[17] See Richard L. Merritt's study of West and East Berlin, *Divided City*, forthcoming.

It must be recognised that in the course of the 1950s average annual growth rates in East Germany have been not far below those of the Federal Republic, the figures are estimated at about 8.5 and 10.3 per cent respectively for the period 1950–57. On a per capita basis—population having declined in the East and increased in the West—there is probably little difference in East and West German growth rates between 1950 and 1957. Of course, the continuing depressed level of East German living standards should be noted; on the other hand, it is likely that this disparity will lessen and a distinct possibility that East Germany may for a while actually register higher future per capita rates than the Federal Republic.[18]

In the course of the 1960's, some of the factors retarding the economic growth of the GDR, relative to that of the Federal Republic, were likely to weaken. The effects of the Soviet reparations policies of 1945–53 would undoubtedly diminish while the flow of American dollars into West Germany would likely decline—on a per capita basis and perhaps even absolutely. The large-scale migration of German-speaking labor, much of it skilled, from Eastern Europe into the Federal Republic likewise had come to an end, and the building of the wall around West Berlin in August, 1961, ended the chances of any sizable flow of refugees from the GDR into West Germany. Planning methods and the competence of planners in the GDR would probably improve with experience.

The international environment of the two rival German states also seemed less likely to favor the Federal Republic as strongly as it had in the past. If the Soviet Union and its bloc of East European countries prospered, as they had been doing during the 1950's, they would be able—if their governments consented —to offer more rewarding trade opportunities to the GDR; on the other hand, if the economic boom in Western Europe and the

United States slid into a business slump, then the pace of West German economic growth would lessen. This possibility materialized in 1961, when the annual economic growth rate of the Federal Republic fell to 4.5 per cent— about average for the non-Communist world in the later 1950's, but well below West Germany's earlier performance.

A serious economic depression in the West might, of course, make things much worse for the Federal Republic; and such a possibility seemed less remote after the American stock market decline during the first half of 1962 than it had seemed in earlier years. Even without any more drastic economic troubles, however, a prolonged period of slowed-down growth in the Federal Republic would give the forced-draft planned economy of the GDR a chance to catch up eventually with the per capita income levels of its Western rival. This threat seemed remote in mid-1962, but if it did materialize there seemed to be little that Bonn could do about it.

Early in 1963, the GDR was still without diplomatic recognition by most governments outside the Communist block. In accordance with the "Hallstein Doctrine"—named after the German diplomat and former professor, State Secretary Walter Hallstein—the Federal Republic announced that it would break off its diplomatic relations with any state that recognized the GDR. Only the U.S.S.R. was exempted from this principle of West German foreign policy. In 1957, when Yugoslavia recognized the GDR, Bonn somewhat reluctantly did break off diplomatic—though not trade— relations, and the doctrine has been cited as one of the main reasons why the Federal Republic still had no diplomatic relations with its eastern neighbors, Czechoslovakia and Poland, whose Communist governments had long recognized the GDR.

Despite this diplomatic deadlock, some form of indirect or *de facto* recognition of the existence of the GDR was under discussion in the West in early 1962. The Communist-ruled GDR continued as the greatest single irritant to the Bonn government, which had been so successful in so many other matters.

[18] Stolper, *Germany between East and West*, pp. 11–12.

Ideology and Opinion

IV

The long and often violent history of the German people has left them with deep-seated memories that have colored their political decisions in the past and will continue to do so for years to come. These memories are embedded in German school books and in learned histories, in words of creative literature and in the minds of individuals. These historic memories recall that for centuries the international environment has not been kind to Germany. From the horrors of the Thirty Years War to the desperate struggles of Frederick II's Prussia and the Napoleonic Wars, foreign economic and military developments are remembered as having threatened or injured Germany, and to this are added memories of the overwhelmingly strong foreign coalitions that united to defeat Germany in World Wars I and II. In such a dangerous world, these memories seem to suggest, Germans should not show any weakness or disunity, or any excessive trust in foreigners or foreign powers. This impression is reinforced by memories of real or imagined exclusion of peaceful German trade from many overseas areas, both before 1914 and between the World Wars—and perhaps today, though to a lesser extent—through the operations of colonial administrations, currency blocs, and various formal and informal controls over credit and trade, all of which were believed to have functioned somehow to the disadvantage of Germany.

In the past, many Germans believed that they worked harder and more efficiently than the members of any other great industrial power in Western Europe, and many also believed that for their efforts they received relatively less in terms of real income, domestic living standards, and international prestige. Members of other nations could move about distant parts of the globe and yet feel respected and at home in the colonies of their nation, but Germans at best had to enter everywhere as foreigners and always had to adapt themselves to the ways of others.

The German "National Character"

In the face of an environment that thus seemed often less than fair to their aspirations, many Germans felt that they had to hold on to their particular virtues as a people. Outstanding among these virtues was a capacity and liking for hard work. Most people seem to consider the members of their own nation as hard-working, but the Germans do so to a far greater extent. While 68 per cent of American respondents to a UNESCO poll applied this term to their own people in 1948–49, and respondents in six out of seven other countries claimed the same distinction for themselves with lesser majorities or pluralities, the Germans interviewed in the poll proclaimed their faith in the diligence of their own people with a solid 90 per cent majority.[1] Later polls confirmed this image; majorities of 60 per cent in 1955, and 56 per cent in 1956, reiterated in German polls the conviction that their own people were "more efficient and gifted than the other peoples."[2]

There is no doubt that these images are based on very real German virtues. Foreign observers, as well as Germans, have attested time and again to the energy, diligence, and thoroughness of Germans in their work, both physical and intellectual. There is a high degree of care and thoughtfulness in German workmanship; there is steadfastness in the face of difficulty, and great courage and discipline in the face of danger. There is a tradition of selflessness, of readiness to sacrifice and suffer, of solidarity with one's group—national, social, or ideological; there is a serious concern for justice and a deep well of imagination. Not all Germans, of course, have all these virtues at all times; but many Germans have shown them often, and under critical conditions. It is these virtues that stand out in the symbols of German literature and poetry; it is these themes that have moved, and still can move, many Germans in political appeals; and it is these qualities that Germans may still be expected to show often in their actions.

[1] I.W. Buchanan and H. Cantril, *How Nations See Each Other: A Study in Public Opinion* (Urbana: University of Illinois Press, 1953), pp. 46–47.
[2] *Jahrbuch*, II, p. 139; see also Deutsch and Edinger, *Germany Rejoins the Powers*, pp. 32–34.

Yet the German "national character"—or those frequent elements and patterns in German culture, traditions, and personality that have relevance for their political behavior—is more complex. Like similar patterns in other countries, it moves often in polarities, that is, in pairs of opposites. Thus German political and cultural styles have moved between the poles of idealism and materialism. Both German and foreign observers have spoken of a German fascination with abstract doctrines and ideas, and sometimes of the preoccupation of Germans with wealth and material success—as once again today people talk of the "success Germans" of the Bonn Republic.

Other polarities exist between the rival images of German profundity and practicality or matter of factness (*Sachlichkeit*); and between chivalrous romanticism and pedestrian stolidity. A romantic nobleman, Walter Stolzing, is opposed by an obtuse critic, Beckmesser, in Richard Wagner's opera, *Die Meistersinger;* or a romantic, searching scientist, Dr. Faust, is contrasted with his diligent but uncreative assistant, Wagner, in Goethe's *Faust.*

German political styles sometimes have been dominated by similar contrasts, or have oscillated between them. Periods of admiration for grandiose or even demonic heroes have been followed by periods of contentment with solid mediocrity; and periods of great resistance to change have been followed by periods of its over-acceptance. More than once in German history, dependable moderate courses of action were firmly held for years and decades, until some strain became too much, and a rapid and intense realignment of political sympathies and styles of action followed. Thus the "blood and iron" period of Bismarck followed nearly a half-century of predominantly moderate and peaceful politics. Hitler followed the years of moderation under the Weimar Republic (thus it is vital for the peace of the world that the present period of stability under the Bonn Republic should prove to be durable). In this manner, much of German history has been a history of breaks in political style.

German attitudes to politics have often oscillated between an insistence on the virtues of being "non-political" or "above the parties" and a willingness to accept the most extreme partisan commitments of totalitarian fanaticism. Both of these poles derive from the same fundamental view of politics, which sees the world of politics as fundamentally evil, governed by the laws and necessities of what St. Augustine described as the city of robbers; which Machiavelli had seen as ruled by the pragmatic necessities of force and fraud, rather than by traditional morality; and which Luther had seen as a world of Princes who had to be obeyed even if they were immoral, since they were set by Providence to rule over subjects corrupted by original sin.

In fact, this was a very naive version both of actual politics and of the views of Augustine, Machiavelli, and Luther, all of whom had been more complex and subtle thinkers. It was a simplified version, however, which fitted the emotional needs of an educated people who lacked any deep or rich experience of responsible political participation, and who found themselves bewildered by what little of politics they actually saw. To conclude that politics was basically wicked, then, meant that one kept away from it as long as possible, but that—if one had to act in politics at all—one might be quite willing to accept some quite ruthless or extreme political practice or ideology, for that was in any case what politics really was like. By no means have all Germans at any one time been stranded on the poles of this non-political or hyper-political dilemma, but a sufficient number of them have been often enough in the past to give to German political attitudes a characteristic cast and potential.

Some of these polarities perhaps can be traced back to the influences of German history, and so can some of the potential political weaknesses which they imply. German history is rich in memories of authoritarian princes and magistrates, and of the dependence of their subjects on them for protection. Some of this authoritarianism was reinforced by the patriarchal tradition of the pre-industrial West European and German family structure and patterns of bringing up children; and it reinforced in turn this tradition in Germany.

In this way, a stronger element of authoritarianism has been transmitted from generation to generation, and transferred into the formation of German national character and political attitudes. Not all Germans, by any means, are authoritarian, but more of them seem to be so to a higher degree than do most of the people in, say, France, Britain, and the United States.

The Lack of a Strong Commercial Class

Another historic legacy may be the result of the long period of relative weakness of the commercial middle classes in Germany from the mid-sixteenth to the mid-nineteenth century, that is, during a period when these classes became relatively strong in England, France, and the United States. As a result, some of the characteristic political assets of a mercantile civilization may have become somewhat under-represented in German culture. In commerce as in politics, it is important to be able to bargain easily and successfully, without being either duped or angered, and without expecting either to give in or else to have things all one's own way. Merchants learn to accept bargaining and compromise as natural, rational, and honorable, while to aristocrats these two practices may seem frustrating and somehow dishonorable. These two contrasting attitudes may carry over into politics, where the word "compromise" has long had a ring of illegitimacy in German ears.

Merchants also need to be capable of some degree of empathy; that is, it helps them greatly to be able to perceive quickly and accurately the moods of their customers, to put themselves in their customers' place. These skills of perceptiveness, sensitivity, and empathy are common ones for the merchant and the politician—and for the types of diplomats, civil servants, and political leaders that England has long been training at Oxford and

Cambridge—but they have not often been conspicuous in German politics.

German empathy has come more often from imagination than from perception. German rationality has been more often not the rationality of the negotiator but rather that of the soldier, the scholar, and the bureaucrat.

The German lack of a strong mercantile tradition and the German authoritarian heritage do not make it easy for Germans to deal smoothly and effectively with equals, or to feel at ease in relations with them. "It is not easy to come to a strange country," the German poet Bertolt Brecht once wrote; "you do not know at whom you may shout, and before whom you must doff your hat." This difficulty of relating easily to equals has been reinforced by German geography and history. For long periods, Germany's Western neighbors appeared to be clearly richer and more advanced, and thus potential objects of envy, while the peoples to the East seemed clearly poorer and more backward, and thus potential objects of contempt; but there were few, if any, prolonged periods in the history of the German people during which they could look upon any other large nation as just about their equals. Remembering a highly stratified society at home, and an internationally stratified environment abroad, it was difficult for Germans to think of their domestic and foreign policies in equalitarian or democratic terms.

Bonn's Postwar Achievements

In the face of this complex heritage of psychological and political assets, liabilities, and contrasts, the Bonn Republic has done remarkably well. It has gone far towards making the politics of compromise appear both successful and legitimate. It has increased the degree of equality in German society and politics, through nearly full employment, broader educational opportunities, and in many other

ways; and it has acted toward the other countries of Western Europe, and particularly toward France, as an equal. More generally, it seems to have lowered the levels of bitterness and tension that could be found in earlier decades in the life and outlook of the German people; and this seems the more remarkable since tensions might have been expected to rise after a defeat in war.

In the early 1930's, the sharp rise in the frequency of suicides was cited by political spokesmen of various parties as evidence of the increase of such bitterness and desperation. It is not easy to say to what extent changes in the suicide rates do, in fact, reflect changes in the level of tensions and frustrations in a country, but the data in Table 4-1 throw at least a suggestive sidelight on the problem.

TABLE 4-1   *Average Suicide Rates among Men, 1893–1959* [a]

Year	Regime	Suicides among 10,000 men	
1893	Second German Empire	3.5	
1913	"	3.5	
1924	Weimar Republic	3.5	
1928	"	3.6	
1931	"	4.9	
1933	Hitler's Reich	4.1	
1934	"	4.1	
1939	"	3.9	
		Federal Republic	GDR
1955		2.6	3.5
1958		2.6	3.7
1960		2.6	3.5

[a] Sources of data: (1) 1893–1939—Roderich von Ungern-Sternberg, "Die Selbstmordhäufigkeit in Vergangenheit und Gegenwort," *Jahrbücher für National ökonomie und Statistik,* 171:3 (Stuttgart: Fischer, April, 1959), pp. 187–207, especially pp. 198–199. (2) 1955–1960—German Federal Republic, *Statistiches Jahrbuch für die Bundesrepublik, 1961,* pp. 84–85, 566.

The figures suggest that, under the Bonn Republic, suicide rates have fallen by between one-quarter and one-third below their pre-war levels, while they have not done so in the German Democratic Republic under Communist rule.

Most important, perhaps, the Federal Republic has provided time, security, and opportunity for a new generation of young Germans to grow up and to reach the threshold of political life.

It is always perilous to generalize about a

country, a people, or a generation, and yet we cannot avoid putting our impressions into general terms, if we are to think coherently. With all due caution, then, we may conclude this chapter with a few impressions about the young Germans of the early 1960's. They seem to have as many or more of the strong points or virtues of their fathers, and they seem to have them more *sans phrase*—without over-assertion or self-consciousness. They seem more relaxed and more confident; less defensive and less envious; more sensitive and more concerned with moral values; more skeptical of high-sounding phrases, and yet more ready to experiment and innovate. Many of them have played as children in the ruins of their cities; and yet they seem a remarkably hopeful generation to have grown from this heritage. Much may depend on whether they will find time and peace during the next two decades to develop their full contribution to a democratic Germany.

Ideological Cleavages and Groupings

"Ideology" is a name by which we sometimes like to call the belief systems of other people. It is a sobering experience to discover that we, too—every one of us—hold many beliefs that we take for granted; that many of these beliefs are coherent and mutually supporting; that we use this collection of our coherent beliefs as a map of reality, or a frame of reference, on which we enter whatever new information we receive, and by which we try to make sense of it; and that, in short, we, too, each may be said to have an ideology which serves us, and inevitably influences us, both in orientation and in action. It would be utterly naive to deny that ideology exists, and only a little less naive to claim that it exists exclusively in others. To be more realistic, we must try to assess critically ideology and its effects in each case, both in others and in ourselves.

Germany was a highly "ideological" country between 1930 and 1945, with an intense degree of ideological commitment among the Nazis, and on the other side, among their opponents. Between 1945 and the present, the situation has been quite different. Intense ideological fanaticism has been rare; even many of those who were deeply committed to political ideas kept them within the limits of pragmatism and moderation. Under this landscape of moderate and practical politics in the Bonn Republic, however, many ideological commitments and cleavages have persisted, and some of these may show up again in times of political or economic stress. This is true not merely of some older people in holding on to the attitudes of their past. Young people in Germany, too, have political attitudes and ideas that may again sharpen into more intense ideological commitments under the stimulus of some crisis.

The Popular Rejection of Communism

One earlier ideology, however, has practically disappeared from West German politics. The Communists, who attracted an average of 10 per cent of the electorate, and 13 per cent of the votes cast, during the seven national elections between 1924 and 1933, have dwindled into insignificance in the Bonn Republic. This change was complete even before the outlawing of their party in 1956. In the 1949 Bundestag elections, the Communist share dropped to 4 per cent of the electorate, and to less than 6 per cent of the valid votes cast. In 1953, the Communist strength dropped still further, to about 2 per cent, both of the electorate and the votes cast.[3]

The votes in the Land elections confirm this trend. Thus in Bavaria, where the Com-

[3] Pre-war data from **Sydney L. W. Mellen**, "The German People and the Postwar World, A Study Based on Election Statistics, 1871–1933," *American Political Science Review*, 37:4 (August, 1943), Table II, pp. 612–613; postwar data from Erwin Faul, ed., *Wahlen und Wähler im Westdeutschland* (Villingen-Schwarzwald: Ring Verlag, 1960), pp. 321–323. The latter is an outstandingly useful and thoughtful collection of studies on voting behavior in the Federal Republic.

munists received the support of an average of nearly 5 per cent of the electorate in the seven national elections between 1924 and 1929, they again received 4 per cent in the election to the Bavarian Constituent Land Assembly in June, 1946, and this share rose to nearly 5 per cent in the Land election in December, 1946. Their share then dropped, however, to 3 per cent in 1949, and to 2 per cent in 1950; and it remained at or below the 2 per cent level in 1953 and 1954 for the rest of the party's legal existence. In West Berlin, too, the share of the electorate voting for the Communist-led SED party dropped from 12 per cent in 1946 to 2 per cent in 1954 and 1958.[4]

Poll results consistently show the same picture. Expressions of symypathy for the Communist Party, or for the Communist regime in the GDR, are down to, or below, the 2 per cent level, while 96 per cent of West German respondents—a staggeringly high proportion—say they are certain that living conditions in the Federal Republic are better than in Communist-ruled East Germany.

In West German politics, Communism is as unpopular as sin—or, if possible, more so. The reasons for this change from the 1920's are complex. The division and occupation of Germany at the end of World War II and the excesses of Russian troops cannot account for all of it. Communist votes in West Germany were higher in 1946–49, when the memory of any such excesses would have been fresh; they dropped only later, when the events of 1945 were receding into the past. Moreover, in Finland, which also was occupied by Soviet troops and lost important territories to Russia, the Communist Party continued to receive a much higher degree of popular support.[5] Pop-

ular revulsion from Communism in West Germany may have been promoted by the continuing stream of expellees and refugees from Communist-ruled areas; by the inflow of these intensely anti-Communist millions into the least-skilled and worst-paid occupations, where the Communists otherwise might have hoped for converts; and most important of all, by the unprecedented rise and spread of economic prosperity after 1948, combined with effective social welfare legislation.

The Changed Emphasis of Democratic Socialism

Even the democratic version of Marxist ideas, traditional for generations in the Social Democratic Party, has greatly receded. The Social Democrats have always been implacably opposed to Communist ideas of violent revolution and dictatorship, but they had accepted Karl Marx's belief in the central importance of class conflict and in the necessity of a fundamental change in property relations in industry, banking, and large-scale agriculture, to be brought about by far-reaching policies of nationalization. While some ideas of this kind were still voiced in the early years after 1945 by such SPD leaders as Kurt Schumacher, they did not prove popular in the elections of 1949 and thereafter, since they had become associated in popular memory with the economic shortages, austerity, and rationing of the early postwar years. In the 1950's and early 1960's, the SPD tried to change its public image from that of a "workers' party" to that of a "party of all the people," stressing human rights, welfare policies, full employment, and the guidance of a private enterprise economy through tax and credit policies, somewhat in the style of a large part of the Democratic Party in the North of the United States. The "basic program" of the SPD, voted by a special party congress at Godesberg in 1959, formally expressed this change of emphasis; and in 1962, when it was suggested that the customary Socialist form of address, "comrade," be dropped, it was only decided to retain this old salutation "for the sake of long tradition." That this question was raised is one manifestation of the impact of the younger generation on

---

[4] From data in Faul, op. cit., pp. 329–335, 366–367.

[5] These points are made by Juan Linz, The Social Bases of West German Politics (Ann Arbor, Mich.: University Microfilms, Inc.), Columbia University Ph.D. Dissertation, 1959, pp. 64–65.

West German politics. Many of these men and women feel over-saturated with the trappings of close human community in politics, such as political salutations and the ritual use of the familiar "thou," all of which became discredited through their use by the Nazis.

Nazi Ideology and the Extreme Right

Ideologies of the Right have retained greater strength in their extreme versions and even more in their more moderate versions. In the mid-1950's, about one German in twenty could be counted as an intense hard-core Nazi, while one in eight professed explicit Nazi sympathies. Thus in a June, 1956, poll, 12 per cent said they would welcome the attempt of a new Nazi party to seize power; one-fourth of these, or 3 per cent of the total, promised their active support. Answers to the same question in 1953 had revealed 5 per cent Nazi activists, and 13 per cent activists plus sympathizers. Among men in 1956, the share of professed Nazi sympathizers plus activists was 14 per cent; and among young men and women between 18 and 29 years, it was 16 per cent.[6] In repeated polls during the years 1949–58, similar proportions of 7 to 15 per cent (1) said they liked Hitler and his rabid Propaganda Minister Joseph Goebbels, (2) professed Nazi race doctrines about the Jews, and (3) blamed foreign powers, and not Germany, for the outbreak of World War II in 1939.[7] Almost the same proportion of explicit Nazi sympathies has been found among the younger generation. In three polls in 1953, 1954, and 1955 among young people between fifteen and twenty-five, an average of 10 per cent professed favorable opinions of Hitler and of National Socialism.[8] In July 1956, in a special poll of young men, 16 per cent declared without qualification that National Socialism had been "a good idea."[9]

Another 10 to 15 per cent of Germans in the 1950's were unmistakable though less fervent sympathizers of National Socialism or extreme nationalism. Together with the 10 to 15 per cent of professed Nazi sympathizers, they bring up the ideological Right wing of the German electorate to about 25 per cent, or one-fourth of the total. The same proportion, about one-quarter of poll respondents, expressed "predominantly favorable" opinions of Hitler, his deputy, Rudolf Hess, and the Nazi youth leader Baldur von Schirach; rejected in repeated polls the black-red-and-gold flag of the Federal Republic; registered an unfriendly attitude toward democracy; blamed domestic sabotage and treason as the main causes of Germany's defeat in World War II; insisted "unconditionally" that in 1933 Germany had had no other choice except Communism or National Socialism; and wanted to bar from high government positions in the Federal Republic any man who had taken part in the wartime resistance against Hitler.[10]

On many particular issues, a considerably larger proportion of Germans agreed with Nazi views. A number of differently worded polls throughout the 1950's consistently found 30 to 40 per cent of the respondents expressing anti-Semitic views.[11] The reality of the attitudes indicated by these poll results was demonstrated in December, 1959, and January, 1960, when a Jewish tombstone and a synagogue in Cologne were disfigured with painted anti-Jewish slogans and Nazi swastikas. These acts of vandalism received wide and unfavorable publicity in the West Ger-

[6] *Jahrbuch,* II, pp. 277, 279.
[7] On these and the following points, see Deutsch and Edinger, *Germany Rejoins the Powers,* pp. 40–42; and poll data in *Jahrbuch,* I, pp. 126, 132, 136, 138, 174, 276; *Jahrbuch,* II, pp. 141, 277–279.
[8] From data in Rolf Frohner, *Wie stark sind die Halbstarken Dritte Emnid Untersuchung zur Situation der deutschen Jugend* (Bielefeld: Stackelberg Verlag, 1956), pp. 119–121, 305–310.

[9] *Jahrbuch,* II, p. 149.
[10] *Jahrbuch,* I, pp. 135–137; *Jahrbuch,* II, pp. 144, 170, 172–173.
[11] *Jahrbuch,* II, p. 126; Erich Lüth, "Deutsche und Juden heute," *Der Monat,* 10:110 (November, 1957), pp. 47, 49; *The New York Times* (March 28, 1958); Deutsch and Edinger, *Germany Rejoins the Powers,* p. 41.

man press, radio, and television, but were promptly followed within about four weeks by 470 similar incidents, at first particularly in North Rhine-Westphalia, but later, in the wake of the mounting publicity, in all Lands of the Federal Republic. A journalistic survey of crime waves in Germany later cited this chain reaction of outrages as a typical example of "sequential crimes," that is, of cases where an already existing predisposition toward a particular type of crime or psychopathic outrage is triggered off by the news of a similar act having been committed elsewhere. "Just what mobilizes," a caption asked, "latent criminals?" [12] The West German authorities, both Land and Federal, were quick and unequivocal in condemning these outrages, and so were most articulate Germans. Yet the fact that there should be so many latent offenders, ready to commit so many imitative outrages in so short a time, vividly suggests how much tinder there is still amassed beneath the tranquil surface of West German politics.

The 1961 trial in Israel of one of the chief organizers of the mass killing of Jews under Hitler, Adolf Eichmann, seems to have had a distinct impact on German opinion. Eichmann confessed the fact of the organized killings of men, women, and children, but defended himself on the grounds of having obeyed superior orders. The fact that six million Jewish lives were lost as a result of Nazi persecution was established once again by expert testimony at the trial. Earlier, in 1952, about two-fifths of Germans polled had opposed legal punishment for anti-Semitic propaganda; poll results published in 1957 showed that nearly two-thirds of the respondents had rejected a lower estimate of five million Jewish victims of the Nazis as "too high," and that 37 per cent had called it "grossly exaggerated."

By January, 1960, however, only 7 per cent insisted that the perpetrators of hostile actions against Jews should not be punished by the courts, while another 15 per cent avoided a yes-or-no answer to this question. In April, 1961, only 15 per cent wanted a mild judgment for Eichmann, another 19 per cent answered "don't know," 35 per cent demanded the death penalty for the Nazi executioner, and another 31 per cent wanted him to get penal servitude for life. Whether the impact of the Eichmann trial on German opinion has been only temporary, or whether it has contributed to a long-run change, only the future can reveal.[13]

Nazi ideas or practices receive support from a broader sector of the German electorate on a variety of other issues, particularly where national solidarity or military considerations are involved. In many such cases, national solidarity seems to outweigh more universal standards of ethics or morality among a sizable group of voters. Thus, in a poll published in 1961, as many as 36 per cent said that even "if after 1933 a person was firmly convinced that wrongs and crimes were being committed under Hitler," he should not have offered any resistance; and when further asked what such a person should have done during the war, the group rejecting any resistance rose to 49 per cent, with 34 per cent advising the moral objector to "wait until after the war," and another 15 per cent saying simply "neither then nor ever." Earlier, in 1956, the same proportion of 49 per cent opposed the alleged proposal of a city government to name a public school after a well-known hero of the German wartime resistance.[14] Similarly, 39 per cent said in 1954 that anti-Hitler refugees should be barred from high government positions in the Federal Republic; 42 per cent—and 47 per cent among the men—in 1956 declared that "without the war, Hitler would have been one of the greatest German statesmen," ac-

[12] *Der Spiegel*, 16:27 (July 4, 1962), pp. 47–49. According to Arnold Heidenheimer in *The Governments of Germany*, p. 88, the official count of outrages finally rose to 685.

[13] Data in this paragraph from *Jahrbuch*, I, pp. 125–137; Erich Lüth, *op. cit.*, pp. 47, 49; Erich Peter Neumann, *Public Opinion in Germany, 1961* (Allensbach and Bonn: Verlag für Demoskopie, 1961), pp. 48–49.

[14] E. P. Neumann, *op. cit.*, pp. 44–47; and *Jahrbuch*, II, p. 145.

cepting apparently within this judgment his concentration camps, mass murders, and dictatorship; more than 50 per cent in 1951 asked for the lifting of the ban on the wearing of the Nazi war decorations, and opposed their being reissued with the swastikas removed; and 55 per cent in 1953 denied that there had been major war crimes by the German military, and insisted that the German soldiers of World War II had no cause for any self-reproach for their behavior in occupied countries.[15]

Most of the potential strength of the extreme Right-wing ideology in Germany rests upon this partial overlap with the beliefs and attitudes of broader sections of the German people. Ideological hard-core activists have become very few in West Germany, well below 2 per cent of the electorate in the case of the Communists, and about 4 or 5 per cent in the case of the Nazis and related Right-wing extremists. But while much of the Communist ideology implies a sharp break with many popular German traditions and beliefs, the ideology of the extreme Right often represents rather an extreme exaggeration of the popular habits and beliefs. Where the few remaining Communists in West Germany are isolated within a wall of popular rejection and distrust, the hard core of extreme Right-wing and Nazi adherents can be likened to the central layers of an onion, surrounded by layer upon layer more distant from the core, but with few sharp breaks between them. The position in terms of poll results from the early 1950's is summarized in Table 4-2.

In interpreting these data, it must be remembered, of course, that a positive judgment of the legitimacy of a party—that is, of its right to exist as part of an accepted political system—does not necessarily imply any agreement with its views. Thus, while less than 2 per cent of West Germans voted or declared themselves as Communists, no more than 11 per cent would concede them even the right to exist, while 80 per cent rejected them as illegitimate, and only 9 per cent were undecided. The contrast to the popular image of the Right-

TABLE 4-2 *Popular Views of the Legitimacy of Extremist Parties* [a]

	Negative views	Neutral or no opinion	Positive views	Total
Respondents' views of:				
Communists	80%	9%	11%	100%
Right-wing extremists	42	46	12	100

[a] From data in Juan Linz, *The Social Bases of West German Politics* (Ann Arbor, Mich.: University Microfilms, Inc.), Columbia University Ph.D. Dissertation, Mic 59–4075, 1959, pp. 114–116; and E. N. and E. P. Neumann, *Jahrbuch der öffentlichen Meinung, 1947–1955* (*Jahrbuch*, I) (Allensbach am Bodensee: Verlag fur Demoskopie, 1957), pp. 272–275.

wing extremists is striking: only 42 per cent saw them as illegitimate in the Bonn Republic, while a plurality of 46 per cent registered themselves as undecided.

The extreme Right is thus not isolated in West Germany. While the discredited Nazi leaders and symbols cannot be paraded in public with any chance of success, thousands of former Nazis have returned as employees of the government at all levels, or have been elected to various positions of influence. The political significance of the extreme Right-wing ideology is based on this continuity of the contacts of its adherents with broader strata of the West German electorate, with some sections of the West German elites, and with some parts of the West German government.[16]

Very slowly, some of this Right-wing strength is being eroded. The 12 per cent who insisted on a one-party system for Germany in 1959 were the remnant of a larger sector, 22 per cent, who had expressed this view in 1951.[17] We have noted above the decline in overt anti-Semitic responses to polls in the early 1960's. To some extent, this trend to-

[16] For an excellent discussion of these matters, see also Alfred Grosser, *Die Bonner Demokratie* (Düsseldorf: Juhil, 1960), pp. 265–289.

[17] E. P. Neumann, *op. cit.*, pp. 50–51.

Ideology and Opinion

[15] Deutsch and Edinger, *Germany Rejoins the Powers*, p. 42; *Jahrbuch*, II, p. 278.

ward a weaker extreme Right may be counter-balanced by the succession of the age group born between 1912 and 1927 to positions of influence, since among them the effects of Nazi indoctrination were somewhat stronger. And the seniority system in the Civil Service, which will fill most of the top-ranking positions after 1965 with officials first appointed during the Nazi period of 1933–45, may work in the same direction. Yet on balance, the extremist trees are not likely to grow into the sky, and during the first dozen years of the Federal Republic a stronger bloc of adherents to the ideology of democracy has had an opportunity to consolidate itself. Here the search of the younger generation for acceptable values may well prove crucial.

The "All-Weather" Supporters of Democracy

For most purposes, consistent defenders of democracy constitute about one-quarter of the West German electorate, and there is some hope that they may grow in the course of the 1960's to one-third or more. Only on a few issues did the support of the democratic position in the 1950's drop to about one-fifth of the total, as it did on the issues of approving wartime resistance against Hitler and of naming a school after one of the heroes of the resistance. One-fourth of the respondents to polls in 1952 condemned Adolf Hitler without qualification; demanded, in 1954, access to high government offices for members of the anti-Hitler resistance; declared, in 1953 and 1956, that they would do all they could to prevent the return of any Nazi-type movement to power; said, in 1956, that Germany was not better off for having no Jews; and expressed, in the same year, their acceptance of democracy in terms not only of rights but also of duties. A somewhat larger fraction, 29 per cent, approved the Constitution in 1956—the so-called Basic Law of the Federal Republic; and between 30 and 34 per cent, depending on the wording of the question, endorsed in the same year its black-red-and-gold flag—a clear gain from the 25 per cent who had done so in 1954.[18]

On many issues, the hard core of 25 per cent "all-weather" democrats are joined by larger numbers of their countrymen. Thus 38 per cent denied in 1956 that Hitler would have been a great statesman even if there had been no war; 40 per cent in several polls in 1951–54 endorsed peacetime resistance against the Nazi regime; 47 per cent in 1952 recorded a "bad opinion" of Hitler; and the same proportion in 1956 put the main guilt for World War II on Germany—a substantial increase over the 32 per cent who had done so in 1951. Fifty per cent of poll respondents in June, 1956, indicated a clear awareness between dictatorship and acts of violence, "such as in concentration camps"; and 56 per cent rejected one-man rule and chose rather a system of government in which "several people have something to say in the state." Already in 1952, as many as 71 per cent demanded that a good political party should be "democratic"; and in 1959 the multi-party system was endorsed by 77 per cent—a substantial increase over the 61 per cent who did so in 1951.[19]

An Ideology of Cautious Pragmatism

Between the one-quarter of committed democrats and the one-quarter nationalist and Nazi sympathizers, there stands at least one-half of the German people. They include most of the 15 per cent of the electorate who usually stay at home and the additional 25 per cent who vote only occasionally or who tend to switch their votes from one party to another; they also include most of the 5–10 per cent who say "undecided" or "don't know" in the opinion polls. They seem to have no commitments and no ideology, and they have

[18] Deutsch and Edinger, op. cit., pp. 38–41; Jahrbuch, II, pp. 126, 145, 165, 173, 279; communication of poll results from EMNID Institute, Bielefeld, 1957, p. 2.
[19] Jahrbuch, I, 135–139, 251; Jahrbuch, II, 172–173, 278; E. P. Neumann, op. cit., pp. 50–51; Deutsch and Edinger, op. cit., pp. 39–40; Linz, op. cit., p. 116.

been called by many names: "fellow-travelers of democracy," "success Germans," or "the skeptical generation." This group seems larger in Germany than in most other advanced countries. In many ways, then, the Federal Republic is like a ship with one-half of its cargo not secured, ready in stormy weather to slide in any direction.

Yet this group, too, shares to some extent a body of common commitments and a common ideology. They have a lively sense of concrete benefits which they prefer to abstract slogans. In their reactions to political posters, this group showed that they preferred an emphasis on jobs and homes to any more abstract terms such as "socialism" or "free enterprise." They are interested in security and

solidarity, and they are willing to accept and support policies and leaders that seem to promote these values. They find these values clearly embodied in the Western rather than the Eastern and Communist way of life. Even though only 21 per cent in 1955 expected America to be stronger than Russia at the end of the next 50 years—while 16 per cent expected Russia to be stronger—as many as 68 per cent in the same year expected the Western way of life to prevail in Europe, and only 6 per cent thought that the East would win. The trend of changing expectations is shown in Table 4-3.

The figures suggest a declining belief in the superiority of Western power, both immediate and in the long run, and there is

TABLE 4-3   *Expectations about the East-West Contest, 1953–1959* [a]   (Percentage)

	Aug. 1953	Sept. 1954	Oct. 1955	Nov. 1957	Dec. 1958	Oct. 1959
Expected winner, if World War III breaks out now						
America	—	43	—	22	27	—
Russia	—	22	—	20	16	—
Neither, no opinion	—	35	—	58	57	—
Expected to be more powerful 50 years from now						
America	32	—	21	22	—	20
Russia	11	—	16	21	—	23
Both, no opinion	57	—	63	57	—	57
Way of life that will prevail finally in Europe						
Western	72	—	68	—	—	—
Eastern	4	—	6	—	—	—
Other, "don't know"	20	—	24	—	—	—

[a] From data in E. P. Neumann, *Public Opinion in Germany, 1961*, pp. 58–59; E. N. and E. P. Neumann, *Jahrbuch der öffentlichen Meinung*, 1957 (*Jahrbuch*, II), p. 338.

some reason to think that this trend has continued into the early 1960's. But they also show that the faith in the attractiveness and vitality of the Western way of life is vastly greater than the belief in the superiority of Western power, and that with the growing expectation of a power deadlock there has been almost undiminished confidence in the victory of the Western way of life in Europe.

In addition to being overwhelmingly pro-Western, the uncommitted half of the West German electorate is strongly middle class in

outlook. To learn that a politician had a "thoroughly bourgeois outlook" (*eine durchaus bürgerliche Gesinnung*) would have been for 56 per cent of the respondents to a March, 1956, poll a good reason to vote for him, and to learn that a politician's views were "thoroughly un-bourgeois" (*unbürgerlich*) would

Ideology and Opinion

have been for 79 per cent a reason to reject him; only 2 per cent of the voters sampled would have considered a candidate with an "un-bourgeois" attitude worthy of support.[20] Business groups have worked untiringly to reinforce this commitment of between two-thirds and four-fifths of the electorate to middle-class values and attitudes and to minimize dissension between the various "bourgeois parties"—all of whom had to go to the same business-backed "sponsors' associations," "civic associations," and similar disbursing agencies for much of their campaign funds. All this, in turn, contributed to the difficulties of the SPD, both in forming coalitions with other parties and in attracting a larger part of the floating or uncommitted voters, most of whom have been floating only within the non-Socialist camp.[21]

A third characteristic of the uncommitted voters, and of the seemingly non-ideological sector of West German opinion, is the desire for security and the willingness to follow leaders and elites. The main Christian Democratic poster in the 1957 election showed only the sun-bronzed, impressive face of Chancellor Adenauer and the slogan "No Experiments!" It had been developed with the advice of experts in public opinion and persuasion, and it was a resounding success. Even apart from such campaigns, elite opinion may safely depart quite far from mass opinion in many matters, including specific measures of foreign policy and armament—since in the end the majority of the voters may be expected to accept or at least support passively the policies of their betters.

A fourth trait is an interest in national power and prestige, not uncommon among the voters in any modern nation-state, but tempered in West Germany since World War II by a sober sense of realism. The great mass of West German voters will back any government measure that promises to increase German prosperity, security, prestige, or power, provided that its risks are moderate. Since 1945, the West Germans have had no interest in desperate adventures; they very much want peace, and they have shown no inclination to underrate the strength of other countries, either of the United States or of the Soviet Union. Only 26 per cent of respondents in June, 1956, favored fighting an atomic war in defense of democratic freedom rather than let Europe fall under Soviet rule; 36 per cent said they preferred to avoid war even at this price, and the rest were undecided. In March, 1961, a bare majority, 52 per cent, favored retaining the Bundeswehr, while 29 per cent would have preferred to abolish it.[22] Earlier, in February, 1958, 71 per cent had opposed equipping the Bundeswehr with nuclear weapons, and 81 per cent had opposed the installation of launching platforms for nuclear rocket weapons on the territory of the Federal Republic.[23] Together, these attitudes suggest the willingness of the bulk of West German voters to accept defense policies at moderate levels of visible risk, but a distinct unwillingness on the part of the voters to go much further.

Unexpected circumstances could strain or shatter this limited consensus on policies of cautious national advance. The long drawn-out crisis of West Berlin under Soviet pressure has received unceasing publicity throughout the Federal Republic, while the popular sentiment for German reunification seems to have grown somewhat, rather than receded, since the early 1950's. Inflamed by various incidents, these feelings may get out of hand and create situations which the Bonn government may find hard to control, and which

[20] *Jahrbuch*, II, pp. 122–123; see also pp. 116–121, 265–267.
[21] Juan Linz, *op. cit.*, pp. 95–96; U. W. Kitzinger, *German Electoral Politics: A Study of the 1957 Campaign* (Oxford: Clarendon Press, 1960), pp. 130, 202, 207–217; Arnold J. Heidenheimer, "German Party Finance; CDU," *American Political Science Review*, 51:2 (June, 1957), pp. 369–385.

[22] *Jahrbuch*, II, p. 361; E. P. Neumann, *Public Opinion in Germany, 1961*, pp. 52–53.
[23] EMNID poll, communicated by German Federal Consulate, Boston, May 1958, cited in Deutsch and Edinger, *Germany Rejoins the Powers*, p. 27.

may confront its Western allies with agonizing choices. A sharp deterioration of economic conditions or a rapid gain of power and confidence among the West German armed forces if they should acquire nuclear weapons might be other sources of serious instability, as could any sudden major threat or provocation by the Soviet bloc powers. The popular consensus during the 1950's on gradual rearmament and consistent demands for reunification on Western terms seemed likely to lead the Federal Republic to the brink of more than one crisis in the 1960's. How its leaders will succeed in maintaining democracy, moderation, and the limited consensus among the different ideological elements of its population under the difficult conditions of the future may well test their statesmanship.

Social Foundations

V

Germany has long been predominantly urban and industrial, and it became somewhat more so during the 1950's. In 1960, cities and towns contained more than three-quarters of the population of the Federal Republic, excluding West Berlin. Large cities above 100,000 population accounted for 31 per cent; middle-sized cities with 20,000 to 100,000 inhabitants added another 17 per cent. As much as 29 per cent of West Germans outside West Berlin, however, still lived in small towns of between 2,000 and 20,000 people; and the remaining 23 per cent lived in still smaller and for the most part rural communities.[1] No political party stressing mainly rural interests could hope for a majority, but thanks to the relative strength of the small towns, a potential majority of

[1] SJB, 1961, p. 45, Table 7.

52 per cent was available for a combined appeal to rural and small-town values.

The Second World War had left its mark on the population. At the beginning of 1960, there were still 53 per cent women to 47 per cent men in West Germany, and in the important age group between 30 and 40 years, where many men had been killed in the war, women made up 55 per cent. During World War II and the years immediately following it, fewer children were born, so that in 1959 the Federal Republic had more inhabitants aged between 50 and 60 years than it had youngsters between 5 and 15. The somewhat unusual age structure of the population of Germany can be seen from the comparisons in Table 5-1, which shows that the population of the Federal Republic, as well as that of the GDR, is old even by West European standards.

The various political and social attitudes of age groups differ considerably. The younger people are more prosperous and non-political; the oldsters are worse off and more conservative, as is shown in Table 5-2. Instead of leading to any Left-of-center radicalism, economic deprivation in the Federal Republic has mainly hit the older people and has left them as conservative, or moderate Right-of-center, as ever, if not more so.

Special interest also attaches to two particular age groups. The first, aged in 1960 between 45 and 60, includes many who made their careers first during the Hitler years after 1933, when they were between 18 and 33

TABLE 5-1   *Age Groups in Germany
and Other Countries* [a]

A. Five Age Groups in the Federal Republic

Age	Percentage
0–15	21%
15–30	23
30–45	18
45–60	21
60 plus	17

B. Some Summary Comparisons

	Under 15	15–45	Over 45
German Democratic Republic (GDR)	21%	37%	41%
German Federal Republic	*21*	*41*	*38*
United Kingdom	23	39	37
France	26	39	36
Switzerland	24	41	34
Italy	25	34	31
United States	31	40	29
U.S.S.R.	29	47	24
Japan	30	48	22

[a] Source: *SJB, 1961,* pp. 29, 46–49.

years old; the normal retirement of still older men will bring the members of this group into many senior positions by 1965. The second group, aged in 1960 between 30 and 45 years, had to spend a large part of its formative years under Hitler's rule, but it also experienced the failure and collapse of the Nazi dictatorship at an impressionable age; this group is likely to succeed to senior offices in government and private life between about 1970 and 1975. The strength of these age groups in the 1959 population of the Federal Republic, as shown in Table 5-1, was somewhat less than one-fifth for the 30–45 year group (18 per cent), and nearly one-quarter for the 15–30 year-olds (23 per cent). The groups under 15, and between 45 and 60 years, respectively, were about equally strong, with 21 per cent each, and 17 per cent were over 60 years old.

In short, the preference of the West Germans for reconstruction over reproduction between 1945 and 1955 has made West Germany a country with one of the oldest populations among the large nations. Under these conditions, the appeal of youth in Germany is likely to be slightly weaker, and the appeal of age and experience slightly stronger, than

these are, respectively, in the United States. These facts may have had something to do with the seemingly perennial popularity of Chancellor Konrad Adenauer, known in Germany as *Der Alte* or "the old one" (he was 86 in 1962), but they are likely to persist well beyond his eventual retirement from the scene.

The Strength of Occupational Groupings

Nearly one-half of the people of the Federal Republic in 1960 were members of its work force of 25.5 million.[2] The rest are for the most part their dependent children, other family members, and some pensioners.

The Federal Republic is one of the most highly industrialized countries in the world; only 14 per cent of its work force is engaged in agriculture. Nevertheless, only a little less than half its work force—48 per cent—are actually engaged in industry or crafts. The sizable remaining group of 38 per cent is occupied in commerce, transportation, and services, both private and public. There are not enough farmers to bring victory to a traditionalist party, but there are enough to press effectively for special economic and political concessions.

Nor are there quite enough workers to bring success to a straight class appeal. Industry proper absorbs only 30 per cent of the work force; of these about 6 per cent are various kinds of white-collar employees, and only 24 per cent, or about 6 million, are industrial workers of the kind which Karl Marx had expected to become a majority of each industrialized nation. Even if one adds to their number the workers in large enterprises outside of industry, such as those in transporta-

[2] These and the following data are based on figures in *SJB, 1961,* pp. 142, 149, 213–216, unless otherwise indicated.

Social Foundations

TABLE 5-2   *Age Groups and Attitudes* ^a

Attitude reported in polls	Age group			
	18–29	30–44	45–60	60 and over
Personal economic situation (May, 1955):				
Better than pre-war	36%	26%	17%	15%
Worse than pre-war	21	40	50	57
Talk occasionally about politics (June, 1956)	39	57	53	53
Right-of-center in politics (Feb., 1956)	31	39	41	44
Left-of-center	15	22	21	19
Do not know meaning of "Right" and "Left"	37	25	22	24

ᵃ Source: *Jahrbuch,* II (1957), pp. 35, 46, 48.

tion, the proportion of "proletarians," in the Marxist sense of the term, within the West German working population falls far short of a majority. Only by adding to their number all "blue-collar" employees in small businesses, workshops, and service establishments, as well as the few remaining rural laborers (2 per cent), and the 1 per cent registered unemployed, can the aggregate proportion of workers of all kinds be brought to 51 per cent of the work force. By contrast, the workers in factories with over a thousand employees —whom Lenin considered the best prospects for Left-wing radicalism—number only about 3 million, or roughly 12 per cent of the total.

After the 51 per cent workers, the strongest group consists of white-collar employees, who make up about 26 per cent of the working population and who include about 5 per cent public officials and perhaps 1 per cent of high-level employees and managers. Another 11 per cent consists of the self-employed urban middle class and the members of their families assisting them in their enterprises. The main groups within this middle class are small businessmen in commerce and the service industries (6 per cent, including family members), artisans and members of their families (4 per cent), and the small group of professional men (1 per cent). The remainder

are peasants (5 per cent) and family members working on their farms (7 per cent).

These figures show the remarkable strength of the self-employed group. Together with the members of their families working in the family enterprises, they made up an unchanged 23 per cent of the total in 1950 and in 1959—11 per cent in the towns and 12 per cent in the country, and totaling nearly one-half as much as the workers. Under these conditions, the 26 per cent white-collar employees are often likely to prove the decisive group in mass politics: without their support, neither labor nor middle-class appeals are likely to be successful. Moreover, two of the subgroups included among them—the same 5 per cent public officials and somewhat more than 1 per cent soldiers—may actually or potentially carry influence well beyond their mere numbers.

Levels of Education

All West German children must go to school for at least eight years. In 1959, less than one-half were continuing for a ninth year; about one-third were going on for the tenth.[3] Nearly one-quarter (22 per cent) of the sixteen-year olds were getting the *Mittlere Reife,* which is the German counterpart to an American non-academic high school education. This was a considerable improvement

[3] These and the following figures are based on data in *SJB, 1961,* pp. 46, 97, 105, and 108, unless otherwise indicated.

over the education received by their parents. According to polling data from the mid-1950's, only 12 per cent of the general population above 18 years had attained this educational level.[4]

Graduation from a full-fledged German academic high school—the *Abitur*, which is the equivalent of an American junior college—had been achieved by only 4 per cent of the general population in the mid-1950's, but it was being attained by as many as 6 per cent of the 19–20 year-olds in 1959—by about 10 per cent of the men and 2 per cent of the women.[5]

There was similar evidence of substantial broader access to university education. Between 1952 and 1960, the number of university students almost doubled, rising from 112,000 to 201,000, when about 4 per cent of the 19 year-olds were entering the universities —8 per cent of the men and 4 per cent of the women.

Compared to the total population of all ages, about 4 out of every thousand were attending some university or technical college, as against the earlier proportion of 2 per thousand in 1950 and in 1932 at the end of the Weimar Republic, and against only 1 student per thousand population under Hitler's regime in 1938.[6] Quietly and without much rhetoric, the Bonn Republic by 1960 had opened the gates of the German universities about twice as wide as they had ever been. While the West German levels are still well below the United States figure of 18 students per thousand population—and of perhaps 12 American students per thousand above the junior college level which corresponds to the German *Abitur*—and while thus there still was no very broad college-educated group in the West German electorate, the proportion of university-educated men and women had grown significantly, and promised to continue to do so.

The widening of opportunities for higher education also has brought with it a broadening of the social composition of the student body. Nearly one half of West German students now receive modest but effective aid from scholarships under a national foundation; and the top students, approximately one per cent of the total, get more substantial grants. There are probably still not more than 5 to 10 per cent sons of workers among the students at West German universities, but even this proportion is larger than it has been under any previous regime, and it seems likely to grow in the future. Together with the absolute increase in the number of students, the increase of the share of students from poorer families has meant that the total opportunities available to students of, say, working-class background have improved appreciably. At the same time, this process is giving to the Federal Republic a substantially larger share of academically educated voters, recruited from a wider variety of backgrounds; and this may well have some effects on the future style and trend of West German politics.

It is more difficult to gauge exactly the potential political implications of this expansion in the share of the better educated among the electorate. In the United States, college education has been on the whole a liberalizing influence; in many surveys and polls, the college educated have shown a greater interest in facts, a markedly greater tolerance for views other than their own, a greater readiness to compromise on matters of ideology or tradition, and a greater commitment to human rights and civil liberties. In Germany under the Weimar Republic, on the other hand, students and university graduates were on the average more nationalistic, militaristic, and intolerant than the bulk of their countrymen. After 1933, the Nazi government cut university enrollments in half within six years; the Nazis tended to impose political screening upon the remaining students, and even more upon the university faculties and especially upon

[4] *Jahrbuch*, II, pp. xliv and 4.
[5] *Ibid.*, and *SJB, 1961, op cit.*
[6] From same sources as above; and William L. Shirer, *The Rise and Fall of the Third Reich: A History of Nazi Germany* (New York: Simon and Schuster, 1960), p. 252.

new appointees to academic posts. Although these controls were not perfectly efficient, they had their effects. A major survey in 1950 still found pro-Nazi and anti-Western sentiments significantly higher among German holders of academic degrees than among the population at large. The nationalism of German academics, as it appeared in this survey, was only exceeded by that of peasants, and of men with more than six years of military service.[7] The education now offered at West German universities is permeated with a more moderate and democratic spirit, even though among the prominent professors in 1962 still were men with a past record of Nazi sympathies, or party membership, or past public endorsements of Nazi leaders or doctrines. On the other side, there are many German scholars who maintained an honorable record of integrity during the Hitler years, and of opposition to the Nazi tyranny. Quite a few of these men suffered exile, imprisonment, or other persecution. Nevertheless, a survey for the year 1955 did not find among the published biographies of the heads of 38 institutions of higher education a single mention of an anti-Nazi record.[8]

Among the students, the traditional, extremely nationalistic student groups of the drinking and dueling type had been for the most part arch-conservative rather than National Socialist in political outlook. Despite their opposition to the totalitarian claims of the Nazi regime, their past record of hostility to democracy, contempt for Western countries and values, and sympathy for aggressive militarism brought them into discredit and eclipse during the first years after the Nazi collapse in 1945. During the 1950's, however, these dueling fraternities have had a partial revival, strongly aided by alumni in high positions in German industry, business, and to a lesser extent the civil service, who made it known that a student's membership in their old and now reconstituted fraternity might greatly benefit his later career. By the beginning of the 1960's, an estimated 5 per cent of university students were Nazi sympathizers, and another 15 to 20 per cent were members of the revived drinking and dueling fraternities—a proportion corresponding roughly to the 25 per cent share of holders of Right-wing sentiments found among the general electorate.

Whatever the views of German students, they are putting on record their willingness to make sacrifices. While of a sample of young men between 17 and 27 years, only about one-half were willing to admit that there are any goals worth risking one's life for, as many as 80 per cent of the university students in a 1960 poll took this view.[9] There is an interesting difference between the particular values endorsed by the students, on the one hand, and by the general sample of young men, on the other, as is shown in Table 5-3.

TABLE 5-3   *Goals Worth Risking One's Life For* [a]

	As named in 1960 by: Young men 17–27 years	University students
Liberty, human dignity, humanity	7%	35%
Christian religion	–	22
The family, persons near and dear	12	8
Germany, the Fatherland	13	6

[a] Source: Erich Peter Neumann, *Public Opinion in Germany, 1961* (Allensbach and Bonn: Verlag für Demoskopie, 1961), pp. 32–35.

The West German universities, in contrast to the ideological regimentation of their counterparts in the GDR, are still an arena of conflicting ideas and trends. As elsewhere in the Western world, the majority of their students

---

[7] Friedrich Pollock, ed., *Gruppen experiment: Ein Studienbericht*, Frankfurter Beiträge zur Soziologie, Band 2 (Frankfurt: Europäische Verlagsanstalt, 1955), pp. 236–272; see also Deutsch and Edinger, *Germany Rejoins the Powers*, pp. 40–43.

[8] Deutsch and Edinger, *op. cit.*, p. 123.

[9] E. P. Neumann, *op. cit.*, pp. 32–35.

are interested in their personal problems, in their studies and careers, and in the enjoyment of their university years. Nonetheless, they cannot help absorbing, directly or indirectly, political attitudes and values. They express views of their own, and as future opinion leaders they will pass them on to many of their countrymen. On the whole, these student opinions today—as far as the majority is concerned—appear to be considerably more democratic, realistic, internationally oriented, and peaceful than they were at any previous period in this century.

Income Groups, Status Groups, and Social Classes

The distribution of income in the Federal Republic is somewhat more unequal than it is in Britain or in the Scandinavian countries, and the leveling effects of postwar taxation have gone somewhat less far.[10] Nevertheless, income distribution in Germany appears to be less unequal than it is in France, and much less unequal than it is in the Mediterranean countries of Europe.

Under the Bonn Republic, most Germans have been less interested in the just distribution of a fixed income than they have been in seeing this total income increase, and in having their own incomes rise with it. The results are shown in Table 5-4.

TABLE 5-4   *Income Levels, 1950–1961* [a]
(Net monthly income of principal provider, percentage of households)

	1950	1956	Nov. 1960	March 1961
Up to DM 399 ($100)	92%	63%	33%	27%
DM 400–800 ($100–$200)	8	3	58	63
DM 800 and more ($200+)		4	9	10

[a] Adapted from data in E. P. Neumann, *Public Opinion in Germany, 1961*, pp. 20–23; and *Jahrbuch*, II, p. 4.

[10] United Nations, *Economic Survey of Europe in 1956*.

These rising income figures, and the increase in the number of households in the middle-income bracket—during a decade in which German prices did not rise very much—have found tangible expression in the lives of West Germans. In 70 per cent of the households, meat is eaten four times a week. There is an impressive list of durable household goods that have become widespread; to cite a single example, the proportion of households with electric refrigerators rose from 10 per cent in 1955 to 39 per cent in 1961.[11]

Germans have long been a highly status-conscious people, and the distribution of status differs in some respects from the distribution of income. Occupations requiring more education, clerical work, and either private or public trust rank more highly in status than the pay they bring might indicate. A majority of respondents (56 per cent) to a poll in March, 1955, said that the population in general would have more respect for a commercial clerk earning 300 DM ($75) a month than for a foundry worker earning 450 DM ($113). In the same month, nearly one-half—45 per cent—of employed workers in a poll said that they would switch to a clerical job for the same pay, if they should be given the opportunity to do so.[12]

In three polls between 1952 and 1955, over two-thirds of the general population expressed their preference for collaboration between the classes, and so did three-fifths of the workers polled. The idea of class conflict was endorsed only by 15 per cent of the general population and by about one-quarter of the workers.[13] Employers in 1955 were considered efficient, rather than merely greedy, by about one-half of the public, but 52 per cent said in December, 1956, that employers cared only for their profits, and not for the welfare of their em-

[11] *Jahrbuch*, I, pp. 27–28; and E. P. Neumann, *op. cit.*, pp. 14–17, 24–25.
[12] *Jahrbuch*, I, p. 244.
[13] *Ibid.*, pp. 244–245.

TABLE 5-5 *Social Strata in West Germany, 1955* [a]

Population sampling	Present generation	Father's generation
Upper-middle strata:		
Professionals, managers and proprietors of larger establishments, and upper civil servants	4.6%	3.0%
Lower-middle strata:		
Minor officials, clerical and sales persons, small businessmen, and independent artisans	28.0	24.6
Upper-lower strata:		
Skilled workers and employed artisans	13.3	12.4
Lower-lower strata:		
Semiskilled and unskilled workers	34.9	31.6
Farmers	10.6	22.0
Farm workers	3.7	4.6
Unclassifiable [b]	4.9	1.8
Number of cases	(3,385)	(3,385)

[a] Source: Morris Janowitz, "Social Stratification and Mobility in West Germany," *The American Journal of Sociology*, 64:1 (July, 1958), pp. 6–24, Table 3, p. 10; and Deutsch and Edinger, *Germany Rejoins the Powers*, p. 262, and, generally, pp. 36, 260–266.

[b] Includes those war and social security pensioners to whom no occupational position could be meaningfully assigned.

ployees. Two-thirds of the workers thought so, and so did 43 per cent of white-collar employees and public officials, as well as 44 per cent of small business and professional men. A majority of the public—53 per cent—agreed that the employers had to be compelled by law to respond to the wishes of their workers and office employees.[14] The total picture is one of moderate status envy, willingness to cooperate with employers without any great trust in them, and a preference for limited but effective government regulation.

The West German social structure has remained remarkably stable during the last several decades of political convulsions. The actual distribution of classes and status groups in the Federal Republic has changed only a little from that which prevailed in Hitler's Germany; and Hitler's Reich differed in this respect but little from the Weimar Republic. The relative strength of the differing strata among fathers and sons in a large sample of the German population taken in 1955 is shown in Table 5-5.

[14] *Ibid.*, pp. 246–247.

The most important fact is the expansion of the upper middle-class strata, from about 3 per cent among the fathers of the present generation to nearly 5 per cent among this present generation itself. There are more than three upper middle-class jobs available to the present generation for every two such jobs that were within reach of their fathers. Near the other end of the scale, the proportion of farmers and farm workers has contracted. While many of the children of these groups have entered the ranks of unskilled or semiskilled labor, these lower groups of labor have also shrunk a little.[15] There has been a partial but significant upward movement throughout the society. A summary of more complex tables of social mobility across a generation is shown in Table 5-6.

From these figures, it can be estimated that only about one-half of the West Germans of 1955 still were in the same social stratum in which their fathers had been, while as many as 30 per cent reported that they had risen in the world, and only about 20 per cent said that they had stepped down, by one or more steps. With one-half of the adult population having changed its social class within its own

[15] References are those given in Table 5-5.

TABLE 5-6   *A Summary of
Intergenerational Mobility, 1955* [a]

Strata in present generation	Share of present strata in present total	Strata of recruitment from father's generation		
		Lower	Same	Higher
Upper-middle	4.6%	72%	28%	—
Lower-middle	28.0	46	51	3%
Upper-lower	13.3	46	29	25
Lower-lower	34.9	22	57	21
Farmers and farm workers	14.3	—	76	23
Unclassifiable	4.9	—	—	100
Total present generation	100.0			

[a] Sources: The same as in Table 5-5, especially Janowitz, *op. cit.*, p. 12, Table 7; and Deutsch and Edinger, *op. cit.*, pp. 262–263.

lifetime, any political appeal to permanent class interests was likely to find only very limited support. And with nearly one-third of the voters having stepped up in the social scale, their outlook on the Bonn Republic was likely to be at least cautiously optimistic—and perhaps also a little concerned to hold on to the improved social status which they and their families had gained. Appeals to conservatism, moderation, and collaboration among classes might sound more meaningful to them in times of prosperity; and unless new cleavages should open between the classes, appeals to national solidarity and perhaps to nationalism might well move a great many West Germans in times of crisis.

All these effects of social mobility—as well as of geographic mobility—were reinforced in the case of the expellees and refugees and their West German-born children—totaling altogether about 10 million in 1950 and 12 million by mid-1962—who made up nearly one-quarter of the population of the Federal Republic in the latter year. Expellees alone in early 1961, together with their children, numbered nearly 10 million, or over 18 per cent of the total West German population. They had the same share of jobs in the public service, but less than one-half of that share among the self-employed, as well as of the jobs in banking, commerce, and in industrial plants. The only activities in which their share exceeded that in the general population were the receipt of social services (23 per cent) and positions as officials of the Federal government (25 per cent).[16]

There are no such data on the more than two million refugees, but their distribution may well be similar. Together, these newcomers cannot but help to break down the differences between regions, classes, and even religious groups, and to strengthen the patterns of national solidarity, nation-wide mobility, and—particularly as far as the older generation is concerned—a continuing and lively interest in the revision of the frontiers to the East. The children of the expellees, on the other hand, are most interested in making their homes in West Germany where they now live. Despite the strenuous efforts of such expellee and refugee youth organizations as the *Deutsche Jugend des Ostens* (DJO), the rights and wrongs of East European politics are beginning to sound as remote to most of them as the troubles of the Old World used to sound to the children of American immigrants who were little interested in the political claims and quarrels their parents had left behind them.

Regional and Religious Factors

It is said that Chancellor Adenauer once described Germany as being divided naturally into three parts—the Germany of wine, the Germany of beer, and the Germany of schnapps, or hard liquor—and that he expressed his love for the first, his sympathy for the second, and his willingness to do his duty for the third. Much has been written by others about the cultural and psychological differences between the wine-drinking Rhineland,

[16] *SJB, 1961*, pp. 54–55.

Social Foundations

beer-drinking Bavaria, and liquor-drinking northern and eastern Germany; and in less picturesque language, the West, the South, the North, and the Central and Eastern regions are widely accepted as the main geographic subdivisions of Germany. The first three of these now constitute three informal regions of the Federal Republic. The fourth has been turned into the GDR and the Oder-Neisse territories, but it lives on in West German politics through the memories of one-quarter of its population, who are refugees and expellees, and through the memories of an even larger proportion of some of the crucial elite groups of the Federal Republic. Thus in a survey of over 500 members of German foreign policy elites in 1956–57, as many as 41 per cent of the military leaders, 29 per cent of the diplomats, and 41 per cent of the SPD leaders came from the Central and East German areas.[17]

Apart from such memories, however, only West Berlin, at most, represents something like an Eastern German view in West German politics; and even the three other large regions have no legal standing in the political and administrative structure of the Federal Republic. That structure rather is built upon ten states, or "Lands." In some instances, these Lands continue the traditions of earlier German political units, as in the cases of Bavaria, Hamburg, and Bremen, while others, such as North Rhine-Westphalia, Baden-Württemberg, and Lower Saxony, represent postwar creations in which earlier territorial units have been merged.

The ten Lands, and the three regions into which they may be grouped,—let it be repeated, somewhat arbitrarily—are shown in Table 8-1. By far the largest Land is North Rhine-Westphalia. It comprises nearly one-third of the population of the Federal Republic, and it accounts for more than one-

[17] Deutsch and Edinger, *Germany Rejoins the Powers,* pp. 126–127, 134.

third of the national economic activity. The second most populous state, and the largest in area, is Bavaria, followed by Baden-Württemberg and Lower Saxony. All the remaining Lands have less than 5 million population each. Indeed, only Hessen and Rhineland-Palatinate are even middle-sized; the rest each have less than 2.5 million people.

The western part of West Germany, prosperous and densely populated, thus consists of one large state, North Rhine-Westphalia, two middle-sized ones, Hessen and Rhineland-Palatinate, and the small but coal-rich Saarland, which was reincorporated into the Federal Republic only in 1957. South Germany consists of two large Lands, Bavaria and Baden-Württemberg, while North Germany is made up of one large state, Lower Saxony, one small and predominantly rural Land, Schleswig-Holstein, and two old and prosperous city-states, Hamburg and Bremen.

Religious Composition

Western Germany and South Germany have Roman Catholic majorities; North Germany is overwhelmingly Protestant. In the Federal Republic, without Berlin, there are slightly less than 25 million Catholics, who form a strong minority of 47 per cent of the total, while the 26.7 million Protestants comprise just 50 per cent of the population. Most of the remaining 3 per cent do not belong to any religious denomination. Of Jews, less than 16,000 were left in the Federal Republic in 1960, most of them elderly; fewer than 200 Jewish children were born there in that year. The addition of West Berlin would add nearly 2 million Protestants, 300,000 Catholics, and 6,000 Jews to the respective totals.

These figures show a shift from 1955, when among adults a somewhat larger majority of 52 per cent Protestants confronted a minority of only 44 per cent Catholics, while 4 per cent were reported as "other," [18] but most of the difference seems caused by the inclusion of children in the 1958 figures. In the same year, 1958, Roman Catholic baptisms equaled very nearly 50 per cent of the children born in that year, while Protestant baptisms accounted only

[18] *Jahrbuch,* II, p. 3.

for another 45 per cent. There were about 440,000 Catholic baptisms of children in 1958, as against about 400,000 Protestant ones. On the other hand, conversions in the same year brought the Protestants a net gain of about 4,000 converts, as against a net loss of nearly 3,000 Catholics. At these rates, the Protestant majority in the Federal Republic, even without West Berlin, seemed likely to persist for most of the rest of the century, while any reunification with the largely Protestant GDR would increase it substantially.[19]

A Protestant majority of 52 or 51 per cent among the voters in the Federal Republic—as against 45 or 46 per cent Catholics and 3 or 4 per cent unaffiliated or scattered—thus seemed likely to persist well into the 1980's, and perhaps beyond. The Protestant share was substantially larger, however, in a sample of the German upper middle class, where it was as high as 60 per cent in 1955, as against only 31 per cent Catholics, 5 per cent unaffiliated, and 4 per cent other denominations.[20] Since the upward social mobility of Protestants also was found to be somewhat higher than that of Catholics,[21] and since the Catholics generally were represented somewhat more strongly among the less highly skilled and educated strata of the population, the Protestant hold on perhaps three-fifths of the upper middle-class positions in the Federal Republic seems likely to persist.

All these figures thus have political significance. There is evidence from polls that Roman Catholics in the Federal Republic go nearly twice as diligently to church as do Protestants, and that, with much active encouragement from the Catholic Church and lay organizations, they furnished in the mid-1950's, three-fifths of the CDU vote, two-thirds of the steadfast CDU voters, and three-quarters of the CDU membership, as well as two-thirds of the CDU leaders and a majority of the Federal Cabinet.[22] In turn, the CDU, the formal functioning of the Federal and Land governments, and perhaps the informal effects of the regions all contribute something close to majority status upon the Catholic minority. Some aspects of this process are shown in Tables 5-7a and 5-7b.

The West German States or Länder

The figures in Table 5-7 illustrate, first of all, the considerable differences in population, area, and wealth among the Länder. By any account, North Rhine-Westphalia stands out. Together with Bavaria, these two states account for nearly one-half the population of the Federal Republic. The "volume of business" figures, technically called economic turnover, show something of the levels of economic development in each Land. Very roughly speaking, national turnover data for the GFR tend to amount to perhaps three times the national income. The city-states of Hamburg and Bremen are noteworthy, of course, for their high per capita basis, and also the absolute wealth going through Hamburg is impressive. They are followed by North Rhine-Westphalia, with its industry, but all the remaining areas for which we have data are below the national average, with the rural states of Schleswig-Holstein, Rhineland-Palatinate, and Lower Saxony at the bottom of the per capita rank order.

As Table 5-7 further suggests, the postwar arrangement of Länder and regions has been least favorable to North Germany. That region is by far the smallest of the three, yet it

[22] See *Jahrbuch*, II, pp. 77, 264; Juan Linz, *The Social Bases of West German Politics* (Ann Arbor, Mich.: University Microfilms, Inc.), Columbia University Ph.D. Dissertation, Mic 59–4075, 1959, p. 44, with reference to Arnold J. Heidenheimer, *La Revue Française de Science Politique*, 7:3 (July–September, 1957), p. 635; U. W. Kitzinger, *German Electoral Politics*, pp. 223–233, and references in p. 223, n. 1; Deutsch and Edinger, *op. cit.*, pp. 131, 135.

[19] From data in *SJB, 1961*, pp. 59, 94.

[20] Computed from data in Morris Janowitz, "Social Stratification and Mobility in West Germany," *The American Journal of Sociology*, 64:1 (July, 1958), p. 10, Table 3, and p. 15, Table 8; cited in Deutsch and Edinger, *op. cit.*, p. 262, Table II.3, and p. 264, Table II.6.

[21] *Ibid.*, p. 264, Table II.6.

Land and Region	Population 1960 (in millions)	Area (in 1,000 sq. kilometers)	Volume of business, 1959	
			(in billion DM)	per capita (in thousand DM)
North Rhine-Westphalia	15.7	34.0	210.0	13.4
Hessen	4.7	21.1	52.0	11.1
Rhineland-Palatinate	3.4	19.8	25.0	7.4
Saarland	1.1	0.8	n.d.	n.d.
Total: Western Germany	24.9	75.7	287.0 [b]	12.1 [b]
Bavaria	9.4	70.5	79.7	8.5
Baden-Württemberg	7.6	35.8	82.6	10.7
Total: South Germany	17.0	106.3	162.3	9.1
Lower Saxony	6.6	47.4	57.5	8.7
Schleswig-Holstein	2.3	15.7	16.5	7.2
Hamburg	1.8	0.1	53.0	29.4
Bremen	0.7	0.1	13.7	19.6
Total: North Germany	11.4	63.3	140.7	12.3
Total: GFR without Berlin	53.3	245.3	626.2 [c]	11.3 [c]
West Berlin	2.2	0.5		

[a] From data in *SJB, 1961*, pp. 36, 38, 454.
[b] Not including Saarland.
[c] Including West Berlin.

is divided into four states, and the economic "raisins" of Hamburg and Bremen are separated from the "cake" of their hinterland in Lower Saxony and Schleswig-Holstein—in striking contrast to the American practice that has left the tax resources of New York, Philadelphia, Boston, Baltimore, and New Orleans within the respective states whose territories they largely serve. Although rural North Germany is relatively poor, it has received more than its quota of expellees and refugees—33 and 35 per cent, respectively, as against the national average of 25 per cent, and the still somewhat lower levels of North Rhine-Westphalia, Bavaria, and Rhineland-Palatinate. North Germany is the region of Protestantism, and of relatively least support for the CDU, but it is small, divided, partly poor, underrepresented in most national elites, and generally less influential in national affairs than it was under the Hohenzollern Empire and the Weimar Republic.

The German Federal Republic~Chapter V

332

This does not necessarily mean that the present arrangement is unpopular, even in North Germany. The continued separate statehood of Hamburg and Bremen appeals to a proud civic tradition, and it has provided the Social Democrats with excellent opportunities for winning and holding control of the government of these city-states, in partial compensation for their persistent exclusion from federal office. The Protestant Church, finally, and particularly its main constituent bodies, the Lutheran churches, have a double tradition of non-political submission to whatever political authorities there be, and of a deep cleavage between the working classes and the somewhat authoritarian Protestant upper middle classes and their culture—a double tradition that would have reduced the political effectiveness of German Protestants in any case well below the level of their numbers. If the Social Democrats have welcomed their special political opportunities in Hamburg and Bremen, nationalists and conservatives have welcomed to some extent countervailing opportunities for Right-of-center politics in Lower Saxony and Schleswig-Holstein. If some well-informed observers have stressed the considerable uni-

TABLE 5-7b *Länder and Regions of the GFR* [a]   (Social and Political Aspects)

Land and region	Percentage of population Expellees and refugees, 1960	Roman Catholics 1958	Percentage of 1951 votes for CDU/CSU	Seats in Bundes-rat	Governing party or coalition, 1961
North Rhine-Westphalia	24%	55%	54%	5	CDU
Hessen	28	32	41	4	Coalition SPD-Refugee Party
Rhineland-Palatinate	15	58	54	4	Coalition CDU-FDP
Saarland	—	73	55	3	Coalition CDU-FDP
Total: Western Germany	22	52	—	16	—
Bavaria	23	72	57	5	Coalition CDU-FDP-Refugee Party
Baden-Württemberg	25	47	53	5	Coalition CDU-FDP-Refugee Party
Total: South Germany	23	58	—	10	—
Lower Saxony	33	19	39	5	Coalition SPD-FDP-Refugee Party
Schleswig-Holstein	35	6	48	4	Coalition CDU-FDP
Hamburg	28	7	37	3	SPD
Bremen	29	9	30	3	Coalition SPD-FDP
Total: North Germany	32	14	—	15	—
Total: GFR without Berlin	25	47	50	41	Coalition CDU-FDP (late 1961)
West Berlin	9	13	37	4	Coalition SPD-CDU

[a] From data in *SJB, 1961*, pp. 54, 94, 137–139; U. W. Kitzinger, *German Electoral Politics: A Study of the 1957 Campaign* (Oxford: Clarendon Press, 1960), p. 281; and *The Statesman's Year Book, 1961*.

formity of politics in the Federal Republic, and the minor importance of regional differences on many issues,[23] then these views should be qualified in the light of what has just been said, and of the such inter-regional differences in poll data as are shown in Table 5-8.

The poll results in Table 5-8 suggest that North Germany suffered more than the rest of the country in World War II; that it is poorer; and that its people on the whole apparently have no strong attachments to their states. The results also indicate that its voters are more highly aware of politics, more to the Right-of-center, more nationalistic, and more intensely insistent on German reunification than are the voters of the other two regions, and that there is more potential support in North Germany for an active military and political policy toward this end. A part—but not all—of the difference could be accounted for in terms of North Germany's greater share of refugees and expellees, but on several issues

[23] See Linz *op. cit.*, pp. 165–166.

the contrast to the attitudes of South Germany is far greater than would correspond merely to this single factor.

Only West Berlin shares some of the attitudes, but not the poverty, of North Germany. The West Berlin attitudes are almost equally far to the Right; and in some matters of nationalist or reunification policies, the readiness to take risks for more radical steps seems to be still greater. Together with the West Berlin voters' preference for social welfare policies, it is this intense concern with anti-Communism and German reunification which has set the conditions for the political appeal—economically moderate but nationally militant—which Willy Brandt has to make in order to succeed as a national leader of the SPD, but first of all, as the popular Mayor of that embattled city.

Social Foundations

TABLE 5-8 *Some Regional Differences in Opinion Polls, 1956* [a] (Percentage of totals for each region)

Response	National average	West	South	North	West Berlin
Home destroyed in World War II (June)	29%	30%	23%	37%	30%
Running water in present home (March)	84	88	86	73	98
"Can manage well" on income (Aug.)	33	35	32	27	40
Favor separate Land citizenship in addition to Federal (Oct.)	8	5	12	7	3
"Right of center" (Feb.)	38	35	35	47	45
Doesn't know political meaning of "Right" and "Left" (Feb.)	27	28	32	20	17
Favor West German Army (May, 1955)	40	35	39	44	60
Division of Germany "intolerable" (Sept.)	53	56	44	57	84
Demand reunification "again and again" (Sept.)	65	65	59	73	81
Favor moving Federal Government from Bonn to Berlin (Dec.)	44	45	29	55	88

[a] Data from E. N. Neumann and E. P. Neumann, *Jahrbuch der öffentlichen Meinung* (1957), pp. 20, 21, 37, 48, 189, 281, 295, 316.

The South German attitudes usually deviate from the national average in the opposite direction. South Germany suffered least from the war, can manage tolerably on its income, and has little more than a moderate one-third of its voters describing themselves as being to the Right-of-center. Its voters have markedly stronger local attachments, and markedly less interest in general ideological concepts, than do those in the rest of the country. Differently put, social distinctions are more moderate in South Germany, and a larger share of middle-class voters see the center point of the political scale itself a little farther to the left. Like the rest, South German voters favor reunification, but they are much less concerned about it; and only less than a third of them have any use for dramatic and risky gestures that might intensify the struggle for Berlin.

The Western German region, finally, emerges as the one that is most nearly representative of the political attitudes of the entire country. It is less nationalistic and intense than the North, but less locally preoccupied and non-political than is the South. Even its greater prosperity only represents a state of affairs which the other regions wish to reach as soon as possible; and on the general issues, its attitudes are usually closest to the national average. In addition to the size of its population, economic resources, and higher share in important national elites, it is perhaps this representative character of many Western German attitudes that has fitted this region so well for national leadership.

THE IMPORTANCE OF THE LAND GOVERNMENTS. Altogether, the system of Lands and regions has had remarkable political results despite its shallow roots. These roots are shallow, first of all, in the seven of the ten Lands—all except Bavaria, Hamburg and Bremen—that are relatively recent conglomerations with no long and inspiring history of their own. An average of one-quarter of their populations are refugees and expellees and their children, with no old ties to the Land in which they happen to reside; and since an average proportion of about two per cent of the population of the Federal Republic moved from one Land to another in each of the years from

TABLE 5-9 *Budgetary Stakes of Politics in the Federal Republic: National, Regional, and Local, 1959* [a]

	Billion DM	Percentage of national income
National income, 1959	192.2	100%
Budgetary income, Federal government	42.5	22%
Plus Federal railroads, mails, telegraph, etc.	11.9	6
Total: Federal sector	54.4	28%
Budgetary income, Land governments [b, c]	29.7	15
Tax income, municipal governments	8.6	4
Total: Government sector	92.7	47%
Public Expenditures (direct): Federal	30.9	16%
Federal railroads and mail	11.4	6
Total: Federal sector	42.3	22%
Lands [b]	24.3	13
Municipalities	18.8	10
Total: Government spending	85.4	45%

[a] Source: Rounded figures computed from Germany, *SJB, 1961,* pp. 340, 372, 427, 434–436, 544.
[b] Lands include city-states (Hamburg, Bremen, West Berlin).
[c] Land incomes include 5.8 billion DM in Federal grants (4.0) and loans (1.8). This tends to overstate the size of the government total sector.

1955 to 1959—and presumably a similar proportion did so in the preceding years—not much more than 50 or at most 60 per cent of the voters in each Land are likely to be native to it.[24]

Even so, the Lands carry out a large part of the functions of government, and their budgets and payrolls are substantial. In 1959, the Lands received, and then spent, nearly 30 billion DM, or nearly one-third of the nearly 93 billion DM passing through the total government sector—Federal, Land, and municipal—in that year. Since the 1959 national income of the Federal Republic was reported at about 192 billion DM, this would suggest that about 47 per cent of the national income passed through the government sector, and that about 15 per cent of the national income passed through the hands of the Land authorities. Measured by this financial yardstick, the Land governments, taken together, were about one-half as important as the Federal government, including the latter's control of the Federal railroads and the post, telegraph, and tele-

phone service; and the Lands were three or four times as important, in terms of income—though not of spending—as the total of municipal authorities.[25] The relationships are set forth roughly in Table 5-9. The figures in this table involve technical problems of aggregation and should be used with caution, but the relative orders of magnitude are clear.

In terms of employment, the public sector employs about one-tenth of the total work force of the Federal Republic, but it provides more than one-quarter of all the white-collar jobs in the country. Within the government sector, the Lands provide nearly one-half of the official positions, and nearly one-half of the clerical jobs. The majority of the Federal officials are employed by the railroads and mails. The number of other Federal officials is relatively small. The great bulk of official

[25] See sources cited in Table 5-9.

Social Foundations

[24] See migration data in *SJB, 1961,* p. 71.

positions, other than with the railroads or mails, is in the Land administrations and subject to the processes of Land politics. Some details are shown in Table 5-10.

Regional diversities are thus met by the partial decentralization of politics through the institution of the Lands; and this system of Lands, in turn, has enhanced the political

TABLE 5-10 *Public Employment in the Federal Republic: National, Regional and Local, 1960* [a] (In thousands)

Source of employment	Officials	Clerical	Workers	Total	Percentage of work force
Federal	60	66	66	192	
Federal railroads, mails	466	46	345	857	
Other economic institutions	0.1	1	4	5	
Total Federal personnel	526	113	415	1,054	4%
Lands (including city-states)	510	260	98	868	
Land economic institutions	9	11	59	79	
Total Land personnel	519	271	157	947	4
Municipalities	111	228	177	516	2
Total Public employment	1,156	612	749	2,517	10
Total Work force		(6,630)	(13,000)	25,500	100

[a] Source: Computed from data in Germany, *SJB, 1961*, pp. 138, 438. Figures in parentheses are estimates, consistent with those given in the text above.

importance of local and regional politics. The system has helped to adapt government to the inequalities of economic development among the different territories. It has permitted favored regions to retain some of their advantages, while using redistributive taxation to reduce gradually the interregional cleavages. The system has perhaps also served to isolate a part of the Protestant Right in North Germany from the main stream of national politics, while it has amplified the influence of Western Germany, of the Roman Catholic Church, and of the CDU/CSU Party combination.

At the same time, however, regionalism and the system of Land governments have served to protect political diversity and to keep alive a strong and responsible opposition. Excluded from Federal office since the beginning, the SPD has drawn strength and experience from its successes in the government of various Lands. In 1961, the SPD governed Hamburg and was the leading partner in the governing coalitions in Hessen, Lower Saxony, Bremen, and West Berlin. The FDP, which had been excluded from Federal office during 1957–61, the period of a one-party CDU majority in the Bundestag, continued to share in government at the Land level.

By early 1961, the FDP was participating in the governments of seven Lands, and the Refugee Party was doing so in four. Although every party wants to win a share in the Federal government, the opportunities in regional and municipal governments seem substantial enough to keep opposition parties alive, if need be, for an indefinite length of time. In these, and other ways, the opportunities of regionalism and Land government have contributed substantially to the stability and adaptability of the democracy in the Federal Republic.

The Basic Law of the Federal Republic

VI

The Basic Law of the German Federal Republic is its constitution, not in name, but in fact. Its language suggests that it is provisional, and its concluding Article 146 says: "This Basic Law loses its validity on the day on which a Constitution comes into effect which has been freely decided upon by the German people." Yet its principles were intended to be permanent, and, with the passage of time, its provisions increasingly have come to be accepted as permanent.

The fundamental decision to organize a democratic and federal German government in the three Western zones of occupation, and to have it based on a written constitution, drafted by a constituent assembly and confirmed by popular ratification, was taken by the Foreign Ministers of the Western powers at their meeting in London in February, 1948. Machinery to carry out this decision was set in motion when the three Military Governors of the Western Powers met on June 30, 1948. On the following day, July 1, they presented the Ministers President of the German Lands

with documents empowering them to convene a constituent assembly not later than September 1 of that year, and to consider also modifying the boundaries of the then existing German states. A third document dealt with the powers which the Allies intended to reserve for themselves until the occupation should be terminated.[1]

The Ministers President objected on the grounds that they wanted to avoid any hardening of the division of Germany, and they "requested that the new political organization should not bear the character of a sovereign state, and that the procedures followed in its creation should distinctly evidence its provisional status. Following joint Allied-German discussion, it finally was agreed that the German conclave would be called the 'Parliamentary Council' (rather than constitutional convention) and that the constitutive act would be called the . . . 'Basic Law' rather than . . . 'Constitution.' "[2]

Out of such provisional beginnings came a constitutional document embodying an un-

[1] Elmer Plischke, *Contemporary Government of Germany* (Boston: Houghton Mifflin, 1961), pp. 21–22. Despite its conciseness, this is a particularly well-informed account of legal and administrative aspects of the emergence of the Federal Republic.
[2] *Ibid.*, p. 22.

337

common wealth of dearly bought historical experience and expert skill. The Parliamentary Council and its committees had at their disposal the advice of a number of constitutional and political experts, including distinguished specialists from the United States. Nevertheless, and despite the expressed wishes of the occupying powers—particularly France—in favor of a more strongly decentralized and federative solution, there emerged a document that was essentially German in conception and content, and that bore the clear marks both of professional skill and of successful resistance to outside interference.[3]

Unlike the Weimar Republic, the new state created by the Basic Law was to be stable; unlike Bismarck's empire and Hitler's Reich, it was to safeguard the liberty of individuals and groups, and to resist any stampede into dictatorship or aggressive war. It was to be federal so as to resist better any drive toward militarism or dictatorship and so as to win the approval of the Land legislatures, which had delegated the members of the Parliamentary Council and which had to ratify the final document.

Accordingly, the Basic Law decentralized particularly the means of state power and persuasion. It left the Lands with a substantial part of the bureaucratic machinery of administration and left the Federal government dependent on the Lands for the execution of most of its own legislation. The Lands were to be in control of the police, except for very small Federal units that were to be used for special purposes; and the Lands were to have charge of all schools and education and of the bulk of radio and television, for the Basic Law restricted the Federal power to matters expressly delegated to the Federal government, thus leaving—according to some jurists, by

[3] Sigmund Neumann, "Germany," in Taylor Cole, ed., *European Political Systems* (New York: Knopf, 1954), p. 351; Alfred Grosser, *Die Bonner Demokratie*, p. 59.

implication—all residual powers to the Lands.[4]

At the same time, the Federal Republic, as created by the Basic Law, is better equipped than the Weimar Republic to form and maintain a stable political will, that is to say, to formulate and carry out consistent policies and to make specific decisions in accordance with them. The great powers given to the Federal Chancellor, including his effective control over the membership of his Cabinet; the provision that the Chancellor can be ousted from his office by the Bundestag only if the latter can agree on a successor for him—the so-called "positive vote of no confidence"; and the narrow limits set to judicial review of Federal laws and of acts of the government—all these tend to concentrate and stabilize the power of legitimate decision-making on the Federal level. The explicit recognition of political parties in the Basic Law, together with the exclusion by the Electoral Law of splinter parties (those with less than 5 per cent of the valid votes cast in a national election) from the distribution of seats in the legislature (the so-called *Sperrklausel* or Exclusion Clause) likewise tend to encourage the prevalence of large, powerful parties, and particularly of one major government party. Small parties are squeezed out or forced to compromise their differences.

A German Type of Federalism

The same goal—to avoid any dangerous concentrations of power, but to facilitate the formation and execution of a single national political will—is also served by the peculiar German variety of federalism which the Basic Law has adopted. The classic concept of federalism in American, British, and British Commonwealth doctrine and practice has its essence in the simultaneous existence of two governments—federal and state—over the same territories and persons, with each of

[4] Theodor Eschenburg, *Staat und Gesellschaft in Deutschland*, 3rd ed. (Stuttgart: Schwab, 1956), pp. 563, 765. Some conservative German jurists disagree and would assign some of the residual powers to the Federal government.

these two governments impinging directly upon the same individual, with each claiming sovereign power within its sphere of jurisdiction, subject only to judicial review by the highest court.[5]

The type of federalism developed in Switzerland and later adopted in Germany and Austria, and now revived in the Basic Law, is quite different. Here, too, the citizen is subject to two governments, Federal and Land, but these are far more intermingled. In Germany, the Federal authorities in most matters have a clearly superior position. As a matter of general principle, as would be familiar from American experience, the Lands retain the residual powers to legislate about all matters in which the Basic Law itself has not explicitly given exclusive or competing legislative powers to the Federal authorities (Articles 70–72). Whether West German judicial practice will accept the same principles of interpretation still remains to be seen. In any case, the explicit Federal powers are very great, and on many important subjects, the Land administrations serve as the executors of Federal law, guided by Federal administrative directions, and under Federal supervision (Articles 72, 74, 75, 84, 85 of the Basic Law). Substantial spheres of "exclusive" legislation are reserved to the Federal government, and the Lands may legislate only if empowered by specific Federal law (Articles 71, 73). In other areas of "concurrent" legislation, the Lands may legislate only to the extent that the Federal government (called the Federation) does not make use of its own legislative powers (Article 72). In these matters, Federal law overrides Land law (Article 31).

The Federation is thus clearly predominant in the area of legislation, while the Lands retain the greater part of the administrative tasks and personnel. As long as government and politics remain within the confines of legality and legitimacy, the Federal authorities have a clear preponderance of power; in situations of crisis, however, any illegal or illegit-

imate attempts to establish a dictatorship or to stampede public opinion will encounter a major obstacle in the Federal dependence on the administrative cooperation of the Land bureaucracies and governments. This arrangement increases the powers and capabilities of the Federal government for legitimate decision-making, while providing for strong obstacles in the way of any *coup d'etat.*

The Guiding Values: Human and Civil Rights

The first paragraph of Article 1 of the Basic Law proclaims that the dignity of man must not be touched; to respect and protect it is the obligation of every state organ and authority. Article 1 has been interpreted broadly in West German legal thought, as implying in itself many of the more specific basic rights. It is held to outlaw all torture or corporal punishment or any physical or mental ill-treatment of prisoners (a prohibition made explicit in Article 104), such as by excessive deprivation of water or sleep; and it bars similarly the use of "truth drugs" or lie detectors and the use of any evidence obtained with their aid, since all such methods tend to reduce or destroy the freedom of the will—and hence the dignity—of the defendant.[6]

The third paragraph is particularly important, for it directs that the basic rights listed thereafter are to bind all executive and judicial authorities "as immediately valid law." The basic rights are many. They begin with the "free development of one's personality," "life and physical integrity," and "freedom of the person" (Article 2). The first of

[6] Eschenburg, *op cit.,* pp. 417–419, with reference to the Federal Law of Criminal Procedure of 1950, par. 136a, 1 and 2; and to H. J. Abraham, O. Bühler, *et al., Kommentar zum Bonner Grundgesetz* (Hamburg, 1950), Art. 1, p. 3.

The Basic Law of the Federal Republic

[5] For the best development of this view, see Kenneth C. Wheare, *Federal Government,* 3rd ed. (London: Oxford University Press, 1953).

these bars, among other things, any prohibition of writing or painting, such as were imposed upon some artists by the Nazi regime. The second outlaws any sterilization and any medical experiments with prisoners, even in the case of volunteers, since under the circumstances their will cannot be considered wholly free.[7]

Further basic rights include equality before the law, equal rights for men and women, and non-discrimination in regard to sex, descent, race, language, home and origin, or religious or political views (Article 3). This provision may have had special importance in barring any preference for local or West German residents as against expellees or refugees. Article 4 guarantees freedom of religion, conscience, the profession of religious or philosophic views, and the right to refuse armed military service, on grounds of conscience. Subsequent legislation and court decisions require that conscientious objectors must refuse to bear arms for any cause, not just refuse to bear arms in the service of some particular policy, and legitimate conscientious objectors may be required to render an equivalent period of civilian service (Article 12.2).

Article 5 protects the freedom of opinion, research, and teaching, but adds that "the freedom to teach does not absolve from loyalty to the Constitution." Article 6 protects marriage and the family; it declares that "the care and education of children is the natural right of their parents," gives "every mother" a claim to protection and care by the community, and provides legitimate and illegitimate children with an equal claim to legislative protection of their social position and opportunities for personal development. The entire language of Article 6 shows the great interest and influence of religious groups, both Catholic and Protestant, and of the CDU in all matters of

the family and education, with some secondary concessions to the more secular viewpoint represented by the SPD and FDP.

A similar distribution of influence appears in the wording of Article 7, which puts all schools under the supervision of the state (i.e., the Lands, according to Article 70.1). Religious instruction, according to Article 7, is to be a regular subject in the public schools, except for the "non-denominational" schools. Wherever it is taught in public schools, religion must be taught according to the principles of the respective churches. The parents decide about the participation of their child in such instruction, and no teacher may be obligated to give religious instruction against his will. The right to open private schools (including parochial schools) is guaranteed, provided they submit to state supervision, do not fall below the standards of the public schools, do not underpay their teachers, and do not promote a separation of pupils according to income.

The Basic Law goes on to guarantee the right of unarmed assembly without prior permission or announcement (Article 8) and the right to found organizations (Article 9). Here the trade unions get their innings. The right to form economic or occupational interest organizations (such as employers' organizations or labor unions) is guaranteed "for everybody and all occupations." Agreements aimed at limiting or hindering this right are void; measures directed to any such purpose are illegal (Article 9.3). Exceptions to the right of assembly are provided in the case of outdoor meetings, which may be regulated by law (Article 8.2). Organizations whose goals or activities are criminal or "directed against the constitutional order or the idea of international understanding" are prohibited (Article 9.2). The constitutional guarantees of free choice of residence and occupation—particularly valuable to refugees and expellees—have been further enhanced in their importance by the fact that jobs and housing were available, thanks to the prolonged full employment and the great amount of housing construction in the Federal Republic during the 1950's and early 1960's.

[7] Eschenburg, *op. cit.*, p. 424, with references.

The possibility of nationalization is explicitly provided for in Article 15. Land, natural resources, and means of production may be transformed into common property, or into other patterns of a mixed public-private economy, but only by means of a law which regulates the kind and extent of compensation, with the same legal safeguards as in cases of expropriation under Article 14. This article, by implication, guarantees the constitutional legitimacy of socialist aspirations within the democratic order, and of socialist programs and measures, such as those advocated at various times by the SPD.

German citizenship may not be withdrawn in any case. Even involuntary loss of citizenship may only occur on the basis of law and only if the person concerned does not become stateless (Article 16.1). No German may be extradited abroad. The politically persecuted have the right of asylum (Article 16.2). Article 16 thus insures that even Nazi war criminals, if they are Germans, cannot be extradited to the countries demanding their punishment, but must be dealt with by German courts.

Many constitutional rights may be denied to those who misuse them in order to destroy the democratic system. Those who misuse the freedom of speech or of the press, the freedom to teach, the freedom of assembly or of association, the privacy of letters, mails, and telecommunications, the right of property or of asylum will forfeit these basic rights. This forfeiture and its extent will be declared by the Federal Constitutional Court (Article 18). The same Court may outlaw political parties "which, according to their aims, or according to the behavior of their adherents, tend to harm or abolish the basic libertarian democratic order, or to endanger the existence of the Federal Republic." This broad language makes parties liable not only for their programs but for the probable or expectable behavior of their followers (Article 21.2). This clause is influenced by the memory of the disastrous tolerance of Nazi subversion by the Weimar Republic, and by the ever-present shadow of the Communist dictatorship in the neighboring GDR. The provision for the banning of political parties acquired practical significance in the outlawing of the neo-Nazi *Sozialistische Reichspartei* (SRP) in 1952, and of the Communist Party in 1956.

The basic rights listed in Articles 1 to 18 are particularly protected by Article 19 against any later amendments that might destroy them. No part of the Basic Law may be amended except by a law passed by two-thirds majorities of the Federal Parliament (Article 79.2). Article 19 concludes the section labeled "Basic Rights." Additional rights and values, outside the special protection of Article 19, are stated, however, in other sections of the Basic Law. Article 20 fixes the character of the German Federal Republic as a "democratic and social federal state"—a phrase that affirms in the connotations of the German word *sozial* the values of social compassion and of social justice, and that gives special constitutional legitimacy to welfare legislation. The Basic Law further establishes popular sovereignty, representative government, and the separation of powers: "All power of government issues from the people. It is exercised by the people in elections and votes, and through separate organs of legislation, of the executive power, and of the judiciary." (Article 20.1–3.)

The legislative power is bound by the constitutional order, and the executive and the judiciary are bound by law (Article 20.4). No change is permissible in the Basic Law that would infringe the principles stated in Article 20, those in Article 1 (the protection of human dignity and human rights), the division of the Federation into Lands, or the principle of the cooperation of the latter in the legislative process (Article 79.3). Together with the prohibition in Article 19.2 of amendments touching the essential content of any basic right, these are striking and somewhat unusual limitations upon the amending power, which testify to the intense concern and commitment of the drafters of the Basic Law to the future

The Basic Law of the Federal Republic

preservation of a constitutional and legal order.

Other rights or values are more specifically stated. Peace is specially protected. Actions which are both "apt and intended to disturb the peaceful co-existence of peoples, particularly to prepare an aggressive war, are contrary to the constitution. They are to be made subject to punishment" (Article 26.1). There must be no special courts. No one must be denied trial before his legally appointed judge. Courts for particular subject matters may be established only by law (Article 101). The death penalty is abolished (Article 102). There may be neither retroactive punishments nor double jeopardy; an action may be punished only if it was legally punishable before it was committed (Article 103.2), and no one may be punished on the basis of the general criminal laws more than once for the same action (Article 103.3). There is an equivalent to the American right of habeas corpus: personal liberty may be limited only on the basis of law; arrested persons may not be ill-treated, "physically or mentally"; the police may not hold anyone beyond the day after his arrest; on that day, at the latest, he must be produced before the judge who must tell him the charge against him, question him, and give him an opportunity to make objections; the judge then must order him released, or else issue a written order for his arrest, including reasons; of every judicial order of arrest or continuation of custody, notice must be given without delay to a relative of the arrested person, or to "a person whom he trusts"—such as, presumably, his lawyer (Article 104.1–4).

The right to citizenship is regulated in the same spirit. A German, according to the Basic Law and other pending legal regulations, is "anyone who has German citizenship, or who has been received in the territory of Germany within the frontiers of 1937 as a refugee or expellee belonging to the German people, or as his or her spouse or descendant" (Article 116.1). Former German citizens, who during the Nazi regime of 1933–45 were deprived of their citizenship for political reasons, must have it restored to them if they claim it. They are deemed not to have been deprived of their citizenship at all if they have taken residence in Germany after May 8, 1945, and have not expressed their will to the contrary (Article 116.2). The result of these provisions, as well as of legislation in both the Federal Republic and the GDR, is that, "although there are at present two German state executives, two state territories and two state populations, there is only one German citizenship: no German citizen is a foreigner in either of the two presently existing German state formations." [8] Since far more Germans, whenever they had any effective choice, have preferred to live in the Federal Republic, the almost unprecedentedly generous and far-sighted provisions of the Basic Law for their reception as citizens with equal rights, backed by the material opportunities created first by Western economic aid and later by West German economic development, have been of the greatest practical and political significance.

The aggregate of all these rights shows a particular concern to protect individuals and families, largely by restraining the power of the state. There is no catalog of positive rights, such as the right to work or to housing, even though some rights of this kind are mentioned in some Land constitutions. In the ruined and impoverished Germany of 1948, when the Basic Law was drafted, such rights might not have sounded realistic; in the prosperous Federal Republic of the 1950's and early 1960's, they would have seemed to most voters unnecessary. A legal claim to the minimum of material support necessary to sustain an individual's life and dignity—that is, a basic legal claim to welfare support in distress—can be derived indirectly, however, from Articles 1 and 2, and from the characterization in Article 20 of the Federal Republic as a "social" state. Similarly, although the right to strike is not explicitly provided in the Basic

[8] Theodor Maunz, *Deutsches Staatsrecht*, 5th ed. (Munich-Berlin, 1956), p. 27, cited in Eschenburg, *op. cit*, p. 383.

Law, it is held to be implied in the freedom to form economic and occupational interest organizations—the so-called "freedom of coalition"—guaranteed by Article 9. The extensive West German social security, labor, and welfare legislation thus lacks specific constitutional protection in its details. The laws of which it consists could all be changed or abolished by simple parliamentary majorities, at least in theory, but the fact that workers and salaried employees together form the great majority of the electorate informally, yet effectively, guarantees their endurance.[9]

The limited goals embodied in the Basic Law are politically realistic, and they accommodate the aspirations of the major parties. They specifically meet the interest of the CDU in religious instruction and in greater power for the Lands; the interest of the FDP and CDU in safeguards for private property and enterprise; and the interest of the SPD in labor unions and welfare legislation, in the legitimate possibility of nationalization, and in equal rights for unwed mothers and for non-religious pupils and teachers. Even the many members of a silent political group, the former members of the Nazi party, the SS elite guard, the Gestapo secret police, and similar organizations of the Hitler period, all find substantial protection in the Basic Law and in the civil and human rights it guarantees. The Basic Law forbids all blanket discrimination against former members of political parties or organizations. Its Article 131 opened the way to the return of the large majority of former Nazi officials into public service, with the result that out of about 53,000 civil servants removed in the Western zones by denazification procedures, only about 1,000 remained permanently excluded through German official action, while most of the rest were gradually taken back into various official agencies.[10]

Fanatical Nazis, to be sure, remained hostile to the constitutional order despite its tolerance, but they were few. In opinion polls, only 6 per cent of the electorate in 1956 still rejected the Basic Law as "not good," while the usual 29 per cent of determined democrats endorsed it; as to the rest, 14 per cent were undecided and 51 per cent professed their ignorance.[11] Since the number of former Nazi voters and adherents has been well above 40 per cent, of whom roughly one-half were still living in 1962, the poll data suggest that perhaps something like two out of three former Nazis have become reconciled, at least passively, to the system of constitutional government that offered dignity and security also to themselves. In this manner, the Basic Law was not only a response to the ideological cleavages within the German people, which we surveyed in an earlier section, but was also an instrument for their modification. It aimed at establishing standards of legality and human rights that might soon win the respect and acceptance of a majority of the electorate, and eventually the support of the majority, particularly the younger generation.

Although this goal has not yet been reached, the first dozen years of government under the Basic Law have succeeded in bringing the goal substantially nearer. Part of this success has been due to such extra-constitutional factors as prolonged economic prosperity and peace, or at least a tolerably low level of international tensions. Another factor in this success, however, has been the efficiency and the actual functioning of the constitutional system which the Basic Law created. It is these governmental institutions and their functioning that we now must survey.

The Predominance of Federal Powers

In the division of powers between the Federation and the Lands, the Federation

[9] Eschenburg, *op. cit.,* pp. 406, 419, 487–490, with references.

[10] Heidenheimer, *The Governments of Germany,* p. 132, with reference to Taylor Cole, "The Democratization of the German Civil Service," *Journal of Politics,* 14 (February, 1952), p. 7.

[11] *Jahrbuch,* II, p. 165.

has the most important powers, even though, as we have seen, the Lands under some interpretations of the Basic Law have all the legislative and administrative powers of the state, unless they are explicitly assigned to the Federal government (Articles 30, 70). The areas of exclusive Federal legislation are listed in Article 73. They include foreign affairs, defense, federal citizenship, freedom of movement and of internal trade, currency, railroads, mails and telecommunications, and the legal position of Federal employees.

Further Federal powers are in the area of concurrent legislation, listed in Article 74. These include all civil and criminal law and procedure; the regulation of organizations and assemblies; refugees and expellees; public welfare; war damages and restitution; all economic and labor legislation; nuclear energy; social security and unemployment insurance; expropriation and nationalization; prevention of abuses of economic power; agriculture; real estate and housing; health, physicians and drugs; shipping, automobiles, and road traffic. In these areas, the Lands may legislate only until and in so far as the Federation does not make use of its legislative powers (Article 72.1). Concurrent Federal legislation is permitted only, however, in so far as there is a need for it: because the matter cannot be regulated effectively by the legislation of single Lands, or because such a Land law might impair the interests of other Lands or of the community at large, or because Federal regulation is needed to preserve the legal and economic unity of the Federal Republic, particularly the uniformity of living conditions beyond the territory of a Land (Article 72.2). Under the same conditions, the Federation may issue general rules (*Rahmenvorschriften*), but the details of implementation must be filled in by Land legislation for such matters as the legal status of Land and municipal employees, the general legal position of the press and motion pictures, the use of land and water

resources, and the identification and registration of the population (Article 75).

The Federation guarantees the constitutional order in the Lands (Article 28.3). Federal law overrides Land law (Article 30). The Lands execute Federal laws under their own responsibility, except where the Basic Law itself states or permits otherwise (Article 83). The Lands organize their own administrations and appoint and promote officials, but the Federal government may issue general administrative regulations, and it may supervise the legality of the execution of its laws by the Land administrations and may send commissioners to the highest Land authorities and, with the consent of the Bundesrat, also to the lower-level ones. Similarly, the Federal government may be empowered, by a law passed with the consent of the Bundesrat, to give specific directions to Land authorities, even in individual cases (Articles 84, 1–3, 5).

If a Land does not fulfill its obligations under the Basic Law, or under any other Federal law, the Federal government, with the consent of the Bundesrat, may force it to do so by means of "Federal coercion." In carrying out this Federal coercion, the Federal government or its commissioner have the right to issue directives to all Lands and their authorities (Article 37). Whether a Land has violated its legal obligations to carry out a Federal law is determined by the Bundesrat, subject to appeal to the Federal Constitutional Court (Article 84.4). To ward off a threat to the basic democratic order of the Federation, or of a Land, a Land may request the services of the police forces of other Lands; but if the Land, in which the danger is threatening, is either unready or unwilling to combat it, the Federal government may put the police forces of this Land, as well as those of other Lands, under its own direction. This Federal takeover of Land police forces must terminate with the end of the danger, or whenever the Bundesrat so requests (Article 91). In short, the Federal government can do little against any single recalcitrant Land, unless most of the other Lands, through their representatives in the Bundesrat, support it; with such support, however, its powers are overwhelming.

The distribution of financial resources between the Federal government and the Lands is specified in the Basic Law (Article 105–115). The list of taxes reserved to the Federation and the Lands, respectively, appears in Articles 105 and 106. The Federal Republic has thus become probably the only country on earth to enshrine the beer tax in its constitution; Article 106.2.5 reserves it to the Lands, to the joy, presumably, of the Bavarian representatives. Of the more important taxes, the turnover tax is Federal, while the yield of income and corporation taxes is to be divided in the ratio of 35:65 between the Federation and the Lands; before 1958, the Federal share was somewhat lower (Article 106.3). The details of the financial arrangements in the Basic Law and related legislation are very complex, but in one respect the rules are relatively simple: the Federation has legal control over all taxes, except local ones.[12]

The outcome of the system is that taxes are collected in the rough proportion of 60:25:15 per cent by the Federation, the Lands, and the municipalities, respectively. Since a part of the funds collected by the Federal government is transferred for spending to the Lands and municipalities, the actual expenditures at these three levels of government approximate the ratio 50:28:22 per cent. The federal share in total government revenues is thus significantly lower than in the United States.[13] In the general setting of financial policy and in the conduct of the predominant part of financial practice, the Federal controls, direct and indirect, are decisive.

[12] Eschenburg, op. cit., p. 630, with references.
[13] Tax collection ratios for the Federal Republic from Heidenheimer, The Governments of Germany, p. 129; spending ratios computed from data in Table 5-9, above. Here, as everywhere in this study, the city-states of Hamburg and Bremen have been considered as Lands, in accordance with their legal and political position. A somewhat higher Federal share in total government spending—60 per cent, including nearly 5 per cent derived from the equalization of burdens program—is given in Plischke, op. cit., p. 115, and contrasted with a 40 per cent ratio in the Empire before 1914, and a 70 per cent ratio during the last years of the Weimar Republic.

The Bundestag

The main agency of Federal legislation is the Federal Parliament, or Bundestag, established under Articles 38 to 49 of the Basic Law. According to the Electoral Law of 1957, one-half of its members are elected from 247 single-member constituencies by simple majorities or pluralities of the "first votes" cast by the voters in each district for the individual candidate of their choice. The other half of its members are elected from party lists of candidates in each Land, by proportional representation in accordance with the share of their parties in the "second votes" cast by all votes at the same elections for the party of their preference. The outcome is a distribution of seats in fairly close accordance with proportional representation.

Only those parties may obtain seats from this distribution according to party lists which win at least 5 per cent of the valid votes cast in the entire Federal Republic, or whose candidates win majorities or pluralities in at least three single-member districts. This "exclusion clause" eliminates most splinter and regional parties. Each of the remaining parties is entitled to its proportionate quota of seats, which is made up from the party lists to the extent that the party has not already won a sufficient number of seats directly in the single-member constituencies. If a party wins more than its porportionate quota of direct seats, however, it retains these "overhang mandates," so that the final number of Bundestag deputies is usually slightly higher than twice the number of single-member districts. Thus the fourth Bundestag, elected in 1961, had 499 members, not counting the 22 non-voting members from West Berlin.[14] The size and political composition of the four

[14] For a good account of the various stages of West German electoral legislation, see Plischke, Contemporary Government of Germany, pp. 69–71, 157–163.

The Basic Law of the Federal Republic

345

Bundestags elected between 1949 and 1961 are given in Table 6-1.

The figures in Table 6-1 show that minor parties have been effectively eliminated and that no two-thirds majority, required for changes in the Basic Law, can be formed in the Bundestag without the support of members of the SPD.

The Bundestag deputies are elected by general, direct, free, equal, and secret vote, according to Article 38.1 of the Basic Law, but the electoral procedure can be, and has been, changed by ordinary Federal law. According to the same article, the deputies are not subject to directions by anyone. In fact, however, the tradition of party discipline, the power of the parties over the placing of candidates in electoral districts and on Land lists, together with

TABLE 6-1 *Party Representation in the Bundestag, 1949–1961* [a]

	1949	1953	1957	1961
I. Small rightist opposition groups	26	3	0	0
II. Potential government coalition parties				
FDP	52	48	41	67
DP	17	15	17	0
CDU/CSU	139	243	270	242
Refugee Party	0	27	0	0
Actual government coalition	208	333	328	309
III. Opposition				
Small Center-Left groups	22	0	0	0
SPD	131	151	169	190
Communists	15	0	0	0
Total Left Opposition	168	151	169	190
Total voting numbers	402	487	497	499

[a] From data in Plischke, *Contemporary Government of Germany*, p. 71; and *Archiv der Gegenwart*, 31:40 (October 10, 1961), p. 9371C.

the need for funds to meet the costs of campaigning, have made the votes and actions of Bundestag members highly predictable. This is particularly true of the SPD. The CDU and FDP allow their deputies more freedom on what are considered minor matters, but on major issues, particularly on foreign policy, they line up with impressive discipline. Cases of defiance of important party orders by a deputy are rare. The exclusion clause would bar his re-election as an independent, and his chances to found a new party strong enough to surmount its requirements are remote. Many voters, moreover, demand trustworthy party labels as much as or more than strong personalities, somewhat as many housewives prefer well-known brand names to the wares

of less well-known individual tradesmen.

The Bundestag determines when to end and reopen its sessions. Its President may call it into session earlier, and he must do so if the Federal President, or the Chancellor, or one-third of the members demand it (Article 39.3). A Permanent Committee is provided by the Basic Law to watch over the interests of the Bundestag during the intervals between two electoral periods (Article 45). Two other Committees, on Foreign Affairs and on Defense, were provided by constitutional amendment in 1956 (Article 45a). The Permanent Committee and the Defense Committee also have the rights of an investigating committee, that is, they may gather evidence and proofs, by procedures analogous to those of general criminal procedure, including the power to compel testimony. Special investigating committees, on any matter other than defense, must be set up whenever one-fourth of the members of the Bundestag demand it. These committees have the same rights and procedures in regard to evidence and testimony. Their proceedings are public, unless a majority of the committee members vote to make a session confidential (Article 44). Since their composition is proportionate to the strength of the parties in the Bundestag, any strong opposition—e.g., the SPD—can compel the setting up of an investigating committee, even on a subject embarrassing to the government, but the majority of the members of the government coalition on the committee may control much of the proceedings, as well as the language of the majority report, leaving the opposition to make its points by bringing out particular items of evidence and perhaps by issuing a minority report at the end.

Most of the work of the Bundestag is done in committees, to a greater extent even than is the case in the United States Congress. There are more than three dozen committees, each dedicated to some special subject area, from the immunity of deputies and the verification of their mandates to cultural policy, economic policy, questions of German reunification and Berlin, and "atomic questions." [15] Each Committee has between 15 and 31 members, many of whom have been selected by their parties with an eye to their expert knowledge in the area of the committee's jurisdiction. Deputies are paid also for their attendance at committee sessions, as well as at sessions of their "fraction," i.e., of their parliamentary party delegation. As a result, the Bundestag has gone further than the British, French, and United States legislatures in delegating much of its work to committees. In 1954, it held only about 55 plenary meetings, but for every such plenary meeting it also held "no less than twenty Committee and nine Party meetings." [16]

The power of these committees and their members, however, is weaker vis-à-vis the executive than is the case in the United States.

Fixed party positions and tight party discipline rarely leave much scope for individual committee members, except for the influence which these persons gain through their special concern and expertise. Moreover, since committee meetings ordinarily are secret, they cannot be turned easily into instruments for publicity for particular deputies or interests. Each committee may require the presence of any Cabinet member at its meetings, and Cabinet members and civil servants also have their own right of access to committee meetings at any time (Article 43). In contrast to the United States Congress, the Bundestag committees have neither adequate professional experts and staffs of their own nor the aid of an adequate legislative reference service, so that many committee members, despite their experience and partial specialization, often find it difficult to maintain their views against those of the Cabinet ministers, which are bolstered by the expert testimony of the civil servants on their staffs. It is estimated, however, that about one-half of the deputies have some expert help and secretarial assistance available through the offices of interest groups at Bonn.

The chief officer of the Bundestag is its President, who is elected by secret ballot but is taken, in fact, from the strongest party. Three Vice-Presidents are elected by the chamber in the same manner; they are taken from the remaining parties, more or less in order of their strength. A Council of Elders, composed of these officers, together with other representatives of the parliamentary party delegations, is in theory only an advisory committee to the President of the Bundesrat, but is in practice a very important body, somewhat comparable in its power to the Rules Committee of the House of Representatives in the United States. The chairmen of all other committees are not elected but are appointed in effect by the Council of Elders, which also schedules the debates on particular items of

[15] For brief discussions of the committee system, see Eschenburg, *op cit.*, pp. 549–553, with a list of committees; Grosser, *op. cit.*, pp. 93–95; Heidenheimer, *op. cit.*, pp. 111–112.

[16] Heidenheimer, *op. cit.*, p. 111, with reference to comparative statistics in "Wie die Parlamente tagen," *Das Parlament* (December 12, 1960), p. 11.

legislation—sometimes only one hour of plenary session for an important law—and allocates the times and order of speaking to the various parties and speakers.

The major sources of power and action in the Bundestag are the "fractions" or parliamentary party delegations which are recognized by the rules of procedures for every party having at least 15 deputies—another device to discourage splinter groups and minor parties. Only parties strong enough to form a fraction are represented on committees, may count on being assigned speaking time in plenary debates, may effectively initiate bills, direct parliamentary inquiries to the government—in short, take an effective part in the work of the Bundestag. After the 1961 elections, there were only three fractions left, those of the CDU/CSU, the SPD, and the FDP, as shown in Table 6-1. The Bavarian Christian Social Union (CSU), however, received separate representation on the committees and study groups within the joint CDU/CSU fraction.[17]

Each of these three fractions works somewhat like a small parliament. In the internal meetings of each party delegation, which are similar to the caucuses of parties in the legislatures in the United States, the delegations debate and decide whether to support or oppose some particular bill, or demand modifications in it. Individual deputies may vote for or against the proposed policies in the closed meeting of their fraction or caucus, but once a policy has been adopted for the entire party delegation by majority vote, all deputies are expected to support it and to vote for it in the plenum. Thus a bill endorsed originally only by a minority of deputies who form, however, the majority of one or two party delegations could become law through the working of party discipline within each delegation. Since the party delegations themselves

---

[17] For this practice in the 1950's, see Eschenburg, *op. cit.*, p. 534.

are very large, power within them has largely shifted to their executive committees, composed of about two dozen particularly influential deputies. In the SPD and CDU/CSU, power rests with inner executive committees of four or five deputies. In the case of the CDU/CSU, the party's Cabinet Ministers form a still higher layer of influence, superior to or at least equal with the top leadership of the parliamentary fraction.

The leadership groups of each of the fractions, and subsequently the entire fractions, meet before every major decision or debate of the Bundestag in order to set their policy, usually in concert with the leadership of their party outside the Bundestag. Since the parliamentary leadership group is also, as a rule, heavily represented on the national committee of their party, conflicts between national parties and their parliamentary delegations are rare. Together with the decisions of the Cabinet—and primarily of the Chancellor—it is the decisions of these leadership groups of the parliamentary and national parties that have the greatest influence on what happens in the Bundestag, even though many details of legislation still are modified by the suggestions of the civil servants and the political give and take of the legislative process in the Bundestag committees.

Deputies have the usual privileges and immunities, but they are not exempt from responsibility for "slanderous insults" (Article 46.1). They may be arrested or prosecuted only with the permission of the Bundestag or if they are arrested in the act of committing a punishable offense or within a day thereafter; if the Bundestag so requests, however, they must be released at once, and all criminal proceedings against them stopped (Article 46.2–4). They may refuse to name or testify about any persons they have received any information from as legislators or about the content of such information; within this area of privileged communication, no documents may be seized (Article 47).

Bundestag members are only moderately well paid, far less well than their colleagues in France or the United States, where national legislators are paid roughly on the scale of the top levels of the civil service in each country. Since 1958, Bundestag deputies receive a basic salary of about $275 per month, with another $125 per month for living expenses, but with $12 deducted for each unexcused absence.[18] From this, they have to pay certain amounts to their parties, more heavily so in the case of the deputies of the SPD.

By the mid-1950's, the Bundestag and its members still had far to go in order to establish themselves in the awareness and the affections of the German people. In sample polls of West German adults, 69 per cent agreed that a parliament was needed, but only 50 per cent said they would care to listen to a Bundestag debate; 38 per cent were not interested, and a familiar 12 per cent said they would listen only "for amusement." A strong minority—46 per cent—thought in the same year that it required great ability to become a member of the Bundestag, but 37 per cent explicitly opposed this view. Only 38 per cent thought that the deputies were serving primarily the interests of the population, while 17 per cent thought they served chiefly their parties or special interest groups, and 19 per cent accused the deputies of being mainly out to line their own pockets. Only 29 per cent reported a favorable impression of the Bundestag. While expressions of distrust declined somewhat during the 1950's, ignorance persisted. In 1956, no more than 14 per cent knew how the Bundestag works. Less than one German in four knew either the name or the party of his local deputy; only 15 per cent knew about anything he had done recently in the constituency; only 8 per cent knew about anything he had done in Bonn; and only 5 per cent had ever communicated with him— 4 per cent by talking, and 1 per cent in writing.[19] Not only democracy in general, but respect for the national legislature had yet to strike deeper roots, even though these results may compare favorably with what they might have been in the Weimar period.

The Bundesrat

The second branch of the Federal legislature—the Council of Lands, or Bundesrat—is even less well known. In repeated polls, the proportion of West Germans who knew at least roughly "what the Bundesrat is here for," inched up slowly from a mere 8 per cent in 1951 to a still feeble 14 per cent in 1956.[20] Nevertheless, the Bundesrat is a coordinate branch of the Federal legislature and has a significant share in the legislative process, as well as considerable powers in emergencies.

The Bundesrat is the specific organ through which the Land governments cooperate in Federal legislation and administration (Article 50). It is composed of members of the Land governments, that is, ordinarily of Ministers, even though these in turn are represented at many meetings by high-ranking officials of their Ministries. The Ministers do not serve, however, as individual deputies, but as members of the delegation of their Land, which must vote as a unit (Article 51.3). Each Land has at least three votes; Lands with more than two million inhabitants have four votes, and Lands of over six million inhabitants have five votes (Article 51.2). The 1961 distribution of Land votes in Bundesrat was shown in Table 5-7b. If a Land is governed by a coalition of several parties, the entire vote of its delegation is cast as a unit in accord with an agreement of the member parties, usually following the views of the strongest party, which usually is also that of the Land Prime Minister. Bundesrat decisions require at least a majority of its constituent votes, so that abstention from voting on a proposal is equivalent to voting to reject it (Article 52.3). Most of the Bundesrat's work is done by fourteen committees; on these, other members of Land governments may serve, or their depu-

[20] *Jahrbuch*, II, p. 280.

---

[18] Heidenheimer, *op. cit.*, p. 114, with reference to Theodor Eschenburg, *Der Sold des Politikers* (Stuttgart, 1959).

[19] From poll data in *Jahrbuch*, II, pp. 174–178.

The Basic Law of the Federal Republic

ties, such as civil servants from Land administrations. Members of the Federal government have the right and, if requested, the duty to attend any meeting of the Bundesrat or its committees; they must be heard at any time (Article 53).

The Bundesrat has a share in all Federal legislation. For constitutional amendments, a two-thirds majority of Bundesrat votes is required, just as it is of Bundestag members. About half of the remaining legislation is composed of the so-called "federative" or "consent" laws—perhaps something like 60 bills a year. These are all the laws for which Bundesrat consent is explicitly required by the Basic Law. Thanks to a successful broad interpretation of the Basic Law by the Bundesrat, all federal legislation which is to be carried out by the Lands and which thus has implications for their administrative institutions and procedures must also be approved by the Bundesrat. For all other bills, the Bundesrat has a suspensive veto, which the Bundestag may override by simple majority. If the Bundesrat's rejection of the bill was by a two-thirds majority, however, a similar two-thirds majority in the Bundestag is required to override the bill (Article 77.4).[21]

For any kind of bill, the Bundesrat may require within two weeks after its receipt from the Bundestag that it be submitted to a Joint Coordinating Committee of the two chambers, composed of eleven members of the Bundesrat, one for each Land, and an equal number of Bundestag members. In the case of "consent" legislation, the Bundestag itself, as well as the Federal government, may also invoke the procedure before the Joint Coordinating Committee (Article 77.2).

During the first Bundestag period, 1949–53, when 805 bills were initiated—472 by the Federal government, 301 by the Bundestag, and 32 by the Bundesrat—the Joint Coordinating Committee was invoked 75 times. Of these 75 cases, 73 ended by compromise; the Bundesrat cast three suspensive vetoes and was overridden by the Bundestag twice. Of the many bills requiring its consent, the Bundesrat vetoed six; of these, two were passed by it later in amended form, and four failed for good.[22] The power of the Bundesrat is reflected, not in the few vetoes it cast, but in the many compromises which it forced on the Bundestag in the Joint Conference Committee, and in the extent of substantive changes which it thus imposed on the original draft legislation.

Unlike the Bundestag, the Bundesrat also has considerable powers in the area of administration. Its consent is required for all administrative ordinances of the Federal government that are based on "consent" laws, or on the basis of laws which the Lands are required to execute as agents of the Federal government, or that regulate the tariffs or conditions of use of the Federal railroads, mails, and telecommunications.[23]

The role of the Bundesrat is still more significant in emergencies, or in cases of conflict between the Federal government and a Land, or between different branches of the government. Bundesrat consent is required for the initiation of Federal coercion against any Land that fails to fulfill its legal obligations (Article 37), and the Bundesrat alone is competent to determine in the first place that such a failure on the part of a Land to meet its obligations has occurred (Article 84.4). The consent of the Bundesrat is also essential for the proclamation of a "legislative emergency" by the Federal President, in the case of a deadlock between the Chancellor and a negative majority in the Bundestag, and for the enactment of legislation during its duration. The Federal government, without the consent of the Bundesrat, may put Land police forces under its orders to combat a danger threatening the existence of constitutional order of the Federal Republic or of any of the Lands; but any such emergency measure

21 For details, see Plischke, op. cit., pp. 82–83; and Eschenburg, op. cit., pp. 562–563, 620–622.

22 From data in Grosser, op. cit., p. 88; and Eschenburg, op. cit., p. 622.

23 Article 80.2; and Eschenburg, op. cit., p. 622.

must be rescinded whenever the Bundesrat demands it (Article 91.2).

The Bundesrat has important assets to meet its tasks. Its members usually are Ministers in the cabinets of their Lands, and its President—elected for one year and taken by custom in rotation each time from a different Land—usually is the Prime Minister of his Land. They thus have considerable status and prestige, and since the Ministers can draw upon the technical advice of the expert staffs of the Land bureaucracies, they also command a good deal of technical competence.

These assets have brought their temptations. Over the years, the Bundesrat has become increasingly inclined to play down its political and straight legislative role, and rather to stress the technical and administrative aspects of its activities. In practice, this tactic of disguising political wishes or objections in the cloak of technical concerns is said to have been quite effective. Technical arguments thus seem to lend more strength to a proposed course of action than do political ones; and this fact testifies in its own way to a significant trend throughout West German politics: the increasing weight of administrative and bureaucratic considerations and the growing power of the Federal executive.

The Chancellor

The Federal Chancellor holds the most important office in the Federal Republic. In effect, he appoints and dismisses all members of the Federal Cabinet, since his proposals are binding on the President of the Republic, who has the formal power of their appointment and dismissal (Article 64). Informally, the political parties whose deputies are to elect him to his office may stipulate in their agreement of coalition that certain ministerial portfolios should be given to certain individuals or to members of certain parties, but once the Chancellor is appointed, the parties have no effective control over his appointment policies, short of threatening to bring down the government by electing a new Chancellor.

The Chancellor has the power and the responsibility to determine the guiding lines of public policy (Article 65). His virtual subordinate, the Federal Minister of Defense, is commander-in-chief of the armed forces in peacetime, but as soon as the "case of defense" —that is, war or war-like emergency—is declared, the supreme command of all forces is vested in the Chancellor himself (Article 65a, added in 1956). This declaration is made by the Bundestag, or in the case of emergency, by the President of the Republic, with the counter-signature of the Chancellor (Article 59a). Unlike the President of the Republic, the Chancellor cannot be impeached; if a law bearing the required signatures of the Chancellor and President were found illegal, only the latter would be subject to possible impeachment.[24]

The Chancellor has the "competence to determine competence" within the general framework of constitutional provisions—that is, he can assign the jurisdiction of the different Ministries, create new ones, or change their organization. He has the main effective control about personnel policies in the Federal government. There are three ways in which a Chancellor may be elected by the Bundestag: (1) on nomination by the President of the Republic and by the votes of the majority of the members of the Bundestag; (2) in case of the failure of the presidential nominee to win such a majority, someone else may be elected Chancellor two weeks later by a majority of the Bundestag members; (3) if no candidate has been elected within those two weeks, another Bundestag vote must be taken at once, in which that candidate is elected Chancellor who gets the largest number of votes, even short of a majority. If the Chancellor has been elected by such a mere plurality, the President of the Republic must appoint him within seven days or else dissolve the Bundestag and thus bring about national

[24] Eschenburg, *op. cit.*, pp. 634–635.

elections of a new legislature (Article 63).

Once elected and appointed, the Chancellor is very likely to remain in office for the entire four-year period of the Bundestag. A hostile majority of Bundestag members can oust him only by a "constructive vote" of no confidence, that is, by electing another Chancellor, whom the President of the Republic is then obligated to appoint (Article 67). If the Bundestag returns a plain vote of no confidence against the Chancellor, without electing a successor, the Chancellor may remain in office or else the President of the Republic, if the Chancellor so requests, may dissolve the Bundestag within twenty-one days and thus bring about new elections (Article 68).

As long as a recalcitrant majority of the Bundestag cannot agree on a successor to the Chancellor, the latter under certain conditions could govern quite effectively against it. German legislatures traditionally have not had a "power of the purse" comparable to that held by legislators in English-speaking countries. Even if the Bundestag should fail to vote a Federal budget for the coming year, the Federal tax laws would continue to operate until they are specifically repealed, and the Federal government would be entitled to collect taxes and other legal income, to continue to spend public funds in order to meet all obligations, to maintain all institutions, based on existing laws, and to continue to perform all tasks for which any amounts have been voted in earlier budgets. In addition to its continuing sources of income, the Federal government in such a case also has automatic authority to borrow for such purposes up to one-quarter of the total amount of the last preceding budget (Article 111). The Bundestag always retains control, however, over new Federal credits and guarantees that are to extend beyond a single fiscal year, for these must always be based on a Federal law (Article 115).[25]

[25] On the whole problem of budgetary powers, see *ibid.*, pp. 584–591.

The Chancellor may even bring about the enactment of Federal legislation against the will of a hostile but divided Bundestag. If he has been defeated on an important bill, but not removed from office by the election of a successor, and if the Bundestag has not been dissolved by the President, the latter, on the motion of the Federal government and with the consent of the Bundesrat, may declare a "state of legislative emergency" and have the bill pass into law in the form proposed by the Federal government, in so far as it has been approved by the Bundesrat (Article 81.1–2). For a six-month period from the first declaration of such a state of legislative emergency, the Chancellor during his term of office may also cause any other legislative proposal of his government to be enacted in this manner, if it has been turned down by the Bundestag. Only the Basic Law may not be changed or suspended, wholly or partly, by such emergency procedures (Article 81.3–4).

Together, and under favorable political and economic conditions, all these provisions tend to make even a weak Chancellor strong, and a fairly strong Chancellor a great deal stronger. His initial strength depends on his position in his own party and on the strength of that party, or on the strength and stability of the coalition of parties that back him. In time, however, if his administration is successful, particularly if it is further aided by economic prosperity and a favorable international climate, then the continuing concentration of power and publicity in his person will tend to make him a commanding figure in the nation.

Thus Konrad Adenauer, a moderately well-known regional leader of the Catholic Center Party in pre-Hitler days and long-time Mayor of Cologne, was elected Chancellor by a one-vote margin in the Bundestag of 1949, by 202 votes out of 402, but was re-elected with much larger majorities in 1953, 1957, and 1961. During his early years in office, opinion polls showed his popularity trailing behind that of his party, the CDU, but from 1952 on, Adenauer's popularity began to lead that of the CDU, and the party's 1957 electoral campaign exploited this personal leadership appeal with great success.[26] During the electoral campaign of 1961, a number of well-known writers, favoring the SPD, saw in Chancellor Adenauer a powerful personal symbol that would rally votes to the cause of such less popular potential successors as Minister of Defense Franz Josef Strauss and Foreign Minister Gerhard Schroeder.[27] In November, 1961, poll results showed that 50 per cent of the voters still wanted the 85-year-old Adenauer to remain Chancellor, either for a limited period (26 per cent), or indefinitely (24 per cent), at a time when the national vote for the CDU in the September, 1961, elections had declined to 45 per cent.[28]

For a strong Chancellor who appreciates power, the Chancellorship is clearly preferable to the Presidency. In the spring of 1959, Adenauer considered briefly accepting the Presidency of the Republic in succession to Theodor Heuss—an office to which he could easily have been elected if he had so desired. He announced his intention to retain as President a firm hold on German foreign policy and to break in his successor as Chancellor, but on reflection decided to remain Chancellor himself, since that office alone could assure him effective control of policy, and to let a less well-known but well-liked CDU leader, Heinrich Lübke, be elected President.

The power of the Chancellor is enhanced by several agencies which are directly subordinated to him. Foremost among these is the Federal Chancellery (*Bundeskanzleramt*). This is, in effect, a super-ministry, the office of organization and coordination for the entire Federal government. It often has decisive influence on the fate of legislative drafts. Such drafts are proposed by some Ministry, but they need the approval of the Chancellor and Cabinet, and thus the informal approval and guidance of the Federal Chancellery is often sought even in the early stages of drafting. The Federal Chancellery also serves to mediate in conflicts between different Ministries, so that only the most important ones have to be decided by the Chancellor himself. It is headed by a Secretary of State, who is the top administrative aide of the Chancellor and who also may be his chief political assistant. Under the Secretary there are about twenty high-ranking civil servants, each of whom is charged with reporting on the affairs of one Federal Ministry. A strong Chancellor may concede certain Cabinet posts, or even the post of Deputy Chancellor, to members of other factions of his own party or of other parties in the government coalition, but he will seek to keep the Chancellery in the hands of men who are politically and personally close to himself.

Such considerations have long continued to focus attention on Dr. Hans Globke, Secretary of State since 1957, for many years the closest collaborator of Chancellor Adenauer and considered at the beginning of the 1960's by a well-informed French observer "the most controversial and perhaps the most powerful man of the Federal Republic." [29] Globke's position

---

[26] See the opinion data given in Deutsch and Edinger, *Germany Rejoins the Powers*, pp. 65–66, with references; and for important additional data, U. W. Kitzinger, *German Electoral Politics*, pp. 104–105; and E. Faul *et al.*, *Wahlen und Wähler in Westdeutschland* (Villingen, 1960), pp. 89 ff.

[27] Martin Walser, ed., *Die Alternative, oder Brauchen wir eine neue Regierung?* (Reinbek bei Hamburg: Rewohlt Taschenbuch Verlag, 1961), with contributions by Hans Magnus Enzensberger, Günter Grass, Inge Aicher-Scholl, and others.

[28] DIVO Institut für Wirtschaftsforschung, Sozialforschung und angewandte Mathematik, *Bundestagswahl 1961*, Repräsentativumfrage 326, Repräsentativerhebung No. 322, July, 1961; No. 323, September, 1961; No. 326, November–December, 1961; Frankfurt, 1961, multigraphed; henceforth cited as DIVO 322, 323, and 326, respectively. The data cited are from DIVO 326, p. 15, Q.C. 36. The authors are indebted to Dr. Erwin Scheuch of the University of Cologne and Harvard for making these materials available.

[29] Grosser, *Die Bonner Demokratie*, p. 106. Under the Nazi regime, Dr. Globke had written in 1936 for the infamous Nürnberg racial laws an official commentary, the reading of which he later described as repulsive and detestable. According to some writers, his commentary made these laws still more severe; according to others, it tended to narrow their application and thus saved many individuals. The attacks on Globke were not free from politics, and the Chancellor defended his associate to the utmost, taking him everywhere on his major

The Basic Law of the Federal Republic

has been compared with that of former Governor Sherman Adams during some years of the Eisenhower Administration, but his duties also include the supervision of the secret intelligence organization headed by General R. Gehlen.

Another instrument of the Chancellor is the Federal Press and Information Office, which since 1952 has been headed by another close associate of the Chancellor, Felix von Eckardt. The Chancellor also has at his disposal a secret fund which was budgeted in 1955–56 at a little less than three million dollars, and which permits the subsidization of favored periodicals, newspapers, and journalists.[30] The office is particularly effective in influencing the provincial press in rural areas and small towns.

Despite the concentration of powers in the Chancellor and the continuing efforts to enlarge them, it is not impossible that at some future time a Chancellor may be politically weak, without adequate support in his party and in the Bundestag and much in need of cooperation from other factions, parties, and branches of the government. In such a situation, the attitudes and powers of the President of the Republic may well prove crucial.

The President of the Republic

The President is the ceremonial head of the Federal Republic in domestic and international affairs. As such, he has constant opportunities to contribute to the leadership of public opinion and to the setting of the tone and style of politics and culture in the country.

The first President, Theodor Heuss, a distinguished intellectual figure and Professor of Political Science, did much to use these opportunities to elevate the prestige and dignity of republican and constitutional institutions and to anchor them to unambiguously democratic values. His indications of dissent from some of Chancellor Adenauer's foreign and military policies were of little avail, but when he left office after two terms, 1949–59, he had won general popularity and high respect not only for himself as a person, but to a significant degree for the Republic which he had represented. While Heuss, a long-standing leader of the liberal wing of the Free Democratic Party, had been elected President at a time when as yet no single political party or leader dominated the scene, his successor, Dr. Heinrich Lübke, a quiet farm leader who had been imprisoned by the Nazis, was selected for the Presidency from Chancellor Adenauer's own party at a time when the Chancellor's personal prestige and power had long been commanding. For the first three years of his office, President Lübke has fulfilled his functions correctly and with dignity.

The President is elected for a five-year term and may be re-elected for a consecutive term only once. He is elected by a special Federal Convention, composed of the members of the Bundestag and of an equal number of members of Land legislatures elected on the basis of proportional representation, which would bring the total in the early 1960's to about 1,000 persons. Election is by majority vote of the members of this body. If in two votes no such majority has been obtained by any candidate, a plurality in a third vote suffices for election (Article 54). In case of the President's incapacity or of the vacancy of his office before the end of his term, his duties devolve upon the President of the Bundesrat (Article 57).

All Presidential orders and decrees are valid only if countersigned by the Chancellor or by the competent Federal Minister. The Basic Law permits only three exceptions from this requirement: the appointment and dismissal

travels. Thus Globke was received by the Pope, and on September 10, 1955, he was toasted for his birthday by Nikita Khrushchev in the Kremlin. (*Ibid.*, pp. 281–82.) Some observers have seen in Globke a steadfast adherent of the Roman Catholic Church, who had at all times the confidence of its leaders and who remained in his compromising and distasteful job under the Nazis only in order to preserve a significant channel of information for the Church.

[30] Eschenburg, *op. cit.*, p. 749.

of the Chancellor; the dissolution of the Bundestag in the event of its failure to elect a Chancellor by majority vote; and the order to a Chancellor or Federal Minister to carry on the affairs of his office until the appointment of a successor (Article 58).

The President, nevertheless, has important reserve powers. If the Bundestag cannot be assembled in time, it is he who must decide whether to declare, with the countersignature of the Chancellor, that the "case of defense" has occurred, and thus, in effect, to declare war (Article 59.2). He must decide whom to propose first as a candidate for the post of Chancellor to the Bundestag and whether to dissolve the Bundestag if no Chancellor is elected by a majority vote of the members (Article 63). Similarly, he must decide whether to dissolve the Bundestag if it has refused the Chancellor a vote of confidence, but has failed to replace him by another (Article 68), or whether to back a minority Chancellor in such a case by declaring, at the request of the Federal government, a state of legislative emergency (Article 81). The President thus can lend considerable strength to a weak Chancellor, or else he can compel him quickly to resign.

For his actions, the President can be impeached before the Constitutional Court, on the grounds of willful violation of the Basic Law or any other Federal law. Impeachment is voted by the Bundestag or by the Bundesrat, by two-thirds of the members of the former, or of the votes of the latter; the motion to impeach, before it can be considered in either of these bodies, requires the backing of one-quarter of the Bundestag members or of the Bundesrat votes, respectively. After impeachment, the Constitutional Court may enjoin the President from exercising his office; if the Court finds him guilty, it may deprive him of his office altogether (Article 61). These provisions underscore the separate legal responsibility of the President, which is distinct from the political responsibility of the Chancellor, and they tend to strengthen the President's hand in his dealings with the Federal government by stressing the autonomous character of his decisions, signatures, and actions, even in cases where the government has requested them. During the controversy over the ratification of the European Defense Community treaty, in December, 1952, President Heuss came close to setting a precedent when he requested an advisory opinion from the Constitutional Court on the constitutionality of the treaty. After a single interview with Chancellor Adenaeur, however, he withdrew the request, a few hours before the Court's opinion was to be made public.

On the whole, however, no major conflicts between the chief institutions and officers of the Federal Republic have arisen thus far, and the President's reserve powers have remained largely untested. On the other hand, some constitutional experts feel that the legal and political potentialities of the Presidency under the Basic Law have been by no means fully utilized. If Chancellor Adenaeur should be replaced by a somewhat less strong or popular successor, or if there would be a struggle for his succession, the President may play a more important role in politics, either by his actions or else by his omissions. Until that time, most of his activities are likely to be taken up by more formal duties of representation and government routine.

The Mechanics of Law-Making

It may be convenient at this stage to summarize the roles of the different legislative and executive agencies in the normal process of legislation. The simplified flow diagram in Fig. 6-1 should be largely self-explanatory.

Bills can be initiated by the Federal government, the Bundestag, or the Bundesrat. Those initiated by the Federal government—more than one-half the total—first must be submitted to the scrutiny of the Bundesrat, while those few bills originating in the Bundesrat must first be commented on by the Federal government. Then, however, all bills—including the nearly one-half that originated in the Bundestag itself—go through the main legislative process in the Bundestag. This starts with a First Reading and a vote in the full Bundestag —the "plenum"—on the general principles of the bill, followed by intensive work on its details in one of the Standing Committees of the Bundestag, which in its report produces a draft version of the bill. This is succeeded by a Second Reading and a vote in the plenum on the specific details of the bill, and a Third Reading and vote to make sure of the cohesion and consistency of the changed bill that may have emerged.

After adoption by the Bundestag, the bill goes to the Bundesrat, and if not amended there, it passes on directly—as do more than nine-tenths of all bills—to the President of the Republic and to the Chancellor or the competent Federal Minister, for their signatures, and on to promulgation into law. For the one-tenth or less bills that are amended in the Bundesrat, another round of procedures is required, from the working out of a compromise version in the Joint Conference Committee to the approval of the compromise by each of the two chambers, before the approved text is returned to the main track for executive signatures and promulgation.

This formal description understates, however, the true influence on legislation of the Federal and Land Ministries and their officials. Many of the draft bills entered by Bundestag deputies actually have been drawn in some Ministry. Preliminary drafts are worked on in interdepartmental committees where both Federal and Land officials participate, so that the views of the Bundesrat are often taken into account at this stage. Parliament then may make further corrections in these drafts, particularly if the civil servants have in their draft misjudged the political strength of one or more of the interest groups concerned. In general, however, the Bundestag resembles the British Parliament, rather than the United States Congress, in expecting to receive legislative drafts more nearly ready for enactment.

The system looks somewhat cumbersome on paper, but it has worked well in practice, insuring thorough consideration of most measures within a reasonable time. Even in a smoothly working system, however, some deadlocks and conflicts are likely to occur. To deal with these, another set of agencies is provided in the courts.

The Courts

The chief agency for resolving constitutional conflicts is the Constitutional Court, provided for in Articles 93 and 94 of the Basic Law. Broadly speaking, the Constitutional Court is competent to deal with six kinds of cases:

1. The control of the constitutionality of laws. There is a hierarchy of laws, in which the Basic Law ranks highest, other Federal laws next, then come Land constitutions, and finally other Land legislation. Any law thus may have to be scrutinized for its compatibility with a higher one, up to the Basic Law. The Constitutional Court may be invoked for this purpose by any other court of law, where in a pending case a conflict of this kind may have arisen, or by the Federal government, or by any Land government, or by one-third of the members of the Bundestag.

2. Interpretations of the Basic Law, occasioned by disagreements about the limits of the rights and duties of any one of the highest organs of the Federal Republic. Here the Court may be invoked by the President of the Republic, the Bundestag, the Bundesrat, the Permanent Committee of the Bundestag provided for by Article 45 of the Bundestag, the Federal Government, or by certain of the major parts of any of these, such as the one-tenth or one-fourth of the members of the Bundestag who have the right to initiate certain procedures there. In any case, however, the plaintiffs must show their specific legal interest in the case at issue.

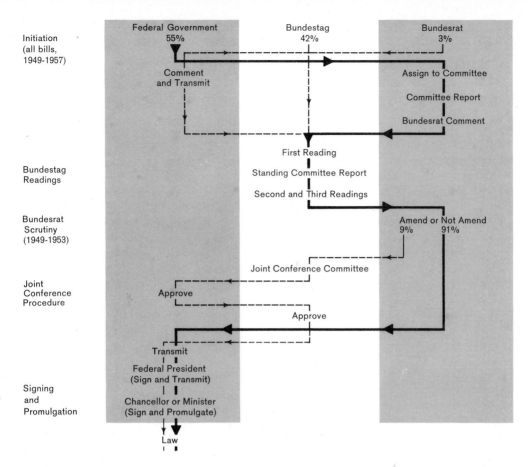

FIGURE 6-1 THE PASSAGE OF ORDINARY BILLS IN THE GERMAN FEDERAL REPUBLIC. *(Heavy line indicates the route of most bills. Data taken from A. Grosser,* Die Bonner Demokratie, *p. 88; E. Plischke,* Contemporary Government of Germany, *p. 81; and T. Eschenburg,* Staat und Gesellschaft in Deutschland, *p. 622.*

3. Disagreements about the rights and duties of the Federal government and the Land governments. Proceedings may be initiated only by the Federal government for the Federal authorities, and only by a Land government for any Land authorities.

4. Formal deprivations of certain constitutional rights, somewhat analogous to criminal proceedings:

a. Forfeiture of Basic rights, on grounds of their anti-constitutional misuse, according to Article 18.

b. Banning of specific political parties as unconstitutional, according to Article 21:2.

c. Impeachment of the President of the Republic by the Bundestag or Bundesrat, according to Article 61, on a motion by the Federal government, or the Bundestag, or the Bundesrat, or by a Land government in the case of parties limited to a single Land.

d. Impeachments of Federal judges, on the motion of the Bundestag, according to Article 98:2.

5. Complaints against decisions by the Bundestag in regard to the validity of an election, or the acquisition or loss of membership in the Bundestag by a deputy or candidate, according to Article 41:2, on the motion of the rejected candidate, or of 101 voters, or

The Basic Law of the Federal Republic

of a Bundestag "fraction," or of one-tenth of the Bundestag members.

6. All constitutional complaints by individuals against any alleged violation of any of their basic rights, or any of the rights contained in Articles 33, 38, 101, 103, or 104 of the Basic Law. Such complaints may be initiated by any individual, but ordinarily he may appeal to the Federal Constitutional Court only after having exhausted his normal legal remedies in the regular courts. The Constitutional Court, however, may accept and decide such a complaint at once, if it deals with a matter of general importance or if the delays of normal legal proceedings through the courts would work serious and unavoidable harm for the plaintiff.

The Constitutional Court, located at Karlsruhe, consists of two chambers or "senates," each composed of ten judges, with the number to be reduced to eight in each senate—or sixteen for the entire Court—in 1963. Originally the First Senate was to deal with conflicts between Federal and Land laws and the Basic Law, and with one another, while the Second Senate was to deal with conflicts between the highest organs of government. Experience soon showed that legal and constitutional disputes of the first kind were frequent, particularly the individual complaints (see point 6, above), while top-level political conflicts of the second type were rare. The Court began to operate in 1951; within the first five years, the First Senate heard nearly 3,000 complaints, while the Second Senate had to deal with about thirty. After the redistribution of the work load in 1956 and 1960, the First Senate now deals mainly with complaints against violations of civil and constitutional rights, leaving most other kinds of cases to the Second Senate, which consequently has somewhat gained in power.

The decisions of each Senate of the Constitutional Court are final. The legal interpretations embodied in them in each case are binding for future decisions by the other Senate. If that Senate wishes to depart from them, the matter must be decided by the full Court—the plenum—which requires for a quorum the presence of at least two-thirds of the members of each Senate. In this way, the unity of decisions by the two Senates of the Court is to be preserved. If a Senate should wish to reverse its own earlier legal interpretation, the matter presumably also might have to be dealt with by the plenum in a similar manner. The aim seems to be, not to make the legal views of the Court immutable, but to make sure that the two Senates of the Court will at all times function as two organs of a single judicial authority.

At times, there has been a tendency in the Federal Republic to pass difficult political problems to the Courts, and particularly to the Constitutional Court, so as to avoid the strains and stresses of handling them through the legislative and executive institutions. As in other countries, this tempting practice has threatened to engage the prestige of the Courts in political controversy, but respect for the Courts has remained high. In a country that still lacks deep-rooted habits and traditions of constitutionalism and democracy, it has been perhaps more necessary to call on the Courts and the respect for law to limit political conflicts, to curb the excessive pragmatism and potential ruthlessness with which interest groups might come to press their claims, and to guard the basic essential rules and procedures of constitutional politics.

In addition to the Federal Constitutional Court, there are six other superior Federal Courts, each of which has the highest jurisdiction over appeals in its special field. The ordinary system of German civil and criminal courts is arranged in three ascending tiers, from the *Amtsgerichte* through the *Landesgerichte* to the *Oberlandesgerichte*. All these are part of the Land jurisdiction, but they apply Federal Law (the German criminal code of 1871 and the civil code of 1900, as amended, are valid in all states), and their decisions are subject to appeal to the Federal High Court (*Bundesgerichtshof*) at Karlsruhe. This Court supersedes the old *Reichsgericht* and is the court of last resort in civil and criminal adjudication, in so far as it does not involve questions of constitutionality. The Federal High Court has three sections of five judges each. These sections deal with civil cases, criminal cases, and treason, respectively; for the last-named, the Court's jurisdiction is original.

The five superior administrative courts include:

1. The Federal Finance Court (*Bundesfinanzhof*) at Munich, dealing with taxes and other fiscal matters;
2. The Federal Administrative Court (*Bundesverwaltungsgericht*) at West Berlin, dealing with disputes among or claims against governments not involving constitutional questions;
3. The Federal Labor Court (*Bundesarbeitsgericht*) at Kassel, which deals with labor affairs;
4. The Federal Social Court (*Bundessozialgericht*) in Essen, which is competent to decide cases arising from social security and public welfare questions;
5. The Federal Court of Discipline (*Bundesdisziplinarhof*) at Frankfurt, which hears appeals from cases against federal public servants under the disciplinary regulations.

The first four of these are provided for by the Basic Law; the last is implied by it (Article 96:1 and 3).

The crowning body for this entire judicial edifice is to be the Supreme Federal Court (*Oberstes Bundesgericht*), which is provided for by the Basic Law (Article 95) and is charged with the task of safeguarding the unity of the application of the laws. Its judges are to be selected by a panel consisting of the Federal Minister of Justice and a special selection committee composed of the Land Ministers of Justice and an equal number of members elected by the Bundestag. After more than twelve years, however, no legislation implementing this complex arrangement has been passed, and the Supreme Federal Court thus far has remained on paper. Even so, the growth in the organization and stature of the West German judiciary has been impressive. In contrast to the Imperial and Weimar period—not to mention the degradation of the

Hitler era—the judiciary under the Federal Republic is separated from the executive power. It is constitutionally protected in its separateness, and so is the independence of the judges. There is a distinct supreme tribunal to deal with questions of constitutionality, and there is an effective doctrine of judicial review, which has subjected the traditional bureaucratic-authoritarian patterns of German government to a far-reaching control by law. Together, these are in many ways far more profound and thoroughgoing changes than those worked by the 1918 revolution.

The changes in the constitutional role of the judiciary contrast with the remarkable continuity of the judges. The personnel of the highest courts, and particularly of the Federal Constitutional Court, have been selected with conspicuous care, both as to their high professional qualifications and their clean political records. Elsewhere in the West German judiciary, as well as among prosecutors and Attorneys General of the Lands, and even of the Federal Government, cases of jurists with Nazi Records kept coming up as late as 1962. In that year, a Federal bill offered early and relatively attractive retirement terms to judges who would admit that they had imposed political death sentences under the Nazi regime, or had collaborated in procuring such death sentences for defendants who would not have been sentenced to death by other than Nazi standards.

A number of judges avoided proceedings by accepting this offer, but others continued to forget or conceal their pasts until confronted with evidence which produced startling headlines in the West German press. The bulk of the judges, however, have not been touched by these spectacular happenings. They are traditionalists and conservatives, not Right-wing radicals. As a group, they are remarkably tightly knit and closely related to the upper middle classes. By duty

The Basic Law of the Federal Republic

and intention, they are to be impartial appliers of the law. By background, marriage, and associations, they are overwhelmingly tied to a single class, and they are almost completely separated from, and uninformed about, that one-half of the German people which consists of workers—skilled, semi-skilled, and unskilled—who are defendants in their Courts.[31] This, however, brings up a matter that goes beyond any problem of legal rules —the crucial question of what persons and interest groups actually operate the West German political system.

[31] See Ralph Dahrendorf, *Gesellschaft und Freiheit* (Munich: R. Piper & Co., Verlag, 1961).

Political Parties and Interest Groups

VII

During the three generations from 1871 to 1961, West Germany has undergone spectacular but uneven changes. Its constitutional arrangements have changed most often and most dramatically. Its political parties have changed somewhat less, and its most influential interest groups have changed relatively least of all. To be sure, the word "relatively" is important here; among the major interest groups, the large landowners and aristocrats who enjoyed such a large share of power and prestige in Imperial Germany, and who still wielded such considerable and even fateful influence in the decline of the Weimar Republic, have disappeared. Most of the other large interest groups of the past, however, have re-emerged, and they pursue with zeal their social, economic, and political interests through the changed party system of the Federal Republic.

With the demise of the landowners, the second traditional great body of interests—big business and industry—has come into its own. For the first time, the business community has no major rival in its relations with the non-socialist parties and in its claims for the solicitude of government. Farmers and labor organizations can and often do exert effective pressure in pursuit of their specific interests; but the very much greater influence and prestige of business in the Federal Republic is conspicuous. When different business groups oppose each other, their influence is weakened, but when business speaks with a united voice, its views, with rare exceptions, weigh heavily in Bonn.[1]

Even the needs and demands of the most powerful interest groups, however, must be translated into political decisions and into administrative and legislative action. They must be made compatible with the interests of other interest groups, so as to secure for them an adequate measure of support, and they may have to be made palatable to potentially opposing interests by a process of

---

[1] The nearest thing to such an exception may have been the German-Israeli Reparations Agreement of 1952, which was opposed by some German business interests, but was pushed through by Chancellor Adenauer for reasons of morality, as well as of foreign policy, and which passed the reluctant Bundestag, thanks only to the solid support of the chief opposition party, the Social Democrats. See Deutsch and Edinger, *Germany Rejoins the Powers*, pp. 168–176; and Kurt R. Grossman, *Germany's Moral Debt: The German-Israel Agreement* (Washington, D. C.: Public Affairs Press, 1954).

political bargaining and mutual concessions. Although the great and persistent interest groups of the country most often get their way, they get it only through the political process, and particularly through the mediation and agency of the political parties.

The Changing Party System

At the first Reichstag elections in 1871, the parties of the Right and Center together won the votes of about 49 per cent of the electorate of Bismarck's Reich.[2] Ninety years later, in 1961, the greatly reorganized and renamed parties of the Center and the Right won the support of approximately 56 per cent of the electorate of the German Federal Republic. During the intervening decades, the joint share of the Right and Center parties dropped to a low of 45 per cent in 1919, and rose to a high of 61 per cent in 1933. Through wars and revolutions, monarchies and republics, the regimes of Bismarck, Ebert, Hitler, and Adenauer, this electoral share of the German Right and Center parties never varied more than 8 percentage points from a mid-point of about 53 per cent of the electorate—a point not too far from their actual share of the electorate in 1961.

At that first election in 1871, only 2 per cent of the electorate gave their votes to the Social Democrats, while another 49 per cent made no use of their franchise. During the decades that followed, however, the voting habit spread. By 1912, a solid 29 per cent of the electorate supported the Social Democrats, while only 15 per cent stayed at home. This broad distribution of the pattern of 1912 was to remain characteristic for much of German politics thereafter. In 1961, the Social Democratic share of the electorate of the Federal Republic stood at 32 per cent, while the share of non-voters had dropped slightly to 12 per cent. Throughout the intervening half-century, with all its dramatic changes, the share of the labor and socialist parties of the Left had only varied between a high of 38 per cent in 1919 and a low of 26 per cent in 1924 and 1949, ranging only 6 percentage points up or down from a mid-point of 32 per cent, where it stood once again in 1961 —with the important modification that this entire share now is concentrated once again in a single party, the SPD, as it was in 1912; in the elections from 1919 to 1953, however, it was split between Social Democrats and Communists, and sometimes also Independent Social Democrats. Finally, the percentage of non-voters ranged between a high of almost 26 per cent in prosperous 1928 to a low of 12 per cent in the crisis election of 1933, and again in the civic-minded Federal elections of 1961. The share of non-voters thus also varied within a range of only about 7 percentage points up or down from a mid-point of 19 per cent (the level attained in 1930).

Within the first two of these three broad divisions—Center-plus-Right, Left, and Non-Voters—the shifts have been considerably more dramatic. The Right, including both Conservatives and National Liberals, started out with 27 per cent of the electorate in 1871. The share of its successor parties dropped to a low of 12 per cent in 1919, to rise again to a spectacular 47 per cent in 1933, and to dwindle to an insignificant 2 per cent of the electorate in 1961; this 2 per cent supported small rightist parties, all of which, thanks to the 5 per cent clause, failed to win representation in the Bundestag. The non-socialist parties of the Middle started with 22 per cent of the electorate in 1871, rose to 33 per cent in both 1912 and 1919, but dropped to a fatally low 14 per cent in 1933. These parties of the Middle, however, rose spectacularly under the Federal Republic, when they inherited the votes of most of the politically homeless former supporters of the discredited Right. As early as 1949, in the first Federal election, 49 per cent of the electorate gave its

[2] For these and the following data, see Table 7-1 below.

TABLE 7-1 *Electoral Shares of German Parties and Groupings, 1871–1961* [a]
(By approximate percentage)

	1871	1912	Jan. 1919	June 1920	May 1924	May 1928	Sept. 1930	Nov. 1932	Mar. 1933	Aug. 1949	Sept. 1953	Sept. 1957	Sept. 1961
Citizens entitled to vote (in millions)	7.7	14.4	36.8	36.0	38.4	41.2	43.0	44.4	44.7	31.2	33.1	35.4	37.4
Valid votes cast (in millions)	3.9	12.2	30.4	28.2	29.3	30.8	35.0	35.5	39.3	24.5	28.5	31.1	31.3
1. Far Right:													
Nazis	—	—	—	—	5	2	15	26	39				
Conservatives	12	11	8	13	19	14	10	7	7	DP and DRP			
2. Moderate Right:		DVP											
National Liberals	15	12	4	11	6	6	3	2	1	4	4	4	1
(1919–33: DVP)													
Subtotal RIGHT	27	23	12	24	30	22	28	35	47	4	4	4	1
3. Progressives and Democrats (1928: State Party)	8	10	16	7	6	10	9	2	2	FDP 9	9	6	11
4. Center and Bavarian Peoples' Party	10	14	16	14	13	11	12	12	12	CDU 24	36	43	38
5. Particularists	4	9	1	1	1	1	1	2	0	13	7	5	2
Subtotal CENTER	22	33	33	22	20	22	22	16	14	49	52	54	51
6. Social Democrats	2	29	32	17	15	22	20	16	16	22	25	27	31
Independent Social Democrats	—	—	6	13	1	—	—	—	—	—	—	—	—
7. Communists	—	—	—	2	10	8	11	13	11	4	2	—	1
Subtotal LEFT	2	29	38	32	26	30	31	29	27	26	27	27	32
8. Non-voters	49	15	17	22	25	26	19	20	12	24	17	15	16
Total	100	100	100	100		100	100	100	100		100	100	100

[a] Sources: Dolf Sternberger, *et. al., Wahlen und Wähler in Westdeutschland* (Villingen/Schwarzwald: Ring Verlag, 1960), pp. 321–323; Sidney Mellen, "The German People and the Postwar World," *American Political Science Review*, 37:4 (August, 1943), 601–625. The elections of December, 1924, and July, 1932, have been omitted; their inclusion would not change any of the major trends. Because of rounding, all figures are approximate.

support to a number of such non-socialist middle-of-the-road parties. By 1961, a much diminished number of such parties was backed by 54 per cent of the registered voters, with 51 per cent concentrated on only two parties, the CDU, supported by 38 per cent, and the FDP, backed by about 11 per cent of the electorate. These and additional data are shown in greater detail in Table 7-1.

Throughout the days of the Empire and of the Weimar Republic, the voting strength of the Center and the Right had been scattered over many parties, with the only exception being in 1933 when the Nazis united a large part of it for their adventure in extremism. Never before the days of the Federal Republic had a moderate party succeeded in uniting under its leadership the bulk of

this potential Right and Center vote, let alone in keeping it together through election after election. All this the CDU has accomplished, and in so doing it has become Germany's first example of a moderate and successful party of political integration.

The Christian Democratic Union (CDU)

The Christian Democratic Union, CDU, together with its Bavarian sister party, the Christian Social Union, CSU, is the successor of the old Catholic Center Party, as well as of some small Protestant non-socialist parties, such as the Christian Social People's Service (*Christlichsozialer Volksdienst*), and of parts of several middle-class and moderately conservative parties, such as the German People's Party (*Deutsche Volkspartei*), and others. For the first time in the history of German political parties, the CDU/CSU has succeeded in uniting strongly committed Catholics and Protestants, together with voters of less intense religious feelings, in a single large party. At the same time, it has united rural and urban voters, farmers and businessmen, artisans and white-collar workers, professionals and housewives, employers and labor-union members, into a single broad party, which has succeeded in maintaining its significant appeal to every one of these diverse interests and groups.

All of these groups have, in fact, responded by giving a substantial part of their votes to the CDU, and they have continued to do so through four Federal elections and a much larger number of elections in the Lands. They have differed significantly, however, in the measure of their support. The extent of these differences near the end of the 1950's is shown in Table 7-2, and there is good reason to think that these differences have persisted.

The figures in Table 7-2, as well as additional survey data, show that the CDU is getting nearly twice as much support from Roman Catholics as it does from Protestants —a fact which becomes particularly evident when it is recalled that the proportion of regular churchgoers—who, in turn, vote still more solidly for the CDU—is much higher among Roman Catholics than it is among Protestants.[3] It also seems clear that the CDU

[3] For data from 1953 surveys, showing much the same picture, with a minor increase in Catholic preferences for the CDU since 1953, see Juan Linz, *The Social Bases of West German Politics*, pp. 181–187, and esp. p. 185, n.l.

is getting most of the votes of farmers, civil servants, and businessmen, both big and small. It gets more of the votes of the wealthy and the well-off, but it does fairly well in every income group. It has a strong appeal for voters over 60 years of age, who, we may recall, are more numerous in Germany than in many other countries. It gets above average support from white-collar employees, housewives, and women in general, as well as from members of the professions, once these decide to support any party at all. The CDU does least well, but still not too badly, among non-churchgoing Protestants, skilled workers, Protestants in general, non-skilled workers, respondents under 20 years of age, and rural laborers, in that order.

The sources of the CDU's electoral support are reflected in the composition of the leading bodies of the party. The formal decision-making body of the party, its national executive (*Bundesvorstand*), mirrors the diversity of the party's supporters and its strong local roots, particularly in Southern and Western Germany. Formal power in this executive is divided between leaders of regional organizations (*Landesverbände*) and the party's chief representatives in the Federal government and in the Bundestag, between Protestants and Catholics, and between trade-union leaders and representatives of business and industry. More relevant for policy decisions, particularly in regard to foreign policy, has been an inner elite of the CDU. At the end of 1956, this group was composed of Chancellor Adenauer, the party chairman and the four vice-chairmen of the CDU, its cabinet ministers, and its parliamentary leaders, consisting of the chairman of the CDU delegation in the Bundestag and his two deputies, the chairman of the CSU delegation and his deputy, and the chairmen of the five major Bundestag committees concerned with foreign affairs, who also were CDU deputies.[4] For other policy decisions, chairmen of some other Bundestag committees might be more relevant; and there have been some changes in

[4] For these and the following data, see Deutsch and Edinger, *op. cit.*, pp. 66–69.

TABLE 7-2 *Major Party Preferences, Fall, 1958* [a] (Summary of 3 consecutive surveys. Asterisk marks percentages at least 2 points *above* average for total sample.)

Categories	CDU	SPD	Others	No Preference	Total of group
1. Total respondents	35%	23%	4%	38%	100%
2. Occupations:					
Independent farmers	59 *	3	4	46 *	100
Civil servants	43 *	11	8 *	38	100
Employers and self-employed	40 *	8	10 *	42 *	100
White-collar employees	37 *	20	5	38	100
Housewives	36	20	3	41 *	100
Free professions	33	5	10 *	52 *	100
Pensioners, and trainees	33	26 *	5	36	100
Rural laborers	31	19	4	46 *	100
Unskilled workers	28	32 *	3	37	100
Skilled workers	26	38 *	2	34	100
3. Income (monthly):					
700 DM and above	41 *	22	6 *	31	100
500 to 699 DM	34	26 *	5	35	100
300 to 499 DM	32	30 *	4	34	100
Up to 299 DM	33	26 *	3	38	100
No income data	34	11	3	52 *	100
4. Age:					
60 and older	39 *	21	3	37	100
50 to 59	34	25 *	3	38	100
40 to 49	35	22	5	38	100
30 to 39	34	24	5	37	100
21 to 29	34	25 *	5	36	100
Up to 20	30	18	5	48 *	100
5. Sex:					
Men	33	27	5	35	100
Women	35	19	4	42 *	100
6. Religion:					
Roman Catholic	47 *	15	2	36	100
Protestant	26	28 *	6 *	40 *	100
Others and no denomination	18	38 *	5	39	100
7. Church attendance:					
Catholic regular churchgoers	57 *	9	2	32	100
Other Catholics	28	27 *	3	42 *	100
Protestant regular churchgoers	32	20	6 *	42 *	100
Other Protestants	24	30 *	6 *	40 *	100

[a] Source: DIVO Institut, *Umfragen: Ereignisse und Probleme der Zeit im Urteil der Bevölkerung* (Frankfurt: Europäische Verlagsanstalt, 1959), pp. 54–56. For 1960 and 1961 data, confirming this general picture, see also Viggo Graf Blücher, *Der Prozess der Meinungsbildung dargestellt am Beispiel der Bundestagswahl 1961* (Bielefeld: EMNID, 1962).

composition of the CDU cabinet ministers and Bundestag committee chairmen between 1956 and 1962, but the general character of the party has remained sufficiently constant to make the picture of its inner elite still relevant for the 1960's.

This inner elite group in 1956 numbered 23 persons. It was composed overwhelmingly of West and South Germans (87 per cent), and of nearly two-thirds Roman Catholics (65 per cent). It was relatively old—52 per cent had grown up under the pre-1918 Empire. Its members were well-educated; two-thirds had attended a university and nearly half of these had won doctorates. About 61

Political Parties and Interest Groups

per cent were military veterans; 39 per cent had served in the First World War and 22 per cent in the Second. Nearly two-fifths (39 per cent) had been prominent members before 1933 of the Catholic Center party or of its affiliate, the Bavarian People's Party. None had gone into exile during the Nazi era, but 35 per cent had been imprisoned for anti-Nazi activities, 39 per cent had an anti-Nazi record, and only 4 per cent had served the Nazi regime in any official capacity. Three-quarters were of middle-class origin (74 per cent); nearly one-quarter (22 per cent) reported a labor background; only 4 per cent—or one man—could be counted an aristocrat.

A similar composition was found among the 250 CDU and CSU deputies who sat in the Bundestag between 1953 and 1957. They were more than three-quarters middle class and nearly two-thirds Roman Catholic. They were less well educated—30 per cent had no formal education beyond the primary level. Far fewer—only 13 per cent—had any clear-cut anti-Nazi record of arrest or imprisonment, and not one reported having been in exile. Since the middle-level leaders, such as these Bundestag deputies of the mid-1950's, are a likely source of new top leaders, it seems plausible that the proportion of top CDU leaders with clear-cut anti-Nazi records will decline. The characteristics of these two CDU elites, and of their SPD counterparts, are summarized in Table 7-3.

The data presented thus far do not tell us which specific interest groups are represented within the CDU, nor by what particular arrangements their influence is exercised. Some inferences may be drawn, however, from general studies of interest representation in the Bundestag in which the CDU deputies comprised at all times a large part, and an absolute majority from 1953 to 1961. Thus, of the 467 deputies in the 1957–61 Bundestag, at least 13 per cent—or some 60 deputies—

openly represented business interests; another 13 per cent represented farmers and their associations, while 10 per cent were officials of trade unions and social welfare organizations.[5] Of the last of these groups, a majority doubtless were members of the SPD, while the bulk of employer and farm representatives were members of the CDU and FDP fractions. Since the CDU delegation outnumbered that of the FDP about 5 to 1, some 40 to 45 employers' representatives presumably were sitting as CDU deputies, forming roughly one-fifth or one-sixth of the total delegation of that party. This proportion holds even if we assume a still higher concentration of employers' representatives—perhaps as high as 31 per cent—among the deputies of the FDP, which was the proportion of such employers' representatives found by a survey in the FDP delegation in an earlier Bundestag.[6]

Despite the reality of direct and indirect interest representation in its councils—including such powerful interests as the Roman Catholic Church, big business and industry, farm groups, small businessmen's and employer's organizations, Protestant Church leaders, and Christian trade unionists—the very multiplicity of these interests and the breadth of the party's electoral support give the CDU and its leaders a measure of independence against any single pressure group. The same facts, however, also increase the importance of the highly visible national leaders, who, after years of successful performance in government, have become unifying symbols for their party and its electorate, or for large parts of it. Chancellor Adenauer's power over his party is well known, but Minister of Economics Ludwig Erhard, Defense Minister Franz Joseph Strauss, and Foreign Minister Gerhard Schröder all have endeavored to build up significant personal reputa-

[5] Deutsch and Edinger, op. cit., p. 91; "Die interessante Zahl," Junge Wirtschaft, V (December, 1957), 522; Heinz Hartmann, Authority and Organization in German Management (Princeton: Princeton University Press, 1958).

[6] Ibid., pp. 91, 94; Rupert Breitling, Die Verbände in der Bundesrepublik (Meisenheim: Hain, 1955), pp. 102–109.

TABLE 7-3 *A Comparison of Party Leadership Groups, 1956*[a]

(Data in percentages)

Characteristic and classification	CDU		SPD		Bundestag[b]	
	Party elite 1956	Bundestag delegates 1953–57	Party elite 1956	Bundestag delegates 1953–57	Legislative elite 1956	Total deputies 1953–57
Total number analyzed	23	250	29	162	44	507
Age structure: [c]						
−1890	17	14	3	11	14	13
1891–1900	35	35	28	28	39	33
1901–1910	26	33	52	36	34	34
1911–1920	22	15	17	20	11	17
1921–1930	0	3	0	5	2	3
1931–1940	0	0	0	0	0	0
1941–	0	0	0	0	0	0
NI	0	0	0	0	0	0
Total	100	100	100	100	100	100
Religion:						
Protestants	35	38	35	32	43	43
Roman Catholics	65	62	0	14	34	37
Others and none	0	0	9	34	5	12
NA and NI	0	0	55	20	18	8
Total	100	100	100	100	100	100
Education: [d]						
Primary	17	30	28	56	11	34
Secondary	9	14	31	16	18	22
University	70	52	35	28	66	42
NA and NI	4	3	7	0	5	2
Total	100	100	100	100	100	100
Anti-Nazi record (political persecution):						
Arrest, prison	35	13	26	32	14	18
Exile	0	0	33	16	5	5
NI or NA	65	87	41	52	82	77
Total	100	100	100	100	100	100
Early training, or social origin: [e]						
Aristocracy	4	n.a.	3	n.a.	0	n.a.
Middle class	74	78	28	55	68	74
Labor	22	21	48	44	30	25
NI (or none)	0	1	21	1	2	1
Total	100	100	100	100	100	100

[a] Source: K. W. Deutsch and L. J. Edinger, *Germany Rejoins the Powers* (Stanford: Stanford University Press, 1959), p. 68.

[b] All computations for Bundestag delegations taken from Martin Virchow, with the collaboration of Rudolf Holzgräber, "Die Zusammensetzung der Bundestagsfraktionen," in Wolfgang Hirsch-Weber and Klaus Schuetz, *Wähler und Gewählte*, pp. 353–92.

[c] Age structure for Bundestag delegations was computed from ages given in ten-year periods, e.g., 50–59 as of December 31, 1953. Even distribution was assumed over the decade so represented, and to make the figures comparable with the figures in this table, the numbers were prorated as in the following example: 30 per cent of those who were 50 to 59 years old as of December 31, 1953, plus 70 per cent of those 40 to 49 equals the number of delegates born between 1901 and 1910.

[d] No information concerning doctorates was discovered for the delegates. Otherwise, figures are comparable with elites.

[e] For Bundestag delegates, information concerns "Early training." There is therefore no data applicable for "Aristocracy."

tions that would make each of them an effective contender for the Chancellorship at some time in the future, provided only that the CDU maintains its unity and its predominant hold on the government of the Republic.

This unity of the CDU has never been effectively threatened. All interest groups within the party stand to gain little and to lose much if it were lost. Some Protestant members may chafe at the predominance of Catholic politicians in the inner councils, but the CDU provides more patronage for middle-class Protestants than the latter would be likely to secure by any voting strength which they could command by their own unaided efforts. Many Protestant workers vote in any case for the SPD; and the CDU policy of allocating national regional and local patronage roughly in proportion to the over-all strength of the denominations, with only minor deviations in favor of Catholics, also gives the CDU Protestants the benefit of the quota of those Protestants who have been voting for the SPD.

Something similar applies to other groups. Catholic trade unionists have been dissatisfied with the steady rightward drift of the CDU, which has moved from stressing social reform and the acceptance of moderate socialism in the party's *Ahlener Programm* of 1947 to the conservatism and increasing identification with the views of business enterprise during the Adenauer era. Yet, as committed Catholics, these unionists are unlikely to join the SPD, and they have no realistic alternative to staying in the CDU. Farm groups likewise have found that they can get much through the CDU—including substantial farm price supports as well as the prestige of having a farm leader, Heinrich Lübke, as President of the Republic—and any alternative political alignment they might make would offer them much less.

The relative satisfaction of all these groups with the CDU during the years of mounting

prosperity has tended to restrict the political chances of the SPD, almost regardless of the policies or skills of its leaders; but the slowing down of this prosperity in the 1960's, together with the demands for a more equitable distribution of some of the gains that are still being made, may offer the SPD new opportunities to compete with the CDU for more broadly based electoral support.

The CDU has been one of the most successful political parties in the world. Starting from a coalition of diverse elements, it has held them together and led them to many electoral victories; once, in 1957, the party won an absolute majority of the valid votes cast—which amounted to 43 per cent of the total electorate—something never before achieved in German history by a single party in a free election. Although it could not hold its 1957 share of the vote, by 1961 and 1962 it had consolidated many of its gains at a level of 40 per cent of the electorate or more and seemed likely to remain the largest West German party for the indefinite future.

Within this spectacularly successful party, however, distinctive elements have persisted. One bloc of voters follows closely the direct and indirect lead of the Roman Catholic Church in political affairs; the stability of this group's commitment is strengthened not only by the influence of the clergy, but also by that of many local and community leaders who as youths were influenced by the various Roman Catholic lay organizations, which many of the leaders are still active in. Particularly important elements among these stable Catholic CDU supporters are rural groups and Catholic trade-union members. Similar but much smaller groups of strongly committed Protestant voters are also reliable CDU supporters. All these stable groups back the CDU regardless of the party's current electoral propaganda or of its financial resources.

These groups that consistently vote for the CDU are not adequate to maintain a large party and give it a good chance to win each election. Many of the voters who ordinarily cast their ballots for the CDU pay little attention to politics. They must be aroused anew at each election and brought to the polls in just the right kind of mood. All this costs a remarkable amount of money—far more than the CDU can collect from its members. Although the CDU/CSU in 1957 polled over 15,000,000 votes, the party had only about 250,000 members, or 1 member for every 60 votes. Annual membership fees are estimated to have brought in less than $300,-000. About another $400,000 per year came in from levies on Bundestag and Landtag deputies of the party, and the remaining $400,000 or $500,000 needed to make up the $1.1 to 1.2 million necessary to run the party organization even in a non-election year had to come from private donations.

In the 1957 election, however, the private campaign expenditures on behalf of the CDU/CSU by the party itself and through parallel campaigns—e.g., the special campaign on behalf of Dr. Ludwig Erhard—totaled perhaps $9.0 million. This was about eight times the amount of off-year spending; by comparison, in Britain, a country with a comparable number of voters, the Conservative Party spent about $1.8 million in the 1955 election. In other words, the CDU collected on the average a little more than $1 from each of its members, while spending about $4 per member in an off-year, and about $36 per member—or about $.60 per vote obtained—in the 1957 election. These per capita figures approach American levels of campaign expenditure, in a country with less than one-half the American per capita income.[7]

In contrast to the CDU, the SPD, in 1957, with 600,000 members—or 1 for every 16 votes—collected about $2 million in dues, or an average of more than $3 per member; it spent less than $2.4 million in the election, corresponding to roughly $4 per party member and $.25 per vote obtained.[8] In short, the

[7] For detailed figures, see U. W. Kitzinger, *German Electoral Politics*, pp. 202–203, and 312, n.l. Kitzinger's careful calculations are lower than the off-year figures computed in Arnold J. Heidenheimer, "German Party Finance: the CDU," *American Political Science Review*, 51:2 (June, 1957), 369–385. The figures alleged in SPD publications are substantially higher; for details see Kitzinger, *op. cit.*, pp. 304–312.

[8] Kitzinger, *op. cit.*, pp. 202–204.

CDU in the 1957 election outspent the SPD by more than 2:1 per vote, by about 4:1 in total campaign expenditures, and by 8:1 per member. There is little reason to think that these conditions have not persisted in the 1960's.

Much of this money is raised from economic interest groups, primarily from those in industry, commerce and banking; the continuing need for money of this kind makes the CDU, and the FDP as well, more dependent on the support of organized business interests, and particularly of big business, than are comparable parties in England and the United States. As we shall see below, business interests in the German Federal Republic have special centralized institutions—the Sponsors' Associations and the Civic Associations—whose contributions are mostly tax-deductible and who get the most political value for their money.

One further source of influence on the CDU should be noted here. The figures for its 1957 campaign expenditures thus far have not included any sums spent by the Federal government at the time of the electoral campaign to popularize its policies, nor do they include the services of government personnel, who also happen to be chiefly CDU members, loaned to the CDU for campaign purposes. The SPD alleged that government spending in 1957 on what was in effect campaign propaganda for the CDU amounted to another 40 million DM, or $10 million. On this point, the cautious judgment of U. W. Kitzinger deserves citation:

It was generally admitted that Government funds were used on a large scale before and during the election to propagate the Government's foreign, military, and domestic policies among the electorate. The Chancellor's fund of 11 million DM per annum was one of the chief sources of finance for such activity, the Press and Information Office with its annual budget of 20 million DM used a certain proportion of its funds in a similar direction, and the information budgets of the various ministries, particularly that of the Ministry of Defence, which amounted to 6 million DM per annum, were also used in part for overt and indirect activity of this kind. But no useful purpose would be served by attempting to calculate a wholly arbitrary figure of Government expenditure incurred more or less directly to return the Government parties to power. The line between propaganda for a government and its policies and for the Government parties and their personalities is not easy to draw in a State where the Opposition rejects such important parts of Government policy as was the case in the Federal Republic. This undoubted fact was used (even perhaps abused) by supporters of the Government to defend its information policy; but it is also a source of very real difficulty for any attempt at a break-down of information accounts for the purposes of political studies.[9]

If, nevertheless, we do try to estimate the size of this indirect government intervention in the campaign, we might perhaps deflate the SPD's estimate about one-half, that is, by the same ratio by which Mr. Kitzinger's careful estimates reduced the SPD allegations of the electoral expenditures by the CDU and parallel campaigns by private groups. This would leave us with another $5 million of effective pro-CDU campaign expenditure by the government, or somewhat more than one-half of all other campaign spending by or on behalf of that party.

If the government support of the CDU is anywhere near this sizable, the CDU would be in an uncomfortable financial position if it ever lost control of the Federal government. The old Center Party of Imperial and Weimar days was uncommonly stable, almost regardless of its political fortunes, but the CDU seems far more dependent on a good deal of money and thus on the continued support of business and government in order to hold its many diversified and partly indifferent voters together.

[9] Ibid., p. 311.

The Social Democratic Party (SPD)

The leaders and many of the members of the SPD think of it as a grand old party with a great tradition, going back for nearly a century to the days of Ferdinand Lasalle, August Bebel, and even—although this is stressed less often—to Karl Marx. They are particularly proud of the party's long record of firm commitment to democracy, maintained in the years of Nazi persecution, as well as against all appeals and threats of Communism, in both West and East Germany and in besieged West Berlin, whose people have been electing SPD majorities for a long time.

Although the party has long shed much of the vocabulary of Marx, much of its concern for ideology, and much of its old, sharply focused class appeal to industrial labor, the fact is that many of its old symbols—the red flag, the old labor songs, and the salutation "comrade"—still remind the members of the hope for a bright and fraternal future. The party has largely de-emphasized or dropped its former demands for nationalization of industries and has replaced them by a stress on indirect economic controls, reminiscent of Keynesian economics and the American New Deal and New Frontier ideas. It is trying to become a "people's party," rather than the party of a single class, and to break through the "forty per cent barrier," within which its share of votes in the Federal Republic and in most of the Lands has been so long confined.

If the party has achieved this changed image in the eyes of many of its own members, it has not done so in the view of many of its more fundamentalist stalwarts or in that of a large part of the electorate. To most middle-class voters, the party still is "red." To the Catholic Church, the SPD's treatment of religion as a strictly private matter, coupled with the actual religious indifference or heterodoxy of many party leaders, has remained unsatisfactory. To those of a conservative temper, including a great many women voters, the party still appears suspect. While the SPD can change many of the sharp edges of its political style, it cannot shed its character as a party that is advocating more comprehensive reforms than is its counterpart, the CDU; only when a majority of the German electorate becomes once more interested in any such reforms are the efforts of the SPD at acquiring a more popular image likely to carry it closer to possible majority status. In the meantime, the SPD continues to derive its most reliable voting support from trade-union members, skilled workers, unskilled workers, non-churchgoers, men, big-city residents, pensioners and trainees, and the lower middle and low income groups—in roughly that order.[10]

The party is based on a strong and disciplined membership. In 1932, before the Nazi dictatorship, the SPD had had about 980,000 members; in 1946, the re-emerging party in the much smaller Federal Republic had already 710,000 members, or proportionately nearly the same number. This membership then rose to a peak of 840,000 in 1948, to decline to a stable 600,000 by 1957. During the same period, the annual membership dues collected rose from $1.6 million in 1949 to over $2 million in 1957—a clear indication of the consolidation and loyalty of the membership and a guarantee of the substantial financial independence of the party.[11]

Compared to these levels of income from membership dues, the income from special donations, advertisements, election contributions and the like, including the contributions from municipalities with SPD majorities, cooperatives, and party-controlled publishing enterprises has been relatively minor. In the 1957 election, it amounted to little more than $1.1 million, or about one-half the total SPD

expenditures in that campaign. None of its diverse sources seemed likely to exert effective influence or pressure on the party. The trade unions continue to be the main interest group of whose views the SPD is likely to be mindful. In contrast to the Weimar period, however, the major labor unions united in the German Trade Union Federation (DGB) include not only Social Democrats but also the former Christian Trade Unions, whose members and functionaries support the CDU and who would oppose any strong partisan commitment by their organization. (The somewhat greater pro-SPD activity of the DGB in the 1953 elections ended in embarrassing political defeat.) For these and other reasons, the trade-union support for the SPD in the 1957 campaign remained peripheral.

A major source of strength for the SPD, together with its membership, are its functionaries—the chairmen of local party organizations, the party representatives elected to seats in the local and municipal governments, the national and district secretaries of trade unions, of cooperatives, and of the SPD itself. These people are committed to the SPD, sometimes with all their bureaucratic virtues and weaknesses—steadfastness, discipline, and loyalty to a centralized hierarchy and routine; the party frequently insists that newcomers serve long political apprenticeships at low levels in the organization and is unwilling to let brilliant "young men in a hurry" make dazzling careers in the party.

The highest authority of the SPD is its biennial Congress, but the real power lies in the party's national executive committee—the *Parteivorstand*—and in the leadership group of the SPD delegation in the Bundestag. This executive committee is effectively in control of the party. Regional leaders have far less power than they do in the CDU. The Bundestag delegation has no tradition of open disagreement with the national executive commit-

[10] See DIVO and EMNID data cited in note to Table 7-2 above; and *Jahrbuch,* I, p. 264.

[11] See Erich Matthias, "Die Sozialdemokratische Partei Deutschlands," in Erich Matthias and Rudolf Morsey (eds.), *Das Ende der Parteien 1933* (Düsseldorf: Droste Verlag, 1960), p. 119, n.2, with references; A. Grosser, *Die Bonner Demokratie,* p. 139; U. W. Kitzinger, *German Electoral Politics,* p. 204.

tee of the party. The most prominent SPD parliamentarians are members of the party executive as well, and many deputies are also employees of the party, or of some organization under its control. The SPD executive committee forms a fairly homogeneous group. Data for its membership in late 1956 may still give us some insight into the nature of the SPD leadership.

The SPD leaders in 1956 formed a relatively unified group, clearly linked to the traditions of their party: 72 per cent had been active in the party before 1933, 20 per cent in major positions. During the Nazi regime, 24 per cent had been in prison or concentration camps, at least 33 per cent had been in exile, and altogether 70 per cent had anti-Nazi records. Of the former exiles, a majority had worked together abroad against Hitler. Quite unlike the CDU leaders, none of the SPD leaders professed the Roman Catholic faith; while 35 per cent were recorded as Protestants, the remaining 65 per cent did not report any religious affiliations. The SPD group was strongly linked to the issue of reunification: 41 per cent came from German territories now under Communist control. Northern Germany contributed another 14 per cent to the group, and, in contrast to the CDU leaders, only 38 per cent came from Western and Southern Germany. The SPD elite was younger and less formally educated than that of the CDU: only 31 per cent had spent their youth in pre-1914 Germany; 69 per cent grew up during or immediately after World War I; 59 per cent had not gone beyond the secondary school level of formal education, and only 14 per cent held doctorates. Unlike the CDU leaders, they did not show a military past: 10 per cent had served in World War I, only 14 per cent in World War II, and another 3 per cent—or one man—had served in both; but more than 72 per cent reported no military service. No record was found of any member of the 1956

SPD Central Committee ever having served the Nazi regime in any official capacity.[12]

The 162 SPD deputies in the 1953–57 Bundestag constitute a part of the middle-level leadership of the party, and can be compared to the Central Committee of the SPD, on the one hand, and to the CDU/CSU parliamentarians, on the other. The SPD deputies were somewhat older than the top party leaders, and less well educated. A majority —56 per cent—had not gone further than through primary school, as against only 28 per cent whose formal education had stopped at that level among the top leaders. A majority of SPD deputies—55 per cent—reported middle-class origins, in contrast to only 28 per cent among top leaders, among whom, however, another 21 per cent were silent on this point.

In contrast to the CDU, the domestic anti-Nazi record of the SPD deputies was even stronger than that of the top leaders of their party: 32 per cent of the Bundestag delegation, as against 26 per cent of the top leaders, had been arrested or imprisoned by the Nazi regime. Fewer of the SPD deputies, however, had been in exile: only 16 per cent, as against 33 per cent of the top leaders. Altogether, the middle-level leaders of the SPD seemed to be as strongly and personally committed to an anti-Nazi stand as were the members of the Central Committee. If the top leadership of the party should in time come to be replenished from among the members of this middle-level group, the intense anti-Nazi commitment of the party will be likely to persist.[13]

The SPD has had a more intense interest than the CDU in German reunification and the recovery of the present DDR territories, from which before 1933 much of the SPD strength was traditionally drawn. The party was cool toward the NATO military alliance with the West and would have preferred to buy German reunification at the price of Ger-

[12] Deutsch and Edinger, *op. cit.*, pp. 72–73.
[13] *Ibid.*, p. 73; and Martin Virchow, "Die sozialdemokratische Fraktion," in Wolfgang Hirsch-Weber and Klaus Schütz, *Wähler und Gewählte: Eine Untersuchung der Bundestagswahlen 1953* (Berlin: Vahlen, 1957), pp. 366–377.

man neutrality and continued disarmament, provided only that reunification should bring genuinely free elections in the DDR areas. This, however, the government of the Soviet Union has never been willing to concede, and thus the SPD willingness during the 1950's to accept some limited compromises with the Soviets has remained somewhat unreal. Gradually, the party has come to accept all the essentials of Chancellor Adenauer's proclaimed foreign policy, including German membership in NATO and in the Common Market and the policy of firm alliance and increasing integration with the West. In June, 1960, this acceptance was formally put on record by the National Party Secretary, Herbert Wehner, speaking for the SPD in the foreign-policy debate in the Bundestag. Willy Brandt, the young and popular governing Mayor of West Berlin, who led the national SPD ticket in the 1961 elections, has become a living symbol of this new SPD course toward greater stress on national unity. The SPD has remained less enthusiastic, however, about the pace and scope of German rearmament, and has retained a distaste for nuclear armaments on German soil, or in the hands of German troops. Although the SPD and the CDU were thus united in the early 1960's on basic foreign policy, the SPD position continued to be slightly more moderate and flexible than the rigidly uncompromising "hard line" of the Bonn government.

Within the SPD, there are fewer distinct interest groups than there are in the CDU. Labor unions and consumers' cooperatives, however, are directly represented in the party leadership and in the SPD delegation in the Bundestag, through members who are or have been their paid functionaries. Another interest group is composed of the many SPD functionaries and deputies who are linked to the municipal governments dominated by the party. These include such men as Mayors Wilhelm Kaiser of Bremen and Max Brauer of Hamburg, who may express to some extent also the interests of these municipalities in the councils of the party. Finally, there are the expellees and refugees, who are now represented among the deputies of both major parties. Within the SPD, their representation is particularly effective through such leaders as Bundestag Deputies Ernst Paul and Wenzel Jaksch—the latter a co-author of the successful "Hessen Plan" for the resettlement of expellees. Jaksch was one of the eleven top SPD leaders selected for Willy Brandt's "shadow cabinet" or leadership team in the 1961 campaign; the chief German refugee organization, in turn, elected Jaksch to one of its highest offices, with an unusually high majority.

The Free Democratic Party (FDP)

The last of the minor parties to survive in the Bundestag after 1961, the Free Democratic Party (FDP) has a somewhat divided character and heritage. It continues from Weimar days the tradition both of the liberal-progressive Democratic Party and of the moderate-conservative German People's Party (DVP), which in turn had been a successor to the National Liberals of the pre-1914 era. The progressive tradition of the party links the FDP to the liberal middle-class Protestants of South Germany, and the conservative tradition ties it to the Protestant and anti-clerical business and professional elements in the North and West of the country. To the adherents of other parties, the FDP appears as a party somewhat to the Left of center, but its own supporters see it as a party of the Right. The latter view is the more realistic. Power within the FDP has shifted from the liberal wing represented by the first President of the Republic, Dr. Theodor Heuss, to the somewhat more nationalistic and business-oriented views of the present party leader, Erich Mende.

At a time when both the CDU and the SPD have succeeded in winning support from a wide range of social groups and strata, the FDP alone, in the words of a recent German study, "today still can be characterized as a class party." [14] It has remained largely a party of the middle classes, of employers and of business management. Accordingly, it has sharply criticized the economic and social welfare policies of the CDU. While it has agreed with the SPD in favoring the separation of religion and politics and in opposing the extension of Church influence in education, public life, and government administration, the FDP has not been able to agree with the SPD on economic policy at the national level. No national coalition between the FDP and the SPD has thus been possible. In Bonn, the FDP has often functioned as a political reserve of the CDU, available for a coalition with it, but unavailable to its SPD rivals. This tactic reflects the interests within the FDP. In proportion to its size, the party and its Bundestag delegation include more representatives of business interests than does the CDU, while in contrast to the CDU's trade-union wing, the influence of labor in the FDP is negligible.

The existence of the FDP offers business interests a second channel of representation in the political arena in addition to the CDU. The result is that the business interests, which support both parties, do not want the FDP to fight the CDU too hard, and they certainly do not want the FDP to form a coalition with the SPD in Bonn—which would be precisely the calamity that business contributions to political parties are intended to prevent. To the major business interests, the FDP often has offered a kind of elite or "quality" version of the same basic policies espoused by the CDU. Lacking, however, the religious motivation and the sociological breadth of the CDU, the FDP is far more unstable. Its gains in the 1961 Federal election were lost again

[14] Viggo Graf Blücher, *Der Prozess der Meinungsbildung dargestellt am Beispiel der Bundestagswahl 1961* (Bielefeld: EMNID, 1962), p. 116; see also *ibid.*, pp. 31, 55–56.

within a year in the North Rhine-Westphalia Land election of 1962. Since it won less than 7 per cent of the valid votes cast in the 1962 election, the FDP is once again dangerously close to that "5 per cent clause" which may yet bar it from further parliamentary representation and thus from effective political life.

Interest Groups and Elites

The Business Interests

The business groups in the Federal Republic are organized into three major organizations or *Spitzenverbände*: the Federation of German Industries (BDI), the Diet of German Industry and Commerce (DIH), and the Federal Union of German Employers Associations (BDA). In addition, there are separate associations for banking, insurance, wholesale and foreign trade, retail trade, shipping, transportation, handicrafts, and others. Serving as a coordinating committee for all these central associations is the Joint Committee of German Trades and Industries (*Gemeinschaftsausschuss der deutschen gewerblichen Wirtschaft*). In the 1950's, this Joint Committee ironed out difficulties among its member organizations and provided public representation for the business community as a whole. Its staff was small and was headed by Dr. Paul Beyer, who was also managing director of the Diet of German Industry and Commerce.

The wealthiest, most influential, and most active of the three top organizations is the BDI. Its membership consists of 36 nationwide industrial trade organizations which in turn are subdivided into more specialized organizations. The BDI has 12 regional offices which coordinate activities of the trade associations at the Land level and conduct public relations and lobbying vis-à-vis the Land government. Policy for the BDI is set by its Assembly, in which its 36 member associations are represented with a voting strength roughly proportional to the total number of employees employed by the member firms of each association. Under this arrangement, the heavy industry of the Rhine-Ruhr area has the greatest voting strength in the Assembly.[15]

The BDI is governed by its Central Committee, which elects a smaller Executive Committee, and this body in turn elects a Presidium of 16 members which seems to be the most important of the elective bodies for day-to-day decisions and which is empowered to make decisions for the Federation in an emergency. Finally, the BDI has a large professional staff, directed by a general manager and by the President of the Federation, Fritz Berg. The BDI is thus far more inclusive and more centralized than is its counterpart in the United States, the National Association of Manufacturers (NAM). Power in the BDI is concentrated in its central organs, in its permanent bureaucracy, and in its 36 constituent trade associations which are themselves highly centralized. Since its formation in 1949, the BDI has been under the control of a moderate, pro-Adenauer leadership, despite a minority which has been demanding a more nationalistic foreign policy and a stronger line toward labor.

The contacts of the BDI with the government have been direct and effective. As one observer has pointed out, the BDI committees and their staff have direct access to their opposite· numbers in the Bundestag committees and the Ministries:

> In the fiscal year 1954–55, around 200 formal communications were submitted to these agencies by the BDI. . . . One cannot escape the impression . . . that there is a constant stream of influence from the professional staffs of the BDI and the trade associations directly into the appropriate units in the ministerial bureaucracies charged with the recommendation of legislative policy, the formulation of regulations, and the execution of public policy.[16]

A more specialized organization is the Federal Union of Employers Associations (BDA), which concentrates on matters of labor and welfare policy. This group is also organized on a regional and functional basis. Its units do not themselves carry on collective bargaining, but develop the employer's position for this purpose and mobilize support for industries affected in the event of a strike. As in the DBI, the regional and central organizations of the DBA between them attempt to influence relevant legislation at the Federal and Land levels.

For major tasks of public relations, the DBI and the DBA collaborate in employing the German Industry Institute (DII). The DII disseminates the views of industry through a large number and variety of publications. These range from books to two semi-monthlies, three weeklies, a semi-weekly service for the press, and a daily sheet for radio stations. Special publications are directed to the business community itself, such as the "Letters to Entrepreneurs" (*Unternehmerbriefe*) and the "Lecture Series," which have exhorted businessmen to become more active in politics. The DII, like other business organizations, generally favors the Adenauer government and its policies. In 1957, the "Letters to Entrepreneurs" urged its readers to "see to it by all permitted and available democratic means that . . . no party cheats the voter by a pact with socialism after the election." [17]

Another public relations organization disseminating the viewpoints of business management was founded in 1952 and styled "The Scales (*Die Waage*), League for the Promotion of Social Equity." This organization specialized in placing paid advertisements in the press, on a very large scale. These advertisements were uniform, and they were published in time of labor disputes or impending "collectivist" legislation. By 1954, the organization claimed that its advertisements had appeared in 70 per cent of all German newspapers, comprising 90 per cent of total newspaper circulation. During electoral campaigns, these somewhat weighted "Scales"

[17] *Unternehmerbriefe*, May 23, 1957, cited in Kitzinger, *op. cit.*, p. 246.

---

[15] For these and the following points, see Gabriel A. Almond, "The Politics of German Business," in Hans Speier and W. Philip Davison, *West German Leadership and Foreign Policy* (Evanston, Ill.: Row, Peterson, 1957), pp. 212–217.

[16] Almond, *op. cit.*, p. 214.

aided the major non-socialist parties by taking large amounts of advertising space for brief statements in support of the Adenauer coalition's policies, without mentioning the parties by name.[18]

The main financial organs of the business community in dealing with political parties in the 1950's were the Sponsors' Associations (*Förderergesellschaften*), and their more modern version, the Civic Associations (*Staatsbürgerliche Vereinigungen*). Sponsors' Associations were founded in 1952 for the purpose of mobilizing the financial resources of business for the 1953 electoral campaign, to strengthen the position of businessmen against the competing claims of the various non-socialist parties, and to make their political contributions tax deductible. All these purposes were served effectively. Far greater sums than in 1949 were made available to the CDU, and appreciable support was given to the FDP and the small conservative *Deutsche Partei* (DP). Instead of being asked for support by several parties, many businessmen could make their main contributions in a single payment, and perhaps obtain better political conditions for their money. The Sponsors' Associations were in a position to check on the proposed expenditures of each party that asked for their support, to insist that the non-socialist parties should not waste their money in fighting one another during the campaign, and to demand at least informal assurances that none of these parties would enter a coalition with the SPD on the Federal level.[19]

Tax exemption for political contributions from the business community was assured first by treating the Sponsors' Associations formally as trade associations which raised their income by a fixed membership levy, usually in proportion to the payroll of each

member firm, amounting, for example, to $.25 per employee per year. In May, 1952, the Federal Fiscal Court decided that political contributions forming a subordinate proportion of the budget of such associations—in practice, up to one-fourth or one-third of their total spending—would be tax exempt. Additional sums could be spent, however, on ostensibly non-political "educational" campaigns which would endorse particular policies and thus indirectly aid the parties espousing them. A Federal law, passed by the Adenauer majority of the Bundestag in 1954, made all donations for political purposes tax deductible.

To take advantage of the new law, Civic Associations were founded to replace or supplement the old Sponsors' Associations, and these new bodies could use the whole of their income for political purposes and all of it would be tax deductible. During the 1957 campaign, 45 per cent of all political contributions made by business corporations were thus paid, in effect, by the state, in the form of lost tax revenue. In 1958, the Federal Constitutional Court, acting on a complaint of the Social Democratic Land Prime Minister Georg August Zinn on behalf of the Land of Hessen, threw out this provision of the 1954 law as unconstitutional, too late to make any difference to the massive use of money in the 1957 campaign.[20]

Regardless of changing legal and organizational details, it seems certain that relatively centralized political spending by business organizations of this type will continue in the 1960's as a major influence in German politics. As such, it will tend to increase the electoral prospects of the non-socialist parties, to enhance the solidarity among them, and to discourage any minor party, such as the FDP, from breaking lightly its coalition with the CDU in favor of any possible cooperation with the SPD in Bonn. In addition, these arrangements will continue to increase the bargaining power of centrally organized business interests vis-à-vis the political parties sup-

---

[18] Almond, *op. cit.*, pp. 215–216; see Kitzinger, *op. cit.*, pp. 304–305.

[19] Kitzinger, *op. cit.*, pp. 207–218.

[20] *Ibid.*, pp. 203–213.

ported by them, and to enhance the prospects of specific industries or business groups to obtain specific favors.

A survey of 47 leaders of German business organizations in 1956 revealed a group of relatively old men (two-thirds had been born before 1900), predominantly Protestant (with professed Protestants outnumbering Catholics two to one), strongly recruited from Western Germany (38 per cent), well educated (44 per cent with a university education), but with only a very doubtful anti-Nazi record: only two men claimed such a record, while three listed themselves as prominent business leaders during the Hitler period, and the remaining 42 kept silent on this point.[21]

Farmers' and Artisans' Organizations

The chief farm organization is the League of German Farmers (*Deutscher Bauernverband*), which in 1952 reported 1.3 million members, comprising 77 per cent of all independent farmers. German farm organizations have considerable political influence, which has been directed effectively toward specific demands such as agricultural subsidies and prices. As a result, German farming has been remarkably well protected and it has been effectively compensated for its high costs. Accordingly, in the fall of 1962, wheat prices in West Germany were almost 30 per cent higher than in the Netherlands, and almost 50 per cent higher than in France. The proposed Common Market price for wheat in Western Europe was set provisionally at only 13 per cent below the German level, and the establishment of a common price for farm products was postponed until July, 1963.[22]

The main organization of independent craftsmen is the League of German Artisans (*Zentralverband des deutschen Handwerks*), with 864,000 members, which includes almost all independent artisans in the Federal Republic. Despite its numerical strength, however, the political influence of this organization is quite limited.

The Labor Unions

In the mid-1950's, althogether 35 per cent of the wage earners, 20 per cent of the white-collar employees, and 84 per cent of the civil servants of the Federal Republic were organized in three large organizations. The most important of these was the German Confederation of Trade Unions (*Deutscher Gewerkschaftsbund*, DGB) with 6.1 million members (1955), comprising about 35 per cent of all wage earners, 12 per cent of all white-collar employees, and 41 per cent of all civil servants. Since the wage earners are much more numerous than the other groups, they form 83 per cent of the DGB membership, with white-collar employees furnishing another 11 per cent and the civil servants the remaining 6 per cent. The Confederation is dominated by the large wage-earners' unions, and it tends to stress the similarities between the wage earners and the white-collar employees and the civil servants in regard to their interests in the labor market. Within the Confederation, the large enterprises are most thoroughly organized and most highly represented. The member unions of the Confederation follow industrial or craft lines. The strongest industrial union, IG Metall, accounts for 25 per cent of the membership of the entire Confederation.

Second in size to the Confederation among white-collar employees is the German Employees Union (*Deutsche Angestelltengewerkschaft*, DAG), with some 425,000 members (1955), or about 8 per cent of all white-collar employees. This union has tended to stress the quasi-professional characteristics of white-

---

[21] Deutsch and Edinger, *op. cit.*, p. 100. On the relations of the German business community to the Nazi regime, see John D. Montgomery, *Forced to Be Free* (Chicago: University of Chicago Press, 1957), pp. 94–125; and Franz Neumann, *Behemoth* (New York: Oxford University Press, 1942), passim.

[22] See Deutsch and Edinger, *op. cit.*, p. 103; *Der Spiegel*, 16:41 (October 10, 1962), p. 24:3.

collar employees, their separate status and their distinct interests, in contrast to those of the wage earners. Nevertheless, in practice the DAG has found itself often pressing economic demands very similar to those advocated by the DGB.

The German Federation of Civil Servants (*Deutscher Beamtenbund*) is the most nearly professional and non-political of the three great interest organizations. With 517,000 members in 1955, it included about 43 per cent of all civil servants.

A sample of 16 leaders of the major West German trade unions in 1956 showed them slightly younger than the employers' representatives. Half of the union leaders came from Western Germany, another fifth from South Germany. Protestants and Catholics were evenly divided between the few union leaders who indicated their religious preference. Nearly one-third (31 per cent), of the union leaders had an anti-Nazi record.[23]

The fact that, just as in many other countries, only a minority of wage and salary earners in the Federal Republic are actually organized as union members weakens the voice of the unions in German politics. Since the majority of the German Confederation of Trade Unions, consisting of the old secular, SPD-oriented unions of the Weimar period, is offset by a minority, consisting of the bulk of the former Catholic unions, it is impractical for the Confederation to lean quite so heavily and openly toward the SPD as was the case in the Weimar period. Nevertheless, the SPD has remained the main channel of trade-union representation in West German politics. About 40 per cent of all Bundestag members in 1957–61 were union members; 30 per cent were in the ranks of the SPD deputies, and another 10 per cent were union members in the CDU delegation, where they formed the core of a Left wing within the party. Of all trade-union deputies in the

[23] Deutsch and Edinger, *op. cit.*, p. 102.

Bundestag, four-fifths were members of the German Confederation of Trade Unions.[24]

The Churches

Other groups besides economic interest groups have contributed major influences to recent German politics; foremost among them have been the churches. Since the role of religious groupings has been discussed earlier, only a few facts need to be recalled here. Although there are somewhat fewer Roman Catholics than Protestants among the population of the Federal Republic, there are far more Catholics than Protestants in church on most Sundays, and there are far more Catholics effectively organized for political action. Between 50 and 60 per cent of nominal Catholics attend church once a week, while only about 10 per cent of urban Protestants—and 20 per cent of rural Protestants—attend church at least once a month.[25]

About 11 million Catholics, or one-quarter of the German electorate, can be found at mass on any Sunday in the year. The Catholic clergy thus can reach every week a larger audience than all German politicians taken together could secure by their own efforts. The 10 million weekly circulation of the Catholic Church press reinforces these possibilities, and the 3 to 5 million Catholics who are adherents of Catholic lay organizations or youth groups are ten times as numerous as the total membership of the CDU. During electoral campaigns, these Catholic audiences are vigorously exhorted by bishops, the clergy, the Church press, and lay organizations to vote, to vote as a duty to their conscience, to remember the great merits of the Adenauer government, and not to vote for irreligious parties, such as the SPD and the FDP. In effect, they are being urged to vote for the CDU, and the evidence for the continuing effectiveness of the appeal seems overwhelming. [26]

Catholic groups in West Germany embrace almost all activities from cradle to grave—from

[24] Heidenheimer, *The Governments of Germany*, p. 83.
[25] Kitzinger, *op. cit.*, p. 223.
[26] *Ibid.*, pp. 225–228.

Catholic kindergartens to Catholic young farmers' leagues, traders' associations, a Catholic Woman's League, and many more. Outstanding among these for their political potential are the Catholic Workers' Movement and the Kolping Family. The Catholic Workers' Movement (*Katholische Arbeiterbewegung,* KAB) has been directly active in electioneering, particularly in North Rhine-Westphalia, where four-fifths of its 150,000 members are concentrated in the three dioceses of Münster, Paderborn, and Cologne. Thirty members of the KAB were elected to the 1957–61 Bundestag. The German Kolping Family—called before 1933 the "League of Catholic Artisan Journeymen"—is the counterpart of the KAB on the skilled worker-to-lower-middle-class level. It has about 210,000 members, nearly as many as the CDU. Since half of the Kolping members are unmarried young men, they are able to lend very active support to the CDU; and the ways in which they could and did do so have been discussed in the literature of their movement. In the 1957 campaign, their help appears to have been effective: 32 of their members entered the Bundestag. Since 11 of them were at the same time also KAB members, the combined Bundestag strength of these two organizations consisted of 54 members.[27]

The Protestant Churches are unlikely to have had more than 2 million people in church on any Sunday during the month before the 1957 election, and the weekly circulation of their church press was below 5 million. Moreover, no organ of the Evangelical Church government issued any statement in support of any of the parties during the election.[28] A relatively large number of the top leaders of the Protestant Churches come from East or Central Germany, and many have strong anti-Nazi records. Their Churches have remained far more concerned with the political issues of peace and reunification, because these Churches include the Protestants of both West and East Germany—with about 25 million being in the Federal Republic, 1.6 million in West Berlin, and 15.5 million

in the GDR. Major support from church-going Protestants has been going to the CDU, which counts among its members such well-known Protestants as Bishop Otto Dibelius of Berlin-Brandenburg and Dr. Eugen Gerstenmaier, who was the Speaker of the Bundestag during the later 1950's. The SPD included among its Bundestag deputies such Protestant ministers as Pastor Hans Merten and Pastor Fritz Wenzel, and prominent Protestant laymen such as Dr. Adolf Arndt and Dr. Gustav Heinemann, former Minister of the Interior in Adenauer's Cabinet and President of the Synod of the Evangelical Church from 1948 to 1955. Although the Protestant Churches were represented in all major parties, their political influence has been relatively weak, but they have retained some potential influence on certain sectors of public opinion.

The Mass Media of Communication

Germany is a country of newspaper readers. In the mid 1950's, 91 per cent of all adults in the Federal Republic read a newspaper at least once a week, while 55 per cent, two-thirds of them men, read one every day. Three-quarters of West Germans polled in March, 1955, said that they followed local news; less than one-half—or 46 per cent—followed domestic politics; and less than two-fifths—only 39 per cent—followed political news from abroad. The difference between the sexes, however, was striking. While 70 per cent of the men followed domestic politics and 64 per cent paid attention to international events, the corresponding figures for women were only 26 and 18 per cent, respectively. An important part of the solid electoral support for Chancellor Adenauer's foreign policy between 1949 and 1962 thus came from women who paid relatively little attention to its details.[29]

By 1960, readership of newspapers had

[29] *Jahrbuch,* I, pp. 53–56; *Jahrbuch,* II, p. 51; Deutsch and Edinger, *op. cit.,* pp. 112–113.

[27] *Ibid.,* pp. 230–231.
[28] *Ibid.,* p. 239.

further increased: 72 per cent of all adults between 16 and 70 years, 76 per cent of the men and 68 per cent of the women, were reached every day by some newspaper, and about 78 per cent of such adults—women almost as much as men—read each month at least one copy of some periodical.[30] The radio audience was, if anything, somewhat larger. In the mid-1950's, about 80 per cent of adults listened for at least an hour each day; 79 per cent said they liked to listen to newscasts; 46 per cent paid attention to political commentaries, but only 33 per cent cared to listen to reports of events abroad.[31] Television is less well established. In 1960, only 30 per cent of respondents had watched a telecast on the preceding day, but 72 per cent had done so at least once during the preceding four weeks.[32]

The West German press, which in the mid-1950's consisted of more than 1,400 dailies with a total circulation of nearly 16 million —or 318 per 1,000 West Germans—thus still represented the major channel of political information in the early 1960's. The editors of the largest dailies and periodicals—those with over 100,000 circulation—formed a relatively small group. Together with the editors of a few smaller but influential periodicals and a few directors of radio networks, this group in 1956 numbered 41 persons and constituted a fair sample of the mass communications elite of the Federal Republic. On the whole, this elite was younger and markedly more liberal than the business and CDU elites, or than the bureaucratic elite surveyed later in this chapter. About 92 per cent had at least secondary school training, and 42 per cent held doctorates. Only 22 per cent claimed

military service, 10 per cent in the First and 12 per cent in the Second World War. As many as 42 per cent had major anti-Nazi records; 38 per cent had been imprisoned by the Nazis and another 5 per cent had been in exile.[33]

The composition of this elite group bears the marks of earlier Allied, and particularly American, influence. During the years of military occupation, licenses to publish newspapers were given mainly to persons with clear anti-Nazi records. Later, when licensing ceased in the early 1950's, many of these publishers and editors maintained themselves by means of their ability and their established position in the field, and during earlier years also by means of continuing Allied, and particularly American, support. This support was given through a Newspaper Leases Control Board, controlled by the Allies, which watched over printing contracts of newspapers whose printing plants might be owned by old-line nationalistic or pro-Nazi interests, and further help was given to pro-Western papers through a Press Fund, supported largely through money provided by the United States government.[34]

Not surprisingly, the leaders of the West German press and of many of the radio networks are on the whole more in tune with mass opinion than are the members of the bureaucratic and the business elites, and they reflect in part also the views of that majority of West German voters who did not vote for the CDU/CSU in 1961. The mass media are more energetic in opposing any remnants of Hitlerism, in demanding the dismissal of Nazis who have slipped back into high-level public service positions by concealing their records, and in pressing for the prosecution and punishment of Nazis who are found to have committed wholesale murders, acts of torture, and similar crimes under the Hitler regime. Significant parts of the press are also more critical of the Federal government, the

[30] DIVO-Institut, *Der Westdeutsche Markt in Zahlen* (Frankfurt: Europäische Verlagsanstalt, 1962), pp. 151–154.

[31] Deutsch and Edinger, *op. cit.*, p. 116; *Jahrbuch*, I, pp. 62–75; *Jahrbuch*, II, pp. 63, 79.

[32] DIVO-Institut, *Der Westdeutsche Markt*, p. 156.

[33] Deutsch and Edinger, *op. cit.*, pp. 120–121.

[34] *Ibid.*, p. 119; Henry P. Pilgert, *Press, Radio and Film in West Germany, 1945–1953*, Historical Division, Office of the Executive Secretary, Office of the U. S. High Commissioner for Germany, 1953, pp. 21, 43, 50–52, 64, 101.

military establishment, the demands for nuclear weapons for the Army, and they criticize what some of them consider the unnecessarily rigid policies of Bonn toward Britain and the United States, as well as vis-à-vis Eastern Europe and the Soviet Bloc.

A Test Case of Elite Conflict: The Spiegel Affair

In October, 1962, the West German Federal Police arrested Rudolf Augstein, the publisher of the well-known West German news magazine, *Der Spiegel*. This periodical—a kind of stepped-up counterpart to *Time* magazine—was somewhat closer to the views of the FDP than to those of any other party, but it had built up its half-million circulation by sensational though generally well-informed reporting in a hard-boiled and iconoclastic style, well suited to the skeptical and disillusioned mood of many of its readers.[35]

The journal had long carried on a feud against Defense Minister Franz Joseph Strauss. In its issue of October 10, 1962, *Der Spiegel* featured a report of instances of inefficiency or unpreparedness in the West German armed forces as allegedly revealed in recent NATO maneuvers. So serious were these faults, the paper claimed, that "the Bundeswehr" today—after almost seven years of rearmament, and after six years of tenure in office of its Supreme Commander Strauss —still bears the lowest of (four possible) NATO ratings: "conditionally suited for defense."[36]

The response of the Federal authorities was spectacular. During the night of October 26 —by coincidence, at a time of extreme international tension over the Cuban crisis between Russia and the United States—agents of the Federal police raided and sealed the editorial offices of the *Spiegel* in Bonn and Hamburg, and they arrested the publisher, Rudolf Augstein, and four other executives of the magazine, on charges of treason and bribery. Bail was refused them, on grounds

of possible collusion, and thus they faced the prospect of being kept in jail on suspicion until their trial, which might be months away.

The Federal Prosecutor's office could have treated the charges made by the magazine as untrue, and prosecuted its publisher and editors for slander, or for undermining the morale of the armed forces. Instead, the authorities chose to prosecute for violation of state secrets, taking the view that some of the details of the charges must have come from secret West German military documents which the paper could have obtained only by bribery. Judged by American standards, this legal interpretation seemed to admit that there might be some truth to some of the facts alleged by the paper, but it threatened its publisher and staff members with far more severe penalties for treason.[37] Actually, West German law uses the label of "treason" far more loosely, including under it also the publication of any untrue statement which, if it were true, would injure, in the opinion of the Federal government, the interests of the Federal Republic. The language of the law is so broad that it could be used to punish many journalistic practices which in the United States would be considered lawful and a legitimate exercise of the freedom of the press. In the case of the German law, much depended on the spirit in which it would be applied, and the *Spiegel* case might well become a precedent of far-reaching importance.

The *Spiegel* affair dramatically posed four issues before the public. The first of these, common to all free countries, was the issue of legitimate government secrecy, particularly in matters of defense, as against legitimate journalistic enterprise in getting out the news, and in taking advantage of whatever documents some individuals or factions within

---

[35] For a critical review, see Hans Magnus Enzensberger, "Die Sprache des Spiegel," in his *Einzelheiten* (Frankfurt: Suhrkamp, 1962), pp. 62–87.

[36] *Der Spiegel*, 16:41 (October 10, 1962), p. 33:1.

[37] *The New York Times*, November 3, 1962, pp. 1, 2, 3; November 5, 1962, 3:13; *Der Spiegel*, 16:45, November 7, 1962; *Time*, 80:19, November 9, 1962.

the bureaucracy may be "leaking" to the press. This issue would be for the courts to decide, where *Der Spiegel,* with its long record of disrespect for authority and of frequent attacks on members of the judiciary with a Nazi past, could count on very little sympathy from the usually conservative judges.

The second issue was one of the police methods used. Henceforth, "the man who presses our doorbell in the early morning hours," said the *Frankfurter Rundschan,* "is not necessarily the milkman. It might be the political police."[38] In a country where people remembered all too well the night raids of the Nazi Gestapo and were well aware of the continuing police-state methods in the Communist-ruled GDR to the East, these methods seemed "wholly repugnant—and wholly unnecessary—in a democratic society."[39]

The third issue was political, and in the end it brought down the Adenauer Cabinet. The prosecution had been set in motion, and the raids and arrests had been carried out without the knowledge of the Minister of Justice, FDP member Wolfgang Stammberger, under whose responsibility the matter ordinarily belonged. Minister of Defense Strauss had delegated his responsibilities in the matter to his subordinate, State Secretary of Defense Volkmar Hopf, in order to avoid, as he said, any appearance of his personal bias against the magazine that had attacked him. Subsequently, as *The New York Times* reported, State Secretary Hopf "has assumed the responsibility for having told" the State Secretary of Justice, Dr. Walter Strauss—who is not related to the Defense Minister—that he should not inform his superior, Minister of Justice Stammberger, of the planned raids and arrests.[40]

[38] Cited in *Time, op. cit.*
[39] *Ibid.*
[40] Sidney Gruson, "Adenauer Trying To Save Coalition," *The New York Times,* November 5, 1962, 1:3 and 3:1–3.

The Minister of Justice thus had been bypassed in his own Department by his subordinates, and possibly with the knowledge of some Cabinet members and perhaps the Chancellor. Minister Stammberger thereupon submitted his resignation; the FDP threatened to withdraw its four ministers from the Cabinet and to bring down the government coalition which since the 1961 election again depended on the votes of the FDP delegation for its Bundestag majority. The FDP insisted not only on the dismissal of the two State Secretaries, Walter Strauss and Wolfgang Hopf, by way of satisfaction for the humiliating treatment meted out to its Minister of Justice, but it also demanded new guarantees that its voice henceforth "would be heeded in the Cabinet, and that Dr. Stammberger would be placed in charge of the investigation into *Der Spiegel.*"[41]

The FDP, in short, saw the issue as a threat to its equality of status as a coalition partner. The acceptance of its demands would leave intact the government coalition and the Cabinet, but it would lead to a stronger political position of the FDP within them. Should its protests be ignored, however, and should the FDP accept the humiliation of such an outcome, then it might lose much of its remaining prestige in the eyes of the voters as a visible third party, and another long step toward the complete predominance of the CDU/CSU in the Bonn government would have been taken.

The fourth and last issue posed by the *Spiegel* affair was that of the relative power and prestige of two contending elites, the government bureaucracy, civilian and military, on the one hand, and the press, on the other. In the United States, the press is highly respected, not only in terms of its acknowledged power but also in terms of the status and respect accorded to its publishers and writers. The American division of powers between the legislative, executive, and judicial branches of the government, together with a long tradition of press freedom, further guarantees and enhances this freedom and high status of the press in American politics, so-

[41] *Ibid.*

ciety, and culture. In West Germany, by contrast, there is no such long tradition of a free press. Under the parliamentary system of Bonn, there is far less of a separation of powers between the Federal government and the Bundestag dominated by the government parties, and the German judiciary traditionally has regarded itself not so much as a coordinate and equal branch of the government, but rather as a subordinate part of the executive power.

Civil servants, military officers, and judges all traditionally had served the same monarch. From this old tradition, many of these groups still derive social status, prestige, and solidarity. Newspapers and journalists, on the contrary, traditionally had been looked down upon in Germany as creatures of the gutter and spokesmen for the mob. Often they had been considered failures who lacked the brains, character, or breeding to qualify as civil servants, and who thus had become hack writers in the hire of commercial purveyors of cheap gossip and sensations. This traditional contempt for newsmen has been dying very hard, although it is deeply inimical to the effective functioning of democracy. By 1962, despite the American-backed innovation of judicial review and stronger press freedom, these traditions of democracy were still young and weak in Germany. Many judges still saw themselves as servants of the executive power, and a large part of the public still looked upon journalists as impudent upstarts who deserved a sharp rebuke.

By the end of 1962, the *Spiegel* affair had already produced a number of changes in West German politics. A wave of popular protest against any revival of high-handed police methods had arisen, cutting across party lines and insisting on greater respect for the freedom of the press. In an opinion poll, 54 per cent of respondents demanded the resignation of Defense Minister Franz Joseph Strauss; only 31 per cent wanted him to stay in office; the rest were undecided or uninformed.[42] The Federal Cabinet resigned. Chancellor Adenauer formed a new one, sup-

ported by the same coalition, but with one-third of the old Ministers dropped, including both Franz Joseph Strauss and Wolfgang Stammberger. Strauss' post as Defense Minister went to a North Protestant CDU leader, Kai-Uwe von Hassel, who until then had been Prime Minister of Schleswig-Holstein and who had a reputation for correctness in his administrative methods and for right-of-center sympathies in politics. Stammberger was replaced as Minister of Justice by another FDP member, the South German Liberal, Dr. Ewald Bucher, with a reputation of particular concern for civil liberties. Most of the new Ministers were a good deal younger than their predecessors. The party and denominational balance of the Cabinet was preserved, except that the influence of the Bavarian CSU seemed somewhat weakened.[43] Chancellor Adenauer had promised publicly to resign after the summer of 1963. This was widely interpreted as a promise to resign in September, 1963; and Ludwig Erhard seemed most likely to succeed him by that time, but Chancellor Adenauer soon was hinting again that he might not feel obligated to vacate his office by any fixed date, and he began to express his hopes for the return of Franz Joseph Strauss to a prominent role in national politics.

Before the reorganization of the Cabinet, the Chancellor and the CDU had negotiated with the Social Democrats about a possible "grand coalition" of the two major parties and about a possible change in the electoral law which would wipe out the FDP. This threat in turn made the FDP more willing to enter the new Cabinet and to accept the continuing predominance of the CDU within it. The results of the affair thus included the temporary eclipse of Franz Joseph Strauss; a slight increase in the political stature of

[43] See German press commentaries in *The German Tribune*, Hamburg, 1:39 (December 29, 1962), pp. 3–5.

Political Parties and Interest Groups

[42] *The New York Times*, November 24, 1962.

the SPD, which had been treated publicly as a possible partner in the national government; a limited gain in the stature of the FDP, offset in part, however, by the threat of a possible "grand coalition" of the CDU and SPD that might lead to practically pure two-party systems; and, perhaps most important of all, a definite upsurge of public opinion in favor of press freedom, democracy, and constitutional legality—a striking affirmation of the deep changes that had occurred in German political culture since 1945.

In the meantime, the *Spiegel* case itself was still pending, and the manner and substance of its outcome were likely to have far-reaching effects. It would sharply illuminate the continuing struggle between the old and new traditions. If the paper were squelched quickly, it would serve as a warning to all others. Journalists and publishers would then walk in greater fear, and government officials in greater assurance. If the paper should win its case, or lose it only after a scrupulously fair trial, free from any taint of high-handed methods, a free press and the right of citizens and of minority groups and parties might emerge strengthened. Whatever the outcome of this particular confrontation between opposing political forces, others were likely to follow. For the time being, the *Spiegel* affair showed once again how much the balance of power between the different West German elites was still in flux, how much the political culture and traditions of the Bonn Republic were still the subject of struggle, but also how significantly popular attachment to democratic liberties had grown in strength.

The Common Characteristics of Bonn's Elites

The elites that we have surveyed vary widely in their composition, interests, and outlooks. Yet there are a number of significant views which they share with one another,

as well as with a majority of mass opinion in the country. No major elite group has any illusion that it alone could run the country, or that Germany alone could have her will prevail in Europe or the world. There is a sober recognition in each group that it must live in an environment of other groups and interests with whom it must make the best terms it can get. No group has cut itself off from reality, by wrapping itself into some impenetrable private ideology or doctrine. The groups share many of their images of reality. Even· those critical of the United States remain mindful, for the most part, of the vast American capabilities. Even the most intense anti-Communists—and almost all West Germans are anti-Communists to some degree—do not ignore or deny the reality of very substantial Soviet strength. All groups are aware of the limitations of their power, both in domestic and international affairs. All feel that they have much to lose, and that changes should be approached with caution.

Yet, all these groups are moving toward change. They are moving toward it, not necessarily by choice, but by the logic of events. In economics, the growth of the West German economy has made it more competitive in world trade, but also more vulnerable to the fluctuations of the business cycle. The institutions of the 1950's, which dealt successfully with the limited foreign trade problems and the moderate waves of boom and recession of that period, may not prove sufficient for the greater international economic problems and for the possibly more severe bouts of recession or depression that the 1960's seem likely to bring. More powerful institutions of international economic cooperation and of domestic economic guidance and control may have to be devised, and it will be the task of West Germany's political parties, interest groups, and elites to work out the new political consensus needed to devise and sustain these new policies and institutions.

In the military field, West Germany is moving ever closer to becoming a sizable, and eventually a major, military power. This is already obvious in the field of conventional weapons; it seems no less true of the ever more pressing West German demands for nuclear weapons for its forces, as a NATO nuclear deterrent or in whatever other political form may prove serviceable at the time. Yet West Germany's growing conventional military strength may intensify her political pressure on the GDR and, with it, increase the likelihood of incidents that sooner or later may get out of hand. West German nuclear armament might have far stronger effects; it might precipitate preventive Soviet military actions and thus set off World War III. Few men, if any, want such an outcome. But rearmament and the pressure for the acquisition of nuclear weapons, unremitting since the mid-1950's, gradually are moving the country toward the edge of this problem. If West German politics between 1949 and 1962 have looked as cool and stable as a glacier, they may also be moving slowly like a glacier toward the edge of a cliff.

Unlike a glacier moving slowly toward a precipice, human affairs have a much wider range of freedom. Men may recognize the dangers of their situations and act in time to change them. Even the situation itself may change. The arms race may be moderated, controlled, or stopped. The Soviet bloc countries may become more diversified among themselves, or more tolerant of other cultures and regimes. The inner characteristics of the Soviet Union may change, and so may those of other powers. Just which of these changes will come, and how soon, no one can say; but that some changes of this kind will come seems almost certain. Most important, West Germany herself may change. Despite more than a thousand years of German history, Germany today is still very much an unfinished country. It is a young country, in the sense that so much still seems possible for it, so many alternatives are still open. Which of these she will take, it is still too early to say. Nonetheless, not only her political leaders, but even more her artists and writers are beginning to give us an indication of the possible shape of things to come.

The Bureaucratic, Diplomatic, and Military Elites

There are roughly 1.1 million professional civil servants employed at the national, Land, and local levels of government in the German Federal Republic, in addition to another 1.3 million clerical and manual workers in public employment below the formal level of civil servant.[44] These civil servants have a strong, caste-like sense of tradition, responsibility, and privilege. Many of them are skeptical of democracy, of popular participation in government, and of outsiders entering the service.[45] This bureaucracy is the only social group that has retained its substantial share of power without major interruption from the days of the late nineteenth-century German empire through two World Wars and three changes of political regime. Its members have become more pliable and more willing to serve efficiently and conscientiously whatever regime may be in power. They are less apt to insist on any old traditions of monarchist, nationalist, or ultra-conservative ideology, but they have retained their sense of role and duty, of separateness as a social group, of revulsion from Communism, and of distrust against Western liberal and democratic innovations.

They are more strongly organized in defense of their immediate interests, such as career security, pensions, salaries, status, and prestige, than any other large social group in the country. As we saw above, 84 per cent of their number are organized in two organiza-

---

44 See Table 5-10 above.
45 For these and some of the following points, see the revealing study by John H. Herz, "Political Views of the West German Civil Service," in Horns species and W. Phillips Davison (eds.), *West German Leadership and Foreign Policy* (Evanston, Ill.: Row, Peterson, 1957), pp. 96–135; also Karl Hochschwender, *German Civil Service Reform after 1945*, Ph.D. thesis, Yale University, 1961.

Political Parties and Interest Groups

tions: 43 per cent in the somewhat exclusive German Federation of Civil Servants (*Deutscher Beamtenbund*), and another 41 per cent in the German Confederation of Trade Unions. Beyond this, however, they have demonstrated a good deal of informal but effective solidarity. Thus they have successfully opposed and eventually rendered ineffective a great part of the Allied efforts at denazification and Civil Service reform, and they have preserved largely intact their hold on the higher ranks of public employment.

Surveys of 67 high civil servants, 44 diplomats, and 54 high-ranking military men in the mid-1950's showed several similar traits for each of these three groups. They were well-educated and recruited largely from families of a similar background. They included a relatively large share of Protestants and of natives of Central and East Germany. They included very few persons—12 per cent of the diplomats, 4 per cent of the military, and 2 per cent of the civil servants—who reported in their biographies any major anti-Nazi background, but many of them had served the Nazi government—including one-half of the diplomats in the sample and all of the military leaders.[46] The political opinions of these bureaucratic and military elite groups differ markedly from the mass opinion recorded by the usual public opinion surveys. They are more strongly in favor of German rearmament, of Germany's membership in the Western alliance, of the major treaties pointing toward Western European integration.[47]

[46] For details, see Deutsch and Edinger, *op. cit.*, pp. 80–86, 133–140, 270–275; also Montgomery, *op. cit.*, pp. 73–83; and the excellent brief study by Ralf Dahrendorf, "Deutsche Richter: Ein Beitrag Zur Soziologie der Oberschicht," in his *Gesellschaft und Freiheit* (Munich: Piper, 1962), pp. 176–196.

[47] Surveys by Daniel Lerner and Suzanne Keller, MIT Center for International Studies, October, 1957, multigraphed, cited in Deutsch and Edinger, *op. cit.*, p. 215.

There are some indications that these elites favor particularly those policies that will preserve for the Federal Republic the shelter of the American, NATO, and West European Alliances, as well as the economic opportunities of the Common Market, as long as these increase the national capabilities of the Federal Republic in economic as well as military matters. The demands of Defense Minister Franz Joseph Strauss for nuclear weapons for the Army, either under collective NATO auspices or as an eventual part of West German national military equipment, has found some support among the military, even though the much discussed "Generals' Memorandum" in 1960 on this topic actually seems to have represented an effort on the part of the civilian Strauss to bolster his previously expressed views by inducing the generals under his authority to produce the kind of expert memorandum he wanted.[48]

In any case, the political and economic weight of the West German military elite seems certain to grow, as the defense sector grows within the German economy, as the Army approaches its half million manpower goal planned for 1963, and as West German troops come to outnumber the American and British forces in the territory of the Federal Republic. The collaboration in the fall of 1962 between the ambitious political leader, Defense Minister Strauss, the intensely motivated key military figure, General Friedrich Foertsch, and a well-organized military public relations organization under the able Press Officer, Lieutenant Colonel Gerd Schmückle, suggests how much political influence such a combination eventually might be able to generate.

[48] Helmut Schmidt, *Verteidigung oder Vergeltung: Ein deutscher Beitrag zum strategischen Problem der NATO* (Stuttgart: Seewald, 1961), pp. 197–199.

The German Federal Republic
Today ... and Tomorrow

VIII

In the 1960's, Germany must make basic decisions about its economic and employment policies, its labor relations and welfare services, and it must adapt its economy to a world market that may be more competitive, to the underdeveloped countries that may need more economic aid, and to a business cycle that may be more severe in its downswings. It must also establish a military policy. Will Germany accept as her share in the common defense effort of the West the provision of moderately strong conventional forces within the limitations of her treaties of the 1950's? Or will she press for nuclear weapons and a more competitive role toward other Western powers?

One of the most prominent spokesmen for the nuclear armament of Western Germany, Defense Minister Franz Joseph Strauss, made it clear that this policy did not necessarily imply any inclination toward military adventures, despite repeated charges to that effect

from Soviet bloc sources. All that it does imply, Strauss has insisted, is a desire to make West Germany so strong as a military and nuclear power that she will become an indispensable partner or party in all future confrontations or negotiations between East and West. In Strauss' words:

A policy of strength in the age of the hydrogen bomb means in no case that one wants to use military pressure, with the risk of a third World War, in order to bring about some territorial changes, if necessary even by force. A policy of strength means rather that one's own freedom of decision cannot be influenced by pressure from hostile or unfriendly quarters. . . . *Germany . . . must become so indispensable to her Western friends, and so respectable for her potential adversary, that both will value her presence in the negotiations.*[1]

Inevitably, however, the same military strength that would make Germany an indispensable and influential party at all future top-level negotiations would also make her a high-priority target in any atomic war that might follow upon a failure of negotiations.

[1] Franz Joseph Strauss, "Sicherheit und Wiedervereinigung," *Aussenpolitik,* 6:3 (March, 1957), 140–147. Italics supplied.

387

In practice, most of the likely uses of any increased bargaining power of a strongly re-armed Germany would involve heightened risks to that country, to her neighbors, to world peace, and to the cohesion of her alliance with the West.

The foreign-policy objectives for which the military and diplomatic power of the Federal Republic might be committed in the 1960's are likely to be shaped by the popular expectations that have been formed in the preceding decade. These popular expectations of the 1950's have included notably the liberation of Eastern Europe, of the GDR, and of East Berlin, the breakdown or abolition of Communist rule in these areas, the eventual recovery of the formerly German Oder-Neisse areas to the East, and the return of the Sudeten Germans and other expellees to their former districts, homes, and properties in Eastern Europe. For more than a dozen years, from the late 1940's to the early 1960's, hopes of this kind have been kept alive by the deeply felt wishes of many Germans and by a succession of specific hopes. The success of the Marshall Plan, it was hoped, would produce in the middle of Europe such a contrast between Western prosperity and Eastern poverty as to make Communist rule untenable. Stalin's death or some other inner crisis, it was hoped, might fatally weaken the Communist grip on the territories under their power.

As these hopes faded, there still remained the firm insistence of the Allies on treating the Potsdam agreements and the distribution of governments and territories resulting from them as merely provisional. The Allied refusal to accept the post-1945 state of affairs, by means of a peace treaty, as in any way legal or legitimate came to appear to many West Germans as an implied promise that some day, somehow, as West Germany and the entire West grew stronger, this Western strength would be used to sweep away the post-1945 divisions, frontiers, and regimes in Eastern Europe and to restore both German national unity and some of the ancient German positions in Eastern Europe. No West German government or major political leader has dared publicly to renounce these claims or hopes. Opinion polls continue to show German reunification as the top-ranking issue in the minds of the young as well as of the old, and they show very high majorities insisting on a deferred but undiminished German claim to the Oder-Neisse territories.

For more than ten years, the West German government not only has refused to recognize the GDR, but under the "Hallstein doctrine" has even declined to have normal diplomatic relations with the governments of Poland, Yugoslavia, and other East European states which had recognized the East German regime. For the same reason, the Bonn Republic has avoided entering the United Nations—except for special U.N. organizations—in order not to offer the GDR an opportunity to enter that world body with the aid of the Soviet Union, which seemed certain to use its veto power to insist on the admission of "two Germanies" or none.

Yet all these hopes for liberation and reunion, and the policies based on them, cannot be kept up indefinitely without at least tokens of their eventual fulfillment. By late 1962, no such tokens were discernible. As year after year of the 1960's pass, as the Berlin Wall continues to stand as a symbol of East German fear and West German frustration, the government and people of the Bonn Republic will eventually have to decide what to do about a political quest that offers little hope for success through conventional political methods. At that time, the West Germans will have to choose whether to make some reckless bid to attain their goals by a policy of deliberate risk or open force, or whether to accept some unsatisfactory compromise arrangement with the Soviet bloc, leaving the latter with most of its conquests, or whether, finally, to settle down to an indefinite period of frustration in the East, while transferring most of their attention, their hopes, and their dreams to the more promising developments of

Western Europe and of Western European integration.

Other possible basic strategies besides the three just sketched may present themselves, or there might be possible combinations among them. But by commission or omission, choices will have to be made, and the Federal Republic will have to make them in the 1960's. In one way or another, these choices will involve two crucial ones: whether to press or to postpone the claims to German reunification and the restoration of formerly German territories and properties in Eastern Europe, and whether to limit the German share in the ongoing process of Western European integration to the point where it might remain compatible with the strongest development of German national capabilities; whether, in other words, to throw the resources and institutions of the Bonn Republic more fully into the melting pot of the emerging West European Federation, at the price of sacrificing not just the trappings but the substance of German national sovereignty in favor of the new union. Next to the decisions about war and peace, these decisions between partial and full commitment to West European Federation may well be among the most important decisions any German government and electorate have ever made.

The Decision about Western European Federation

All the great steps toward West European integration during the 1950's and early 1960's—the European Coal and Steel Community, the European Atomic Energy Agreement, the European Common Market—still remained in their results at the margins of the national economies of the participating countries. The flow of trade between Germany and France had increased only moderately between 1913 and 1954. They had grown in absolute amounts, as had the national incomes of both countries, but French exports to Germany had risen only from 13 per cent of all French exports in 1913 to 14 per cent in 1959, while German exports to France had somewhat more steeply grown from 7 per cent to 12 per cent during the same period.

Only if we compare the share of each country in the exports of the other with the percentage of world exports which the same country accepted in the same year can we demonstrate the substantial increase in mutual preference for one another's goods that has occurred. In 1890, France and Germany bought such relatively large shares of total world exports that the total amount of goods which they bought from each other was 35 per cent *less* than what it would have been if they had been merely quite indifferent to one another and had bought each other's exports in strict proportion to their total purchases in the world market. By 1959, however, other countries had greatly increased their shares of the world market, while the share of world exports purchased by France and Germany had shrunk. Thus already in 1954, when the percentages of the *national* exports of each country, sent to the other, were the same as in 1890, they now represented a much higher degree of mutual preference. Germany now bought from France 46 per cent *more* than she would have done on the basis of mere indifference; and France bought 30 per cent *more* goods from Germany than would have corresponded to the general French share of goods accepted from the world market. In 1959, the Indices of Relative Acceptance for the trade between the two countries were still higher. Some further details and references are given in Table 8-1. Here it must suffice to say that the analysis in terms of Indices of Relative Acceptance shows that substantial strides toward limited French-German economic integration have been taken since the end of World War II.

The figures in Table 8-1 show the gains in aspects of integration between Germany and France, as the key example of the inte-

TABLE 8-I *Two Measures of German-French Trade Integration, 1890–1959*

Year	1890	1913	1928	1938	1954	1959
Average percentage of mutual share in each other's mail [a]	15 [b]	12	5	4	4 [c]	9 [d]
Average percentage of national exports: [e]						
France to Germany	9	13	11	7	9	14
Germany to France	7	8	7	4	7	12
Index of relative acceptance (percentage plus or minus of amount exportable under conditions of indifference):						
France to Germany	−35	−27	+0.008	−27	+46	—
Germany to France	−35	−9	+3	−25	+30	—

[a] Mail figures from K. W. Deutsch, "Towards Western European Union: An Interim Assessment," *The Journal of International Affairs*, 16:1 (January, 1962), pp. 89–101.

[b] 1888.

[c] 1952.

[d] 1958.

[e] Trade figures from Karl W. Deutsch and I. Richard Savage, *Regionalism, Trade and Political Community*, forthcoming. For the "Index of Relative Acceptance," see also K. W. Deutsch, "Toward an Inventory of Basic Trends and Patterns in Comparative and International Politics," *American Political Science Review*, 54:1 (March, 1960), pp. 34–57, and especially 46–48; and I. Richard Savage and K. W. Deutsch, *Econometrica*, 28:3 (July, 1960), pp. 551–572.

gration between Germany and all the other Common Market countries. They show that these gains are real but limited. Thus far, these advances are much more limited than the enthusiastic publicity for the integration of Europe would suggest—a publicity that is understandably inclined to take future aspirations for present accomplishments.

The gains appear still more limited if we consider that in large, highly developed countries, such as Germany and France, exports represent only a fraction of the gross national product. Trade with France, taking both imports and exports together, amounted in 1959 to less than 3 per cent, and trade with the entire Common Market to less than 10 per cent, of the gross national product of the Federal Republic.

To date, the freeing of trade under the Common Market has not affected the ability of the Federal authorities to maintain acceptable levels of employment, prices, availability of credit, and general stability and rate of economic growth. In the boom years of the 1950's, relatively little government action was required for these ends, and the powers of the Bonn government—and thus indirectly of

The German Federal Republic~Chapter VIII

the West German electorate—were ample for the purpose. As Western European integration progresses through the 1960's, however, the time will arrive when the powers of the Bonn government and the national institutions of the Federal Republic no longer will suffice to maintain the levels of prices, employment, credit, and value of the national currency, in the face of possible fluctuations. By that time, the business cycle may put more severe demands on the capabilities of the Federal government to conceive, execute, and maintain effective policies of economic stabilization. But by that time, European integration may have so weakened the powers of national governments, including the powers of the Federal Republic, that only common West European institutions, supported by the common will of the West European elites and electorates, would be able to take the necessary action.

How willing are the West German voters to accept such common European institutions and to surrender their national sovereignty to them, both in form and in substance? In 1955, only 32 per cent of poll respondents were willing to cede the ultimate power of decision to a European parliament; a larger number, 42 per cent, insisted on reserving that power to a German Parliament, and 26 per cent were indifferent or uninformed. In 1960, a somewhat differently worded question left only 8 per cent undecided. The rest were divided in nearly the same proportion, between 42 per cent adherents of a European government and 50 per cent presumably upholders of national sovereignty. Between 1955 and 1960, the net proportions between the "Europeans" and the defenders of the nation-state had shifted only by about 2 per cent, an insignificant amount in view of the different wording of the question. By contrast, during the same period the very high majority in favor of German reunification rose still further, from 79 to 87 per cent. The contrasting attitudes are shown in Table 8-2.

TABLE 8-2 *Attitudes toward German Reunification and European Integration, 1955–1960* [a]

Attitude	1955	1960
Ultimate decisions by European Parliament	32%	—
Common European Government	—	42%
Ultimate decisions by German Parliament	42	—
Each country to keep Government for itself	—	50
Don't know; no opinion	26	8
Total	100%	100%
For German reunification	79%	87%
Against German reunification	3	
Indifferent; don't know; no opinion	18	13
Total	100%	100%

a Sources: Elisabeth Noelle Neumann and Erich Peter Neumann, *Jahrbuch der öffentlichen Meinung, 1947–9155*, (*Jahrbuch*, I) 2nd ed. (Allensbach: Verlag fur Demoskopie, 1956), p. 341; DIVO Institut, *Umfragen*, Vol. 3–4 (Frankfurt: Europäische Verlagsanstalt, 1962), pp. 18, 36.

The idea of a common European government was not more popular in 1960 among the young between 16 and 25 years old than it was among the population at large, where a strong minority of 42 per cent backed it. The idea was favored somewhat more often by adherents of the CDU/CSU—51 per cent as against only 38 per cent among the sympathizers with the SPD—and by those with at least a secondary education (52 per cent).

There were sharp differences between regions. Hessen, Rhineland-Palatinate, and the Saarland had strong pro-European majorities of 61, 57, and 55 per cent, respectively, while Bavaria, Lower Saxony, and Schleswig-Holstein were least European-minded, with only 29, 37, and 37 per cent in favor in each case.[2]

Taken together, all these figures suggest two conclusions. The first is optimistic. The idea of actual European integration, here and now or in the near future, is becoming a meaningful issue in West German politics. Never in German history before World War II has so large a minority of Germans backed it. The second conclusion sounds a caution. National sovereignty still seems to be insisted on by fully one-half of the German voters. Clearly, the country is not yet ready, politically and psychologically, for the decisive steps toward European integration and the transfer of most of national sovereignty to European institutions. Several more years, perhaps one or more decades, may be needed to bring about a popular West German majority large enough to undertake and consolidate these crucial changes in the future.

In the meantime, it seems doubtful whether the Bonn government will be able to afford politically an indefinite continuation of its rather rigid policy of 1961–62 toward the entry of Britain into the Common Market. During these years, the governments at Paris and Bonn insisted that Britain accept in essence their policies and bow to their will. Britain, they seemed to insist, should drop most of her ties to the Commonwealth and to the United States, and she should expect that her entry into the Common Market should be only a prelude to her early surrender of a substantial part of British sovereignty to a European political union, shaped largely in accord with French and West German desires.

These demands of the French and German

2 DIVO Institut, *Umfragen*, Vol. 3–4, pp. 19–20.

Today . . . and Tomorrow

governments, together with their refusal of any major concessions to special British needs, delayed the entry of Britain into the Common Market through the fall of 1962, and allowed France to veto Britain's entry without arousing strong German opposition. German readers smiled broadly at cartoons showing the German Chancellor guarding the raised drawbridge which was keeping the British troubadour out of the castle of Europe. Some of them now felt a thrill of power over Britain, who had been a victor in World War II and one of the occupying powers of Germany until the 1950's. Yet neither the economic nor the political institutions of the German Federal Republic had as yet shown anything like the stability of their British counterparts, which had stood the tests of boom and depression, of defeats and victories, with unwavering firmness. This contribution of tested and dependable stability, and of "unflappable" good sense, even more than Britain's military contributions at Berlin and at the Rhine, still seemed essential for the security and stability of Europe, and not least of West Germany.[3] For years to come, West Germany would still need the stabilizing support of the Allies, until the growth of her own democratic forces could in time become deepened and consolidated.

The Political Dreams of the New German Literature

On the surface, and to its critics, the Bonn Republic looks prosperous and stolid, enthusiastically dedicated to economic success, to conventional middle-class values, to a fair amount of efficient mediocrity, to a fear of innovation and experiment, to a longing for protection by superior authority, to the

[3] See Viggo Graf Blücher, *Der Process der Meinungsbildung* (Bielefeld: EMNID, 1962), pp. 118–119.

solidarity of its national in-group, and to a prudent disinclination to probe or question too deeply its own past, present, or future. But after all these reassuring successes, there recurs the little question: "And then . . .?" What is there to dream about, to remember from the past, or to long for in the future? If men must seek a wider horizon and a deeper meaning for their lives, they must reach out beyond the conventions and taboos that have become installed in much of West German life together with the "economic miracle." This broadening of perspectives is just what a new generation of West German writers is trying to do. They question the past and insist that it be brought up again for unflinching examination. Writers born in 1929, like Günter Grass, who were adolescents when Hitler's regime fell, now recreate in their writings the years in the early 1930's when the Nazis rose to power. They portray, as in an X-ray picture, the sick culture that produced these events, and they and their readers seem to think that these are relevant things to write and think about amidst the prosperous forgetfulness of Bonn.

Here, again, we encounter the problem of differential rates of change. The economic, political, and military burdens on the Federal Republic, and on the consensus among its citizens, may grow faster than the Republic's capabilities to meet them, or faster than its citizens can initiate and carry through needed policies in time. Since we can at present only guess at the speed with which men learn to act effectively and in concert to attain the goals and values they already seek, so we can also only guess at the speed and direction of their movement toward new goals and new values.

This subtle shift toward new goals and new values may be one of the least conspicuous and yet most important aspects of West German politics. Individuals, groups, and whole nations sometimes change their goals and even their character. When they do so, changes in their actions follow. Are there any signs of such changes in the German Federal Republic? If so, her artists and writers might be most likely to give us some hints of the changes that are now going on quietly but that may become manifest later. Theirs are more than merely private dreams. Their books are very widely read, and thus they also say something about the minds of their countrymen who find their writings relevant.

The images of the new writers usually are not images of Europe or of the Atlantic world. Rarely are they dreams of a reunited Germany. Most often—as in Uwe Johnson's *The Third Book about Achim*—they are poignant visions of the mounting barriers to understanding that are rising between the two parts of one people that are becoming every day more different from one another. Johnson communicates his revulsion at the regimented life under the East German dictatorship, but he insists that a new generation of non-fanatical but committed collectivists is growing up there, and he conveys his longing to understand them and to keep open the last remaining opportunities for communication between them and their neighbors to the West. Johnson's book is more subtle and penetrating than those of the more popular writers on the German East-West problem. Among the latter, Hans Helmut Kirst, author of an earlier best-selling trilogy of war novels, has written, in *The Seventh Day,* an uncomfortably plausible scenario of an East German uprising, followed by a border clash between West German and East German troops and ending in the destruction of Europe by the nuclear weapons of the allies of both sides.[4]

Most often, the new writers deal with West Germany herself and with the people and the spirit that are developing within her borders. They begin with the insistent demand that Germans face the hidden and intolerable past. The past is brought back by Günter Grass in the persistent rhythms of *The Tin Drum,* which has been struck through the years of Hitler, war, and postwar Germany by a stunted child who has refused to grow up into this kind of adult world, and whose piercing cry has gained the power to shatter glass and illusions. Postwar Germany is portrayed there in the image of the elegant "onion bar" at Düsseldorf, where prosperous executives and intellectuals pay for a serving of breadboards, knives, and large raw onions, which they chop up, in order to regain their lost capacity for shedding tears.[5]

A Catholic writer, Heinrich Böll, introduces us to a civil engineer and structural expert who deliberately blew up the great abbey which his father had designed and built, and whose son now in turn hesitates to accept the offer of a job to rebuild the structure. In the same novel, *Billiards at Nine Thirty,* one meets the successful organization man and police torturer of the Nazi era, now once again a high-level executive, offering small favors to those of his victims who happened to survive.[6]

In Gerd Gaiser's *Final Ball,* Soldner, the demobilized veteran and teacher without certificate, observes, in the teeth of the economic miracle of the city of Neu-Spuhl, that "an automobile is a means of transportation; the utterly ignorant consider it a badge of rank." Later, Soldner walks out on teaching and on his love, and prospers in business. "I go along with being rich," he says, "until the next time of poverty comes."[7] And there is Gaiser's final symbol, "the day of the dragonflies."

Suddenly I noticed that something was moving in the morass: unrecognizable dirty life. . . . I suddenly saw that an apparent twig, covered with mud, was in reality a large ugly larva. The larva pushed with an awkward unquenchable force to a dry place and lay there in obvious exhaustion.

Many such larvae are crawling out of the mud. And now something happens to one of them.

[5] Günther Grass, *Die Blechtrommel* (Darmstadt: Luchterhand, 1960).
[6] Heinrich Böll, *Billiard um halbzehn* (Köln-Berlin: Kiepenhenen & Witsch, 1959).
[7] Gerd Gaiser, *Schlussball* (Frankfurt: Fischer Bücherei, 1961).

[4] Uwe Johnson, *Das dritte Buch über Achim* (Frankfurt: Suhrkamp, 1961); Hans Helmut Kirst, *Und Keiner kommt davon* (Munich: Desch, 1957), English translation, *The Seventh Day* (New York: Doubleday and Ace Books, 1959).

Today . . . and Tomorrow

The grey husk burst, and a body, gleaming wetly, arched itself with blue and green rings. Then with a quick pull, it came long and slim out of the tube; a dragonfly was sitting on the stalk and trembling imperceptibly. Its tremendous, rapacious eyes still seemed dead, while from somewhere, perhaps out of the air, substance seemed to flow into the slack body and helped fill it. In the air there also were hardening the crumpled, finely veined wings; they began to stretch out, taut and brittle. The eyes began to shine, as if some blinding dust was disappearing from them. They became illuminated from within. Finally I saw the first dragonfly hovering above the water. A flash; it stood hovering; it sped away, a blue spark. . . . Wherever we looked, we saw pushing and slipping out. The brown pool seemed a place of transformation. They crawled and rose. Everywhere a straining upward and a slipping out. . . . We saw newly emerged ones laboriously straining, and we saw others spread their wings that had turned hard and glassy, and saw others shoot upward with a whir. *Imago.* This is the way it will be.

The image is compelling and ambiguous. Is it to be once again the emergence of something long and slim, tremendous and rapacious, hard and glassy out of the warm mud of the money-minded city of New Spuhl? Gerd Gaiser is a former fighter pilot of the Luftwaffe of World War II. Does he envision the metamorphosis of an insect which emerges from its husk only as an exact repetition of the pattern of the preceding generation? Is this a poetic way of saying: "The day will come"—*Es Kommt der Tag*—when the uniforms, the machine guns, the pistols, and the fighter planes come once again? Or is this meant to be an image of the rebirth of human beings and of a human community, a human spring beyond the fatal repetition of the biological cycle of the seasons and the dragonfly

—a truly new birth and a new beginning?

No one inside or outside Germany can tell for certain. The riddle of her future is part of the riddle of our own. At the beginning of the interplanetary age, all the world's nations are unfinished once again. Their past is inescapably real, and yet the meaning and power of that past is in question. Their national institutions are once again being melted and recast. Their political bodies and souls are strained by the pressures for change, and they may yet be born again. More or less, this is true of all the great nations—but perhaps it is most true of Germany, the Germany beneath the surface of its so recently consolidated institutions and behind the highly gifted German people of whom no one, not even they themselves, yet know what they will be.

Some of mankind's greatest treasures of integrity, courage, and kindness have persisted in Germany—among the German prisoners in her concentration camps, among the members and martyrs of her resistance, among those who preferred danger or exile to acquiescence in injustice, and among those, young and old, political and non-political, who throughout the years of trial retained an honest mind, a sensitive heart, and a helping hand for others. In today's Germany, these treasures have increased. Among her people, and most of all among her youth, there is a more sober but profound commitment to spiritual and human values than before. On the frontier between two bitterly competing social systems, the people of the German Federal Republic are one of the great and perhaps decisive partners of Western democracy and of the future of mankind.

Bibliography

General

The following are general accounts of West German politics, or of some of their major aspects. They are relevant for several or all of the chapters, but they will not be repeated in the special bibliographies for each chapter.

Blücher, Viggo Graf, *Der Prozess der Meinungsbildung chargestellt am Beispiel der Bundestag wahl 1961* (Bielefeld: EMNID, 1962). Important recent public opinion data.

Deutsch, Karl W., and L. J. Edinger, *Germany Rejoins the Powers: Mass Opinion, Interest Groups and Elites in German Foreign Policy* (Stanford: Stanford University Press, 1959). Gives detailed data and critical discussion of German public opinion and elites, together with some studies of foreign policy decisions.

DIVO Institut, *Umfragen: Ereignisse und Probleme der Zeit im Urteil der Bevölkerung* (Frankfurt: Europäische Verlagsanstalt, 1959). An important summary of opinion data.

German Federal Government, *Facts about Germany* (Bonn: Press and Information Office, 1957).

Germany, Federal Republic of, *Statistisches Jahrbuch für die Bundesrepublik* (SJB), 1961.

Grosser, Alfred, *Die Bonner Demokratie* (Düsseldorf: Rauch Verlag, July 1960). Also available in French. The best general treatment available at full length.

Heidenheimer, Arnold J., *The Governments of Germany* (New York: Crowell, 1961). An excellent survey.

Kitzinger, U. W., *German Electoral Politics: A Study of the 1957 Campaign* (Oxford: Clarendon Press, 1960). An outstanding election study by a British author that tells much about the background of German politics.

Linz, Juan, *The Social Bases of West German Politics*, Ph.D. dissertation, Columbia University, 1959, Mic. 59–4075, Ann Arbor, Michigan, University of Michigan Microfilm, 1959. Contains a wealth of relevant and well-chosen material.

Neumann, E. P., *Public Opinion in Germany, 1961* (Allensbach and Bonn: Verlag für Demoskopie, 1961). Contains a brief English summary of highlights of recent poll data.

Neumann, Elisabeth Noelle, and Erich P. Neumann, *Jahrbuch der öffentlichen Meinung (1947–1955) Jahrbuch I & Jahrbuch II* (Allensbach: Verlag für Demoskopie, 1957). The two most extensive collections of important German poll data that have been published.

Plischke, Elmer, *Contemporary Government of Germany* (Boston: Houghton Mifflin, 1961). The best brief treatment in English of legal and constitutional aspects of German politics, and of the role of the American occupation.

Pollock, James K., and Homer Thomas, *Germany in Power and Eclipse* (New York: Van Nostrand, 1952). An important book by a major American adviser in postwar economic reconstruction.

Speier, Hans, and W. P. Davison (eds.), *West German Leadership and Foreign Policy* (Evanston, Ill.: Row, Peterson, 1957). Very informative research essays edited by two top experts of the RAND Corporation.

Stahl, Walter (ed.), *Meet Germany* (Hamburg: Atlantik-Brücke, 1958).

U.N. Economic Commission for Europe, *Economic Survey of Europe*, 1953, 1955, published in Geneva; 1956, 1960, published in New York. A basic source of comparative economic data.

Chapter I

Almond, Gabriel A., *The Struggle for Democracy in Germany* (Chapel Hill: University of North Carolina Press, 1949).

Federal Ministry for Expellees, Refugees, and War Victims, *Facts*, Bonn, 1961.

United Nations, *Yearbook of National Account Statistics*, New York, 1961.

Chapter II

Barraclough, G., *Origins of Modern Germany* (Oxford: Blackwell, 1946).

Bracher, Karl D., *Die Auflösung der Weimarer Republik*, Eng. trans., *The Dissolution of the Weimar Republic*, 3rd ed. (Villingen: Ring Verlag, 1960).

Bracher, Karl Dietrich, W. Sauer, G. Schulz, *Die Nationalsozialistische Machtergreifung: Studien zur Errichtung des totalitären Herrschaftssystems* in *Deutschland 1933/34* (Köln and Opladen: Westdeutscher Verlag, 1960).

Craig, Gordon A., *The Politics of the Prussian Army* (New York: Oxford University Press, 1956). The best and most balanced historical treatment through 1918.

Erikson, Erik H., *Young Man Luther* (New York: Norton, 1958).

Fay, Sidney Bradshaw, *The Rise of Brandenburg-Prussia to 1786* (New York: Holt, 1937).

Fried, Hans, *The Guilt of the German Army* (New York: Oxford University Press, 1942). Stresses the German military's share of responsibility for the Nazi regime.

Holborn, Hajo, *Modern Germany: Vol. I, The Reformation* (New York: Knopf, 1959).

Hughes, Stuart, *Consciousness and Society* (New York: Knopf, 1959). An outstanding discussion of European intellectual developments, 1890–1930, notably including Germany.

———, *The United States and Germany* (Cambridge: Harvard University Press, 1948).

Kohn, Hans, *German History: Some New German Views* (Boston: Beacon Press, 1954).

———, *The Mind of Modern Germany* (New York: Scribners, 1960).

Kracauer, Siegfried, *From Caligari to Hitler: A Psychological History of the German Film* (New York: Noonday Press, 1959).

Krieger, Leonard, *The German Idea of Freedom* (Boston: Beacon Press, 1957).

Lowie, Robert H., *The German People: A Social Portrait to 1914* (New York and Toronto: Farrar and Rinehart, 1945).

———, *Toward Understanding Germany* (Chicago: University of Chicago Press, 1954).

Matthias, Erich, and R. Morsey (eds.), *Das Ende der Parteien 1933* (Düsseldorf: Droste Verlag, 1960).

Neumann, Franz, *Behemoth* (New York: Oxford University Press, 1942).

Parsons, Talcott, "Democracy and Social Structure in Pre-Nazi Germany," in *Essays in Sociological Theory*, rev. 2nd ed. (Glencoe, Ill.: Free Press, 1954). A brief but important essay.

Pinson, Koppel S., *Modern Germany, Its History and Civilization* (New York: Macmillan, 1954).

Reinhardt, Kurt, *Germany: 2000 Years*, rev. ed. (New York: Unger, 1961).

Rothfels, Hans, *The German Opposition to Hitler* (Chicago: Regnery, 1948).

———, *Zeitgeschichtliche Betrachtungen* (Göttingen: Vandenhoeck & Ruprecht, 1959).

Scholl, Inge, *Die weisse Rose* (Frankfurt: ·Fischer Bücherei, 1955). The story of the wartime re-sistance of Munich students against the Nazi regime.

Shirer, William L., *The Rise and Fall of the Third Reich: A History of Nazi Germany* (New York: Simon and Schuster, 1960).

Thyssen, F., *I Paid Hitler* (New York: Farrar and Rinehart, 1941).

Zink, Harold, *The United States in Germany, 1944–1955* (New York: Van Nostrand, 1957).

Chapter III

Deutsch, K. W., and A. Eckstein, "National Industrialization and the Decline of the International Economic Sector, 1890–1959," *World Politics*, 13:2 (January, 1961).

Frankfurter, Rundschau, January 5, 1960.

Germany, Federal Republic of, Bundesministerium für wirtschaftliche Zusammenarbeit, *Der europäische Wirtschaftsraat*, OEEC Handbuch, 1956.

Germany, Federal Republic of, *Germany Reports*, 1953.

Merritt, Richard L., *Divided City: The Political Community of West Berlin and East Berlin*, (forthcoming).

Stolper, Wolfgang, *Germany Between East and West* (Washington, D. C.: National Planning Association, 1960).

———, *The Structure of the East German Economy* (Cambridge: Harvard University Press, 1960).

Chapter IV

Buchanan, J. W., and H. Cantril, *How Nations See Each Other: A Study in Public Opinion* (Urbana: University of Illinois Press, 1953).

DIVO Institut-für Wirtschaftsforschung, Sozialforschung, und angewandte Mathematik, *Bundestagwahl 1961*, Repräsentativumfrage #326 Nov.–Dec., 1961, #322 July, 1961, #323 Sept., 1961 (lithoprint).

Mellen, Sydney L. W., "The German People and the Postwar World, A Study Based on Election Statistics, 1871–1933," *American Political Science Review*, 37:4 (August, 1943).

Faul, Erwin (ed.), *Wahlen und Wähler in Westdeutschland* (Villingen-Schwarzwald: Ring Verlag, 1960).

Fröhner, Rolf, *Wie stark sind die Halbstarken: Dritte EMNID Untersuchung zur Situation der deutschen Jugend* (Bielefeld: Stackelberg Verlag 1956).

Heidenheimer, Arnold J., "German Party Finance: the CDU," *American Political Science Review*, 51:2 (June, 1957).

von Schmertzing, Wolfgang P., *Outlawing the Communist Party—A Case History* (New York: The Bookmailer Co., 1957).

von Ungern-Sternberg, Roderich, "Die Selbstmord bäufigheit in Vergangenheit und Gegenwart,"

Jahrbücher für Nationalökonomie und Statistik 171:3 (April, 1959), Stuttgart: Fisher.

Chapter V

Anger, Hans, *Probleme der Deutschen Universität* (Tübingen: J. C. B. Mohr (Paul Siebeck), 1960).

Heidenheimer, Arnold, "La structure confessionelle, sociale et regionale de la CDU," *Revue Française de Science Politique,* 7:3 (July–September, 1957).

Janowitz, M., "Social Stratification and Mobility in West Germany," *The American Journal of Sociology,* 64:1 (July, 1958).

Pollock, Friederick, *Gruppen Experiment: Ein Studienbericht,* Frankfurter Beiträge zur Soziologie, Band 2, Frankfurt, Europäische Verlagsanstalt 1955.

Chapter VI

Archiv der Gegenwart, Bonn, 32:4 Jan. 21–26, 1962, #9636 y; 32:1 Jan. 6, 1962, #9584 A; 31:40 Oct. 10, 1961, #9371 C.

Abraham, H. J., and O. Bühler, *et al., Kommentar zum Bonner Grundgesetz* (Hamburg: Hansischer Gildenverlag, 1950).

Cole, Taylor, "Democratization of the German Civil Service," *Journal of Politics* (February 14, 1952).

Eschenburg, Theodor, *Staat und Gesellschaft in Deutschland,* 3rd ed. (Stuttgart: Schwab, 1956).

———, *Der Sold des Politikers* (Stuttgart: Seewald, 1959).

Heidenheimer, Arnold J., "Wie die Parlamentetagen," *Das Parlament* (December 12, 1960).

Leibholz, Gerhard, *Struktur Probleme der Modernen Demokratie* (Karlsruhe: C. F. Müller Verlag, 1958).

Maunz, Theodor, *Deutsches Staatsrecht,* 5th ed. (Munich-Berlin: Beck, 1956).

Neumann, Sigmund, "Germany," in Taylor Cole (ed.), *European Political Systems* (New York: Knopf, 1954).

Walser, Martin (ed.), *Die Alternative, oder brauchen wir eime neue Regierung?* (Reinbeck bei Hamburg: Rowohlt Taschenbuch Verlag, 1961).

Wheare, Kenneth C., *Federal Government,* 3rd ed. (London: Oxford University Press, 1953).

Chapter VII

Breitling, Rupert, *Die Verbände in der Bundesrepublik* (Meisenheim: Hain, 1955).

Dahrendorf, R., "Deutsche Richter: Ein Beitrag zur Soziologie der Oberschicht," in his *Gesellschaft und Freiheit* (Munich: Piper, 1961).

DIVO Institut, *Der Westdeutsche Markt in Zahlen* (Frankfurt: Europäische Verlagsanstalt, 1962).

Enzensberger, Hans M., "Die Sprache des Spiegel," *Einzelheiten* (Frankfurt: Suhrkamp, 1962).

Grossman, Kurt R., *Germany's Moral Debt: The German-Israel Agreement* (Washington, D. C.: Public Affairs Press, 1954).

Hartmann, Heinz, "Die interessante Zahl," *Junge Wirtschaft* (December, 1957).

———, *Authority and Organization in German Management* (Princeton: Princeton University Press, 1958).

Hirsch-Weber, W., and K. Schutz, *Wähler und Gewählte: Eine Untersuchung der Bundestagwahlen 1953* (Berlin: Vahlen, 1957).

Hochschwender, K., *German Civil Service Reform after 1945,* Ph.D. thesis, Yale University, 1961.

Lüth, Erich, "Deutsche und Juden heute," *Der Monat,* 10:110 (November, 1957).

Mellen, Sydney L. W., "The German People and the Postwar World, A Study Based on Election Statistics 1871–1933," *American Political Science Review,* 37:4 (August, 1943).

Montgomery, John W., *Forced to be Free* (Chicago: University of Chicago Press, 1957).

The New York Times: Nov. 3, 1962; Nov. 5, 1962; Mar. 28, 1958.

Pilgert, Henry P., *Press, Radio and Film in West Germany, 1945–1953,* Historical Division, Office of the Executive Secretary, Office of the U. S. High Commissioner for Germany, 1953.

Schmidt, H., *Verteidigung oder Vergeltung: Ein deutscher Beitrag zum strategischen Problem der NATO* (Stuttgart: Seewald, 1961).

Sternberger, Dolf, *Wahlen und Wähler in Westdeutschland* (Villingen/Schwarzwald: Ring Verlag, 1960).

Time, 80:19 (November 9, 1962).

Chapter VIII

Böll, Heinrich, *Billiard um halbzehn* (Köln-Berlin: Kiepenheuer & Witsch, 1959).

DIVO Institut, *Umfragen,* Vol. 3–4 (Frankfurt: Europäische Verlagsanstalt, 1962).

Deutsch, K. W., and R. Savage, "A Statistical Model of the Gross Analysis of Transaction Flows," *Econometrica,* 28:3 (July, 1960).

———, *Regionalism, Trade and Political Community* (forthcoming).

Deutsch, K. W., "Towards Western European Integration: An Interim Assessment," *The Journal of International Affairs,* 16:1 (January, 1962).

———, "Toward an Inventory of Basic Trends and Patterns in Comparative and International Politics," *American Political Science Review,* 54:1 (March, 1960).

Gaiser, Gerd, *Schlussball* (Frankfurt: Fischer Bücherei, 1961).

Grass, Günter, *Die Blechtrommel* (Darmstadt: Luchterhand, 1960).

Hallstein, Walter, *United Europe: Challenge and Opportunity* (Cambridge: Harvard University Press, 1962).

Johnson, Uwe, *Das dritte Buch über Achim* (Frankfurt: Suhrkamp, 1961).

Kirst, Hans H., *Und Keiner kommt davon*, Eng. trans., *The Seventh Day* (Munich: Desch, 1957); (New York: Doubleday and Ace Books, 1959).

Leibholz, Gerhard, *Sovereignty and European Integration: Some Basic Considerations* (Leyden: A. W. Sÿthoff, 1960).

Der Spiegel, October 10–November 15, 1962; 16:41, October 10, 1962; 16:45, November 7, 1962; 16:27, July 4, 1962.

Strauss, Franz Joseph, "Sicherheit und Wiedervereinigung," *Aussenpolitik*, 6:3 (*March*, 1957).

VERNON V. ASPATURIAN

The
Soviet Union

Introduction

I

In 1848, when two young German intellectuals, Karl Marx and Friedrick Engels, both in their mid-twenties, wrote the *Communist Manifesto,* Communism was simply a startling idea, but one which the two youthful authors declared was "a specter haunting Europe," destined to inspire a fundamental reorganization of society which would sweep away the civilization created by capitalism. Within the short space of fifty years, Marxist Communism had spawned influential Socialist and Social Democratic Parties in Western Europe and a multitude of splinter and sectarian political groups. One of them—the Bolshevik or radical wing of the Russian Social Democratic Party (later renamed the Communist Party), led by Vladimir Ilyich Lenin—used the ideas of Marx to shape a revolutionary party that seized power in one of the great nations of the world, the Russian Empire. For the first time, the world witnessed the establishment of a social, economic, and political system that was frankly and boldly patterned after the ideas expressed in the *Communist Manifesto.*

The Bolshevik Revolution of 1917 constitutes one of the great watersheds in the evolution of human history. The multiple revolutions and transformations that have taken place throughout the world in the past four decades have been profoundly shaped and influenced by the ideas of the Bolshevik Revolution and the power of the Soviet state which it brought into being. In the 1960's, a little more than a hundred years after the appearance of the *Communist Manifesto,* Communism is no longer a simple idea, but is a way of life embracing thirteen states with a population of nearly a billion people, occupying approximately one-third of the earth's total land surface. Within this bloc of nations are to be found over 200 different nationalities and ethnic and linguistic groups, most of the races of mankind, and numerous cultures and religions. Furthermore, Communist Parties, large and small, exist in seventy-five additional countries on five continents, ranging from miniscule illegal groups to large mass parties like those found in France, Italy, and Indonesia. All these parties are dedicated to establishing Communism as a way of life in their own countries.

The Soviet Challenge

In forty years, Communism has transformed Russia irrevocably, but in the process the ideas of Communism have also been subjected to a profound revision. The Communism that haunts or challenges the world in the mid-twentieth century is not the utopian vision of Marx and Engels, nor even the modified version conjured up by Lenin, but rather the concrete realities of the new social order forged in the Soviet Union during the past four decades.

The Soviet challenge has a dual character. First of all, the Soviet system emerges as a rival *process* of industrialization and modernization, a process which before the success of the Soviet system was historically the monopoly of capitalism. Secondly, it is a rival *way of life* to that of the West, whose civilization and institutions it seeks to supersede. Thus, the Soviet challenge is simultaneously a promise and a threat. What Communism has done for Russia during the past forty-five years is to enable it to meet successfully the challenge of rapid modernization, which excites underdeveloped countries eager for quick modernization and industrialization, but repels the advanced and modernized societies, which prefer their own social and political systems to that developed in Russia.

Soviet Russia as a
Former Underdeveloped Country

Before 1917, Russia was a giant with feet of clay. Although a huge sprawling empire stretched across both Europe and Asia and one of the great powers of Europe, its prestige was in rapid decline because it failed to meet the imperatives of the modern industrial era. The most significant feature of the

Imperial Russian state was not that it was a despotic autocracy, but that it was a country with a great potential which remained unrealized. In both Germany and Japan, autocratic governments took the initiative in adapting their societies to the industrial age, but not in Russia.

In 1914, Russia ranked last among the great industrial states of the world, but by 1960, the Soviet Union had already surpassed all the great industrial powers of Western Europe (and Japan) in the basic indicators of industrialization, and was second only to the United States, which it avowedly aims to equal and overtake.

In 1914, Russia was militarily weak; she had suffered defeat in one war after another after 1850, and in 1905 was humiliatingly beaten by an upstart Japan. Her rapidly declining military strength was further verified by defeat, occupation, and revolutionary convulsions during World War I. In the 1960's, however, Russia rivals the United States for military supremacy and in some areas appears to be clearly in the lead.

In 1914, Russia had a vast unskilled and illiterate population. She produced a few outstanding individual scientists, but in general was lagging far behind the rest of Europe in educational, technological, and scientific advancement. By 1960, the Soviet Union had achieved virtually 100 per cent literacy. Today, the Soviet Union has four times as many students enrolled in higher education as Great Britain, France, Italy, and West Germany *combined*. It now annually graduates more than three times as many engineers as the United States. In many respects, it has established an educational system second to none.

The story is virtually identical in the field of social services, particularly in medicine. In 1914, Russian medical science was woefully retarded, and medical care was available only to the very wealthy. The number of physicians and dentists before the Revolution was 28,000. By 1960, it was nearly 375,000, which gives the Soviet Union today the largest number of doctors in proportion to the population of any country (except Israel) in the world, including the United States. Today, every Soviet citizen is entitled to free medical care. Life expectancy in Russia has gone up from an average age of 32 before the Revolution to 68, which gives Russia one of the longest average life expectancies in the world. The number of hospital beds has also increased: from 207,300 before the Revolution to nearly one million and a half in 1960.

As in many pre-industrial societies, pre-Revolutionary Russia did not provide many opportunities for women. Today in the Soviet Union, 53 per cent of all Soviet citizens with some secondary education are women. Before the Revolution, 10 per cent of the medical doctors were women; today, more than 75 per cent of all physicians in the Soviet Union are women. The situation with respect to teachers is almost identical. Women are to be found in all walks and all levels of Soviet cultural, professional, and scientific life in increasing numbers and in higher proportions than in any other country.

These are substantial achievements, and they transcend ideologies or social systems, for industrial power, military strength, literacy and education, scientific and technological progress, medical care, and the emancipation of women are universally desired goals. These are the undeniable marks of a modernized, industrialized, and Westernized society. They symbolize power, prestige, and dignity for the communities which bear them. The underdeveloped countries are interested in results, for they have no vested interest in doctrines or dogmas, and they are attracted to that process which promises to accelerate their entry into the modern technological age. In the Soviet experience, they see the concrete fulfillment of the dreams and aspirations of a previously underdeveloped country.

Also significant is the fact that the Soviet achievement was not only spectacularly quick, but was practically a do-it-yourself operation against overwhelming odds. For more than thirty years, Bolshevik Russia was an isolated pariah in a world of antagonistic capitalist states. The Bolsheviks inherited a country ravaged by war, occupation, and economic disorganization. She industrialized herself in the face of severe external impediments and in-ternal convulsions. After 1933, she was the avowed object of conquest by Germany and Japan; she survived the Nazi attack, and, although most of her developed areas (virtually one-half of European Russia) were occupied and despoiled, she was able to mobilize a counterattack which broke the back of the German Army and set the stage for Germany's ultimate defeat.

Soviet Communism thus emerges as a process for the rapid transformation of backward agrarian and semifeudal states into advanced industrial societies. It is a process that promises quick transformation of illiterate populations into educated communities, rapid conversion of raw unskilled peasant hands into skilled technicians and workmen, quick elimination of disease, the early emancipation of women, and rapid improvement in the standard of living. But, above all, it promises the rapid acquisition of power, influence, and dignity for emerging national communities, whose aspirations currently exceed their capacities. The larger the population of a given underdeveloped country and the more diversified and extensive its natural resources, the more applicable the Soviet experience is apt to be. The largest underdeveloped national community in the world, China, has already embarked on the same process. China, under Communism, enjoys greater power and prestige in world affairs than at any time in the past 200 years.

In short, Soviet Communism offers a seductive and effective way to meet the demands of the "revolution of rising expectations" that is sweeping the underdeveloped lands.

The Main Features of Soviet Totalitarianism

The Soviet social order, taken as a whole, is unique, but its political system has certain features in common with both modern and ancient autocracies and dictatorships. Un-

FRANCE
Paris
GERMANY
Berlin
DENMARK
NORWAY
SWEDEN
Prague CZECH
Vienna AUSTRIA
Budapest HUNGARY
YUGO.
RUMANIA
Kishenev
MOLDAVIAN S.S.R.
Bucharest
Budapest
POLAND
Warsaw
KALININGRAD OBLASI (for R.S.F.S.R.)
Kaliningrad
Vilna
LITHUANIAN S.S.R.
Kaunas
LATVIAN S.S.R.
Riga
ESTONIAN S.S.R.
Tallinn
Helsinki
FINLAND
KARELIAN A.S.S.R.
Petrozavodsk
Archangel
Murmansk
NOVAYA ZEMLYA
FRANZ JOSE. LAND
Leningrad
Kalinin
Smolensk
Moscow
Minsk
BELO-RUSSIAN S.S.R.
Kiev
Kharkov
UKRAINIAN S.S.R.
Dnieper
Odessa
Sea of Azov
Sevastopol
BLACK SEA
ROSTOV Don
KABARDINO-BALKAR A.S.S.R.
ADYGEI A.R.
KARACHAI-CHERKESS A.R.
KALMYK A.S.S.R.
Volga
Saratov
MORDVIN A.S.S.R.
CHUVASH A.S.S.R.
Gorky
Volga
KIROV
MARI A.S.S.R.
Kazan
TATAR A.S.S.R.
KOMI-PERM. N.A.
Perm (Molotov)
UDMURT A.S.S.R.
BASHKIR A.S.S.R.
Ufa
KOMI A.S.S.R.
Pechora
NENETS N.A.
Vorkuta
YAMALO-NENETS N.A.
KHANTY-MANSY N.A.
Ob
Sverdlovsk
Chelyabinsk
Magnitogorsk
Irtysh
Ob
Omsk
Petropavlovsk
Barnaul
Novosibi.
Stal.
KHAKAS A.R.
GORNO-ALTAI A.R.
Urumchi
SINKIANG
RUSSIAN SOCIALIST F
TURKEY
GEORGIAN S.S.R.
S. OSSETIAN A.R.
ADJARIAN A.S.R.
ABKHAZIAN A.S.S.R.
Batumi
Poti
Tbilisi
ARMENIAN S.S.R.
Yerevan
NAKHICHEVAN A.S.S.R. (to Azerbaidzhan)
NAGORNO-KARABAKH A.R.
AZERBAIDZHAN S.S.R.
Baku
N. OSSETIAN A.S.R.
CHECHEN-INGUSH A.S.S.R.
DAGESTAN A.S.S.R.
Astrakhan
Guryev
CASPIAN SEA
Krasnovodsk
TURKMEN S.S.R.
Ashkhabad
IRAN
Tehran
IRAQ
Persian Gulf
KAZAKH
Volgograd (Stalingrad)
Kuibyshev
Aral Sea
Syr Darya
KARA-KALPAK A.S.S.R.
UZBEK S.S.R.
Amu Darya
Bukhara
Samarkand
Stalinabad
Kabul
AFGHANISTAN
TADZHIK S.S.R.
GORNO-BADAKSHAN A.R.
Tashkent
Frunze
KIRGIZ S.S.R.
Alma Ata
Semipalatinsk
Karaganda
S. S. R.
Balkhash
Lake Balkhash

Miles
0   100   200   300   400   500

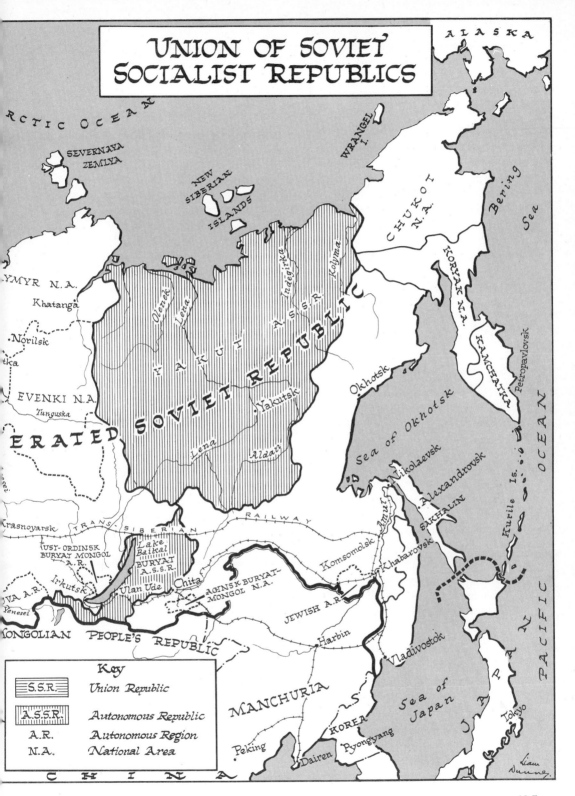

UNION OF SOVIET SOCIALIST REPUBLICS

ALASKA

ARCTIC OCEAN

SEVERNAYA ZEMLYA

NEW SIBERIAN ISLANDS

WRANGEL I.

CHUKOT N.A.

Bering Sea

...YMYR N.A.

Khatanga

Norilsk

...tka

EVENKI N.A.

Tunguska

KORYAK N.A.

KAMCHATKA

Petropavlovsk

Olenek

Lena

YAKUT A.S.S.R.

Indigirka

Kolyma

Okhotsk

SOVIET REPUBLIC

Yakutsk

Sea of Okhotsk

...ERATED

Lena

Aldan

Nikolaevsk

Alexandrovsk

SAKHALIN

Amur

Kurile Is.

PACIFIC OCEAN

Krasnoyarsk

TRANS-SIBERIAN RAILWAY

Komsomolsk

Khabarovsk

UST-ORDINSK BURYAT MONGOL A.R.

Lake Baikal

BURYAT A.S.S.R.

...VA A.R.

Yenesei

Irkutsk

Ulan Ude

Chita

AGINSK BURYAT-MONGOL N.A.

JEWISH A.R.

...ONGOLIAN PEOPLE'S REPUBLIC

Harbin

Vladivostok

Sea of Japan

J A P A N

Tokyo

MANCHURIA

KOREA

Pyongyang

Peking

Dairen

C H I N A

Liam Dunne.

Key

S.S.R.	Union Republic
A.S.S.R.	Autonomous Republic
A.R.	Autonomous Region
N.A.	National Area

due preoccupation with the political institutions and practices of the Soviet system in isolation from its social institutions and ideological goals serves to place the Soviet dictatorship in the company of the Nazi and fascist totalitarian systems. While the Soviet Union shares with these two systems certain political practices, the ideological principles and social goals of the Soviet state are sharply divergent from those of the Nazi and fascist orders. A proper understanding of the Soviet system, therefore, requires that its political system be examined within the context of its ideological goals.

Modern dictatorships that mobilize and manipulate the masses and demand their active support are called "totalitarian dictatorships," to distinguish them from the traditional personal dictatorship or dynastic autocracy which sought to justify or preserve their rule without the active involvement of the masses.

While Soviet spokesmen reject the label of personal dictatorship, they accept the notion of a "class" dictatorship and even define the Soviet regime as a "dictatorship of the proletariat." But they claim that the dictatorship of the proletariat is essentially democratic, since it embodies a system in which a majority (the workers and their allies) rule over a minority. Indeed, they reject the Western idea of democracy as being a "bourgeois" or capitalist democracy, that is, democracy for the few—the capitalists. In their eyes, then, Western democracy is a dictatorship over the working masses, while Soviet democracy is a dictatorship over the former capitalist ruling class.

Democracy as a symbol has always played an important role in Soviet policy and doctrine because of its obvious appeal. Even at the height of the Stalinist terror, Soviet authorities described the Soviet system as "the most democratic system" in the world. After Stalin's death, however, Khrushchev conceded that the Soviet Union under Stalin, at least

from 1934–53, was in fact a personal dictatorship.

The political life of the Soviet Union is monopolized by a single party, the Communist Party of the Soviet Union, which is the only legal political organization in the country. Highly centralized in its organization, the party, as the custodian and interpreter of the official ideology, actually governs the country. Its membership currently amounts to only 5 per cent of the total population, but it furnishes or selects the key personnel in all political, economic, military, and cultural institutions. Thus not only is the official ideology "total," but control is total as well, since the party does not permit the appearance of any political or social force that could challenge its monopoly of power in the Soviet system.

The Soviet economy is also "total" in the sense that it is almost entirely public in character. In response to the ideological norms of Marxism, the Soviet state owns outright all the land, water, natural resources, industrial establishments, and financial institutions of the country. None of these can be privately owned. Virtually the entire urban working population is employed by the state or by state- and party-directed institutions. In the countryside, most of the rural population works on collective farms, which are theoretically cooperative enterprises. The state owns the land, however, and the collective farms are closely governed by state laws and regulations.

Control of the economy is considered to be an indispensable prerequisite to a centrally directed and planned economy. The Soviet state, upon instructions from the party, determines the economic development of the country. The state decides what shall be produced and how much. It sets the market price of commodities as well as the wages and salaries of employees and managers. Collective bargaining and strikes are unknown in the Soviet Union. Everything is determined from the top and at the center.

No less under the control of the Soviet state than the economy is the cultural life of the country. The party and state institutions own or control all the media of communications and distribution, all schools and universities, museums and recreational facilities, libraries, newspapers, printing and publishing establishments, radio and TV stations, motion-picture studios, and theaters. Control over culture and communications insures that the party and state can condition and manipulate the minds of their citizens by controlling their access to information. In the Soviet Union, it is assumed that the interests of society must prevail against those of the individual and that the latter can find true freedom only as a member of society. The individual, by definition, thus cannot have rights and interests in opposition to those of the state and, in the event of conflict, those of the individual must give way.

The decision of the party under Stalin to modernize and industrialize Russia quickly collided with the inertia and interests of vast sectors of the population. In order to impose the state's ideological goals upon an unwilling population in the name of building a socialist and Communist society, Stalin resorted to the use of terror and violence. The modernization of Russia was quickly achieved, but at tremendous cost in human lives and liberty. Soviet Russia became a vast police empire of terrorized citizens, whose main incentive for working was not the prospect of a better life but sheer survival.

Since Stalin's death in 1953, the terroristic aspects of the Soviet system have been largely eliminated. The secret police have been considerably reduced in numbers, many of their veterans have been removed or executed, and the concentration camps have been emptied of their prisoners. Soviet citizens are allowed considerably more freedom of thought and movement, but the basic features of the Soviet dictatorship and the fundamental structure of society remain fundamentally intact.

The Soviet system, with all its drawbacks, however, still offers a route for overcoming the poverty, illiteracy, and backwardness of the underdeveloped countries. It is a short-cut process for transforming retarded agricultural countries into modernized industrial states, but a process which exacts a terrible tribute for its advantages. Soviet leaders boast that in the twentieth century all roads lead to Communism because it has already demonstrated its superiority in achieving concrete results. Unless the Western world, led by the United States, is able to renovate and export the values and institutions it cherishes and can demonstrate an alternative that will deliver both the quick results of the Soviet pattern and the freedoms of Western civilization, then the attractiveness of Communism, and with it its international impact, will grow.

The purpose of this essay is to give the reader an objective and detailed account of the Soviet political system, so he may be in a better position to follow the competition between the "Western" and the "Soviet" models —a contest, as was pointed out in the introduction to this book, that will determine the nature of our world for many centuries to come. It is not our purpose to make value judgments, but rather to dissect carefully the Soviet political system—its ideology, its power structure, its social configurations, and the recent trends that are noticeable since Stalin's death in 1953. Total objectivity is perhaps impossible, and the reader will quickly sense the author's preference for democratic values. But while it is easy to extol these values, the study of foreign governments should give the reader a new perspective and force him to reassess these values and be less complacent about them.

Introduction

407

The Russian Political Heritage

II

When Lenin and the Bolsheviks overthrew the Provisional Government in November, 1917, and established the Soviet System, they thought that the umbilical cord with the past was irrevocably severed. The Soviet system was to begin with a *tabula rasa;* Russia's past was to be repudiated, and the future would be inspired by the ideological vision of Karl Marx in which nations would melt into one another to produce an authentic international community.

The Russian "National Character"

Nations, however, cannot dispose of their heritage so easily. The latitude of action permitted to the Bolsheviks was severely limited by the human and physical resources with which they had to work. The Soviet state,

territorially, was a truncated version of the Russian Empire; it inherited the same geographical location, the same exposed frontier, and the same enemies, who still looked upon her territories with envy. Most importantly, Soviet Russia inherited the same population, most of whom were Russians. The people of Russia, then, with their religions and languages, knowledge and ignorance, skills and superstitions, memories, fears, anxieties, and customs were the raw human material out of which a Communist society was to be fashioned. The Bolsheviks also inherited Russia's potential, and this was enormous both in terms of natural resources and of population. The most tenacious element of the legacy the Bolsheviks inherited was that elusive thing called the Russian "national character." Russia presents a unique illustration of both the tenacity and plasticity of national character and traditions. An avowed objective of the Bolsheviks was to transform the people of Russia by radically reorganizing the country's social and economic order. Yet many of the qualities of pre-revolutionary Russia persist in contemporary Soviet society. Indeed, the Russian culture has been extended to nearly 100,000,000 non-Russians within the Soviet system.

Being the most numerous and influential element in the population, the Russians inevitably became the instruments for disseminating the culture, language, and traditions of the Communist doctrine to the non-Russian nationalities. The Russian language became the *lingua franca* of the Union, while the

Cyrillic alphabet (in modified form) became the vehicle for reducing other languages to writing. Of all the nationalities of the U.S.S.R., only the three Baltic nations, Georgia, and Armenia (whose numbers total only 10 out of 215 million) do not use the Cyrillic alphabet. Russian cultural attainments have become the common treasures of all the peoples of Soviet Russia, and while their own cultures, languages, and traditions have also been permitted to flourish (within definite limits, however), they have been relentlessly exposed to Russian cultural norms for more than four decades. The Soviet Union today is thus simultaneously more "Russian" and less "Russian" than ever before, because, under Soviet rule, Russian culture has been converted from a purely national phenomenon into a multi-national civilization. The only conspicuously Russian cultural institution which has not been universalized is the Orthodox Church.

The Historical Background

The Autocratic Tradition

Indigenous Slavic states of a tribal character flourished on the soil of modern Russia as early as the seventh century, but it was the Kievan state of Rus, founded by Norse marauders under Rurik the Red in the ninth century, that marks Russia's formal entry into recorded history. The Kievan state, located in the territory of the present-day Ukraine, was in every way comparable in the development of its civilization to that of the feudal states of Western Europe, but its principal outside contacts were with the Byzantine Empire, with which it quickly established intimate and fruitful commercial, political, and cultural connections.

THE BYZANTINE LEGACY: CAESARO-PAPISM AND THE MESSIANIC IDEA. The Byzantine influence on Russia was the earliest and most pervasive of all alien influences on Russian political development. Byzantine culture was an amalgam of Roman, Greek, and Near Eastern elements. From Rome, through Byzan-

tium, Russia inherited the imperial title of "Tsar," a corruption of "Caesar"; from the Greeks, the Russian language gained the Cyrillic alphabet; from the Near East, Russia adopted the institution of the God-Emperor in its specific Byzantine Christian adaptation known as Caesaro-Papism, whereby the authority of the Pope and the Emperor are amalgamated in the person of the Tsar.

A further important Byzantine influence on Russia was the notion of Messianic orthodoxy, or the idea that the orthodox faith was the one and only vehicle of eternal salvation, to be extended dogmatically and with undiminished fervor. The Byzantine Empire, like its contemporaries, the Holy Roman Empire and Islam, was a potentially universal state with a divinely ordained mission to extend its "truth" to the entire world. Constantinople was the "second Rome," the second capital of the universe and its Emperors the successors to the Roman Empire. Twenty years after the fall of Constantinople to the Turks (1453), the Grand Dukes of Moscow proclaimed themselves as successors to the Tsars of Byzantium, arrogated the headship of the Orthodox Church, proclaimed Moscow to be the "Third Rome," pre-empted the Byzantine double-headed eagle, and invested themselves with the title, "Tsar, autocrat, chosen by God."

The Church of Old Rome fell [wrote the Russian monk Theophilus shortly after the fall of Constantinople] because of its heresy; the gates of the Second Rome, Constantinople, háve been hewn down by the axes of the infidel Turks; but the Church of Moscow, the Church of the New Rome, shines brighter than the sun in the whole Universe. . . . Two Romes have fallen, but the Third Rome stands fast; a fourth there cannot be.[1]

MONGOL-TATAR DOMINATION: THE INSTITUTIONALIZATION OF BARBARISM. The second

[1] Cited in Arnold J. Toynbee, *Civilization on Trial* (New York: Oxford University Press, 1948), p. 171.

major alien influence on Russia was that of the Mongols and Tatars. The Kievan state of Rus was easily overwhelmed and destroyed in the thirteenth century by the Mongol conquest, and the Russian lands passed under control of the Khans from 1234 to 1460. Mongol-Tatar rule was indirect; native princes and bishops, if they chose to cooperate, were reduced to vassalage but allowed to rule their own subjects and to maintain their property and serfs. They were forced to deliver annual tribute to the Khans, which they exacted from their own subjects with the same cruelty and barbarism they experienced in dealing with their masters.

The two hundred years of Mongol-Tatar domination not only re-enforced the despotic qualities borrowed from Byzantium, but it also cut Russia off from contact with Western Europe, retarding not only her social and economic development, but also insulating her from the liberating currents of the Renaissance and the Reformation which swept through the West. Relative to Western Europe, Russia was set back nearly two centuries in its development, and one of the perennial objectives of subsequent Russian rulers was to narrow the gap by administrative decrees. The grim realities of this legacy were recognized by Stalin himself, in 1931, when he stressed the necessity to make up quickly and ruthlessly for Russia's retardation:

To slacken the tempo would mean falling behind. And those who fall behind get beaten. But we do not want to be beaten. No, we refuse to be beaten. One feature of the history of old Russia was the continual beatings she suffered for falling behind, for her backwardness. She was beaten by the Mongol Khans . . . the Turkish Beys . . . the Swedish Feudal lords . . . the Polish and Lithuanian gentry . . . the British and French capitalists . . . the Japanese barons. All beat her—for her backwardness: for military backwardness, for cultural backwardness, for political backwardness, for agricultural backwardness. She was beaten because to do so was profitable and could be done with impunity. Do you

remember the words of the pre-revolutionary poet: "You are poor and abundant, mighty and impotent, Mother Russia". . . . We are fifty or a hundred years behind the advanced countries. We must make good this distance in ten years. Either we do it, or they crush us.[2]

The chief legacies of Mongol-Tatar domination were essentially psychological and administrative: the refinement of despotic arts; the cultivation of cruel and insensitive methods of rule and rebellion; the premium placed on centralization of power, enforced national unity, and ideological conformity; the tradition of backwardness and the efforts of the rulers to overcome it.

THE LEGACY OF MUSCOVITE ABSOLUTISM. Under the Khans, Russia's center of political gravity shifted to the Moscow region, whose princes gradually rose to prominence beginning in the twelfth century. A succession of unusually able but unscrupulous rulers expanded Moscow's power over the other princes and enhanced its influence at the Tatar court. Ivan I, known as *Kalita* or "Moneybags" (1325–41), maneuvered himself into the job of collecting the tribute from the other princes for the Khans, and his successor, Simeon I (1341–53), managed to be appointed Chief Prince over the others. As Muscovite absolutism increased, the power of the Khans was correspondingly eroded. Ivan III, the Great (1462–1506), finally overthrew the Tatars completely in 1480. Ivan continued Moscow's expansion, and under his rule all of Moscow's rivals were subdued and Muscovite absolutism firmly secured and established. In 1472, Ivan married Sophia, the niece of the last Byzantine Emperor, and thus claimed succession to the Byzantine Emperors.

Centralization of political power and its absolute exercise—two persistent features of contemporary Soviet rule—thus have an ancient legacy. Only through ruthless centralization of power could Moscow overthrow the Khans, and subsequent history has demonstrated that when this power was fragmented or seriously challenged by an internal opposition, Russia

[2] J. V. Stalin, *Leninism: Selected Writings* (New York: International Publishers, 1942), p. 200.

was exposed to invasion and defeat. The idea that decentralization is tantamount to anarchy and weakness and that dissent is treason is firmly rooted in Russian history. Stalin recognized the importance of this tradition on the occasion of Moscow's eight hundredth anniversary in 1947:

Moscow's service consists first and foremost in the fact that it became the foundation for the unification of a disunited Russia into a single state with a single government, a single leadership. . . . Only a country united in a single centralized state can count on being able to make substantial cultural-economic progress and assert its independence.[3]

The Consolidation
of Autocratic Rule

All attempts to limit the absolute power of the Tsar throughout Russian history failed, and the Russian autocracy was preserved virtually intact down to the 1917 Revolution itself. As in other feudal societies, the monarch could be effectively opposed only by the hereditary nobility, whose members jealously sought to cultivate authority in their own domain, and occasionally to aspire to the throne itself. Sharing power with the Tsar was the Duma of Boyars, comparable to the House of Lords in Britain. The boyars struggled against the absolutism of the Tsars for their own personal and class advantage, but met their match in Ivan the Terrible (1533–84), that half-mad genius, both feared and beloved by the common people as their protector against the cruel boyars. He eventually broke the power of the boyars by various stratagems, including the formation of the first Russian secret police organization, the dreaded Oprichnina, which ruthlessly liquidated opposition to the Tsar.

Ivan also introduced an embryonic "House of Commons," the Zemsky Sobor, in 1549, a quasi-representative assembly made up of the lesser nobility, upper clergy, landed gentry, and urban bourgeoisie, to counterbalance the strength of the boyars. The Zemsky Sobor successfully limited the power of the boyars, and during the "Time of Troubles" (1584–1613), it played a significant role in governing

Russia, when the country was plagued by false pretenders to the throne and threatened with foreign intervention by the Poles. Its most important act was the election of Prince Michael of the Romanov family as Tsar in 1613. The Zemsky Sobor was unable to maintain its authority and degenerated in a manner similar to the French Estates-General. Both it and the Duma of Boyars gradually deteriorated and were abolished by Peter the Great.

Subsequent attempts to limit the power of the Tsar were either instituted by the Tsar himself or forced upon him by revolutionary pressures. Peter the Great (1689–1725), for instance, sought to "Westernize" and modernize the autocracy so as to increase the power of Russia and render its absolute government more efficient. He introduced a bureaucratic system based on merit, and faithful service to the state by the landowners or gentry could earn them titles of nobility or promotion to higher status. A hierarchy of fourteen ranks was organized for the armed services, the courts, and the civil service, each with its own distinctive status, with promotion awarded to the most able. The system, eventually corrupted by nepotism, bribery, and favoritism, lasted down to 1917, when it was abolished, only to be resurrected in new and expanded form by Stalin in 1943, when all branches of the Soviet bureaucracy were once again organized into ranks, replete with uniforms and special privileges.

Peter also created the Imperial Governing Senate in 1711 to replace the Duma of Boyars. Officially an advisory body, akin to a Cabinet, made up of nine members appointed by the Tsar to coordinate and direct the administration of the state, including the royal governors of the provinces, it was actually a supine creature of the Tsar. Directly under the Senate were eight departments of government, each run by a committee of three to five men, which reduced the possibility that any one person would become too powerful in administering

The Russian Political Heritage

[3] *Pravda*, September 11, 1947.

the country. Peter abolished the Russian Patriarchate and placed the Church under the direction of a Holy Synod (1721), which was dominated by the "eyes and ears" of the Tsar, the Procurator, a trusted layman. Much of Peter's reforms served to strengthen both the autocracy and the country as a whole. Under Peter, Russia continued her expansion in all directions and finally absorbed St. Petersburg and thus acquired her long-sought "window" on the Baltic.

Under Catherine the Great (1762–96), elective municipal councils (*dumas*) were established, although the elections were severely limited to the propertied classes. The most important development after Peter, however, was the steady infiltration of German ideas and bureaucrats into Russia. The process was accelerated under Catherine the Great, herself a German Princess, and the Romanov dynasty was soon all but Germanized.

During the reign of Alexander I (1801–1825), Michael Speransky was commissioned to draw up an elaborate plan of governmental reform providing for the indirect election of local, intermediate, and provincial assemblies, ultimately to be climaxed with a National Duma or Parliament. Speransky's efforts led only to the creation of a marginal organ, the Imperial State Council, half of which were appointed by the Tsar, and the other half elected by special social groups. Virtually all its members were drawn from the nobility, and it merely served as another administrative coordinating body. After 1905, it became the Upper House of the Imperial Legislature.

In the middle of the nineteenth century, a system of local self-governing bodies (the Zemstvos), based on popular elections, was established, but their powers were limited and their authority restricted essentially to such local matters as sanitation, roads, hospitals, schools, etc. Elections were frequently rigged, and the Zemstvos were usually dominated by the local gentry. Under Alexander III (1891–

1894), the executive committees of the Zemstvos were controlled by provincial governors. They continued to attract reform-minded and progressive members of the nobility, and they constituted the only school of local self-government in the entire history of the Russian autocracy.

The Fear and Attraction of Anarchy

Throughout the history of Russia runs an elusive but detectable thread of anarchism. Superficially, this seems to contradict the spirit of absolutism that has animated Russia's rulers, but, in fact, the two may be complementary. The relaxation of authority has, in the past, threatened to plunge the country into anarchy, so a strong central government has been necessary to keep the people under control. During the nineteenth century, latent anarchistic forces gave rise to various movements designed to destroy the state, in the hope that society would reformulate itself spontaneously into a stateless socialistic community. It is perhaps more than fortuitous that Marxism emerged as an ideology tailor-made to fit the contradictory impulses of both absolute order and anarchy, for Lenin's Bolshevism imposed the necessary order, while Marx's vision of a classless society promised a community in which the state would ultimately "wither away."

The Revolutionary Tradition

The concentration of absolute power in the hands of the Tsar meant that change and reform could come about only by initiative from above or revolution from below. Reforms from above were few and far between and usually followed by a period of repression. As the pressure built up for revolution, underground groups increased their violent and terroristic methods. All the accumulated resentments, disappointments, sufferings, and sublimated hopes of nearly a thousand years seemed to explode in the Revolutions of 1917.

The Revolutions of 1917 did not develop without precedents. Previous revolutions, however, were limited in character, either geographically or socially. Characteristically, down to the twentieth century, revolutions were directed against the harsh social and economic order. The Tsar and the autocratic system itself were by and large immune, for the Tsar was viewed as a benevolent patriarch who would have instantly intervened had he known the miseries and agonies of his people. In times of external crises, the Tsar was a powerful symbol around whom all classes of Russians rallied.

The Russian faith in the autocracy was re-enforced by a deep and primitive faith in the power and majesty of God, from whom the Tsar claimed divine sanction. The Orthodox Church had been completely subordinated to the state after a brief and unequal struggle between the Patriarchate and the Tsar, and it became one of the basic instruments of autocratic rule. The Orthodox priests cultivated in the minds of the Russian peasants a fatalism about their earthly conditions of life and thus increasingly became a principal bulwark of the autocracy, blessing and sanctifying its endeavors and activities, even to the extent of pressuring ordinary priests into the service of the secret police. The ferocity of the Bolshevik reaction against the Orthodox Church must always be assessed with this perspective in mind, for the Orthodox Church was not a "free church," but an indispensable and willing instrument of the autocracy in its oppressive rule over the people of Russia.

IVAN THE TERRIBLE'S "REVOLUTION FROM ABOVE." The earliest popularly supported "revolution" in Russia was, in fact, a "revolution from above," executed by Ivan the Terrible. In 1564, as a consequence of his conflict with the boyars, led by Prince Kurbsky, Ivan abandoned Moscow for a small village and denounced the boyars and upper clergy as traitorous, corrupt, and evil, at the same time absolving the urban bourgeoisie and the common people. Ivan, without abdicating, announced that he had given up his kingdom and would let God determine his future course. When Ivan was asked to return, by a delegation sent by the middle classes and the common people, he laid down a number of conditions, including the right to establish a special institution called the Oprichnina, over which he would have personal jurisdiction. In effect, the Oprichnina became a vast secret police empire, untrammeled by law and subject only to the jurisdiction of the Tsar.

The ultimate objective of the Oprichnina was to destroy the power of the boyars, by arresting and exiling them to remote parts of the country and expropriating their estates. The methods and tortures employed by the Oprichniki were worthy precedents for the subsequent secret police systems in Russia: the Imperial Okhrana, and the Soviet Cheka, GPU, NKVD, MGB, and the current KGB. Ivan's measures against the boyars were by no means unpopular among the common people, who saw in the Tsar their protector against the hated landlords.

Ivan's assault against the boyars set the stage for the gradual destruction of an independent Russian nobility, whose power and status stemmed not from the grace of the Tsar, but, like the Tsar's, from divine right transmitted by heredity from one generation to the next. Many of the boyars were scions of princely families, who considered themselves to be the peers of the dynastic line itself, and, in fact, challenged the existing dynasty in its right to rule. Through the Oprichniki, Ivan inundated the ranks of the boyars by creating a new landed aristocracy and court nobility, the *pomeshchiki* and the *dvoriane,* who were obligated to render service to the state in return for their grants of land and serfs, seized either from the boyars or newly conquered territories. Unlike the boyars, the new nobility owed both its power and status to the Tsar. This nobility was further expanded by Peter the Great, who swelled its ranks with additional recruits who had performed with loyalty and competence either on the field of battle or in the state bureaucracy. Thereafter, the Imperial land-owning nobility never constituted a threat to the power of the Tsar.

The Russian Political Heritage

THE DECEMBRIST REVOLT. Of much greater significance was the so-called Decembrist Revolt of December 26, 1825, which was a movement directed against the autocracy itself rather than against "abuses" and "corruption." The Decembrist uprising was an attempted palace revolution by the officers in the Tsar's own Guards. Inspired by the ideas of both the American and French Revolutions and organized into secret societies and conspiracies, these liberal-minded, but politically unsophisticated, young officers were united in a common determination to sweep away the autocracy as the chief obstacle to progress in Russia. They were not clear about what should replace it, however. Some advocated a constitutional monarchy, others a republic; some wanted to retain a centralized state, others argued for a federation; still others agitated for a democracy, while some demanded a benevolent dictatorship.

THE REVOLUTIONARY INTELLIGENTSIA. The Decembrist Revolt was quickly crushed by the new Tsar, Nicolas I, and Russia was subjected to a renewed period of reaction and oppression. The Revolt became, however, the inspiration for many revolutionary movements and terroristic groups, all of which had to go underground because political parties and movements were outlawed by the autocracy. Hounded and infiltrated by the Tsarist secret police, provoked to premature action by *agents provocateurs,* many of these revolutionary groups were driven to extreme and violent action because of the unhealthy atmosphere in which they were forced to operate. Their agents, in turn, infiltrated the Tsarist secret police, and double-agents and even triple-agents were not unusual. A few individuals did not really know whether they were primarily revolutionaries or agents of the Tsarist police.

The most oppressive institution in early nineteenth-century Russian society was that of serfdom, which embraced most of the rural population of Russia. The serfs tilled the soil and were owned by the landed aristocracy. Extensive studies of the condition of the serfs had been commissioned by the Tsars, but little had been accomplished to alleviate their virtual slavery.

It was only in 1861 that serfdom was abolished by the liberal-minded Tsar, Alexander II. Although its abolition was an important step in the social evolution of Russia, it did little to stem the growing tide of revolutionary sentiment that had gripped the Russian intellectuals and university circles, which became increasingly inspired by the ideas of the French Revolution, the idealistic philosophies of Fichte, Schelling, Kant, and Hegel, and the utopian socialism of the French philosophers.

The intelligentsia was drawn from all classes of Russia—the bureaucracy, the gentry, the peasantry and working class, the merchants and professions—but they considered themselves to be without class, irrespective of their social origins. They were united not so much by common ideas or philosophy, but by a common passion to reform the social order, so that Russia might fulfill her physical and spiritual potential. Some thought that Russia's best course would be to adopt the technology, philosophy, and institutions of the West, and they were called Westernizers. Others emphasized the unique spiritual and psychological traditions of Russia and insisted that Russian civilization was actually superior to Western culture, and that the country's salvation lay in freeing the true Russia which had been all but suffocated by successive layers of foreign ideas and institutions. These members of the intelligentsia were labeled Slavophils. Still others of the intelligentsia maintained a foot in each camp, trying to bridge the two in an endeavor to create a synthesis made up of the best of both worlds. Both groups were essentially utopian in outlook, and the Slavophils were also profoundly messianic in their orientation, for some felt that Russia had a mission to emancipate not only herself but the entire world from the materialistic philosophy of the West. Yet, even the Westernizers reflected a messianic faith in Russia's destiny. Thus Chaadayev could write:

I am deeply convinced that we Russians are destined to solve the greatest number of problems of the social order, to bring to a conclusion the greater part of the ideas which arise in the old societies, to answer the most important questions troubling mankind.[4]

And the great Russian critic, V. G. Belinsky, wrote these prophetic words in 1840:

We envy our grandchildren and great grandchildren who are destined to see Russia in 1940— standing at the head of the educated world, laying down the law in science and art and receiving the reverent tribute of respect from the whole of enlightened mankind.[5]

The same spirit animated Stalin in 1917, before the Revolution, when he argued against the notion that Russia had to take second place to the industrialized countries in blazing the path to socialism:

The possibility is not precluded that Russia will be the country to lay the road to socialism. . . . We must cast aside the obsolete idea that only Europe can show us the way.[6]

THE NARODNIK MOVEMENT (POPULISTS). Intellectual ferment gave way to political organization after the emancipation of the serfs, principally in the Narodnik movement, whose various sects and factions were influenced by the ideas of both the Westernizers and the Slavophils. The Narodniki were initially drawn from student and intellectual groups who were motivated by a desire to achieve an agrarian socialist society uncorrupted by Western industrialization, capitalism, and materialism. According to the Narodniki, the Russian peasant, organized in the ancestral *mir*, or village commune, was naturally socialist in his inclinations, and once the oppressive autocratic system and the iniquitous feudal order were destroyed, Russia would spontaneously be reorganized as a vast association of agrarian cooperative communities. The Narodniki favored appealing directly to the people living in their village communes, enlightening and educating them, ministering to their wants, winning their confidence, and inspiring them to revolt against the existing order.

The peasants, however, viewed many of the Narodniki who settled in the villages as teachers, nurses, and counselors with deep mistrust and suspicion, often reporting their activities to the Tsarist authorities and, in some instances, taking direct action against them. The failure of the peasantry to respond to their good intentions and the increasingly repressive measures employed by the government resulted in fragmenting the Narodnik movement into a variety of underground and illegal organizations, ranging from pacific anarchism to terroristic nihilism. The more the peasants failed to respond to the Narodnik program, the more convinced were the reform leaders that the revolution could be accomplished only by a militant elite—a view which later powerfully influenced Lenin's brand of Marxism.

REVOLUTIONARY VIOLENCE AND TERRORISM. Broadly speaking, the revolutionary groups emerging out of Narodism tended either toward some brand of anarchism or to the view that some sort of progressive state was necessary to replace the Tsarist autocracy. Part of these groups advocated peaceful measures, but the rest cried for violence and even individual acts of terrorism. The peaceful anarchists wanted to dissolve the state in favor of a giant association of peasant communes. The best-known representatives of violence were Peter Tkachev and Bakunin and his protégé Nechayev, whose views were grimly set forth in the *Catechism of the Revolutionist:*

The revolutionist is a doomed man. He has no personal interests, no affairs, sentiments, attachments, property, not even a name of his own. . . . He despises and hates the present-

[4] Cited in Joshua Kunitz, *Russia, The Giant That Came Last* (New York: Dodd, Mead, 1947), p. xiv.
[5] V. G. Belinsky, *Selected Philosophical Works* (Moscow, 1948), p. xlix.
[6] J. V. Stalin, *The Road To Power* (New York: International Publishers, 1937), pp. 20–21.

day code of morals with all its motivations and manifestations. To him whatever aids the triumph of the revolution is ethical; all which hinders it is criminal. . . . All tender softening sentiments of kinship, friendship, love, gratitude, and even honor itself must be snuffed out in him by the one cold passion of the revolutionary cause. . . . The Association has no aim other than the complete liberation and happiness of the masses.[7]

The first revolutionary party, *Zemlya i Volya* (Land and Freedom), was oriented toward violence. It in turn split into two factions, the *Narodnaya Volya* (People's Will), which specialized in bombings and assassinations, and the *Chorny Peredyel* (Black Redistribution), which called for the peasants to seize the land from the landlords. Members of the first group were responsible for the assassination of Alexander II in 1881, and to this movement belonged Lenin's older brother Alexander Ulyanov, who was excuted in 1887 for complicity in a plot to assassinate Alexander III. The execution of his brother profoundly intensified Lenin's own political fanaticism.

The *Chorny Peredyel* is noteworthy because the first Russian Marxists were among its members. Because Russia was essentially an agrarian society, the ideas of Karl Marx appeared to be largely irrelevant to her social and economic problems. Before 1865, the working class in Russia was virtually non-existent, and a political movement dedicated to representing the interests of the proletariat would have been an anomaly. After the emancipation of the serfs, opportunities were created for the development of capitalism in Russia, and by 1890 the new social class of proletarians numbered some 2,400,000 people (up from 200,000 in 1865). Mostly concentrated in St. Petersburg, Moscow, Baku, and the Donetz Basin, this class was quickly courted by revolutionaries disillusioned by the political inertia of the peasantry.

[7] Cited in Max Nomad, *Apostles of Revolution* (Boston, 1939), pp. 228–233.

The Development of Marxism in Russia

The first Russian Marxist organization was founded abroad in 1883 by George Plekhanov, Vera Zasulich, Axelrod, and Deutsch and called itself the Emancipation of Labor. It translated the works of Marx and Engels into Russian, struggled against the views of the Narodniki, repudiated the whole concept of Russian agrarian socialism, and maintained that the industrialization of Russia would soon create a revolutionary proletariat; it wrote off the revolutionary potential of the peasants and advocated instead an alliance between the liberal middle class and the working class to bring about a revolution to establish a middle-class constitutional and representative democracy.

Marxist groups sprang up in the urban centers of Russia between 1883 and 1894, including one in 1895 in St. Petersburg, headed by Lenin. During the same period, Joseph Dzhugashvili (Stalin) was active in Tiflis and the Caucasus, while Leon Bronstein (Trotsky) was to become politically active a few years later in St. Petersburg. In 1898, representatives of some of these groups convened a "Congress" in Minsk, attended by nine people, which issued a manifesto announcing the formation of the Russian Social Democratic Party, modeled after the one in Germany. Although no party was actually organized and no program was issued, the foundations were prepared for active Marxist political organization and agitation.

The growth of industry in Russia and the attraction of Marx's ideas all but obliterated the Narodnik movement. Those who still retained faith in agrarian socialism merged in 1901 to form the Social-Revolutionary Party, whose program of land redistribution represented the interests of the peasantry more than that of any other party.

Middle-class intellectuals, members of the professions, and progressive elements of the bourgeoisie and nobility supported the formation of an association called the Union of Liberation, under the leadership of Paul Milyukov. Because they favored essentially a renovation of the autocracy into a constitutional monarchy patterned after the British model, they later adopted the name Constitutional Democrats or Cadets. A middle-class party, par excellence, it played a significant role during the decade of the Duma that followed the Revolution of 1905 and in the events leading to the March Revolution of 1917.

BOLSHEVIKS AND MENSHEVIKS. At the second Congress of the Russian Social Democratic Party, which was held first in Brussels and then in London in 1903, with both Lenin and Trotsky in attendance as delegates, the Party split into two factions over questions of membership, organization, and principles of action. Because Lenin managed to secure a small majority as a result of procedural technicalities, the faction led by him was called the Bolsheviks (majority), as opposed to the Mensheviks (minority). The labels stuck, and the two wings of the Social Democratic Party were to be known henceforth as the Bolsheviks and the Mensheviks. Ironically, it was the Bolshevik faction that was subsequently most often in the minority.

Lenin presented a proposal based on his work *What Is To Be Done?* that had been published just prior to the meeting. In essence, he called for an entirely new kind of nonparliamentary party, one whose objective was not to win votes at the ballot box (which in any event did not exist in Russia at the time), but to seize power on behalf of the working class and to establish a "dictatorship of the proletariat." The party was to be restricted to a hard-core elite, made up of professional revolutionaries and organized along militant lines rather than as a mass party. Its guiding principle was "democratic centralism," whereby the authority of the party was to be concentrated in the hands of its central committee, in which, in turn, the minority would bow to the majority. According to Lenin's view, only that party which possessed unity of action, forbade the organization of dissenting factions, and acted as a monolithic unit could achieve its objectives. Thus, in *What Is To Be Done?* Lenin wrote:

I assert: (1) that no movement can be durable without a stable organization of leaders to maintain continuity; (2) that the more widely the masses are spontaneously drawn into the struggle and form the basis of the movement and participate in it, the more necessary it is to have such an organization, and the more stable must it be (for it is much easier for demagogues to sidetrack the more backward sections of the masses); (3) that the organization must consist chiefly of persons engaged in revolutionary activities as a profession; (4) that in a country with an autocratic government, the more we *restrict* the membership of this organization to persons who are engaged in revolutionary activities as a profession and who have been professionally trained in the act of combating the political police, the more difficult will it be to catch the organization; (5) the *wider* will be the circle of men and women of the working class or of other classes of society able to join the movement and perform active work in it.[8]

Lenin pressed his views in the newspaper *Iskra (The Spark)* and in numerous pamphlets. He eventually succeeded in creating just such an organization of dedicated professional revolutionaries, while his rivals in the Menshevik faction continued to emphasize democratic principles of organization and nonviolent principles of action. Although the two factions constituted distinct organizations, both continued to operate within the framework of a single political party. As long as neither was in power, Lenin's principles were restricted only to his group. Individuals freely migrated from one faction to the other, while some, like Leon Trotsky, remained suspended between the two during the years before 1917. Once the Bolsheviks seized power, however, Lenin's ideas were applied to the entire country, and the foundations of totalitarian politics were firmly laid. The ban on factional opposition was transformed into a prohibition of other political parties and organizations; the principle of the subordination of the minority to the majority was converted into a con-

8 V. I. Lenin, *Selected Works,* II (New York: International Publishers, n.d.), pp. 138–139.

The Russian Political Heritage

demnation of dissenting political views; terrorist and conspiratorial methods used in pursuing the revolution were transformed into instruments directed against counter-revolution. What were originally the principles governing a small sectarian party were eventually extended to command the lives of millions in a vast empire.

The Revolution of 1905

After 1900, Russia was once again on the verge of revolution. A severe economic crisis stimulated strikes in the cities and rebellions in the countryside; police measures were intensified as *agents provocateurs* and spies proliferated. Thousands of real and suspected revolutionaries were imprisoned or exiled either abroad or to Siberia.

The Japanese attack on Port Arthur in 1904 temporarily postponed the inevitable revolutionary outburst, but on January 9 (Bloody Sunday) of the following year, when soldiers fired on a peaceful procession of workers bearing a list of grievances to the "Little Father" (the Tsar), killing hundreds and wounding thousands, an amorphous revolt broke out in the capital. The workers went out on a general strike; the sailors on the ship *Potemkin* mutinied; and peasants rebelled in scattered rural localities. Soviets, or workers' councils, were established in the cities to direct the strike. The most important council was the St. Petersburg Soviet, one of whose leaders was a youthful 26-year-old revolutionary, Leon Trotsky. The St. Petersburg Soviet called for the amelioration of social and economic conditions and for moderate political reforms: a constitution, elections, a national parliament, and freedom for political parties. The aim of the 1905 Revolution was to achieve middle-class political reforms comparable to those that had been won in Western Europe.

THE REFORMS OF 1905: THE DECADE OF THE DUMA. The revolution was easily quashed,

but not until after a frightened Monarch issued his famous October Manifesto, promising a constitution, political parties, elections, a national Duma, and civil liberties. Although the reforms that followed were more formal than real, differences in political conditions before and after 1905 were substantial and should not be minimized. The open organization of political parties and national elections in themselves were important achievements, even if the Duma was more a debating society than a law-making body and the Tsar's absolute power remained virtually intact. The introduction of such civil liberties as freedom of speech, assembly, worship, and movement, the relaxation of censorship, parliamentary immunity, and political agitation, while frequently violated in practice, made the Russia after 1905 a less oppressive society than the Russia before. Besides the political parties already mentioned, political organizations of the Right also materialized, ranging from the conservative Octobrists to the reactionary Union of the Russian People.

In addition to the popularly elected Duma, the Tsar established the Council of State as an upper chamber, half of whose members were appointed by the Tsar and the other half by the bureaucracy, upper clergy, and nobility. The Council of Ministers, the bureaucracy, and the armed forces remained under the control of the Monarch. All bills, before they could become law, had to have the approval of the Council of State and of the Tsar, who retained the power of absolute veto. The Tsar kept the exclusive right to initiate modifications of the fundamental law and controlled the Duma through his power to convene or dissolve it at his discretion. He also retained the title of Supreme Autocrat and in this capacity could govern by decree during periods of emergency, which he had the authority to declare.

The first Duma was elected in 1906, but was dissolved after 73 days because it outspokenly advocated further and immediate reforms. A limited agrarian reform program, however, was implemented by decree. The government tried to control the elections to the second Duma, but it proved to be even more radical than the first, and it, too, was dissolved after 103 days of existence. A new electoral law, adopted in violation of the constitution, severely limited the suffrage in favor of the propertied classes and served as the basis for the election of the third Duma. The fourth Duma, elected in 1912, demonstrated considerable vitality in spite of its overwhelmingly conservative character. The Constitutional Democrats, particularly, were active far out of proportion to their numbers, and criticism of the government by opposition radical and reform parties was spirited.

The outbreak of war in 1914 once again arrested the eruption of revolutionary violence, for all the parties, with the exception of the Bolsheviks, supported the war against Germany in an outburst of patriotic feeling. The incompetence of the government in prosecuting the war was quickly revealed as Russia suffered severe reverses at the front. The Duma was convened to deal with the situation, but its suggestions for military, economic, and political reforms were disregarded. The Imperial Court was dominated by the Siberian Monk Rasputin through his influence over the Tsarina, and his venality infected every agency of the state, including the military. Ministers were appointed and dismissed upon his advice, and even strategic war plans were influenced by his "nocturnal visions." Russia's difficulties, however, had more profound causes, and Rasputin's assassination in 1916 did little to help the deteriorating situation.

The Revolution of 1917

Defeat in war, repressive measures at home, the incompetence and corruption of the Court, the ineptitude of the Tsar, espionage, bribery and treason in high places, general war weariness, the disaffection of the border nationalities, the breakdown of the transportation system, bread riots and strikes in the cities, demoralization and desertion at the front, and peasant rebellions in the countryside climaxed a millennium of frustration and resentment, which erupted in the violent upheavals of 1917.

The occasion was characteristically inauspicious. When the "Progressive Bloc" in the Duma, made up of liberal and moderate elements, demanded that the Duma be given more power in order to restore the confidence of the country in the government, the Tsar refused and, instead, ordered the Duma dissolved. Refusing to disband, the leaders of the Duma organized a provisional executive committee. The Tsar was advised to abdicate in favor of his brother, who declined to accept the throne. As a consequence, the provisional committee of the Duma became the Provisional Government of Russia, and the Revolution became an accomplished fact. The Bolsheviks played no direct part in the "overthrow of Tsarism," for all their leaders were either in exile or were imprisoned in Siberia, although they were soon allowed to return to the capital by the political amnesty issued by the Provisional Government.

During the first days of the Revolution, local revolutionary councils, or soviets, sprang up all over Russia, in villages, towns, and in the armed forces. Unlike the soviets of 1905, which were restricted to the workers, those of 1917 also included soldiers and peasants, and accurately reflected the revolutionary mood of the country. The most significant of the soviets was the Petrograd Soviet, controlled by the moderate Left. (St. Petersburg, the Imperial capital, was renamed Petrograd in 1914; after Lenin's death in 1924; it was renamed Leningrad, and the Bolsheviks re-established Moscow as the capital of Russia in 1918.) From the very beginning, the Petrograd Soviet proved to be a formidable rival to the Provisional Government, an essentially middle-class regime whose goal was political reform and a constitutional monarchy rather than the profound social and economic changes and the creation of a republic demanded by the Soviet. The immediate consequence was dual power, a dyarchy in which political power was divided between a legal Provisional Government and a spontaneous representative institution, the Soviet. The Provisional Government actually enjoyed little popular support, and in an endeavor to eliminate the awkward dyarchy, it invited Alexander Kerensky of the Petrograd Soviet to join the Government as Minister of Justice.

Although the Soviet voted confidence in the Provisional Government, Lenin's return to Russia in April produced an explosive crisis. Met at Petrograd's Finland Station by a delegation from the Provisional Government, who asked him to join the Government, Lenin, instead, issued his famous April Theses in which he denounced the Provisional Government, called for its overthrow and the immediate transformation of the "bourgeois-democratic revolution" into a "proletarian" revolt. Lenin's defiance caused great consternation among the other revolutionary parties and even among his own followers in the capital, including Stalin, who had been supporting the Provisional Government in *Pravda*, the Bolshevik newspaper. Lenin demanded immediate land reforms and Russia's withdrawal from the "imperialist" war. "Land, Peace, and Bread" became his social program and "All Power to the Soviets" his political objective. Lenin recognized in the soviets the future institutions and organs of the "dictatorship of the proletariat" and exhorted the Bolsheviks to infiltrate and win them over:

This extremely peculiar circumstance, unparalleled in history in such a form, has led to the *interlocking of two dictatorships:* the dictatorship of the bourgeoisie (for the Provisional Government . . . is a dictatorship, i.e., a power based not on law, nor on the previously expressed will of the people, but on seizure by force, accomplished by a definite class, namely, the bourgeoisie) and the dictatorship of the proletariat and peasantry (the Soviet of Workers' and Soldiers' Deputies).[9]

The Bolshevik program of land for the peasant, bread for the worker, and peace for the soldier hit a responsive chord in the masses.

[9] Lenin, *Selected Works*, VI, pp. 48–49.

The Provisional Government's determination to carry on the war, while popular with Russia's allies, was becoming increasingly unpopular at home. Its ambiguous position on land reform also earned it the distrust of the peasants, who were already seizing the property of the landlords and wanted their expropriations legalized. By July, Kerensky had become Minister of War in the Provisional Government; the influence of the Octobrists had vanished, while that of the Constitutional Democrats was waning. Clearly, the program of moderate, constitutional reform was too little and too late. With the installation of Kerensky as Prime Minister, the Provisional Government faced the increasing discontent of the Soviets.

The Bolsheviks stepped up their activities, encouraging the soldiers to desert, the workers to strike, and the peasants to expropriate land. In July, Lenin was indirectly implicated in an attempted revolt by unruly and hungry soldiers and workers in Petrograd, and an order went out for his arrest. He fled to Finland and temporarily directed operations from there. The Bolshevik strategy was to use the soviets, which came increasingly under their control, to dislodge the Provisional Government. The doom of the Kerensky Government was sealed in August, when his army commander, General Kornilov, demanded that the soviets be abolished and attempted to overthrow the government in favor of a Right-wing dictatorship. Kerensky had few reliable troops at his disposal and was compelled to ask Lenin's Red Guards to aid him in suppressing the military coup. Once the Petrograd and Moscow Soviets passed to the Bolsheviks, Lenin knew that the time was rapidly approaching when the Bolsheviks could make an open bid for power.

Kerensky tried to stave off the inevitable by introducing more reforms. More Socialists and Mensheviks were brought into the Government, a Provisional Republic was formally proclaimed, reactionary organizations and groups were disbanded, political prisoners of the radical Left were turned loose, and, finally, the Duma itself (elected under the rigged electoral laws before the war) was dissolved. New elections were scheduled for November to elect a Constituent Assembly. All to no avail. On the night of November 6–7,[10] Lenin ordered the Red Guards to surround all government buildings and arrest the members of the Provisional Government. Only Kerensky managed to escape.

The Provisional Government was dissolved, and Lenin proclaimed that all power had passed to the Soviet and its Central Executive Committee. A Council of People's Commissars, with Lenin as Chairman, Trotsky as Commissar of Foreign Affairs, and Stalin as Commissar of Nationalities, was established, and the Soviet Republic was born. Only the Left wing of the Social Revolutionary Party supported the Bolsheviks. The elections for a Constituent Assembly took place in the fol-

lowing month. Of the 808 deputies elected in Russia's only democratically organized election, the Bolsheviks had only 168 members. In January, 1918, they disbanded it!

The Bolsheviks, contrary to official mythology, did not displace an oppressive Tsardom but a democratic regime that had allowed the greatest amount of political and civil liberty in the entire history of Russia during its brief period of existence. By postponing reform, the Provisional Government lost the support of the masses, and it lost the confidence of the Russian nationalists and the army through its inability to prosecute the war successfully. The only realistic alternatives to the Kerensky Government appeared to be either a dictatorship of the Right or the Left. The Right made its bid for power in August and lost; the Bolsheviks succeeded two months later. There seemed to be no middle ground between the Rightists, who promised despotism and order, and the Bolsheviks, who promised despotism and social justice. No strong liberal middle class had developed in Russia.

---

[10] At the time, Russia was using the old Julian Calendar which differed by 13 days from the present one. Thus the Bolshevik Revolution occurred on October 24–25 of the old calendar (Old Style) and on November 6–7 of the new (New Style). Similarly, the first Revolution of 1917 took place in February or March, depending on the calendar employed.

The Foundations of Soviet Politics

III

exposed of that of any state, totaling nearly 38,000 miles in extent.

Inside the Soviet Union are to be found an extraordinary diversity and range of climates, land features, and natural resources, more variegated than that of any other state in the world. In many ways, the Soviet Union is a microcosm of the world.

Economic Foundations

Natural Resources

Russia is one of the richest countries in the world in natural resources and is considered second only to the United States in natural potential; new finds of mineral deposits are discovered virtually every year, and it is not inconceivable that she may soon exceed the United States in known deposits of strategic minerals. Russia possesses deposits of almost every important mineral, and, like the United States, is practically self-sufficient in food.

According to a report submitted to the American government in October, 1960, "Russia has nearly twice the conventional energy sources of the entire free world, without considering recent oil discoveries in the Soviet Union." [1] Imperial Russia's known coal deposits amounted to only 3 per cent of the world's total, but today the U.S.S.R. claims 57 per cent of the world's coal deposits and 60 per cent of its peat. Recent oil discoveries raise Russia's share of known oil reserves from

The Soviet Union, like the Tsarist Empire it superseded, is the largest intercontinental state in the world. Sprawling across two continents, Russia embraces the eastern half of Europe and nearly the entire northern half of Asia. Within the boundaries of some 8,500,000 square miles (approximately one-sixth of the total land surface of the earth) are to be found more than 200,000,000 people, representing more than 100 different racial, ethnic, national, and linguistic groups, which range from the most advanced level to the most primitive nomadic tribes. At its widest point, the Soviet Union stretches some 6,000 miles around the Northern Hemisphere or about twice the distance from New York to San Francisco, while from north to south the maximum points are about 3,000 miles apart. More than a dozen states border on the Soviet Union, whose frontier is the longest and most

422

[1] *The New York Times*, January 22, 1961.

55 per cent to nearly two-thirds of the world's reserves. She also claims 28 per cent of the world's water power and one-third of its timber resources.

Russia's reserves of minerals and chemicals are no less impressive. Pre-revolutionary Russia's iron-ore deposits amounted to less than 4 per cent of the world's total, but today she claims 53.5 per cent, more than the rest of the world combined and three times as much as the United States, Britain, France, and West Germany together. She claims no less than 88 per cent of the world's manganese, 54 per cent of its potassium salts, 30 per cent of its phosphates, and claims to be first in the known reserves of copper, lead, zinc, nickel, bauxite, tungsten, mercury, and sulphur. The only major resources that she lacks in quantity are tin and natural rubber. Russia's vast resources have enabled the U.S.S.R. to achieve second place only to the United States in the production of steel, pig iron, coal, and oil. (Since geological explorations continue on a massive scale, these statistics are subject to constant revision upwards.) Yet about 25 per cent of the Soviet territory remains geologically unexplored, and geological investigation of the enormous territories of her Chinese ally are just beginning. Within Russia's borders are also to be found nearly 250 million acres of rich black soil.

As the Soviet resources are converted into production, the entire political and economic balance of power in the world may be fundamentally altered. Already, the Soviet Union has invaded the world oil market, backed by her tremendous reserves and accelerated production (3,000,000 barrels per day in 1960, exceeded only by that of the United States), and undersells the prevailing market price by from 20 to 30 per cent. From shipments of only 35,000 barrels a day in 1953, the Soviets exported at the rate of 500,000 barrels per day in 1961.[2]

Industrial Growth and Power

The foundation of modern national power is industrialization, a fact which Joseph Stalin,

the architect of Russia's modern power, recognized at an early date. Soon after he established his control over the Soviet state, Stalin introduced an ambitious Five Year Plan in 1928 designed both to socialize and industrialize Russia in order to secure national strength and to provide a strong base from which the ideological goals of world Communism could be pursued.

The first of the three pre-war Five Year Plans was supposed to concentrate on heavy industry, the second (1933–38) on consolidating the gains of the first, and emphasizing quality, while the third (1939–44) was to shift over to light industry and the production of consumer goods. The rise of Hitler in Germany and the designs of Japan in the Far East, however, forced Stalin to alter this program of industrialization in favor of accelerating the expansion of heavy industry and increasing the military capacity of the Soviet Union. The Third Five Year Plan was disrupted by World War II and was never completed. After the war, Stalin inaugurated a new series of three Five Year Plans, designed, respectively, to repair the war devastation and restore the country to a sound state, to overtake the advanced industrial states of Western Europe, and, finally, to close the gap between the Soviet Union and the United States.

By 1951, the Soviet Union had fully recovered from the destruction of the war and had already developed an atom bomb and was on the verge of producing the hydrogen bomb. Although Soviet recovery was hastened by the 10 billion dollars in reparations exacted from Germany and her exploitation of the satellite states of Eastern Europe, the recovery was largely dependent on her own resources. The rapid postwar recovery of the Soviet economy is even more remarkable in light of the damages suffered not only by the economy during the war but by the population as well. The Germans occupied fully one-half of European Russia, including some of her most important

The Foundations of Soviet Politics

423

2 *The New York Times,* January 13 and 22, 1961.

industrial centers and food-producing regions. Judging from the 1959 census (the first in twenty years), the Soviet Union lost more than 25 million killed, plus the 20 million or so who were not born as a result of the deaths and dislocations of the war. These war losses were concealed by Stalin to prevent the exposure of Soviet weakness to the outside world.

Only in 1961 did the Soviet government permit the publication of statistics showing the magnitude of the damage to Russia by the war (see Table 3-1). By 1942, the second year

TABLE 3-1 *Indexes of Basic Industrial Production in the U.S.S.R., 1913–1965* [a] (In millions of tons)

Item	1913	1928	1940	War years	1950	1955	1959	1965 (planned)
Steel	4.2	4.3	18.3	8.0	27.3	45.3	60.0	86–91
Pig iron	4.2	3.3	14.9	—	19.2	33.3	43.0	65–70
Iron ore	9.2	6.1	29.9	18.0	39.7	71.9		
Rolled steel	3.5	3.4	13.1	—	20.9	35.3	49.0	65–70
Coke	4.4	4.2	21.1	—	27.7	43.6		
Coal	29.1	35.5	165.9	75.0	261.1	391.3	507.0	600–612
Oil	9.2	11.6	31.1	—	37.9	70.8	129.6	230–240
Gas [b]	17.0	336.0	3,392.0	—	6,181.0	10,356.0	37,200.0	150,000.0
Peat	1.7	5.3	33.2	—	36.0	50.8	60.5	
Electricity [c]	1.9	5.0	48.3	—	91.2	170.2	265.0	500–520
Cement	1.3	1.8	55.7	—	10.2	22.5	38.8	75–81
Machine tools (1,000 units)	1.5	2.8	63.1	—	79.6	136.5	175.8	226–236
Gross national product [d]								
Total					115	155	200	280
Per capita					632	783	858	899

[a] *Narodnoye Khozyaistvo SSSR v 1959 Godu* (Moscow, 1960).
[b] Millions of cubic meters.
[c] Billions of KWH.
[d] Total in billions of dollars; per capita, in dollars.

of the war, industrial production dropped to a level about equal to that of 1928–32. Steel production dropped from 18,300,000 metric tons to 8,000,000. By 1944, it rose to nearly 11,000,000 tons. The production of iron ore, as vital as steel in modern war, dropped from about 30 million metric tons in 1940 to 22 million tons in 1942, and to little more than 18 million in 1943–44. Coal production was also cut in half, from 166 million tons to 75, although by 1944 it rose to more than 121 million tons.[3]

The losses in agriculture were equally severe. Only 60 per cent of the area sown in 1940

[3] *The New York Times,* January 2, 1961.

The Soviet Union~Chapter III

was planted in 1942, while livestock suffered a sharp decline in numbers. Pigs were reduced from 27.5 million in 1941 to a low of 5.6 million in 1944; horses from 21 million to less than 8 million; cows from nearly 28 million to less than 14 million in 1943, to 16.5 million in 1944. The number of sheep and goats declined from 91.6 million to a low of 62 million in 1943, while cattle dropped from 54.5 million to a low of 28.4 million in 1943. In view of these admissions, the 11 billion dollars of lend-lease aid that had been given to the U.S.S.R. by the United States may well have provided the margin of survival.

By the time of Stalin's death, however, in March, 1953, the Soviet Union was well on the road to becoming the second industrial power in the world and the first in space and rocket technology. In 1946, Stalin announced what in retrospect appear to be modest industrial goals to be achieved by 1961. Steel production was set at 60 million tons, pig iron at 50 million, oil at 60 million, and coal at 500 million tons. These projections were ridiculed by many foreign observers as ambitious and unrealistic, designed primarily for propaganda purposes. Yet some of these goals were exceeded by 1960—steel production, for instance, was 71.5 million tons. By 1959, oil production in the Soviet Union reached 129 million tons, and coal production totaled 507 million tons.

The growth of the national power of the Soviet Union is systematically planned. The equilibrium between production for national power and private consumption is tightly controlled and manipulated by the state. Under Stalin, the public sector of the economy was developed at the expense of the private sector. Consequently, the Soviet standard of living lagged far behind the rate of technological advance. Since the death of Stalin, his successors have devoted more attention to raising the standard of living, although it remains a poor second to the country's capital investment in national power.

Although the total production of goods and services in the United States is three times that of the Soviet Union, a substantial proportion is devoted to private consumption, while the amount devoted to maintaining and enhancing national power is only about equal to that of the Soviet Union in absolute terms and in some key areas is actually less. Thus the standard of living in the Soviet Union is artificially depressed, while that in the United States is almost frivolously exaggerated because of the different ratios established for the public and private sectors of the economy. The implications of this contrast are discussed below.

Khrushchev has promised that the new Seven Year Plan will pay greater attention to raising the standard of living. Real wages for factory and office workers will be upped 40 per cent, while basic food production will be enhanced by more than 50 per cent. The housing shortage will be attacked more vigorously, and the production of textiles and clothing will enjoy a comparable increase. At the same time, the work week was to be reduced to 40 hours by 1962 (it was reduced to a seven-hour, six-day week of 42 hours in 1960) and to only 35 hours by 1965. Medical and educational facilities will continue to be expanded at a rapid rate. Foreign travelers to the Soviet Union consistently report a steady and appreciable rise in the Soviet standard of living every year, and this increase will continue to be steady and modest, but certain.

The Soviet leaders plan for the Soviet Union to catch up and surpass the United States in the major indexes of production by 1975. It is the opinion of some American economists that if the Soviet annual growth rate is sustained at 9 per cent while that of the United States remains at 3 per cent, the Soviet Union will equal the United States in total industrial output by 1972.[4] Since it has been the fashion to deprecate Soviet capacity in the past, it would be the better part of wisdom to assume that the Soviet growth rate will remain at a high figure.

The difference between a vigorous and expanding Soviet economy and a stagnating American level of productivity at a relatively high plateau is caused not by economic considerations, as is often assumed, but by political and ideological factors. The steel *capacity* of the United States in 1961, for example, stood at more than 151,000,000 tons, yet the production of steel in 1957–60 averaged about 95 million tons and in some months dropped close to 60 million tons. Steel production in this country thus operates well below its total capacity, sometimes as low as 50 per cent, while Soviet steel production operates at maximum capacity. Whether a nation decides to utilize its full capacity or not is ultimately a

[4] See the collection of studies issued by the Soviet Economic Committee of the Congress of the United States, *Comparison of the United States and Soviet Economies* (Washington, D.C.: Government Printing Office, 1960), in three parts. Hereinafter cited as *Joint Economic Committee Studies.*

political question, not an economic one. Just as Tsarist Russia chose not to exploit its natural potential, a country like the United States can choose not to utilize its total productive capacity, but in the long run it must accept the social and political consequences of its choice. The Soviet government has as its avowed ultimate objective the liquidation of capitalism, by demonstrating that the Soviet system is superior in its ability to mobilize national power and to exploit natural resources for social purposes.

Agriculture and Food Production

Soviet and non-Soviet observers universally agree that agriculture constitutes the Achilles heel of the Soviet economy. While Soviet industrial production, science, technology, and education have registered virtually uninterrupted progress, Soviet agriculture has failed to keep pace and has stagnated at a fairly low level of production. An adequate food supply is just as vital as industrial production in contributing to national power, but agricultural production is not as susceptible to rational planning and control as is industrial production.

The weaknesses of Soviet agriculture are not all due to the vagaries of the climate. The very process of rapid industrialization and urbanization within the span of a single generation was bound to dislocate the equilibrium between town and country life. Top priority was given to industrialization, in accordance with Marxist principles, at the expense of agriculture and the peasants if necessary. Badly needed factory workers were drawn from the farms. Since the Soviet regime could not secure financial assistance from the capitalist countries in the form of loans or gifts, it had to rely on agricultural exports to accumulate enough capital to import foreign machinery and technicians to start the industrialization of Russia. The diminishing labor supply in

the countryside and the drain of agricultural exports reduced the country's food supply to below the subsistence level.

Stalin was thus confronted with a dilemma of serious proportions, a dilemma that inevitably confronts every underdeveloped country wishing to industrialize rapidly. How to resolve it is one of the supreme political problems of the modern age. Stalin's method of increasing agricultural production consisted of three parts: collectivization, mechanization, and political control. Collectivizing the farms satisfied both the Marxist demand for the socialization of agriculture and the demands of efficiency, for small individual farms were replaced by large state-supervised collective farms. Mechanization of farm equipment helped compensate for the reduced labor supply, and the state's retention of the ownership of the land and agricultural machines, together with its exclusive power to set agricultural prices and buy agricultural commodities, insured that the peasants would remain under the thumb of the government.

The net result of Stalin's program was a disaster for rural Russia. The Kulaks (the wealthy peasants) ferociously resisted collectivization; they burned their crops, slaughtered their livestock, and destroyed their implements rather than surrender them to the state. From 1930 to 1934, the Soviet state was locked in a virtual civil war with a substantial part of the peasantry. What crops were produced, including the seed grain, were seized by Communist Party brigades and shipped to the cities to feed the workers and for export abroad. The food supply diminished catastrophically. The disaster was magnified by the world-wide economic depression which knocked the bottom out of the market prices for agricultural commodities, causing the Soviets to export more for less return. During the height of the crisis, a severe drought hit the Ukraine, which further reduced agricultural production. Famine stalked rural Russia as millions died of starvation, and vast numbers of Kulaks were "liquidated." According to Stalin, the struggle against the Kulaks' resistance was a greater crisis for his regime than the war against Germany.

Rural Russia has never fully recovered and Soviet agricultural production has only recently exceeded the production registered in 1916. Per capita production for the total population is still not much better than nearly 50 years ago and lags considerably behind that of the United States. The number of livestock, in particular, dropped tremendously, and only after 1950 did the Soviet Union manage to reach the figures of 1916.

The Soviet government has endeavored to raise agricultural production through more intensive use of existing farm lands and by an expansion of the acreage under cultivation. In attempting to get more productive use of present farm lands, the Soviet government has steadily enhanced the mechanization of agriculture, fostered greater scientific research, and increased the production of fertilizer, even copying some techniques from the United States.

The most ambitious attempt to expand the area under cultivation has been underway since 1955, when Khrushchev inaugurated the so-called "virgin lands" project whereby enormous tracts of uncultivated lands in western Siberia and the Central Asian Republic of Kazakhstan were plowed up and planted. The program involves enormous risks, because the climate on these plains is so unpredictable. A large amount of capital has been invested in the program, and energetic efforts and inducements have been made to get farmers to settle in the new lands. Every year hundreds of thousands of Komsomols (members of the Communist youth organization) and university students "volunteer" to spend a year or two working in the area. Life is very hard, and even the modest amenities of ordinary Soviet life are largely absent in the great tent cities that have been erected on the Central Asian steppes.

The virgin lands program has undoubtedly increased the total production of grain, but whether on balance it has been worth the effort and cost is still debatable. Three crops years out of the first five were adjudged failures, and the careers of important Communist Party and government officials have suffered with each failure.

Population

A nation's demographic configuration reveals a great deal about its power and potential. If we examine the size and growth of the Soviet population, its territorial distribution, sex and age, skills, talents and literacy rates, social composition, and finally its ethnic diversity, we will learn much about the current capabilities as well as the future prospects of the U.S.S.R.

At the outset, perhaps we should outline the general profile of the present Soviet population. As a result of World War II, today there are 45,000,000 fewer citizens of the U.S.S.R. than there might have been had there been no war. Whereas before the war the population of Russia was 46 per cent larger than that of the United States, presently it is only 18 per cent larger. During the entire era from 1914 to 1960, Russia's population rose from 159 million to 209 million, an increase of only 50 million. During this same period, the population of the United States shot upward from 92,000,000 (census of 1910) to 180,000,000 (census of 1960). World War II left the Soviet Union with 20,000,000 more women than men (the most unbalanced ratio of any country save East Germany), and this has resulted in social, economic, and military problems of an acute character. The age structure of Russia's population was also drastically altered. In the United States, the war produced a "boom" in babies, but the precise opposite took place in Russia, which, consequently, faces a diminished supply of workers and soldiers during the years of the immediate future.

Because of advances in science, medicine, and sanitation, the life expectancy of the Soviet citizen has increased to the point where it equals that of the United States and is one of the highest in the world. This means that

The Foundations of Soviet Politics

the future population of Russia will show a higher proportion of old people. Although the birth rate has declined, while that of the United States has gone up, the Soviet birth rate is still higher than ours. Industrialization has brought about a revolution in the urban-rural ratio of the Soviet population. Today, 48 per cent of Russia's population is urbanized (that is, lives in towns with over 3,000 population), and the Soviet educational effort has transformed a nation of illiterates into one of the most literate countries in the world. The Soviet Union now has virtually 100 per cent literacy, and all children attend school.

Besides the population movement from country to town, there has been a corresponding movement of population eastward. The over-all population increase from 1939 to 1959 was only 9.5 per cent, but all the regions east of the Urals registered increases of more than 30 per cent, with the Soviet Far East showing a high of 70 per cent. Some of the western border regions, however, have actually decreased in population, owing both to the war and migrations eastward. One result of this movement eastward has been the spread of the Slavic nationalities among the non-Slavic populations of Central Asia. In the Kazakh Republic, according to the census of 1959, the Kazakhs have been reduced to a minority in their own Republic.

Perhaps the most unique characteristic of the Soviet population is its ethnic diversity. The people of the Soviet Union remain divided among more than 100 different nationalities, of which the Great Russians account for more than half the total. The language and literacy data of the 1959 census reveal two important modifications of the ethnic situation in the Soviet Union. The first is the increasing "russification" of many of the smaller non-Russian nationalities; the second is the virtual establishment of Russian as a second spoken language for all non-

Russians. An impressive number of small non-Russian nationalities had more than 50 per cent of their members list Russian as their mother tongue. The compulsory teaching of Russian in all non-Russian schools has resulted in a bilingual population, virtually all of whom speak and read Russian in addition to their native language. The Soviet population, in spite of its ethnic diversity, is thus a far more homogenized population than it was two decades ago.

Size and Growth

For all practical purposes, the Soviet Union and the United States are in the same population class, both being considerably overshadowed by two demographic giants, China and India. Since the gap between the population of the U.S.S.R. and that of the United States has decreased over the past decades, the competitive struggle and rivalry between the two countries will increasingly turn on which country most effectively marshals and mobilizes its human and natural resources. The population of the United States is not expected to reach the current Soviet size before 1970, and because of the slightly higher increase of births over deaths in Russia, the Soviet Union is expected to widen its margin in the next several decades. With immigration into the United States practically at a standstill, the United States must now rely on natural increases to replenish its demographic resources.

According to current projections, the population of the United States in 1965 will approximate 196 million, while that of the Soviet Union should total 234 million in 1966 (Table 3-2). In 1957, the rate of natural increase for the United States was 15.7 per thousand per year, as compared with 17.5 per thousand for Russia. When compared with the 1940 rates of 8.6 and 13.4, respectively, we see the remarkable advance chalked up by the United States. The Soviet increases were caused by a rapid decline in the death rate and a slight decline in the birth rate; the increases for the United States according to an authoritative source resulted not only from a declining death rate but

TABLE 3-2   *Population Growth of the U.S. and U.S.S.R.,*
1913–1966 (In millions)

	1913	1920	1926	1930	1940	1950	1960	1965	Over-all rate of increase
U.S.	96 [a]	106		123	132	151	180	196	104%
U.S.S.R.	159		147 [b]		191	179 [c]	209	234 [d]	47%

[a] Interpolated from 1910 and 1920 census returns.
[b] Applies to Soviet boundaries existing before September, 1939.
[c] Estimated.
[d] 1966 projection.

from a 30 per cent spurt in birth rates.[5]

Age and Sex

The ratio of men to women in the Soviet population has steadily decreased since World War I. In 1926, the number of males per 100 women was 93.4; in 1939, 91.9; and, according to the 1959 census, the percentage has dropped to 81.9. During the same period, the number of males per 100 females in the United States declined from a small surplus of 103.1 to a small deficit of 98. The lack of men in Russia deprives approximately 21 million women of husbands and children and forces many women into heavy manual labor and other unskilled work, a situation that often shocks western observers.

Equally if not more serious is the aging of the Soviet population. Because of the deficit in births caused by World War II, the Soviet Union will experience serious shortages of manpower during the early 1960's. The most serious deficiency, as of the 1959 census, was in the 10–15 age group, which amounted to only 60 per cent of the number in this age group in 1939 (Table 3-3). Note that the number of people over 70 in 1959 was 179 per cent of that in 1939, the sharpest increase of any age group.

Distribution

The population of neither the United States nor the Soviet Union is distributed equally throughout the country. In the United States, the bulk of the population is found east of the Mississippi; in the U.S.S.R., the over-

TABLE 3-3   *Age Structure of the Soviet Population, 1939 and 1959* [a]

	(Number of people in millions)		Percentage of total		1959 percentage
Age	1939	1959	1939	1959	of 1939
0–9	43,476	46,363	22.8%	22.2%	107%
10–15	28,365	17,133	14.9	8.2	60
16–19	13,030	14,675	6.8	7.0	113
20–24	15,786	20,343	8.3	9.7	129
25–29	18,520	18,190	9.7	8.7	98
30–34	15,598	18,999	8.2	9.1	122
35–39	12,958	11,590	6.8	5.6	89
40–44	9,603	10,408	5.0	5.0	108
45–49	7,776	12,264	4.1	5.9	158
50–59	12,533	19,146	6.6	9.2	153
60–69	8,535	11,736	4.5	5.6	137
Over 70	4,462	7,972	2.3	3.8	179

[a] Source: *Narodnoye Khozyaistvo SSSR v 1959 Godu.*

whelming proportion of the population is west of the Urals. In both countries, there has been a steady movement of people from the more densely populated areas to those relatively sparse in people. Vast stretches of territory remain virtually unpopulated in both countries. Much of Soviet Asia is inhospitable and incapable of supporting large populations.

Excluding the ancient settled regions of Central Asia, Russia east of the Urals, including Kazakhstan, around the turn of the century contained a little more than 8 million people. By 1926, it had more than doubled to 17.4 million. In 1939, it had risen to 22.7 million, and, according to the latest census

The Foundations of Soviet Politics

[5] See *Joint Economic Committee Studies,* I, pp. 31–94.

(1959), the total population of Siberia and Kazakhstan is now approximately 34 million. These increases are almost all due to the migrations from the western regions of Russia.

Since the Revolution, the Soviet government has sedulously planned the movement of the population eastward, for essentially three reasons: (1) to increase the proportion of European Slavs in Soviet Asia and thus to reduce the possibility that the non-Russian groups in Asia would defect; (2) to more effectively tap the rich natural resources of the region; (3) to protect Soviet Asia against the ambitions of a predatory Japan and against the possibility of population pressures from China. Much of the Soviet Far East was once a nominal part of China, which lost its hold on the area largely because of the activities of various Russian adventurers, beginning in the seventeenth century and continuing down into the nineteenth.

Russian population movements eastward have, by and large, not been voluntary migrations on the part of people in search of new opportunities, as was the case in the westward movement in the United States. A substantial part of the shift resulted from forcible deportations. During the Stalinist era, millions of Russian and Ukrainian peasants were deported to Central Asia and the Soviet Far East, and millions were herded into vast concentration camps. When released, most of the ex-prisoners were obliged to remain in the area, or found it convenient to begin life anew in Russia's Asian provinces.

Since Stalin's death, most of the slave-labor camps in the Soviet Union have been disbanded, and compulsory emigration to Soviet Asia has been stopped. Now the government is inducing people to move eastward, especially to the "virgin lands" of the Kazakh Republic and western Siberia, by offering them long-term financial support on generous terms, large and potentially fertile farm lands, wage bonuses, and other rewards.

In spite of these impressive attempts to spread Soviet population to the east, nearly 70 per cent of Russia's population is still found west of the Urals. Soviet Asia, with 75 per cent of the land area of the Soviet Union, supports only about 25 per cent of the population or 49 million people (compared with only 14 million in 1897). The Soviet government intends to continue the migration eastward, and the current Seven Year Plan allocates substantial capital investments for the development of Soviet Asia, which also reflects the government's anxiety about Communist China's possible desires on the scantily populated regions of the Soviet Union bordering on her territory.

URBAN-RURAL DISTRIBUTION. More dramatic than the movement of the Soviet population from west to east has been the shift of people from country to town. In 1926, the total urban population of the country was only 26 million, which by 1939 had grown to more than 60 million (Table 3-4). In 1949, the urban population of Russia amounted to nearly 100 million, or 48 per cent of the population. Urbanization has taken place throughout the country, but in the Asian regions, it has increased by more than 100 per cent. The Soviet Far East and some of the Central Asian Republics have registered increases of 150 per cent, as against an average of 30 per cent for the western areas.

Between 1939 and 1959, 503 new cities and 1,354 new urban-type settlements were created. As an indication of the continuing character of Soviet urbanization, 128 cities and 499 urban settlements came into being during the three years between 1956 and 1959. Today, the Soviet Union has a larger number of cities with a population of 50,000 or more than has the United States. Of cities with populations in excess of 500,000 in 1960, the U.S.S.R. had 25, while the United States had only 21. The United States leads in super-cities, however; we have five with 2 million inhabitants or more to Russia's two, Moscow and Leningrad. It should be emphasized that the Soviet government has, by law and administrative action, prevented the development of overcrowded and swollen city

TABLE 3-4   *Urban Growth in the U.S.S.R., 1926–1959* [a]

Settlements	1926	1939	1941	1951	1956	1959
Cities	709	923	1,241	1,451	1,566	1,679
Urban-type settlements	1,216	1,450	1,711	2,320	2,423	2,940
Cities						
(50,000–100,000)	60	94	——	——	138	156
(100,000–500,000)	28	71	——	——	113	123
(Over 500,000)	3	11	——	——	22	25
Total urban population	26,300,000	60,400,000	60,600,000	71,400,000	86,600,000	99,778,000

[a] Source: *Narodnoye Khozyaistvo . . . v 1959 Godu.*

populations. Moscow today has slightly less than 5 million people, Leningrad a little more than 3 million, followed by Kiev and Baku, with 1 million and 900,000, respectively.

Thus, while the increase in population from 1939 to 1959 was only 9.5 per cent, the urban population during the same period increased by 65 per cent. Between 1926 and 1959, villages of mud huts and straw-covered houses were transformed into modern towns, and the empty plains and valleys of Soviet Asia saw the erection of giant new cities, whose populations were busily exploiting the natural resources of Siberia. Imposing industrial centers like Karaganda (375,000) and Magnitogorsk (290,000) did not even exist before 1926.

Although the image of the Soviet Union as a vast land populated by peasants has long been out-dated, the rural population of Russia still accounts for 52 per cent of the population, or about 109 million people.

Ethnic Composition and Distribution

Like Imperial Russia before it, the Soviet Union is a country of many nationalities and tribal groups who speak a variety of languages and dialects. The 1959 census tabulates more than 100 nationalities, tribes, and linguistic groups. This ethnic heterogeneity renders any purely quantitative analysis of Soviet population based on size, growth, territorial distribution, age structure, sex ratios, etc., grossly misleading unless it is accompanied by an ethnic analysis as well.

The Great Russians occupy the continental interior of Eurasia, and they are fringed on all sides by a belt of non-Russian nationalities that forms a buffer around the borders of the Soviet Union. Most of the Baltic coast is inhabited by Estonians, Latvians, and Lithuanians, while the Byelorussians, Ukrainians, and Moldavians occupy the territories bordering Poland, Czechoslovakia, and Rumania. In the Caucasus, the Georgians, Armenians, and Azerbaidzhani Turks inhabit the regions next to Turkey and Iran. In Central Asia, the Turkmen, Uzbeks, Kazakhs, and Kirgiz live in the border areas adjacent to Iran, Afghanistan, and the Sinkiang Province of China, and a multitude of Turkic, Mongol, and Tungusic tribes occupy the border regions near Outer Mongolia. Only in the Soviet Far East do Great Russians inhabit territories adjacent to the international frontiers of the U.S.S.R., and this is a region remote from the heartland of the Russian nation.

Of the more than 100 nationalities enumerated in the 1959 census, 22 number more than 900,000 each, and these account for 95 per cent of the total population (Table 3-5). The other 80 nationalities amount to less than 10 million.

The demographic contours of the Soviet population thus vary widely from one ethnic group to another, and this unevenness is of fundamental significance in assessing Soviet power and political behavior. The mosaic of nationalities in Russia has had, and continues

The Foundations of Soviet Politics

TABLE 3-5   *Major Nationalities of the U.S.S.R., 1939 and 1959* [a]

Nationality	1939	1959
Russians	99,019,000	114,500,000
Ukrainians	28,070,000	36,981,000
Byelorussians	5,267,431	7,829,000
Uzbeks	4,844,021	6,004,000
Tatars	4,300,000	4,969,000
Kazakhs	3,098,000	3,581,000
Azerbaidzhanis	2,274,805	2,929,000
Armenians	2,151,884	2,787,000
Georgians	2,248,566	2,650,000
Lithuanians	——	2,326,000
Jews	3,020,141	2,268,000
Moldavians	——	2,214,000
Germans	1,423,534	1,619,000
Chuvash	1,367,930	1,470,000
Latvians	——	1,400,000
Tadzhiks	1,928,964	1,397,000
Poles	626,905	1,380,000
Mordvins	1,451,429	1,285,000
Turkmen	811,769	1,004,000
Bashkirs	842,925	983,000
Kirgiz	884,306	974,000
Estonians	——	969,000

[a] Source: *Narodnoye Khozyaistvo . . . v 1959 Godu.*

to have, an important impact on the foreign policy of the Soviet Union, its internal constitutional structure and political processes, and its social and cultural development. The geographical balance and distribution of the Russian versus the non-Russian nationalities of the Soviet Union is thus of crucial importance. The Great Russians occupy the continental interior of Eurasia, and they are fringed on all sides with a virtually uninterrupted belt of non-Russian nationalities who form a buffer separating the Russian inhabited territories from the international borders of the Soviet Union. Because of the strategic location of the border nationalities, the loyalty and reliability of these nationalities to Moscow and their relationship to the Russian people have always been a vital factor in Russian and Soviet security considerations. The failure of the Tsars to earn the loyalty of the non-Russian nationalities contributed significantly to the military inefficiency of Russia during

World War I, and their dissatisfaction under Tsarist rule contributed materially to the Revolution, while Bolshevik promises of national self-determination was an important factor in Lenin's successful seizure and preservation of power. The nature and intensity of the loyalty and political reliability of the various nationalities of the Soviet Union vary from nationality to nationality, with the Russians—as would be expected—being the most intensely loyal and patriotic. During the war, Stalin retaliated against five of the very small nationalities by dissolving their autonomous Republics and deporting their populations to Siberia, on grounds that they went over to the Germans. This action was denounced by Khrushchev in 1956, and their Republics have since been revived and their populations relocated.

Literacy and Education

According to the census of 1959, the Soviet Union has achieved virtually 100 per cent literacy, with less than two million people between the ages 9–59 reported as being unable to read and write. This cultural revolution in Russia during the past forty years is one of the most significant transformations achieved in the social history of any nation. "In the organization of a planned society in the U.S.S.R.," reads the 1959 report of the first United States official educational mission to the U.S.S.R., "education is regarded as one of the chief resources and techniques for achieving social, economic, cultural and scientific objectives in the national interest. . . . They are convinced that time is on their side and that through education and hard work they can win their way to world acceptance of communist ideology." [6] The Soviet Union has recently established seven years as the minimum schooling for children. Until a few years ago, the government was able to guarantee only a four-year education in many of the rural areas of the country.

Another feature of the Soviet educational effort merits attention: adult classes. An adult-

[6] *Soviet Commitment to Education* (Washington, D.C.: U.S. Department of Health, Education and Welfare, 1959), p. 1.

education program, on the job and in the evening, was inaugurated soon after the Revolution to combat illiteracy. That battle having been won, its place has been taken by factory schools, correspondence courses, and evening classes, whose primary purpose is to provide opportunities for working people to learn new skills or improve old ones. It is perhaps worth noting that Nikita Khrushchev could neither read nor write until he was over twenty years old and thus owes his rise to this adult-education program of the Communist Party. In 1960, the total Soviet student enrollment in higher educational institutions was nearly two and a quarter million, less than two-thirds that in the United States but four times that of Great Britain, West Germany, Italy, and France combined.

Before the Revolution, 76 per cent of the people were illiterate, including 88 per cent of the women. Virtually complete illiteracy prevailed among the indigenous populations of Siberia and Soviet Central Asia. Indeed, more than 40 languages had not been reduced to writing at all. Prior to the Revolution, only 290,000 Russians possessed any kind of higher education, whereas the 1959 census reported that more than 13 million citizens had some higher or specialized secondary education, and more than 45 million people had 7–10 years of education.

Before the Revolution, 80 per cent of the children of Russia were deprived of educational opportunities, and all instruction, with but few exceptions, was in the Russian language. Today all Soviet children must attend school, and instruction is provided in no less than 59 indigenous languages, although Russian is the universal and virtually obligatory second language. Raising the literacy rate from 24 per cent to 98.5 per cent within the span of a single generation for more than 200,000,000 people would be an achievement in itself if only one language were involved, to say nothing of the severe problems posed by a multilingual society.

In 1914, only 127,000 students were enrolled in 95 institutions of higher learning; in 1960, there were nearly 2.4 million enrolled in some 766 institutions of higher education, 3,346 technicums (non-professional technical colleges), and other specialized secondary schools (Table 3-6). Over 50 million people were enrolled in all types of schools in 1960 as compared with 10.6 million people in the years 1914–15.

TABLE 3-6 *School Enrollment in the U.S.S.R., 1914–1959* (In thousands)

Schools	1914–15	1927–28	1940–41	1945–46	1956–57	1960–61
General schools	9,656	11,638	35,552	26,808 [a]	30,127 [a]	36,186
Grades 8–11	152	170	2,571	1,091 [a]	6,136	5,121
Technical and special secondary schools	54	189	975	1,008	2,107	2,060
Higher education	127	169	812	730	2,001	2,396

a Low figures represent birth-deficit years caused by World War II.

Educational institutions of every level have been established in all the Republics and in areas inhabited by other major nationalities (Table 3-7). Instruction is offered in both the native language and in Russian. The quality of these institutions varies considerably, with the venerable Universities of Moscow and Leningrad setting the highest standards of excellence in the country. Although a non-Russian can acquire a higher education in his native language, it is to his advantage to master Russian if he wishes to enter one of the national universities, apply for the diplomatic service, or work outside his native Republic.

To detail the massive character of the Soviet

The Foundations of Soviet Politics

TABLE 3-7   *Institutions of Higher Learning in the Non-Russian Republics, 1914–1960* [a]

Republic	1914	1927	1940	1945	1957	1960
Ukraine	27	39	173	154	138	135
Byelorussia	None	4	25	24	24	24
Uzbek	None	3	30	33	32	30
Kazakh	None	1	20	24	26	28
Georgia	1	6	21	20	19	18
Armenia	None	2	9	13	12	10
Azerbaidzhan	None	3	16	17	15	12
Lithuania	—	—	7	10	12	12
Latvia	—	—	7	8	9	10
Estonia	—	—	5	5	6	6
Moldavia	—	—	6	6	8	6
Tadzhik	None	None	6	7	8	6
Kvgiz	None	None	6	6	9	8
Turkmen	None	None	5	6	6	4

[a] Does not include technical or special secondary schools. Source: *Narodnoye Khozyaistvo . . . v 1959* and *. . . v 1960 Godu*.

educational effort in Central Asia, the Uzbek Republic, which is the most advanced of the Central Asian areas today, as it was in pre-revolutionary Russia, provides an apt illustration. Before the Revolution, only 2 per cent of the population was literate. There were no native engineers, doctors, or teachers with a higher education. In short, Central Asia was no different in this respect from most of the colonial dependencies of the European powers and worse off than many.

Today, in the Uzbek Republic alone, there are 30 institutions of higher learning, 100 technicums, 50 special technical schools, 12 teachers' colleges, and 1,400 kindergartens. More than 1,500,000 children attend school, and 50 per cent of the 80,000 teachers have had some higher education.[7] In addition, the Republic has an Academy of Science and an Academy of Agricultural Sciences. The rate of literacy is over 95 per cent. The Republic before the Revolution possessed no public libraries; today there are 3,000. The number of books printed in the Uzbek language in 1913

was 118,000; today it approaches 22 million. When this record is compared with that of Iran, Afghanistan, the Arab countries, the states of Southeast Asia, or even Turkey, all of which were at a comparable or more advanced level of educational attainment in 1914, the achievement is impressive.

Not only has the Soviet government assiduously developed the human potential among the non-Russian nationalities, but it has also paid serious attention to the education and training of women. In 1960, 49 per cent of all Soviet citizens with some higher education were women, and 53 per cent of those with some secondary education were also women. In 1957, women accounted for 52 per cent of all students in special secondary schools, 51 per cent of enrollment in higher education, and 29 per cent of all post-graduate students. Soviet women are being educated in practically all fields of science, culture, technology, and the professions in rapidly increasing numbers.

[7] *Ibid.*, p. 3.

Communications Media

One of the earliest acts of the Bolshevik regime was to abolish the private ownership of newspapers, book publishing firms, radio stations, and other mass communications media and subject them to the control of the Soviet state. Although Article 125 of the Soviet Constitution guarantees the Soviet citizen, "freedom of speech . . . press . . . assembly, including the holding of mass meetings . . . street processions and demonstrations," the exercise of these "rights" is severely limited by the constitutional admonition that these rights shall be allowed only "in conformity with the interests of the working people, and in order to strengthen the socialist system." All media of public communication in the Soviet Union are thus directly or indirectly owned or controlled by agencies of the government and the Communist Party, whether they be national or local in scope.

Soviet Control of Information and Opinion

Within the framework of the Soviet system, communications media, like the educational system, are considered instruments of indoctrination and propaganda rather than vehicles of information and recreation, and they are utilized to reshape the minds of the Soviet people into the mold of Communist ideology. All information coming from abroad is rigorously censored by the government, and information originating within the U.S.S.R. is revised to further the objectives of the system.

As the Soviet system increases in power and stability, the mass media are allowed to relax their drive for indoctrination. Ownership and control, however, remain in the hands of the state and the party, although greater latitude may be permitted individual editors and writers who can be relied on not to publish anything that would consciously injure the Soviet system. But the party remains vigilant and has the last word.

By the time of Stalin's death, the widening gap between an increasingly educated public and a communications system dedicated to propaganda and monotonous indoctrination could no longer be perpetuated without seriously damaging the Soviet system. Stalin's successors have been more lenient because they have greater confidence in the political reliability of the Soviet people and their loyalty to the system. Since 1953, publishers and journalists have been permitted a wider range of discretion, and some have produced works they knew beforehand would not be welcomed by the regime. Errant writers are no longer likely to be expelled to Siberia or executed, although they are still often subjected to harsh criticism and are asked to revise their material.

Newspapers and Magazines

Newspapers and magazines are the chief printed media for the dissemination of information and propaganda in the Soviet Union. The printed word in the U.S.S.R. appears in nearly 70 different languages, 60 of them being in tongues spoken by Soviet nationalities. In 1959, no less than 10,463 newspapers were published, with a combined circulation of 59,300,000, or approximately one copy for every three Soviet citizens. Since Stalin's death, a calculated effort has been made to infuse greater liveliness and individuality into periodicals, but variety is still depressingly absent.

Of the more than 10,000 newspapers in Russia, less than 25 are national in character, and they account for more than one-third of the total circulation. Of these, the most important and well-known are *Pravda* (the official organ of the Central Committee of the Communist Party) and *Izvestia* (the official journal of the government). *Pravda's* circulation in 1957 was listed as 5,500,000, *Izvestia's* 1,550,000. The organ of the Young Communist League, *Komsomolskaya Pravda,* under the aggressive editorship of Alexei Adzhubei, Khrushchev's son-in-law, managed to outstrip *Izvestia's* circulation and hit nearly 2,000,000 in 1957. (Adzhubei has since become editor of *Izvestia.*)

Every Union Republic, national ethnic group, and all large cities publish their own local newspapers. The overwhelming number of Soviet journals are local publications, in-

TABLE 3-8 *Production and Number of Radio and TV Sets in the U.S.S.R., 1940–1959* [a] (In thousands)

Item	1928	1940	1945	1950	1955	1958	1960
In use							
Radios	70	1,123	475	1,767	6,097	9,500	10,000
Wired speakers	22	5,853	5,589	9,685	19,544	27,000	30,800
TV sets	—	0.4	0.2	15	823	3,000	4,800
Production							
Radios					3,530	3,900	4,165
TV sets					496	1,000	1,726

[a] Source: *Narodnoye Khozyaistvo . . . v 1960 Godu.*

cluding nearly 3,000 collective-farm newspapers. National, or all-Union, newspapers are essentially organs of various organizations: *Krasnaya Zvesda* is published by the Red Army, *Literaturnaya Gazeta* by the Union of Writers, *Trud* by the trade unions. *Pravda,* as we have seen, is the official organ of the Communist Party, *Izvestia* of the government. All Soviet newspapers must thus speak for some legally recognized group, since privately owned newspapers are prohibited. Dissident elements are thereby effectively deprived of any opportunity to employ the printed word. Needless to say, the policies of the state are never subject to attack except in the rare instance when the leadership is divided and various newspapers are controlled by contending factions. Once the struggle for power is resolved, total conformity is again imposed.

Russia is a land not only of newspapers, but of periodicals as well—political, scholarly, and popular. In 1958, Soviet sources reported the publication of 3,824 periodicals (total circulation: 637 million), of which about 800 were magazines, the others being bulletins, circulars, and throw-aways. Soviet magazines are published in nearly 60 languages, of which 41 are languages of Soviet nationalities. Like the newspapers, magazines in the Soviet Union are printed and published by recognized organizations and agencies.

Radio and Television

From the very inception of the Soviet regime, radio was envisaged as one of the most important instruments of indoctrination and propaganda. The Soviets zealously began to construct broadcasting facilities and to produce radios and distribute them to the people. They even devised a method to prevent the Soviet public from hearing foreign radio broadcasts, by creating elaborate systems of wired speakers in central meeting and assembly areas that could receive only official programs. As more people acquired their own sets, however, this system became increasingly inadequate. Today, the government relies largely on jamming unwanted foreign broadcasts, but this is an extremely costly and often ineffective device. Even as late as 1958, however, there were less than 10,000,000 receivers in the Soviet Union capable of independent reception, as opposed to nearly 31,000,000 wired speakers in 1960 (Table 3-8). In the same year, over 70 per cent of the receivers produced were wired speakers. Although the government continues to jam broadcasts made by the Voice of America and other overt propaganda programs beamed at the Soviet Union from abroad, Soviet citizens today are free to tune in on *foreign language* broadcasts that emanate from the outside. For the millions of Soviet citizens who understand English, French, German, and Spanish, listening to these foreign programs has become a favorite pastime.

Television is still in an infant stage of development in Russia. As of 1960, there were less than 5 million sets in use, with more than 67 television centers and 80 relay stations in operation. Television transmission is still limited to the large cities, but the government is planning a rapid expansion of television broadcasting, since not only does it offer greater political and educational possibilities than radio, but is less subject to outside intrusion, at least in the present state of electronic technology.

Ideological Foundations

IV

The Philosophy of Karl Marx

The official ideology of the Soviet Union is called Marxism-Leninism to distinguish it from other varieties and interpretations of Marxism. As a philosophical system, Marxism owes its origin not only to the great fund of accumulated Western philosophy, but more immediately to many of the currents and ideas that were prevalent in the nineteenth century. The century that produced Marx also produced Comte, Darwin, J. S. Mill, Spencer, and others, all of whom were preoccupied with the development of comprehensive theories about history and society. Marx and his followers imagined that just as Darwin had discovered the "laws" of evolution, Marx had discovered the "laws" governing the development of history and society.

Three ideological strands merged into Marxism: (1) German philosophical idealism, particularly that of Hegel, from whom Marx derived his dialectical method of history; (2) French revolutionary and utopian doctrines, to which Marxism owes its revolutionary militancy and its doctrine of a classless and stateless society; (3) British classical economic theory, especially that of Ricardo, from whom Marx appropriated his labor theory of value. As a comprehensive philosophy, Marxism purports to explain everything. It encompasses theories of human nature, society, history, economics, politics, ethics, esthetics, knowledge, and logic. It simultaneously seeks to explain the world (a theory of analysis or reality) and to change it in conformity with certain preconceived social norms (a normative theory or theory of utopia). Thus Marx boasted before he was thirty years old that "the philosophers have *interpreted* the world in various ways; the point however is to *change* it." [1]

The Dialectical Process

Dialectics is a process of discovering the truth (intellectual or factual) by revealing the contradictions in an opponent's argument or ideas, or in nature itself. Hegel's dialectic gave primacy to the inner conflict of ideas and their synthesis within the recurrent triadic formula of thesis (idea), anti-thesis (counter-idea), and synthesis (fusion of idea and counter-idea), which automatically becomes a

[1] Karl Marx, *Selected Works,* I (New York: International Publishers, n.d.), p. 473.

438

new thesis. For Hegel, the conflict of ideas shaped the development of the physical world, which was its reflection, and thus Hegel's system is sometimes called *dialectical idealism* to distinguish it from Marx's *dialectical materialism*. The chief characteristic of the dialectic is its dynamic quality, for the world is viewed as being in a state of constant transformation and motion, in contrast to the normal tendency to view reality as static or evolutionary. Thus Marx describes the dialectical process as "the science of the general laws of motion—both of the external world and of human thought." [2]

In contrast to Hegel's dialectic, whose movement was divinely inspired, Marx's dialectic is *naturalistic* in that change is inherent in reality itself and results from the energies released by internal contradictory forces, not from something external, like a prime mover or God.

The Marxist Theory of History

Marx appropriated Hegel's dialectic, but gave it a materialistic content. Claiming that he found Hegel's system standing on its head and restored it right side up, Marx asserted that instead of the earthly world being a reflection of the dialectical development of ideas in conflict and synthesis, the ideas were in fact a reflection of the dialectical process working itself out in the physical world. Marx at one time wrote:

My dialectical method is not only different from the Hegelian, but is its direct opposite. To Hegel, the life process of the human brain . . . is the demiurgos [creator] of the real world, and the real world is only the external, phenomenal form of "the Idea." With me, on the contrary, the ideal is nothing else than the material world reflected by the human mind, and translated into forms of thought. . . . With him it is standing on its head. It must be turned right side up again, if you would discover the rational kernel within the mystical shell. [3]

The application of Marx's dialectical method to the study of history and society is called *historical materialism*. For Marx, history moves neither in a straight line nor in a circle nor fortuitously, but rather moves upward through predetermined stages. By apprehending the laws of social development, it is possible, on the basis of the past and present, to predict several stages of development in the future.

Each succeeding stage of history is more progressive than the preceding one, and hence the special meaning of "progress" in Marxist-Soviet terminology must be understood in terms of movement along the historical dialectic. Thus a slave society is more progressive than primitive Communism, a feudal society superior to a slave-based economy, a capitalist society preferable to a feudal order but in turn inferior to a socialist society, which in turn is less progressive than a Communist society. Accordingly, each historical stage contains the seeds of its own destruction and constitutes the womb out of which its successor emerges. Each phase makes its contribution to civilization, a part of which is carried over from one stage to the next, thus giving an organic unity to the historical movement and to human civilization.

The Class Struggle

The fuel that powers the historical dialectic is manufactured by the class struggle. The two conflicting classes are those who own the land and the means of production and those who must work and operate them in order to live. Those without property are forced to deliver their labor in return for a bare subsistence living. According to Marx's "surplus labor" theory of value, all value is created by labor, which is expropriated by those who own the means of production, who pay out in wages just enough to keep the workers alive. This is the Marxist meaning of "exploitation of man by man." Thus an irreconcilable conflict between classes prevails which is resolved by revolution, only to reappear in new form. Capitalism, Marx wrote, is the last historical society in which exploitation of man by man

[2] Cited in Lenin, *Selected Works*, XI, p. 17.
[3] Karl Marx, *Capital* (New York: Modern Library, n.d.), p. 25.

Ideological Foundations

will exist. With the advent of the proletarian revolution, the expropriation of the capitalists, and the establishment of socialism, humanity will finally emancipate itself from exploitation and the class struggle. In the words of the *Communist Manifesto:*

The history of all hitherto existing society is the history of class struggles. Freeman and slave, patrician and plebeian, lord and serf, guildmaster and journeyman, in a word oppressor and oppressed stood in constant opposition to one another, carried on an uninterrupted, now hidden, now open fight, a fight that each time ended, either in a revolutionary reconstruction of society at large, or in the common ruin of the contending classes. . . . In our epoch . . . society as a whole is more and more splitting up into two great hostile camps, into two great classes directly facing each other—bourgeoisie and proletariat.[4]

Economic Determinism

The specific form of the class struggle is determined by the way in which society organizes the instruments and means of production. Thus, in the Marxist scheme, the given economic order constitutes the foundation of society and determines the character of the social, political, ethical, and legal "superstructure" which it supports. When the economic foundations change, the "superstructure" inevitably crumbles, to be re-established in conformity with the contours set by the new economic relations. At any given stage of history, those who own the instruments of production constitute a ruling and exploiting class, which seeks to preserve the given economic order from which it benefits.

But the economic foundations of society are fluid and cannot remain fixed, for, in accordance with the dialectical laws of contradiction, man, in his eternal search for more efficient instruments of production, renders the existing system increasingly obsolete and automatically subverts the prevailing order. Those who stand to gain most from the new methods of

production are inevitably shaped into a class hostile to those who benefit from the existing system. The class struggle is thus joined. The old class is overthrown; the new is enthroned, and the entire superstructure of society—social relations, political institutions, morals, etc., is then automatically adjusted to correspond with the new economic foundations of society. In a famous passage from Marx:

In the social production of their means of existence men enter into definite, necessary relations which are independent of their will, productive relationships which correspond to a definite state of development of their material productive forces. The aggregate of these productive relationships constitutes the economic structure of society, the real basis on which a juridical and political superstructure arises, and to which definite forms of social consciousness correspond. The mode of production of the material means of existence conditions the whole process of social, political and intellectual life. It is not the consciousness of men that determines their existence, but, on the contrary, it is their social existence that determines their consciousness. At a certain stage of their development the material productive forces of society come into contradiction with the existing productive relationships, or, what is but a legal expression for these, with the property relationships within which they had moved before. From forms of development of the productive forces these relationships are transformed into their fetters. Then an epoch of social revolution opens. With the change in the economic foundation the whole vast superstructure is more or less rapidly transformed.[5]

It must be understood that these changes in the fundamental economic structure of society, according to Marx, proceed irrespective of man's will or cognizance and can be determined with scientific accuracy.[6] They are inevitable, and movement from one stage of history to the next cannot be prevented, although man can intervene to speed up or delay the process, providing he has become aware of the dialectical laws governing the movement of history. Marx called his socialism "scientific," because the socialist society which he had been anticipating was destined to come inevitably,

[4] Marx, *Selected Works,* I, pp. 205–206.

[5] Emile Burns, *A Handbook of Marxism* (New York: Random House, 1935), pp. 371–372.
[6] See Friedrich Engels, *Socialism: Utopian and Scientific* (New York: International Publishers, n.d.).

not because of man's hopes, dreams, and wishes (as would be the case in utopian socialism).

The Proletarian Revolution

The most relevant aspect of Marxism for us here is, of course, the transition from capitalism to socialism and the processes by which this is accomplished. Under capitalism, according to Marx, society is divided into two great contending classes: the capitalists—owners of factories, business enterprises, financial institutions, and other means of production—who become constantly smaller in numbers as they grow wealthier, and the proletariat, which becomes more impoverished as it grows more numerous. With the increasing concentration of wealth into fewer hands and the increasing misery of the vast majority, the downtrodden proletariat becomes conscious of its historical mission, which is to overthrow the capitalist ruling class, not only in its own interests but in the interests of society as a whole:

Along with the constantly diminishing supply of the magnates of capital, who usurp and monopolise all advantages of this process of transformation, grows the mass of misery, oppression, slavery, degradation, exploitation; but with this too grows the revolt of the working class, a class always increasing in numbers, and disciplined, united, organized by the very mechanism of the process of capitalist production itself. The monopoly of capital becomes a fetter upon the mode of production, which has sprung up and flourished along with, and under it. Centralization of the means of production and socialization of labour at last reach a point where they become incompatible with their capitalist integument. This integument is burst asunder. The knell of capitalist property sounds. The expropriators are expropriated.[7]

The proletarian revolution was thus supposed to take place in an advanced industrialized society, in which "the lower strata of the middle class—the small tradespeople, shopkeepers, and retired tradesmen generally, the handicraftsmen and peasants—all these sink gradually into the proletariat . . . and . . . the proletariat is recruited from all classes of the population."[8] In contrast to "all previous historical movements [which] were movements of minorities, or in the interest of minorities . . . the proletarian movement is the self-conscious, independent movement of the immense majority, in the interest of the immense majority."[9]

The consequence of the revolution is the elevation of the proletariat as the ruling class and the establishment of a "dictatorship of the proletariat," whose primary purpose is to expropriate the capitalists in favor of the state and to suppress the overthrown bourgeoisie and eliminate it as a class, as a prelude to the elimination of classes, class struggles, and exploitation generally. Ultimately the state would "wither away."

The Theory of the State

"The State," wrote Lenin, "inevitably came into being at a definite stage in the development of society, when society had split into irreconcilable classes . . . ostensibly standing above society," but in fact protecting the interests of the property-owning classes. According to Marx:

The antique state was . . . the state of the slave-owners for the purpose of holding the slaves in check. The feudal state was the organ of the nobility for the oppression of the serfs and dependent farmers. The modern representative state is a tool of the capitalist exploiters of wage-labor.[10]

All states, therefore, are class states, i.e., they are instruments of the ruling economic class, whose interests they serve. The idea that the state is an impartial agent standing above society and classes as a referee or umpire is rejected as a myth inspired and perpetuated by the ruling class as part of the prevailing ideology. A society's legal system and courts, its philosophy, religion, education, morality, and even art all play their role in disguising the class nature of the state by rationalizing, justifying, and sanctifying the existing social order.

[9] *Ibid.*, p. 217.
[10] Lenin, *Selected Works*, XI, pp. 35–36.

Ideological Foundations

[7] Marx, *Capital*, pp. 836–837.
[8] Marx, *Selected Works*, I, p. 213.

The state, with its legal monopoly of the instruments of coercion (army, police, law, courts, etc.) preserves the *status quo*, by force if necessary.

Just as the bourgeoisie uses the state to preserve the capitalist system, the proletariat, when it gains power, will establish a proletarian state, whose purpose is to serve the working class. What we call Western democracy is termed "bourgeois democracy" by the Soviets, on the grounds that it constitutes democracy only for the ruling class, whereas it is, in fact, a dictatorship over the proletariat. Communists do not draw fundamental distinctions between states based on different institutions and processes, but rather define states only on the basis of their social and economic order. The "dictatorship of the proletariat" is, consequently, the bourgeois state turned upside down: democracy for the proletariat and dictatorship for the bourgeoisie.

Accordingly, ideas such as "freedom," "justice," "law," "morality," and "democracy" do not exist for the Marxists as absolutes, but rather have relativistic meanings, depending on the prevailing class structure of society. The pertinent question for the Marxist is this: freedom, justice, democracy, and morality for what class? Freedom for the slave-holder, for example, meant deprivation of freedom for the slave. With the emancipation of the slaves, the slave-holder lost his "freedom" and his "right" to own slaves. Thus, according to Marx, one social system's immorality may become the morality of the succeeding social order.

Lenin:
The Emergence of Voluntarism

The dialectical movement of history was asserted by Marx to be inevitable—that is, independent of man's will. It is this imperative of inevitability which imparts to Marxism its predictive or scientific quality. For if history indeed moves along a predetermined arc, knowledge of the "laws" governing this movement will enable men to predict the future. But to "predict" human history means also to "control" and manipulate history. It is precisely this manipulative quality of Marxism which was in direct conflict with the scientific theory of inevitability. The idea that events can be shaped and determined by the will of man is called voluntarism, which is considered by Marxists to be the diametric opposite of determinism. Voluntarism, however, is more than implicit in Marxism. If determinism was necessary to impart to the system its pseudo-scientific character, voluntarism was just as indispensable to guarantee that the scientifically predicted future would come about.

"Give me an organization of revolutionists," Lenin boasted, "and we shall overturn the whole of Russia." Later, he asserted that "politics cannot but have precedence over economics. To argue differently means forgetting the ABC of Marxism." [11] Under these conditions, Marxism was transformed from a "science" into a self-fulfilling prophesy in which men organize to achieve events which theory postulates to be inevitable!

Lenin's Theory
of Party Organization

Nothing illustrates better the influence of voluntarism than Lenin's theory of the Communist Party. By 1900, most of the socialist political parties inspired by the ideas of Karl Marx had abandoned active revolutionary objectives in favor of becoming parliamentary parties seeking to win control of the government at the ballot box or by some other legal means. In France, Germany, and elsewhere, powerful Socialist or Social Democratic Parties played a responsible role in the political life of the country and became reformist parties seeking to introduce socialism by reform and not revolution. The Marxist notions of a proletarian revolution to smash the "bourgeois bureaucratic state machine," and establish a "dictatorship of the proletariat" had been largely abandoned. Even the idea of the "class

[11] Lenin, *Selected Works*, IX, p. 54.

struggle" had been considerably de-emphasized in favor of political and parliamentary maneuvering.

The mellowing impact that parliamentary institutions had on Marxist parties in the West, however, was notably absent in Imperial Russia, where neither a parliament nor legal political parties existed before the Revolution of 1905. Thus a greater profusion of terroristic and conspiratorial political groups sprang up in nineteenth-century Russia than in the West. As we have already pointed out, the early Marxist organizations in Russia evolved out of the native Russian revolutionary-conspiratorial movements, and since political parties were illegal in Russia before 1906 and barely tolerated afterwards, it was virtually inevitable that Marxist movements in Russia would in some measure retain the kernel of their terroristic origins.

This was particularly true of the Bolshevik wing of the Russian Social Democratic Party, which emerged as a distinct organizational movement under Lenin's leadership after 1903. It was Lenin's view that a proletarian revolution was not likely to come about spontaneously, but rather through the calculated efforts of a professional and militant organization acting in behalf of the proletariat. The historical mission of the proletarian class was thus to be guided by a revolutionary elite, whose primary purpose was not to express the momentary whims of the masses, or to win votes at ballot boxes, or to engage in parliamentary maneuvering or debates, but rather to execute the pre-ordained mission of the proletariat by mobilizing the masses in a revolutionary assault against the capitalist ruling class. Lenin therefore placed great emphasis on leadership and discipline, on a militant spirit and on effective political organization.

Since the proletariat had a single purpose, the party could have only a single will; it could not be divided into factions and converted into a futile debating society. The minority view would always have to be subordinated to the will of the majority in accordance with what Lenin called the principle of "democratic centralism," which meant that the authority of the party would come to rest in its executive bodies. When Lenin first revealed his ideas on the party in 1903, Leon Trotsky (only 23 years old at the time) subjected it to scathing and prophetic criticism:

> The organization of the Party takes the place of the Party itself; the Central Committee takes the place of the organization; and finally the dictator takes the place of the Central Committee.[12]

Although its primary purpose was to maximize the effectiveness of revolutionary action, the principle of "democratic centralism" harbored the germ of what subsequently emerged as Soviet totalitarianism, because after the Revolution the principles of Bolshevik Party organization were extended to the whole of society.

Lenin's Theory of Revolution in Russia

Lenin was primarily interested in bringing about a proletarian revolution in Russia. But Russia was overwhelmingly backward culturally, and it had basically an agricultural economy and was feudal in its political organization and practices. Marx had predicted that the proletarian revolution would take place initially in advanced industrial societies like England and Germany.

Lenin, however, argued that since the revolution was inevitable, it was unnecessary to await the full maturation of capitalism. Rather than wait for the proletariat to grow and develop a class consciousness, which might take an intolerably long time, the party could act *for* the proletariat, and thus a proletarian revolution could take place as soon as any society embarked upon the road of capitalist development. This doctrine was little more than a disingenuous rationalization for a revolution in Russia, at a time when the country had just entered the phase of capitalism.

In order to compensate for the fact that the

---

[12] Cited in Bertram D. Wolfe, *Three Who Made A Revolution* (New York: Dial Press, 1948), p. 253.

Russian proletariat was no less a minority of the population than the bourgeoisie and to provide moral justification for a revolution executed on behalf of a minority class, Lenin contrived the formula of an "alliance" between the working class and the peasantry. The Communist Party could then carry out a revolution on behalf of the proletariat in alliance with the peasants. In this way, Lenin sought to impart the color of "democracy" to the Revolution. It was not his intention, however, that the peasants would share power with the proletariat or its party, for although a government of workers and peasants would be established, the party would retain a monopoly of power on behalf of the proletariat and would dictate the policies of the government.

Lenin's Theory of Imperialism

One of Lenin's most significant contributions to Marxist doctrine was his theory of imperialism, formulated just prior to the Revolution while he was in exile in Switzerland. While his short book, *Imperialism, the Highest Stage of Capitalism,* relies for most of its factual information on the work of the British liberal, Hobson, and much of the interpretation is taken from the works of the German Marxists, Rosa Luxembourg and Rudolf Hilferding, the synthesis he produced remains of utmost importance because not only did it provide Lenin with a further rationalization of the revolution in Russia, but it also served to explain why certain of the Marxist predictions about revolutions did not materialize in Western Europe. Lenin's *Imperialism* remains one of the basic documents upon which the Soviet perception of the world still rests, and it has become particularly relevant in understanding Soviet policies in the underdeveloped and ex-colonial countries of the world.

According to Lenin's *Imperialism,* Western capitalism had managed temporarily to delay its inevitable doom through revolution by the device of colonial imperialism. By establishing

overseas dependencies, the major capitalist powers of Europe were able to invest capital in the colonies and, in return, receive raw materials for processing which were then re-exported as manufactured goods. In this way, Lenin concluded, new outlets were found for surplus capital, old jobs were preserved for the workers and new ones created, and new markets were found for goods which could not profitably be absorbed in domestic markets.

The transformation of capitalism into imperialism, Lenin wrote, resulted in several important consequences. (1) The standard of living of the upper strata of the working class in the major capitalist countries was raised, thus blunting their class consciousness and diverting them away from revolution into trade unions and preoccupation with higher wages and better conditions of work. According to Lenin, these elements of the working class had become unwitting allies of the capitalists in exploiting the colonies and could no longer be relied upon to bring about a revolution. (2) The socialist revolution in the advanced countries was temporarily delayed, but new internal strains and stresses were introduced into the capitalist system, which was transformed from a national system in each individual country into an international system, involving the entire world, both backward and advanced areas. In Lenin's view, imperialism was the final, overripe stage of world capitalism, the phase in which all the devices contrived to prolong the existence of capitalism were exhausted, making it ready for revolutionary conflagration. (3) The internationalization of the capitalist system created entirely new revolutionary possibilities completely unforeseen by Marx and Engels. The class struggle, instead of now being the individual affair of each country, was internationalized, and the focus of revolutionary contradictions shifted away from the advanced industrial centers to their periphery in the colonial and semi-colonial societies, which were subjected to ruthless exploitation by international capitalism. (4) The division of the world into colonial empires of the various capitalist states not only internationalized the class struggle, but wars as well, which were transformed into world-wide conflicts as the capitalists fought over the division and redistribution of markets and colonies.

In accordance with this analysis, Lenin maintained that prior to the existence of imperialism, the class struggle and the impetus to revolution proceeded more or less independently in each country, depending on its economic development. Now, however, capitalism had become world-wide through the formation of international monopolies and cartels, and the advanced countries used their advantage to arrest the development of the less advanced regions of the world. The greatest possibilities of revolution were to be found, not in the industrial countries, but at the "weakest link" in the world capitalist chain, where the "front" of capitalism was exposed and the revolutionary ferment was most intense. Not the size of the proletariat, but its revolutionary consciousness and zeal would determine the location of proletarian revolutions.

Lenin believed that Russia was in 1917 this "weakest link" and that an uprising in Russia could plunge the entire world into a revolutionary convulsion. The "imperialist" war (World War I), he thought, could be transformed into a world-wide civil war in which the proletariat of Europe would join with the colonial populations against their imperialist rulers. The failure of the revolution to spread, however, soon produced a new crisis in the theory of Communism.

Stalin: The Hardening of Totalitarianism

Lenin died in 1924, and his successors were confronted with an uncertain future. Neither Marx nor Lenin had provided a precise blueprint for maintaining a revolution in isolation in a predominantly agricultural country. If Lenin converted Marxism into a revolutionary formula for seizing power in virtually any society with a vast dispossessed and discontented population, it was left to Joseph Stalin to further transform Marxism

into an instrument of industrialization and modernization of backward societies.

"Socialism in One Country"

The idea of building a socialist society in a backward country like Russia seemed to some of the Bolshevik intellectuals and leaders, particularly to Leon Trotsky, as both impossible and a deviation from Marxism. Stalin, however, was a man endowed with extraordinary talents for organization, administration, and political intrigue. He occupied the post of General Secretary of the party, which he quickly converted into a powerful and strategic springboard for seizing control of first the party apparatus, then the party itself, and then the state. Considered by most of his colleagues to be an intellect of mediocre calibre, Stalin possessed a sharp mind with a firm grasp of the situation. He understood power and men and possessed an exceptional ability to size up a situation immediately, reach quick decisions, and implement them with an implacable determination.

To silence his opponents, Stalin contrived the idea of "socialism in one country" and shrewdly ascribed the theory to the dead Lenin, whose loyal and faithful disciple he repeatedly claimed to be. The theory found a responsive echo not only among the Communist rank and file, but among ordinary citizens of the country as well. They preferred constructive promises linked with Russia's national security and national development to the anxieties and turmoil promised by the policy of "permanent revolution" advocated by Trotsky, in which Russia was to spearhead revolution in the name of Communist internationalism. The people of Russia were tired of war and revolution; they wanted peace and an opportunity to reconstruct their homes and country.

Stalin was determined to modernize and industrialize Soviet Russia, not only that it might become a powerful country in its own right, but also that it might serve more effectively as a base for expanding the Communist revolution. Socialism was to be developed through a series of five-year plans, which required singleness of purpose and concentrated effort for their successful fulfillment. Stalin's modernization program was based on three principles. (1) First priority went to the construction of heavy industry, which would not only enhance the military power of the state, but would also provide the basis for consumer-goods industries at a later stage. (2) Agriculture was to be collectivized and mechanized in order to destroy the capitalist system of private farming in the countryside, increase agricultural production, and permit the siphoning off of labor into the cities and factories. (3) A large reservoir of scientific personnel and skilled workers was to be created through a centrally planned and directed program of education. Once the state-owned heavy industrial base had been constructed and stabilized, the farms collectivized, and an appropriate level of educational and technological achievement had been reached, Soviet Russia would automatically enter an era of socialism.

Stalin's powerful resolve to impose his program of "socialism in one country" against all opposition, internal and external, profoundly affected the entire theoretical structure of Soviet Marxism, to say nothing of its concrete application. The Marxist-Leninist doctrines on the organization and functions of the party, the nature and role of the state in a socialist society, the destiny of the world revolution, and the delicate balance between Communist internationalism and Russian nationalism were all subjected to radical revision.

From Party Dictatorship to Personal Dictatorship

In 1903, Trotsky had predicted that Lenin's theory of party organization and leadership logically would culminate in the establishment

of a personal dictatorship. Under Stalin, this is, in fact, what actually happened. In his secret speech before the Twentieth Party Congress in 1956, Nikita Khrushchev finally conceded what had been widely known and acknowledged both outside and inside the U.S.S.R., that the Soviet Union under Stalin was governed by the most brutal and capricious form of personal dictatorship, masquerading as a "dictatorship of the proletariat" under the leadership of the party.

Before the party seized power in 1917, those guilty of violating the principle of "democratic centralism" (i.e., the minorities that refused to abide by the majority decisions) were told either to mend their ways or suffer expulsion from the party. Expulsion was not a fatal punishment, because the Bolshevik Party was just one revolutionary movement among many. After the party seized power and established a monopoly over all political activity and organization, however, expulsion brought profoundly different consequences. Since all rival parties were dissolved and declared illegal, the only opposition to the party line could come from within the party itself, and, as a result, various factional groupings, "oppositions," and deviations developed within the party against that of the majority view. As long as opposition was expressed *before* a decision had been taken on a particular question, it was considered by Lenin to be legitimate, but once a vote had been taken, the minority was duty-bound to subordinate its views to the majority. Infractions of "democratic centralism" ultimately resulted, as before the Revolution, in expulsion from the party, which in fact meant abstention from all political activity, since it was illegal to agitate or organize outside the party itself. The twin rules governing party organization—internal discipline and political monopoly—thus constituted the foundation of the complete autocracy of the party.

Stalin started out in the same way, but once he had solidly entrenched himself in power, he applied measures reserved by Lenin for the enemies of the system to his rivals *in* the party. His major theoretical contribution in this connection, if it can be so described, was the concept of the "enemy of the people," which meant that any person so designated was charged with counter-revolutionary and treasonable activities and then executed, imprisoned, or banished, with or without trial. Thus, according to Nikita Khrushchev's indictment of Stalin before the Twentieth Party Congress:

Stalin . . . practiced brutal violence, not only toward everything which opposed him, but also toward that which seemed, to his capricious and despotic character, contrary to his concepts. Stalin acted not through persuasion, explanation and patient co-operation with people, but by imposing his concepts and demanding absolute submission to his opinion. . . . Stalin originated the concept "enemy of the people." This term automatically rendered it unnecessary that the ideological errors of a man or men engaged in a controversy be proved; this term made possible the usage of the most cruel repression, violating all norms of revolutionary legality, against anyone who in any way disagreed with Stalin, against those who were suspected of hostile intent, against those who had bad reputations.[13]

It should be noted, however, that despite what developed in practice, Stalin never repudiated the principle of "collective leadership," but always maintained that he was simply the spokesman for the Central Committee or the Politburo of the party. Nor did he countenance the formulation of a theory of personal rule, although in practice and in ceremony, he both fostered and demanded sychophantic adulation, which, in the words of Khrushchev, transformed him "into a superman possessing supernatural characteristics akin to those of a god. Such a man supposedly knows everything, sees everything, thinks for everyone, can do anything, is infallible in his behavior." [14]

Stalin's Theory of the Soviet State

The 1936 proclamation of socialism in the U.S.S.R. required some fundamental revisions of the basic doctrine of the state. Since, theoretically, the class struggle and exploitation by the ruling classes had been eradicated, what was to be the function of the Soviet state? In 1930, at the Sixteenth Party Congress, Stalin boasted that the Soviet state was the mightiest in all history and that before it could "wither away," it had to become even more powerful. But the issue of a mighty leviathan in a socialist society continued to haunt the Communist Party. Stalin himself raised the problem at the Eighteenth Party Congress in 1939:

It is sometimes asked: We have abolished the exploiting classes; there are no longer any hostile classes in the country; there is nobody to suppress; hence there is no more need for the state; it must die away. . . . Now, the Marxist doctrine of the state says that there is to be no state under communism. Why then do we not help our socialist state die away? [15]

Stalin then proceeded to review the Marxist literature on the "withering away" of the state and concluded that classical Marxist doctrine is applicable when socialism has been established in a number of countries simultaneously, but it is not applicable when socialism is being built in just a single country. By 1950, in another major theoretical disquisition, Stalin finally concluded that the Soviet state represented the interests of society as a whole. Indeed, under Stalin major emphasis was put on strengthening the state. Thinly veiled threats warned Soviet intellectuals that exaggerated preoccupation with the "withering away" of the state might be construed as prima-facie evidence of treason. This view was grimly reiterated by Georgi Malenkov at the Nineteenth Party Congress (the last meeting attended by Stalin) when he asserted that "the enemies and vulgarizers of Marxism advocated the theory . . . of the weakening and withering away of the Soviet state."

[15] Stalin, *Leninism: Selected Writings*, pp. 468–469.

[13] Khrushchev's secret speech on "The Cult of Personality," full text reprinted in Bertram D. Wolfe, *Khrushchev and Stalin's Ghost* (New York: Praeger, 1957).
[14] *Ibid.*

Stalin and World Revolution

Stalin's doctrine of "socialism in one country" was not a repudiation of world revolution. As long as Soviet Russia was weak, Stalin believed, it could not actively promote world revolution. But if Russia were transformed into a strong industrial and military power, it could effectively support revolutionary movements elsewhere, with the assistance of the Red Army if necessary. To insure that Russia would be converted into a base for world revolution, the Communist International (Comintern) and Communist Parties in all countries were required to give first loyalty to the Soviet Union as the only fatherland of the world proletariat and were thus forced to submit to the complete discipline of Moscow. Those foreign Communists who resisted the centralization and domination of the Comintern by the Soviet Party were expelled, and gradually the Comintern was completely subjugated to the dictates of Stalin; foreign Communist Parties became willing instruments of Soviet policy, and acted as fifth columns by engaging in espionage and subversion.

Stalin proclaimed that the world revolution was impossible without the Soviet base and that consequently the interests of the world revolution were identical with the interests of the Soviet Union. Therefore, anything that strengthened the Soviet Union promoted the world revolution; anything that reacted adversely against Moscow retarded the world revolution. In this way, the interests of the Soviet Union as a state were irrevocably fused with the interests of promoting world revolution, and the interests of all Communists in the world were tied to the preservation of the Soviet nation state.

After World War II, when Communist Parties were installed in power in Eastern Europe, Stalin insisted that Communist leaders would have to continue to sacrifice the interests of their own countries to the greater glory and power of the Soviet Union, which remained the base of the world revolutionary movement. Marshal Tito of Yugoslavia rebelled against this view in 1948, advocating instead that individual Communist parties owed first loyalty to their own country; otherwise the Stalinist principle of "proletarian internationalism" would be nothing short of Soviet imperialism, with the most powerful Communist country exploiting the weaker and smaller ones. Communist leaders in the other satellite states of Eastern Europe who were suspected of harboring views similar to those of Marshal Tito were removed (many were imprisoned or executed, after the manner of Stalin's earlier victims), although they were leaders of foreign countries. Between 1948–52, a succession of bloody purges and execution swept the entire satellite world.

Stalinism and the Russian Heritage

Not only did Soviet totalitarianism reach its full flowering under Stalin, but the doctrine of "socialism in one country" also caused the traditional cultural and historical forces of Russia to blend with the new dynamics of Marxism. Marxism profoundly altered Russia, but itself was profoundly altered in turn. Marxism gave order to the primitive anarchical impulses of Russia, while Russian traditionalism succeeded in channeling Marxism into a unique secular religion, at once both terrifying and effective.

Many of the influences of the Russian tradition upon Marxism were inevitable. After all, socialism was not being built in a vacuum but in Russia—in historic Russia, with its cultural traditions, geography, and people. The language of Russia became the language of socialism and Communism, and the vanguard of the world proletariat was to become the Russian working class, with its own memories and responses. A backward country, Russia was to be transformed into the *first* country of socialism. In order to tap the spiritual and physical resources of the Russian people, Stalin, beginning in 1934, systematically resurrected Russia's past glories and grandeur, even to the point of retrospectively refurbishing her Tsars and territorial conquests with progressive intentions and consequences. In his characteristically ingenious way, Stalin saw in Russian nationalism the ultimate key to the success of his policies. With the support of the Russian people, his program might succeed; without that support, it was doomed. Russia's past was rewritten as a reflection of the Soviet present, and both Ivan the Terrible and Peter the Great were recreated in Stalin's image. In this way, Stalin was made into a legitimate extension of Russia's long history.

The revival of Russian nationalism reached its zenith during World War II, when the very survival of the Stalinist regime depended on the loyalty and patriotism of the Russians, which could be most effectively exploited by an appeal to Russian nationalism rather than by Marxist slogans. Virtually all the old Marxist clichés vanished, while Russia's past heroes and their military exploits were resurrected. Traditional ranks and titles were reinstituted in the Civil Service, diplomatic corps, and military and police forces, and gilt-edged shoulder-boards reappeared on Tsarist-type uniforms. Numerous medals were struck honoring the generals and admirals of Russia's past, and Stalin himself was appointed first a Marshal of the Soviet Union and then Generalissimo of the armed forces. The war itself was called the Second Great Patriotic War of the Soviet Union, the first being the national resistance against Napoleon in 1812. "The war you are waging is a war of liberation," Stalin urged four months after the German attack. "Let the manly images of our great ancestors—Alexander Nevsky, Dmitri Donskoi, Kuzma Minin, Dmitri Pozharsky, Alexander Suvorov, Mikhail Kutuzov—inspire you in this war!" [16]

Soviet Ideology since Stalin

The death of Stalin unleashed new ideological forces in the Soviet Union which cracked the shell of Stalinist dogma. Innovations in both internal and foreign policy took place almost immediately after his death, culminating in the denunciation, at the Twentieth Party Congress in 1956, of the old tyrant himself and of the personal dictatorship and terror which he established (called the "cult of personality" in Soviet jargon).

The Post-Stalin Party and State

The repudiation of the "cult of personality" and the so-called restoration of "collective leadership" required no modifications of doctrine, since Stalin had always presented himself as simply the "wisest of the wise" in the executive organs of the party and claimed that all his policies represented the decisions of the party and its Central Committee rather than his personal whim. Khrushchev's concept of leadership is closer to the Leninist concept of "collective leadership" than to "one-man rule." The dictatorship was continued, but in the form of an ever-rotating and expanding oligarchy rather than an absolute autocracy.

Two important Stalinist doctrines were renounced—the concept of the "enemy of the people" and the theory that the class-struggle became more intense as Soviet society moved closer to its ultimate objective of Communism. Both ideas were important props supporting the Stalinist terror. When the Molotov-Malenkov-Kaganovich faction in the Party Presidium failed to oust Khrushchev in June, 1957, the plotters were removed from the leading organs of the party, not as "enemies of the people," but as an "anti-party group." They were neither expelled completely from the party, nor imprisoned. All have since been given important, although demeaning (in view of their past eminence), positions in accordance with their specialties. And the members of the "anti-party group" were given the opportunity to propound their views before a special meeting of the Central Committee, which issued the order of expulsion.

At the Twenty-Second Party Congress,

[16] J. V. Stalin, *The Great Patriotic War of the Soviet Union* (New York: International Publishers, 1945), pp. 37–38.

Khrushchev introduced some new theoretical refinements concerning the nature and destiny of the Soviet state, which can be summarized as follows:

1. The dictatorship of the proletariat has fulfilled its historic mission and is now being gradually transformed into "a state of the entire people . . . expressing the interests and will of the people as a whole."
2. The dictatorship of the proletariat is withering away, but "the state as an organization of the entire people will survive until the complete victory of Communism."
3. The organs and institutions of the state will be gradually converted into "organs of public self-government" as it embarks upon the road to oblivion.
4. In the meantime, government officials will be systematically rotated out of office at every election and at all levels, so that leading officials as a rule will hold office for not more than three consecutive terms, unless they are unusually gifted.
5. The military power of the Soviet state will continue to be strengthened to fulfill "its international duty to guarantee . . . the reliable defense and security of the entire socialist camp."

Soviet Ideology and the External World

The most dramatic and immediate modifications were made in Stalinist views of the outside world; of greatest significance was the abandonment of the Stalinist dogmas of "capitalist encirclement" and of the "inevitability of wars" and of his view that the world is divided into two camps, poised in military readiness for the inevitable armageddon that would decide the issue of Communism versus capitalism with finality.

The doctrine of "capitalist encirclement" was one of the foundations of the Stalinist terror, since the danger of "capitalist attack" justified the brutal and ruthless dictatorship. Although the expansion of Soviet power into Eastern Europe after World War II and the Communist victory in China created a buffer against "capitalist encirclement," Stalin refused to alter his position and, instead, extended the terror to the entire Communist orbit. To abandon the idea of "capitalist encirclement" would deprive the Soviet dictatorship of its principal theoretical justification.

Closely related to the idea of "capitalist encirclement" was the Leninist-Stalinist doctrine that wars are inevitable as long as capitalism and imperialism continue to flourish. Stalin insisted on this dogma even when nuclear weapons introduced a factor unforeseen by Marx or Lenin. As far as Stalin was concerned, nuclear technology was simply another stage in the development of weapons and could not in any way alter the course of historical development, whose direction was irrevocably determined by scientific and objective laws discovered by Marx and Engels.

Wars, according to Stalin, were neither the result of accident nor of human will, but were rooted in the capitalist system itself. They would end only with the elimination of capitalism. Speaking soon after the end of World War II, on February 9, 1946, Stalin reaffirmed this doctrine and provided the theoretical basis of the "cold war," which was to dominate the affairs of the postwar world.

It would be wrong to think that the Second World War was a casual occurrence or the result of mistakes of any particular statesmen, though mistakes undoubtedly were made. Actually, the war was the inevitable result of the development of world economic and political forces on the basis of monopoly capitalism. . . . The fact is, that the unevenness of development of capitalist countries usually leads in time to violent disturbances of equilibrium in the world system of capitalism, that a group of capitalist countries which considers itself worse provided than others with raw materials and markets usually attempts to alter the situation and repartition the "spheres of influence" in their favor by armed force. The result is a splitting of the capitalist world into two hostile camps and war between them.[17]

Stalin's postwar policy was thus predicated on an inevitable conflict with the West, which was clearly going to be led by the United States. At the founding convention of the Cominform in 1947, Stalin's associate on

[17] J. V. Stalin and V. M. Molotov, *The Soviet Union in World Peace* (New York: New Century Publishers, 1946, pp. 5–6.

the Politburo, Andrei Zhdanov, provided the authoritative Soviet interpretation on the emerging bipolarization of world power and its consequences:

The fundamental changes caused by the war on the international scene and in the position of individual countries have entirely changed the political landscape of the world. A new alignment of political forces has arisen. The more the war recedes into the past, the more distinct become two major trends in postwar international policy, corresponding to the division of the political forces operating on the international arena into two major camps; the imperialist and anti-democratic camp, on the one hand, and the anti-imperialist and democratic camp, on the other. The principal driving force of the imperialist camp is the U.S.A. . . . The cardinal purpose of the imperialist camp is to strengthen imperialism, to hatch a new imperialist war, to combat Socialism.[18]

Both the doctrines of "capitalist encirclement" and the "inevitability of wars" were repudiated at the Twentieth Party Congress. "The period when the Soviet Union was . . . encircled by hostile capitalism now belongs to the past," [19] a reluctant Molotov was forced to say at the Congress, and in March, 1958, Khrushchev added a new twist to the entire encirclement concept:

At the present it is not known who encircles whom. The socialist countries cannot be considered as some kind of island in a rough capitalist sea. A billion people are living in the socialist countries, out of a total of 2.5 billion. . . . Thus, one cannot speak any more about capitalist encirclement in its former aspect.[20]

The Stalinist "two-camp" image was replaced by a "three-camp" image. A third "anti-imperialist" group of powers, which had been released from the decaying colonial empires but had not joined the Communist cause, was recognized by Khrushchev at the Twentieth Party Congress. Stalin's inflexible two-camp image needlessly threatened to alienate these new states and force them back into the bosom of capitalism.

The Soviet leaders hoped to woo the underdeveloped world first into the Soviet diplomatic orbit and then eventually into the Communist ideological camp. Anticipating that the demands of the emerging nations for rapid modernization and industrialization would conflict with the interests of the capitalist powers, the Soviet leaders expect that the hostile or apathetic reaction on the part of the West will drive the poorer countries into their arms. Castro's Cuba is considered to be the prototype of this kind of process. According to the Soviet view, Cuba has moved from being dependent on the United States through a non-capitalist, non-Communist stage, and is now being forced toward the Communist orbit because of the hostility of the United States.

The new Soviet leaders have scrapped Stalin's bellicose policy in favor of a formula of "peaceful coexistence" between capitalism and Communism, which calls for non-violent forms of competition between the two forces until Communism wins its inevitable victory. Wars are still considered to be possible, because of the instability of the capitalist system and the chance that war might be triggered accidentally, but they are not thought to be inevitable. Russia still intends to remain strong militarily, and her leaders believe that the development of their rocket and nuclear technology and the psychological impact of their space achievements have given them an irreversible advantage in the cold war. In Khrushchev's view, the capitalist countries will not resort to war, not because they have become more humanitarian, but because they realize that the Soviet Union is capable of laying waste the entire American landscape. Soviet leaders think that victory for them is only a matter of time; as Khrushchev succinctly has stated:

The situation in the world has fundamentally changed. Capitalist encirclement of our country no longer exists. There are two world social systems: capitalism which is coming to the end of its

---

[18] Strategy and Tactics of World Communism (Washington, D.C.: Government Printing Office, 1948), pp. 216–217.

[19] Moscow Radio, February 20, 1956.

[20] Interview with Serge Groussard in Le Figaro, March 19, 1958.

days, and socialism in the full flood of its growing forces, on whose side are the sympathies of the working people of all countries. Just as any other socialist country, the Soviet power is not guaranteed from possible aggression on the part of the imperialist states. However, the correlation of forces in the world is at present such that we will be able to rebuff any attack by any enemy. The danger of the restoration of capitalism in the Soviet Union has been excluded. This means that socialism has triumphed, triumphed fully and finally. Thus, it can be considered that the problem of building socialism in one country, of its complete and final victory, has been solved by the world-historic progress of social development. The victory of socialism in the U.S.S.R. and the creation of a world socialist system are incalculably strengthening the forces of the international workers movement and opening up new prospects for it. "The issue of struggle," Lenin said, "depends in the final analysis on the fact that Russia, India, China, and so forth form an immense majority of the population," and it is precisely this majority of the population which has been drawn at an exceptionally rapid pace in the past few years into the struggle for its liberation, so that in this respect no shadow of doubt can remain as to the final outcome of the world struggle. In this respect the final victory of socialism is fully and unconditionally insured.[21]

The ultimate objective of Soviet policy remains the attainment of world Communism, by peaceful means or violent, by fair methods or foul, although the current Soviet view is that it can be achieved non-violently. Khrushchev's formula of "peaceful coexistence" is simply another strategy for burying the Western world as painlessly as possible.

[21] *Pravda,* January 28, 1959.

The Soviet Social Order

V

In the Soviet Union, private owner-ship of the land, of the means of production, and of distribution has been abolished in favor of total and permanent public ownership. Ownership is permanently vested in an insti-tution, the state, or in an abstraction, "society." The state, however, is the executive and ad-ministrative arm of the Communist Party, which allegedly represents the social will of the working class and is the source of all policy formulation. Control of the party assures con-trol of the state, and through it control of the land, the economy, the coercive instruments of society (the armed forces, police, courts, and legal system), the means of transportation and distribution, and the media of communication. No matter who controls the party, *ownership* of the means of production is never an object of the struggle for power, for it remains perma-nently vested in the state.

According to Article 1 of the Soviet Consti-tution, "the Union of Soviet Socialist Re-publics is a socialist state of workers and peas-ants," which is defined in Article 12 as a society in which "work . . . is a duty and a matter of honor for every able-bodied citizen," and which is organized in accordance with two principles: "He who does not work, neither shall he eat," and "From each accord-ing to his ability, to each according to his *work*." According to official dogma, the Soviet Union has been a socialist society since 1936 and is now well advanced on the road to Com-munism, in which distinctions between "workers" and "peasants" will cease to exist and society will be governed by the principle of Communism: "From each according to his ability, to each according to his *needs*."

Contrary to a widespread misconception, the Soviet Union does not claim to be an egalitarian society; social differentiation exists, and definite and often rigid hierarchical lines divide one social group from another. Soviet society is not defined as a *classless* society, but is officially described as a society in which *class conflict* and exploitation of man by man have been eliminated. Two classes are recognized, the workers and peasants, and they are sup-posed to work together in harmony and peace; the intelligentsia, which is not mentioned in the Constitution and is not officially desig-nated as a class, is a part of the upper social layer of the working class. The intelligentsia, however, constitutes the social and political elite of Soviet society and from its ranks spring those who struggle for control of the party, the state, and the economy. Although the state is a "dictatorship of the proletariat," it is defined constitutionally as a "socialist state of workers and peasants," which, according to Article 2, "grew and became strong as a result of the overthrow of the power of the landlords and capitalists."

The Soviet state is a "proletarian democracy" organized as a "dictatorship of the proletariat," whose primary function is to express the interests of the working class, which is the dominant class in Soviet society, just as all "bourgeois democracies" are essentially "dictatorships of the bourgeoisie" over the proletariat. The initial function of the Soviet "dictatorship of the proletariat" was to establish proletarian control over the former ruling bourgeois class in order to eradicate it as a class and pave the way for a classless society in which the state would ultimately "wither away." This becomes possible only when the proletariat seizes power and nationalizes all means of production. Article 4 of the Soviet Constitution states:

The economic foundation of the U.S.S.R. is the socialist system of economy and the socialist ownership of the instruments and means of production, firmly established as a result of the liquidation of the capitalist system of economy, the abolition of private ownership of the instruments and means of production, and the elimination of exploitation of man by man.

Article 6 further specifies that:

The land, its mineral wealth, waters, forests, mills, factories, mines, soil, water and air transport, banks, communications, large state-organized agricultural enterprises (state farms, machine and tractor stations, and the like), as well as municipal enterprises and the bulk of the dwelling-houses in the cities and industrial localities are state property, that is, belong to the whole people.

Aside from state-owned property, the Soviet Constitution recognizes cooperative and collective-farm property as a form of socialist ownership, since it is collectively exploited by groups. All land, however, belongs to the state and is only leased to cooperative and collective groups "in perpetuity." Private property exists only in two forms: (1) individual peasants' and artisans' establishments in which production is based on the owner's own labor (hiring others for personal gain is constitutionally defined as "exploitation" and is severely punished as one of the most serious crimes against society) and (2) personal property, including individual homes, articles of personal and household use, and savings.

The current organization of Soviet society, however, is as much an outgrowth of the social realities of Russia at the time of the Revolution as it is of the social theories of Marx and Lenin. "Socialism" in Russia is the society that emerged as a result of Stalin's industrial and agricultural transformation of a backward rural nation within the span of a single generation. Its characteristics are as unmistakably Russian as they are Marxist.

The Social Transformation of Russia

Before the Revolution, Russia was a semi-feudal society with rigidly distinct class divisions. At the top was a small stratum composed of the landed gentry, court nobility, upper clergy, and the Imperial Family, which together owned most of the arable lands of the country and controlled the state. At the bottom was a large land-hungry, superstitious, illiterate, and sullen peasant population, only recently emancipated from serfdom, whose ugly moods periodically threatened to disrupt the social order. Sandwiched between the top and bottom was a small middle class, made up of merchants, civil servants, professional people, intellectuals, and students, who, however, did not constitute a true bourgeoisie in the Marxist sense (capitalists who owned the means of production), because most of the industrial and financial enterprises in Russia were owned by foreign capitalists. Alongside the small middle class was a slightly larger working-class population, recently uprooted from the countryside, alienated from society, and living in incredible squalor in Moscow, St. Petersburg, Baku, and the Donetz Basin.

In 1913, more than 78 per cent of the population was made up of peasants, divided between those with no land or small plots (about 66.7 per cent of the population) and rich peasants or kulaks (about 11.3 per cent). Of the 367 million hectares of agricultural land owned before the Revolution (within the pre-1939 borders of the U.S.S.R.), the poor and moderately well-off peasants possessed altogether only 135 million hectares, while the great landlords, the Imperial Family, and the Orthodox Church, amounting to only 3 per cent of the population, owned 152 million hectares (1 hectare = 2.471 acres). The rich peasants owned the remaining 80 million hectares. Thirty per cent of the peasants possessed no land whatsoever, while another 34 per cent owned no agricultural implements or livestock. The middle class accounted for about 6 per cent of the population, while the urban workers amounted to about 13 per cent of the total.

"War Communism" and the NEP

The original intention of the Bolshevik regime was to establish a Communist society by an executive fiat nationalizing all the land, natural resources, financial institutions, and factories of the country, thus expropriating the land-owning and capitalist classes. All class distinctions were abolished, as were the official ranks in the government and the armed forces. Workers and peasants were instructed to seize the factories and lands on behalf of the state and were ordered to establish direct control over production and distribution. During this initial period of "War Communism," equality was the rule: equality of social status and equality of income, irrespective of the quality and quantity of work performed.

Under these conditions, the economy of the country was reduced to a shambles as the workers proved incompetent to manage factories and other enterprises. They embarked upon a "Roman holiday," voting themselves unrealistic increases in wages and absurdly numerous holidays. The economy in the cities came to a virtual halt; workers threatened riots when the customary pay day arrived and the payroll did not materialize. Famine once again stalked the streets of the urban areas as the peasants refused to accept the worthless printing-press money of the state and demanded manufactured goods of comparable value, which were being turned out in increasingly diminished quantities.

Lenin called a halt to "War Communism" in 1921, and introduced the so-called New Economic Policy, or NEP, which authorized the temporary revival of small-scale capitalist enterprises. Small factories and retail establishments, privately operated and based on incentives, quickly sprang up and flourished in the cities. Equally desperate was Lenin's decision to abolish state-imposed prices for agricultural goods in order to spur agricultural production. The peasants were required to deliver a certain amount of grain to the state, but they then could sell whatever they produced in excess of this amount on the open market at whatever price they could exact. This program resulted not only in reviving the economy, but also in the re-emergence of a small entrepreneurial class, the Nepmen, in the cities, and a powerful, and numerically significant rich-peasant or kulak class in the countryside.

The NEP was introduced as a purely temporary measure and was not intended to be permanent. The state retained the "commanding heights" of the economy, from which it subsequently descended upon the hapless Nepmen and kulaks. Banks, large industrial and economic enterprises, communications media and transportation systems, foreign trade, natural resources, and the ownership of land remained in the hands of the state. This guaranteed that the state would at all times be complete master of the situation. But it was becoming increasingly clear that either the NEP would have to become a permanent characteristic of the Soviet system or it would have to be abandoned in favor of socialism. After the death of Lenin, a "great debate" ensued among his successors as to Soviet Russia's future course, and this issue became an integral part of a complicated struggle for power.

Stalin emerged as the new Soviet leader, outmaneuvered his opposition, and, by 1927, felt sufficiently confident to press for an ambitious Five Year Plan designed to erect a heavy industrial foundation for Russia's economy and to mechanize and collectivize agriculture—in short, to bring about a cultural and technical revolution in the U.S.S.R. The scope of his plan, particularly with respect to the peasants, brought him into direct conflict with the more conservative members of the party, who wanted to proceed cautiously in the countryside, even at the expense of delaying industrialization. Stalin had the majority, however, and administrative measures were initiated against the kulaks, who were withholding grain from the market, threatening the cities with famine. Originally, the Five Year Plan called for the collectivization of only 20 per cent of the country's agriculture, but Stalin changed his mind once the program was under way and decided to destroy all the kulaks.

The "Revolution from Above" (1928–1933)

The over-all objective of the Five Year Plan that came into effect in 1928 soon became nothing less than a "second revolution," whose goal was to completely transform Russia from a backward agrarian country into an industrialized and modern socialist society. Stalin had to achieve eight objectives if his ambitious project were to succeed: (1) the elimination of the residual capitalist classes, in particular the kulaks; (2) the collectivization of agriculture; (3) the creation of a large army of industrial workers out of raw, untutored peasants; (4) the creation of a heavy industrial base; (5) the creation of a corps of cultural and technical specialists out of the working class who would be capable of coping with the demands of an industrialized society; (6) the rapid mechanization of agriculture to make up for the reduced rural labor supply necessitated by the industrialization program; (7) the cultural and educational transformation of Russian society; (8) the preservation of his own power at all costs.

Stalin realized this period would not see a rise in the standard of living, for it was to be a period of sacrifice, with the possibility that food, shelter, and clothing would be reduced to a bare subsistence level. The magnitude of Stalin's ambitions was matched only by the forces that almost overwhelmed him: (1) the hostility of the capitalist world, which hopefully expected him to fail; (2) the opposition of the peasants, particularly the kulaks, to collectivization; (3) the opposition of his rivals within the party; (4) the shortage of foreign exchange which was required to purchase necessary machinery and to hire foreign technicians and specialists and which could be earned only by selling agricultural commodities on the world market, thus further reducing the home supply; (5) the fundamental inertia of a backward, illiterate, superstitious, and overwhelmingly agricultural population.

Stalin's plan succeeded, but at a tremendous cost. Millions died through starvation, exposure, deportation, and execution so that Russia might be industrialized. Since most of those who suffered were peasants, the modernization of Russia was accomplished largely at the expense of the peasant population, which still remains the most exploited and downtrodden of Soviet Russia's social classes.

The estimates of the number of people who died during the farm-collectivization program range from 3,000,000 to 15,000,000, and Russia's total population deficit for this period is set at about 20,000,000. The catastrophe was further intensified by a drought which blighted the land during the height of the collectivization drive and by the world economic crisis which depressed the world market price for grain. The memories of this era are indelibly etched in the minds and psychology of the Soviet population in both town and country, while the physical scars are still evident in lagging production statistics, the depressed living conditions of the peasantry, the decimated livestock population, and the sullen and passive resistance of the collective farmer.

By 1934, the kulaks had been destroyed and 90 per cent of the peasants transformed from a class of individual farmers into a collectivized group held in bondage by the state. The transformation was later described as a "second revolution" or a "revolution from above," because it was stimulated by the government against the people rather than generated from below against the regime. It was indeed the second great bloody surgical amputation of a class from the social body, following the expropriation of the bourgeoisie. With the collectivization of agriculture and the liquidation of the kulaks, the residual manifestations of private ownership over the means of production had been eliminated. Stalin could thus report in 1935:

> The landlord class . . . the capitalist class . . . the kulak class . . . and the merchants and profiteers . . . have ceased to exist. Thus all the exploiting classes have now been eliminated. There remains the working class . . . the peasant class . . . the intelligentsia.[1]

The "second revolution" introduced a new dynamic quality into what had been essentially a static society. By 1937, the working class was nearly double that of 1928, while the intelligentsia was nearly quadrupled during the same period. The number of the peasantry was reduced by about 20 per cent.

The Stratification of Soviet Society

Officially, there are only two classes in present-day Soviet society, the working class and the collective farm peasantry. The intelli-

gentsia is not called a "class" but a "stratum" and is considered the upper layer of the working class. Yet it is this "stratum" which is the most significant social group in Russia today and is itself divided into a number of substrata or elites. The relative numerical size and political influence of these three social groups have been in a state of flux since 1928 and are continually changing.

Since the Revolution, the industrialization of Russia has increased the size and the skills of the working class, and the cultural and educational advances have expanded the intelligentsia and enabled them to become the social and political elites (Table 5-1). In the process, the number of peasants has been drastically reduced by nearly one-half.

Rural Society: The Farms

According to the 1959 census, 52 per cent (108,848,955) of the Soviet population is still rural in character, although only 31.4 per cent (65,500,000) consists of collective farmers and their families and 0.3 per cent (600,000) of individual farmers and artisans. The remaining 20 per cent (42,800,000) that makes up the rural population represents the category "workers and employees" and their families, which includes workers on the state-owned farms and other state-owned agricultural institutions and members of the rural intelligentsia and their families.

The two main rural institutions of Soviet society, then, are the *kolkhoz* or collective farm and the *sovkhoz* or state-owned farm. The collective farm, or kolkhoz, is considered by Communists to be a relatively low form of socialist organization in contrast to the more ideal commune and sovkhoz, which the regime originally supported as the more suitable forms for a socialist society.

THE KOLKHOZ. The dominant type of collective farm, the kolkhoz, is neither a genuine cooperative nor a state-owned enterprise. It can

[1] Stalin, *Leninism: Selected Writings*, p. 382.

TABLE 5-1 *Changing Social Structure in the U.S.S.R., 1913–1960* [a] (In percentages)

Class	1913	1928	1937	1939	1955	1959	1959 numerical totals
Nobility, upper-class bourgeoisie, clergy, military officers, etc.	3.0	0	0	0	0	0	(zero)
Kulaks	11.3	4.6	0	0	0	0	(zero)
Middle class and intelligentsia	6.0	0	0	0	0	0	(zero)
		4.0	14.0	17.5	58.3	22.8	47,600,000
Workers	13.0	13.6	22.2	32.2		45.5 [b]	95,100,000
Collective farmers	0	2.9	57.9	47.9	41.2	31.4	65,500,000
Individual peasants and artisans	66.7	74.9	5.9	2.6	0.5	0.3	600,000

* Sources: *Narodnoye Khozyaistvo . . . v 1959 Godu; Vestnik Statistiki*, No. 12, 1960, pp. 3–21.
[b] Includes several million Sovkhoz workers and other "rural working-class" elements.

be best described as a cooperative that has been established and is supervised and controlled by the state. Most of the agricultural land is pooled together, but the peasant is entitled to retain his own house and a small garden plot, upon which he can grow vegetables and fruits to sell in the open market. The peasant is also authorized to keep small flocks of fowl and a private cow. Under no circumstances can the peasant hire anyone but members of his own immediate family to work in this private garden. The existence of these private gardens and the time which peasants spend on them have been a source of continuing anxiety and concern to the regime and have even been responsible for heated ideological controversies in the highest councils of the state and party. The chief worry is that it keeps alive feelings of private ownership and capitalist psychology which the regime would like to eradicate.

The kolkhoz is supposed to be governed by its members, who meet in a general assembly that is theoretically empowered to elect an executive committee and a chairman or director to manage the farm. The general meeting, according to the kolkhoz charter, sup- posedly confirms the farm's production plan, admits or expels members, and establishes the general regulations governing finance and ad- ministration. Actually, the director is "elected" after he is appointed by party and state offi- cials. Soon after the replacement of Malenkov as Premier in 1955, some 30,000 new collec- tive-farm chairmen were appointed in ac- cordance with a directive from Moscow, and all were duly "elected" by their respective collective farms. The executive committee is normally selected or confirmed by local party and state officials.

The "voluntary" character of the collective farm and the theoretical control of the general meeting by the peasants are easily refuted by an examination not only of how the system works in practice but also of the freedom allowed to it by law. The first legal restriction is that the land is owned by the state. In re- turn for its use, the farms, before 1957, were forced to deliver a certain quota of their output to the state, at prices fixed by the state that were well below the price at which the state resold the commodities on the market. Forced deliveries were abolished in 1957, and the state has warned the farms that they no longer can be assured an automatic market; the state now purchases only what it needs at competitive prices. As long as agricultural commodities are in short supply, however, it is unlikely that collective farms will remain without buyers, and the farms have been receiving higher prices than before.

Before 1958, there was a second restriction on the initiative of the farms, in the form of state-owned Machine and Tractor Stations (MTS), which "rented" their heavy agricultural machinery to the farms under "contract" in return for payment in kind. Thus, the state owned not only the land but the principal means of production as well. The power to withhold an MTS contract gave the state an effective instrument of control over the farms, since the state had to be satisfied with a farm's work norms, plan schedules, programs of forced deliveries, and use of scientific techniques before it would grant the farm a contract. The MTS were abolished in 1958 and their equipment sold to the collective farms, but the farms must now first pay installments to the state for the machinery and meet all other financial obligations to the state for loans, technical assistance, and new types of seed before they can distribute the "profit" of the farm among its members.

The peasant receives payment in cash and kind for his services on the farm, in accordance with the number of "labor-day" units he has accumulated during the year. The "labor day" is an arbitrarily fixed production norm established by law and is based on a complicated formula involving both quantity and quality of work performed. All income is computed in terms of "labor days," which need not correspond to the actual labor performed during a work day, but it does provide a basic unit which can be readily divided and multiplied and applied to various types of rural labor. In 1948, nine different labor-day norms were established, the lowest being rated at one-half a "labor day" for a whole day of actual work for the least skilled work performed on the farm and the highest being set at 2.5 "labor days," or five times that of the lowest.

Since the peasant can make more by intensively working his own tiny garden plot, sometimes illegally expanded by various ingenious devices, the state in 1939 made it compulsory for the peasant to meet his "norm," or suffer criminal and financial penalties, and to accumulate a minimum number of "labor-day" credits during the year or face exile to Siberia. The criminal penalties were abolished in 1956, but not the financial ones. Even with financial penalties, some peasants still find it more profitable to work their own plots, where they can grow whatever they wish to fulfill consumer demand and sell it on the open market for high prices. The peasant lovingly cultivates his own plot, and what he produces is often of much higher quality than that produced by the farm, where he grudgingly reports for work. In some categories of agricultural production, the tiny plots altogether produce more than the collective farms themselves—for instance, they account for 67 per cent of the potatoes produced, 87 per cent of the eggs, 57 per cent of the milk, and 55 per cent of the meat!

The peasant's income is thus made up of the cash and produce he receives as his share of the profits on the farm plus what he raises, for his own consumption or sale, on his garden plot. His income is still pitifully small, and his wife and older children must usually work in order to make ends meet. The highest-paid individual on the farm is normally the director, who receives a certain number of "labor-day" units to begin with, based on his experience and on the size and type of farm he manages. Like the factory manager, he can earn bonuses and other financial rewards for exceeding production norms. The rural intelligentsia, "stakhanovites" (workers who habitually exceed their norms by substantial amounts), and other skilled workers are also relatively well paid.

THE SOVKHOZ. The state farm is described as the highest form of socialist agriculture in Soviet society and is the regime's favored form of agricultural organization, but the peasants hate and fear it even more than they do the collective farm. Whereas the average collective farm embraces about 5,000 acres, the average sovkhoz runs to about 15,000 acres (Table 5-2). The tendency is for the collective farms to become larger and the sovkhozes to diminish in size, so that eventually distinctions in size will be rendered irrelevant. The sovkhoz is managed by a director, who is appointed by the Minister of Agriculture, and his status is comparable to that of a large factory manager and is usually more important than that of the kolkhoz director. He is also likely to have more experience and formal education than the kolkhoz director. Workers are hired directly by the state and receive wages. They are not described as peasants in the official literature but are listed among "workers and employees." Several farms may be grouped together in a larger administrative unit, the trust.

TABLE 5-2 *Kolkhozes, Sovkhozes, and MTS, 1928–1960* [a]

	1928	1940	1953	1957	1959	1960
Kolkhozes	33,300	236,900	93,300	78,200	54,600	44,900
Sovkhozes	1,407	4,159	4,857	5,905	6,496	7,375
MTS	6	7,069	8,985	7,903	34	23

[a] Source: *Narodnoye Khozyaistvo . . v 1959 Godu.*

Many of the sovkhozes are located in remote areas, and most of the new lands brought under cultivation, e.g., the "virgin lands," are organized into state farms. Like the collective farm, the sovkhoz is a self-contained rural community with its own recreation centers, schools, medical clinics, laboratories, agricultural machinery, animals, and implements. Many sovkhozes specialize in certain crops and often are centers of agricultural experimentation, with their own scientific and technical personnel.

Rural Social Stratification

Five distinct social strata flourish in Soviet rural society; about 60 per cent of the rural population are ordinary peasants, and the remaining 40 per cent consist of the rural intelligentsia, rural foremen, rural "working class," and farmers on the sovkhozes.

THE DIRECTORS. The rural social pyramid has at its apex the directors of the collective farms and the sovkhozes, who are invariably not native to the locality in which they serve. The director, whether of the kolkhoz or the sovkhoz, represents the interests of the party and the state, to which he is beholden for his position, his salary and bonuses for superior production records, and his professional and political future. His primary goal is thus to satisfy the demands of the party and the state and not the peasants, who often become mere instruments of production. The director usually cultivates the popularity of the peasants and caters to their interests only if it will enhance production and is conducive to efficient management. As an agent of the regime, the director is responsible for seeing that the state receives its proper share of farm produce, that the property of the state is safe from pilferage, and that an indoctrination program is given the peasants (in cooperation with the local party organization) to insure that they faithfully execute all the state and party directives.

The director is often the most powerful administrative and political personage in the rural locality, not excluding the local party secretary and the chairman of the local soviet, with whom he shares local political power. The latter two individuals have powerful inspection and auditing powers, and they are also responsible for the formal transmission of party and state directives, but they are not invested with managerial or administrative authority over the farms. The director himself is frequently the most powerful political individual in a local district by virtue of his long experience and membership in the party. In 1960, more than 95 per cent of the directors were party members. The director, party secretary, and soviet chairman often constitute a local "troika" or directorate, and the three together virtually pre-empt all political power in the rural locality.

Increasingly, directors are graduates of agricultural institutes, but they are typically of rural origin rather than from the cities. More than 55 per cent of the directors in 1960 had a higher or specialized secondary education, while more than 56 per cent had more than three years' experience as farm managers. The fact that nearly 45 per cent of the directors in 1960 had less than three years' experience is testimony to the rapid turnover in this important position.

In 1959, the number of kolkhoz chairmen and their deputies was given as 102,800, but by April, 1960, in conformity with the planned amalgamation of collective farms, the number had been reduced to 71,829, of which 46,169 were listed as directors and 23,785 as deputy directors. As the collective farms are increased in size, the complexities of management and the importance of political reliability increase. The amalgamation process, which has been under way since 1950, does much to explain the higher percentages of technically qualified and politically motivated collective-farm directors. Since the number of sovkhozes in 1960 was given as 7,375, the number of sovkhoz directors and their deputies must number between 15,000 and 18,000, for some of the larger state farms have more than a single deputy director.

THE PEASANTS. The ordinary peasantry itself is divided into three groups, the first being those who work on the sovkhozes (about 4,000,000), most of whom possess some specialization. The second group consists of about one million collective farmers who also pursue some type of specialization in crop production, while the third group is made up of some 24,000,000 muzhiks without any type of specialization, who constitute the overwhelming bulk of the collective farmers and rest at the bottom of the rural social structure, and indeed at the bottom of the Soviet social and economic order as a whole. The sovkhoz farmers enjoy the highest status of the three. Their cash income is much higher than that of the kolkhoznik, although on some of the rich collective farms, the collective farmers may be better off.

The Soviet peasantry in its entirety, numbering over 70,000,000 people (including families) on both collective and state farms, still rivals the working class as the largest single social class in Soviet society. Although the peasant works longer and harder than his urban counterpart, he receives less than any other class in terms of education, medical care, sanitation, transportation and communication facilities, consumer goods, recreational facilities, and other ordinary amenities of Soviet life. In terms of real income, even Soviet data reported in 1956 that the income of the Soviet peasant "in cash and kind" was only three times that of the peasant before 1913, which was described as "extremely low." This indicates that millions of peasants today earn little more than the subsistance amount represented by the current legal Soviet minimum wage of 27–35 rubles (30–38 dollars) per month.

As a political force, the peasantry has little direct influence. Unlike the workers and various sections of the intelligentsia, who not only have their trade unions and various guild and professional organizations, the only legal rural organization permitted is the collective farm, and thus the Soviet peasantry is deprived even of the Soviet version of a "pressure group." His only recourse is to malinger, refuse to meet his quotas, spend more time on his own little garden plot, and in general "to drag his feet," all of which he has been doing very well. The situation had become so serious by mid-1962 that the regime ordered an extraordinary increase in the price of butter and meat. This increase, which represented a 25–30 per cent rise, offered the collective farms higher prices for their commodities as a spur to greater production.

In the meantime, social mobility on the farm has become sluggish. With the end of the era of rapid industrialization, economic and social opportunities have seriously decreased. Peasant youth are no longer encouraged to migrate to the cities; in fact, urban dwellers are urged to move back to the farm. Since educational opportunities for the children of collective farmers are less than those for workers and the intelligentsia, the peasantry is entering a period of social stagnation.

Opportunities for direct movement from the peasantry to the intelligentsia within a single generation are few. The ranks of the intelligentsia are being filled increasingly from within itself and from the workers. Since mobility from peasant status to that of worker is itself becoming more difficult, direct movement from the peasantry to the intelligentsia is virtually impossible. Although the seven-year school was recently made compulsory for all rural areas, in the cities the ten-year school is the rule, with ample opportunities for attendance at institutions of higher learning or specialized secondary schools. Table 5-3 literally speaks for itself.

TABLE 5-3   *Urban-Rural Educational Levels, 1939–1959* [a]   (In millions of people)

Educational level	1959 total	1959		Percentage rural		Per 1,000 1959		Per 1,000 1939	
		urban	rural	1959	1939	urban	rural	urban	rural
Complete higher	3,778	3,170	608	16%	20%	32	5.6	16	1.7
Incomplete higher	1,738	1,332	406	23					
Specialized secondary	7,870	5,446	2,424	31	30	344	188	162	37
Complete secondary	9,936	7,426	2,510	25					
Incomplete secondary	35,386	20,254	15,132	45					

[a] Source: *Narodnoye Khozyaistvo . . . v 1959 Godu.*

The Workers

According to the census of 1959, the social category "workers and employees," together with their families, accounted for nearly 143,000,000 people, or more than 68 per cent of the Soviet population. This represented an increase of 16 per cent over 1939. The 1959 census reported a total of 99,000,000 people actually employed (about 42.7 per cent of the population), with more than 81 per cent of all employed people being engaged in "productive" work and 14.6 per cent involved in services and other non-productive labor. Of the total employed, 78,635,000 (79.3 per cent) were engaged in physical labor, while 20,495,000 (20.7 per cent) were engaged in "mental work." Women accounted for 48 per cent of all those employed and 54 per cent of those engaged in intellectual labor. In the Soviet Union, virtually the entire adult population of the country is gainfully employed, with 54 per cent of all males and 41.5 per cent of all females actively working.

The size of the Soviet "working class" can be established only by statistical distillation. Of the 78,635,000 reported in the category of "physical labor," some 33,893,000 are classified as engaged in agricultural labor, leaving a total of nearly 44,742,000 non-agricultural "physical workers," including members of the armed forces. A tabulation of the non-agricultural workers by industry and occupation adds up to a total of 43,053,400. To this 43,053,400 base figure for the Soviet working class proper, we can add the 2,576,000 tractor and combine operators and other rural mechanical and repair personnel and raise the total to about 45.5 million.

A close scrutiny of the category of "mental workers" reveals a large number of lower-level "white-collar" and "blue-collar" workers, whose economic and social status is more comparable to that of the working class. This heterogeneous aggregation of foremen, teachers, librarians, rank-and-file government and other clerical workers, accountants, bookkeepers, auditing and accounting personnel, draftsmen, non-professional technicians, etc., amounts to about 10,500,000 people.

The largest single component of the working class is found in industry, which numbers approximately 20,000,000 workers, whereas industry, construction, transportation, and communications together account for more than 33,000,000 workers (Table 5-4). The various service workers and those without designated occupations, numbering about 10,000,000 people in all, round out the urban working-class proper. Of this number, some 15,000,000 are described as possessing special qualifications and skills; about 20,000,000 people appear to have semi-skilled occupations, while the remainder, amounting to about 8,000,000 workers, are unskilled or have skills of a very low order.

The Soviet working class has grown rapidly with the industrialization of the country. The number of workers and employees in 1928 was 10.8 million, which was more than doubled to 22.8 million by 1932 and had reached 27.8 million in 1938. With the territorial annexations of 1940, it was increased to 31.5 million, dropping to 19.3 million in 1943 during the height of the war, and rising again to 28.3 million in 1945. By 1960, "workers and employees" numbered 57 million and are scheduled to total 66.5 million in 1965.

TRADE UNIONS AND MANAGEMENT. The Soviet working class is organized into trade unions, but unlike workers' organizations in most other countries, Soviet trade unions are not autonomous organizations representing the economic, social, and often political interests of the workers, but mass organizations under the complete control and supervision of the state and party. During the early days of the regime, the trade unions made an attempt to survive as independent agencies representing the economic and social interests of the workers. This view was condemned by Lenin, who felt that spontaneous and independent trade unionism diverted the working class from its historic mission, and he thus maintained that unions should be controlled by the party. Under Stalin, the leaders of the trade unions tried to use them as an instrument in the struggle for power, and they were destroyed. The labor organizations were reduced to pliable instruments of the regime, devoid of any separate existence of their own.

Membership in Soviet trade unions is "voluntary" and currently exceeds 50,000,000, but the advantages of membership are so obvious that it is virtually universal. Actually, some of the so-called social and economic rights guaranteed to the Soviet citizen by the Constitution can only be exercised by joining a trade union. Union members receive twice the sickness and disability benefits paid to other workers, they can apply for special loans and grants from union funds, and their likelihood of spending a vacation at one of the various sanatoria and health resorts on the Crimean or Caucasian shores of the Black Sea is also greater. Trade unions also maintain an elaborate network of cultural, educational, and recreational facilities, in the factories and elsewhere. Soviet labor organizations thus cannot have a role in political life outside the framework of the Communist Party.

Workers do not strike in the Soviet Union, not because they "own" the factories as Khrushchev and other Soviet leaders fatuously maintain, but because they would suffer

The Soviet Social Order

TABLE 5-4 *Distribution of Soviet Workers by Industry and Occupations, 1959* [a]

Occupation	1939	1959	Percentage increase
Total non-agricultural physical workers		44,742,000	
(military "physical workers")		(1,689,000)	
Industry and Construction		24,772,500	
Power plants, etc.	585,500	1,721,000	294%
Miners	589,000	1,187,100	203
Metal and metallurgical	4,358,500	9,304,000	213
Machine operators		1,551,000	
Metal fitters		3,202,000	
Tool and die workers		239,000	
Tool and punch-press operators		131,000	
Assemblers		1,290,000	
Mechanics		594,000	
Chemicals	209,500	395,000	188
Minerals (extraction, etc.)	240,000	538,500	224
Lumber	808,600	751,000	93
Woodworking and furniture	989,900	1,406,800	142
Machine operators	90,700	189,500	209
Framers	20,100	150,800	751
Carpenters, cabinet makers	488,700	778,400	159
Paper	22,100	36,500	166
Printing	163,100	212,000	130
Textiles	1,059,800	1,130,100	107
Spinners	115,500	127,900	111
Weavers	213,700	251,900	118
Knitters	90,200	86,500	96
Clothing	728,300	1,302,300	179
Machinists, machine operators	72,300	249,800	346
Tailors, sewers	483,800	840,200	174
Cutters	19,300	76,100	394
Leather	196,200	145,200	74
Footwear	510,900	372,200	73
Food	692,800	815,400	118
Fishing	185,400	127,600	69
Construction	2,478,700	5,094,200	206
Excavator operators	9,000	124,000	1,400
Machinists and operators	1,700	116,500	7,000
Unskilled workers	321,800	180,300	56
Masons	176,100	723,500	411
Carpenters	1,273,500	2,092,000	164
Plasterers	147,400	518,900	352
Painters	176,200	430,000	244

violent repression. Strikes are not technically illegal, but the penalties for "sabotage" and "counter-revolutionary activity" are very severe, and strikes called without the approval of party or trade-union authorities would be so designated. Workers are relatively free to pick their own jobs, unlike in the grim days of

the Stalin era when many workers were prevented from leaving their places of work or were assigned to new jobs and locations for trivial infractions such as absenteeism and being late for work.

The paramount objective of the plant union leader is identical to that of the plant director and the factory party secretary. This factory "troika" encourages the workers to fulfill or exceed production goals established by the regime, so the workers and the "troika" can collect bonuses and enhance their professional

TABLE 5-4 *Distribution of Soviet Workers* (continued)

Occupation	1939	1959	Percentage increase
Transportation			
Rail transport	939,000	1,664,100	177
Machinists, steam and diesel locomotives, etc.	164,500	314,600	191
Machinists, electro-locomotive	8,100	78,400	974
Water transport	160,300	244,300	152
Auto and municipal transport	800,900	3,395,100	424
Chauffeurs and operators	725,000	3,174,200	438
Other transport	2,714,800	2,721,900	100
Postal workers	181,200	242,900	134
Restaurants, etc.	577,800	783,600	136
Cooks	354,400	522,500	147
Waiters	185,300	183,800	99
Communal, custodial, janitorial	4,556,200	5,024,900	110
Sanitary and hospital orderlies	428,700	894,900	209
Store workers	722,500	904,700	125
No designated occupations	1,047,000	2,462,100	235
Unaccounted for (probably military)		1,688,000	

Summary, The Soviet Working Class by Sectors

Physical workers (urban)	43,053,000
Rural working class	2,576,000
White- and blue-collar "mental" workers [b]	10,500,000
Total	56,129,000

[a] Source: *Vestnik Statistiki*, No. 12, 1960.
[b] The white- and blue-collar workers were calculated on the following basis. The Soviet data give a total of 20,495,000 as "mental" workers in both town and country and in the military. Of these, 8,000,000 are further identified as specialists with higher or specialized secondary education (not including the military). Assuming that about 1,000,000 mental workers without higher education have important positions, this allows a residue of 10,500,000 white- and blue-collar workers in both town and country.

careers. The unions also engage in a sham "collective bargaining" and actually sign a "contract" with the director covering working conditions, individual grievance procedures, and the general administration of a specific plant or enterprise. Under no circumstances are the workers allowed to complain against the established economic or labor policies of the government, but they may "expose" corruption, collusion, inefficiency, and negligence on the part of management if they feel sufficiently courageous. Since Stalin's death, workers have more often exercised their right to complain about work norms, pay, promotions, etc.

The administration of the factory is the sole responsibility of the director, and although his performance is watched and checked by both the plant party secretary and the trade-union leader, they cannot interfere with his direction unless they wish to make formal charges of mismanagement. The three normally work cooperatively with one another and are not ordinarily in professional competition with

The Soviet Social Order

each other. The plant director is normally a technically trained specialist (usually an engineer); this is not the usual background of the party and union official.

Although the worker has a formal "pressure group" in the form of a union, he is shorn of any independent political leverage. But because of his close proximity to the centers of power and his access to party membership, he has an opportunity to exert individual pressure through his union, local party organization, local soviet, or simply by writing a letter to the newspapers. As a social group, the working class enjoys far greater representation in the party than does the peasant, and the opportunities for working-class children to move upward socially via higher education are definitely superior to those of the peasant.

INCOME AND WAGES. In industry, the quality and number of skills have gradually expanded through on-the-job training and special vocational schools, which continue to train millions of new workers every year. The more skilled, talented, and educated the worker, the greater is his reward. The ideal citizen of the future in the Soviet vision is the worker-engineer who works with both hands and brain.

Like others in Soviet society, workers are paid according to the skill and amount of their work. Each skill has its basic pay scale, based on production norms established by the regime, with extra pay for fulfillment and overfulfillment of the quotas. The minimum wage established by law in 1957 is 35 rubles per month. About 8 million workers were making less than 35 rubles per month in late 1956, and the 1957 law raised their pay to the new minimum. A range of 50–70 rubles per month plus incentive bonuses appears to be the norm of the urban worker. While income distribution is a guarded state secret, one scholar has devised a breakdown based on projected tax decreases per income group by

1965. According to J. A. Newth, income distribution in the Soviet Union, as of 1960, approximates the following: [2]

Income per month (current rubles) [a]	Number
under 50	unknown
50– 60	13,000,000
60– 70	8,000,000
70– 80	9,000,000
80– 90	8–9,000,000
90–100	6,000,000
100–120	7,000,000
120–140	4,000,000
140–160	2,000,000
160–200	under 2,000,000

[a] Official rate of exchange: 1 ruble = $1.11.

Pay scales vary from industry to industry, depending not only on the skill and performance of the workers, but also on whether the regime wishes to spur production in a particular sector of the economy. In recent years, the pay-scale ratio between the highest- and lowest-paid workers has been reduced from 1 to 4 to less than 1 to 3. All workers, from the lowest ranks to the managers, engineers, technicians, office personnel, and foremen, can earn extra amounts over their base pay. An individual can receive a bonus, if he meets or surpasses his production quota, and all the workers in a particular plant get a bonus when the plant exceeds its over-all quota. No individual may receive more than 150 per cent of his basic salary from bonus payments. Managers receive bonuses for more efficient management, for reducing production costs, for using new methods of work, and for various other kinds of improvements.

THE SOVIET STANDARD OF LIVING. The worker's standard of living is still appreciably higher than that of the peasant and lower than that of the intelligentsia. In Soviet society, the spread between the few who receive the highest income (about 2,000 rubles per month) and those who receive the lowest (about 27 rubles per month) is very wide

[2] J. A. Newth, "Income Distribution in the U.S.S.R.," *Soviet Studies*, October, 1960.

(Table 5-5). The mean Soviet income seems to be around 85 rubles per month for all classes. The maximum Soviet annual income, which is about $26,400, from which about $3,000 are deducted in taxes, allows the *highest* members of the Soviet elite to live at a level only comparable to that of the American or Western European upper middle class. This income is very modest compared to that for top American executives, and there are no Soviet citizens whose income or standard of living even approaches that of the big executive or successful performing artist in America.

A definite ceiling is established on the Soviet standard of living, irrespective of income, for it is limited by the quantity, quality, and diversity of goods, services, and housing that are available, all of which are controlled by the Soviet government. Housing, for example, is quite cheap, but it is in desperately short supply and accommodations are apt to be very dreary.

The average urban family would consider itself fortunate if it had two small rooms to itself and shared a kitchen and bath with one or more other families, but the norm is a single room of about 240 square feet per family. In many crowded metropolitan areas, the apartments would be considered slums or substandard housing in the United States and Western Europe. Sometimes, two or even three families may each have a corner of one large room, divided by sheets strung across ropes.

Housing is assigned usually in accordance with the individual's status in the economy and social hierarchy. Needless to say, the intelligentsia monopolizes the most decent housing in the cities, but even this is quite modest. Even the best-paid members of Soviet society rarely have apartments exceeding four or five rooms. Yuri Gagarin, the first Soviet astronaut, for example, was moved from an old two-room apartment to a new four-room dwelling after his venture into space. The Soviet worker spends about 50 to 70 per cent of his income for food, while the peasant spends virtually none. Food prices for ordinary staples are cheap, but the staples are not always available.

TABLE 5-5 *Monthly Incomes of Representative Occupations in Soviet Society* [a]

Occupation	Rubles [b]
Intelligentsia	
Top party and state leaders	–2000
Scientist (academician)	800–1500
Minister or department head	700
Opera star	500–2000
Professor (science)	600–1000
Professor (medicine)	400– 600
Docent (assistant professor)	300– 500
Plant manager	300–1000
Engineer	100– 300
Physician, chief	95– 180
Physician, staff	85– 100
Teacher (high school)	85– 100
Teacher (primary school)	60– 90
Technician	80– 200
Bookkeeper	110– 115
Working Class	
Office clerk	80– 90
Skilled worker	100– 250
Semi-skilled worker	60– 90
Unskilled worker (cleaning woman, cook)	35– 50
Peasant	27– 50

[a] Source: *Monthly Labor Review*, April, 1960.
[b] In "hard rubles" introduced in 1961. Official rate of exchange is 1 ruble = $1.11.

The intelligentsia can afford more and better food, not only at home, but in restaurants, where prices are very high.

The Soviet Intelligentsia

The Soviet intelligentsia consists of remnants of the pre-revolutionary intelligentsia and their children and the children of parents of working-class and peasant origin. Fewer and fewer members of the intelligentsia are being drawn from the third category. The tendency of the individual members of the intelligentsia to transmit their status to their children is closely watched by the regime, and energetic measures are periodically taken to prevent the establishment of a self-perpetuating privileged stratum.

The Soviet concept of the intelligentsia embraces not only members of the arts, sciences, and professions, but engineers, lawyers, technicians of various kinds, government officials, doctors, journalists, and university students. The intelligentsia are all considered to be "mental workers," and the group includes a wide spectrum of "white-collar" employees.

After the Revolution, the intelligentsia was to be made to serve the new ruling class—the proletariat. Virtually all "non-political" technical and specialist posts were filled with members of the old intelligentsia, pending the creation of a new corps of technicians and specialists from the proletariat. The government bureaucracy, the Army, and educational and medical establishments continued to rely on the old intelligentsia for their operations. As the new Soviet intelligentsia grew in numbers, the remnants of the old were gradually retired, purged, or isolated in innocuous enterprises. Surprisingly, however, the suspicions of the working class, the peasantry, and the regime against the intelligentsia did not abate completely, and the existence of a privileged stratum in a society that cherishes the cult of equality continues to nag the system.

Both Lenin and Stalin repeatedly stressed the altered character of the intelligentsia in Soviet society, but these protestations were constantly negated by the regime itself, which periodically purged, castigated, and cajoled the intelligentsia. Thus, in 1935, Stalin asserted that:

> The intelligentsia . . . is no longer the old hidebound intelligentsia which tried to place itself above classes, but which actually, for the most part, served the landlords and the capitalists. Our Soviet intelligentsia is an entirely new intelligentsia, bound up by its very roots with the working class and the peasantry. In the first place, the composition of the intelligentsia has changed. People who come from the aristocracy and bourgeoisie constitute but a small percentage of our Soviet intelligentsia; 80 or 90 percent of the Soviet intelligentsia are people who have come from the working class, from the peasantry, or from other strata of the working population. Fi-

nally, the very nature of the activities of the intelligentsia has changed. Formerly it had to serve the wealthy classes, for it had no alternative. Today it must serve the people, for there are no longer any exploiting classes. And that is precisely why it is now an equal member of Soviet society, in which, side by side with the workers and peasants . . . it is engaged in building the new, classless, socialist society.[3]

In spite of this sanguine and premature tribute to the loyalty of the Soviet intelligentsia, Stalin, during the purges which immediately followed, decimated the ranks of the intelligentsia,. particularly those of the older generation.

In the past twenty years, the Soviet intelligentsia has steadily increased in size and prestige. Since 1939, it has more than doubled in number from 9,600,000 to 20,500,000, with the greatest increments being registered in the lower ranks (Table 5-6). It occupies a powerful position in the Soviet economy. Virtually all economic and political power is concentrated in this group. Those who control the party and state are automatically part of the intelligentsia. All the managerial, technical, and scientific skills are concentrated in the intelligentsia, for, by definition, any person who possesses these skills is a member of the intelligentsia. The intelligentsia plans production, establishes national goals and purposes, allocates rewards, and makes, executes, and enforces the law.

If the intelligentsia were in permanent control of the economy and other institutions of society and could transmit this control from one generation to the next, it would meet all the formal requirements for being a "ruling class," but it does not have this power. Its individual members have no legal right to their social status, nor can they hope to keep it through material wealth; to belong to the intelligentsia, one must actively perform certain specialized functions and demonstrate ideological conformity.

WOMEN IN THE INTELLIGENTSIA. Women make up 54 per cent (11,055,000) of the "mental workers," while they account for 59

[3] Stalin, *Leninism: Selected Writings*, pp. 475–476.

TABLE 5-6   *Soviet "Mental Workers" (Intelligentsia), 1939–1959* [a]

	1939	1959
Totals	9,600,000	20,495,000
Executives in state administration, public organizations, and their departments	445,000	392,100
Executives of enterprises and their departments	757,000	955,000
Collective-farm chairmen and their deputies	(278,800)[b]	(102,800)
Engineering and technical personnel	1,656,500	4,205,900
Engineers (excluding executives)	(247,300)	(834,300)
Designers and draftsmen	(103,900)	(297,100)
Foremen	(267,000)	(753,500)
Technicians	(274,000)	(513,000)
Laboratory assistants	(156,500)	(436,200)
Agronomists, zootechnicians, vets, foresters	294,900	477,200
Scientists and educators in higher education	111,600	316,400
Heads of educational institutions	(73,100)	(114,900)
Other teachers, educators, scientific workers	1,368,400	2,403,700
Senior physicians and medical executives	46,500	44,000
Physicians	122,300	337,900
Dentists	14,000	31,700
Interns, midwives, nurses	332,400	1,058,200
Planning, auditing, accounting personnel	3,102,000	3,501,900
Economists, planners, statisticians	(282,100)	(308,300)
Accountants, bookkeepers	(1,785,400)	(1,816,900)
Cashiers, clerks	(279,300)	(413,500)
Inspection and audit personnel	(755,200)	(963,200)
Literature and publishing	58,000	104,100
Cultural workers	285,000	462,000
Librarians	(87,000)	(239,000)
Arts	143,300	190,600
Lawyers, judges, prosecutors	82,600	101,700
Communications personnel	265,400	476,400
Trade, restaurants, etc.	1,626,000	2,268,220
Directors, etc.	(244,900)	(334,800)
Secretarial personnel	489,400	535,900
Public and social services personnel	202,500	277,100
Agents and expediters	176,400	146,000
Unaccounted for (probably includes military, etc.)		1,875,000

[a] Source: *Vestnik Statistiki*, No. 12, 1960.
[b] Figures in parentheses are included in the total of the general category.

per cent (4,798,615) of all "specialists in the national economy" with higher or specialized secondary education. Within the intelligentsia itself, women are overwhelmingly represented in some sectors, only sparsely in others. Among state, party, and economic executives, the number of women is very small, while in areas like teaching, medicine, and in the offices of economic planning bodies, they dominate. But when these categories are more closely scrutinized, we find that whereas 70 per cent of the teachers are women, only 22 per cent of the school principals are women; although 36 per cent of the scientific workers are of the female sex, women account for only 7 per cent of the professors (but 51 per cent of their assistants).

Although women account for 75 per cent of the physicians and 92 per cent of all medical specialists, most of the important administrative positions in medical establishments are occupied by the few men in the field.

Thus, while individual women can aspire to any social level in Soviet society, from membership in the Party Presidium or a government Ministry to the lowest cleaning occupations, the more significant the political or power implications of the position, the nar-

The Soviet Social Order

rower their opportunities. As in most societies, women have virtually no access to the main instruments of coercion in Soviet society, the armed forces and the secret police.

NATIONALITY COMPOSITION OF THE INTELLI-GENTSIA. Although the Russians account for 55 per cent of the total population of the U.S.S.R., they make up more than 62 per cent of the intelligentsia. Of the other nationalities, only the Georgians and Armenians reflect a higher ratio in the composition of the intelligentsia than their share of the population. The other nationalities, in varying degrees, are underrepresented, the most extreme cases being in Central Asia. Tremendous progress, however, has been registered in creating a national intelligentsia for each nationality, as is shown in Table 5-7.

Social Mobility in the Soviet Union

Every society develops its own special avenues to higher rewards and status, although as the society "matures" and the opportunities for its evolution and differentiation within the existing socio-political framework are narrowed, these roads tend to be blocked by law, custom, and advantages of birth. During the early years of the Soviet regime, when it was struggling for survival and political loyalty and ideological conformity were at a premium, virtually the only channel for social movement upwards was through active political activity and ideological conformity. Access to positions of responsibility and to higher education and training was through the party or its preparatory institutions. Once it was realized that political loyalty and ideological conformity were insufficient to insure the technical competence or professional knowledge necessary for the economic and cultural transformation of society, political and ideological tests were

TABLE 5-7 *Distribution of the Soviet Intelligentsia by Major Nationalities, 1959* [a]

Nationality	Number
Great Russians	5,014,000
Ukrainians	1,219,200
Byelorussians	235,000
Georgians	145,800
Armenians	121,000
Tatars	120,000
Azerbaidzhani	89,600
Uzbeks	86,100
Kazakhs	68,700
Lithuanians	66,000
Latvians	57,800
Estonians	45,200
Chuvash	33,800
Moldavians	28,500
Tadzhiks	22,000
Turkmen	17,900
Mordvins	17,800
Kirgiz	17,000
Daghestani	16,400
Ossetians	16,100
Bashkirs	14,900
Komi	14,500
Udmurts	12,600
Total	8,017,000

a Does not include members of the armed forces. Includes only those with higher or specialized secondary education working in the national economy.

de-emphasized for positions which were relatively non-political in character, but required special ability, knowledge, and skill. It was only demanded that the individual not be actively hostile to the regime. Naturally the rarer the skill and the knowledge and the fewer the individuals with special aptitudes, the greater the immunity from political and ideological tests.

Political Conformity and Professional Competence

In due time, two separate but parallel avenues of social advancement were established: those of political loyalty and technical competence. When the two are combined, success is virtually assured in the Soviet system. Competence alone, however, is sufficient to assure high status and rewards, but not the highest; loyalty alone is rarely sufficient, since, by itself, it is always in plentiful supply. However, whether one embarks on the ideological-political or technical-professional road to success, higher education is the common vestibule through which all must first pass. Access to higher education, and the rewards it promises, is thus fundamental, since mobility upwards in Soviet society is almost impossible without it.

The best possibilities of social mobility are still through politics, but the risks are correspondingly higher. The more remote one is from politics, the more secure his status. For this reason, many people eschew "political" careers entirely, immersing themselves in the sciences and mathematics, the study of foreign languages, ancient history, literature, and a host of other fields widely divorced from political reality. High social rewards in Soviet society are thus possible in certain technical and specialized areas, even without membership in the Communist Party. Large numbers of outstanding scientists, professors, and artists deliberately remain outside the Communist Party and consciously avoid involvement in politics, relying only upon their abilities and talents to achieve success.

Even within the sciences and professions and arts, however, there is the "political" scientist, professor, or artist, who may have achieved some distinction in his field, but is not of outstanding caliber and propels his movement upward by joining the party and accepting the inherent risks and corresponding opportunities. Administrative and supervisory positions in bodies like the Academy of Sciences are likely to be bestowed upon the savant who chooses to become involved in party activities, rather than the most eminent personalities in the given field of endeavor.

If loyalty and competence are the two primary personal factors involved in social mobility, there are a number of peripheral or secondary considerations which can affect social mobility adversely or advantageously. They are: social origins, nationality, and sex.

SOCIAL ORIGINS. Social origin plays a crucial role in relation to accessibility to higher education and one's advancement after its attainment. During the early years of the regime, social origin played an important negative role, with definite preferences being shown toward those of working-class and peasant parentage. Today, having a kulak, priest, merchant, or even a nobleman as an ancestor is no longer a social crime, although it is slightly more respectable to be of working-class, peasant, or "toiling intelligentsia" background.

Social origin, once again, is assuming an important influence on the contours of social mobility. All things being equal, the children of members of the intelligentsia will have greater opportunities for remaining in the privileged stratum or advancing upward within it than children of working-class and peasant parents. As Soviet society becomes more routinized and stabilized, the normal patterns of family connections and favoritism inevitably exact their tribute in gaining admission to schools, acquiring preferred geographical assignments, and gaining promotions. Children of "working-class" origin still have ample opportunity for higher education, provided they have demonstrated ability, but they labor under the normal disadvantage of not having the superior cultural, environmental, and psychological preparation which the children of the intelligentsia enjoy.

Children of peasant origin, particularly on the collective farms, have fewer and fewer opportunities. Although compulsory education in rural areas is now seven years, this is insufficient to allow them to compete equally with children in the urban areas who are now assured of ten years of schooling. Most of the children of peasant parentage are doomed to stay on the farm and can hardly aspire to more than a modest advance into the rural "working-class" or rural foreman group.

NATIONAL ORIGIN. Even if not admitted, national origin does influence the social mobility of an individual. Membership in certain nationalities automatically creates definite limitations, while membership in other nationalities provides better opportunities which are equally accidental in character. All things being equal, a Great Russian is endowed with greater advantages than citizens of other nationalities. Russian is the official language of the party and state, the medium of instruction in all of its most important institutions of higher learning, the language of the most numerous and powerful nationality, the language of the most influential culture. An absolute command of the Russian language is an indispensable prerequisite for social mobility beyond the purely local national level, and this is a special barrier which the native Russian does not have to overcome. The opportunities for Ukrainians are also fairly large. Smaller nationalities, like the Georgians, Armenians, Jews, and Germans, have also enjoyed special advantages because of a relatively higher rate of educational attainment and acquired skills, although both Jews and Germans have suffered discrimination and prejudice for political reasons—namely, suspicions of divided ideological and psychological loyalties. While many Jews are found in the arts, sciences, and professions, they appear to be systematically excluded from sensitive areas like the diplomatic service, and informal quotas have been established limiting their numbers in institutions of higher learning.

The Moslem nationalities have had fewest opportunities of all, not only because of a heritage of backwardness (which was real enough), but also because of suspected political unreliability and the inevitable residual cultural prejudices which continue to divide Christian and Moslem nationalities. With the accelerated educational and cultural transformation of these nationalities, their opportunities have correspondingly increased, and prejudices resulting from national origins will continue to diminish progressively in the future.

The Communist Party

VI

Ultimate power in Soviet society is vested in the Communist Party of the Soviet Union. Political action outside the framework of the party is illegal and thus subject to the harshest penalties. The monopoly position of the party in the Soviet system is given juridical expression in Article 126 of the Soviet Constitution:

The Communist Party of the Soviet Union . . . is the vanguard of the working people in their struggle to build communist society and is the leading core of all organizations of the working people, both public and state.

As the ultimate repository of power in the Soviet system, the symbol of legitimacy, and the organization through which are disseminated the policies of the Soviet leadership, the Communist Party of the Soviet Union emerges as the arena in which social, ideological, and political conflicts are resolved into decisions. Although the nature and composition of the party have undergone significant change, there has been little alteration in its formal organization and structure. The membership of the party has been substantially expanded,

its institutions and organs have been periodically rearranged, and qualifications for membership adjusted, but in its outward form and in its basic principles of organization, the party shows remarkable continuity.

The Leninist conception of the party as an organization in which the party's will would be democratically determined and autocratically executed remains intact. In fact, Khrushchev maintains that the Stalinist period was an aberration that distorted the Leninist norms of party life, which, since Stalin's death, have been restored. Thus, according to F. R. Kozlov:

Having overcome the consequences of the cult of J. V. Stalin, the Party has fully restored the Leninist norms of Party life and the principle of collective leadership. . . . The Party's organizational structure is firmly based on the Leninist principle of democratic centralism, which harmoniously combines a high degree of organization and the strictest discipline with the broadest inner-Party democracy.[1]

Article 19 of the new party statutes outlines the principal characteristics of party organization as follows:

The guiding principle of Party organizational structure is democratic centralism, which means:

[1] *Pravda,* October 29, 1961.

473

a. Election of all leading Party organs, from the lowest to the highest organ.

b. Periodic accountability of Party organs to their Party organizations and higher organs.

c. Strict Party discipline and subordination of the minority to the majority.

d. The decision of the higher organs are absolutely binding on lower organs.

The principal "democratic" feature of the party organization is the theoretical right of the rank-and-file membership of the party to elect the representatives of the lowest party organs directly; those lower organs in turn select representatives to the next higher body and so it goes on up through the pyramidal structure of the party, culminating in the Central Committee, the Presidium, and the Secretariat.

At the bottom of the party pyramid are the myriads of primary party organs, which remain the only party units organized along functional lines (Fig. 6-1). The structure of the party follows the territorial-administrative pattern of the state, which is divided into both territorial-administrative and ethno-administrative units, which frequently overlap. Thus, whereas the primary party units elect delegates to the next higher territorial organizations— the rayon party conference in rural areas and the city party organizations in urban regions— the rayon and city organs may send delegates directly to oblast, Autonomous Oblast, kray, or Autonomous Republic party conferences, as the case may be. In the case of some of the smaller Union Republics, the territory is divided simply into rayons, and the rayon organizations elect delegates directly to the Union Republic Party Congress.

Theoretically, each party organization, at whatever level, elects its own executive officials and secretaries, but they are held to be accountable not only to the organ which elects them but to the next higher organ as well. Since the party rules read that "the decisions of the higher organs are absolutely binding on lower organs," officials and secretaries of

lower organs reflect the will, not of the bodies which elected them, but of the organ directly above them. Accountability of officials to their own party organizations thus amounts to little more than faithful and efficient execution of decisions handed down from above.

The total number of party organizations in 1962 was about 300,000, embracing 8,872,516 party members and 843,489 candidate members, for a total membership of nearly 10 million people, an increase of about 2,500,000 since the Twentieth Party Congress in 1956. The party organizations in 1962 were distributed as follows: [2]

Organization	Number
Union Republic	14
Kray	7
Autonomous Republic	20
Oblast	108
Autonomous Oblast	8
National District	10
City	602
Borough	343
Rayon	3,202
Primary party organizations	296,444

Between 1956 and 1961, the number of party organizations was reduced by 55,000, of which more than 1,000 were at the rayon level or above. This reflects the effort to consolidate and increase the size of the smaller party units as membership grows.

The Primary Party Organizations

The primary party organizations (P.P.O.), formerly called party cells, are found at every level of Soviet society. Ranging in membership from 3 to 3,000 people, they are formed at place of work, except in rural areas where they may be organized at place of residence or in housing administrations. These party cells are found in factories, farms, schools, universities, research institutes, stores, cultural institutions, government bureaus and offices, armed forces and police units; in any

[2] *Partiinaya Zhizn*, No. 1, January, 1962, pp. 44–54.

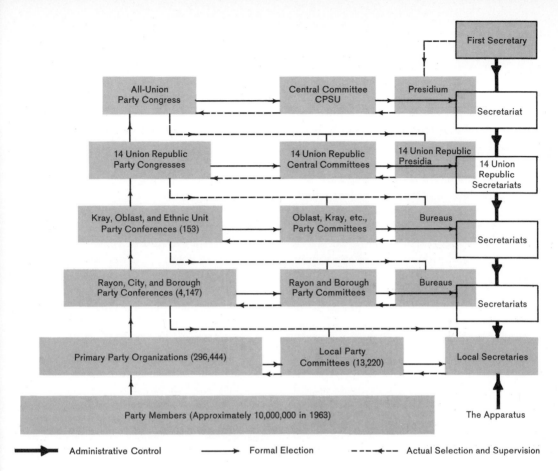

FIGURE 6-I   THE ORGANIZATIONAL STRUCTURE OF THE COMMUNIST PARTY OF THE SOVIET UNION.

Soviet institution or enterprise in which there are at least three party members, a primary organization may be formed.

As the basic unit of party organization, the party cells are in direct contact with the rank-and-file membership of the party and are thus the final organs for the dissemination of party policies and decisions. In the performance of this function, the party cell "carries out mass agitation and propagandist work, educates the masses in the spirit of communism," and further "organizes workers to implement communist construction tasks, leads socialist competition to implement state plans and pledges, mobilizes the masses . . . and strives to strengthen labor discpline, achieve a steady increase in labor productivity and improvement of production standards, and to protect and in-

crease communal property in enterprises and on collective and state farms." Primary party organizations also check to insure that the enterprises or institutions in which they are located are performing in accordance with party dictates, and the cells are supposed to "promptly inform the Party organs of any shortcomings in the work of the establishment or individual workers, regardless of their positions."

Communist Party cells thus resemble permanent vigilante committees; they must show more zeal and enthusiasm for the Soviet cause

The Communist Party

475

than ordinary citizens, and very often their self-righteous exhortations irritate many sectors of the Soviet population. Since many Soviet citizens become party members for opportunistic reasons, their ideological enthusiasm is often superficial. The meetings, lectures, parades, and cultural programs constantly being organized by party cells to disseminate the party's ideological propaganda are not always well attended and are far from popular.

Since the size of the primary party units varies so much, their organization must be somewhat flexible. The constituent body of the P.P.O. is the general meeting, which is supposed to meet every month. Primary units with 15 or more members are authorized to elect a bureau; those with less than 15 are authorized to appoint a secretary and an assistant. Primary organizations with 50 or more members can elect a shop committee, which has the status of a full P.P.O. and is itself authorized to elect a bureau and secretaries. In 1962, 103,800 such shop committees existed (up from 26,900 in 1956). If the primary organization has more than 150 members, the secretary is a full-time, paid official of the party, who supervises the work of the unit and handles its administration. Units with more than 300 members may be broken down into smaller sections. Where the membership of the primary organization is 300 or more, the general meeting assembles at the call of its committee or at the request of several sections of the unit. In 1962, more than 23,000 primary party organizations were endowed with party committees.

Regional and Union Republic Party Organizations

All party organizations above the primary units are territorial in character and parallel the territorial-administrative divisions of the Soviet state; they supervise and inspect

the work of all Soviet institutions, enterprises, and activities within their territorial unit.

The U.S.S.R. is divided into 15 Union Republics, which are the highest territorial-administrative divisions in the country. The larger Republics are divided into *oblasts*—the basic provincial unit—and some also include lesser nationality units called Autonomous Republics, Autonomous Oblasts, and National Districts, in descending order of importance. The smaller Republics and the oblasts are divided into rural units called *rayons* and city administrations. Normally, the administrative chain of control would be from All-Union to Republic to oblast to rayon and city. The largest Republic, the R.S.F.S.R., also has six special territorial units called *krays,* which are indistinguishable from the oblast except that five of them contain National Autonomous Oblasts. Autonomous Republics and Autonomous Oblasts are subordinate directly to the Union Republic or kray within whose boundaries they are located.

The organizational hierarchy is thus from primary party organizations to rayons and city organizations, to oblast, Autonomous Republic, and kray organizations, then, to the 14 Republic party organizations, one for each of the non-Russian Republics. The R.S.F.S.R. does not have a separate party organization, and its party affairs are directed by a special Bureau of the Central Committee, whose chairman is Nikita Khrushchev.

All party organizations contain five organs: (1) a constituent body, "the highest governing organ of Party organization," which is called the "general meeting" in the primary party organizations, the Party Conference at the rayon, city, oblast, and kray levels, and the Party Congress at the Union Republican and All-Union levels; (2) a delegated governing body—called a "committee" at lower levels and the Central Committee at Republic and All-Union levels—which is elected by the constituent body to act for it between its sessions; (3) an executive decision-making organ—called the "bureau" at all levels except that of the All-Union and in the Ukrainian Party organization, where it is called the Presidium—which is elected by the appropriate delegated governing body, for which it substitutes when that body is not in session; (4) a permanent administrative organ, called the Secretariat (elected by the appropriate committee or central committee), consisting of several secretaries and their staffs, including a First and Second Secretary at higher levels, which handles the day-to-day work of the party organization and makes up the powerful network of permanent officials called the "party apparatus"; (5) a body called the "auditing commission" at lower levels and the Central Auditing Commission at the All-Union level, which inspects the work of the party organization itself.

To understand properly the formal structure of party organization, at the local and state level, the following points should be kept in mind:

1. While constituent bodies are called the "highest governing authority" of party organizations and theoretically "elect" their committees, the members of the committees are, in effect, selected by the bureaus and secretaries from among the most prominent government, party, cultural, and economic personalities in the area under their jurisdiction.

2. Since constituent bodies and their committees meet only infrequently and are relatively large and cumbersome, they abdicate their authority to the bureaus and secretaries. The bureaus and secretaries are themselves selected by the next higher party organization.

3. The members of the bureaus who are not party secretaries normally have other administrative responsibilities which occupy most of their time and efforts. These members thus do not exercise continuous administrative control over their party organization.

4. The party secretaries are full-time party officials and are the most permanent officials in the party. They are frequently members of the committee of the next higher organization and thus constitute a bridge between higher and lower organs.

5. As the permanent official of the party organization, the party secretary speaks and acts for the organization more or less continuously.

6. Since the party secretary is selected by the next higher secretary in the hierarchy, he tends to look up to him for instructions and advice rather than to his own committee, to which he transmits orders from above.

7. As the permanent links between higher and lower organizations, the secretaries make up a chain of power that becomes the master of the party rather than its servant. This chain of power is called the "apparatus," and its members are called the *apparatchiki*.

8. The decisions of higher organs are absolutely binding on lower organs, which means the decisions of higher secretaries, beginning with the First Secretary of the CPSU [Communist Party of the Soviet Union] (Nikita Khrushchev), are absolutely binding on lower party secretaries.

Inner-Party Democracy: Party Elections

All elections within the party are theoretically by secret ballot. Each candidate is supposed to be voted upon separately and is considered elected if he receives at least 50 per cent of the vote. In practice, however, all candidates are approved by officials of the next higher organization.

The new party rules adopted in 1961 introduced some innovations in elections which may eventually be of great significance. To frustrate the revival of "the cult of personality" (dictatorship), the "principle of the systematic renewal of the membership of party organs" has been incorporated into the party statutes. At least one-fourth of the membership of the All-Union Central Committee and its Presidium must be changed at each election. Presidium members "as a rule" are to be elected for not more than three *consecutive* terms (a total of 12 years), although certain "outstanding" leaders may be elected for more than three consecutive terms if they receive not less than three-quarters of the vote. At least one-third of the membership of the Central Committees of the Union Republics and of the oblast and kray committees and at least one-half of the committees of lesser organizations must be changed at every regular election. The general restriction to three consecutive terms (a total of 6 years) applies here, with the same reservations with respect to "deserving" leaders.

The Communist Party

These new restrictions do not apply, significantly, to secretaries except those of primary party organizations, who cannot be re-elected for more than two consecutive terms. Expulsions from Central Committees and committees are decided by a two-thirds majority, which is the procedure carried over from the preceding party rules.

According to F. R. Kozlov's commentary on the new party statutes at the Twenty-Second Party Congress:

. . . the systematic turnover of the membership of Party agencies precludes excessive concentration of power in the hands of individual officials. . . . The proposed procedure for systematic turnover of the membership of Party bodies . . . is at the same time aimed against people who have grown conceited and who violate the norms of inner-Party life, as well as against weak-willed workers lacking initiative.[3]

It is, of course, too early to assess the full implications of the new party rules, since past party history indicates that the party is run by those who control the "apparatus," irrespective of the formal rules and procedures that may be on the books. Clearly, however, Khrushchev is trying to make a clean break with the Stalinist system, and the rules are designed to govern party processes not so much while he is still alive but to provide a more stable procedure after his death. The new provisions do provide a *legal* basis for removing leaders who abuse their position; in the event the attempt is successful, these provisions will legitimize any successful move against despotic abuses, but they cannot ensure the success of any such venture.

The provisions for systematic rotation of leading officials stabilize the political system and signify that the Soviet system is maturing; the purge machinery is becoming "civilized," for party leaders who are slated for removal can be quietly rotated out of office in accordance with the party rules. Khrushchev,

[3] *Pravda,* October 29, 1961.

in his report to the Twenty-Second Party Congress, noted that:

. . . the failure to reelect a party member to a Party body because he has completed the established period in office should not serve as a basis for discrimination against the Party member. If a communist has worked well for the established tenure in a post entrusted to him, honor and glory to him.[4]

Inner-Party Democracy: Criticism and Self-Criticism

The party rules have always stipulated that party members have both rights and duties. The cherished Bolshevik principle of "criticism and self-criticism" is conceived as the self-regulating mechanism that prevents a party with a monopoly of power from degenerating into a static, complacent, and corrupted organization; at the same time, it is supposed to preserve the "democratic" character of the party. As a duty, party members are obliged "to develop criticism and self-criticism, boldly expose shortcomings and work to eliminate them, fight against exhibitionism, conceit, complacency, and localism, decisively rebuff all attempts to suppress criticism, and oppose any activities prejudicial to the Party and report them to the Party organs, right up to the CPSU Central Committee."

Under the section on the rights of party members, the party statutes authorize the party member

to discuss freely at Party meetings, conferences, congresses, Party committee meetings, and in the Party press questions regarding Party and practical activities, submit proposals, and openly express and defend his opinion before the organization adopts a decision. . . .

Elsewhere, Paragraph 27 of the new party rules reads:

Free and businesslike discussion of the questions of Party policy in individual Party organizations or in the Party as a whole is an inalienable right of a Party member and an important prin-

[4] *Pravda,* October 19, 1961.

ciple of inner-Party democracy. Criticism and self-criticism can be developed, and Party discipline . . . strengthened, only on the basis of inner-Party democracy.

Since the accession of Khrushchev to power, the bounds of discussion have been widened considerably. The new rules thus reflect not only the altered situation since Stalin's death, but spell out what rights of criticism the party members have, although a nebulous area of ambiguity still exists between what is permitted and what will not be tolerated, between the imperative of inner-party democracy and the imperative of monolithic and centrally executed will.

The incompatibility of democracy and centralism under conditions of a one-party monopoly remains as valid as before; the real difference is not that there is more democracy under Khrushchev, but rather that centralism is implemented less barbarously and in more humane and rational ways. The Soviet system and party life remain as undemocratic as before, but the terroristic aspects of Bolshevik totalitarianism have been lifted or suspended. The right of those in control to stigmatize undesirable criticism and discussion as "anti-party" in character, while not as grim in its consequences as Stalin's formula of "enemy of the people," preserves for them the ultimate authority to narrow or expand the area of discussion and criticism at will.

The Central Institutions of the Party

In the Soviet system, a functional division of labor exists between the institutions of the party and the state, which are interlocked at every level of power and administration. The function of the party is to translate ideological norms into policies and decisions, which are then transmitted to the organs of the state for their execution and administration as formal laws and official acts of the state. The party performs a further function in supervising and checking on the execution of its decisions through corresponding state institutions. The party, however, is warned "not [to] supplant administrative, trade union, cooperative, and other social organizations of working people and not [to] tolerate confusion between the functions of the Party and other organs, or superfluous parallelism in work." However, it has not always been easy to separate the functions of the party from government and other institutions, and the relationship between party and state organs has exhibited remarkable fluidity in the past, depending on personalities, problems, and events.

The Communist Party's function of translating ideological, policy, and personality conflicts into decisions is performed by the All-Union organs of the party, which stand at the pinnacle of the party pyramid. These decisions are then transmitted to the central institutions of the state for their execution and administration as formal acts and laws of the state. The interlocking of state and party organs is symbolized by the dual position of Nikita Khrushchev as First Secretary of the party and Chairman of the Council of Ministers. This interlocking relationship at the highest level was temporarily interrupted after Stalin's death, when the post of First Secretary was separated from that of Premier during the years 1953–57, but their fusion was resumed in 1958 when the Khrushchev faction of the party felt sufficiently powerful to assert its dominance.

At the summit, the party is divided into the same five functional divisions of responsibility as are the lower party organizations. These are (see Fig. 6-2): (1) a constituent body, the All-Union *Party Congress;* (2) a delegated constituent body, the *Central Committee;* (3) an executive decision-making organ, the *Presidium* (called *Politburo* before 1952); (4) a permanent administrative body, the central *Secretariat,* headed by the First Secretary; and (5) a self-inspecting body, the *Central Auditing Commission.*

The Communist Party

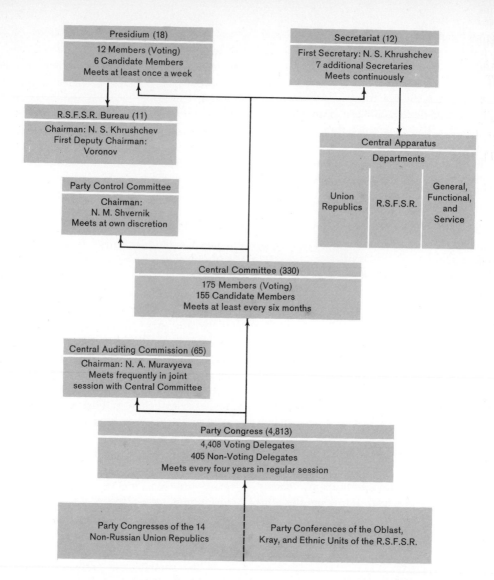

FIGURE 6-2   THE CENTRAL ORGANS OF THE COMMUNIST PARTY OF THE SOVIET
UNION, 1963.

The Party Congress

In theory the most exalted, but in practice the most impotent of the central party institutions is the All-Union Party Congress, which is described in the party statutes as "the supreme organ of the Communist Party of the Soviet Union." Traditionally, the most important pronouncements on Soviet ideology and policy are reserved for meetings of the Party Congress which, according to the party statutes, "determine the Party line on questions of domestic and foreign policy and examine and decide on the most important problems in the building of communism." In actual fact, the Party Congress is little more than a rubber stamp whose delegates have been carefully picked and screened from above through the apparatus of the party, and thus it simply confirms decisions made by the party leadership, adopts resolutions introduced from above, and, in general, provides the ritual of ideological sanctification demanded by the Soviet system.

The formal authority of the Party Congress has remained relatively unchanged throughout the history of the party and is reflected in article 33 of the 1961 party statutes as follows:

The Congress: (a) hears and approves the reports of the Central Committee, the Central Auditing Commission, and other central organizations; (b) reviews, amends, and approves the Party program and statutes; (c) determines the Party line on questions of domestic and foreign policy and examines and decides on the most important problems in the building of communism; (d) elects the Central Committee and the Central Auditing Commission.

According to the party statutes, the Congress must be convened regularly every four years. The Congress is considered to possess full authority if at least one-half the party members are represented in it. Special sessions of the Congress may be convened by the Central Committee on its own initiative or at the request of one-third of the party members represented at the last Party Congress. Convocations of regular Congresses must be announced at least six weeks in advance; extraordinary sessions can be convened on two months' notice.

Representation in the Congress is based on territorial constituencies. Each Party Congress of the 14 non-Russian Republics sends a delegation, as do the Conferences of Oblast, Kray, and Autonomous Republics of the R.S.F.S.R., which does not have a separate Party Congress. Moscow and Leningrad were authorized to send delegates to the Twenty-Second Party Congress (1961), who were elected by borough and rayon conferences. Members of the armed forces are represented through delegations from the territorial constituency in which they are stationed, while those stationed abroad are allowed separate unit representation.

The statutes read that "the proportion of representation at the Party Congress is estab-lished by the Central Committee," which means that the latter body possesses the authority to define the territorial constituencies which shall elect delegates as well as the size of the Congress itself. Delegates are of two types: (1) those with full voting rights, representing members, and (2) those representing candidate members who have participating rights only (and are hence called candidate delegates). As the size of the party has increased, so has the Congress itself. At the Congresses held in 1952 (19th) and 1956 (20th), delegates (both voting and non-voting) were elected on the basis of one seat for each 5,000 party members and candidate members, respectively. At the extraordinary Twenty-First Party Congress held in 1959, the ratio was one delegate per 6,000 members. The Twenty-Second Party Congress (1961) reflected a radical change in the ratio of representation, whose full significance remains to be evaluated. Although membership in the party reached the record level of nearly 10,-000,000, instead of reducing the ratio of representation so as to keep the size of the Congress uniform, the ratio of representation was stepped up to one delegate per 2,000 members and one non-voting delegate per 2,000 candidate members. This raised the size of the Party Congress to 4,813 delegates (of which 405 were non-voting), no less than three and a half times the size of the three preceding Congresses!

As the Congress has grown in numbers, and hence grown increasingly unwieldy, its significance and power have correspondingly diminished (Table 6-1).

During the Leninist era, the Party Congress met every year (1918–25), but after 1925 the intervals between each succeeding Congress were extended, first to two years, then to three and finally to four, which remains the current rule. In patent violation of his own rules, Stalin not only shot a majority of the delegates to the Seventeenth Party Congress, but

The Communist Party

TABLE 6-1   *Party Congresses and Party Membership, 1918–1961*

Congress	Year	Size of Congress [a]	Party membership [b]
Seventh	1918	46 + (58)	145,000
Eighth	1919	301 + (102) [c]	313,766
Ninth	1920	554 + (162)	611,978
Tenth	1921	694 + (296)	732,521
Eleventh	1922	522 + (165)	532,000
Twelfth	1923	408 + (417)	386,000
Thirteenth	1924	748 + (416)	735,811
Fourteenth	1925	665 + (641)	643,000 + (445,000)
Fifteenth	1927	898 + (771)	890,000 + (350,000)
Sixteenth	1930	1,268 + (891)	1,260,874 + (711,609)
Seventeenth	1934	1,225 + (736)	1,874,488 + (935,298)
Eighteenth	1939	1,574 + (466)	1,588,852 + (888,814)
Nineteenth	1952	1,192 + (167)	6,013,259 + (868,886)
Twentieth	1956	1,349 + (81)	6,795,896 + (419,609)
Twenty-First	1959 [d]	1,269 + (106)	7,622,356 + (616,775)
Twenty-Second	1961	4,408 + (405)	8,872,516 + (843,489)

[a] Candidate delegates in parentheses.
[b] Candidate members in parentheses.
[c] These are the figures given in J. V. Stalin, *History of the Communist Party of the Soviet Union* (New York: International Publishers, 1939). Another source, N. Popov, *Outline History of the CPSU*, Vol. II (New York: International Publishers, n.d.), gives the figures as 286 and 100, respectively.
[d] Extraordinary or Special Congress.

refused to convene a Party Congress after 1939 (18th) until 1952—an interval of 13 years—although the party rules still required a session every four years.

In recent years, the main constitutional and reviewing activity of the Congress has been to act as a sounding board for the speeches delivered by members of its Central Committee and Presidium, which are duly ratified and approved unanimously. The agenda of the Congress is set by the Central Committee, and every regular Congress includes a Report of the Central Committee (called the Main Report), which is divided into three parts on the (a) external situation, (b) internal situation, and (c) state of the party. This Report is normally delivered by the most important figure in the party hierarchy. A second report, which appears regularly, is that of the Central Auditing Commission, which is perfunctory and technical in character. A third regular item is the election of central party organs. Other business on the agenda is determined by the Central Committee and can include virtually anything. The only special Congress in the history of the party, the Twenty-First, held in 1959, listed only one item on its agenda, the goals for the seven-year economic plan (1959–65).

Since 1930, all decisions by the Congress have been unanimous. By approving the "reports" and resolutions introduced by the leadership and by confirming all acts performed in the name of the party since the preceding Congress, the Congress "establishes the line" of the party.

The Congress elects the Central Committee and the Central Auditing Commission, supposedly by a secret ballot cast individually for each candidate. Voting is held behind closed doors, and the precise electoral procedure remains a secret. Members of the Congress have the right, under party rules, to reject candidates and to criticize them in open discussion. Under the revised rules, the Congress determines the size of the Central Committee and the Central Auditing Commission, with all candidates receiving more than a majority of the Congress vote being considered elected. The Twenty-Second Congress established the rule that at least one-fourth of the Central Committee membership be retired at each election and that any person who has been a member for three consecutive terms can be elected only if he receives three-quarters of the vote.

The Party Congress no longer functions as a constituent body for the party in a real sense. Its present size, nearly 5,000 members, clearly precludes that function, as did, indeed, its more modest size of about 1,400 members at preceding Congresses. Its role has become ritualized as a sounding board for important ideological and policy pronouncements, as a vehicle for disseminating the party line at home and abroad, and as an occasion for formally altering the leadership of the Central Committee and the Presidium. Thus, at the Twentieth Party Congress, in 1956, Khrushchev used the occasion to introduce radical innovations in doctrine such as repudiating the Stalinist concepts of "capitalist encirclement" and the "fatal inevitability of wars." The Twenty-Second Party Congress was also used as a platform for denouncing the leaders of the Albanian Party for their adherence to Stalinist positions, for provoking a public ideological dispute with Communist China, and for excoriating once again the "anti-party group" led by Molotov.

The Congress serves a further function as an institution which imparts formal legitimacy to the acts and decisions of the Central Committee and its Presidium. The nearly fourfold increase of the size of the Congress at the Twenty-Second Party Congress thus simultaneously signals its demise as a legislative organ of the party and hails its formal reconstruction as a rubber-stamp organization.

The Central Committee

With the increasing size of the Party Congress and the diminishing frequency of its meetings, the significance of its delegated body, the Central Committee, increased for a brief period in the late 1920's and early 1930's. As discussion and debate vanished from the Congress, it slipped behind the closed doors of the Central Committee, where sharp exchanges continued down to about 1936. They were stifled after Stalin who, according to Khrushchev's account, "arrested and shot" 98 of the 139 members and candidate members (70 per cent) of the Central Committee elected by the Seventeenth Party Congress.

According to the party statutes, the Central Committee "during the intervals between Congresses directs all Party activities and local Party organs," and "directs the work of the central state and social organizations." It also "selects and distributes leading cadres . . . organizes various organs, establishments, and institutions of the Party and directs their activities; appoints the editorial staff of central papers and journals functioning under its control; and . . . represents the CPSU in its relations with other parties." In actual fact, the Central Committee is invested with virtually the plenary powers of the Congress during the four-year intervals between its sessions. The Committee is empowered to meet every six months, which it neglected to do in the later years of Stalin's life. The Central Committee has also gradually grown in size until in 1961 its total membership exceeded that of Party Congresses elected during the early years of the Soviet regime.

As it has grown in size, so has its importance diminished. In 1918, the Central Committee consisted of only 15 members and 8 candidate members. In 1927, the Fifteenth Party Congress fixed its membership at 71 full members and 68 candidate members. It was almost doubled in size by the Nineteenth Congress in 1952, when its membership was raised to 125 full members and 111 candidates. It was increased slightly in size at the Twentieth Party Congress (1956) to a total of 255 full and candidate members, but more significantly, during the interval between the two Congresses nearly one-half of its membership was replaced, a reflection of the grim power struggles which had ensued. The Twenty-First Special Congress did not elect a Central Committee, but at the Twenty-Second Congress (1961), the size of the Central Committee was expanded to 175 full members and 155 candidate members, for a total of 330 members.

Candidate members are authorized to participate in deliberations of the Committee, but do not possess voting rights. According to the party rules, the full members of the Committee are replenished from among the candidate members in the event of vacancies caused by expulsion, resignation, or death. Meetings of the Central Committee are called plenums, and frequently joint meetings are held with the Central Auditing Commission.

As Stalin's grip on the party apparatus tightened, plenary sessions were called infrequently, and during Stalin's later years, meetings were not even held with the regularity required by the party statutes. Its records and proceedings for this period remain generally unpublished, except for publicly announced reports delivered by Stalin and resolutions adopted by the Committee. After 1936, the Central Committee, like the Congress, was reduced to a sounding board, and its decisions were in all likelihood unanimous. According to Khrushchev's secret report at the Twentieth Party Congress:

Whereas, during the first few years after Lenin's death, Party Congresses and Central Committee plenums took place more or less regularly, later, when Stalin began increasingly to abuse his power, these principles were brutally violated. This was especially evident during the last 15 years of his life. Was it a normal situation when over 13 years elapsed between the Eighteenth and Nineteenth Party Congresses. . . .? It is true that there was an attempt to call a Central Committee plenum in October 1941, when Central Committee members from the whole country were called to Moscow. They waited two days for the opening of the plenum, but in vain. Stalin did not want to meet and talk to the Central Committee members.[5]

There is no question but that the Central Committee proved to be as superfluous as the

[5] Khrushchev's Secret Speech, in Wolfe, *op. cit.*

Congress for Stalin, and between March, 1946, and October, 1952, this "directing organ" of the party was convened only three times. Since Stalin's death, its role has been enhanced and its power revitalized. While it failed to meet with the regularity required by the party statutes before Stalin's death, since then it has met more often than required. Thus it was convened five times in 1953; twice in 1954, in 1955, and in 1956; four times in 1957; six times in 1958; and twice in 1959 and in 1960. Since Stalin's death, the typical plenum has lasted two days, with the shortest being a single day and the longest lasting eight days. This eight-day plenum, which ousted the "anti-party group" from the Central Committee, the Presidium, and the Government in June, 1957, has been the most significant of any during the post-Stalin era.

From the evidence of several published records of Central Committee plenums in the post-Stalin period, the proceedings of the Central Committee appear to deviate little from those of other party bodies. The First Secretary delivers a report on the main item on the agenda, which is then "discussed" by other members. The "discussions" assume the form of speeches delivered by members, which are freely interrupted by the First Secretary, who affirms, criticizes, warns, and even threatens the speakers, who in return meekly make the appropriate gestures. One lower-ranking member of the Central Committee revealed at the Twentieth Party Congress:

At plenums of the Central Committee . . . its First Secretary, Comrade Khrushchev and other members of the Presidium . . . corrected errors in a fatherly way when we individual members of the Central Committee have made mistakes, correcting us regardless of our posts or reputations.[6]

At the December, 1958, plenum, 75 speakers "discussed" Khrushchev's report, and Bulganin used the opportunity to denounce himself for his complicity in the "anti-party group" conspiracy to oust Khrushchev from power

[6] Speech of Z. I. Muratov at the Twentieth Party Congress, Moscow Radio Broadcast, February 21, 1956.

the preceding year, after scathing condemnation by other members of the Committee.[7]

The more or less placid character of the Central Committee plenums reflected in the published proceedings can be quite misleading, since it is known that many of the post-Stalin plenums have been characterized by stormy controversy and fierce infighting between various cliques and factions. Perhaps the stormiest of the post-Stalin plenums was its longest, held in June, 1957, when the so-called "anti-party group" of Molotov, Malenkov, Kaganovich, Bulganin, and Voroshilov, together with Pervukhin and Saburov—a clear majority of the Presidium members—was overruled by the Central Committee in its attempt to oust Khrushchev as First Secretary of the party. It was officially reported that 60 members delivered speeches and 115 filed statements in an authentic and acrimonious debate preceding the vote, whose unanimity was tarnished by a single obstinate abstention cast by Molotov—the first and only publicly admitted dissident vote in a Central Committee meeting in almost thirty years.[8]

Other plenums, such as those that ousted Malenkov as Secretary of the party in March, 1953, that expelled and ordered the trial of Beria in July, 1953, that denounced Molotov's foreign-policy views in July, 1955, and that reversed economic policies in December, 1956, and February, 1957, were also charged with violent conflict and clash of opinion. Since the expulsion of the "anti-party group" in June, 1957, the Central Committee meetings have been marred by the expulsion of Marshal Zhukov from the Presidium, by controversy over the pace and tempo of the de-Stalinization program, and by the ideological controversies with China and Albania over foreign policy and the world Communist movement.

The most important decisions and policies of the party are issued in the form of Resolutions and Decisions of the Central Committee. In times of crisis, or on particularly significant occasions, joint Decrees are issued with the Council of Ministers, which ha the force of state law. Immediately a Stalin's death, for example, an extraordinary joint Decree was issued over the combined authorities of the Central Committee, the Council of Ministers, and the Presidium of the Supreme Soviet, in order to insure total ideological legitimization and legalization of the actions taken by the Soviet leadership in reorganizing the party and the state in the absence of both a Party Congress and a Supreme Soviet session, i.e., the constituent and legislative organs of the party and state.

The Central Committee remains a potentially powerful institution and, far more than the Party Congress, constitutes a body with authority and power in its own right. This stems from the fact that selected for membership in this body are the most powerful and influential elites and groups in Soviet society. In the Central Committee are to be found the members and candidate members of the Presidium, the members of the Secretariat, the important Ministers of the government, the First Secretaries of the Republic party organizations and Second Secretaries of important Republic party organizations, First Secretaries of important oblast, kray, and other regional organizations, the most important government officials of the Union Republics, marshals, generals, admirals, ambassadors, trade-union and Komsomol officials, and leading party ideologists and cultural celebrities. More than any other designation, membership in the Central Committee imparts status and recognition in the Soviet system. While increasing the size of the Central Committee may tend to diminish its power, it also widens the ambit of recognition and status.

Members and candidate members of the Central Committee can be removed only by the Central Committee itself (and, of course, by the Congress), but not by the higher organs, the Presidium and Secretariat. According to the party statutes, a member or candi-

---

[7] *Plenum Tsentralnovo Komiteta Kommunisticheskoi Partii Sovetskovo Soyuza 15–19 Dekabrya 1958 g.* (Moscow, 1958).

[8] See *The New York Times,* July 6, 1957.

date member of the Committee who "injures his honor and dignity . . . cannot remain in the body of the Central Committee," but can be removed only by a two-thirds vote of a Committee plenum in a closed and secret ballot. Like its two inner organs, the Presidium and the Secretariat, the Central Committee has been subjected to a thorough purge since the rise of Khrushchev. No less than 64 per cent of the members of the 330-member Central Committee elected by the Twenty-Second Party Congress are new to this body. Over 50 per cent of the members of the 1956 Central Committee and Central Auditing Commission have been dropped.

The Presidium

There is no question but that the most important decision-making organ in the party and state is the Presidium of the Party (called Politburo before 1952). In accordance with the principle of "democratic centralism," the ultimate authority of the party is entrusted to this organ, although its decisions may be overruled by the Central Committee. Since the party statutes instruct the Presidium to direct the work of the Central Committee between plenums, the Presidium is the supreme policy-making body of the Soviet Union. Members are elected by a majority vote of the Central Committee, although under the new rules, one-fourth of its membership must be renewed at every regular election, and members who have served three or more consecutive terms must receive a ¾ majority for re-election.

COMPOSITION. Membership in the Presidium, however, is determined in fact not by the Central Committee, but by the Presidium itself, which is a self-perpetuating body. The Central Committee merely ratifies the candidates offered by the ruling Presidium, the nominees reflecting the equilibrium of power existing within the Presidium itself. This equilibrium is, of course, further reflected

in the candidates put forward for election to the Central Committee and selection for the Party Congress. Thus, whenever a change in the distribution of power takes place in the Presidium, this is eventually registered downward through the various party echelons.

Like other party bodies, the Presidium has both full members and candidate members. Only full members are entitled to vote; candidate members are entitled to take part in the discussions. The membership of the Presidium and its predecessor, the Politburo, has varied considerably, as has the ratio between full and candidate members. Stalin kept the membership of the Politburo at about a dozen members, but reduced and expanded it at will and appointed and expelled members according to his whim or fancy. At the Nineteenth Party Congress, he unexpectedly abolished the Politburo and replaced it with an enlarged Presidium of 25 members and 11 candidate members. According to Khrushchev, this change "was aimed at the removal of the old political Bureau members . . . and a design for the annihilation of the old political Bureau members." The post-Stalin Presidium was reduced to ten full members and four candidate members. At the Twentieth Party Congress in 1952, its size was set at eleven full members and six candidate members; after the expulsion of the "anti-party group," it was reconstructed at fourteen full and eight candidate members; at the Twenty-Second Party Congress, it was once again reduced to eleven full and five candidate members, but by early 1963 membership had been expanded to twelve full members and six candidates.

In between regular elections, the size of the Presidium has expanded and contracted in response to the struggle for power. Expulsions and elections to the Presidium are technically made by the Central Committee, but, in fact, the Committee merely ratifies whatever changes have been made by the controlling factions in the Presidium. Removals and appointments, however, are formally announced after Central Committee plenums, the regular election being at the plenum held by the new Central Committee elected by a Party Congress.

The Presidium of the party represents the fusion of party and state authority at the highest level, as reflected in the interlocking character of its membership. Some members are virtually ex officio, like the First Secretary, the Premier, the Chairman of the Presidium of the Supreme Soviet, the First Secretary of the Ukrainian Party, and the Premier of the R.S.F.S.R. Other members are drawn from the Secretariat, the Council of Ministers, and key Republic party and government officials. The precise distribution reflects the equilibrium of power that exists among the various elite groups at any given time. Since the ascendancy of Khrushchev, and particularly since the expulsion of the "anti-party group," the party apparatus has been the dominant elite represented in the Presidium.

Under Stalin, all important and many trivial decisions were made by him. Rival and dissident views were quashed and their adherents liquidated. He appointed and removed members of the Politburo at will and had them shot, imprisoned, or exiled without resort to the procedures and institutions which he himself had fashioned. Stalin, in Politburo meetings, could either announce his decisions and expect unanimous approval, submit them for examination and ask for a discussion with or without a vote, simply act without consulting his colleagues, or consult with various members on certain questions to the exclusion of others.

During the decade since Stalin's death, there has been a remarkable rotation of personalities at the pinnacles of Soviet power, but virtually no alteration in institutional forms (Fig. 6-3). Since 1952, 52 individuals have sat on the Presidium, either as full or candidate members. The number of individuals admitted to membership and candidate membership in the Central Committee must come to nearly a thousand. More than 30 Soviet citizens who have experienced the dizzying heights of the Presidium are now in less responsible positions. This fact alone is a remarkable demonstration of the evolving maturity and stabilization of the Soviet political order, since, under Stalin, expulsion from the Politburo nearby always meant an early and untimely death.

HOW THE PRESIDIUM FUNCTIONS. The post-Stalin Presidium, according to a remark by Khrushchev in 1957, "meets regularly, not less than once a week." In its deliberations, it tries to arrive at a consensus by discussion, but in the event of disagreement, questions are resolved by a simple majority decision. Only full members are entitled to vote, although candidate members participate in debate and discussion. According to Khrushchev and Mikoyan, most decisions are adopted unanimously, and this is undoubtedly true, but the revelations of the circumstances surrounding the expulsion of the "anti-party group" indicate that many Presidium meetings have been stormy and, inconclusive.

As an institution, the Presidium, like the Central Committee, has recovered much of its former prestige and authority. It is no longer a mere façade for a one-man dictatorship, but functions as an institution in its own right. The First Secretary, who presides over its meetings as its chairman, continues to be the most powerful and influential personality, but he is more likely to represent a particular faction rather than function as an absolute autocrat. The strong representation of the Secretariat in the Presidium since 1957 betrays the dominant role of the party apparatus at the present time.

The Presidium's procedure has also been changed considerably since Stalin's death. Present indications are that the Presidium works from an agenda prepared in advance, containing items suggested by members of the Presidium that may have in turn been prompted by subordinates and government Ministers. Since all Presidium members have administrative responsibilities in the government or the party, they must rely on their professional and technical staffs to control the flow of information and problems that reach them from the lower levels of the state and the party. Greater delegation of responsibility to subordinates has also been the rule since

The Communist Party

487

FIGURE 6-3 EVOLUTION OF THE PARTY PRESIDIUM IN THE SOVIET UNION, 1952–1963.

		July, 1952	October, 1952	March, 1953	February, 1955	February, 1956	June, 1957	December, 1959	January, 1963
FULL-TIME PARTY FUNCTIONARIES	*Secretariat*	(Politburo) STALIN MALENKOV KHRUSHCHEV *Suslov* *Ponomarenko*	STALIN ARISTOV KHRUSHCHEV MALENKOV MIKHAILOV PONOMARENKO SUSLOV *Brezhnev* *Ignatov* *Pegov*	KHRUSHCHEV *Ignatyev* *Pospelov* *Shatalin* *Suslov*	KHRUSHCHEV *Suslov* *Pospelov*	KHRUSHCHEV SUSLOV *Brezhnev* *Furtseva* *Shepilov* *Belyayev* *Aristov* *Pospelov*	KHRUSHCHEV SUSLOV BELYAYEV ARISTOV BREZHNEV FURTSEVA KUUSINEN *Pospelov*	KHRUSHCHEV KIRICHENKO SUSLOV ARISTOV BREZHNEV FURTSEVA KUUSINEN MUKHITDINOV IGNATOV *Pospelov*	KHRUSHCHEV KOZLOV SUSLOV KUUSINEN Demichev Ilyichev Shelepin Ponomarev
	Party Control Committee	ANDREYEV	SHKIRYATOV			*Shvernik*	SHVERNIK	SHVERNIK	SHVERNIK
	Provincial Party Secretaries		ANDRIANOV MELNIKOV *Patolichev* *Puzanov*	*Melnikov* *Bagirov*	*Ponomarenko*	KIRICHENKO *Mukhitdinov*	IGNATOV KIRICHENKO KOZLOV *Kainberzin* *Kirilenko* *Mazurov* *Mukhitdinov* *Mzhavanadze*	BELYAYEV *Kirilenko* *Mazurov* *Mzhavanadze* *Podgorny*	PODGORNY VORONOV KIRILENKO *Mazurov* *Mzhavanadze* *Rashidov*
FULL-TIME GOVERNMENT FUNCTIONARIES	*Central Government Officials*	STALIN MOLOTOV BERIA VOROSHILOV KAGANOVICH BULGANIN MIKOYAN KOSYGIN *Shvernik*	STALIN SHVERNIK BERIA BULGANIN IGNATYEV KAGANOVICH MALENKOV MALYSHEV MIKOYAN MOLOTOV PERVUKHIN PONOMARENKO SABUROV VOROSHILOV *Kabanov* *Kosygin* *Tevosyan* *Vyshinsky* *Zverev*	BERIA BULGANIN KAGANOVICH MALENKOV MIKOYAN MOLOTOV PERVUKHIN SABUROV VOROSHILOV *Ponomarenko*	BULGANIN KAGANOVICH MALENKOV MIKOYAN MOLOTOV PERVUKHIN SABUROV VOROSHILOV	BULGANIN VOROSHILOV KAGANOVICH MIKOYAN MOLOTOV PERVUKHIN SABUROV MALENKOV *Zhukov*	BULGANIN VOROSHILOV MIKOYAN ZHUKOV *Kosygin* *Pervukhin*	KHRUSHCHEV KOZLOV MIKOYAN VOROSHILOV *Kosygin* *Pervukhin*	KHRUSHCHEV BREZHNEV MIKOYAN KOSYGIN
	Provincial Government Officials		KOROTCHENKO KUUSINEN				Korotchenko	Polyansky Korotchenko Kainberzin	POLYANSKY Shcherbitsky
MISCELLANEOUS			CHESNOKOV KUZNETSOV MIKHAILOV *Yudin*		*Shvernik*				*Grishin*

SMALL CAPITALS: Full Member, Presidium, Soviet Communist Party.
Italic type: Candidate member, Presidium, Soviet Communist Party.
Roman type: Not Presidium members.

Stalin's death, and many problems originating at lower levels of administration are decided before they reach the top.

Specialists and experts, as well as bureau and department heads, are often invited to Presidium meetings when technical or specialized advice is required by the Presidium. Questions relating to party matters flow up through the party apparatus into the Secretariat, where they are handled by the appropriate sections or dispatched upward to the individual members of the Secretariat, some of whom are also Presidium members. Problems relating to some aspect of state administration similarly move upward through the echelons of the given Ministry. Some Ministries, like the Foreign Ministry and perhaps the Defense Ministry, report regularly to the Presidium, although in recent years neither Minister has been a Presidium member.

The functioning of the Presidium also varies in accordance with the nature of the outside responsibilities of its members. Whether it operates on the basis of a quorum is not known; it is apparent that some Presidium members are normally located in Moscow, while others are assigned to regional responsibilities, such as the First Secretary of the Ukrainian Party Organization or the First Secretary of the Kazakh Party. Consequently, informal communication among Presidium members is more likely to be restricted to those whose outside responsibilities keep them in Moscow rather than in provincial areas.

Another aspect of the Presidium's style of work which distinguishes the present body from those of Stalinist days is the activity of individual members of the Presidium. During the Stalinist era, neither Stalin nor other members of the Politburo engaged in "grass-roots" politics or barnstormed through the provinces to contact the lower echelons of the bureaucracy or the masses of Soviet citizenry. This practice has now become widespread, and Khrushchev and other Presidium members are on the move continuously, speaking at local conferences and meetings, collective farms, and professional and cultural assemblies, from one end of the country to the other. There is no question but that all this activity has served to bring both the party and the state closer to the Soviet people, giving them a deeper sense of personal involvement, participation, and commitment to both institutions.

The Secretariat and the Central Apparatus

The Secretariat, as an institution, was established in 1919 along with the Politburo and the Orgburo, and with Stalin's appointment as General Secretary, in April, 1922, he became the only important party leader who was a member of all three bodies. The functions of the Secretariat were largely undefined, and they evolved in response to Stalin's personality and ambitions. The reputation of the Secretariat as a power base was imparted to it by Stalin, since at the time of his appointment, the General Secretary's position was considered to be a purely innocuous and administrative body. Within the year, Lenin, in his so-called "Testament," written on December 25, 1922, warned that Stalin had already used the position to accumulate unprecedented power:

> Comrade Stalin, having become General Secretary, has concentrated enormous power in his hand; and I am not sure that he always knows how to use that power with sufficient caution.

In a postscript to the "Testament," dated January 4, 1923, Lenin suggested that Stalin be removed from this post:

> Stalin is too rude, and this fault entirely supportable in relations among us Communists, becomes insupportable in the office of General Secretary. Therefore, I propose to the comrades to find a way to remove Stalin from that position and appoint to it another man who in all respects differs from Stalin in one superiority—namely, that he be more tolerant, more loyal, more polite and more considerate to comrades, less capricious, etc.[9]

[9] Full texts of "Testament" and "postscript" are printed in Wolfe, *Khrushchev and Stalin's Ghost*, pp. 260–263.

The growth of the party was accompanied by an increase in the activities of the Central Apparatus and in the size of its staff, but the Secretariat typically consisted of the General Secretary (Stalin occupied this post until his death in 1953) and three or four other secretaries, of which the majority were usually members of the Politburo and the Orgburo as well. As a normal rule, Stalin's closest and most trusted cronies were to be found in the Secretariat, but because of its pivotal position as a possible springboard to power, they were often transformed, in Stalin's suspicious eyes, into impatient and impudent successors to his power, who had to be liquidated.

The size of the Secretariat has fluctuated erratically in response to the continuing struggle for power, dropping to a low point of only three members in 1953–54 and reaching its post-Stalinist highpoint of 12 members in December, 1962. At the Twenty-Second Party Congress (1961), the number had been reduced to nine. It continues to fluctuate and to reflect the shifting individual fortunes of Soviet leaders in the struggle for power and influence.

According to the party statutes, the members of the Secretariat are elected by the Central Committee "to direct current work, mainly in the selection of cadres and organization and supervision over fulfillment of Party decisions." The membership of the Secretariat is not subject to the principle of "systematic renewal" of leading party organs, and the statutes are silent concerning the majorities necessary for election to the Secretariat.

As the administrative center of the party, the Secretariat supervises a large and variegated central apparatus, which serves as the staff and technical departments of the Central Committtee. Each secretary is in charge of a group of related departments and sections, which are organized along both functional and geographical divisions. Although no formal ranking of the secretaries exists, aside from that of First Secretary, there is reason to believe that an informal ranking does apply, comparable to the second and third secretaries at lesser organizational levels. Normally, the second-ranking man in the Secretariat, the informal second secretary, as it were, handles general administrative supervision over the apparatus under the First Secretary.

As the chief administrative organ of the party, the Secretariat supervises the execution and fulfillment of the party's policies and decisions in all administrative, economic, military, social, cultural, and professional institutions, organizations, and establishments in all parts of the country and at every level, through the hierarchy of secretaries which makes up the corps of full-time professional party functionaries. What emerges as the *de facto* policy of the party is in large measure what the party apparatus implements in its day-to-day activities.

The Secretariat thus maintains an organizational and hierarchical network of professional functionaries that constitutes a powerful instrument for seizing and maintaining control of the party, the state, and the entire Soviet system itself. In a real sense, it constitutes an *imperium in imperio,* for, in the words of Stalin, "The Party cadres constitute the commanding staff of the Party; and since our Party is in power, they also constitute the commanding staff of the leading organs of the state. . . . Party cadres become the decisive force in the work of guiding the Party and the State."

In its operations, the party apparatus gives concrete shape to the decisions and policies of the party because it not only implements the decisions of the party but checks on their execution by other organs, institutions, and establishments. Thus, in summary, the Secretariat and the apparatus perform the following functions: (1) they determine key appointments in all party, state, economic, social, cultural, and military institutions at every level; (2) they explain and implement the policies of the state and party in all sectors of Soviet life; (3) they check and insure the fulfillment of party and state directives; (4) they mobilize and manipulate the energies and pressures required for the implementation of the party's will; (5) they accumulate and organize information and prepare reports and recommendations for action, which are transmitted to the Presidium; (6) they keep a close tab on public moods and sentiments, report their impressions to the central authorities, and maintain an extensive file of dossiers on party members.

Although the formal authority to make policy is vested in the Presidium, this power is clearly shared with the Secretariat, which at times tends to overshadow the Presidium. The balance of power between the two organs is reflected in the degree of interlocking membership between them. The rise of Khrushchev to primacy has been accompanied by an increase in the number of secretaries who are also members of the Presidium. Thus, in 1953–54, Khrushchev was the only secretary in a Presidium of ten full members. After the Twentieth Party Congress (1956), however, the Secretariat was expanded to eight members (five of them new to this body), with five being simultaneously elected to a Presidium of 11 full and 5 candidate members. With the expulsion of the "anti-party group" in July, 1957, all eight secretaries were elected to membership in an expanded Presidium of 15 full and 9 candidate members. The ten secretaries appointed at the Twenty-First Party Congress (1959) were also elected members of the Presidium. Even more important, of the fourteen full or voting members of the Presidium, no less than nine were also members of the Secretariat. This meant, in effect, that the policies and decisions of the Presidium were in reality those of the Secretariat, and that the division of functions between the two organs had been all but obliterated.

The composition of the Secretariat and its interlocking membership with the Presidium began to change soon after the Twenty-First Party Congress. Having defeated his Stalinist contemporaries, Khrushchev moved to consolidate his power by purging his own supporters, some of whom may have been overly ambitious or whose loyalty was not matched with competence. Between 1959 and 1961, three powerful secretaries (Kirichenko, Belyayev, and Aristov) were dropped from both bodies for various reasons, while three more (Ignatov, Furtseva, and Mukhitidinov) were expelled from the Secretariat and Presidium at the Twenty-Second Congress (1961). All six had been key supporters of Khrushchev in his bid for power against the older members of the Presidium. Nine new faces were introduced to the summit at this Congress—four in the Presidium and five in the Secretariat—but none of the nine were appointed to simultaneous membership in both organs. The interlocking membership between these two bodies was reduced to four veteran leaders (Khrushchev, Kozlov, Suslov, and Kuusinen), and, with Khrushchev firmly in charge of both the Presidium and the Council of Ministers, the Secretariat could be reduced to its function of executing the policies of the Presidium instead of making them.

On the whole, however, leaders who made their way to the summit through the party apparatus continue to dominate the Presidium, and they constitute an absolute majority of its membership. Powerful as the party apparatus is, its relative strength in the Soviet political structure has diminished in response to the steady growth of the economic and military power of the Soviet Union. This growth has resulted in the creation of several parallel hierarchies and structures of power in the Soviet system that challenge the supremacy of the apparatus in the party and compete with it for control over the party and its symbols of authority and legitimacy. It is within the context of this rivalry that conflicts within the party are institutionalized and resolved into concrete decisions.

The Communist Party

The Social Composition of the Communist Party

VII

In all social systems, the social structure has a profound influence on the political dynamics of the system, irrespective of formal institutions and processes. The Soviet Union is no exception to this rule. Since the Communist Party is the only legal political organization in the country, the struggle for power in the Soviet system inevitably resolves itself into a struggle for control of the party. During the early years of the Soviet regime, the struggle proceeded from very narrow social foundations, but after Stalin's death, the conflicting demands made upon the system by the new social groups created by the great transformations of the past four decades erupted into factional strife within the Presidium. Inconclusive struggle in this body led the rival factions to seek support in the Central Committee, below which controversy has not been permitted to filter down. If the factional divisions within the Presidium were formalized, they would crack the party pyramid down to its base and open the way perhaps to an eventual evolution toward a two or more party system operating within the framework of Marxist-Leninist ideology.

Under the Soviet one-party system, factional rivalry at the party summit becomes a crude surrogate for a two-party contest, while the relationship between the Central Committee and its Presidium is the nearest approximation to a system of institutional responsibility and accountability.

The sharp divisions in the Presidium have caused the moribund Central Committee to be revived. Factional differences have been displayed before plenums of the Central Committee, where the actions of the Presidium have been appealed by the opposition for reversal or revision. The symbolic importance of the Central Committee is further reflected in the revelation at the Twenty-Second Party Congress that Molotov, who had been condemned in June, 1957, for "anti-party" factional activity, had sent a letter to the Central Committee in October, 1961, just before the opening of the Twenty-Second Congress, in which he criticized the policies of the Khrushchev leadership.[1] Although the text of the letter was not published and Molotov was not given a hearing, the mere existence of the

[1] See speech by P. A. Satyukov at Twenty-Second Party Congress, *Pravda*, October 27, 1961.

letter indicates the continuing role of the Central Committee as a body to which various factions may appeal.

Conflicts within the party arise as a result both of personal ambitions for power and of differences over doctrine and policy. Personal rivalries and policy disputes are so intricately interwoven that attempts to isolate the two are bound to be a sterile exercise. The rival cliques within the party hierarchy that were formed during Stalin's later years, and may have indeed been encouraged by him in his efforts to play off subordinates against one another, evolved into factions, each with its own aspirations and social foundations of power outside the party structure.

Factionalism in Soviet Society

Contrary to the official Soviet view that factions within the party do not arise from social conflicts within Soviet society but are rather the deviationary expressions of personalities seeking power, it is obvious that factions could neither arise nor flourish unless they received nourishment from powerful social forces in Soviet society. Just as party factions do not organize themselves into separate political organizations to challenge the supremacy of the party for political power, so social groups with their own interests do not form separate social bodies to demand formal representation in the party, but rather seek to make their demands on other groups in the party.

Within the context of Marxist-Leninist ideology, a social group with its own distinctive interests is automatically designated a social class that is, by definition, in conflict with the interests of other classes. After the Revolution, the interests of the working class alone, as determined by the party, were considered to be legitimate, and the interests of other classes were suppressed. Factional groupings within the party during the pre-1936 era were ascribed by Stalin to the attempts of classes slated for oblivion to worm themselves into the party, while deviations were described as ideological expressions of these classes articulated through the party. In 1936, Stalin pro-

claimed that class conflicts in Soviet society had been eradicated. The Communist Party was verbally transformed from a party representing only the interests of the working class into one representing the interests of all Soviet social groups. Consequently, Soviet ideology and party doctrine continue to deny the legitimacy of competing interest groups and refuse to tolerate their autonomous existence.

Although the Soviet intelligentsia consists of a number of elite groups, all its members have a common desire to perpetuate the Soviet system from which they have sprung and in which they benefit as a privileged group. Within this broad common framework of interests, however, these elites are concerned pre-eminently with the social status of their own group, and they seek to shape doctrine and policy according to their own special interests. They are officially recognized as occupational and professional categories, but they do not enjoy official or ideological sanction and thus cannot formally organize themselves into political organizations outside the party or as explicit factional groupings within the party. They must exert their influence and make their demands only as amorphous entities inside the Communist Party. Since they cannot legitimately articulate a separate interest inside or outside the party, they are inevitably forced into competing for control of the party's decision-making organs and into presenting their interests in terms of the party and the society as a whole.

Because Soviet ideology demands conformity, conflicts among social elites and their representatives in the party's leading organs cannot be resolved within an institutionalized framework of political accommodation and compromise. Rather, one interest group or faction must assert its supremacy over the others and impose its interests as those of all of society. If one group is unable to subdue the others, an uneasy and temporary coexistence ensues, and the party, under the pressures of diverse groups seeking political articulation, becomes a cover for a conglomeration of interests whose incompatibilities are only partially and temporarily obscured by a transparent veneer of "monolithic unity."

The Composition of the Party

The relationship between social structure and political power in the Soviet system is eloquently revealed by the social configuration of the Communist Party as a whole. From about 1930 until 1962, precise data on the social composition of the party were officially suppressed, because its representation as a working-class party was totally out of character with its social composition. The presence of working-class elements in the party was little more than an embarrassing reminder of its theoretical class character, as it increasingly was transformed into an organization whose membership was overwhelmingly drawn from the intelligentsia, which at times accounted for more than 70 per cent of the total membership. Representation of the peasantry in the party virtually disappeared.

In 1961, party membership was predominantly Great Russian (64 per cent), male (80 per cent), urban (82 per cent), middle-aged (52 per cent), and intelligentsia (48 per cent). Since Stalin's death, the social profile of the party has changed substantially in the direction of diminishing its character as a Russian, male, urban, middle-aged, and intelligentsia organization, and this trend appears to be continuing.

The Shifting Composition
of the Party, 1905–1962

The proportion of workers, peasants, and intelligentsia in the party has varied considerably during its existence. Before the Revolution, workers consistently accounted for 60 or more per cent of the party, while the intelli-

gentsia, which provided virtually the entire leadership of the party, made up about one-third of its membership. The peasants, who were neither attracted to the party nor actively recruited, furnished from 5 to 8 per cent of the party down to the time of the Revolution. After the Revolution, the balance among these three social groups underwent a substantial shift. From 1917 to 1920, the proportion of the working class was systematically reduced until it reached a low point of 33 per cent, while that of the peasantry rose to nearly 37 per cent to constitute the largest single social group to be represented. The proportion of the intelligentsia also suffered some reduction. The year 1920 was the high point of peasant representation in the party.

The party experienced its first purge in 1921, when party membership was nearly halved from 732,521 members to 401,000, and the social composition of the party was subjected to new and radical alterations. From 1922 to 1931, the proportion of workers was steadily increased until it reached a high of 66.6 per cent, while that of the peasantry was trimmed to 22.3 per cent and that of the intelligentsia was slashed to 11.1 per cent, to be cut further to 7.7 per cent in the following year. These changes in social composition were a consequence of two factors: (1) the classification "worker" was given a broader definition to include also those who were workers at some time in their life, which inflated the worker category by about 15 to 20 per cent of the total; (2) the party increased in size from 401,000 in 1922 to 3,172,215 in 1932, and, during this period, not only were energetic measures taken to recruit workers into the party, but the intelligentsia itself came under suspicion, and their entry into the party became subject to stringent qualifications and requirements.

After 1932, data concerning the social composition of the party were suppressed, and for good reason. During the period of the Five Year Plans, the role of the intelligentsia in the industrialization and modernization of Russia was of crucial significance, and, within the complex of incentives and rewards introduced by Stalin, membership in the party assumed cardinal importance. The barriers erected against the intelligentsia were gradually relaxed and finally eliminated in 1939. Because of their education and abilities, the members of the intelligentsia easily met the formal qualifications for membership and quickly moved upward in the party hierarchy and soon monopolized all positions of importance and influence; the proportion of party members drawn from the intelligentsia swelled to well over 50 per cent of the total.

The "proletarian" character of the party was partially restored during World War II, when workers and peasants in uniform were almost indiscriminately recruited into the party, and the percentage of workers may have risen once again to about one-third of the total member-

ship. Immediately after the war, however, another purge hit the party and those who were hastily recruited into the party during the war were mustered out, most of those expelled being workers and peasants. The intelligentsia in all probability accounted for nearly 70 per cent of the total at this time.

In January, 1962, Soviet authorities published the first comprehensive social breakdown of the party in three decades, probably because for the first time since 1933 the proportion of the intelligentsia in the party dropped to below 50 per cent of the total. As of July, 1961, according to the official data, workers accounted for 34.5 per cent of the total membership and peasants accounted for 17.5 per cent (Table 7-1). "Employees and all

TABLE 7-1 *Social Composition of the Communist Party, 1905–1961*

Social category	1905	1917	1920	1932	1956	1961
Workers	61.7%	60.2%	33.2%	64.5%	32.0%	34.5%
Peasants	4.7	7.6	36.9	27.8	17.1	17.5
Intelligentsia	33.6	32.2	22.1	7.7	50.9	48.0
Total	8,400	23,600	612,000	3,172,215	7,173,521	9,176,005

others accounted for 48 per cent, a category which includes the intelligentsia and perhaps the members of the armed forces. The statistics for 1956 were also divulged, and these were 32 per cent workers, 17.1 per cent peasants, and 50.9 per cent "employees and all others." [2] In spite of this influx of workers and peasants in the party, the intelligentsia, which together with their families account for only 18 per cent of the total population, still provides nearly 50 per cent of the membership of the party.

Rural Representation in the Party

The party is predominantly urban in character, with more than 80 per cent of its membership being drawn from the cities (urban workers and intelligentsia). Before the death of Stalin, the party may have been actually

more than 90 per cent urban in character at times. The party has always been weakly organized in the countryside, not only because of built-in ideological biases, but also for the following reasons: (1) the agricultural and rural proportion of the population has been in steady decline since 1928 and this decline is continuing; (2) educational opportunities in rural areas are limited, and the quality of literacy and cultural life is much lower than in the cities; hence most collective farmers cannot meet the qualifications for membership; (3) incentives on the farms are very low, with the result that most of the ambitious and capable elements of the rural population migrate to the cities.

In 1934, for example, more than 50 per cent

[2] *Partiinaya Zhizn,* No. 1, January, 1962, pp. 44–54.

of the collective farms did not have a single party member, while by 1939, only 5 per cent of the 243,000 collective farms had primary party organizations, with the membership on these farms accounting for only 153,000 out of a total party membership of almost 2,500,-000. With the amalgamation of the collective farms, the proportion with party organizations increased, until by 1953, 85 per cent of the farms had party organizations. At the Twentieth Party Congress, further progress was registered, but more than 7,300 collective farms were still without primary party organizations. Virtually all state and collective farms were reported as having party organizations in 1958, and by 1961 primary party organizations were to be found on 41,387 collective farms, 5,721 of which were large enough to have party committees, while 9,206 primary units were located on state farms, of which 2,718 were large enough to have party committees.

The rural population was officially estimated at 107,878,000 people in June, 1961, about 50 per cent of the total Soviet population. Rural party membership, however, accounted for only 23.5 per cent of the total party membership and was spread unevenly among the different social groups in Soviet rural society (Table 7-2). Thus while more than 95 per cent of the collective-farm chairmen and virtually 100 per cent of the sovkhoz directors were party members, only two to three per cent of the ordinary collective farmers were to be found in the party.

Of the 1,700,000 collective farmers reported to be in the party in June, 1961, 220,000 were, in fact, equipment operators and mechanics who were formerly with the Machine and Tractor Stations, which were dissolved. Another 22.6 per cent, or 384,000, are listed as holding administrative posts or being on pensions. This leaves only 1,100,000 collective farmers as party members, of which brigade leaders and heads of farm sections account for

a substantial proportion.[3] The leverage that rural society in general, and the peasantry in particular, has in the Soviet political process

TABLE 7-2   *Social Composition of the Communist Party in Rural Areas, 1961*

Sovkhoz directors	9,000
Collective-farm directors	40,000
Rural intelligentsia and pensioners	384,000
Sovkhoz farmers and workers	557,000
Equipment workers on kolkhozes	220,000
Collective farmers, including rural foremen	1,100,000
Total rural Communists	2,310,000 (23.5%)

is thus very low, and this has been consistently reflected in the low priorities and rewards which have been allocated to the farm areas in Soviet society.

Urban Representation in the Party

As we have seen, the working class has always occupied a significant role in the doctrine and practice of the party. During the period of the great social and economic transformation of the Soviet social order between the two World Wars, the party underwent a profound change. The most able and ambitious members of the working class acquired new skills and education and thus mustered themselves out of the working class into the "ruling class" in the Soviet system. While expelling them from the party or erecting barriers to reduce their ratio of membership might satisfy the official myth, it would effectively destroy the incentive of the workers. The requirements of reality had to be reconciled with the imperatives of ideology, and the intelligentsia was redefined as a "working" or "toiling" intelligentsia, whose social origin was predominantly proletarian or peasant in character. Thus, at the Eighteenth Party Congress (1939), Stalin etched a social dilemma, which continues to disturb the regime:

Hundreds of thousands of young people coming from the ranks of the working class, peasantry

[3] *Ibid.*

and the working intelligentsia entered the universities and technical colleges, from which they emerged to reinforce the attenuated ranks of the intelligentsia. . . . As a result, we now have a numerous, new, popular, socialist intelligentsia fundamentally different from the old, bourgeois intelligentsia both in composition and in social and political character. . . . It is therefore all the more astonishing and strange that . . . people should be found within our Party who . . . it appears, assert that workers and peasants who until recently were working in Stakhanov fashion in the factories and collective farms, who were then sent to the universities to be educated, thereby ceased to be real people and became second-rate people. So we are to conclude that education is a pernicious and dangerous thing. We want all our workers and peasants to be cultured and educated, and we shall achieve this in time. But in the opinion of these queer comrades, this purpose harbors a grave danger; for after the workers and peasants become cultured and educated they may face the danger of being classified as second-rate people. The possibility is not precluded that these queer comrades may in time sink to the position of extolling backwardness, ignorance, benightedness and obscurantism. It would be quite in the nature of things. Theoretical vagaries have never led, and never can lead, to any good.[4]

The ideological guilt feelings aroused by the transformation of the party into a party of the Soviet intelligentsia was clearly betrayed by the nearly three-decade refusal to reveal the social composition of the party. According to the data released in 1961, the working class accounted for more than one-third (34.5 per cent) of the total membership, an increase from 32 per cent in 1956. But this category not only includes industrial foremen, who make up a substantial proportion of the party membership, but also nearly 500,000 workers on sovkhozes, who are classified as workers in Soviet practice. Of the 43,000,000 urban workers in Soviet society, less than 2,000,000 belong to the Communist Party, that is, less than five per cent of the workers in urban areas. This compares with the more than 22 per cent of the intelligentsia who belong to the party. In recent years, emphasis has been placed on recruiting party members from

"branches of material production," which includes workers, peasants, and intelligentsia occupied in producing goods as distinguished from those in "non-productive" or service enterprises and occupations. As of 1961, 71.4 per cent of all members were engaged in production, while 28.6 per cent were in non-productive spheres of the economy.[5]

The Social Pyramid of Power

The Distribution of Elites in the Party

As of July 1, 1961, 48 per cent of the Communist Party was made up of the category "employees and all others," which includes the intelligentsia, perhaps members of the armed forces (unless they were distributed by occupation), and university students. In 1961, more than three million members of the party were classified as "specialists with higher or specialized secondary education," 47.8 per cent of whom were engineers, technicians, or agricultural specialists.

The Soviet "ruling elite" corresponds approximately to the more than 4,600,000 Communists who are drawn from the various categories of the intelligentsia. The changes in social distribution between 1956 and 1961 demonstrate the calculated shift in emphasis within the intelligentsia to recruit more heavily from those elites who are engaged in the material branches of the economy and to reduce the relative representation of the executives and managers as well as those in the service branches of the economy. All decision-makers in the Soviet system are selected from among these 4,600,000 party members who are classified as intelligentsia, for only they possess the requisite skills to operate the complex machinery of an expanding industrial and technological empire (Table 7-3).

[5] *Partiinaya Zhizn, op. cit.*

[4] Stalin, *Leninism: Selected Writings,* pp. 476–477.

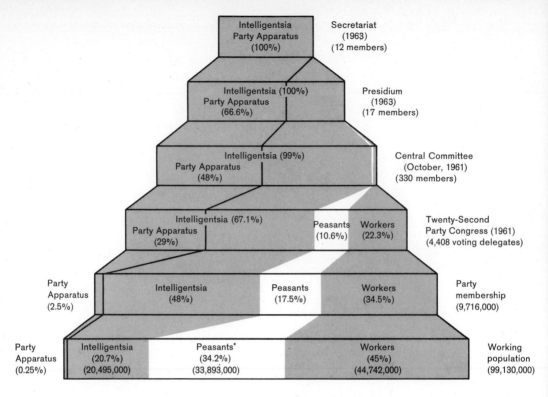

Party Apparatus	Intelligentsia		Peasants	Workers	

Intelligentsia Party Apparatus (100%) — Secretariat (1963) (12 members)

Intelligentsia (100%) Party Apparatus (66.6%) — Presidium (1963) (17 members)

Intelligentsia (99%) Party Apparatus (48%) — Central Committee (October, 1961) (330 members)

Intelligentsia (67.1%) Party Apparatus (29%) | Peasants (10.6%) | Workers (22.3%) — Twenty-Second Party Congress (1961) (4,408 voting delegates)

Party Apparatus (2.5%) | Intelligentsia (48%) | Peasants (17.5%) | Workers (34.5%) — Party membership (9,716,000)

Party Apparatus (0.25%) | Intelligentsia (20.7%) (20,495,000) | Peasants* (34.2%) (33,893,000) | Workers (45%) (44,742,000) — Working population (99,130,000)

FIGURE 7-I   THE SOCIAL PYRAMIDIZATION OF POWER IN THE SOVIET SYSTEM.

The Social Composition of Party Congresses

Throughout the party's history, the largest social groups in the Soviet Union have had the narrowest representation at the top of the party pyramid. Conversely, the groups with a narrow social base have dominated the party. Thus, even in 1905, when 62 per cent of the party was made up of workers, 93 per cent of the delegates to the Party Congress were classified as intelligentsia and only 4 per cent were listed as peasants. Of the 15 members on the Central Committee in 1918, only one was classified as a worker; about 40 per cent of the Party Congress, however, was composed of workers.

In 1952, the percentage of workers, including foremen, in the Party Congress was less than 8 per cent, while the intelligentsia accounted for more than 84 per cent of the delegates (Table 7-4). The situation has improved substantially since Stalin's death. The proportion of workers elected to the Twenty-Second Party Congress (1961) was nearly three times that in 1952, but the number of delegates to the Congress had quadrupled. While the percentage of workers was tripled, the increase in delegates from the intelligentsia was little short of astronomical—in absolute numbers, the increase in the number of delegates from this class was from about 1,114 members to nearly 3,000.

The Khrushchev regime has tried to give greater representation to workers, peasants, women, and the agricultural sectors of Soviet life. Most of the delegates representing the workers and peasants in the Congresses are

TABLE 7-3   *The Distribution of the Intelligentsia in the Communist Party, 1961*

Category	Party membership	Percentage	Total size of elite	Percentage of elite in party
Intelligentsia	4,600,000	48.0%	20,500,000	22.2%
Executive and managerial	460,000	10.2	1,347,000 [a]	34.0
Engineer, technical	1,380,000	29.2	4,683,000 [b]	29.0
Cultural-professional	989,000	21.5	5,991,000 [c]	16.5
Trade, etc.	230,000	4.9	2,268,000	10.0
Accounting, clerical, and other office workers	552,000	11.9	4,461,000	12.3
Other employees	1,100,000	22.3	Indeterminate	
Workers (urban and rural)	3,400,000	34.5	46,000,000	7.4
Peasants	1,700,000	17.5	31,000,000	5.5

[a] Includes 392,100 state, party, and public organization executives and 955,200 economic executives, including farm directors.
[b] Excludes executives, but includes agricultural specialists.
[c] Includes medical, educational, legal, cultural personnel.

TABLE 7-4   *Social Composition of Party Congress, 1952–1961*   (Voting delegates only)

	1952 Number	Percentage	1956 Number	Percentage	1959 Number	Percentage	1961 Number	Percentage
Total	1,192		1,355		1,269		4,408	
Workers		7.8% [a]		12.2%			984	22.3%
					399	32.0%		
Peasants		7.8 [b]		4.9			469	10.6 [c]
Intelligentsia		84.4		82.9	870	68.0	2,955	67.1
Party apparatus			526	37.3 [d]	456	36.0	1,262	28.7 [e]
State officials			177	13.1	147	11.5	465	10.5
Managerial-technical					126	10.0	667	15.0 [f]
Cultural-professional					50	4.0	235	5.3
Military			116	8.5	91	7.0	305	7.0 [g]
Other							21	0.5
Women		12.3	193	14.2	222	17.5	1,073	22.3

[a] Includes foremen.
[b] Includes farm directors and rural intelligentsia.
[c] Includes farm directors.
[d] Includes 20 trade-union and Komsomol officials.
[e] Includes 104 trade-union and Komsomol officials.
[f] Includes 260 agricultural specialists.
[g] Includes police officials with military rank.

foremen or supervisory personnel rather than ordinary workers or collective farmers. Even at the level of the Congress, in spite of the ornamental additions of representatives of workers and peasants, imbalance between the size of the class and its power in the party emerges. The intelligentsia as a whole, which accounts for about 21 per cent of the working population, comprised almost 50 per cent of the party membership in 1961 but accounted for 67 per cent of the delegates to the Congress (although the percentage was down, from 84.4 per cent in 1952). (See Figure 7-1 at the top of page 498.)

Social Composition of Communist Party

The Distribution of Elites in the Central Committee and Presidium

Although "workers" and "peasants" are sprinkled throughout party committees at lower levels of organization, their numbers thin out progressively as one moves up the party pyramid, and disappear completely at the level of the All-Union Central Committee (Table 7-5). Even at the lowest levels, only 37.9 per cent of the members of city and borough party committees were "workers" and "peasants," while 26.3 per cent were from the local party and governmental bureaucracies, 17.4 per cent were engineers, technicians, and professional workers, 10.1 per cent were industrial and farm executives, and 8.3 per cent were from other agencies (probably including the military).

TABLE 7-5   *Social Composition of the Central Committee, 1952–1961*   (Members and candidates)

Social category	1952	1956	1961
Party apparatus	103	117	158 (48%) [a]
State and economic officials	79	98	112 (34)
Military officers	26	18	31 (9.3)
Cultural and scientific	—	—	18 (5.4)
Police	9	3	2
Other	19 [b]	19 [b]	9 [c] (3.3)
Totals	236	255	330

[a] Includes 9 trade-union and Komsomol officials.
[b] Includes cultural and scientific personnel.
[c] Includes a few "workers" and "peasants."

At the level of the Central Committee in 1961, the party apparatus accounted for nearly one-half the total membership, while the state bureaucracy, including both administrative and managerial officials, comprised about one-third. Thus the state bureaucracy remains the chief rival of the party apparatus for control of the party, and the power struggles since Stalin's death can be charted

through the changing balance and distribution of the elites in the Central Committee and its Presidium. The Secretariat, by its very nature, remains the exclusive domain of the apparatus, and the distribution of power at the summit is reflected in the degree of interlock between state and party officials in the Presidium. Since Stalin's death, the pattern of distribution in the Party's highest body has been as shown in Table 7-6.

The Nationality Composition of the Party

It has not always been easy to assess the importance of nationality within the party, for official information has been fragmentary and unreliable. Great Russians are found in substantial numbers in many of the non-Russian party organizations, and, since the organizational and political requirements of party leadership have priority over balanced ethnic composition, it has not been unusual for party organizations in some of the non-Russian Republics to be actually controlled by ethnic Russians, who might make up a small fraction of the population in the areas.

The degree of Russian presence in non-Russian party organizations has varied considerably over time. In all Republics, with the exception of the Georgian and Armenian, Russians occupied the commanding heights of Republic party organizations under Stalin, although indigenous communists may have actually held the post of First Secretary from time to time.

The distribution and influence of various nationalities within the party at the national level has been highly uneven. In sheer numbers, Great Russians have always dominated membership in the party. Whereas Russians accounted for only 53 per cent of the population in 1926, they made up 72 per cent of the party only two years earlier. The Ukrainians, in contrast, who provided more than 21 per cent of the population, made up only 6 per cent of the party members. In 1962, the first complete national breakdown of the party in decades was published. Great Russians still accounted for 64 per cent of the total; the decrease in percentage resulted from a deter-

TABLE 7-6   *Distribution of Elites in the Presidium, 1952–1963*

Category	October 1952	March 1953	February 1956	July 1957	July 1961	October 1961	January 1963
Party apparatus [a]	13 (5) [b]	2 (2)	4 (3)	10 (6)	10 (3)	7 (3)	8 (4)
State bureaucracy							
Economic	5 (4)	4	4	1 (2)	2 (1)	2	2
Non-economic	4 (2)	3 (1)	3 (1)	3	2 (2)	2 (2)	2 (2)
Professional							
Military	0	0	0 (1)	1	0	0	0
Police	2	1 (1)	0	0	0	0	0
Cultural							
intelligentsia (ideologists)	1 (1)	0	0 (1)	0 (1)	0 (1)	0	0
Totals	25 (11)	10 (4)	11 (6)	15 (6)	14 (7)	11 (5)	12 (6)
Women	0	0	0	1	1	0	0

[a] State and police officials, ideologists, and others who were appointed to government positions from the party apparatus are included in this category rather than in their official position. Main career experience determines classification. Thus, M. A. Suslov is classified with the party apparatus rather than with the cultural intelligentsia.
[b] Figures in parentheses are candidate members.

TABLE 7-7   *Nationality Distribution of the Party, July, 1961*

Nationality	Party members	Percentage	Total number	Percentage
Russians	6,116,700	64.0%	114,114,000	55.0%
Ukrainians	1,412,200	14.7	37,253,000	18.0
Byelorussians	287,000		7,913,000	3.6
Georgians	170,400		2,692,000	1.3
Armenians	161,200		2,787,000	1.3
Kazakhs	149,000		3,662,000	1.7
Uzbeks	142,000		6,015,000	3.0
Azerbaidzhani	106,000		2,940,000	1.4
Lithuanians	42,000		2,326,000	1.2
Latvians	33,900		1,400,000	0.7
Tadzhiks	32,700		1,397,000	0.7
Turkmen	27,300		1,002,000	0.5
Kirgiz	27,300		969,000	0.46
Moldavians	26,700		2,214,000	1.1
Estonians	24,100		989,000	0.48
Others	866,100			
Totals	9,626,700		208,827,000	

mined effort on the part of the regime to increase the representation of other Republics. More than 100 nationalities were represented in the Party as of July 1, 1961. The distribution of the various nationalities is shown in Table 7-7.[6]

The representation of the non-Russian nationalities in the higher organs of the party has varied considerably over the years. A score or more nationalities have been represented in the Central Committee of the party since 1952. Although the proportion of non-Russians, especially Ukrainians, has been steadily increasing since Stalin's death, the Russian presence has been overwhelming, rising as high as 80 per cent of the total membership. At the apex of the party, the proportion of Russians has been smaller, but only 9 non-Russian nationalities have found representation on the party's highest body. Of the 78 members or candidate

Social Composition of Communist Party

[6] *Ibid.*

members who have served on the Party Presidium and its predecessor, the Politburo, for any length of time, 47 have been Great Russians. Other nationalities have been distributed as follows:

Nationality	Full	Candidates	Total
Great Russians	37	10	47
Ukrainians	6	4	10
Jews	5	3	8
Georgians	3	1	4
Armenians	1	1	2
Uzbeks	1	1	2
Latvians	1	1	2
Karelo-Finns	1	0	1
Azerbaidzhani	0	1	1
Poles	1	0	1
Totals	56	22	78

Statistics alone, however, do not tell the complete story. Although the Ukrainians constitute the second largest nationality in the Union, not a single Ukrainian was admitted to the party's highest body between the years 1938 and 1952. The first Moslem to be admitted was an Azerbaidzhani crony of Beria's, who was appointed a candidate member in 1953, only to be executed about a year later. The first Central Asian, an Uzbek, was admitted to the Presidium in December, 1956, and was replaced by another in 1961. Under Stalin, the Politburo was in fact dominated by the Great Russians and the Caucasian nationalities, the latter constituting from one-third to one-fourth of the total membership.

The Soviet Constitutional Order

VIII

The Soviet system during its more than four decades of existence has operated under three different constitutions. The first constitution, which was restricted only to the Russian Republic—the R.S.F.S.R.—was promulgated on July 10, 1918; it was superseded by the first Constitution of the U.S.S.R., which came in force officially on January 3, 1924. The present Constitution was promulgated on December 5, 1936, and has remained in force since, although it has been amended frequently, especially in recent years. It is virtually impossible to secure an up-to-date text of the Soviet Constitution, whose versions now appear with the frequency of a periodical. Amendments to the Soviet Constitution are not conveniently enumerated, as is the case in American constitutional practice, but rather the alterations are inserted directly into the text, so that amendments can only be detected by examining various versions of the Constitution itself. The situation has become so bewildering that on more than one occasion after Stalin's death Khrushchev has called for

its drastic overhaul or replacement with a new document. On April 26, 1962, Khrushchev proposed before the Supreme Soviet that a new draft of the Soviet Constitution be undertaken. A Drafting Commission was quickly appointed with Khrushchev serving as its Chairman.

Khrushchev's main point in calling for a new constitution was that the existing one "conformed to the period of the consolidation of socialism and the basic completion of the construction of a socialist society [and] . . . the chief provisions of this constitution are now obsolete." [1] Trying to patch up the already battered and mutilated Stalin Constitution, he noted, "would be nothing but adding new wings to an old building." The new Constitution would reflect a society in which "socialism had achieved full and final victory [and] . . . has entered the period of full-scale communist construction," during which time "the state of the dictatorship of the proletariat has evolved into a socialist state of all the people" and "has emerged from capitalist encirclement," to lead "a great community of socialist states." [2]

[1] *Pravda*, April 25, 1962.
[2] *Ibid.*

503

The Functions and Principles of the Constitution

The Soviet Constitution performs the four universal functions of constitutions everywhere: (1) it legalizes the existing social order and makes explicit its ideological principles; (2) it establishes a framework of government and administration; (3) it regulates social and institutional behavior; (4) it enumerates normative Soviet goals and aspirations. In addition, the Soviet Constitution performs another function: (5) it serves as a propaganda document for export abroad.

The Constitution gives legal expression to the basic ideological norms of Soviet doctrine that have been concretely implemented. The most important of these are: (1) the abolition of private ownership of the means of production in favor of state or public ownership; (2) the collectivization of agriculture; (3) the nationalization of natural resources; (4) a centrally directed planned economy; (5) mandatory employment, in accordance with the formulas, "He who does not work, neither shall he eat" and "From each according to his ability, to each according to his work"; (6) the legal monopoly of the Communist Party.

Among the normative goals, which are essentially hortatory in character, are: (1) "the aim of increasing wealth, of steadily raising the material and cultural standards of the working people" (Article 11); and (2) "the steady growth of the productive forces of Soviet society, the elimination of the possibility of economic crises, and the abolition of unemployment" (Article 118). These are general aspirations, expressing hope rather than concrete fulfillment.

Some normative goals in the Constitution, however, have been realized to some degree: (1) "the right to rest and leisure"; (2) "the

right to maintenance in old age and also in case of sickness and disability"; (3) "the right to education." In the same category is the principle that "women in the U.S.S.R. are accorded equal rights with men" (Article 122) and the principle of national and racial equality, which asserts the "equality of rights of citizens . . . irrespective of their nationality or race," violations of which are "punishable by law." The implementation of these doctrines has been extremely uneven, often capricious and unreliable. The regime's record concerning the non-Russian nationalities, for instance, has been exemplary in some areas and deplorable in others.

Other principles of the Soviet Constitution can be dismissed as transparent propaganda clichés which are essentially meaningless. Among these are the assertions that: (1) the Soviet Union "is a socialist state of workers and peasants"; (2) "all power in the U.S.S.R. belongs to the working people"; (3) the Soviet Union is "a voluntary union of equal . . . Republics"; (4) the Republics have "the right to freely secede from the U.S.S.R."; (5) "the highest organ of state power in the U.S.S.R. is the Supreme Soviet."

Another category of unrealized principles are those which are purely declaratory in character. These are the principles dealing with political rights of Soviet citizens and the manner in which they are to be exercised. Thus Article 125 asserts that Soviet citizens "are guaranteed by law . . . freedom of speech . . . of the press . . . of assembly, including the holding of mass meetings . . . of street processions and demonstrations," provided that these freedoms are exercised "in conformity with the interests of the working people, and in order to strengthen the socialist system." With similar reservations, Article 126 reads that Soviet citizens "are guaranteed the right to unite in public organizations: trade unions, cooperative societies, youth organizations, sport and defense organizations, cultural, technical and scientific societies," *but not in political parties or organizations.* Article 126 does not give Soviet citizens even the right to join the Communist Party, which is reserved only for "the most active and politically conscious citizens," and "is the core of all organizations . . . both public and state."

Article 124, concerning the exercise of religion, provides for "freedom of religious worship and freedom of anti-religious propaganda." This means that freedom of "religious propaganda" is not guaranteed in the Constitution and, in fact, constitutes a crime under separate legislation. On the other hand, the full power and apparatus of the state and party are mobilized on behalf of "anti-religious propaganda," which is a basic freedom in the Soviet Constitution obviously superior to freedom of religion. Since virtually all physical property in the Soviet Union belongs to the state, churches and religious institutions are either non-existent or in a state of decay and disrepair; clergymen are hounded and persecuted, while "believers" find themselves harassed and insulted and discover that their opportunities in Soviet society are severely limited. "Freedom to worship," in effect, means freedom to worship silently, inconspicuously, and in isolation.

Another group of principles covers "rights" that have been continuously and grossly violated. Article 127 reads that "citizens of the U.S.S.R. are guaranteed inviolability of the person [and] no person may be placed under arrest except by decision of a court or with the sanction of a prosecutor," while Article 128 asserts: "the inviolability of the homes of citizens and privacy of correspondence are protected by law."

These are "rights" that Soviet jurists now acknowledge were systematically outraged during the entire period of the Stalinist regime. Ironically enough, the very moment these "rights" were promulgated as sacred provisions of the "most democratic" Constitution in the history of mankind, they were being violated by the secret police, which arrested, tortured, and executed hundreds of thousands of ordinary citizens and state and party officials of the highest rank, without benefit of public trial, legal counsel, or formal arraignment as provided by the Constitution and legal codes. Since 1956, Soviet jurists have been actively engaged in disavowing the Stalinist violations of the "norms of socialist legality," the secret police has been shorn of its powers and dismembered, the concentration camps have been emptied of political prisoners, and the criminal and procedural codes have been revised in an effort to provide some concrete fulfillment of these universally cherished human rights.

Soviet Federalism: Theory and Practice

The Soviet Union is constitutionally described as "a federal state formed on the basis of a voluntary union of equal Soviet Socialist Republics." Although, juridically, the U.S.S.R. resembles more a confederation than a federation, in practice it is organized as a tightly centralized monolithic system.

The Origins of Soviet Federalism

The Soviet federal system does not spring from Marxist doctrine, but rather has its source in the ethnic legacy left by the collapse of the Tsarist system. The Bolsheviks fell heir to a land with more than 100 races and nationalities, which had been absorbed but never digested by the expanding Russian Empire. Long exposed to "russification" and aggression, these peoples smoldered with discontent, and their hostility constituted one of the chief political problems of the Imperial system which was never satisfactorily resolved.

Federalism as an idea was anathema to both Marx and Lenin, for it seemed to be incompatible with the imperative of central economic planning. Furthermore, nationalism —and its moral justification, national self-determination—contravened the Marxist emphasis on class solidarity and a unified international proletariat. In spite of these ideological prejudices against nationalism,

Lenin demonstrated his flexibility by recognizing that in the light of the experiences of the nations of the Russian Empire, no political movement could succeed without allowing for the nationalistic impulses which motivated the non-Russian minorities. In 1903, Lenin espoused the principle of national self-determination in spite of his ideological reservations. At first, he tried to interpret it in such a way that it would exclude the right of secession and independence, but by 1913, Lenin recognized that national self-determination "cannot be interpreted otherwise than in the sense of *political* self-determination, i.e., the right of secession and formation of an independent state," a view echoed by Stalin, the party's emerging expert on the nationalities question.[3] From that point on, the right of the nations of Russia to secede became a declaratory principle that appears in every Soviet constitutional document.

The Bolshevik stand, it should be made clear, was dictated by tactical expediency, as Lenin frankly admitted:

We, on our part, do not want separation at all. We want as large a state as possible. . . . We want a voluntary amalgamation and that is why we are obliged to recognize the freedom of secession.[4]

Wherever it could, however, the Soviet regime used the power of the Red Army to prevent secession and to reconquer those areas of the former Russian Empire which took the Bolshevik position seriously and tried to secede. Those border regions that managed to make good their separation, even in the face of an attempted Soviet conquest (i.e., Poland, the three Baltic States, and Finland), remained outside the Soviet Republic.

[3] Lenin, *Selected Works*, VII, p. 123.
[4] V.I. Lenin, *Collected Works*, XVI, (New York: International Publishers, 1945), p. 507. See also V.V. Aspaturian, "The Theory and Practice of Soviet Federalism," *Journal of Politics*, Vol. 12, 1950, 20–51.

The Principles of Soviet Federalism

The federal structure of the Soviet state, therefore, is dictated more by historical necessity than by ideological inspiration. In general, the trend has been toward greater *juridical decentralization accompanied by tighter ideological and political centralization.* While Soviet federalism reflects a conventional pattern of organization in its purely juridical dimension, it also exhibits five characteristics which are unique. These are:

1. Soviet federal units are based on nationality rather than on regional, economic, or historical distinctions. All federal units are nationality units; hence the Soviet system is primarily a *multi-national* federalism.

2. Not all nationality units possess the same degree of national autonomy, but rather a hierarchy of national units exists, with the highest being called a Union Republic and the lowest a National District (okrug).

3. The highest federal units, the Union Republics, have a juridical right to secede, as the ultimate manifestation of their national autonomy.

4. Since February 1, 1944, all Union Republics are constitutionally endowed with the power to engage in diplomatic relations, to sign international agreements, and to maintain separate troop formations. Thus, juridically, foreign affairs and defense are decentralized. Although two Republics, the Ukraine and Byelorussia, are members of the United Nations and engage in limited diplomatic activity and all Union Republics have Foreign Ministries, the diplomatic powers of the Republics remain potential rather than real. In the matter of defense, not a single Republic has ever established a Defense Ministry, appointed a Defense Minister, or organized a separate army.[5]

5. Since December, 1958, the collective

[5] V.V. Aspaturian, *The Union Republics in Soviet Diplomacy* (Geneva: Libraire Droz, 1960); and "The Union Republics and Soviet Diplomacy: Concepts, Institutions and Practices," *American Political Science Review* (June, 1959), 383–411.

head of the Soviet state, the Presidium of the Supreme Soviet, must have as many Vice Chairmen as there are Union Republics. By custom, the Chairmen of the Presidia of the Union Republics are ex officio Vice-Chairmen of the Presidium of the Union. Similarly, the Chairmen of the Council of Ministers of the Union Republics are ex officio members of the All-Union Council of Ministers. Thus, in the Soviet pattern, the basic federal units have representation in the central executive and administrative organs of government.

Aside from the unique departures enumerated above, Soviet federalism in its formal dimensions is quite conventional. It follows the principle of federal supremacy, in that all Republic constitutions must be in conformity with that of the U.S.S.R., and federal laws take precedence over Republic laws.

The Hierarchy
of National Units

As the Constitution of a federal state, the Soviet Constitution establishes a system of multiple jurisdiction and shared sovereignty. In a strictly technical sense, the federal character of the Soviet Union is restricted to the relationship between the Soviet Union and the Union Republics, of which there are currently fifteen. Lesser national units enjoy narrower degrees of autonomy. The Union Republics vary in size from the R.S.F.S.R.—which embraces three-quarters of the territory of the U.S.S.R., stretches from the Baltic to the Pacific, and includes 55 per cent of the population of the Soviet Union—to Estonia, the smallest in population (1.2 million), and Armenia, the smallest territorially. According to existing Soviet doctrine, first enunciated by Stalin in 1936, a national territory must meet three physical criteria in order to qualify as a Union Republic:

Since the Union Republics have a right to secede from the U.S.S.R., a republic . . . must be in a position logically and actually to raise the question of secession from the U.S.S.R. . . . Of course none of our republics would actually raise the question of seceding from the U.S.S.R. But since the right to secede from the U.S.S.R. is reserved to the Union Republics, it must be so arranged that this right does not become a meaningless scrap of paper [sic].[6]

The right to secede, of course, is illusory. No Republic has ever attempted it, although non-Russian Soviet leaders have been tried and executed allegedly for plotting to take various Republics out of the Union!

Since the Republics are juridically organized as national states, each has a constitution, a government, and a flag, and also a coat of arms that is a variation of that possessed by the Union. Each Republic has a Supreme Soviet (unicameral instead of bicameral, however), a collective head of state called the Presidium of the Supreme Soviet, a Council of Ministers with a Chairman (Premier), a Supreme Court, a Procurator, a Foreign Ministry, and provisions for a Defense Ministry. Union Republics have 25 deputies in the Council of Nationalities—the second "federal" chamber of the Supreme Soviet.

Immediately below the Union Republic in the Soviet federal hierarchy is the Autonomous Republic, which is reserved for moderately large nationalities that are "culturally advanced" but cannot meet the criteria for Union Republic status laid down by Stalin in 1936. Autonomous Republics, of which there are 20, resemble Union Republics in almost all particulars. They have constitutions and governments virtually indistinguishable from those of the Union Republics, but they do not have the juridical right to secede, are subject to the jurisdiction of a Union Republic rather than to that of the Soviet Union directly, are not endowed with international responsibilities, do not enjoy a Vice-Chairmanship on the All-Union Presidium nor ex officio membership on the All-Union Council of Ministers, and are entitled to only 11 deputies in the Council of Nationalities.

The Autonomous Oblasts, of which there were 8 in 1962, are populated by smaller na-

[6] Stalin, *Leninism: Selected Writings*, p. 400.

The Soviet Constitutional Order

tionalities, and their juridical status and powers are considerably less than those of the Union and Autonomous Republics. The Autonomous Oblasts are entitled to 5 deputies in the Council of Nationalities. The lowest national units are the National Okrugs, of which all 10 were located in the R.S.F.S.R. in 1961. These units are populated by very small national, ethnic, or linguistic groups, numbering in the thousands. Altogether, 53 national groups are organized into units. National units can move up or down in the federal hierarchy, but the usual procedure is promotion to higher status: National Oblast to Autonomous Republic, or Autonomous Republic to Union Republic.

Soviet Federalism in Perspective

Since Soviet federalism arose neither as a practical device to restrain the power of the central government nor in response to an ideological compulsion, its true significance is not likely to be found in its functional attributes, but rather in its role as a device for organizing many national groups under a uniform ideology. Federalism is still viewed in Soviet doctrine as a transitional device to centralization, although it has undoubtedly influenced Soviet administration in ways not originally intended. Soviet federalism is a very weak restriction against the power of the central authority. Since the Constitution itself is not designed as a limiting instrument, it is not likely that the federalism it establishes can become an effective limitation on the central government.

While the Soviet policy on nationalities is deficient in many particulars, the Soviet multinational system is a unique experiment. Western criticism of Soviet nationality policy and Soviet federalism is leveled principally at the uniform ideological content of Soviet life, the totalitarian character of Soviet rule, and the inadequacies of Soviet federalism as a limita-

tion on the state. It remains true, nonetheless, that nationalities were given a modicum of administrative authority and that their cultural self-expression was respected and at times even restored. The party, on the other hand, is anti-federal, and transcends the Constitution itself; it is the single thread that weaves together the entire Union into a compact political monolith. This unification is enhanced by the centralization of economic planning and by the socialization of the means of production by the Soviet state.

The Soviets under the 1936 Constitution

The 1936 Constitution established a pseudo-parliamentary system, although the term "soviet" was retained. All soviets (people's legislative bodies) are elective. All electoral discriminations were abolished in favor of equal, direct, and universal suffrage. Soviets (which literally means "councils") exist at all territorial-administrative levels, from the village through the towns and cities, rayons, oblasts, krays, Autonomous Oblasts, and Autonomous Republics, Union Republics, and finally at the Union level. The soviets at the Union, Union Republic, and Autonomous Republic levels are called Supreme Soviets, while the lesser bodies are called oblast, rayon, city, etc., soviets.

Every soviet elects an executive committee to function as an administrative and supervisory body, with a chairman, who in effect functions as the chief administrative officer of the unit concerned. At the Union, Union Republic, and Autonomous Republic levels, instead of an executive committee, there is an elected Presidium and Council of Ministers, each with a chairman. The soviets are the ultimate repositories of "state power" for the territorial unit which they administer, and in this capacity they exercise control over the courts as well as over the executive, legislative, and administrative branches of local government.

The total number of soviets in 1957 exceeded 60,000 in the localities alone, and included more than 1,500,000 deputies. These bodies varied in size from 40 to 80 in districts, 70 to 150 in rayons, 50 to 700 in cities, with

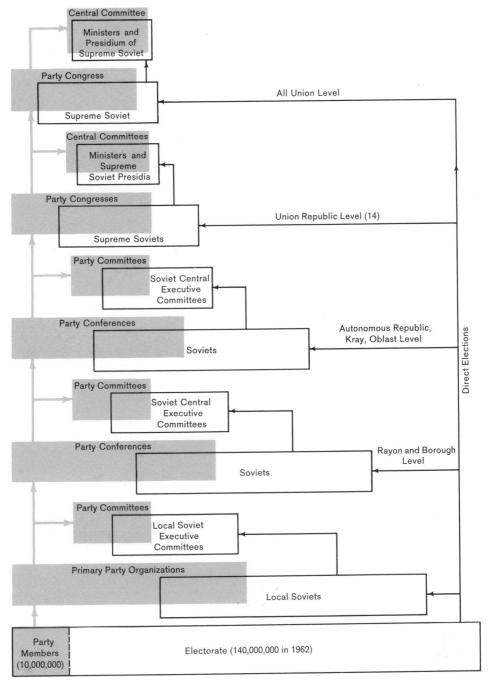

FIGURE 8-1 INTERLOCKING PARTY AND STATE STRUCTURES.

as many as 850 in large metropolitan areas. Unwieldy in size and meeting irregularly, they delegate their authority to the smaller executive bodies, whose chairmen are high party officials and whose members are full-time paid officers of local administration. The executive committees exercise the powers of the soviets between sessions and are responsible not only to the soviet but to the executive committee of the higher territorial unit. In instances where the executive committee itself is fairly large, a bureau or presidium serves as an inner executive body.

It should be noted that the soviets parallel and virtually duplicate the party organizations at all levels, and a close and continuing relationship exists between the two (Fig. 8-1). In theory, the soviets represent the "masses," since they are elected by all citizens, whereas the party represents the "vanguard" or leading element in the population. Consequently, at all levels of organization there is an overlapping between party and soviet organizations. Party membership among deputies to local soviets in 1957 ranged from an average of 32 per cent in Lithuania to nearly 60 per cent in Armenia. As a general rule, the higher the administrative level of the soviet, the greater the proportion of party members, which at the All-Union Supreme Soviet level in recent years has varied from 70 to 85 per cent. Since the soviets represent the masses, it is only appropriate that a certain proportion of deputies at all levels be ordinary non-party citizens.

Soviet Elections

Under the 1936 Constitution, Soviet elections are direct, universal, equal, and "secret," but since there is only one candidate for each elective position, elections are obviously not designed to provide the electorate with a choice of representatives, but merely a

superficial opportunity to ratify and approve the policies of the Communist Party. The Soviet electorate, of 140,000,000 (1962), is one of the largest in the world, with the minimum voting age set at 18. Even though Article 141 of the Constitution stipulates that "the right to nominate candidates is secured to public organizations, trade unions, cooperatives, youth organizations and cultural societies," candidates are, in fact, selected and screened by the appropriate organs of the party, although they may encourage other groups to suggest names as possible candidates.

Elections in the Soviet Union have more the character of a festive occasion than of a serious political event. Since no contest exists, artificial stimulants are required to create a feeling of public participation. Rallies and assemblies are held, "campaigns" are conducted, slogans are coined, speeches are made, banners and pins are distributed, and get-out-the-vote drives are organized. Elections are normally scheduled on a holiday or non-working day in order to assure maximum turnout. Election commissions consisting of representatives of the party and other organizations are established at all levels, from the precinct to the Union; they administer and supervise elections, certify candidates, register voters, examine complaints, check "irregularities," count the votes, and report the results—in a solemn and serious manner. The number of citizens involved in these electoral bodies runs into the millions.

In order to adhere to the constitutional imperative of a "secret" ballot, polling booths are provided for the voters at voting stations, but since only one candidate exists for each position, the normal procedure is for the voter to simply fold his ballot and drop it in the ballot box in full view of the voting officials. His other choices are not to vote at all or to cross the name off the ballot as a gesture of disapproval. The latter would require that the voter utilize the polling booth. Since use of the booth would arouse suspicion, it is infrequently used; under Stalin, resort to the booth often signified the last election in which the voter would participate for some time. If more than 50 per cent of the voters scratch a candidate's name, he fails election, but rejection by the voters is a rare occurrence and happens only at lower levels and only when officially inspired.

Voter participation in Soviet elections is very high, since the social and political pressures to vote are intense. Failure to vote may provoke social criticism and penalties, although it is not against the law to abstain. In a system that relishes and demands unanimity, deliberate abstention is tantamount to a negative vote. Whereas in earlier years the proportion of eligible voters who participated was less than 50 per cent, it has been more than 95 per cent since 1937, reaching 99.97 per cent in 1958 and 99.95 per cent in 1962. In the local soviets, more than 99 per cent of the eligible voters ordinarily cast their ballots.

Since neither in theory nor in practice is it the purpose of Soviet elections to choose a government, what functions are performed by these elections and why are they held with so much fanfare and expense? As we shall see, several very useful purposes can be served by even these manipulative and staged elections.

1. The elections provide a façade of legitimacy and legality for the Communist regime. Since the Soviet system claims to be the most "democratic" in the world, some external evidence of democratic "choice" must be demonstrated. And since the regime is controlled by an elite party that makes up but a small fraction of the total population, there is a compulsion to provide unanimity in elections to render emphatic the ratification of the party's policies and identify them with the will of the "masses."

2. Soviet elections also impart to the population a feeling of participation and involvement in the political process, and they mobilize the energies and enthusiasms of the people and imbue them with a sense of Communist civic responsibility, i.e., the opportunity to vote for the candidates presented by the regime.

3. Soviet elections can also serve as useful barometers of dissatisfaction for the regime and act as warning devices. While to the uninitiated eye, the dreary unanimity of the voting may be unenlightening, the smallest variation from one section of the country to another in the total number of abstentions and negative votes can be very revealing to the regime.

4. Elections also provide ceremonial occasions for the leaders of the regime to make speeches and pronouncements, to establish contact with the general population, to disseminate and popularize the policies of the regime, and to provide a stage for the announcement of new policies and major shifts of personnel in the government.

5. Finally, Soviet elections perform a valuable external propaganda device by providing a spectacular occasion for disseminating propaganda abroad concerning the Soviet Constitution and Soviet electoral procedures and democratic institutions. While these gestures may register little impact on countries that enjoy free and periodic elections, their effect on countries that do not have elections, or whose elections are narrowly restricted or corrupt, may be substantial.

The Supreme Soviet of the U.S.S.R.

According to Article 30 of the Soviet Constitution, "the highest organ of the state power in the U.S.S.R. is the Supreme Soviet of the U.S.S.R.," which means that all the constitutional powers in the Soviet system are vested in this body. Elected for a term of four years, the Supreme Soviet superficially resembles a bicameral legislative body of an ordinary federal state (Fig. 8-2). One chamber—the Soviet of the Union—is elected directly by the people, while the other—the Soviet of Nationalities—includes representatives from the federal units. The Constitution specifies that "the legislative power of the U.S.S.R. is exercised exclusively by the Supreme Soviet of the U.S.S.R."

The Supreme Soviet is an institution that

The Soviet Constitutional Order

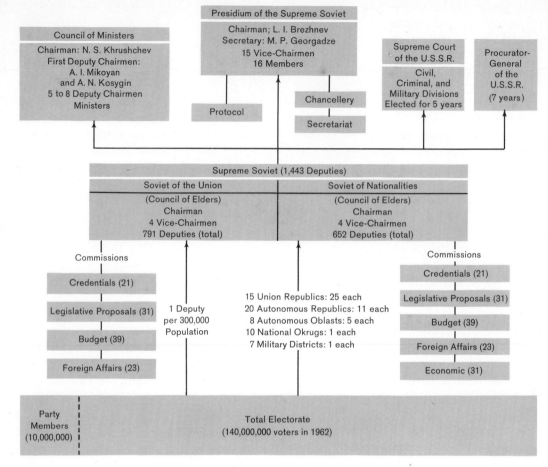

FIGURE 8-2 CONSTITUTIONAL STRUCTURE OF THE SOVIET STATE.

formally symbolizes democracy and legality. It transforms the will of the party into laws enacted by the "representatives" of the masses. The Supreme Soviet is the custodian, not of supreme power in Soviet society, but of supreme *state* power. Although it is the highest legal organ, the real source of Soviet power and legitimacy, as we have seen, is the Communist Party. The Supreme Soviet, therefore, is an institution designed to lead the masses into thinking that they participate in government.

The Soviet Union~Chapter VIII

The Supreme Soviet "at Work"

The Supreme Soviet is composed of two chambers, constitutionally of equal power: the Soviet of the Union and the Soviet of Nationalities. By custom, however, the Soviet of the Union carries the highest prestige and ranks in protocol over the Soviet of Nationalities. The Soviet of the Union is composed of deputies elected from single-member districts, in the ratio of one deputy per 300,000 population. As a general rule, the Soviet of the Union includes among its deputies a larger proportion of high party and state officials than does the Soviet of Nationalities.

The Soviet of Nationalities is elected on the basis of nationality units; identical national units have equal representation, irrespective of geographical or demographic size. Each Union Republic is entitled to 25 deputies; each Autonomous Republic is assigned 11 deputies, while Autonomous Oblasts are allotted 5 deputies each, and National Okrugs 1 apiece. The Soviet of Nationalities is thus both federal and multi-national. The Supreme Soviet is the largest elected legislative body in the world; in 1962, it consisted of 1,443 deputies, of which 791 were members of the Soviet of the Union and 652 members of the Soviet of Nationalities.

Each chamber has a Council of Elders (*Sovet Stareishin*), which is an informal and quasi-secret body made up of senior deputies that makes the preliminary arrangements for the organization and procedure of each chamber, prepares the agenda for the opening session, and seems always to be consulted in moments of crisis. Constitutionally, each chamber is provided with a Chairman and four Vice-Chairmen, who constitute the Presidium of each house (not to be confused with the Presidium of the party) and preside over its meetings. The chambers may sit jointly or separately. Sessions of both chambers begin and terminate simultaneously, and virtually all sessions are held jointly.[7]

According to the Constitution, the Supreme Soviet is convoked into regular session by its Presidium and can be convened into special session at the direction of the Presidium or upon the demand of one of the Union Republics. In actual practice, until 1955 the Supreme Soviet was normally convened only

[7] Even the agendas of the two chambers are identical. Thus, at the opening session of the Supreme Soviet elected in March, 1962, a spokesman for each chamber, "speaking on behalf of the Council of Elders," introduced the following agenda for each house (quoted in *Pravda*, April 24, 1962):
1. Election of the Credentials Committee.
2. Selection of standing committees.
3. Ratification of decrees of the Presidium of the U.S.S.R. Supreme Soviet.
4. Selection of the Presidium of the U.S.S.R. Supreme Soviet.
5. Report on negotiations in Geneva.
6. Formation of the U.S.S.R. Government and the U.S.S.R. Council of Ministers.
7. Selection of the U.S.S.R. Supreme Court.
8. Working out the draft of the new U.S.S.R. Constitution.

once a year, and the character and durat' its sessions were extraordinary by any st. ard. Between 1946 and 1954, this "highest organ of state power" sat for a total of 45 days, with the longest session lasting 7 days and the shortest exactly 67 minutes (to confirm the changes made after Stalin's death). Since 1955, a determined effort has been made to use this body more often, and although its sessions still last for only 4 to 7 days, they have taken place at the regular intervals required by the Constitution.

The Supreme Soviet is not a deliberating body: the deliberations take place elsewhere. Nor is it a debating assembly; debates, too, are held elsewhere, if at all. Neither does it formulate policy. It functions essentially as a listening assembly, and most of its "working" time is preoccupied with hearing reports from government Ministers. It listens attentively and with conditioned enthusiasm; if requested, it enacts legislation with rare dispatch, whether the subject be fundamental or trivial. "Debate" is ritualized; proposals and comments from the floor are prearranged with consummate precision. Panegyrics are delivered by a dozen or more carefully selected deputies; the appropriate personalities and actions of the past are roundly condemned, while the wisdom and correctness of the government is widely praised. During the entire existence of the Supreme Soviet, there has never been a single negative vote (or abstention) cast in either chamber, and no disagreement between the two bodies has ever occurred.

The Powers and Functions of the Supreme Soviet

Some powers are entrusted exclusively to the Supreme Soviet. Only the Supreme Soviet can pass "laws" or statutes, called *zakons*; only the Supreme Soviet can "amend" the Constitution (Article 146); only the Supreme Soviet, in joint session, "elects" the Presidium of the Supreme Soviet; "appoints" the government of the U.S.S.R. (the Council of Ministers); "elects" the Supreme Court of the U.S.S.R. (Article 105), and "appoints" the Procurator-General of the U.S.S.R. (Article 114). It also possesses exclusive authority to enact legislation concerning the judicial system, judicial procedures, criminal and civil codes, Union citizenship, rights of foreigners, and the determination of the "principles" governing marriage and the family.

The Constitution, however, is deliberately ambiguous on the precise demarcation of authority between the Supreme Soviet and its Presidium, since Article 14 assigns powers not only to the Supreme Soviet, but also to the "higher organs of state power," which also include the Presidium. Thus the Supreme Soviet must share authority with the Presidium in the following important spheres.

FOREIGN AFFAIRS AND NATIONAL SECURITY. Representation of the U.S.S.R. in international relations; conclusion, ratification, and denunciation of treaties; questions of war and peace; organization of national defense and security; direction of foreign trade on the basis of a state monopoly.

CONSTITUTIONS. Control over the observance of the Constitution and insuring the conformity of the Union Republic constitutions with the All-Union document; admission of new republics; confirmation of boundary changes between Union Republics and other administrative-territorial boundary alterations.

ECONOMICS. Determination of the national economic plan; approval of the consolidated state budget; allocations of taxes and revenue between the Union and local budgets; determination of land tenure and use of natural resources; administration, organization, and/or direction of banks, financial, credit, and mone-

tary institutions; administration of economic enterprises, transport, communications, state insurance, and the organization of a uniform system of national-economic statistics.

EDUCATION AND WELFARE. Determination of the "basic principles" of education and public health; determination of the principles of labor legislation.

Normally, sessions of the Supreme Soviet are not devoted to passing "laws," but to confirming the executive orders (*ukazes*) of the Presidium, and this it can do quickly. Thus, on a single day—April 26, 1954—the Supreme Soviet managed to ratify 40 *ukazes* of the Presidium, most of which had altered the Constitution. This was accomplished with neither debate nor extensive "discussion." Aside from *zakons* which merely confirmed the decrees of the Presidium and introduced minor constitutional alterations of an administrative character, the Supreme Soviet between 1938 and July, 1956, enacted only a total of less than 25 *zakons* (laws).[8]

The Supreme Soviet, although an impotent body, represents primarily the privileged elites of Soviet society and largely duplicates the social membership and even the personnel of the hierarchies in the party, state, economic, and military establishments. For this reason, it should not be surprising that the policies of the party are adopted by the Supreme Soviet with neither questions nor criticisms.

Since 1955, when Malenkov announced his resignation before the Supreme Soviet, calculated efforts have been made to enhance its prestige and to give it a more conspicuous role in the policy process. Meetings of the Supreme Soviet have been more frequent, and it is employed more often as a sounding board for policies which require dramatization and public dissemination. But the Supreme Soviet continues to be a captive of the party and will remain so unless, an unlikely prospect, it becomes useful in the struggle for power by one of the Soviet elites against the party apparatus.

[8] *Sbornik Zakonov SSSR i Ukazov Prezidiuma Verkhovnovo Soveta SSSR, 1938–1956* (Moscow, 1956).

The Presidium
of the Supreme Soviet

The Presidium of the Supreme Soviet is defined in the Constitution as one of the "higher organs of state power" and is vested with a wide and impressive range of both ceremonial and substantive powers, combining executive, legislative, diplomatic, military, and judicial functions. It functions as the collegial or plural chief of state of the Soviet Union, whose closest counterpart in the West is the Swiss Federal Council; otherwise, it is distinctively Soviet in character and is an expression of the party principle of collective leadership and responsibility. The Chairman of the Presidium acts as the ceremonial head of the Soviet Union.

The Presidium is elected by the Supreme Soviet in joint session at the first meeting after new elections, and its tenure is identical with that of the Supreme Soviet which elected it. It is composed of 33 members: 15 Vice-Chairmen, a Secretary, and 16 additional members. Since December, 1958, each Republic is entitled to a Vice-Chairman. Before 1958, the allocation of a Vice-Chairman to each Republic was customarily accomplished by electing the Chairman of a Republic Presidium as Vice-Chairman of the All-Union Presidium, and this is still governed by custom. An examination of the composition of the Presidium since its establishment in 1938 reveals that among the ordinary members are to be found high-ranking military officials, representatives of Autonomous Republics, high party officials of Republic organizations, and from 4 to 6 full or candidate members of the Party Presidium.[9] As a rule, the First Secretary of the party is elected as an ordinary member of the Presidium when he does not occupy an executive

or administrative position in the government. Thus both Stalin and Khrushchev were ordinary members of the Presidium during the period when they held no other government office. This practice invests the party leader with a high official status which can be held in reserve and employed when demanded by protocol.

The Chairman of the Presidium is its most conspicuous member, but not necessarily the most powerful one. Only four individuals have occupied this position. The first was the veteran old Bolshevik and long-time Politburo member, Mikhail Kalinin, who served as the ceremonial chief of state from 1919 until his death in 1946. His successor, Nikolai Shvernik, was a relatively low-ranking member of the party hierarchy (a candidate member of the Politburo) and was picked by Stalin, no doubt, because of his apparent passion for anonymity. He was replaced after Stalin's death by Marshal Voroshilov, a popular military-political leader. Marshal Voroshilov announced his retirement in 1960, but apparently he was forced out because of his complicity in the plot to unseat Khrushchev in June, 1957. His successor is a veteran party functionary and loyal Khrushchev supporter, Leonid Brezhnev who, like Voroshilov and Kalinin, was a full member of the party's highest body at the time of his appointment.

The Chairman of the Presidium is frequently, but incorrectly, referred to as the "President of the Soviet Union." Under the Constitution, his powers are no greater than those of other members. Normally, the Chairman performs all the symbolic and ceremonial acts in the name of the Presidium as a whole, and enjoys the prestige and prerogatives normally enjoyed by a titular chief of state. He presides over sessions of the Supreme Soviet, signs the decrees and other acts issued by the Presidium, and formally promulgates laws of the Supreme Soviet with his signature. He dispatches ambassadors and ministers, receives

---

[9] See *Pravda,* April 25, 1962, for the composition of the Presidium. Four members were full or candidate members of the Party Presidium; two were also members of the party Secretariat. F. R. Kozlov was the only member with simultaneous membership in the Party Presidium and Secretariat. Of the remaining members, sixteen were also full or candidate members of the Central Committee.

the credentials of foreign emissaries, and issues acts of pardon and amnesty.

The powers of the Presidium under Article 49 are very broad, but they are even broader in actual practice. As a "higher organ of state power," the Presidium is, in effect, a working legislature and to all intents and purposes exercises the entire spectrum of state power during intervals between sessions of the Supreme Soviet. It is, in the words of one Soviet authority, "the *highest permanently functioning organ of state power of the Soviet Union*." [10] It issues decrees, which have the force of law throughout the Union, although in theory these decrees must be based on laws enacted by the Supreme Soviet.

Just as it shares legislative authority with the Supreme Soviet, its executive powers overlap those of the Council of Ministers. In its executive capacity, the Presidium convenes and dissolves the Supreme Soviet, annuls decisions and orders of the Council of Ministers of the U.S.S.R. and of the Union Republics (if they do not conform to law), institutes and awards decorations and titles of honor, and, during intervals between sessions of its parent body, releases and appoints Ministers of the U.S.S.R. on the recommendation of the Council of Ministers, subject always to subsequent confirmation by the Supreme Soviet.

The Presidium's diplomatic and military powers are very extensive. It can order general or partial mobilization, proclaim martial law in separate localities or throughout the Union, create military titles, diplomatic ranks, and other special titles, appoint and remove the high command of the armed forces, and, in between sessions of the Supreme Soviet, is empowered to declare a state of war in the event of military attack or to fulfill treaty obligations.

The role and function of the Presidium in practice and its relationship to the Supreme

[10] V. Karpinsky, *The Social and State Structure of the U.S.S.R.* (Moscow, 1951), p. 122.

Soviet is precisely the reverse of that in theory. Since both the Supreme Soviet and its Presidium are creatures of the party, the relationship between the two bodies depends on the requirements and conveniences of the party. As is the case with the Supreme Soviet, the Presidium is the captive of the party. It is the chief legalizing instrument of the party, since its membership overlaps that of the Party Presidium and the Secretariat. Party policies and decisions can be almost instantaneously promulgated as decrees of the Presidium. Normally, the Chairman and up to a half dozen members of the Presidium are drawn from the party summit, while another dozen or more are members of the party Central Committee.

The Council of Ministers

The Council of Ministers is described by the Constitution (Article 64) as "the highest executive and administrative organ of state power" in the U.S.S.R. The Council of Ministers, also called the "Government," is invested with the principal responsibility for the *execution* and *administration* of policy, as distinct from its *formulation*, which is, of course, the province of the party summit. The Council is nominally accountable to the Supreme Soviet and its Presidium, but in fact is an administrative arm of the Party Presidium, with which its membership overlaps. In actuality, the relationship between the Party Presidium and the Council of Ministers in the decision-making process depends more on the degree of interlocking membership between the two organs than on constitutional norms.

Under Stalin, particularly after he became Chairman of the Government in 1941, interlocking membership was virtually complete and was designed to insure maximum harmony and coordination between party policy and state administration. Distinctions between formulation and execution of policy were blurred and rendered irrelevant, since the Politburo of the party and the Presidium of the Council were almost identical in membership. Stalin, by a simple motion, could transform the same group of individuals from one body to another, since he was the head of both.

The chairmanship of the Government and the leadership of the party were first united under Lenin, but after Lenin died, the two positions were separated, and Stalin established control of the Soviet system through his position as General Secretary of the party. Between 1924 and 1941, Stalin chose to rule from his post in the Secretariat of the party, and was thus completely separated from the formal organs of the state and the administration. Mistakes and errors could be conveniently ascribed to the state agencies and officials. The Chairman of the Council during this period was simply a shadow of the party Secretary, and state institutions were distinctly inferior to the organs of the party.

Shortly before Germany attacked the Soviet Union in 1941, Stalin, sensing an imminent crisis, suddenly assumed the chairmanship of the Council, relegating Molotov—its incumbent since 1930—to full-time duty as Commissar of Foreign Affairs. From being a secondary institution, the chairmanship was immediately invested with an authority that it had possessed only under Lenin. Stalin retained his post as General Secretary. Thus, as head of both party and Government, he made policy in one capacity and executed it in the other! The elaborate duplication of decision-making institutions between the party and the Government became a handicap. As a consequence, the decision-making institutions and procedures of the Politburo and the Central Committee of the party withered away, as Khrushchev so plaintively revealed at the Twentieth Party Congress. Stalin steadily enhanced the status and prestige of the state and its institutions, at the expense of the party. The exalted prestige imparted to the state by Stalin was probably a major factor in Malenkov's decision to fill Stalin's boots as Chairman of the Council rather than don his tunic as First Secretary of the Party. Legally, as head of the Government, he would have under his control the two principal instruments of violence, the police and the armed forces, and in addition would have administrative supervision and direction of the economic and industrial establishment and legal ownership of the means of production. The party seemed to have been left with little more than a vestigial remnant of its former eminence as the sole custodian of the symbols of revolutionary legitimacy, despite the fact that the Party Congress had been convened only six months earlier by Stalin, after an interval of 13 years.

The separation of the First Secretariat from the Premiership after Stalin's death once again drove a chasm between the organs of the state and the party. But Khrushchev's assumption of the chairmanship of the Council of Ministers in March, 1958, while still retaining his post of First Secretary, signified that the functions of policy formulation and administration could once again be reunited in a single person. Since March, 1958, the conflict between the organs of policy formulation (the party) and state administration (the Government) has been reduced to a minimum, with Khrushchev standing at the apex of both structures.

The Council of Ministers, which superficially resembles a cabinet in a Western parliamentary system, is constitutionally subordinate to the Supreme Soviet, which "appoints" it in joint session (Article 56). It is also "responsible and accountable" to the Presidium of the Supreme Soviet when the Soviet legislature is not in session, which, of course, means about 350 days out of the year. Executive authority in the Soviet government is formally distributed between the Presidium and the Council, with the former exercising appointive, ceremonial, and titular functions and the latter being charged with the actual execution of the law. Administrative power, however, is vested exclusively in the Council, and although it is formally accountable and responsible to the Supreme Soviet and/or its Presidium, the Council is in reality independent of both organs in the exercise of its authority. Only lip service is paid to the fiction of accountability to the Supreme Soviet.

The Soviet Constitutional Order

517

Under Article 68 of the Constitution, the Council is empowered to: coordinate the work of ministries and other organs of administration under its jurisdiction; direct the work of the national economic councils through central and Union Republic institutions; execute economic plans; administer the budget, credit, and monetary system; adopt measures for the maintenance of public order, state security, and the rights of citizens; exercise general guidance in foreign relations; fix the annual contingents to be conscripted into the armed forces and direct the general organization of the military forces. It is also empowered to establish special committees and central administrative organs under its jurisdiction for economic, cultural, and defense matters.

The functions and powers of the Council so modestly outlined in the Constitution are, in fact, only a small part of what the Council of Ministers actually does. The magnitude of its responsibilities is like that the President of the United States and his Cabinet would have if they had responsibility not only for federal administration but for the duties now performed by the states and also by private businesses and trade unions.

The Council of Ministers is thus the most important organ of the Soviet state and is the chief administrative instrument of the party summit. Under the Constitution, it is empowered to issue decrees and orders in carrying out its functions, but these must be in conformity with laws in operation. It is charged with checking the execution of its own acts, but both the Supreme Soviet and the Presidium are authorized to annul decrees and orders of the Council if they are in conflict with existing law, or for any reason whatsoever, although no decree or order of the Council has ever been overruled in the entire history of the Soviet system. The decrees and orders of the Council, which are binding throughout the Union, constitute the overwhelming bulk of legislation in the Soviet Union. Although the Council of Ministers, constitutionally, is not a legislative body, it is the chief source of law in the Soviet state.

The composition, but not the operational structure, of the Council of Ministers is established by the Constitution, and these provisions of the Constitution have been subject to more emendations, perhaps, than any other. The Council is directed by a smaller decision-making body called the Presidium of the Council of Ministers (not to be confused with either the Presidium of the Supreme Soviet or the Presidium of the party) and consists of the Chairman and his Deputies, which, as of 1963, included two *First* Deputy Chairmen and eight deputies of lesser party rank. The 71-member Council of Ministers, appointed in April, 1962, was made up of the following categories: [11]

1. *Presidium:* One Chairman; 2 First Deputy Chairmen; 5 Deputy Chairmen; Chairman of Commission on Foreign Economic Problems.

2. *Ministries:* Six All-Union Ministries (Transport Construction, Electric Power Station Construction, Merchant Marine, Foreign Trade, Railroad Communications, Medium Machine Building [Atomic Energy]; 9 Union Republic Ministries (Foreign Affairs, Defense, Finance, Culture, Health, Agriculture, Higher and Specialized Secondary Education, Postal Services and Telecommunications, Geology and Mineral Resource Conservation).

3. *State Planning Committee (Gosplan):* Two First Deputy Chairmen; 2 Deputy Chairmen; and 1 Department Head.

4. *State Committees, Boards, Councils, etc.:* Twenty-seven Chairmen or Deputy Chairmen at the All-Union and Union Republic levels (including: Foreign Economic Relations, Shipbuilding, Atomic Energy, State Bank, Cultural Ties with Foreign Countries, Labor and Wages, State Security and State Control).

5. *Ex officio:* The 15 Republic Premiers.

The enormous size of the Council of Ministers has been accompanied by a correspond-

[11] *Pravda,* April 25, 1962.

ing decrease in its power and significance as a deliberating organ. In fact, the Council rarely meets as a body and, when it does, betrays little more animation than listening and applauding various reports. The decision-making functions of the Council have been preempted by the Presidium of the Council of Ministers.

*The Chairman
and Presidium of the Council*

The Presidium of the Council is the principal administrative decision-making organ of the Soviet state. It presides over the Ministries and other administrative organs of the government, supervises their work, coordinates their activities, settles jurisdictional conflicts, and decides questions of a general administrative character. Decrees (*postanovleniya*) of the Council of a general character are issued by the Presidium in the name of the Council and signed by the Chairman or First Deputy and countersigned by the Administrator of Affairs, who is in charge of the drafting and other housekeeping agencies of the Council. Orders (*rasporyazheniya*) of the Council, which are decisions more operational and current in character, can be signed by the Chairman, First Deputy, or a deputy. Individual Ministers are empowered to issue instructions and regulations that are administratively binding within the agencies under their jurisdiction.

The most influential member in the Council of Ministers is its Chairman, who has always been in the highest rank of the party hierarchy. This office has been occupied by only seven men since its establishment on the day after the Revolution: Lenin (1917–24); Rykov (1924–30); Molotov (1930–41); Stalin (1941–53); Malenkov (1953–55); Bulganin (1955–58); Khrushchev (1958–). Of these, all but Lenin, Rykov, and Stalin are still alive; except for Lenin all of the past occupants of this post, whether dead or alive, are in disgrace. Rykov was executed in 1938 after the last of the notorious purge trials; Stalin's corpse has been banished from Lenin's mausoleum and his memory defiled; Molotov,

Malenkov, and Bulganin have been disgraced.

The size and composition of the membership of the Presidium has varied in response to the vagaries of factional politics. Under Stalin, the Council's Presidium consisted of a dozen or more members, most of whom, after 1949, did not carry ministerial portfolios. Apparently, Stalin operated through an even smaller body, the "Bureau" of the Presidium, whose existence, but not composition, was revealed only after Stalin's death. Immediately after Stalin's death, the secret "Bureau" was abolished, the Presidium was reduced in size, and First Deputies were restored to various consolidated portfolios, as were other members of the party Presidium in the Government. In the first post-Stalin Government, the Presidium consisted of the Chairman (Malenkov), 4 First Deputies (Beria, Molotov, Kaganovich, Bulganin), and one Deputy (Mikoyan)—all of whom were full members of the Party Presidium. The size of the Presidium increased and reached a peak after February, 1955, when Bulganin displaced Malenkov as Premier. Bulganin's Presidium in 1956 consisted of 5 First Deputies (all members of the Party Presidium) and 8 Deputies (including the disgraced Malenkov, who remained a full member of the Party Presidium), and the Council itself expanded to include more than 50 Ministries.

In the following year, however, after the economic reorganization acts of May, 1957, the abolition of 25 economic ministries and other ministerial reorganizations reduced the number of Ministries to less than 20. By 1962, the Ministries had been reduced to 15, but the size of the Council expanded to more than 70 members because of the admission of other agencies and organs.

Khrushchev probably assumed the office of Chairman because of its magnetic attraction for those who already exercise supreme power from another vantage point. The prestige with which Lenin and Stalin endowed this position converted it into a powerful counterpoise to the First Secretary, and Khrushchev apparently considered it too risky to permit a continued separation of the two offices. The post of Premier serves to legalize the First Secretary's power, while the First Secretary's position gives him a solid control of the party. Thus party and state are once again embodied in one person.

Ministries and Other Departments

Ministries in the central government are of two types: All-Union and Union Republic. The All-Union Ministries, of which there were six in 1962, are administrative agencies which are completely centralized in the federal government and are limited to matters which are incapable of being decentralized, such as foreign trade, merchant marine, etc. The Union Republic Ministries are departments dealing with matters in which jurisdiction is shared between the center and the circumference. According to Soviet constitutional doctrine and administrative practice, the Union Republic Ministries are governed by a system of dual subordination. The Ministry exists at two levels: in Moscow and in each of the 15 Union Republics. Constitutionally, each Union Republic Ministry is responsible to its corresponding supreme organ of state authority, but, administratively, the Union Republic Ministries in the Republics are subordinated to their counterparts in the central government.

The Union Republic Ministries are primarily functional in character and include what are normally considered to be the most important departments of government: foreign affairs and defense. The Union Republic Ministries are useful devices for decentralizing administration and responsibility, without, at the same time, relinquishing control of policy from the center. Thus, whereas the Union Republic Minister in Moscow is appointed by the All-Union Supreme Soviet and the Union Republic Ministers in the Republics are appointed by their respective Supreme Soviets, Article 76 of the Constitution specifies that the Moscow Ministries direct the activities of the Union Republic Ministries in the Republics. In the case of foreign affairs, this division of authority is only a matter of form, and in the case of defense does not go beyond the printed words of the Constitution. For the Ministries of Culture, Health, Higher Education, and Agriculture, however, genuine deconcentration of administrative personnel and responsibility can be usefully introduced.

The Ministries at one time were the chief administrative agencies of the Government, but in recent years, they have been eclipsed in numbers by various State Committees, Boards, Councils, etc. The State Committees are organized much like the Ministries and are of two types: All-Union and Union Republic. The main difference is that the department is directed by a Committee rather than by a Minister, although in some cases the Chairman may carry the title of Minister. With one or two exceptions (notably the Committee for State Security), the Committees deal with matters which cut across various departments and agencies and thus require coordination, such as Science and Technology, Automation, and Machine Building, etc. Some Committees were formerly Ministries, and the reasons for their transformation are not always clear. The conversion of the Ministry of State Security (the secret police) into a State Committee was calculatedly designed to dismantle the dangerous apparatus built by Beria and to insure that it could not again become an instrument of a single individual.

The National Economic Councils (Sovnarkhoz)

In May, 1957, virtually the entire network of economic ministries was set aside and their powers deconcentrated into more than 100 regional economic councils, with complete authority over all industrial enterprises within their territorial jurisdiction. Under the ministerial pattern, industrial administration was vertically organized, with all enterprises of a given type centrally directed from Moscow, no matter where they might be located. Enterprises belonging to different Ministries in the same locality could not deal directly with one another, but had to communicate through their respective Ministries in Moscow. These cumbersome bureaucratic procedures, while effective in centralizing control, resulted in intolerable red tape and inefficiency. Frequently, managers, in order to fulfill their production norms, would establish informal and illegal arrangements with other enterprises in the locality belonging to another Ministry. The organization of the regional economic councils was designed to provide greater coordination between various economic enterprises within a given locality and to bring administration nearer to the enterprises that were being administered.

All the councils were established within the boundaries of Union Republics, in order not to offend local sensitivities, although this created problems of an economic character. Large Republics are divided into several regions, while the smaller Republics constitute a single *sovnarkhoz*. In order to overcome the drawbacks of drawing economic regions to correspond with political divisions, in May, 1961, the 100 or so economic regions were grouped together into 17 main economic regions, which still respected Republic boundaries but did enable the grouping of entire Republics within single major regions. The R.S.F.S.R. was divided into 10 major regions and the Ukraine into 3, while the Baltic Republics were grouped into a single major region, as were the 3 Transcaucasian Republics and the 5 Central Asian Republics.

In May, 1962, Councils for Coordination and Planning were established for each of the major economic regions, made up of party, state, and economic officials from the center as well as from the localities, to coordinate the work of the various *sovnarkhozes* under its jurisdiction. Technically, the *sovnarkhoz* is a Republic organ. Its Chairman and members are appointed by the Republic's Council of Ministers, to which it is responsible, and the Chairman may enjoy ministerial standing in the Republic Council of Ministers. The *sovnarkhoz* is divided into branch and operational administrations and is charged with planning and coordinating administrative functions. It is empowered to issue decrees and orders to carry out its work. The councils are also subordinated to the over-all planning operations of the State Planning Committee, which operates through corresponding State Planning Committees in the Union Republic; the work of several contiguous *sovnarkhozes* is coordinated by the Planning and Coordinating Councils of one of the seventeen major economic regions. Since Soviet industrial administration is currently in a stage of radical reorganization, the network of communications and responsibilities between various agencies at different levels is still transitional and extremely complicated.

How "New" Governments Are Formed

Since the Soviet governmental machinery is organized along pseudo-parliamentary lines, it is not surprising that the relationship between the Council of Ministers and the Supreme Soviet imitates those of parliamentary systems. In the Soviet system, there are four formal occasions when the formation of a "new" government is required: (1) after the election of a new Supreme Soviet (regularly every four years); (2) when the Chairman of the Council resigns; (3) when the Chairman dies or becomes incapacitated; (4) when the Chairman loses the confidence of the Supreme Soviet.

The last occasion has never materialized, but it remains a possibility. From 1941, when Stalin replaced Molotov as the head of the Government, until Stalin's death in March, 1953, only the first occasion arose. At the initial meeting of a newly elected Supreme Soviet, Stalin would submit a written statement "surrendering" the powers of his Government to the Supreme Soviet, meeting in joint session, which would be accepted. Almost simultaneously, the Supreme Soviet would then commission Stalin to submit proposals for a "new" Government. At the "next" joint sitting (the following afternoon or day), the Chairman of the Presidium would announce the "new" Government proposed by Stalin. The announcement would be greeted by an outburst of prearranged odes to Stalin by selected deputies, whereupon Stalin's "new" Government "was then voted upon as a whole and unanimously adopted amidst loud applause passing into an ovation in honor of Comrade Stalin, who was elected Chairman of the Council of Ministers of the U.S.S.R." [12]

Stalin's sudden death in March, 1953, confronted his successors with the problem of devising a formula for organizing a "new" Government for the first time since Lenin and Stalin had ceased dominating the scene. Orderly procedure gave way to procedural chaos. The crisis clearly required supra-constitutional procedures, whose only counterpart elsewhere is the *coup d'état*. In other words, the vacuum created by Stalin's death could only be filled outside the Constitution, because it was a question of power and not a question of law. Before orderly constitutional processes could be observed in the Soviet system, the question of succession in the party had first to be settled. On March 7, 1953, an extraordinary joint decree was issued over the names of the Party Central Committee, the Council of Ministers, and the Presidium of the Supreme Soviet, which cleverly embraced every conceivable instrument of legitimacy and legality in the Soviet system and included all possible contenders for power.

[12] Karpinsky, *op. cit.*, pp. 123–124.

The Presidium of the Supreme Soviet received a new Chairman and Secretary (although the Constitution specifies that the members of the Presidium can only be elected by the Supreme Soviet). Malenkov was advanced to Stalin's vacated post of Premier, and other members of the Party Presidium were appointed First Deputies, Deputies, and ordinary Ministers. One week later, on March 15, 1953, the Supreme Soviet, in a breathless session of 67 minutes, approved the *fait accompli*, and the bare bones of constitutional procedure were thus preserved.

"New" Governments following resignations of the Chairman have been nominated twice, the first time on February 8, 1955, when a statement was read by the Chairman of the Council of Union on behalf of Malenkov before the Supreme Soviet at 1:00 o'clock in the afternoon, in which he submitted his resignation on grounds of administrative inexperience and incompetence. The Premier of the R.S.F.S.R. moved that the resignation be accepted, which was unanimously approved, and in less than 10 minutes the session was adjourned. At 4:00 o'clock in the afternoon, the Supreme Soviet was reconvened, and Khrushchev, the first speaker, proceeded to nominate Nikolai Bulganin as Malenkov's successor. Five minutes after the session started, Bulganin was unanimously approved as the new Chairman. On the next day, Bulganin delivered his acceptance speech and submitted his list of proposed Ministers.

The second resignation took place in March, 1958, when Bulganin submitted his resignation, which was accepted unanimously. Khrushchev's name was placed in nomination by Marshal Voroshilov, the Chairman of the Presidium of the Supreme Soviet. The First Secretary was approved as the new Premier unanimously by acclamation, and the "new" Government was in business less than 24 hours after the convocation of the Supreme Soviet.

The precision and rapidity with which the Supreme Soviet accepted resignations and approved "new" Governments, with neither advance notice nor deliberation, is sufficiently eloquent by itself to demonstrate the nature of the responsibility and accountability of the

Council to the Supreme Soviet. Needless to say, the smoothness of the changeovers simply reflects the fact that all the basic questions were decided in the Party Presidium and were then simply formalized in the presence of the Supreme Soviet. In a strictly technical sense, the procedure seems to resemble the manner in which governments are chosen by party caucuses or executive committees in democratic countries, which are then ratified by parliaments, with the very significant exception that the Party Presidium is, as we have seen, the only "party caucus" tolerated in the Soviet system.

The Soviet Union Today ... and Tomorrow

IX

Although the Soviet system is now nearly a half-century old, any attempt to determine with precision its definitive contours would still be premature. Soviet society has been subjected to a continuous process of social and political convulsions that have been engineered from the top in an attempt to achieve the ideological goals of the party leadership. Still Soviet society today remains an unfinished social order. From the standpoint of the party leadership, current Soviet society represents simply another way-station on the road to Communism. Changes, radical and trivial, will continue to be initiated from above, following the needs of the moment, although what in fact emerges will continue to represent a balance between the imperatives of ideology and the resistance of internal and external forces to change.

In the evolution of Soviet society, significant groups with an interest in arresting further social transformations have continuously emerged, and the present state of things is no different except that the social groups which today have a vested interest in maintaining the present *status quo* are more differentiated, influential, and more firmly rooted than in previous periods. It would be a mistake, however, to assume that they will necessarily be any more successful in arresting further social transformations. External impediments, in the form of differently perceived interests by various Communist states, particularly China, and the successful resistance of the non-Communist world to the expansion of the Communist sphere are just as likely to force a reshaping of the ideological goals of Soviet society as are internal forces. Soviet society thus remains in a condition of flux.

Certain features of the Soviet system have achieved a degree of permanence because they satisfy not only the requirements of ideology, but have won genuine popular acceptance: the public ownership of the means of production, natural resources, and financial institutions, and state control of communications, information, health, education, welfare, and culture are two examples. The collective-farm system, on the other hand, seems to be universally disliked and represents an unwelcome burden on agriculture and the peasantry. The one-party system finds wide acceptance, although the people would prefer more flexibility in nominations and elections and would like more than one candidate to stand for political office. It might also be noted that some nationalities, particularly the three Baltic countries, would prefer to be outside the Soviet community altogether, and tensions continue to arise over the Communist failure to reconcile completely the conflicts between national dignity and Soviet patriotism, between local national pride and Great Russian nationalism.

Problems Ahead

The dilemmas of the Soviet system thus derive from the failure of social realities to correspond with desirable ideological goals which were promised or are claimed (democracy, freedom, etc.), and from the state's efforts to impose undesirable ideological goals (collectivized agriculture, for example) or to transform existing institutions and processes which are acceptable into unacceptable patterns. These dilemmas and problems can be grouped into four general categories: (1) problems arising out of the necessity to falsify or rationalize reality (ideological distortion or false perception); (2) problems arising from the failure to legitimize or legalize the transfer of power; (3) problems of social equilibrium and stabilization; (4) problems arising from the utilization of economic resources and production. Implicit also is the fundamental problem arising from the conflict between the requirements of internal stability and the ideological goals of foreign policy.

Ideological Distortions

The Soviet system continues to be plagued by the agonies of what we might call false perception resulting from ideological distortions of reality. While many of these problems appear esoteric, they are of crucial significance in a society in which a systematically articulated ideology is officially enshrined. In some instances, Soviet leaders and citizens appear to believe many things to be true which are in fact false, and this results in a condition known as "false consciousness," an aberration which infects all societies, but one to which the Soviet is especially prone.

Soviet society is described as "free," "demo-cratic," and without class hostility, although this is patently untrue. It is asserted that the Communist Party represents the monolithic will of all classes, whose interests are unified and harmonious, whereas in fact social groups in Soviet society perceive their interests differently, and the Communist Party articulates the will of the elites rather than that of all social classes. Formulating policy and social behavior in accordance with beliefs which are out of focus with reality results in distorted perceptions of problems and situations and gives rise to misdirected or inappropriate solutions and responses. Problems which in fact exist remain unnoticed and without solutions, while problems which do not exist appear as real and are met with artificially contrived solutions.

Legitimacy and Succession

A perennial and still unresolved problem in the Soviet system is that of the institutionalization and legitimization of political power. Theoretically, the problem does not exist, and, in official doctrine, Soviet leaders and citizens must behave as if the problem is non-existent. Theoretically, power is lodged in the party and is then delegated to the central organs of the party, which exercise this power in a collective or institutional rather than personal capacity. Power, however, cannot be exercised impersonally, but must be possessed and exercised by individuals, who may be members of bodies or groups.

At any given time in the Soviet system, the institutional seat of power can be defined, but the particular personalities who hold the reins of power cannot. Thus, while Stalin was alive, power theoretically rested in the Presidium of the party, but in fact was vested in Stalin as a person. When Stalin died, theoretically no power vacuum existed, since the Presidium as a body continued to function. In fact, a profound vacuum resulted because no orderly process had been devised for transferring power. The official ideology refused to recognize the existence of such a problem. In the absence of a legal or predetermined succession procedure, the problem was resolved informally by a struggle for supremacy among various personalities, cliques, and groups, although the existence of such a struggle was itself repeatedly denied. The composition of various party and state organs changed with each phase of the struggle, but no actual transfer of power in the party hierarchy was officially recognized, since, theoretically, the power of the party was always lodged in its central organs.

Although certain unwritten ground rules seem to be developing governing the struggle for power, these do not enjoy official recognition nor are they explicitly articulated, and unless an orderly system for transferring power is devised, a dangerous vacuum will continue to exist at the very apex of the Soviet system.

Another closely related problem of power is the precise relationship that exists between the party and the state. Again, in theory, no problem is supposed to exist: the party devises policy and transmits it to the state for execution and implementation as law. In fact, however, tensions appear between the two not only because this functional division of labor is impossible to sustain in a meaningful sense, but also because each inevitably becomes the instrument of power of those who control it. This tension, in practice, is resolved only when both institutions are under the control of a single center of power, reflected usually in the unification of the highest post in the government with the highest post in the party in a single person. Thus, as did Lenin throughout his lifetime and Stalin from 1941 to 1953, Khrushchev since 1958 has held the position of party leader and Premier of the Government. As long as the problems of power and succession are not dealt with in their realistic, as opposed to their ideologically distorted, dimension, the Soviet system will con-

tinue to be threatened with instability at the very pinnacle of power, and each succession crisis carries in it a potential of disaster.

Social Stratification and the Party

The Communist Party is being increasingly transformed into an arena in which the various Soviet elites make known their demands on one another, articulate their special interests, and try to impose their desires as the unified will of society as a whole. It is clear that one of the most substantial problems of the Soviet social order is how to reduce the inevitable tensions between the desire of a privileged group, the Soviet intelligentsia, to preserve its special status, and the ideological imperative of a classless society to which the party leadership is committed. While theoretically the intelligentsia as an entity is committed to a classless society, in actual fact only the party apparatus appears to have an enduring interest in it. The very function of the party apparatus is to preserve the purity and integrity of the Communist doctrine. Besides, the apparatus's political power is not likely to be undermined by the implementation of Communist egalitarian principles. On the contrary, it would probably be enhanced since egalitarian reforms would tend to undermine the position of non-party privileged groups.

According to Soviet doctrine, the intelligentsia is destined to dissolve into the society as a whole. Hence, the idea of recognizing distinct groups within the intelligentsia—although they exist in actuality—is in flagrant conflict with Marxism-Leninism. But since future Communist development will be determined by the ideological commitment of the party *and* the attitude of social groups, the study of social structure and social stratification is extremely important. There is no question but that the several elites which have crystallized within the Soviet intelligentsia have, on the whole, a vested interest in preserving largely intact the *de facto* social order which exists in the Soviet Union today. They would like nothing better than to receive official recognition guaranteeing the *status quo*. While quasi-autonomous interest groups flourish within the intelligentsia, they do not enjoy either legal or ideological recognition and hence the fiction must be preserved that they do not exist. Only the intelligentsia as a whole enjoys ideological acceptance as a stratum of the working class. Thus a constant friction and conflict between the upper social groups in the intelligentsia and the party apparatus is likely to be the rule in the Soviet society for some time to come. The party leaders will attempt to undermine the vested interests of the intelligentsia, while the latter will try to buttress its social position either by constitutional reform or by capturing the very citadel of political power—the leadership of the party.

The regime clearly recognizes the existence of the tensions between the desire of social elites to maintain their privileges and the ideological imperative of a classless society. The ideological key to the resolution of this dilemma is to raise the level of productivity to the point where it meets total social demand, which then automatically renders superfluous all necessity for establishing priorities in the distribution of rewards. The economic transformation of society, according to the Soviets, will bring about the necessary psychological transformation of man so that "it will become a habit to work to the best of one's ability, not only as a duty, but also as an inner urge," and then both the material and psychological prerequisites for a classless society will have been met. In Soviet jargon, this means that distinctions between physical and mental labor and between rural and urban life must be eliminated so that "the activity of all workers of Communist society will be a combination of physical and mental work."

It can be safely assumed, therefore, that existing social distinctions and differentials in rewards and status will persist for some time and that privileged elites will endeavor to maintain their privileges, but it can also be expected that the regime will take periodic measures to curb these tendencies so that social mobility in Soviet society will remain relatively high. The intelligentsia will continue to expand in numbers and occupations. It seems hardly credible that privileged elites

will disappear voluntarily in Soviet society. Yet the ultimate goal is precisely that. "With the victory of communism," writes one authority, "there will be no intelligentsia as a separate social stratum."

Raising the Standard of Living

Raising the standard of living in the Soviet Union has crucial ideological significance, since Communist society requires an economy of abundance to provide the material basis for the psychological and moral transformation of man. The tremendous effort devoted to enhancing the productive forces of the country, however, are not all directed to raising the standard of living, for the regime is still determined to enhance Soviet military power and promote the ideological goal of world Communism. Consequently, the major Soviet economic effort is directed toward three fields, which results in a certain amount of conflict since the Soviet economy is not capable of satisfying the needs of all three simultaneously. The three fields are: (1) heavy industry—the goal is to maintain a high rate of industrial growth for prestige purposes and to accomplish foreign policy objectives; (2) military power—again for purposes of prestige as well as national security and for the promotion of ideological objectives, in part through foreign military assistance to various countries; and (3) consumer goods and food production.

Production for the consumer has always received the lowest priority in the Soviet Union, particularly in agriculture, and one of the basic tensions of contemporary Soviet society stems from the desire of the people for a more rapid improvement in their standard of living, as opposed to the regime's insistence on assigning priority to heavy industry and military power. Since Stalin's death, greater attention has been devoted to raising the standard of living, and substantial progress has been made, but this has merely whetted the public's appetite rather than satisfied it. Furthermore, the

The Soviet Union Today . . . and Tomorrow

527

Russian people are now more aware that the standard of living could be even higher if less effort and investment were channeled into the production of heavy industry and rockets.

Agricultural production, particularly, has always lagged far behind industrial growth. While industrial goals are consistently achieved and sometimes exceeded, agricultural production almost always falls short of planned targets. This has created a serious imbalance in the Soviet economy, and, while the Soviet public is not undernourished or on the verge of a subsistence diet, the agricultural sector of the Soviet economy remains a jerry-built structure which can crumble in the face of a serious crisis.

The inefficiency of agricultural production in the Soviet Union stems from two causes: (1) the low priority it receives in terms of investment and effort; (2) the collective farm system. Admittedly, food production could be significantly increased if the state funneled greater resources in that direction, but this would be at the expense of heavy industry and armament. In early 1962, Khrushchev publicly rejected this alternative in favor of boosting prices for meat and dairy products by 25–30 per cent as an inducement to the farmers to produce more in exchange for greater profits.[1] This will serve only to raise slightly the peasant's standard of living at the expense of the urban standard of life and cannot be regarded as an effective solution.

Altering the structure of Soviet agriculture could also result in greater food production, but again at the expense of redistributing income between town and country. Incentives for greater production within the collective farm system have just about reached their maximum point, and the regime is now confronted with the major decision of accepting stagnation in agriculture or stimulating further growth by greater investment at the expense of industry and armaments or radically revising the collective farm system to give the peasant greater incentives for greater effort.

One of the great anomalies of the Soviet system is the vast disparity between its low material standard of living and its high level of culture and education. This asymmetry produces psychological tensions which cannot be sustained over a long period of time. As the intelligentsia becomes acutely aware of the imbalances and incongruities of the Soviet system, particularly as it gains knowledge of how its social counterparts in other industrial societies live, it may think in terms of solutions outside the framework of official doctrine, especially if the further implementation of doctrinal goals would have an adverse effect on its station in society. Already there are important signs which indicate that the educated elite of the coming generation will be less inclined to accept at face value the ideological goals of the regime and will be even less predisposed to accept the frequently disingenuous rationalizations and explanations which are advanced to justify existing policies and conditions. While the satisfactions, on the whole, outweigh the tensions in Soviet society, and violent internal upheavals against the regime are not likely, the possibility of a silent revolution which will transform both the internal and external goals of the Soviet system in the direction of greater social stability, greater freedom, and more attention to concrete and material (rather than ideological) problems is a real one.

[1] At the November, 1962, Plenum of the Central Committee, Khrushchev announced a 30 per cent increase in agricultural investment over 1962.

Bibliography

Chapter I

Berdyaev, Nicolas, *The Origins of Russian Communism* (London: Geoffrey Bles, 1948).

——————, *The Russian Idea* (New York: Macmillan, 1948).

Black, C. E., ed., *The Transformation of Russian Society: Aspects of Social Change since 1861* (Cambridge: Harvard University Press, 1960).

Carr, E. H., *A History of Soviet Russia: The Bolshevik Revolution, 1917–1923*, 3 vols. (New York: Macmillan, 1951–1953).

Chamberlin, W. H., *The Russian Revolution, 1917–1921*, 2 vols. (New York: Macmillan, 1935).

Florinsky, M. T., *Russia: A History and an Interpretation* (New York: Macmillan, 1953).

Karpovich, M., *Imperial Russia, 1801–1917* (New York: Macmillan, 1932).

Kennan, G. F., *Russia Leaves the War: Soviet American Relations, 1917–1920* (Princeton: Princeton University Press, 1956).

Maynard, John, *Russia in Flux* (New York: Macmillan, 1948).

Pares, Sir Bernard, *A History of Russia*, 5th ed. (New York: Knopf, 1947).

Pipes, R., *The Formation of the Soviet Union* (Cambridge: Harvard University Press, 1954).

Schuman, F. L., *Russia since 1917* (New York: Knopf, 1957).

Seton-Watson, Hugh, *The Decline of Imperial Russia* (New York: Praeger, 1952).

Sukhanov, N. N., *The Russian Revolution, 1917: A Personal Record* (New York: Oxford University Press, 1955).

Trotsky, Leon, *The History of the Russian Revolution*, 3 vols. (New York: Simon and Schuster, 1936).

Chapter II

Balzak, S. S., V. F. Vasyutin, and Y. G. Feigin, *Economic Geography of the U.S.S.R.* (New York: Macmillan, 1949).

Barghoorn, F. C., *Soviet Russian Nationalism* (New York: Oxford University Press, 1956).

Bereday, G. Z. F., and J. Pennar (eds.), *The Politics of Soviet Education* (New York: Praeger, 1960).

Campbell, R., *Soviet Economic Power* (Boston: Houghton Mifflin, 1960).

Comparisons of the United States and Soviet Economics, Parts 1–3 (Washington, D.C.: Government Printing Office, 1959).

Counts, G. S., and N. Lodge, *The Country of the Blind* (Boston: Houghton Mifflin, 1949).

DeWitt, N., *Soviet Professional Manpower* (Washington, D.C.: Government Printing Office, 1955).

Education in the U.S.S.R. (Washington, D.C.: Government Printing Office, 1957).

Inkeles, A., *Public Opinion in Soviet Russia* (Cambridge: Harvard University Press, 1949).

Jorré, G., *The Soviet Union, the Land and its People* (London: Longmans, Green, 1950).

Kolarz, W., *Russia and Her Colonies* (New York: Praeger, 1952).

Nove, Alec, *The Soviet Economy* (New York: Praeger, 1961).

Schwartz, H., *Russia's Soviet Economy*, 2nd ed. (Englewood Cliffs, N.J.: Prentice-Hall, 1954).

Shabad, T., *Geography of the U.S.S.R.* (New York: Macmillan, 1951).

Chapter III

Aspaturian, V. V., "The Contemporary Doctrine of the Soviet State and its Philosophical Foundations," *American Political Science Review* (December, 1954).

Daniels, R. W. (ed.), *A Documentary History of Communism* (New York: Random House, 1960).

Gruliow, Leon (ed.), *Current Soviet Policies, I, II, III, IV* (New York: Praeger, 1953, 1957, 1960, 1962).

Haimson, L. H., *The Russian Marxists and the Origins of Bolshevism* (Cambridge: Harvard University Press, 1955).

Hook, Sidney, *From Hegel to Marx* (New York: The Humanities Press, 1950).

Hunt, R. N. C., *The Theory and Practice of Communism*, 5th ed. (New York: Macmillan 1957).

Leites, N., *A Study of Bolshevism* (Glencoe, Ill.: The Free Press, 1953).

Marcuse, H., *Soviet Marxism* (New York: Columbia University Press, 1958).

Meyer, Alfred G., *Leninism* (Cambridge: Harvard University Press, 1957).

——————, *Marxism: The Unity of Theory and Prac-*

tice (Cambridge: Harvard University Press, 1954).

Plamenatz, J., *German Marxism and Russian Communism* (London: Longmans, Green, 1954).

Simmons, E., *Continuity and Change in Russian and Soviet Thought* (Cambridge: Harvard University Press, 1955).

Wilson, E., *To the Finland Station* (New York: Harcourt, Brace, 1940).

Wolfe, B., *Three Who Made a Revolution* (New York: Dial Press, 1948).

Ulam, Adam B., *The Unfinished Revolution* (New York: Random House, 1959).

Chapter IV

Bauer, R., *The New Man in Soviet Psychology* (Cambridge: Harvard University Press, 1952).

Berliner, Joseph S., *Factory and Manager in the U.S.S.R.* (Cambridge: Harvard University Press, 1957).

Curtiss, John S., *The Russian Church and the Soviet State* (Boston: Little, Brown, 1953).

Deutscher, I., *Soviet Trade Unions* (London, 1950).

Dinerstein, H. S., *Communism and the Russian Peasant* (Glencoe, Ill.: The Free Press, 1955).

Djilas, M., *The New Class* (New York: Praeger, 1957).

Granick, D., *The Red Executive* (Garden City, N.Y.: Doubleday, 1960).

Inkeles, A. and R. Bauer, *The Soviet Citizen* (Cambridge: Harvard University Press, 1959).

Inkeles, A., R. Bauer, and C. Kluckhohn, *How the Soviet System Works* (Cambridge: Harvard University Press, 1956).

Inkeles, A., and K. Geiger, *Soviet Society* (Boston: Houghton Mifflin, 1961).

Jasny, N., *The Socialized Agriculture of the U.S.S.R.* (Stanford, Calif.: Stanford University Press, 1949).

Laird, Roy D., *Collective Farming in Russia* (Lawrence, Kansas: University of Kansas Publications, 1958).

Laqueur, W. and L. Labedz (eds.), *The Future of Communist Society* (New York: Praeger, 1962).

Moore, B., *Terror and Progress: U.S.S.R.* (Cambridge: Harvard University Press, 1954).

Pipes, R. (ed.), *The Russian Intelligentsia* (New York: Columbia University Press, 1960).

Schwarz, S. M., *Labor in the Soviet Union* (New York: Praeger, 1952).

Vucinich, A., *Soviet Economic Institutions* (Stanford, Calif.: Stanford University Press, 1952).

Wolin, S. and R. Slusser (eds.), *The Soviet Secret Police* (New York: Praeger, 1957).

Chapter V

Brzezinski, Z., *The Permanent Purge* (Cambridge: Harvard University Press, 1956).

Carr, E. H., *The Interregnum* (New York: Macmillan, 1954).

————, *Socialism in One Country*, Vols. 1 and 2 (New York: Macmillan, 1958, 1960).

Deutscher, I., *The Prophet Armed: Trotsky, 1879–1921* (New York: Oxford University Press, 1954).

————, *The Prophet Unarmed: Trotsky, 1922–1929* (New York: Oxford University Press, 1959).

Jacobs, Dan N. (ed.), *The New Communist Manifesto and Related Documents*, 2nd ed. (Evanston, Ill.: Row, Peterson, 1962).

Leites, N. and E. Bernaut, *The Ritual of Liquidation* (Glencoe, Ill.: The Free Press, 1954).

Reshetar, J., *A Concise History of the Communist Party of the Soviet Union* (New York: Praeger, 1959).

Rush, M., *The Rise of N. S. Khrushchev* (Washington, D.C.: Public Affairs Press, 1958).

Schapiro, L., *The Communist Party of the Soviet Union* (New York: Random House, 1959).

————, *The Origin of the Communist Autocracy* (Cambridge: Harvard University Press, 1955).

Stalin, J. V., *History of the Communist Party of the Soviet Union* (New York: International Publishers, 1938).

Treadgold, D., *Lenin and His Rivals* (New York: Praeger, 1960).

Chapter VI

Arendt, H., *The Origins of Totalitarianism* (New York: Harcourt, Brace, 1951).

Armstrong, John A., *The Soviet Bureaucratic Elite* (New York: Praeger, 1959).

————, *The Politics of Soviet Totalitarianism* (New York: Random House, 1961).

Brumberg, A., *Russia under Khrushchev* (New York: Praeger, 1962).

Conquest, R., *Power and Policy in the U.S.S.R.* (New York: St. Martin's Press, 1961).

Dallin, D. J., *The Changing World of Soviet Russia* (New Haven: Yale University Press, 1956).

Deutscher, I., *Stalin* (New York: Oxford University Press, 1948).

Fainsod, M., *Smolensk under Soviet Rule* (Cambridge: Harvard University Press, 1958).

————, *How Russia Is Ruled* (Cambridge: Harvard University Press, 1953).

Friedrich, C., and Z. Brzezinski, *Totalitarian Dictatorship and Autocracy* (Cambridge: Harvard University Press, 1956).

Kulski, W. W., *The Soviet Regime*, rev. ed. (Syracuse: Syracuse University Press, 1959).

Mead, M., *Soviet Attitudes toward Authority* (New York: McGraw-Hill, 1951).

Moore, Barrington, *Soviet Politics—The Dilemma of Power* (Cambridge: Harvard University Press, 1948).

Rostow, W. W., *The Dynamics of Soviet Society* (New York: Norton, 1953).

Wolfe, B. D., *Khrushchev and Stalin's Ghost* (New York: Praeger, 1957).

Chapter VII

Aspaturian, V. V., *The Union Republics and Soviet Diplomacy* (Geneva, Switz.: Libraire Droz, 1960).

Berman, H. J., *Justice in Russia* (Cambridge: Harvard University Press, 1950).

Carson, G. B., Jr., *Electoral Practices in the U.S.S.R.* (New York: Praeger, 1956).

Guins, G. C., *Soviet Law and Soviet Society* (The Hague: Martinus Nijhoff, 1954).

Hazard, J. N., *The Soviet System of Government*, rev. ed. (Chicago: University of Chicago Press, 1960).

Kelsen, H., *The Communist Theory of Law* (New York: Praeger, 1955).

Meisel, J. H., and E. Kozera (eds.), *Materials for the Study of the Soviet System* (Ann Arbor, Mich.: George Wahr, 1953).

National Policy Machinery in the Soviet Union (Washington, D.C.: Government Printing Office, 1960).

Scott, Derek, J. R., *Russian Political Institutions* (New York: Praeger, 1961).

Towster, J., *Political Power in the U.S.S.R., 1917–1947* (New York: Oxford University Press, 1948).

Turner, J., and H. McCloskey, *The Soviet Dictatorship* (New York: McGraw-Hill, 1960).

Vyshinsky, A. Y. (ed.), *The Law of the Soviet State* (New York: Macmillan, 1948).

Werth, A., *Russia under Khrushchev* (New York: Crest Books, 1962).

ROY C. MACRIDIS

Epilogue

In studying the political institutions of Great Britain, France, West Germany, and the Soviet Union, we have been concerned primarily with "advanced" political societies, where there seems to be widespread acceptance of the system by the majority of the people; where illiteracy is virtually non-existent; where the government enjoys stability and legitimacy; where the party system helps to translate the demands of various interests into policy and often to articulate them into decisions; where bureaucracy has developed into a special organization composed of skilled individuals who perform agreed-upon tasks; where political roles seem to be clearly perceived so that the administrator, the party leader, the legislator, and the Army officer have clearly assigned functions within the system.

We have further studied the basic functions performed by these political systems. They provide the services and satisfy the demands of individuals and groups; they have institutions through which decisions are made in a manner that appears to be accepted by the great majority of citizens; they provide stable instruments through which the perennial conflicts between various interests and points of view are reconciled; they devise ways by which the political leaders are selected and held accountable.

With increased modernization and industrialization, not only in Germany and in England—the latter being after all the first country to industrialize—but also in Russia and France, certain common patterns can be identified.

One of them is the decrease in intense political emotions and in ideological conflict. In Germany, this new empiricism has been translated into a two-party system and a marked governmental stability. In Russia, despite the lip service that is paid to Marxism and Leninism, there is also an increased tendency toward political pragmatism. In agriculture, in industry, and in trade in the Soviet Union, the emphasis is being put on performance and prosperity, and the best ways of implementing them are often unrelated to the Bible of Marxism, which has undergone many changes. In all the systems we have covered, politics becomes increasingly a matter of *more* or *less,* thus opening the way to compromise solutions.

The decline of political passions and conflicts is noticeable in the attitudes held by the citizens in France and England about the scope of state action. In these two countries, it is now widely accepted that the role of the state is to provide citizens with at least a minimum of social and economic welfare, even by means of the nationalization of key economic activities if necessary. Transport, electricity, gas, coal, education, and health are matters that have been moved out of political controversy to become public services. To some extent, public investment in the social sector of the economy in research, economic development, and economic growth is also generally considered to be a legitimate concern of the state.

With modernization has come a progressive trend toward social equality. The old class divisions—manifested in dress, speech, degree of leisure, housing, etc.—are giving place to a growing uniformity among all groups of the population. This has been the result of two converging factors: industrialization and prosperity on the one hand and social mobility on the other. The two, of course, are different sides of the same coin, since prosperity implies not only higher per capita income but also growing opportunities for advancement that break down the barriers of class. Greater mobility is being made possible by the opening of educational opportunities to the children of the underprivileged, giving them access to higher-status jobs and incomes.

Modernization and prosperity, therefore, tend to overcome the nineteenth-century class conflicts and to produce a society in which the social and economic conditions of the majority of the citizens are, relatively speaking, not markedly different. A mass society—consisting of undifferentiated individuals who seek and get equal opportunities—is in the process of developing even in Western Europe and England, where old feudal structures and traditions had inhibited the process for so long. The growth of mass media of communications and adult education, through such technological improvements as television and radio, is a contributory factor.

Social homogeneity produces a citizenry that is drawn closely together in the sense that all begin to enjoy many of the same material benefits and to share relatively similar expectations. The public begins to show less variety and to become progressively more middle class in its outlook. An inevitable corollary of prosperity seems to be a certain degree of political apathy. Old clashes over principles give way to common strategies on how to gain specific advantages. Issues become increasingly technical and thus are "depoliticized." The apathy apparent among the citizens of many prosperous Western democracies—including the United States—however, has nothing in common with the apathy of many groups in the backward or primitive communities. It is apathy born of success, fulfillment, and com-

monly shared goals and values, not from exclusion, alienation, or downright ignorance.

Similarities and Differences

Needless to say, the modern political systems we have examined also show great differences among themselves. It was precisely the task of our country-by-country study to underline these differences. We have seen one-party, two-party, and multi-party systems in operation; we have noted varying degrees of legitimacy and varying types of executive-legislative relations. We have discovered that interest groups are organized in many different ways. And we have found how the pervasive elements of ideology and political tradition work to shape the broad contours of political action and to influence the manner in which political elites perceive the world. In examining these four modern political communities, we have seen that they divide into "types" and "sub-types" of political organization.

Britain, France, and West Germany, despite numerous differences, are democracies. Their political systems are characterized by a relative openness in the power conflict among various groups, freedom in the expression of opinions and ideas, the sharing of power among many governmental agencies, and the presence of political leaders who are ultimately responsible to the community through periodic, free, and open elections. The Soviet Union, on the other hand, is the prototype of a totalitarian, one-party political system. The struggle for power is ever present in the Soviet system, although it is restricted to a small group of the population—the Communist Party; even decisions within the party are made by a very small group and are binding on the rest of the party members. Soviet political leaders do not allow the community at large to speak in an open and free election. Responsibility of the governors to the governed—the keystone of a democratic society—does not exist in the Soviet Union. The leaders are accountable only to the party and especially to those who represent the higher echelons of the party machinery.

To identify similarities and differences

among the political systems investigated in this book we have used some broad descriptive categories: (1) *ideology,* which, in rather loose terms, includes history, political tradition, and "national character"; (2) *decision-making,* which primarily involves the relations between executive and legislature; (3) *consensus,* which designates the degree of legitimacy that exists in a given country; and (4) *interest groups and political parties,* through which the citizenry tries to achieve its political desires.

Ideology

History, tradition, and ideas form the environment that nourishes and sustains a nation's political institutions. The study of a country's "ideology," then, should enable us to comprehend its special political character. France under the Fourth Republic was prey to intense ideological conflicts, which accounted and will continue to account for a multi-party system, a divided legislature, and a weak executive. The same conflicts produced the instability of the Weimar Republic. The search for national unity in both France and Germany has resulted in a borrowing from the traditions of the past, including the traditions of strong executive leadership and a certain degree of personal government. In Britain, on the other hand, the continuity of parliamentary institutions, the commitment to party government, and the dominance of the executive (although qualified by parliamentary control), have been so pervasive and profound that British political institutions are now deeply interwoven with British political ideas and culture.

Reference has frequently been made in the preceding essays to a French, a British, a Russian, or a German "national character." We use this rather ambiguous term as a shorthand way of designating attitudes about authority and government that have grown out of the political, economic, military, and social history of a nation. Differences in national character stem from concrete historical factors. The ambivalence of the French to political authority is the result of continuous conflicts about authority; the deference of the British to the Monarch and their pragmatic and con-

crete approach to the game of politics is the result rather than the cause of the successful operation of their political institutions over a long period of time. The fact that Germany attained its national unity late in history and the harsh manner in which it was realized left a legacy of a strong and united German Empire which imparted to the Germans a taste for centralization and authority that often transcended consideration of individual freedom and rights.

National character is a convenient way to evoke history and tradition. It is a generalization that is lacking in desired precision, but still it conveys a complex of attributes that must be taken into consideration in the study of all political societies. And, as all the authors have made abundantly clear, "national character" shows a great deal of plasticity. The passage of time, changing economic and social conditions, modifications in social structure, and the general "winds of change" in the world are gradually transforming the stereotypes of "national character"—and will continue to do so, perhaps at an accelerating rate.

Decision-Making

In the three democracies we have studied, we have attempted to categorize the decision-making procedures. Britain has a "strong executive" type of government. This means that the Cabinet is assured of stability and has considerable leeway in making decisions because it knows its decisions will be respected and enforced. The same thing applies, to a lesser extent, in West Germany today and in France under de Gaulle. This situation, however, did not obtain under the Weimar Republic and under the French Fourth Republic, where the executive was weak, unstable, and could not expect to see its decisions readily enforced or accepted. Both countries suffered under what may be called a "weak executive" type of government or an "assembly government." Under the French Fourth Republic and the German Weimar Republic, the "weak executive" governments were based on coalition Cabinets (composed of the leaders of many parties) that often reflected the divisions of the representative assemblies; since the coalitions were susceptible to pressures on the part of interest groups and had to share power among many political and non-political groups —legislative committees, interest groups, promotional associations, the Civil Service, the Army, etc.—they were highly unstable.

Political Parties

What accounts for "strong executive" and "weak executive" types of government? Much of the cause seems to lie with the political parties. In parliamentary governments, a strong executive exists when there are two disciplined political parties (or more than two if they have a tradition of fully ironing out their differences and allowing an effective Cabinet to be formed, as is the case in some Scandinavian countries). This is certainly the situation in England and, to a great extent, in West Germany today. The stability of the French Cabinet in the Fifth Republic has been somewhat illusory. France under de Gaulle has moved in the direction of a "presidential" system in which one man, by virtue of his overwhelming popularity, has been able to govern and impart an unprecedented degree of continuity and stability to the government as a whole. Even in France, however, the role of the President and of his Cabinet was considerably strengthened by the existence in Parliament of a political party—the UNR— which represented about two-fifths of the Assembly members and which remained loyal to General de Gaulle and his Cabinet. On the other hand, the "weak executive" governments of the Weimar Republic and of the French Fourth Republic clearly resulted from the existence of a multi-party system and the inability or unwillingness of the parties to come to terms and support a strong executive.

The perceptive reader will want to know more. Granting, he will say, that weak and strong executives generally correspond to two-party and multi-party systems, respectively, what accounts for the nature of the party systems? To answer, we must again return to the individual countries and search for the causes of the fragmentation of parties. Is it ideology? Social structure and class configuration? Does it stem from ethnic diversities or is it due to the electoral system? The important thing is to find an *individual* explanation: the electoral system under the Weimar Republic; the perennial ideological divisions in France sustained by a highly diversified and fragmented social configuration; the sharp delineation, until recently, of class structure in England. In other words, *individual* differences must be traced to specific *individual* factors, something that we would have been unable to do if we had not started with some general propositions.

The concepts of ideology, "national character," parties, and decision-making are also helpful in the study of the Soviet system. Lenin's ideology, for instance, was grafted onto Russia's past revolutionary tradition, and Marxism, despite its revolutionary aspirations, had to adjust to the realities of Russian history and to the need to provide a strong authoritarian system of government in order to spur industrialization—something which was also attuned to Russian political tradition. Another observation is of great relevance to our understanding of the political process in the Soviet Union. Many professional and business groups and emerging working-class groups did not have access to the political process in Russia and were not allowed to participate in it under the Tsarist regime, despite certain half-hearted reforms made in 1905. The success of the Bolshevik Revolution was due, at least in part, to the fact that peaceful and open channels for change were not available within the Russian society. We might state this observation in the form of a general proposition: *Whenever emerging groups are not given access to political power, they will resort to violence.* Thus in Britain, where the new groups emerging as a result of the Industrial Revolution in the late eighteenth and the nineteenth century were effectively given a share of political power through the extension of the franchise, a stable political system evolved. This, again, was not the case in France, and, as a result, the working class developed a revolutionary spirit.

Consensus

Another concept we used in our political analyses is "consensus." Consensus means a general agreement on the goals and the procedures of government. In some societies, and this is especially true in Britain, agreement on the procedures of government—on the fundamental rules by which decisions will be made, agreement in other words on what we generally call the constitution—is intensely felt and shared by the vast majority of the citizens. In Britain, such institutions as the Monarch, Parliament, periodic elections for the choice of a new governmental majority, and individual rights are deeply respected. "Consensus" in Great Britain applies also to certain major economic and welfare institutions, such as the National Health Service and the nationalization of some of the key means of production and transportation. In other words, even certain substantive policy questions are so overwhelmingly accepted that they cease to be a matter of political dispute. British society, therefore, appears to be solidly in agreement: social divisions are not sharp; the decision-making process is relatively smooth; and law enforcement is easy.

In contrast, both Germany and France in the course of their history have had political institutions that were not widely accepted and governments whose decisions were constantly and bitterly contested. We may say that such societies are "fragmented" and that they enjoy a low degree of legitimacy. These societies are characterized by frequent changes in the fundamental law—the constitution—and by intensely ideological conflicts about both political means and ends, as both the French Fourth Republic and Weimar Germany demonstrate; in these systems, there is relative difficulty in reaching decisions and enforcing them. Social groups and classes tend to become both polit-

ically and ideologically differentiated, and the result inevitably is a multi-party system.

Some of the many causes of the fragmentation of a society are: conflicting myths about authority; the inability of a system to give access to new social groups; a tradition of violence; the existence of a lower middle class that feels threatened by modernization—and all of these can be found in French history. Both the access of new groups to political power in Britain and the effective working of the parliamentary system account for the development of a broad consensus in England. On the other hand, the Great Depression of 1929 split the fragile agreement underlying the Weimar Republic wide open. The Algerian war in France brought about the downfall of the Fourth Republic, whose Constitution and institutions had progressively lost favor with the French public. In contrast, neither in modern Britain nor in the United States have similar crises resulted in a direct challenge to the symbols and processes of government.

It is not surprising that the Communist Party of the Soviet Union has striven to create a "consensus" in the Russian body politic. The party has tried to devise acceptable symbols of government, to fashion stable processes of decision-making, and to inculcate loyalty to Communist principles on the part of the citizenry. The discussion of "elections" in the Soviet Union is extremely interesting in this regard. Elections do not divide the people as they do in democracies, since they do not involve choice. On the contrary, they are more in the nature of civic ceremonies in which the loyal participation of the body politic is both expected and commanded. An election is a ritual through which unity is expressed. Its purpose is not very different from that of the various national holidays that prevail in a democracy. In some democracies, political unity is so strong that hotly contested elections do not constitute a real threat to its

Epilogue

existence. This is notably the case in England, the United States, Switzerland, and in some of the democratic countries of Scandinavia. It is certainly less true in Italy, France, and perhaps even Germany. In the majority of the other political systems of the world, however, elections are sharply divisive.

The one-party systems in the Soviet Union and elsewhere keep the decision-making machinery in the hands of the few and do not allow political divisions to endanger the newly established regime. The one-party systems in the Soviet Union and the newly developed states, then, may be simply serving the same historical role that kings, the aristocracy, churches, and, later on, the predominantly middle-class parliaments played in the West. All of these ruling institutions the Soviets have telescoped and combined in their one-party system. As a symbol of unity, an instrument of decision-making, and a channel for public participation, the one-party system molds a national consensus before the regime can indulge in the luxury of allowing free choice.

This historical analogy is strengthened by a look at economic history. Whereas Western democracies embarked on the road of industrialization more than 150 years ago and were able to overcome the ensuing social and political cleavages, for the new nations (for which the Soviet Union is a prototype), modernization and industrialization have been chosen as goals to be achieved as rapidly as possible, regardless of the disrupting effects on their society. To achieve their purpose, these new nations cannot afford the time the West took to modernize nor can they allow the shifts and changes that political divisions entail. Again history has been telescoped, and the one-party governments have had to play the role that individual entrepreneurs and powerful corporations played in the West.

While it is not always easy to measure the degree of consensus in any given political sys-

tem, its absence is a matter of empirical observation. Government instability, recurrent changes of the constitution, overt acts of violence by dissident groups, widespread evasion and disobedience of the law, and the inability of the law-enforcing agencies to carry out their duties are some obvious manifestations. Equally important—though more difficult to assess—are two other phenomena: the low esteem held by the citizenry of the symbols of the state and the public's withdrawal from political participation and involvement. The most extreme form of the absence of consensus is, of course, civil war.

If we were to range the systems we have studied on the basis of the degree of legitimacy, we would rank them in the following order: Britain, West Germany, and France. As for the Soviet Union, it is still in the process of fabricating a consensus. On two occasions, however—during World War II and upon the death of Stalin—the Soviet system might have been expected to demonstrate some of the symptoms associated with lack of consensus. The fact that no serious symptoms appeared indicates that consensus in the U.S.S.R. is far stronger than one might have earlier believed.

Future Trends

On the basis of our discussions of the systems of Britain, France, West Germany, and the Soviet Union, what can we foresee of the future, barring a major international conflict? First, there is every reason to expect that all these systems, including the Soviet Union, will continue on the road of economic modernization, which means they should maintain a high level of prosperity. If our general theory is correct, these countries should experience a further decrease in internal ideological conflict and a greater degree of governmental stability.

Second, the trend in favor of increasing state intervention in economic matters—in production, social welfare, and economic growth —will continue in Britain and France and will inevitably begin to influence the politics of the German Federal Republic. Contrary to the theories of the nineteenth century, the state has emerged as the dispenser of welfare services and the custodian of the social sector of the economy—of schools, hospitals, health, highways, housing, urban development, and the like. The trend is toward more "statism," which brings in its wake an enlarged Civil Service and a new group of state economic "managers." Economic planning (direct or indirect) will become increasingly the rule. In fact, increasing state intervention in the Western democracies undoubtedly will gradually make the difference between capitalism and socialism even less meaningful.

Third, modernization and economic planning will continue to dissolve social inequality in two ways: by decreasing the disparity between poor and rich and by widening educational opportunities to provide for greater social mobility. Societies will thus become increasingly undifferentiated and egalitarian. This, in turn, is bound to further decrease political and ideological conflict.

Fourth, the complexity of social and economic problems will call for more decisions on the part of the executive. As issues become more technical, solutions will almost necessarily become more administrative in character. When basic decisions about the distribution of national wealth and the objectives of economic planning and activity have been made by the community through the electoral or the legislative process, implementation will be left increasingly to the administrative and executive organs of the state. This will inevitably weaken the legislature as a deliberative and decision-making body.

Modern democracies are likely to fashion stronger bonds between the electorate and a personal political leader, who will head the executive in order to implement specific policies. The trend may be toward more "presidential government." Interest groups are then likely to direct their efforts more toward the executive, by forming advisory councils and professional representative bodies. These interests will attempt to influence policy through a method of consultation with the executive rather than by operating in a piecemeal way on the various stages of the legislative process.

Similar trends are taking place in the Soviet system. The present policies of the state toward economic planning and controls, equality, social mobility, and personal leadership is likely to continue. The real question is for how long and in what form totalitarian controls will be maintained. Will the system shed some of its authoritarian characteristics and allow increasing participation in the broad decision-making processes and perhaps even allow a choice between alternate policies? Such a development may be accompanied by a greater tolerance of genuine criticism and may even lead to the establishment of constitutional rules and processes that guarantee individual rights and freedoms now denied in the Soviet Union. The one-party system may be made to accommodate more and more debate and criticism, more and more conflict among competing points of view, thereby approximating the two-party systems of the West, at a time when, as we have noted, differences between social and political groups in the West are decreasing in sharpness. If this loosening up of political control were to happen in the Soviet Union—and arguments against such a trend are both numerous and extremely cogent—then perhaps the differences between Western democracies and Soviet totalitarianism will become less important.

The conflict between the democracies and Soviet totalitarianism may well continue for other reasons, but since both systems are moving toward increased political modernization and greater equality and stability, more of the desires of the citizenry in both the West and in the Soviet Union may be peacefully channeled through the government, rather than allowed to boil up in revolutionary fervor. Perhaps we may be so bold as to hope that conflicts among these systems may be reduced in intensity. Compromises and agreements among these states may replace, as has occurred in domestic politics, ideological conflicts that demand violent solutions.

Epilogue

541

General Bibliography

Almond, Gabriel A., and James S. Coleman, *Politics of the Developing Areas* (Princeton: Princeton University Press, 1960).

Asher, Robert E., *Development of the Emerging Countries* (Washington, D.C.: Brookings Institution, 1962).

Braibanti, Ralph, and Joseph J. Spengler (eds.), *Tradition, Values and Socio-economic Development* (Durham: Duke University Press, 1961).

Brinton, Crane, *The Anatomy of Revolution*, rev. ed. (Englewood Cliffs, N.J.: Prentice-Hall, 1952).

Catlin, George E. G., *Systematic Politics* (Toronto: Toronto University Press, 1962).

Dean, Vera M., *The Nature of the Non-Western World* (New York: New American Library, 1957).

Deutsch, Karl W., *Nationalism and Social Communication: An Inquiry into the Foundations of Nationality* (New York: Wiley, 1953).

Duijker, H. L. J., and N. H. Frijda, *National Character and National Stereotypes* (Amsterdam: North Holland Publishing Company, 1960).

Duverger, Maurice, *Political Parties: Their Organization and Activity in the Modern State* (New York: Wiley, 1954), translated by Barbara and Robert North.

Easton, David, *The Political System: An Inquiry into the State of Political Science* (New York: Knopf, 1953).

Eckstein, Harry, and David Apter (eds.), *Comparative Politics: A Reader* (Glencoe, Ill.: The Free Press, scheduled for publication in 1963).

Eckstein, Harry, *Pressure Group Politics: The Case of the British Medical Association* (Stanford: Stanford University Press, 1960).

Ehrmann, Henry W. (ed.), *Interest Groups in Four Continents* (Pittsburgh: Pittsburgh University Press, 1958).

Emerson, Rupert, *From Empire to Nation: The Rise to Self-assertion of Asian and African Peoples* (Cambridge: Harvard University Press, 1960).

Finer, Herman, *The Theory and Practice of Modern Government*, rev. ed. (New York: Holt, 1949).

Fortes, Meyer, and E. E. Evans-Pritchard (eds.), *African Political Systems* (London: Oxford University Press, 1940).

Freeman, Edward A., *Comparative Politics* (London: Macmillan, 1873).

Friedrich, Carl J., *Constitutional Government and Democracy: Theory and Practice in Europe and America*, rev. ed. (Boston: Ginn, 1950).

Friedrich, Carl J., and Z. K. Brzezinski, *Totalitarian Dictatorship and Autocracy* (Cambridge: Harvard University Press, 1956) (New York: Praeger, 1961).

Galbraith, John K., *Economic Development in Perspective* (Cambridge: Harvard University Press, 1962).

Hecksher, Gunnar, *Comparative Politics and Government* (London: Allen and Unwin, 1957).

Hoselitz, Bert F. (ed.), *The Progress of Underdeveloped Areas* (Chicago: Chicago University Press, 1952).

Hyman, Herbert, *Political Socialization: A Study in the Psychology of Political Behavior* (Glencoe, Ill: The Free Press, 1959).

Johnson, John J. (ed.), *The Role of the Military in Underdeveloped Countries* (Princeton: Princeton University Press, 1962).

Kaplan, Morton A., *The Revolution in World Politics* (New York: Wiley, 1962).

Kautsky, John, *Political Change in Underdeveloped Countries* (New York: Wiley, 1962).

Laqueur, Walter Z. (ed.), *The Middle East in Transition* (New York: Praeger, 1958).

Lasswell, Harold D., and Abraham Kaplan, *Power and Society: A Framework for Political Inquiry* (New Haven: Yale University Press, 1950).

Lasswell, Harold D., Daniel Lerner, and C. Easton Rothwell, *The Comparative Study of Elites: An Introduction and Bibliography* (Stanford: Stanford University Press, 1952).

Lerner, Daniel, *The Passing of Traditional Society: Modernizing the Middle East* (Glencoe, Ill.: The Free Press, 1958).

Levy, Marion J., Jr., *The Structure of Society* (Princeton: Princeton University Press, 1952).

Lipset, Seymour, *Political Man: The Social Bases of Politics* (Garden City, N.Y.: Doubleday, 1960).

Macridis, Roy C., and Bernard E. Brown, *Comparative Politics: Notes and Readings* (Homewood, Ill.: The Dorsey Press, 1961).

Macridis, Roy C. (ed.), *Foreign Policy in World Politics* (Englewood Cliffs, N.J.: Prentice-Hall, 1958).

————, *The Study of Comparative Government* (Garden City, N.Y.: Doubleday, 1955).

Marx, Fritz Morstein, *The Administrative State: An Introduction to Bureaucracy* (Chicago: Chicago University Press, 1957).

MacIver, Robert M., *The Web of Government* (New York: Macmillan, 1947).

McClelland, David C., *The Achieving Society* (Princeton, N.J.: Van Nostrand, 1961).

Merton, Robert K., *Social Theory and Social Structure* (Glencoe, Ill.: The Free Press, 1949).

Michels, Robert, *Political Parties* (New York: Dover, 1959).

Millikan, Max F., and Donald L. M. Blackmer (eds.), *The Emerging Nations* (Boston: Little, Brown, 1961).

Moore, Barrington, Jr., *Political Power and Social Theory* (Cambridge: Harvard University Press, 1958).

Neumann, Sigmund (ed.), *Modern Political Parties: Approaches to Comparative Politics* (Chicago: University of Chicago Press, 1956).

Parsons, Talcott, *Essays in Sociological Theory: Pure and Applied* (Glencoe, Ill.: The Free Press, 1949).

————, *The Social System* (Glencoe, Ill.: The Free Press, 1951).

Parsons, Talcott, and Edward A. Shils, *Toward a General Theory of Action* (Cambridge: Harvard University Press, 1951).

Rokkan, Stein (ed.), "Citizen Participation in Political Life," *International Social Science Journal*, Vol. XII, No. 1 (1961).

Rostow, W. W., *The Stages of Economic Growth, A Non-Communist Manifesto* (Cambridge: Cambridge University Press, 1960).

Rustow, Dankwart A., *Politics and Westernization in the Near East* (Princeton: Princeton University, Center of International Studies, 1956).

Sellin, Thorsten, and Richard D. Lambert (ed.), "Asia and the Future of World Leadership," special issue of the *Annals of the American Academy of Political and Social Sciences*, Vol. 318 (July, 1958).

Siffin, W. J. (ed.), *Toward a Comparative Study of Public Administration* (Bloomington: University of Indiana Press, 1957).

Staley, Eugene, *The Future of Underdeveloped Countries: Political Implications of Economic Development*, rev. ed. (New York: Praeger, 1961).

Ulam, Adam B., *The Unfinished Revolution* (New York: Random House, 1960).

Wheare, Kenneth D., *Modern Constitutions* (New York: Oxford University Press, 1951).

Comparative Tables of Statistics

The following six tables furnish specific insights into the relative levels of performance and development of the twenty-six societies under consideration in *Modern Political Systems: Europe* and *Modern Political Systems: Asia*. Figures for the United States have been added to provide a further measure of comparison. In compiling tables of this sort, we must always question what particular types of indicators are most meaningful. A great many more than we have used are available. This particular selection represents our best judgment of the measurements that are most useful in our comparative study of the socio-economic development of political systems that are experiencing varying degrees of modernization. The tables should also provide the reader with a ready source of reference for the basic statistical facts about the countries under consideration. Thus they complement the more detailed tables and charts that appear under the various countries and regions in the two volumes.

A word of caution is in order about the actual figures contained in the tables. They have been derived or calculated from the most reliable and authoritative sources available to the authors. But in many cases, their accuracy is still questionable. On the U.S.S.R. and the Chinese Peoples Republic, for example, many of the data sought are still regarded as state secrets. The figures used, therefore, are either official and, in some instances, suspect or the result of calculations by outsiders based on incomplete and unsatisfactory information. This does not mean that they are necessarily inaccurate or without value. In most cases, they represent the best approximations that are publicly available and probably do convey a satisfactory notion of at least the order of magnitude involved.

In the case of the newer states of Asia, we encounter a different sort of statistical problem. In some instances, these countries have not yet developed a fact-gathering and analyzing apparatus of sufficient sophistication or reliability to provide much insight into national circumstances. Who knows the basic statistics about Yemen, for example? Sometimes, for political reasons, these countries are not interested in compiling or making public such information. With the statistics of these nations, then, we are in the same position as we are with those of the totalitarian states. We use the best estimates available, but with caution and with a knowledge of their shortcomings.

One further aspect of the tables should be noted. The figures used in a given column or section are apt to derive from many different dates. It would be very convenient if all nations had compatible decennial or quinquennial-censuses. Unfortunately, they do not. The Chinese Peoples Republic has not had a census since 1953, for example, and, as a result, we do not really know, within a margin of error of forty million people or more, the present population of China. Laos or Yemen have never had a real census. As a consequence, some incompatibility of base dates for the data set forth will be encountered. Wherever this is important, an attempt has been made to provide the base dates concerned.

Finally, having offered these qualifications, the editors would like to say that they feel that these tables do provide useful insights into the relative levels of performance of these societies and that they furnish a valuable basis for the type of comparisons and generalizations that are set forth in the conclusions of both volumes.

TABLE I *Comparative Table of National Populations and Areas* *

Country or area	Year of census or estimate	Population	Estimated annual percentage population increase	Percentage of population in communities of 100,000 and more and 20,000 and more inhabitants			
				100,000 and more		20,000 and more	
				Year	Percentage	Year	Percentage
Asia							
Japan	1960	93,418,501	1.0%	1959	41.2%	1955	65.7%
Chinese People's Republic	1958	669,000,000	2.3	1953	8.3	—	
India	1961	438,000,000	2.3	1960	8.6	1951	12.0
Pakistan	1961	93,831,982	2.4	1961	7.3	1951	8.0
Burma	1959	20,457,000	1.0	1958	5.3	1953	8.2 [1]
Cambodia	1959	4,845,000	—	1959	8.7	—	
Indonesia	1961	95,189,000	2.2	1959	9.4	—	
Laos	1959	1,760,000	3.2	1956	6.3	—	
Federation of Malaya	1959	6,698,000	3.0	1957	10.8	1958	20.8
Philippine Republic	1960	27,455,799	3.2	1960	9.9	1948	55.6
Thailand	1960	26,257,848	4.3	1947	9.9	—	
South Vietnam	1959	13,790,000	5.9	1959	10.8	—	
Afghanistan	1959	13,150,000	—	—		—	
Iran	1960	20,633,000	2.4	1960	18.1	—	
Iraq	1959	6,950,000	3.1	1957	14.5	—	
Israel	1961	2,170,082	3.6	1959	34.3	1955	56.3
Jordan	1961	1,690,123	3.1	1952	8.1	—	
Lebanon	1958	1,550,000	2.8	1958	33.2	—	
Saudi Arabia	1956	6,036,000	—	1956	8.4	—	
Syria	1960	4,555,267	3.5	1955	28.9	—	
Turkey	1960	27,829,198	2.9	1960	12.1	1955	18.2
Yemen	1949	4,500,000	—	—		—	
U.S.	1960	179,323,175	1.7	1960	28.4	1960	44.5 [1]
Europe							
France	1959	44,097,000	0.9	1954	16.8	1954	33.3
West Germany	1959	52,785,000	1.2	1959	30.7	1950	41.5
Great Britain	1961	52,675,556	0.5	1958	51.0	1951	70.8
U.S.S.R.	1959	208,826,650	—	1959	23.5	1959	35.5

* Compiled from United Nations, *Statistical Yearbook, 1961; F.A.O. Production Yearbook, 1961;* and United Nations, *Demographic Yearbook, 1961.*
[1] Communities of 25,000 or more.
[2] Jewish population.

Appendix

548

TABLE I *Comparative Table of National Populations and Areas (cont.)*

Country or area	Total area (sq. km., 1959)	Inhabitants per sq. km.	Year	Arable area as percentage of total area	Inhabitants per sq. km. of arable area	Period	Expectation of life at age 0 (male—female)
Asia							
Japan	369,661	252	1960	14.0%	1,805	1960	M 65.37 F 70.26
Chinese People's							
Republic	9,561,000	68	1954	11.2	612		—— ——
India	3,262,980	134	1958	49.0	274	1961	M 46.8 F 48.2
Pakistan	946,719	98	1957	26.1	351		—— ——
Burma	678,033	30	1957	12.7	238		
Cambodia	172,511	28	1956	11.4	242	1958–59	M 44.2 F 43.3
Indonesia	1,491,564	62	1954	11.9	507		—— ——
Laos	236,800	7	1956	4.3	173		
Federation of							
Malaya	131,313	51	1958	16.7	298	1956–58	M 55.78 F 58.19
Philippine Republic	299,681	93	1957	24.4	376	1946–49	M 48.81 F 53.36
Thailand	514,000	51	1957	15.2	327	1947–48	M 48.69 F 51.90
South Vietnam	170,806	81	1958	18.2	404		
Afghanistan	650,000	20	1954	13.9	146		—— ——
Iran	1,648,000	13	1950	10.3	120		—— ——
Iraq	444,442	16	1955	12.3	121		—— ——
Israel	20,700	102	1958	19.6	508	1959–60	M 70.67 F 73.47 [2]
Jordan	96,610	17	1954	9.2	183		—— ——
Lebanon	10,400	149	1958	26.7	558		—— ——
Saudi Arabia	1,600,000	4	1952	0.13	2,874		—— ——
Syria	184,479	25	1957	24.9	99		
Turkey	780,576	35	1958	31.8	113	1950–51	M 46.00 F 50.41
Yemen	195,000	26		—	—		
U.S.	9,363,389	19	1954	20.1	95	1959	M 66.5 F 73.0
Europe							
France	551,208	82	1958	38.9	210	1960	M 67.2 F 73.8
West Germany	247,960	213	1958	35.1	601	1959–60	M 66.69 F 71.94
Great Britain	244,022	215	1958	29.0	732	1960	M 68.3 F 74.1
U.S.S.R.	22,402,200	10	1956	9.4	94	1958–59	M 64 F 72

TABLE II Comparative Table of Indexes of Industrialization *

| Country or area | Year | Distribution of labor force | | | Per capita energy consumption [6] (1960, kilograms) | Year | Total production electric energy (million KWH) |
		Percentage primary industry [1]	Percentage secondary industry [2]	Percentage tertiary industry [4]			
Asia							
Japan	1959	36.5%	26.0%	37.5%	1,164	1960	115,489
Chinese People's Republic	—	—	—	—	—	1959	41,500
India	1958	71.2	12.9	15.9	140	1960	19,685
Pakistan	1954–56	65	13	22	67	1960	1,450
Burma	—	—	—	—	55	1960	396
Cambodia	—	—	—	—	34	1960	57
Indonesia	—	—	—	—	134	1959	1,081
Laos	—	—	—	—	31	1960	12.8
Federation of Malaya	1957	58	12	30	241	1960	1,190
Philippine Republic	1958	58	15	27	138	1959	2,286
Thailand	1954	88	3	9	63	1957	468.6
South Vietnam	—	—	—	—	52	1960	306
Afghanistan	—	—	—	—	14	1959	82.6
Iran	—	—	—	—	366	1959	907
Iraq	—	—	—	—	430	1960	852
Israel	1958	17	31	52	1,266	1960	2,312
Jordan	—	—	—	—	190		—
Lebanon	—	—	—	—	596	1960	350
Saudi Arabia	—	—	—	—	229		—
Syria	—	—	—	—	289	1960	368
Turkey	1955	77	8	15	237	1960	2,886
Yemen	—	—	—	—	6		—
U.S.	1961	7.6	— [3]	— [3]	8,013	1960	840,946
Europe							
France	1957	26	36	38 [5]	2,402	1960	72,118
West Germany	1957	16	47	37 [5]	3,651	1960	116,418
Great Britain	1951	5.4	47.4	47.2	4,920	1960	136,666
U.S.S.R.	1959	38.8	36.7	19.8	2,847	1960	292,274

* Compiled from United Nations, *Statistical Yearbook, 1961; Demographic Yearbook, 1961;* and ILO, *Yearbook of Labor Statistics, 1959* and *1961.*
[1] Agriculture, hunting, fishing, forestry.
[2] Mining, manufacturing, construction.
[3] Secondary and tertiary industries combined accounted for 92.4 per cent of the U.S. labor force in 1961.
[4] Trade, utilities, finance, communications, etc.
[5] Includes the unemployed.
[6] Quantities in kilograms of coal equivalent.

Appendix

TABLE II *Comparative Table of Indexes of Industrialization (cont.)*

Country or area	Crude steel production (1960, 1,000 metric tons)	Crude steel consumption (1960, kilograms per capita)	Cement production (1960, 1,000 metric tons)	Year	Volume of railway traffic (millions of: A—Passenger km.; B—net ton km.)	
					A	B
Asia						
Japan	22,138	208	22,538	1960	159,260	53,859
Chinese People's Republic	18,450	27	12,500	1959	45,670	265,260
India	3,287	11.4	7,835	1959	74,135	82,002
Pakistan	7	5.0	1,138	1960	11,035	8,215
Burma	——	—	45	1960	1,528	776
Cambodia	——	2.2	——	1960	83	74
Indonesia	——	3.1	387	1959	6,627	1,046
Laos	——	—	——		——	——
Federation of Malaya	——	29	286	1960	612	706
Philippine Republic	——	15	788	1959	824	193
Thailand	——	8.4	440	1960	2,353	1,138
South Vietnam	——	4.5	406	1960	542	141
Afghanistan	——	—	37		——	
Iran	——	25	782	1959	1,997	1,928
Iraq	——	33	487	1959	656	768
Israel	——	170	806	1960	350	220
Jordan	——	—	165		——	
Lebanon	——	107	854	1960	5	36
Saudi Arabia	——	9.5	——			
Syria	——	23	489	1960	42	107
Turkey	266	22	2,038	1960	4,396	4,322
Yemen	——	—			——	
U.S.	90,067	501	56,063	1960	34,216	835,421
Europe						
France	17,281	306	14,349	1960	32,040	56,886
West Germany	34,100	525	24,905	1960	38,583	56,437
Great Britain	24,695	425	13,501	1960	34,677	30,496
U.S.S.R.	65,300	296	45,520	1960	170,800	1,504,400

TABLE III *Comparative Table of Educational Attainment and Circulation of Mass Media* *

| Country or area | Percentage of literacy [1] | | School enrollment ratios | | | | |
	Year of census or survey	Percentage of total population	Year	Primary [6] 5–14 years	Secondary 15–19 years	Total 5–19 years	Adjusted school enrollment ratio (primary and secondary levels)
				Unadjusted school enrollment ratios [5]			
Asia							
Japan	1948	98%	1960	62	109	77	96
Chinese People's Republic	1950	50	1955	36	7	28	35
India	1961	23.7	1958	24	35	28	35
Pakistan	1951	19	1958	20	15	19	29
Burma	1954	58	1958	31 [7]	16	27	45
Cambodia	1958	33	1959	44	6	33	38
Indonesia	1950	15–20	1959	39	13	31	39
Laos	1950	15–20	1958	24	1	17	20
Federation of Malaya	1957	47 [2]	1960	58	25	50	62
Philippine Republic	1958	75	1958	56	26	48	72
Thailand	1956	64	1959	51	23	44	55
South Vietnam	1950	15–20	1958	32	11	26	
Afghanistan	1950	1–5	1959	4	1	3	4
Iran	1956	15	1959	26	13	22	28
Iraq	1947	31	1959	36	19	31	42
Israel	1948	94 [3]	1959	80	36	69	86
Jordan	1950	15–20	1959	51	33	46	63
Lebanon	1950	45–50	1959	56	32	49	61
Saudi Arabia	1950	1–5	1959	5	1	4	5
Syria	1950	25–30		—	—	—	—
Turkey	1955	39	1959	37	14	31	42
Yemen	1950	1–5	1958	5	0.3	4	5
U.S.	1959	98	1957	88	71	83	104
Europe							
France	1946	97	1959	76	75	76	94
West Germany	1950	98–99 [4]	1959	68	81	73	84
Great Britain	1950	98–99	1958	67	75	70	81
U.S.S.R.	1959	98	1959	67	24	53	79

* Based on UNESCO, *Basic Facts and Figures, 1961* (Paris, 1961); United Nations, *Statistical Yearbook, 1961* (New York, 1962); UNESCO, *World Illiteracy at Mid-century, a Statistical Study* (Paris, 1957); and United Nations, *Demographic Yearbook, 1961* (New York, 1962).

[1] Literacy is defined as the ability to read and/or write.

[2] Including Singapore.

[3] Jewish population only.

[4] Including East Germany.

[5] Unadjusted school enrollment ratios represent percentages of enrollment related to the population of the relevant age groups, i.e., 5–14 years inclusive for the primary level, 15–19 years inclusive for the secondary, and 5–19 years inclusive for the total column. Since the age levels of pupils actually enrolled in a given country do not exactly correspond to these arbi-

TABLE III *Comparative Table of Educational Attainment and Circulation of Mass Media (cont.)*

Country or area	Year	Daily general-interest newspaper circulation per 1,000 inhabitants	Radio sets per 1,000 inhabitants	Year	Number of domestic letters sent and received (thousands)
Asia					
Japan	1958	398	157	1960	6,796,000
Chinese People's Republic	1955	20	10		———
India	1959	48	4	1959	3,378,000
Pakistan	1955	9	2.9	1960	541,165
Burma	1958	8	2.4		———
Cambodia	1959	5	3.9		
Indonesia	1958	11	9.0	1960	213,792
Laos	—	—	—		———
Federation of Malaya	1959	34	35	1960	78,555
Philppine Republic	1956	19	22		———
Thailand	1958	8	4.4		
South Vietnam	1958	28	6.8	1960	34,848
Afghanistan	1959	5	1.5		———
Iran	1959	5	42	1956	125,135
Iraq	1957	10	14	1953	16,825
Israel	1957	210	194	1960	97,609
Jordan	1959	19	37	1958	4,171
Lebanon	1959	97	52	1960	12,028
Saudi Arabia	1959	2	12		———
Syria	1958	19	57		
Turkey	1959	45	45	1960	172,976
Yemen					———
U.S.	1959	328	948	1960	62,072,000 [8]
Europe					
France	1959	243	239	1960	5,733,000
West Germany	1959	313	289	1960	7,739,000
Great Britain	1959	582	287	1960	10,082,000
U.S.S.R.	1959	160	194	1956	3,896,000

trary age groups and since the length of schooling varies widely from one country to another, the respective school enrollment ratios must be interpreted in the light of actual age ranges and the duration of primary and secondary schooling in each country. This accounts for the fact that ratios for some countries exceed 100 and that ratios at the secondary level occasionally exceed those at the primary level. The adjusted school enrollment ratios attempt to compensate for such variations by relating total enrollment, not to the arbitrary age group of 5–19 years, but to the population more nearly corresponding to the actual duration of schooling in each country.

[6] It should be noted that in all cases in this column, except Great Britain, these percentages tend to understate actual performance since the states concerned have normal school-enter ing ages of 6 or 7 rather than 5.

[7] Public schools only.

[8] Domestic and foreign mail.

TABLE IV   *Comparative Table of Gross, and per Capita National Products, 1960* [*]

Country or area	"Money" GNP		"Real" GNP		GNP per capita in dollars	
	Billions of dollars	Precentage of world total	Billions of dollars	Percentage of world total	"Money" GNP	"Real" GNP (1961)
Asia						
Japan	36.0	2.6%	58.0	3.3%	383.0	613.0
Chinese People's Republic	58.0	4.2	116.0	6.6	83.0	167.0
India	29.6	2.1	59.2	3.4	69.9	139.8
Pakistan	5.6	0.4	11.2	0.6	62.4	124.8
Burma	1.3	0.1	2.6	0.1	60.6	121.2
Cambodia	0.4	—[1]	0.8	—[1]	77.4	154.8
Indonesia	9.2	0.7	13.7	0.8	98.6	147.9
Laos	0.1	—[1]	0.2	—[1]	52.0	104.0
Federation of Malaya	2.6	0.2	3.9	0.2	368.3	552.4
Philippine Republic	4.8	0.3	7.2	0.4	188.2	282.3
Thailand	2.3	0.2	4.6	0.3	101.2	202.4
South Vietnam	1.5	0.1	2.9	0.2	110.7	210.3
Afghanistan	0.8	0.1	1.5	0.1	58.5	117.0
Iran	2.5	0.2	3.8	0.2	120.3	180.4
Iraq	1.1	0.1	1.6	0.1	160.9	225.3
Israel	1.7	0.1	2.4	0.1	733.4	1,026.8
Jordan	0.2	—[1]	0.3	—[1]	126.3	189.4
Lebanon	0.5	—[1]	0.8	—[1]	319.5	479.2
Saudi Arabia	1.2	0.1	1.7	0.1	169.8	254.7
Syria	0.8	0.1	1.2	0.1	173.3	259.9
Turkey	6.3	0.5	9.4	0.5	222.5	333.7
Yemen	0.2	—[1]	0.5	—[1]	80.2	160.4
U.S.	515.0	37.3	515.0	29.4	2,790.0	2,790.0
Europe						
France	55.3	4.0	66.4	3.8	1,200.0	1,440.0
West Germany	65.7	4.7	89.5	5.0	1,170.0	1,590.0
Great Britain	70.4	5.1	91.5	5.2	1,340.0	1,740.0
U.S.S.R.	176.0	12.7	212.0	12.1	818.0	986.0

[*] Compiled with the assistance of Professor P. N. Rosenstein-Rodan and based on M. F. Millikan and D. L. M. Blackmer (eds.), *The Emerging Nations* (Boston, 1961), pp. 150–151; and P. N. Rosenstein-Rodan, "International Aid for Underdeveloped Countries," *Review of Economics and Statistics* (May, 1961), p. 126–127.
[1] Less than 0.05 per cent.

TABLE V   *Comparative Table of Industrial Origin of Gross Domestic Product* *

| Country or area | Year | Percentage distribution | | |
		Primary industry [1]	Secondary industry [2]	Tertiary industry [3]
Asia				
Japan	1960	15%	38%	47%
Chinese People's Republic	1956	48	32	20
India	1959	48	18	34
Pakistan	1960	54	13	33
Burma	1960	42	19	39
Cambodia	1959	41	12	47
Indonesia	1959	56	10 [4]	34 [4]
Laos	—	—	—	—
Federation of Malaya	1960	45	10	45
Philippine Republic	1960	34	23	43
Thailand	1960	36	20	44
South Vietnam	—	—	—	—
Afghanistan	—	—	—	—
Iran	—	—	—	—
Iraq	—	—	—	—
Israel	1959	12	29	59
Jordan	—	—	—	—
Lebanon	1958	17	17	66
Saudi Arabia	—	—	—	—
Syria	1959	32	18	50
Turkey	1959	44	22	34
Yemen	—	—	—	—
U.S.	1960	4	37	59
Europe				
France	1960	10	45	45
West Germany	1960	7	52	41
Great Britain	1960	4	45	51
U.S.S.R.	—	—	—	—

* Compiled from United Nations, *Statistical Yearbook, 1961.*
[1] Agriculture, hunting, fishing, and forestry.
[2] Mining, manufacturing, and construction.
[3] Trade, utilities, finance, transportation, communications, public administration, defense, etc.
[4] Construction is included in the tertiary category.

TABLE VI   *Comparative Table of Exports and Imports*
as a Percentage of Gross National Product *

Country or area	Year	Exports	Imports
Asia			
Japan	1959	10.5%	11.1%
Chinese People's Republic	—	—	—
India	1958	5.7	8.7
Pakistan	1958	(6.9)	(9.1)
Burma	1959	19.9	21.8
Cambodia	1956	—	—
Indonesia	—	—	—
Laos	—	—	—
Federation of Malaya	1957	44.4	35.3
Philippine Republic	1959	12.1	10.9
Thailand	1957	21.7	23.1
South Vietnam	1956	—	—
Afghanistan	—	—	—
Iran	—	—	—
Iraq	1956	48.9	32.5
Israel	1959	12.5	25.1
Jordan	1954	(5.7)	(40.2)
Lebanon	1958	(7.6)	(51.2)
Saudi Arabia	—	—	—
Syria	1957	(25.0)	(26.8)
Turkey	1959	1.7	2.8
Yemen	—	—	—
U.S.	1959	4.2	4.7
Europe			
France	1959	14.2	12.5
West Germany	1959	24.3	20.6
Great Britain	1959	14.6	16.8
U.S.S.R.	—	—	—

* Compiled from United Nations, *Yearbook of National Accounts Statistics, 1960;* International Monetary Fund, *International Financial Statistics, June, 1961;* and other sources.
  Parentheses indicate percentage of national income rather than of gross national product.

Index

A

Abitur (German junior college), 325

Abrams, Dr. Mark, 36–37, 39, 76–77

Adenauer, Konrad: Berlin crisis, 300–301; *Der Spiegel* affair, 382–384; election, 295; European Common Market, 392; Franco-German relations, 248, 256, 297; on German regions, 329; popularity, 323, 352; power, 352–353, 368; rearmament, 297

Administrative class: British, 109–111; French, 203–206; German Democratic Republic, 302–303; German Federal Republic, 351, 353–354, 383; Soviet, 460–461

Adzhubei, Alexei, 435

Afghanistan, 434

Agriculture, British: Common Market effect on, 126; National Farmers Union, 41, 44

Agriculture, French: communism, appeal of, 156; economic foundations (*table*), 149; farmers (*table*), 155–156; farmers, decrease in (*table*), 152; interest groups, 166–167; legislation, recent, 250; political orientation, 156; problems under Fifth Republic, 250; resistance to new techniques, 149

Agriculture, German: European Common Market, 299–300; political influence, 377; social strata (*table*), 328–329; tractors (*table*), 304

Agriculture, Soviet: collectivization, 446; directors, farm, 460–461; Five Year Plan, 456–457; inefficiency of production, 528; the kolkhoz, 457–459; Machine and Tractor Stations, 459; peasant population, 455; social conditions, 495; the sovkhoz, 459–460; weaknesses, 426–427

Albania, 483, 485

Alexander I (Russian), 412

Alexander II (Russian), 414, 416

Alexander III (Russian) 412

Algeria: emigration of settlers, 247; and Fifth Republic, 245–246; and French Algeria, 228; and French army, 162; independence, 247; military government, 201; modernization, 246; rebellion under Fourth Republic, 200–201; refugee problem, 250; and Sahara, 246; student attitude, 170; in the United Nations, 254

Allied Control Council, 294, 295

Allied High Commission, 295

Allied Kommandatura (Berlin), 294-295

All-Union Party Congress (Soviet), 480–483

All-Union Supreme Soviet, 510; Ministries, 520

Amery, L. S., 25

Ancien Régime, French, 138, 140; changes since, 147; legacy of, 143; and Poujadists, 190

Anglican Communion, 22

Anti-Semitism, German: decline in, 317–318; in German Federal Republic, 315–316; Nazi concept, 287; Nazi extermination, 290; *Protocols of the Elders of Zion,* 286

Aristotle, 138, 158

Armenia, 507, 510

Asquith, Herbert, 52

"Association for the Fifth Republic," 235

Association of the British Chambers of Commerce, 42

Attlee, Clement, 54, 70

Attlee, Earl, 104

Augstein, Rudolf, 381

Auschwitz concentration camp, 291

Australia, 19, 127

Autonomous Republics, Soviet, 507–508

B

Bach, Johann Sebastian, 280

Baden-Württtenberg, Germany, 330–333

Baldwin, Stanley, 99

Balfour, Arthur, 59

Bank of France, 151

Basic Law of the German Federal Republic, 295; Allied powers in, 338; Bundesrat, 349–351; bureaucratic power under, 339; Chancellor, 338, 351–354; civil rights, 339–343; Constitutional Court, 356–358; and *Der Spie-*

Basic Law of the German Federal
Republic (*Cont.*)
  gel affair, 381–384; drafting of,
  337–338; executive, power of,
  338; Federalism, 338–339, 343–
  345; popular support, 318; Presi-
  dent's powers, 354–355; "state
  of legislative emergency," 352;
  treason, 381
Bavaria, Germany, 330–333
Belinsky, V. G., 415
Belleville Program, 181–182
Beria, Lavrenti, 502, 519, 520
Berlin: Allied division of, 294;
  blockade, 295; wall, 300, 307,
  388; *see also* East Berlin; West
  Berlin
Bevan, Aneurin, 54, 65
Beveridge, Sir William, 122
Beveridge Report (*1942*), 122
Bevin, Ernest, 91, 104
Bismarck, Otto von: "blood and
  iron" period, 310; as Chancellor,
  281–282
"Bizonia" (Germany), 294–295
Blum, Léon, 178, 180
Board of Trade, British, 114
Böll, Heinrich, 393
Bolshevik Revolution, 419, 420–
  421
Bonaparte, *see* Napoleon I
Bonapartism, 138–139; and de
  Gaulle, 244; and Gaullism, 224;
  and Independent parties, 186;
  recurrence, 189; revival in *1958*,
  202; twentieth century, 139
Bonham, John, 76
Bonn Constitution, *see* Basic Law
  of the German Federal Republic
Bourbon restoration, 138, 140
Brandenburg-Prussian monarchy,
  see Prussian State
Brandt, Willy, 333, 373
Brecht, Bertolt, 312
Bremen, Germany, 330–333
Brezhnev, Leonid, 515
British Broadcasting Corporation,
  31, 112
British Employers' Confederation,
  41
British Medical Association, 42,
  44, 46
British Overseas Airways Corpo-
  ration, 112

Bruning, Heinrich, 289
Buder, Dr. Ewald, 383
Bulganin, Nikolai, 484–485, 519,
  522
Bundesrat (German Council of
  Lords), 281; and Federalism,
  344; Länder representation (*table*), 333; law-making in, 355–
  356; power of, 350; status of,
  351
Bundestag, German Federal Republic: Chancellor, 351–352;
  CDU majority in, 336; committees, 346–347; Communist
  strength, 313; Council of Elders,
  347; fiscal powers, 352; formation of, 295; "fractions," 348;
  legislative process, 356; and military service, 298; party strength
  (*table*), 362–363; President of,
  346–347; and President of the
  Republic, 354–355; and pressure groups, 366; rearmament,
  297; representation in (*table*),
  345–346; union members in,
  378
Bundeswehr (West German
  Army), 320
Bureaucracy, German: authoritarianism of, 277; characteristics,
  385–386; court control of, 359;
  and *Der Spiegel* affair, 382–383;
  increasing influence, 351; and
  Nazis, former, 386; power under
  Basic Law, 339; rise of, 277;
  Social Democratic Party, 371;
  tradition of, 277; and university
  training, 278
Butler, R. A., 94
"Butskell, Mr.," 94
Byelorussia, 506
Byrnes, James F., 294
Byzantine culture, 409

C

CDU, *see* Christian Democratic
  Union
Caesaro-Papism, 409
Cabinet, British: Agenda, 104–
  105; committees, 105; and the
  Constitution, 23–24; control of,
  92–93; coordination within the
  Executive, 107–108; formation,
  102; *vs.* French, 50–51, 197;
  membership (*table*), 53; offices,
  103; Opposition Party pressure,
  94–95; policy, transmitting, 109;
  and pressure groups, 44; Prime

Cabinet, British (*Cont.*)
  Minister, 103–104; Privy Coun-
  cillor's oath, 105; Queen's prerogatives, 99; responsibilities,
  81–83; Secretariat, 104–105;
  and two-party system, 50; votes
  of confidence, 92
Cabinet, French: and "absolute
  majority," 195; *vs.* British, 50–
  51; communist opposition, 174;
  and English Cabinet, 50–51,
  197, 205; under Fifth Republic,
  214; under Fourth Republic,
  195–196; instability of, 139–
  140; and National Assembly,
  195; and the President, 213; and
  the Prime Minister, 213; "relative majority," 195
Cabinet, German Federal: and
  Bundestag, 348; CDU control
  of, 297, 348; Chancellor, 338;
  Der Spiegel affair, 382–384;
  growing independence, 298; religious composition, 331
Campaign for Nuclear Disarmament (British), 42–43, 128
Canada, 19, 127
Capitalism: British, 35–36;
  French, 148–149, 157–158; Soviet, 454–456, 458
Catechism of the Revolutionist,
  415–416
Catherine the Great (Russia),
  412
Catholic Church in Britain: break
  with Rome, 22; membership,
  30
Catholic Church in France, 138;
  conservatism of, 156; and education, 143, 159; "indifferent"
  members, 158; political distribution, 156; priesthood, 159–160;
  schools, 251; youth organizations, 160
Catholic Church in Germany:
  Basic Law, influence in, 340;
  and Bundestag, 378–379; Center Party, 283; CDU, power in,
  364–366, 368; in German Federal Republic, 330–331; Hitler's
  Concordat with Vatican, 289;
  influence of, 378–379; and
  Länder system, 336; medieval,
  275; Nazi persecution, 291;
  Peace of Augsburg, 277; political affiliations (*table*), 364–365;
  the Reformation, 276
Catholic Workers' Movement
  (German), 379
Center groups, French: and Alge-

Center groups, French (*Cont.*)
ria, 201; and communism, 193;
history, 181–182; internal division, 198; organization, 182;
program, 183–184; strength,
183

Center Party, German, 283, 289

Central African Federation, 19

Central Committee, Soviet; character, 485–486; importance,
483–484; Molotov's letter, 492–
493; nationality distribution,
501; and the Secretariat, 490;
social composition (*table*), 500

Central Electricity Board (British),
55, 112–113

Ceylon, 19

Chairman of the Council of Ministers, Soviet, 519–520

Chamberlain, Austen, 59, 104

Chamberlain, Joseph, 52

Chamberlain, Neville, 53, 93, 95,
104

Chancellor, German Federal Republic: Adenauer, Konrad, 295,
352–353; Bundestag influence,
348; and Cabinet, 351; election
of, 351; powers, 338, 351–352;
press influence, 354

China, Communist, 69, 403, 430,
483, 485

Chorny Peredyel (Black Redistribution), 416

Christian Democratic Union
(CDU), German: and Ade-
nauer, 352–353; Basic Law,
influence on, 340, 343; in
Bundestag (*table*), 346; conservatism, increased, 368; *Der
Spiegel* affair, 382–384; in East
Zone 302–303; election expenses, 368–370; elite, 364–366;
heritage, 364; and Länder system, 336; middle-class appeal,
320; in North Germany, 332;
organization of, 364–365; patronage, 368; power within,
348; and prosperity, 368; religious composition (*table*), 364;
success of (*table*), 362–363

Christian Social Union (CSU),
German, 364; *see also* Christian
Democratic Union

Church of England, 22, 54

Churchill, Winston, 91, 93, 95,
99, 104

Civic Associations, German, 376

Civil Service, British: and Acts
of Parliament, 106; administrative class, 109–111; coordina-

Civil Service, British (*Cont.*)
tion, 107–108; departmental
structure, 106–107; public-
school men, 40–41; within the
Executive, 106; interdepartmental consultation, 108–109;
and pressure groups, 46; as
pressure group check, 46; Prime
Minister's control, 103; responsibilities, 111; Treasury, 108

Civil Service, French: and the
Council of State, 206; employees (*table*), 204; political
neutrality, 205; tradition since
Napoleon, 203; traditionalism,
145

Civil Service, German: Allied reforms, failure of, 386; Bundestag committees, 347; characteristics, 385–386; "denazification," 295, 343; expellees, 329;
Federal Chancellery, 353; Federal Court of Discipline, 359;
legislation, influence on, 348,
356; Nazi leadership, 318; unions, 377–378

Class structure, British: Conservative Party attitude, 55; and
education (*tables*), 33–35; in
the Labour Party, 68–69; mobility, 124; by occupation, 33;
political role, 39–41; social, 36–
38

Class structure, French: since
Ancien Régime, 147; Center
parties, 181–184; and Communist Party, 173–177; farmers
(*table*), 152–153; and Independent parties, 186–188; middle-class, 157–158; and MRP,
184–185; and Poujadists, 190–
191; and RPF, 188–189; social
foundations, 147–148; Socialist
Party, 177–181; workers, 155

Class structure, German: bureaucracy, rise of, 277; commercial
class, 311–312; elite, 385–386;
in German Federal Republic,
323–324; and political allegiance (*table*), 364–365; stability (*table*), 327–328

Class structure, Soviet: and the
classless society, 526–527; conflict, elimination of, 453–454;
directors, rural, 460–461; factionalism, 493–494; family connections, 471; and housing, 467;
intelligentsia, 467–470; Lenin's
theory, 444–445; Marxist theory, 439–440; party (*table*),

Class structure, Soviet (*Cont.*)
494–495; Party Congresses
(*table*), 498–499; peasants,
461–462; pre-revolution, 454–
455; social movement, 470–472;
stratification, 457; workers, 462–
463

Cobbett, William, 121

Cold War, 450–451

Collectivization, Soviet: directors,
460–461; farmers, 457–460;
Five Year Plan, 456–457; and
party membership, 496

Colonialism, *see* Empire

Committees, in the House of Commons, 85–86

Common law, British, 17, 24

Common Market, *see* European
Common Market

Commons, House of: adjournment
motions, 90–91; Allocation of
Time Order, 83–84; backbencher's role, 93; Cabinet responsibility to, 82; censure, vote of,
91–92; closure, 83; committees,
85–86; constitutional principles,
88; discipline, 117–118; Estimates, 118; Estimates, voting on,
91; evolution, 23; executive,
control of, 89; expenditures, 89;
financial legislation, 88–89;
franchise expansion, effect on,
23; French counterpart, 257;
function, 83–85; "honorable
members," 84–85; importance
of, 92–93; "kangaroo," 84; law-
making, 86–88; Opposition
Party, 93–95; parliamentary
questions, 89–90; pressure
groups, 44; Prime Minister's
control of, 103–104; private
bills, 87; privileges of members,
84–85; public acts, 86–87; public corporation's policy, 112;
Queen's function, 99; Queen's
Speech debates, 91; Speaker,
85; subordinate legislation, 87–
88; Supply Days, 88–89, 91;
taxation cycle, 88

Commonwealth of Nations: British export surplus, 125–126; and
the Common Market, 126; members, 19; Prime Ministers, 103;
Queen as link, 99–100

Commonwealth Relations Office, British, 19
Commune of Paris, 139, 143
Communism: *vs.* authoritarianism, 12–13; and socialism, 453; "War Communism," 455
Communist International, 448
Communist Manifesto, 440
Communist Party, Albanian, 483
Communist Party, British, 51
Communist Party, French: class warfare, 155; configuration (*table*), 176; cooperation with other parties, 242; de Gaulle, opposition to, 225; diversity, 177; election gains, 235; fascism, opposition to, 173–174; and the Fifth Republic, 224–225; under Fourth Republic, 173–176; Fourth Republic, opposition to, 197–198; history, 173–174; ideology, 176–177; influence (*table*), 242; losses in *1938,* 220; membership, original, 144; membership, since the Liberation, 173; middle-class votes, 158; Nazi occupation, 174; organization, 174–175; as protest party, 177; rural support, 176; and the Soviet Communist Party, 174; stability, 161; unity in, 174–175; victories (*table*), 243; voters, 175
Communist Party, German: in Bundestag (*table*), 346; electoral strength (*table*), 362–363; emergence, 282–283; and the Nazis, 287, 289; rejection in German Federal Republic, 298, 313–314, 341; in Soviet Zone, 302–303; in Weimar Republic, 284, 313
Communist Party, Soviet: All-Union Party Congress, 480–483; anti-federalism, 508; Central Apparatus, 490–491; Central Committee, 483–486; constitutional monopoly, 473; directors, rural, 461; and elections, 510; elections within, 477–478; factionalism, 492–494; formal structure, 477; interest groups within, 526–527; issuing decisions, 485; Lenin's theory,

Communist Party, Soviet (*Cont.*) 442–443, 473; membership (*table*), 482; organization units (*chart*), 474; Party Congress, social composition (*table*), 498–499; Presidium, 486–489; and the Presidium of the Supreme Soviet, 516; primary party organizations, 474–476; ruling elite (*table*), 497–498; rural representation, 495–496; Secretariat, 489–491; self-criticism, 478–479; social composition, 494–495; and social rewards, 471; and soviets, parallel to, 510; and state institutions, 479; structural pyramid (*Illus.*), 474–475; and the Supreme Soviet, 512; territorial party organizations, 476–477; urban representation, 496–497; world communism, 401–402; World War II character, 495; world revolution, 448
Community, French, 210, 244–245
Comparative politics, 6–14
Concentration camps, German, 290
Confederation General des Travailleurs Unitaire (CGTU), 173
Congo, 64
Conseil d' Etat (Council of State), 205–206
Consensus, as concept, 539–540
Conservative Party, British: and big business, 47–49; capitalism reaccepted, 35–36; Central Office, 58; colonial independence policy, 129–130; and the Common Market, 126–127; Conference, 58–59; constituency associations, 57–58; economic policy, 113–114; election expenditures, 73; formation, 52; future of, 119–120; heritage, 54; ideology, 55–56; image, 54–55; Leader, 58; Lords, House of, 97; nationalization policy, 112–113; National Union, 56–57; Parliamentary Party, 59–60; pressure groups, 44; problems, 60–61; regulating nationalization expenditures, 118; Right wing, 60; social class voting (*table*), 39–40; state and industry, 55; structure, 56–60; voter identification, 76–77; welfare state, 122–123

"Constantine Plan," 246
Constitution, British: and the Cabinet, 102–103; characteristic features, 24–25; and Commons, House of, 88; conventions, 24; de Gaulle's remarks, 131; evolution, 22–25; Settlement of *1689,* 23
Constitution, French: amendments, 217; and Cabinet, 215–216; legislature, 214–217; major features (*table*), 208; popular sovereignty, 210; and the President, 210–213; principles, 217–218; republican tradition, 209–210; weak parliament, 207
Constitution, German Federal Republic, *see* Basic Law of the German Federal Republic
Constitution, Second German Empire, 281, 283
Constitution, Soviet: amendments, 503; communications control, 434–435; and the Council of Ministers, 517–518; early versions, 503; electoral system, 510–511; function, 504; on Ministries, 520; monopolistic position of the party, 473; nationalization of production, 454; Presidium of the Supreme Soviet, power of, 515; principles, 504–505; secrecy about, 503; socialism, 453; supra-constitutional procedures, 522; Supreme Soviet, 511
Constitution, Weimar, 282–284
Constitutional Council, French, 217–218
Constitutional Court, German, 356–358
Co-operative Party, British, 42
Council of Lands, German, *see* Bundesrat
Council of Ministers, Soviet: composition, 516–518; functioning, 519–520; and the *sovnarkhoz,* 521; and the Supreme Soviet, 513
Council of State, French, 205–206
County Councils Association (British), 45
Cripps, Sir Stafford, 125
Cromwell, Oliver, 20
Crown, British: and the Constitution, 22–23; contrasted to French President, 212; prerogatives, 98–99
Cuban Crisis: and France, 233;

Cuban Crisis (*Cont.*)
    and Germany, 381; and the So-
    viet Union, 451
Curzon, Lord, 99
Cyprus, 19, 82, 130
Cyrillic alphabet, 409
Czars, *see* Tsars, Russian

D

Daily Express (London), 129
Daily Herald (London), 31
Daily Mail (London), 31
Daily Telegraph (London), 31,
    75
Daily Worker (British), 31
Dante Alighieri, 275
Darwin, Charles, 287, 438
Debré, Michel, 239; Cabinet
    (*table*), 255–256; and the Con-
    stitution, 207–208; endorse-
    ments (*1959*), 229; as Prime
    Minister, 213; resignation
    (*1962*), 230
Decembrist Revolt, 414
Declaration of the Rights of Man
    (*1789*), French, 209
de Gaulle, Charles: Algerian crisis,
    201; and Berlin, 248; on Brit-
    ish Constitution, 131; Cabinet,
    256; and Civil Service, 205; and
    the Constitution, 254–255; de-
    pendency of Fifth Republic on,
    192, 252; the monarchical tradi-
    tion, 145; nationalization policy,
    150; and NATO, 248; opposi-
    tion to, 229; opposition to, in-
    crease in, 240; opposition to, vic-
    tory over, 231–232; parliamen-
    tary democracy, 4–5; popularity,
    3–4; as President, 210–213; and
    RPF, 188–189; Referendum of
    October 28, 1962, 233; return
    to leadership, 202; successor to,
    244, 261–263; as symbol, 244;
    world power of France, 247;
    in World War II, 161
Democracy, British: and the aris-
    tocracy, 96; pressure group serv-
    ices, 45–46; public participation,
    26–27
Democracy, French: constitu-
    tional, 210; instability of, 5; tra-
    dition of the French Revolution,
    143
Democracy, German: in Basic
    Law, 341; Bundestag popular-
    ity, 349; and bureaucracy, 385–
    386; *Der Spiegel* affair, 381–

Democracy, German (*Cont.*)
    384; German Federal Republic,
    312, 318; Heuss' efforts for,
    354; Hitler, popularity after
    World War II, 290; Länder
    system, 336; weak tradition, 5,
    312
Democracy, Soviet: constitutional
    guarantees, 505; criticism, inner-
    party, 478–479; distortions, 525;
    elections, inner-party, 477–478;
    elections, staged, 511; forming
    "new" governments, 522–523;
    information control, 434–437;
    Lenin's theory, 444; in party
    organization, 474; as symbol,
    406
Der Alte, see Adenauer, Konrad
Der Spiegel affair, 381–384
Deutsche Jugend des Ostens
    (DJO), 329
Deutsche Partei (DP), 376
Dialectical process, 438–439
Diet of German Industry and
    Commerce, 374
Dietrich, Otto, 288
Directorate, French, 138
Disraeli, Benjamin, 51, 94, 129
Dreyfus, Alfred, 161
Dugdale, Sir Thomas, 82
Duma, Russian, 418–419
Dynamics of politics, 9–10

E

EEC, *see* European Common Mar-
    ket
East Berlin: "Berlin crisis," 300;
    Ebert as mayor, 303; ties with
    West Germany, 307; wall,
    388
East Germany, *see* German Demo-
    cratic Republic
Ebert, Friedrich, 303
École National d'Administration,
    204
École Polytechnique, 204
Economic and Social Council,
    French, 217
Economic determinism, Marxist
    theory, 440–441
Eden, Anthony, 54, 60, 99, 104
Education, British: and class struc-
    ture, 33; party attitudes, 56;
    "power elite," 40–41; social
    class differences, 37; as a social
    service, 114–115; student as-
    sistance, 123–124; university ad-
    missions, 34–35

Education, French: Catholic
    schools, 251; interest groups,
    164; problems, 251; student or-
    ganizations, 169–170
Education, German: and the Basic
    Law, 340; and class structure,
    327; German Democratic Re-
    public reforms, 324–327; under
    Nazis, 325–326; of political
    leaders (*table*), 367; of press
    elite, 380; and religion, 331;
    university enrollment, 278, 325;
    and values (*table*), 326–327
Education, Soviet: character of,
    432–434; literacy rate, 428;
    rural opportunities, 495; urban-
    rural levels (*table*), 462; Su-
    preme Soviet control, 514
Eichmann, Adolf, 316
Eisenhower, Dwight D., 247
Elections, British: campaigns, 74–
    75; conducting, 72–73; fran-
    chise, 72; franchise extension,
    23; General Elections, future,
    130–131; General Election turn-
    out, 26–27; Liberal Party, effect
    on, 79; party statistics (*table*),
    54; pressure groups, 44–45; pub-
    lic participation, 26–27; and
    social class (*tables*), 39–41;
    "swings," 75; voting habits (*ta-
    ble*), 75–77
Elections, French: ballot results
    (*table*), 221; Fifth Republic
    (*table*), 222–223; and the Presi-
    dent, 231; traditional voting pat-
    tern, 241
Elections, German: Bundestag,
    345; Catholic Church influence,
    378; and the Chancellor, 351–
    352; costs, 368–369; govern-
    ment propaganda, 369–370
Elections, Soviet: constitutional
    function, 510; in the kolkhoz,
    458; party, 477–478; purpose of,
    511
Electoral Law, German, 338
Electricity Board for Northern Ire-
    land, 112
Elizabeth II (England): position
    in Commonwealth countries, 19;
    Royal title, 98
Empire, British: colonization, 19;
    Conservative Party attitude, 61;

Empire, British (*Cont.*)
emancipation resistance, 129–130; Labour Party attitude, 64; and party policy, 129–130; "white" population, 130
Empire, French, 138; colonial independence, 244–245; *see also* Algeria
Empire, German, *see* First German Empire; Second German Empire
Enabling Bill, German, 289
Entente Democratique, 222, 227, 231
Erhard, Ludwig, 367–368, 383
"Establishment," (British), 120–121
Estonia, 507
European Atomic Energy Agreement, 389
European Coal and Steel Community, 297, 389
European Common Market, and Britain: British economic decline, 126; Conservative Party attitude, 56; Liberal Party support, 79; as political issue, 130–131; right-wing reaction, 61
European Common Market, and France: commitments, 249; Fifth Republic, attitude of, 248; economic life, stimulus to, 153; Radical Socialist Party, 183
European Common Market, and Germany: admission of Britain, 300; agriculture, protection of, 377; benefits (*table*), 389–392; role of Germany, 299; SPD acceptance, 373
European Defense Community (EDC), 199
European Recovery Program, 294
Evian agreements (French), 246, 252

F

FDP, *see* Free Democratic Party, German
Fabian Society, 61, 62
Fairlie, Henry, 121
Federal Chancellery (*Bundeskanzlerant*), 353–354

Federal Council, German, *see* Bundesrat
Federal High Court (*Bundesgerichtshof*), 359
Federal Union of German Employers Associations (BDA), 374
Federalism, German: in Basic Law, 338–339; Bundesrat powers, 350; in German Federal Republic, 343–345
Federalism, Soviet: Constitution of 1936, 508, 510; hierarchy, 507–508; interlocking structures (*table*), 509; origins, 505–506; power struggle, 526; principles, 506–507; significance, 505
Federation of British Industries, 41–42, 45, 47
Federation of German Industry (BDI), 374
Federation of National Education (FEN), French, 165
Fellowship for Freedom in Medicine (British), 46
Fifth Republic, French: activist formations, 228–229; agriculture, 250; Algeria, 245–247; Algerian refugees, 250; atom bomb, 248; Bonapartist tendencies, 140; budget, 216–217, 257; Cabinet, 255–256; Civil Service support, 205; colonial independence, 244–246; committees, 222; Communist Party, 224–225; communist vote (*table*), 242; Constitution, 207–219; crisis in, 232; Debré Cabinet, 229–230; economy, 248–251; education, 251; elections, 222, 236; European Common Market, 248; executive power, 257; foreign policy, 247–249; *vs.* Fourth Republic, 138, 210, 222–223, 262–263; franc, devaluation of, 249; French Empire, 245; future of, 258–263; housing, 249; Independent parties, 228; inflation, 250; legislative elections, 220–223, 234; military budget, 250; as military dictatorship, 261; ministerial cabinets, 205; and the MRP, 226–227; National Assembly (*chart*), 221–223; National Assembly, dissolution of, 232; national product income, 259; Parliament, 229–231, 254–257; parties, failure of, 261; political forces, 223–229; political institutions, 252–

Fifth Republic, French (*Cont.*)
257; powers, reserved and free, 255; and the President, 253, 256–257, 262; Radical Party, 227–228; social forces, 241; Socialist Party, 225–226; transitional period, 261; unemployment, 249; votes of censure (*table*), 230; *see also* de Gaulle, Charles
First German Empire, 274–276
First Republic, French, 138, 140
Five Year Plans, Soviet, 423
Foertsch, General Friedrich, 386
Force Ouvrière (CGT-FO), 155
Fourth Republic, French: Algeria, 200–201; Cabinet (*table*), 195–197; Cabinet instability, 139; Catholic education, 198; Center groups, 198–199; Civil Service, 205; coalition groups, 173; communist opposition, 197–198; Communist Party, 173–176; Constitution, 194; economy, 259; elections, 171–172, 192–194; failure of, 202; "Hexagonal Assembly" (*table*), 194; ideologies, 172; and *immobilisme,* 197–202; leftist organization, 171–172; "negative majority," 198; Prime Minister, 172; proportional representation, 192–193; Third Republic, similarity to, 144, 172; United States government, compared to, 195; and the Vichy government, 138
France: administration, 203–206; administrative continuity, 143; and Algeria, 200–201, 245–246; army, 160–162; atomic power, 248; Bourbon dynasty, 138; Catholic Church, 137, 156–160; Civil Service, 203–206; colonial empire, 137, 139; Communist Party, 173–177; consensus in, 539; constitutional monarchy, 138; Consulate, 138; "crisis of legitimacy," 139; economic foundations, 148–153; employment (*table*), 153; European Common Market, 153; farmers, 155–156; First Republic, 138, 140; future of, 259–263; future trends, 540–541; geography, 137; and Great Britain, 139, 148–149; 171–172, historical foundations, 142–144; ideological structure, 144–146; *immobilisme,* 140; income, individ-

France (Cont.)
ual, 137; income, national (table), 151; Independent political parties, 186–188; industrial production (table), 150; intellectuals, 162–163; interest groups, 163–170; landholdings (table), 155–156; map, 141; the middle class, 156–158; the MRP, 184–186; multi-party system, 171; national unity, 137–138; nationalization, 151; natural resources, 137; political divergences, 139; political instability (table), 137–140; population, 137, 148–149, 152; Poujadists, 190–191; presidential election, 173; Radical Socialist Party, 181–184; republican tradition, 143, 202, 263; the RPF, 188–191; Second Republic, 138–140; social foundations, 147–153; social groups, 154–163; Socialist Party, 177–181; symbolic status, 140; taxation, 151; Third Republic, 143–144, 147; trade unions, 155; workers, 154–155; World War II damage, 138, 148; see also Fourth Republic; Fifth Republic

Franco-Prussian War, 138
Franks, Lord, 109
Frederick II (Prussia), 280
Free Democratic Party (FDP), German: in Bundestag (table), 346; and business interests, 369; Der Spiegel affair, 381–384; electoral strength (table), 362–363; heritage, 373; instability of, 374; in Länder, 336; policies, 374
French Community, 210, 244–245
French Confederation of Christian Workers (CFTC), 155, 160
French Revolution (1789), 137–139, 145
French Union, 219

G

GDR, see German Democratic Republic
GFR, see German Federal Republic
Gaiser, Gerd, 393–394
Gaitskell, Hugh, 66, 71, 94, 127
Gaullism: and Anti-Gaullism, 235,

Gaullism (Cont.)
237; Bonapartism, similarity to, 144; decline, 193; electoral triumph, 240
General Confederation of Labor (CGT), French, 155
"Generals' Memorandum," 386
George I (England), 51
George, David Lloyd, 52
German Confederation of Trade Unions (Deutscher Gewerkschaftsbund), 377
German Democratic Party, 283
German Democratic Republic: and "Berlin crisis," 300–301; citizenship in, 342; economy, 302–305; formation of, 295; future, 307–308; and the German Federal Republic, 304–305, 341, 385; migration to and from German Federal Republic (table), 305–307; population, 303; regions, 330; and the Soviet Union, 302–303; suicide rate, 312; unrest, 305–307
German Economic Council, 294
German Employees Union (Deutsche Angestelltengewerkschaft), 377–378
German Federal Republic: achievements, 312–313; agricultural interests, 377; Allied restrictions, 296; anti-Semitism, 315–316; atomic weapons, 299; Bundesrat, 349–351; Bundestag, 345–349; bureaucracy, 385–386; business interests, 374–377; Chancellor, 351–354; Christian Democratic Union, 364–370; citizenship defined, 342; class structure (table), 327–329; and Common Market, 299–300, 391–392; communism, rejection of, 313–314; consensus in, 539; Constitutional Court, 356–358; crime waves, 315–316; Der Spiegel affair, 381–384; economic growth, 296, 308; elites, 384–385; electorate, uncommitted (table), 318–321; expellees, 296; Federalism, 338–339; foreign policy, 297–298; formation of, 295; and France, 137, 151, 389–390; Free Democratic Party, 373–374; future problems, 301–302; and German Democratic Republic, 295, 304–307; "Hallstein Doctrine," 308; Hitler, attitude towards, 290; Hohenzollern Empire, at-

German Federal Republic (Cont.)
titude towards, 290; income groups (table), 327–329; Korean War, 297; labor interests, 377–378; Länder, 335; law-making (table), 355–359; literature, 392–394; mass media, 379–381; map, 273; military power, 384–385; national income, 300; national prestige, 320; Nazis, attitude towards, 315–318, 341; popular expectations, 388; population, 322; President, 354–355; press influence, 379–381; rearmament, 297–298; refugees, 296; regions, 329–330; religious composition, 330–331; religious influence, 378–379; reunification (table), 391; and the Saar, 298; Social Democratic Party, 370–373; social mobility (tables), 327–329; and the Soviet Union, 297–298; status-seeking, 327–328; "success Germans," 310; suicide rate (table), 312; trends, future, 540–541; and United Nations, 388; Weimar Republic, attitude towards, 290; and Western Europe, 297–300, 389–392
German Federation of Civil Servants (Deutscher Beamtenbund), 378
German Industry Institute, 375
German-Israeli Reparations Agreement, 298, 361 n
German Trade Union Federation, 371
Germany: education, 324–327; First German Empire, 274–276; Länder, 331–336; language, 276; medieval domination of Europe, 274–275; national character, 309–312; partition after World War II, 293–294; population, 322; regional differences, 329–336; religious composition, 330–331; and Western European Federation, 389–392; Second German Empire, 281–282; suicide rates (table), 312; unification under Prussia, 281; urban industrial predominance,

Germany (*Cont.*)
322; Weimar Republic, 282–285; World War I, 282; and world-wide depression, 285; *see also* German Democratic Republic; German Federal Republic

Germany, Allied control of: Berlin airlift, 295; Civil Service reforms, 385; economic mergers, 294–295; foreign debts, 298; Länder, new, 330; newspaper elite, 380; Occupation Statute, 295–296; political parties in East Zone, 302–303; size and territories, 293; Soviet annexation, 293; surrender, 292

Germany, Nazi: atrocities, 291; attempted *coup d'état*, 292; foreign tolerance, 290–291; ideological intensity, 313; national income and foreign trade, 300; rearmament, 291; Russian occupation, 423–424; Sudetenland annexation, 291; suicide rates (*table*), 312; university enrollment, 325; *see also* Nazi movement

Ghana, 19, 100, 126, 130
Gibraltar, 129
Gladstone, William, 51–52
Glass, D. V., 33
Globke, Dr. Hans, 353–354
Goebbels, Dr. Joseph, 290, 315
Goethe, Johann Wolfgang von, 280, 310
Gorer, Geoffrey, 29–30
Grass, Günther, 392–393
Great Britain: administrative class, 109–111; affluence, 35–36; business in politics, 47–49; Cabinet, 81–83; civic groups, 42–43; Colonial Office, 19; colonial emancipation, 129–130; Commons, House of, 83–95; consensus in, 539; Conservative Party, 54–61; Constitution, 22–25; Co-operative Union, 42; cultural achievements, 17; Commonwealth, 18–20; democracy, 3–4; economic decline, 124–127; education, 33–35; elections, 72–77, 130–131; the Empire, 18–20; employers, 41–42; employment, full, 121–122; the

Great Britain (*Cont.*)
"Establishment," 121; and France, 148–149, 171–172; geographical advantages, 20–21; governmental department pressures, 43; H-bomb production, 128; income, national, 3, 29, 32; Industrial Revolution, impact of, 18, 28–29; labor force, 32–33; Labour Party, 61–77; Liberal Party, 77–80; Lords, House of, 95–101; map, 21; military decline, 128–129; military power, 18; monarchical sentiment, 28, 99–101; National Health Service, 115–116; national income, 29; Order of Precedence, 85; participation in public affairs, 26–27; pluralistic government, 27–28; press, 30–31; pressure groups in action, 43–47; Prime Minister, 103–104; professions, 42; public-school men, 40–41; public corporations, 112–113; Queen's speech, 100; radio, 31; religious differences, 30; religious history, 22; social class, 36–37; social mobility, 33–35; social services, 114–116; television, 31–32; trades unions, 42; treasury, 108; trends within, 541; two-party system, 50–51; United Kingdom, 20 *n*; welfare state, 122–123; as world power, 17

Grotewohl, Otto, 303
Guesde, Jules, 180
Guinea, 219, 244

H

Habsburg dynasty, 276–277
Hailsham, Lord, 119
"Hallstein Doctrine," 308, 388
Hamburg, Germany, 330–333
Hardie, Keir, 29
Harrison, Martin, 67
Hegel, G. F., 438–439
Hessen, Germany, 330–333
Heuss, Dr. Theodor, 295, 353, 373
"Hexagonal Assembly," French, 194
High Council of the Judiciary, French, 217
High Court of Justice, French, 217
Hilferding, Rudolph, 444
Hindenburg, Paul von, 289

Historical materialism, 439
Hitler, Adolf: anti-Communism, 291; appointed Chancellor, 289; death, 292; foreign policy, 289; German opinion of, 290; ideas, 286; *Mein Kampf*, 286–287; Norway seizure, 95; personality, 286; popularity in German Federal Republic, 316–317
Hoggart, Richard, 37
Hohenstaufen dynasty, German, 275
Hohenzollern dynasty, German, 279
"Holy Roman Empire of the German People," *see* First German Empire
Hopf, Wolfgang, 382
House of Commons, *see* Commons, House of
Hugenberg, Alfred, 288
Huguenots, 143
Huxley, Aldous, 142
Hyndman, Henry Mayers, 62

I

Immobilisme, 140, 197–202
Imperialism, the Highest Stage of Capitalism, 444
Independent parties, French: Fifth Republic, 228; history, 186; program, 187
Independent Television Authority (British), 31
India, 19, 69, 99, 129
Indochina, 162, 170, 247
Indonesia, 130
Industrialists' Union, German, 288
Industry, British: Industrial Revolution impact, 28–29; industrial supremacy, 18; public corporations, 112–113; slowdown of production, 124–125
Industry, French: decentralization, 204; economic foundations, 148–149; modernization, 259; workers, 154–155, 260
Industry, German: CDU support, 369; and the FDP, 374; Hitler, support of, 288; influence of, 361; Länder distribution (*table*), 331–332; leaders, 377; political pressure groups, 374–377; propaganda, 375–376; recovery in German Federal Republic, 296–297; Soviet expropriation, 302

Industry, Soviet: *vs.* agriculture, 528; growth, 423; and party membership, 494–495; production (*table*), 424; working conditions, 463–466; Seven Year Plan, 425–426; the *sovnarkhozes*, 521

Institute for Consumer's Research (British), 46

Institute of Directors (British), 41

Intellectuals, French, 163, 168

Intelligentsia, Soviet: distribution (*table*), 497–498; influence of, 493; and nationality, 470; Party Congress representation, 499; party membership, 494–495; and peasantry, 462; "revolution from above," 456–457; as ruling class, 468; social stratification, 467–468; Stalin's criticism, 496–497; vested interests, 526–527; women, 468–470

Interest groups, *see* Pressure groups

Iran, 434

Iraq, 129

Ireland: and Great Britain, 20–22; Irish Home Rule, 52; Liberal Party support, 78

Irish Nationalist Party, 73

Iskra (The Spark), 417

Ivan the Great (Russian), 410

Ivan the Terrible (Russian), 411, 413

Izvestia (Russian newspaper), 435

J

Jamaica, 19

James II (England), 51

Japan, 430

Jaurès, Jean, 180

Jeanneney, J. M., 167

Johnson, Uwe, 393

Jordan, 64

"July Monarchy" (French), 138, 140

Junkers, East German, 302, 304

K

Kaganovich, Lazar, 485, 519

Kalinin, Mikhail, 515

Kant, Immanuel, 280

Katanga, 60, 90

Kazakh Republic, 428

Kazakhstan, 427, 430

Kennedy, John F., 256, 300–301

Kenya, 61, 120, 129

Kerensky, Alexander, 420–421

Khrushchev, Nikita: "capitalist encirclement," 451; Central Committee, 484; as Chairman of the Council of Ministers, 519–520; constitutional changes, 503; on the Council of Ministers, 517; discussion, inner-party, 479; dual position, 479; elections within the party, 478; leadership concept, 449; ouster, attempted, 485; Party Congress as platform, 483; "peaceful co-existence," 451–452; and the Presidium, Party, 487–489; in the Secretariat, 491; denounces Stalin, 446–447; theoretical refinements, 450; virgin lands project, 427

Kirst, Hans Helmut, 393

Kolkhoz (Soviet collective farm), 457–459

Konradin, Emperor (German), 275

Korea, 64, 297

Kozlov, F. R., 473, 478, 515 n

Krasnaya Zvesda (Russian newspaper), 436

Kurbsky, Prince (Russian), 413

Kuwait, 129

L

Labor, *see* Trade Unions; Workers

Labour Party, British: antecedents, 61–62; Beveridge Plan revisions, 122–123; and the Common Market, 126–127; Conference, 65–66; early forms, 29; economic policy, 113–114; election expenditures, 73; employment promises, 121; founding, 52–53; and France, 260; future of, 119–120; ideology, 62–64; and Liberal Party, 73–74; Liberal Party merger, 78; Lords, House of, 97; membership (*table*), 63; membership ambiguity, 70; National Executive Committee, 67; nationalization of industries, 112; organization (*illus.*), 65; parliamentary grievances, 117–118; Parliamentary Party, 65–70; pledged candidates, 58; policy ambiguity, 71–72; problems, 69, 119–120; social class voting (*table*), 39; social composition, 68–69; Standing Orders, 68;

Labour Party, British (*Cont.*) structure, 64–68; Trades Unions pressures, 44, 66–67; victory in *1945*, 35; voter identification, 76–77; voting support (*table*), 62; welfare state, 122–123

Labour Representation Committee (British), 62

Laissez faire, 55

Länder, German (*tables*), 330–333; under Allied occupation, 294; and Basic Law, 338; and Bundesrat, 349–351; elections, 313–314; expellees and refugees (*table*), 333; and Federalism, 343–345; financial powers (*table*), 335; government, 334–336; school supervision, 340; social services, 297; as states, 332

Laniel, Joseph, 197

Law, Bonar, 99

Law-making, British: Commons, House of, 86–88; civil servant's role, 111; Commonwealth distinctions, 19; and the Constitution, 24–25; subordinate legislation, 87–88; veto by House of Lords, 97

Law-making, French: the Constitution, 207–210; the Constitution, amendments to, 217; the Constitution, reforms in, 262; under Fifth Republic, 214–217; under Fourth Republic, 195–197; interest groups, 164–165; legislative limitations, 215–216; special presidential powers, 253

Law-making, German: bill passage, 355–356; the Chancellor, 352; Court system, 358–359; *Der Spiegel* affair, 381–384; ex-Nazi judges, 359; Federal and Länder division, 344; judicial review, 338–339; judiciary stature, 359; political contributions, 376; special courts outlawed, 342; Supreme Federal Court, 359

Law-making, Soviet: administrative decision-making, 519; constitutional guarantees, 504–505; Council of Ministers, 518; federal hierarchy, 507–508; federal laws, 506–507; interlocking

Law-making, Soviet (*Cont.*) structures (*chart*), 509; multiple jurisdiction, 507; Presidium of the Supreme Soviet, 516; Soviets, power of, 508; in the Supreme Soviet, 513–514

League of German Farmers, 377

Lenin, Nikolai: as Bolshevik leader, 417; brother's death, 416; as Chairman of the Council of Ministers, 519–520; "democratic centralism," 417; on federalism, 505–506; imperialism, theory of, 444–445; New Economic Policy, 455–456; party organization, theory of, 442–443; denounces the Provisional Government, 420–421; revolution, theory of, 443–444; "Testament," 489; and trade unionism, 463; voluntarism, 442

Liberal Party, British: history, 52–53; nuclear policy, 128; recent gains, 119; revival, 77–80; social class voting (*table*), 39–40; as third party, 73

Lincoln, Abraham, 142

Literaturnaya Gazeta (Russian newspaper), 436

Lithuania, 510

London Passenger Transport Board, 112

Lords, House of: Crown's relation to, 97; as debating chamber, 99; delaying power, 97; duties, 97; historical role, 23; initiating bills, 98; judicial function, 96; peers, background of, 96; power, 96–97; reforming issue, 99; veto, 97

Louis XIII (France), 142

Louis XIV (France), 142

Louis Napoleon, *see* Napoleon III

Louis Philippe (France), 231

Lower Saxony, Germany, 330–333

Lübke, Heinrich, 353

Luther, Martin, 276, 311

Luxembourg, Rosa, 444

M

MRP, *see* Popular Republican Movement

MTS, *see* Machine and Tractor Stations

MacDonald, Ramsay, 53, 99

Machiavelli, *Prince*, 311

Malthus, Robert, 287

Machine and Tractor Stations, Soviet, 459

MacLeod, Ian, 93

MacMahon, Marshal, 143, 235

Macmillan, Harold, 54, 99, 104, 127, 245, 256

Madagascar, 219, 244

Malagasy, 245

Malaya, 19

Malenkov, Georgi, 447, 485, 517, 519, 522

Mallalieue, J. P. W., 69

Malraux, André, 235

Marshall Plan, 174, 294–295

Marx, Karl, 180, 370; theories, 438–442

Marxism: British, 62; class struggle, 439–440; dialectical process, 438–439; economic determinism, 440–441; and Federalism, 505–506; first organization, 416; history, theory of, 439; irrelevance before 1865, 416; and nationalism, 448–449; pragmatic, 535; proletarian revolution, 441; split, 417; Stalin's modifications, 446; the state, theory of, 441–442; terroristic origins, 443

Marxism-Leninism, 438

Mass media: British, 30–32, 37; German, 379–381; Soviet, 434–437

Mazarin, Cardinal, 142

Mein Kampf, 286–287

Members of Parliament, British, 84–85; and the Administrative Class, 110–111; Conservative Party, 60; Question Time, 89–90; salary, 118

Mende, Erich, 373

Mendès-France, Pierre, 183, 194, 197, 199, 227

Mers El-Kebir, 246

Messianic orthodoxy, 409

Middle class, French: and the Communist Party, 158; interest groups, 167–168; number, 157; political distribution, 157–158

Middle class, German: in the CDU, 366; in the FDP, 374; in German Federal Republic, 324; in German Federal Republic, politically uncommitted (*table*), 318–321; income, 327; judges, 359–360; in the princi-

Middle class, German (*Cont.*) palities, 277; religious composition, 331; and the Revolution of 1848, 281; ruined by inflation, 285; Second German Empire, 282; social mobility (*table*), 328; and the SPD, 370; in South Germany, 334; tradition, lack of, 311–312

Middle Class Vote, The, 76

Mikoyan, Anastas, 487, 519

Mill, John Stuart, 158

Milyukov, Paul, 416

Ministers, British: amending bills, 87; backbencher opposition, 59; Cabinet, 102–103; civil service chief, 110–111; committee influence on, 93; parliamentary questions, 89–90; removal by Prime Minister, 103; "Shadow Ministers," 86

Ministers, German: on Bundesrat, 349; under Chancellor, 351; *Der Spiegel* affair, 382

Ministers, Soviet, *see* Council of Ministers, Soviet

Ministers of the Crown Act (1937), 102–103

Ministries, Soviet, 520

Mittlere Reife (German high schools), 324

Mollet, Guy, 200, 226, 238

Molotov, Vyacheslav, 451, 485, 492–493, 517, 519

Mombassa Base, Kenya, 129

Monarchy, British: evolution, 23–24; importance of, 99–100; Queen's prerogatives, 98–99; succession, 98; as symbol, 28

Monarchy, French: changes in, 138; centralized administration, 138; national greatness, 137; traditionalism, 145

Monnerville, Gaston, 232

Monnet, Jean, 150

Monnet Plan, 150, 156, 202

Monopolies Commission, British, 114

Morocco, 162, 247

Morrison, Herbert, 82, 105

Mouvement Républicain Populaire, *see* Popular Republican Movement

Munich Conference, 291

N

NATO, *see* North Atlantic Treaty Organization

NEP, *see* New Economic Policy, Soviet

Napoleon I, 20, 137, 138, 144, 203

Napoleon III, 138, 140, 241

Narodnaya Volya (People's Will), 416

Narvik campaign (Norway), 95

National and Local Government Officer's Association (British), 42

National Assembly, French: after *1962* elections (*tables*), 239–240; seating arrangements (*table*), 222–223; strength in Fourth Republic, 195

National Assistance Board (British), 116, 122–123

National character, as concept, 537

National Council of French Employers (CNPF), 164, 169

National Council of Small and Medium-Sized Business (CNPME), French, 164, 167

National Economic Councils (Soviet), 520–521

National Farmer's Union (British), 41, 44, 126

National Federation of Farmers (FNSEA), French, 164, 167

National Health Service (British), 115–116

National Health Service, A, 122

National School of Administration (French), 204

National Socialist German Workers Party (Nazi Party): absolute power, 289; electoral strength (*table*), 363; after World War I, 282; *see also* Nazi movement

National Student Union (UNEF), French, 164, 169

National Union of British Manufacturers, 42

National Union of Conservative and Unionist Associations (British), 56–58

National Union of Teachers (British), 41, 42, 48

Nationalism: Irish, 73; Welsh, 30

Nationalism, German: in German Democratic Republic, 320; in German Federal Republic, 316–317; Hitler's appeal, 288; medieval tradition, 274–275; regional, 332–333; after Second German Empire, 282; Socialist Imperial Party, 298; in West Berlin, 333

Nationalism, Soviet: and ethnic

Nationalism, Soviet (*Cont.*) diversity, 428; and federalism, 505–506, 508; among non-Russian nationalities, 432; party membership distribution (*table*), 500–501; political representation by nationality, 513; social influence of, 471–472; Stalin's use of, 449

Nationalist Party, German, 289

Nationalized industry, British: Conservative Party attitude, 55; denationalization, 71; Labour Party view, 63–64; public corporations, 112–113; regulation problems, 118; social services, 114–116

Nationalized industry, French, 151

Nationalized industry, German: Basic Law provisions, 341; in East Germany, 302; extent of, 297; SPD ideology, 370

Nationalized industry, Soviet: constitutional provisions, 454; *see also* Collectivization, Soviet

Nazi movement: appeal of, 285; in Britain, 27; compared to Communism, 276; electoral strength (*table*), 363; *Mein Kampf,* 286–287; National Socialist German Workers Party, 289, 363; opinions of, 290; popularity in German Federal Republic, 315–318; purge, 289; "Strength through Joy," 290; World War II propaganda, 291–292

Nazi-Soviet Pact, 291

New Economic Policy, Soviet, 455–456

New Left Review, 27

New Statesman, 27

New Zealand, 19, 127

News of the World (London), 31

Newspapers, *see* Press

Newspaper Leases Control Board, German, 380

Newth, J. A., 466

Nicholas I (Russian), 414

Nigeria, 19, 126

Nilys, Sergei, 286

North Atlantic Treaty Organization: Britain's role, 66, 126, 128; French position, 174, 183, 247–248; and Germany, 372–373

North Rhine-Westphalia, Germany, 330–333

Northern Ireland, 30, 37

Northern Rhodesia, 60, 93

Norway, 95

Nuclear power: British, 64, 79, 128; Soviet, 450

Nyasaland, 95, 120

O

OAS, *see* Secret Organization of the Army

Oblasts, Autonomous Soviet, 507–508

Observer (London), 31

October Manifesto (Russian), 418

"Oder-Neisse Line," 271, 293

Opposition Party, British, 93–95

Oprichnina (Tsar's secret police), 413

Order of the British Empire, 100

Orleanist Monarchy, 138, 140

Orthodox Church, Russian: Messianic orthodoxy, 409; and the Tsar, 413

Orwell, George, 47

Otto the Great (German), 275

P

Pakistan, 19

Palestine, 130

Papen, Franz von, 289

Paris Commune, *see* Commune of Paris

Parliament, British: backbencher's role, 93; and Cabinet, 81–83; and civil servants, 110–111; Commons, House of, 83–95; and the Constitution, 23–24; conventions, 24; criticism of, 117–118; group pressures, 43–44; "honorable members," 84–85; Instruments, 87–88; Lords, House of, 95–101; Opposition rights, 84; pressure groups, 43–44; Prime Minister's control of, 104; privileges, 84–85; Queen's presence at, 100; Queen's Speech, 91; Scrutiny Committee, 88; sovereignty, 24

Parliament, French: budget, 216–217; composition, 214; legislative limitations, 216; "ration-

Parliament, French (*Cont.*) alized," 214–215; *see also* National Assembly, French

"Parliamentary Council," German, 295, 337–338

Parliamentary Conservative Party, British, 59–60

Parliamentary democracy, 17

Parliamentary Labour Party, British, 65–70

Parnell, Charles, 52

Party Congress, Soviet, 480–483; social composition, 498–499

Party system, British: and the Administrative Class, 110; committee influence, 93; and electoral system, 74; history, 51–54; importance, 50; Lords, House of, 97; Opposition Party, 93–95; problems, 119–120; Sovereign, consulting the, 99; third party weakness, 73; *see also* Political parties, British

Party system, French: breakdown, 260–261; diversity and fragmentation, 157; in the Fourth Republic, 171–191; limitations, 207; traditionalism, 261; *see also* Political parties, French

Party system, German Federal Republic: Basic Law provisions, 338; in Bundestag, 346, 348; constitutional curbs, 341; history (*table*), 362–363; Länder influence, 336; popular support for, 318; *see also* Political parties, German

Party system, Soviet, 539–540; "democratic centralism," 446

Pax Britannica, 18

Peasants, Soviet: children's opportunities, 471; in the collective farm, 457–459; Five Year Plan, 456–457; income, 461; "labor-day" units, 459; Party Congress representation, 499; party membership, 494–495; on the party pyramid, 500; social stratification, 461–462; on the state farm, 459–460

Peasants' Revolt, German, 277

Peel, Sir Robert, 51, 94

Peerage, British (*table*), 96

Pervukin, M. G., 485

Pétain, Marshal, 138, 140, 144, 161, 178, 182, 202

Peter the Great (Russian), 411, 413

Pflimlin, Pierre, 201–202

Philip II (Spain), 20

Phillips, Morgan, 66

Pinay, Antoine, 189, 199, 228

Pitt, William, 103

Plaid Cymru, 30

Plekhanov, George, 416

Pluralism, British, 27–28

Political heritage, British: history, 17–18; Liberal and Conservative party, 52; in the nineteenth century, 52–53; pluralism, 27–28; Whigs and Tories, 51–52; United Kingdom, 20–22

Political heritage, French: Bonapartism, 138–139; Bourbon dynasty, 138; Catholic Church, 158–160; constitutional monarchy, 138; Directorate, 138; First Republic, 138–140; Fourth Republic, 192–206; historical foundations, 142–145; ideological foundations, 144–147; *immobilisme*, 140; republican tradition, 143, 202; Second Empire, 138, 140; social foundations, 147–149; Third Republic, 143–144

Political heritage, German: authoritarianism, 311; bureaucratic tradition, 277; First German Empire, 275–276, 281–282; Habsburg dynasty, 276–277; Hanseatic cities, 276; Hitler's rise, 286–289; Hohenstaufen dynasty, 275; medieval power, 274–275; Napoleonic Wars, 280; patterns and polarities, 309–311; Peasants' Revolt, 277; Prussia, 279–280; the Reformation, 276; Thirty Years War, 276, 278; unification, 281

Political heritage, Russian: anarchism, 412; autocratic rule, 411–412; barbarism, 409–410; Bolsheviks, 417; Byzantine legacy, 409; the Duma, 418–419; federalism, 505–506; "House of Commons," 411; influence on Marxism, 448–449; national character, 408–409; Mensheviks, 417; Muscovite absolutism, 410–411; Populists, 415; "revolution from above," 413; Revolution of 1915, 418; Revolution of 1917, 419–421; revolutionary

Political heritage, Russian (*Cont.*) terror, 415–416; secret police, 413; serfdom, 414; social classes, 454–455; Stalin as reflection of, 449

Political parties, British: Communist, 51; Conservative, 54–61; Labour Party, 61–71; Liberal, 52–53, 77–80; structuring, 52–54; Whigs and Tories, 51–52

Political parties, French: Communist Party, 173–174; Independent parties, 186; Radical Socialist Party, 181–182; Rally of the French People (RPF), 188–189; Popular Republican Movement (MRP), 184–185; Poujadists (UFF), 190; Socialist Party, 177–178

Political parties, German: banning of, 357; Christian Democratic Union (*tables*), 364–370; Christian Social Union, 364; Communist Party, 313; extremists (*tables*), 313–318; "fractions," 348; Free Democratic Party, 373–374; in Länder (*table*), 332–333; Social Democratic Party, 370–373; in Soviet Zone, 302–303; in Weimar Republic, 282–284, 289

Pompidou, Georges, 227, 228, 230–232, 238, 242, 256

Popular Front, French, 173, 175, 180, 242

Popular Republican Movement (MRP), French, 158, 160, 166, 178–181; Algerian vote, 253; and de Gaulle, 184; and de Gaulle, hostility to, 226–227; Fifth Republic, 226–227; Fourth Republic, 198–199; history, 184; majority system, opposition to, 193; organization, 185; referendum of 1958, 220–221; strength, 185

Postanovleniya (Soviet decrees), 519

Poujade, Pierre, 168, 190–191, 221, 228

Poujadists (UFF), 167, 181, 252; Algerian integration, 201; "floating vote," 194; and Gaullists, 193; history, 190; "negative vote," 199; organization, 190; and RPF, 194; under referendum of 1958, 220–221; strength, 190–191

Pravda (Russian newspaper), 435

Presbyterian Church of Scotland, 20

President of the French Republic: as arbitrator, 212, 255; and the Cabinet, 213; election reforms, 231; in the Fifth Republic, 210–213, 252–253; monarchical tradition, 212; new powers, 211–212; political powers, 213; under Third and Fourth Republics, 211

President of the German Federal Republic, 346; and the Chancellor, 351–352; impeachment of, 355, 357; powers, 354–355

Presidium, Party (Soviet): composition, 486–487; and the Council of Ministers, 516; factionalism, 492; forming "new" governments, 522–523; functioning, 487–489; nationality distribution (table), 502; and the Secretariat, 491; social composition (table), 500–501

Presidium of the Council of Ministers, Soviet, 518–520

Presidium of the Supreme Soviet: function, 515–516; and the Supreme Soviet, 514, 516; Vice Chairmen, 507

Press: British, 30–31; German, 379–383; Soviet, 435–436

Pressure groups, British: big business, 47–49; major, 41–43; targets, 43–45; value, 45–47

Pressure groups, French: army and veterans, 168; characteristics, 165; middle-class, 167; organization, 163–164

Pressure groups, German: agricultural interests, 377; business interests, 361, 374–377; in Bundestag, 366; Hitler's rise, 289–290; legal curbs on, 358; press, 379–381; and political parties, 369–370; religious interests, 378–379; in Second German Empire, 282, 361; in SPD, 373; trade unions, 377–378; in Weimar Republic, 361

Pressure groups, Soviet: and the classless society, 526–527; peasants, 461–462

Prime Minister, British: forming a Cabinet, 102; powers, 103–104; primacy, 103; Queen's relation to, 99

Prime Minister, French, 139; under Fifth Republic, 213; and Fourth Republic, 195; and the

Prime Minister, French (Cont.) legislature, 216–217; rejection of Communist support, 198

Proletarian revolution: Lenin's theory, 443–444; Marxist theory, 441

Protestant Church, German: anti-Nazi leaders, 379; Basic Law, influence on, 340; in German Federal Republic, 330–331; Peace of Augsburg, 277; political influence, 379; and political parties, 364–365, 373; political submission, 332; the Reformation, 276

Protestantism, British, 22

Protocols of the Elders of Zion, 286

Prussian State, 279–281

Public corporations, British, 112–113

Q

Queen's Speech, 91

Question Time, House of Commons, 89–90

R

RPF, see Rally of the French People

Radio: British, 31; German, 380; Soviet, 436–437

Radical Socialist Party, French: decline, 182; under Fifth Republic, 227–228; history, 181–182; opposition to de Gaulle, 227; organization, 182; strength, 183

Rally of the French People (RPF): history, 188; and the MRP, 184, 186; organization, 189–190

Rasporyazheniya (Soviet orders), 519

Rasputin, 419

Referendum of April 8, 1962 (French), 219, 247, 252

Referendum of January 8, 1961 (French), 219, 245, 252, 262

Referendum of July 1, 1962 (French), 247

Referendum of October 28, 1962 (French), 173, 219, 229, 232–235

Referendum of September 28, 1958 (French), 219–221, 244–245, 262

Referendums under the Fifth French Republic (1958–1962), (table), 234

Reform Act of 1867 (British), 52

Reformation in Germany, 276–277

Refugee Party, German: in Bundestag (table), 346; in Länder, 336

Reichsrat (German Federal Council), 283

Reichstag, German: fire, 289; party strength in (table), 362–363; powers, 281

Reichswehr (German army), 283

Religious intolerance: British, 22; Soviet, 472, 505; see also Anti-Semitism, German

Renault Automobile Co., 151

Republican Front, French, 194

Republics, Soviet, 506–507

Restrictive Practices Act (1956), British, 56

Revolution, French: of 1789, 137–139, 145; of 1830, 138; of 1848, 138

Revolution, Russian: of 1905, 418; of 1917, 419–421

Reunification, German: desire for (table), 391; in literature, 393; popular sentiment, 320; prospects for, 397–398; regional desire for (table), 334; SPD interest in, 372–373

Reynaud, Paul, 231

Rhineland, Germany, 291, 329–333

Rhodesia, 130

Richelieu, Cardinal, 142

Roads Campaign Council (British), 41

Roman Catholic Church, see Catholic Church

Rothschild Bank, 230

Rotten boroughs, 23

Rousseau, Jean Jacques, 143

Rurik the Red, 409

Russell, Bertrand, 120

Russia, Imperial: alien influence, 409–410; autocratic tradition, 409–412; class structure, 454; Communist Party, 494; Decembrist Revolt, 414; federalist ideology, 505–506; Marxism, de-

Russia, Imperial (*Cont.*)
velopment of, 416–418; Mongol-Tatar domination, 409–410; Muscovite absolutism, 410–411; Narodnik movement, 415; national character, 408–409; Oprichnina, 413; parliamentary institutions, 443; reforms of *1905*, 418–419; Revolution of *1915*, 418; Revolution of *1917*, 419–421; revolutionary intelligentsia, 414–415; revolutionary violence, 415–416; *vs.* Soviet Russia, 402–403; Zemsky Sobor, 411

Rykov, Aleksei, 519

S

SPD, *see* Social Democratic Party, German

Saarland, Germany, 332–333
Saburov, M. Z., 485
Sahara, 246
St. Simon, Comte de, 144
Salisbury, Lord, 82, 99
Sawyer, John E., 147
Schirach, Baldur von, 315
Schleicher, Kurt von, 289
Schleswig-Holstein, Germany, 330–333
Schmückle, Gerd, 386
School of National Administration (French), 259
Schroeder, Gerhard, 353, 367–368
Scotland, 37, 61; cultural assimilation, 22; national church, 20; nationalism, 30; peers, 96; Scottish Committee, 85
Second British Empire, 19
"Second Empire," French, 138, 140
Second German Empire: Constitution, 281–282; destruction, 282; North German influence, 332; Prussian dominance, 281; suicide rates (*table*), 312; and World War I, 281–282
Second Republic, French, 138, 140
Secretary of State, German, 353–354
Secret Organization of the Army (OAS), French, 228–229

Senegal, 245
"Settlement" of *1689*, 17–18, 23
Seven Year Plan, Soviet, 425
Shvernik, Nikolai, 515
Siberia, 427
Sierra Leone, 19
Sixth Republic, French, possibility of, 192
Social class, British: differences, 36–38; and education (*tables*), 33–35; party attitudes, 55, 68–69; political role (*table*), 39–40
Social class, French: and the Catholic Church, 156–160; Center parties, 181–184; and the Communist Party, 158, 173–177; farmers, 155–156; ideological distribution, 154–155; and intellectuals, 162–163; in Independent parties, 186–188; political distribution, 157–158; political influence, 139; Poujadists, 190–191; and the Socialist Party, 177–181; workers, 139
Social class, German: bureaucracy, 277, 383–386; commercial class, 311–312; income distribution (*table*), 327–328; journalists' status, 383; Peasants' Revolt, 277; political leaders (*table*), 367; and political party (*table*), 364–365; population breakdown, 323–324; in Prussian State, 279
Social class, Soviet: advancement, 470–471; differentiation, 453–454; directors, 460–461; factionalism, 493–494; frictions, 526–527; and income, 466–467; intelligentsia, 467–470; and national origin, 471–472; Party Congresses (*table*), 498–499; and party membership (*table*), 494–495; peasants, 461–462; and social origin, 471; stratum, 457; under "War Communism," 455; workers, 462–463
Social Democratic Federation (British), 61
Social Democratic Party (SPD), German, 282, 288, 330; Basic Law, influence in, 340, 343; Brandt, Willy, 333; in Bundestag (*table*), 346; in city-states, 332; *Der Spiegel* affair, 383–384; difficulties, 320; in East Zone, 302–303; election expenses, 369; electoral strength

Social Democratic Party (*Cont.*)
(*table*), 362–363; electoral support, 371; and French Socialist Party, 177; functionaries, 371; heritage, 370; in Länder, 336; leadership, 371–372; municipal strength, 373; out of power, 297; power in, 348; and reunification, 372–373; solidity, 371; trade union support, 378; and United States Democratic Party, 371; in Weimar Republic, 283, 289
Social homogeneity, as concept, 536
Social mobility: British, 33–35; French, 152–157; German, 328–329, 331; Soviet, 470–472
Social Security, British, 116
Social welfare, British: acceptance of, 535; Beveridge Plan, 122–123; National Health Service, 115–116; Social Security, 116; welfare state, 122–123
Social welfare, French: attitude towards, 535; farmers, 155–156; under Fifth Republic, 249; middle-class, 157–158; workers, 155–156
Social welfare, German: Basic Law provisions, 343; "equalization of burdens law," 297; Federal Social Court, 359; in Nazi Germany, 290
Social welfare, Soviet: medical advances, 402–403; Ministries, 520; popular acceptance of, 524; and trade union membership, 463
Socialism, British: democratic, 4; Labour Party ideology, 62–64; welfare state, 122–123
Socialism, French, 145
Socialism, German: in Basic Law, 341–342; in German Democratic Republic, 302–303; in German Federal Republic, 297
Socialism, Soviet: constitutional, 453; Five Year Plan, 456–457; proclamation of *1936*, 447; under Stalin, 446
Socialist Congress of Tours (*1920*), 173, 181
Socialist Imperial Party (SRP), German, 298
Socialist Party, French: decline, 180; under the Fifth Republic, 225–226; history, 177–178; membership, 179; opposition to de Gaulle, 226; organization,

Socialist Party, French (*Cont.*) 178–180; program, 180–181; in World War II, 178

Soviet of Nationalities, 512–513

Soviet of the Union (legislative chamber), 512–513

Soviet Union: agriculture, 426–427; All-Union Party Congress, 480–483; as Britain's rival, 18; Central Committee, 483–486; communications media, 434–437; Constitution, 503–505; Council of Ministers, 516–520; culture, 408–409; decision-making, 539–540; democracy, inner-party, 477–479; education, 432–434; elections, 510–511; ethnic distribution, 431; factionalism, 492–494; farms, 457–460; federalism, 505–510; Five Year Plan, 456–457; future of, 524–525; German occupation, 423–424; governmental changes, 521–523; housing, 467; ideological distortions, 525; ideology, recent, 450–452; vs. Imperial Russia, 401–402; industry, 423–426; intelligentsia, 467–470; information control, 434–437; the kolkhoz, 457–459; Kulak crisis, 426, 456–457; "labor-day" units, 459; language, 409; Lenin's theories, 442–445; map, 404–405; Marxist theory, 438–442; Ministries, 520; National Economic Councils, 520–521; nationalistic discrimination, 471–472; natural resources, 422–423; New Economic Policy, 455–456; newspapers, 435–436; ownership controls, 453–454; Party Congress, 480–483, 498–499; "peaceful coexistence," 451–452; political power, transferring, 525–526; population, 427–428; population movement, 430–431; post-Stalin period, 449–450; Presidium of the Party, 486–489; Presidium of the Supreme Soviet, 515–516; primary party organizations, 474–476; private property, 454; problems ahead, 525–528; radio, 436–437; "revolution from above," 456–457; ruling elite (*table*), 497–498; rural social stratification, 460–469; secret police, 520; Secretariat, Party, 489–491; size, 422; social dif-

Soviet Union (*Cont.*) ferentiation, 453–454; social mobility, 470–472; the soviets. 508–510; the sovkhoz, 459–460; Stalin's role, 445–449; standard of living, 466–467; standard of living, raising of, 527–528; Supreme Soviet, 511–514; television, 436–437; territorial party organizations, 476–477; totalitarianism, 405–406; totalitarianism, decreasing, 541; trends, future, 540–541; Union Republics, 506–508; urban-rural distribution, 430–431; "War Communism," 455; World War II losses, 424, 427

Soviets: controlled by Bolsheviks, 420–421; Petrograd council, 419; in the revolution of *1905*, 418

Sovkhoz (Soviet state farm), 459–460

Sovnarkhoz (Soviet Economic Councils), 520–521

Spain, 91

"Spartacus" revolt, 283

Speransky, Michael, 412

Stalin, Joseph: agricultural dilemma, 426; "capitalistic encirclement," 450; and the Central Committee, 484; as Chairman of the Council of Ministers, 519–520; "cult of personality," 449–450; as dictator, 406–407, 446–447; Five Year Plans, 423, 456–457; "inevitability of wars," 450–451; and the intelligentsia, 468, 496–497; Kulak problem, 456; legacy of retardation, 410; Lenin's criticism, 489; Moscow's legacy, 411; on national territory, 507; "new" governments, 521–522; Party Congress, 481–482; party and state administrations, 516–517; population distribution, 430; and the Presidium, 486–489; retaliates against non-Russian nationals, 432; Russian destiny, 415; and the Russian heritage, 448–449; and the Secretariat, 489–490; socialism under, 445–446; state, theory of, 447–448; and trade unionism, 463; and world revolution, 448

Stammberger, Wolfgang, 382

Standing Orders, Labour Party, 68

Statute of Westminster (*1931*), 19

Strauss, Franz Joseph, 299, 353, 367–368, 381–384

Strauss, Walter, 382

"Strength through Joy," 290

Sudetenland, 291, 293

Suez intervention of *1956*: British parties' reaction, 61, 64; French attitude, 247; as political issue, 117; United States' role, 61

Sunday Times (London), 31

Supreme Federal Court, German, 359

Supreme Soviet: constitutional structure (*table*), 511–512; and the Council of Ministers, 517; function, 513–514; Presidium, 515–516; Soviet of Nationalities, 512–513; Soviet of the Union, 512–513

Swiss Federal Council, 515

Syndicalism, British, 62, 115

T

Tanganyika, 19

Television: British, 31–32; German, 380; Soviet, 436–437

Third Republic, French: first president, 143; and Fourth Republic, 193; longevity, 138; successor to the Commune, 139; reaction against, 144

Thorez, Maurice, 225

Thyssen, Fritz, 288

Times, The (London), 46–47, 121

Tin Drum, The, 393

Tito, Marshal, 448

Tkachev, Peter, 415

Tories, history of the, 51–52

Townsend, P., 122

Trade Unions, French: distribution of membership, 155; organization, 155; strength, 226

Trade Unions, German: anti-nationalism, 288; constitutional rights, 340; leaders, 378; organization of, 377–378; political influence, 378; and political parties, 371; and SPD, 371, 373

Trade Unions, Soviet, 463–466

Trades Unions, British: and the

Trades Unions, British (*Cont.*)
Common Market, 126; evolution, 28–29; and the Labour Party, 29; as Labour Party pressure group, 44; Labour Party role, 66–67; party membership ambiguity, 70–71; as pressure group, 42; wage rises, 125

Trades Union Congress (British), 42; authority of, 125; as pressure group, 45; representation (*table*), 28

Treasury, British: and French Ministry of Finance, 205; preeminence, 108; and public corporations, 112

Treaty of Union, 37

Treaty of Versailles, 291

Trinidad-and-Tobago, 19

Trizonal Fusion Agreement, 295

Trotsky, Leon: criticizes party organization, 443; and Marxism, 445; and Marxist factions, 417; St. Petersburg Soviet, 418

Trud (Russian newspaper), 436

Tsars, Russian: Byzantine influence, 409; centralization of power, 410; consolidation of rule, 411–412; and non-Russian nationals, 432; October Manifesto, 418; as symbol, 413

Tunisia, 162, 247

Turkey, 434

Twenty-Second Party Congress, *1961* (Soviet), 480–483

U

UFF, *see* Poujadists

UNR, *see* Union for the New Republic

U.S.S.R., *see* Soviet Union

Uganda, 19

Ukazes (Soviet executive orders), 514

Ukrainia, 502, 506

Ulbricht, Walter, 301, 303

Ulyanov, Alexander, 416

Union and French Fraternity, *see* Poujadists

Union for the New Republic (UNR), French, 194, 220; bloc-status, 241; as center group,

Union for the New Republic (*Cont.*)
222; and de Gaulle, dependence on, 241; and de Gaulle, loyalty to, 224; electoral triumph (*table*), 239; history, 223–225; Paris victories (*table*), 243

Union of South Africa, 120

Union Republics, Soviet, 506–507; Ministries, 520

Unions, *see* Trade Unions; Trades Unions

United Kingdom, *see* Great Britain

United Nations: British party views, 63–64; and France, 245; and German Federal Republic, 388

United Nations Economic Commission for Europe, 296

United States, and Britain: bases in Britain, 64; Cabinet, 81–82; civil service appointments, 107; Congressional committees, 86; H-bombs, 90; health plans, 123; missiles for British bombers, 128; presidential system, 17, 93; spy flights, 95; in Suez crisis, 61

United States, and France: Constitution, 217; Declaration of Independence, 142; elections, 172, 192; Fourth Republic, 195; senators and deputies, 171; industrial concentration, 151; industrial rank, 137; population growth, 149; size, 137

United States, and Germany: aid, 294–296; administrative power, 353–354; authoritarianism, 311; business organization, 375; commercial class, 311–312; the Depression, 285; education, 325; election costs, 369; Federalism, 338–339; government revenues, 345; habeas corpus, right of, 342; legislative bodies, 347, 348; legislative procedure, 356; legislators' salaries, 348–349; legislatures' "power of the purse," 342; population age-groups (*table*), 322–323; press freedom, 382–383; separation of powers, 383; SPD and the Democratic Party, 370; work capacity, 310

United States, and the Soviet Union: baby boom, 427; Con-

United States, and Soviet Union (*Cont.*)
stitution, 503; democratic values, 407; executive responsibilities, 518; population growth, (*table*), 429; production, 425

University Grants Committee (British), 115

Uzbek Republic, 434

V

Vichy government, French: Bonapartist regime, 140; Third Republic, as successor to, 138, 144

Volksdeutsche (German minorities), 293–294

Voltaire, 146

Voluntarism, theory of, 442

Voroshilov, K. E., 485, 515

W

Wagner, Richard, 310

Wales, 20–22, 30, 37

Wallas, Graham, 76

Wehner, Herbert, 373

Weimar Republic: Chancellors, 289; conservative rule, 289; Constitution, 282–284; and Hitler, 288–289, 310; inflation, 284–285; military influence, 283; national income and foreign trade, 300; nationalism, 282; Nazis, tolerance of, 341; North German influence, 332; suicide rates (*table*), 312; United States aid to, 285; university enrollment, 325; unpopularity of, 284; weaknesses, 284

West Berlin: "Berlin crisis," 300; blockade, 295; Brandt, Willy, 333; political outlook (*table*), 333–334; politics, 330; refugees, 305; religious composition, 330; SPD strength, 370; United States aid, 296; United States policy toward, 306

West European Federation, 389–392

West Germany, *see* German Federal Republic

What Is To Be Done?, 417

Whigs, history of the, 51–52

Whips, Parliamentary Party, 59–60

Wilhelm I (Germany), 281

Wilhelm II (Germany), 281–282

Wilson, H. H., 94

Wilson Report, 75

Workers, French: distribution by ideology, 154–155; individualism, 147; instability of, 155; opportunities, 154; political consciousness, 139

Workers, German: constitutional protections, 342–343; educational opportunities, 325; Federal Labor Court, 359; in German Federal Republic, 323–324; public employment (*table*), 335–336; nationalism, 288; Nazi

Workers, German (*Cont.*)
prosperity, 290; party affiliations (*table*), 364–365; social status, 327–328; unemployment, 297; unions, 377–378

Workers, Soviet: distribution (*charts*), 464–465; Five Year Plan, 456–457; on party committees, 500; Party Congress representation, 499; and party interest, 493; party membership, 494–495; pre-revolution, 454–455; social stratification, 462–463; strikes, 463–464; unions, 463–466; wages, 466; "War Communism," 455

Workers Second International, 177

Wylie, Lawrence, 153

Y

Yalta Conference, 293

Yugoslavia, 448

Z

Zakons (Soviet laws), 513–514

Zasulich, Vera, 416

Zemlya i Volya (Land and Freedom), 416

Zemstvos, Russian, 412

Zhdanov, Andrei, 451

Zhukov, Grigori, 485

Zola, Emile, 161, 163

Zollverein (German customs union), 281